MICHAEL CLAYTON

HANCOCK

THE DARK KNIGHT

THE INCREDIBLES

Using popular movies to bring OB to life

ORGANIZATIONAL BEHAVIOR
Improving Performance and Commitment in the Workplace

Second Edition

JASON A. COLQUITT
University of Florida

JEFFERY A. LEPINE
University of Florida

MICHAEL J. WESSON
Texas A&M University

ORGANIZATIONAL BEHAVIOR: IMPROVING PERFORMANCE AND COMMITMENT IN THE WORKPLACE

ISBN 978-0-07-813717-4
MHID 0-07-813717-9

Vice president and editor-in-chief: *Brent Gordon*
Publisher: *Paul Ducham*
Executive editor: *John Weimeister*
Director of development: *Ann Torbert*
Development editor: *Sara Knox Hunter*
Editorial assistant: *Heather Darr*
Vice president and director of marketing: *Robin J. Zwettler*
Marketing manager: *Natalie Zook*
Vice president of editing, design and production: *Sesha Bolisetty*
Senior project manager: *Bruce Gin*
Senior production supervisor: *Debra R. Sylvester*
Designer: *Matt Diamond*
Senior photo research coordinator: *Jeremy Cheshareck*
Photo researcher : *Ira C. Roberts*
Senior media project manager : *Susan Lombardi*
Cover design: *Eric Kass*
Cover image: *Photofest*
Interior design: *Matt Diamond*
Typeface: *10/12 Times New Roman*
Compositor: *Laserwords Private Limited*
Printer: *R. R. Donnelley*

Library of Congress Cataloging-in-Publication Data

Colquitt, Jason.
    Organizational behavior : improving performance and commitment in the workplace/Jason
  A. Colquitt, Jeffery A. LePine, Michael J. Wesson. — 2nd ed.
    p. cm.
  Includes index.
  ISBN-13: 978-0-07-813717-4 (alk. paper)
  ISBN-10: 0-07-813717-9 (alk. paper)
  1. Organizational behavior. 2. Personnel management. 3. Strategic planning. 4. Consumer
  satisfaction. 5. Job satisfaction. I. LePine, Jeffery A. II. Wesson, Michael J. III. Title.
HD58.7.C6255   2011
658.3—dc22
www.mhhe.com

2009039941

Dedication

To Catherine, Cameron, Riley, and Connor, and also to Mom, Dad, Alan, and Shawn. The most wonderful family I could imagine, two times over.

–J.A.C.

To my parents who made me, and to Marcie, Izzy, and Eli, who made my life complete.

–J.A.L.

To Liesl and Dylan: Their support in all I do is incomparable. They are my life and I love them both. To my parents: They provide a foundation that never wavers.

–M.J.W.

About the Authors

JASON A. COLQUITT

Is a Professor in the Management Department at the University of Florida's Warrington College of Business. He received his PhD from Michigan State University's Eli Broad Graduate School of Management and earned his BS in Psychology from Indiana University. He teaches organizational behavior and human resource management at the undergraduate, masters, and executive levels and also teaches research methods at the doctoral level. He has received awards for teaching excellence at both the undergraduate and executive levels.

Jason's research interests include organizational justice, trust, team effectiveness, and personality influences on task and learning performance. He has published more than 20 articles on these and other topics in *Academy of Management Journal, Academy of Management Review, Journal of Applied Psychology, Organizational Behavior and Human Decision Processes,* and *Personnel Psychology.* He is currently serving as an Associate Editor for *Academy of Management Journal* and has served (or is serving) on a number of editorial boards, including *Academy of Management Journal, Journal of Applied Psychology, Organizational Behavior and Human Decision Processes, Personnel Psychology, Journal of Management,* and *International Journal of Conflict Management.* He is a recipient of the Society for Industrial and Organizational Psychology's Distinguished Early Career Contributions Award and the Cummings Scholar Award for early to mid-career achievement, sponsored by the Organizational Behavior division of the Academy of Management. He was also elected to be a Representative-at-Large for the Organizational Behavior division.

Jason enjoys spending time with his wife, Catherine, and three sons, Cameron, Riley, and Connor. His hobbies include playing basketball, playing the trumpet, watching movies, and rooting on (in no particular order) the Pacers, Colts, Cubs, Hoosiers, Spartans, and Gators.

JEFFERY A. LEPINE

Is the Darden Restaurants Diversity Management Professor at the Warrington College of Business, University of Florida. He received his PhD in Organizational Behavior from the Eli Broad Graduate School of Management at Michigan State University. He also earned an MS in Management from Florida State University and a BS in Finance from the University of Connecticut. He teaches organizational behavior, human resource management, and management of groups and teams at undergraduate and graduate levels.

Jeff's research interests include team functioning and effectiveness, individual and team adaptation, citizenship behavior, voice, engagement, and occupational stress. He has published more than 20 articles on these and other topics in *Academy of Management Journal, Academy of Management Review, Journal of Applied Psychology, Organizational Behavior and Human Decision Processes,* and *Personnel Psychology.*

He is currently serving as Associate Editor of *Academy of Management Review,* and has served (or is currently serving) on the editorial boards of *Academy of Management Journal, Journal of Applied Psychology, Organizational Behavior and Human Decision Processes, Personnel Psychology, Journal of Management, Journal of Organizational Behavior, and Journal of Occupational and Organizational Psychology.* He is a recipient of the Society for Industrial and Organizational Psychology's Distinguished Early Career Contributions Award and the Cummings Scholar Award for early to mid-career achievement, sponsored by the Organizational Behavior division of the Academy of Management. He was also elected to the Executive Committee of the Human Resource Division of the Academy of Management. Prior to earning his PhD, Jeff was an officer in the U.S. Air Force.

Jeff spends most of his free time with his wife Marcie, daughter Izzy, and son Eli. He also enjoys playing guitar, avoiding sharks while trying to surf, and restoring his GTO.

MICHAEL J. WESSON

Is an associate professor in the Management Department at Texas A&M University's Mays Business School. He received his PhD from Michigan State University's Eli Broad Graduate School of Management. He also holds an MS in human resource management from Texas A&M University and a BBA from Baylor University. He has taught organizational behavior and human resource management based classes at all levels but currently spends most of his time teaching Mays MBAs, EMBAs, and executive development at Texas A&M. He was awarded Texas A&M's Montague Center for Teaching Excellence Award.

Michael's research interests include organizational justice, goal-setting, organizational entry (employee recruitment, selection, and socialization), person–organization fit, and compensation and benefits. His articles have been published in journals such as *Journal of Applied Psychology, Personnel Psychology, Academy of Management Review,* and *Organizational Behavior and Human Decision Processes.* He currently serves on the editorial boards of the *Journal of Applied Psychology* and the *Journal of Organizational Behavior* and is an ad hoc reviewer for many others. He is active in the Academy of Management and the Society for Industrial and Organizational Psychology. Prior to returning to school, Michael worked as a human resources manager for a *Fortune* 500 firm. He has served as a consultant to the automotive supplier, healthcare, oil and gas, and technology industries in areas dealing with recruiting, selection, onboarding, compensation, and turnover.

Michael spends most of his time trying to keep up with his wife Liesl and son Dylan. He is a self-admitted food and wine snob, home theater aficionado, and college sports addict (Gig 'em Aggies!).

Preface

Why did we decide to write this textbook? Well, for starters, organizational behavior (OB) remains a fascinating topic that everyone can relate to (because everyone either has worked or is going to work in the future). What makes people effective at their job? What makes them want to stay with their employer? What makes work enjoyable? Those are all fundamental questions that organizational behavior research can help answer. However, our desire to write this book also grew out of our own experiences (and frustrations) teaching OB courses using other textbooks. We found that students would end the semester with a common set of questions that we felt we could answer if given the chance to write our own book. With that in mind, *Organizational Behavior: Improving Performance and Commitment in the Workplace,* was written with the following questions in mind.

DOES ANY OF THIS STUFF REALLY MATTER?

Organizational behavior might be the most relevant class any student ever takes, but that doesn't always shine through in OB texts. The introductory section of our book contains two chapters not included in other books: *Job Performance* and *Organizational Commitment.* Being good at one's job and wanting to stay with one's employer are obviously critical concerns for employees and managers alike. After describing these topics in detail, every remaining chapter in the book links that chapter's content to performance and commitment. Students can then better appreciate the practical relevance of organizational behavior concepts.

IF THAT THEORY DOESN'T WORK, THEN WHY IS IT IN THE BOOK?

In putting together this book, we were guided by the question, "What would OB texts look like if all of them were first written now, rather than decades ago?" We found that many of the organizational behavior texts on the market include outdated (and indeed, scientifically disproven!) models or theories, presenting them sometimes as fact or possibly for the sake of completeness or historical context. Our students were always frustrated by the fact that they had to read about, learn, and potentially be tested on material that we knew to be wrong. Although historical context can be important at times, we believe that focusing on so-called "evidence-based management" is paramount in today's fast-paced classes. Thus, this textbook includes new and emerging topics that others leave out and excludes flawed and outdated topics that some other books leave in.

HOW DOES ALL THIS STUFF FIT TOGETHER?

Organizational behavior is a diverse and multidisciplinary field, and it's not always easy to see how all its topics fit together. Our book deals with this issue in two ways. First, all of the chapters in our book are organized around an integrative model that opens each chapter (see the back of the book). That model provides students with a roadmap of the course, showing them where they've been and where they're going. Second, our chapters are tightly focused around specific topics and aren't "grab-baggish" in nature. Our hope is that students (and instructors) won't ever come across a topic and think, "Why is this topic being discussed in this chapter?"

DOES THIS STUFF HAVE TO BE SO DRY?

Research on motivation to learn shows that students learn more when they have an intrinsic interest in the topic, but many OB texts do little to stimulate that interest. Put simply, we wanted to create a book that students enjoy reading. To do that, we used a more informal, conversational style when writing the book. We also tried to use company examples that students will be familiar with and find compelling. Finally, we included insert boxes, self-assessments, and exercises that students should find engaging (and sometimes even entertaining!).

OB ON SCREEN

This feature uses memorable scenes from recent films to bring OB concepts to life. Films like *Slumdog Millionaire, Michael Clayton, The Dark Knight, Star Trek, The Devil Wears Prada,* and *There Will Be Blood* offer rich, vivid examples that grab the attention of students.

"**Very comprehensive.** Well laid-out. **Interesting.** Good mix of theoretical material and practical insights."

OB AT THE BOOKSTORE

This feature links the content in each chapter to a mainstream, popular business book. Books like *Outliers, How the Mighty Fall, Three Signs of a Miserable Job,* and *The 4-Hour Workweek* represent the gateway to OB for many students. This feature helps them put those books in a larger context.

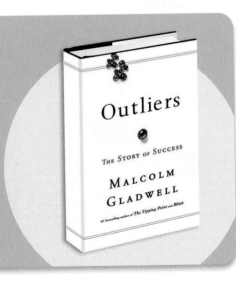

OB ASSESSMENTS

This feature helps students see where they stand on key OB concepts in each chapter. Students gain insights into their personality, their emotional intelligence, their style of leadership, and their ability to cope with stress, which can help them understand their reactions to the working world.

> "The material presented in this chapter is **well balanced**. Again, the **tables**, **charts**, and **figures** help to organize the material for students."

OB INTERNATIONALLY

Changes in technology, communications, and economic forces have made business more global and international than ever. This feature spotlights the impact of globalization on the organizational behavior concepts described in this book. It describes cross-cultural differences in OB theories, how to apply them in international corporations, and how to use OB to manage cultural diversity in the workplace.

End-of-Chapter Sections

TAKEAWAYS

TAKEAWAYS

1.1 Organizational behavior is a field of study devoted to understanding and explaining the attitudes and behaviors of individuals and groups in organizations. More simply, it focuses on *why* individuals and groups in organizations act the way they do.

1.2 The two primary outcomes in organizational behavior are job performance and organizational commitment.

1.3 A number of factors affect performance and commitment, including individual mechanisms (job satisfaction; stress; motivation; trust, justice, and ethics; learning and decision making), individual characteristics (personality and cultural values; ability), group mechanisms (team characteristics and diversity; team processes and communication; leader power and negotiation; leader styles and behaviors), and organizational mechanisms (organizational structure, organizational culture).

1.4 The effective management of organizational behavior can help a company become more profitable because good people are a valuable resource. Not only are good people rare, but they are also hard to imitate. They create a history that cannot be bought or copied, they make numerous small decisions that cannot be observed by competitors, and they create socially complex resources such as culture, teamwork, trust, and reputation.

1.5 A theory is a collection of assertions, both verbal and symbolic, that specifies how and why variables are related, as well as the conditions in which they should (and should not) be related. Theories about organizational behavior are built from a

Students are always asking, "What are the most important 'takeaways' from this chapter?" This section gives a point-by-point review of the Learning Goals found at the beginning of each chapter.

form the beginning point for the scientific method and inspire hypotheses that can be tested with data.

1.6 A correlation is a statistic that expresses the strength of a relationship between two variables (ranging from 0 to ± 1). In OB research, a .50 correlation is considered "strong," a .30 correlation is considered "moderate," and a .10 correlation is considered "weak."

KEY TERMS

KEY TERMS

Summarizes the most critical terms covered in the chapter, with definitions of all terms available in the Glossary.

"Great attention-getting opening section, makes a good case for why students should care about OB, and how the topics have wide-ranging real-world applicability."

DISCUSSION QUESTIONS

Not only for review purposes, our Discussion Questions ask students to apply concepts in the chapter to their own lives and experiences.

DISCUSSION QUESTIONS

1.1 Can you think of other retail businesses that, like the Apple Store, seem to do an effective job with customer service? If you managed a franchise for one of those businesses, which organizational behavior topics would be most important to maintaining that high service level?

1.2 Think again about the worst coworker you've ever had—the one who did some of the things listed in Table 1-1. Think about what that coworker's boss did (or didn't do) to try to improve his or her behavior. What did the boss do well or poorly? What would you have done differently, and which organizational behavior topics would have been most relevant?

1.3 Which of the individual mechanisms in Figure 1-1 (job satisfaction; stress; motivation; trust, justice, and ethics; learning and decision making) seems to drive your performance and commitment the most? Do you think you're unique in that regard, or do you think most people would answer that way?

1.4 Create a list of the most successful companies that you can think of. What do these companies have that others don't? Are the things that those companies possess rare and inimitable (see Figure 1-2)? What makes those things difficult to copy?

1.5 Think of something that you "know" to be true based on the method of experience, the method of intuition, or the method of authority. Could you test your knowledge using the method of science? How would you do it?

CASES

To help bring students full circle, a case appears at the end of every chapter that provides a follow-up to the company highlighted in the Opening Vignette.

CASE: APPLE

Apple's hiring strategy for its retail stores was summarized this way by a journalist who worked part-time at one of the locations: "The company was not looking for great salespeople using sophisticated technology, as one would imagine it easily could; instead it isolates true enthusiasts and true believers in Apple products, of which there are many. . . . As workers all we had to bring to the table was a passion for Apple products; the company supplied the knowledge we needed to teach, share, and sell to customers."[39] Other than that singular focus, the hiring procedures at the Apple Store are fairly typical. Applicants apply online by answering a few questions, pasting in their resume, and selecting the jobs and locations in which they're interested. This process may need to be repeated multiple times before the applicant is contacted by a store. That contact may then lead to one or more face-to-face interviews, perhaps at the store itself or at a local coffee shop.

Two recent decisions, however, signal a departure from Apple's hiring and overall retail philosophies. On the hiring front, Apple recruiters have been spotted handing out black cards to retail employees in other organizations.[40] The front of the card bears the Apple logo and reads, "You're amazing. We should talk." The back of the card reads, "Your customer service just now was exceptional. I work for the Apple Store, and you're exactly the kind of person we'd like to talk to. If you're happy where you are, I'll never ask you to leave. But if you're thinking about a change, give me a call. This could be the start of something great." The card also includes a URL for more information. With respect to its overall retail philosophy, Apple entered into an agreement with Best Buy to create a "store within a store" at select locations.[41] Although it remains a pilot program,

EXERCISES

In addition to the self-assessments within the chapter, we have included exercises at the end of each chapter. Some of them we have created ourselves over the years, but we also feature some "classics" that are tried and true and that nearly everyone we know uses in class.

EXERCISE: IS OB COMMON SENSE?

The purpose of this exercise is to take some of the topics covered in this textbook and examine whether improving them is "just common sense." This exercise uses groups, so your instructor will either assign you to a group or ask you to create your own. The exercise has the following steps:

1.1 Consider the theory diagram shown below. It explains why two "independent variables" (the quality of a movie's script and the fame of its stars) affect a "dependent variable" (how much the movie makes at the box office).

1.2 Now build your own theory diagram about organizational behavior. In your groups,

Supplement Features

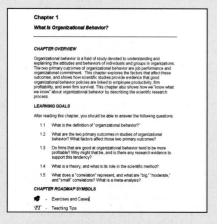

Instructor's Manual

Prepared by Jason Colquitt, this manual was developed to help you get the most out of the text in your own teaching. It contains an outline of the chapters, innovative teaching tips to use with your students, and notes and answers for the end-of-chapter materials. It also provides a guide for the assessments in the book, along with suggestions for additional assessments from the Asset Gallery (see below). The manual also contains additional cases, exercises, and OB insert boxes from the first edition of the book, giving you extra examples to use in your teaching. Find all of these features on our Web site at www.mhhe.com/colquitt.

Testbank and EZ Test Online

TESTBANK: Our Testbank contains a variety of true/false, multiple choice, and short and long essay questions, as well as "scenario-based" questions, which are application based and use a situation described in a narrative, with 3–5 multiple-choice test questions based on the situation described in the narrative. We've aligned our Testbank questions with Bloom's Taxonomy and AACSB guidelines, tagging each question according to its knowledge and skills areas. We have also tagged our questions according to Learning Objective, Level of Difficulty, and Topic.

EZ TEST ONLINE: McGraw-Hill's EZ Test Online is a flexible and easy-to-use electronic testing program. The program allows instructors to create tests from book-specific items, accommodates a wide range of question types, and enables instructors to add their own questions. Multiple versions of the test can be created, and any test can be exported for use with course management systems such as WebCT, BlackBoard, or any other course management system. EZ Test Online is accessible to busy instructors virtually anywhere via the Web, and the program eliminates the need to install test software. For more information about EZ Test Online, please see the Web site at www.eztestonline.com.

PowerPoint Presentation Slides

Based on instructor feedback, the PowerPoint Presentation slides (prepared by Liesl Wesson, Texas A&M University) consist of 2 types of presentations: Outline and Detailed formats that give instructors the flexibility to tailor their presentations to their class needs. The Outline format follows a "don't give them everything" philosophy, which requires students to attend class and take notes to have all the information available to them. The Detailed set builds on the outline format to include full definitions and descriptions for the topics covered. This format is designed for instructors who prefer that the students be listening to them instead of taking basic, definition-oriented notes during class. Each format has advantages and disadvantages, but the provision of multiple sets of slides should make it easier for instructors to access ready-made presentations designed to fit their teaching style.

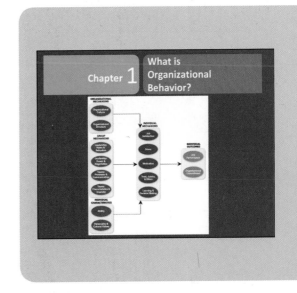

Organizational Behavior Video DVD

(ISBN: 0073337285, 13-digit ISBN: 9780073337289)
For instructors who want to incorporate more "real-world" examples into the classroom, *Organizational Behavior: Improving Performance and Commitment in the Workplace* offers this compilation video DVD, which features news clips on organizational behavior–related topics from NBC, PBS, and BusinessWeek TV. Videos are organized by topic and include such companies as Disney Imagineering, 1154 Lil, Johnson & Johnson, and Xerox, as well as topics such as outsourcing, work/life balance, layoffs and their psychological effects, discrimination, and employees with passion. Instructor Notes can be found in the Instructor Center of the Web site at www.mhhe.com/colquitt.

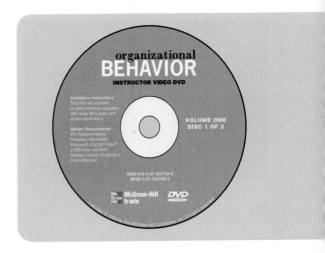

Online Learning Center

www.mhhe.com/colquitt

Separated into both Instructor and Student areas, each section of the OLC holds a variety of material for instructors to develop and use in their course and for students to use to review. Instructors will find supplements, additional course materials including video notes, and a link to the Asset Gallery, a one-stop shop for all your OB needs. Students will find basic material like chapter quizzes and the basic PowerPoint outline slides free to use. For a nominal fee, they can access premium content, which includes access to the student version of the Asset Gallery.

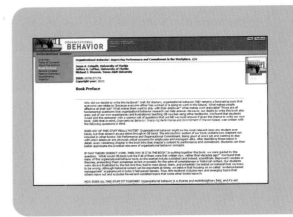

Manager's HotSeat Online
www.mhhe.com/mhs

EXPANDED 6 NEW CLIPS! The Manager's HotSeat offers interactive software that allows students to watch as 21 real managers apply their years of experience to confront these issues. Students assume the role of the manager as they watch the video and answer multiple-choice questions that pop up, forcing them to make decisions on the spot. They learn from the manager's mistakes and successes, then write a report critiquing the manager's approach by defending their reasoning. Reports can be e-mailed or printed out for credit. Access these videos through the McGraw-Hill Asset Gallery or go to www.mhhe.com/mhs for more information.

Asset Gallery

The Management Asset Gallery is McGraw-Hill's new resource portal with convenient access to all of our non–text-specific Management Resources. The vast library of resources includes Self-Assessments, Test Your Knowledge exercises supporting student skill building, videos, Manager's Hot Seat segments, and much more. In addition to finding the resources you need, you will also find supporting instructor materials making integration of those resources virtually flawless: Teaching Notes, PowerPoint slides and Video Cases. Intuitively designed, the Management Asset Gallery may be by one of the 40 management topics or by resource. And there's only one place for your students, too. They access their assigned materials on their textbook's Premium Content.

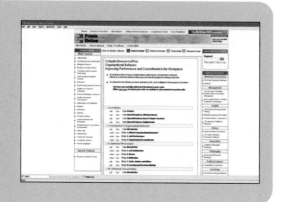

McGraw-Hill Primus Online
Digital Database

You can customize this text. McGraw-Hill Primis Online digital database offers you the flexibility to customize your course, including the material from the largest online collection of textbooks, readings, and cases. Primis leads the way in customized eBooks with hundreds of titles available at prices that save your students more than 20 percent off bookstore prices. Additional information is available at 800-228-0634, or go to primisonline.com.

CONNECT Management™ and CONNECT Management Plus™

McGraw-Hill's Connect Management™ is a comprehensive online learning, assignment, and assessment solution that gives instructors the power to create assignments, practice, tests, and quizzes online, while also saving time! Connect Management™ acts like a navigation system for students by diagnosing where individual students are; providing the fastest, most efficient path to mastering each learning objective; and offering continuous, specific feedback all along the way. Connect™ also grades assignments automatically, provides instant feedback to students, and securely stores all student results. Detailed results let instructors see at a glance how each student performs and easily track the progress of every student in the course. The Connect Management™ grade reports can be easily integrated with WebCT, BlackBoard, and Angel. Connect Management™ is also available with an integrated online version of the textbook.

With a single access code, students can read the eBook, work through practice problems, do homework, and take exams. Ask your sales rep how to incorporate Connect into your course.

Tegrity Campus

This semester, try incorporating Tegrity Campus into your lectures and give your students the opportunity to truly engage in class without the distraction of copious note taking. Tegrity is a simple, one-click start/stop process that automatically captures audio, PowerPoint, Web pages, all computer screens, video, and more. To learn more about Tegrity, go to http://highered.mcgraw-hill.com/tegrity/be.

> "A major strength of this text in general is the **effective use of tables, charts,** and **figures** to help summarize, present, or simplify material for students.

Acknowledgments

An enormous number of persons played a role in helping us put this textbook together. Truth be told, we had no idea that we would have to rely on and put our success in the hands of so many different people! Each of them had unique and useful contributions to make toward the publication of this book, and they deserve and thus receive our sincere gratitude.

We are overly indebted to John Weimeister, our sponsoring editor, for his encouragement to write the textbook and his steadfast belief in our doing things in a more "unorthodox" way at times. John has been taking good care of us all the way back to our graduate school days. Thanks also go out to Sara Hunter, our Development Editor. We also owe much gratitude to our Marketing Manager, Natalie Zook. We also would like to thank Bruce Gin, Matt Diamond, Jeremy Cheshareck, and Susan Lombardi at Irwin/McGraw Hill, as they are the masterminds of much of how the book actually looks as it sits in students' hands; their work and effort were spectacular. A special thanks also goes out to Liesl Wesson (Texas A&M University) for her development of the PowerPoint presentations.

We have also had the great fortune of having had over 40 faculty members from colleges and universities around the country provide feedback on various aspects of the Second Edition of this textbook. Whether by providing feedback on chapters or attending focus groups, their input made this book substantially better:

Kristin Byron, *Syracuse University*

Matthew Eriksen, *Providence College*

Charles R. Foley, *Columbus State Community College*

Janice S. Miller, *University of Wisconsin-Milwaukee*

Nell Hartley, *Robert Morris University*

Lorianne D. Mitchell, *East Tennessee State University*

James P. Morgan, *Columbia College*

Donita Whitney-Bammerlin, *Kansas State University*

Goli Sadri, *California State University, Fullerton*

Arlene S. Kreinik, *Western Connecticut State University*

Barbara Crandall, *Oklahoma City University*

Timothy R. Oxley, *Fairmont State University*

George Knox Pittard, *Tarrant County College*

Bruce Alan Kibler, *University of Wisconsin-Superior*

Rhonda S. Palladi, *Georgia State University*

Jonathon Halbesleben, *University of Wisconsin-Eau Claire*

Gregory J. Schultz, *Carroll University*

Eileen Askey, *SUNY Brockport*

Morgan R. Milner, *Eastern Michigan University*

K. Nathan Moates, *Valdosta State University*

Marla Baskerville, *Northeastern University*

Denise Marie Tanguay, *Eastern Michigan University*

Elisabeth Ryland, *University of California, Riverside*

Jeanine Andreassi, *Sacred Heart University*

Lynn Wilson, *Saint Leo University*

Amy Randel, *San Diego State University*

Muhammad A. Obeidat, *Southern Polytechnic State University*

John W. Michel, *Towson University*

Kenneth Nathan Moates, *Valdosta State University*

Shane Spiller, *Western Kentucky University*

Jonathon R. B. Halbesleben, *University of Wisconsin-Eau Claire*

Judy Bullock, *Keller Graduate School of Management*

Joy E. Beatty, *University of Michigan-Dearborn*

Catherine Marsh, *North Park University*

Jason Kanov, *Western Washington University*

Patrizia Porrini, *Long Island University*

Amanda Starling, *The Fashion Institute of Design & Merchandising*

Kristin Holmberg-Wright, *University of Wisconsin-Parkside*

Dennis P. Slevin, *University of Pittsburgh*

Susan Eisner, *Ramapo College of New Jersey*

We would also like to thank our students at the undergraduate, masters, and executive levels who were taught with early versions of these chapters for their constructive feedback toward making them more effective in the classroom. Thanks also to our PhD students for allowing us to take time out from research projects to focus on this book.

Finally, we thank our families, who gave up substantial amounts of time with us and put up with the stress that necessarily comes at times during an endeavor such as this.

Jason Colquitt

Jeff LePine

Michael Wesson

Brief Contents

Table of Contents

ORGANIZATIONAL BEHAVIOR
Improving Performance and Commitment in the Workplace

chapter 1

What Is Organizational Behavior?

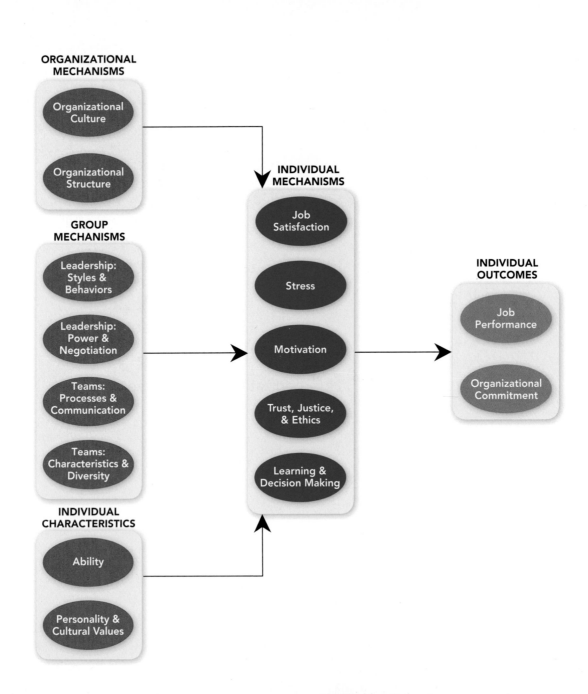

✓ LEARNING GOALS

After reading this chapter, you should be able to answer the following questions:

1.1 What is the definition of "organizational behavior" (OB)?

1.2 What are the two primary outcomes in studies of OB?

1.3 What factors affect the two primary OB outcomes?

1.4 Why might firms that are good at OB tend to be more profitable?

1.5 What is the role of theory in the scientific method?

1.6 How are correlations interpreted?

APPLE

Let's say you're in the market for a new laptop. You'll do some searching online, certainly. But you'll also want to check out your candidates in the brick-and-mortar world to make sure they're not too heavy or too flimsy and that their keyboards aren't too squished together. One of the places you might visit on your journey is the Apple Store. Apple opened the first of its retail stores in McLean, Virginia, in 2001.[1] At the time, Apple's products sold primarily through retailers such as CompUSA and Sears, right alongside competing products from PC makers. Steve Jobs, Apple's cofounder and CEO, reasoned that people would be more likely to buy a Mac if the salesperson showing it to them really loved it (and knew how to use it).

How did Apple design and launch its own stores when the company had no retailing experience? By hiring people who did. Jobs added Mickey Drexler, the CEO of The Gap, to its board of directors, then hired Ron Johnson, head of merchandising at Target. As the team designed its stores, it asked an 18-person focus group to describe the best service experience they'd ever had.[2] Sixteen of the 18 responses referred to a hotel. "Well, how do we create a store that has the friendliness of a Four Seasons Hotel?" Johnson asked. His answer: "Put a bar in our stores. But instead of dispensing alcohol, we dispense advice." Thus was born one of the signature elements of the Apple Store, its Genius Bar, where Apple experts dole out tips, field questions, and perform repairs on Macs, iPods, and iPhones.

The Apple Store's emphasis on friendliness extends beyond the Genius Bar however. Apple Store employees are instructed to treat customers like "season ticket holders"—people who will visit again and again, before and after their purchases.[3] Training procedures encourage employees to "be who you are" and answer difficult questions with, "I don't know, let's find out." That relaxed atmosphere, together with the positive buzz generated by Apple's products, makes the Apple Store a popular place to work. Apple reports that it turns away 90 percent of its applicants. How well is this retail strategy working? Well, at the time that Apple opened its 174th store, with an iconic glass cube entrance on New York City's Fifth Avenue, Apple Stores were generating $4032 in sales per square foot.[4] Want some perspective on that number? The world-famous jeweler Tiffany & Co. sits half a block away and takes in $2666 per square foot.

WHAT IS ORGANIZATIONAL BEHAVIOR?

Before we define exactly what the field of organizational behavior represents, take a moment to ponder the following question: Who was the single *worst* coworker you've ever had? Picture fellow students who collaborated with you on class projects; colleagues from part-time or summer jobs; or peers, subordinates, or supervisors working in your current organization. What did this coworker do that earned him or her "worst coworker" status? Was it some of the behaviors shown in the right column of Table 1-1 (or perhaps all of them)? Now take a moment to consider the single *best* coworker you've ever had. Again, what did this coworker do to earn "best coworker" status—some or most of the behaviors shown in the left column of Table 1-1?

TABLE 1-1	The Best of Coworkers, the Worst of Coworkers
THE BEST	**THE WORST**
Have you ever had a coworker who usually acted this way?	*Have you ever had a coworker who usually acted this way?*
Got the job done, without having to be managed or reminded	Did not got the job done, even with a great deal of hand-holding
Adapted when something needed to be changed or done differently	Was resistant to any and every form of change, even when changes were beneficial
Was always a "good sport," even when bad things happened at work	Whined and complained, no matter what was happening
Attended optional meetings or functions to support colleagues	Optional meetings? Was too lazy to make it to some required meetings and functions!
Helped new coworkers or people who seemed to need a hand	Made fun of new coworkers or people who seemed to need a hand
Felt an attachment and obligation to the employer for the long haul	Seemed to always be looking for something else, even if it wasn't better
Was first to arrive, last to leave	Was first to leave for lunch, last to return

The Million Dollar Question:
Why do these two employees act so differently?

If you ever found yourself working alongside the two people profiled in the table, two questions probably would be foremost on your mind: "*Why* does the worst coworker act that way?" and "*Why* does the best coworker act that way?" Once you understand why the two coworkers act so differently, you might be able to figure out ways to interact with the worst coworker more effectively (thereby making your working life a bit more pleasant). If you happen to be a manager, you might formulate plans for how to improve attitudes and behaviors in the unit. Such plans could include how to screen applicants, train and socialize new organizational members, manage evaluations and rewards for performance, and deal with conflicts that arise between employees. Without understanding why employees act the way they do, it's extremely hard to find a way to change their attitudes and behaviors at work.

ORGANIZATIONAL BEHAVIOR DEFINED

Organizational behavior (OB) is a field of study devoted to understanding, explaining, and ultimately improving the attitudes and behaviors of individuals and groups in organizations. Scholars in management departments of universities and scientists in business organizations conduct research on OB. The findings from those research studies are then applied by managers or consultants to see whether they help meet "real-world" challenges. OB can be contrasted with two other courses commonly offered in management departments: human resource management and strategic management. **Human resource management** takes the theories and principles studied in OB and explores the "nuts-and-bolts" applications of those principles in organizations. An OB study might

 1.1

What is the definition of "organizational behavior" (OB)?

explore the relationship between learning and job performance, whereas a human resource management study might examine the best ways to structure training programs to promote employee learning. **Strategic management** focuses on the product choices and industry characteristics that affect an organization's profitability. A strategic management study might examine the relationship between firm diversification (when a firm expands into a new product segment) and firm profitability.

The theories and concepts found in OB are actually drawn from a wide variety of disciplines. For example, research on job performance and individual characteristics draws primarily from studies in industrial and organizational psychology. Research on satisfaction, emotions, and team processes draws heavily from social psychology. Sociology research is vital to research on team characteristics and organizational structure, and anthropology research helps inform the study of organizational culture. Finally, models from economics are used to understand motivation, learning, and decision making. This diversity brings a unique quality to the study of OB, as most students will be able to find a particular topic that's intrinsically interesting and thought provoking to them.

AN INTEGRATIVE MODEL OF OB

Because of the diversity in its topics and disciplinary roots, it's common for students in an organizational behavior class to wonder, "How does all this stuff fit together?" How does what gets covered in Chapter 3 relate to what gets covered in Chapter 13? To clarify such issues, this textbook is structured around an integrative model of OB, shown in Figure 1-1, that's designed to provide a roadmap for the field of organizational behavior. The model shows how the topics in the next 15 chapters—represented by the 15 ovals in the model— all fit together. We should stress that there are other potential ways of combining the 15 topics, and Figure 1-1 likely oversimplifies the connections among the topics. Still, we believe the model provides a helpful guide as you move through this course. Figure 1-1 includes five different kinds of topics.

1.2

What are the two primary outcomes in studies of OB?

INDIVIDUAL OUTCOMES. The right-most portion of the model contains the two primary outcomes of interest to organizational behavior researchers (and employees and managers in organizations): *job performance* and *organizational commitment.* Most employees have two primary goals for their working lives: to perform their jobs well and to remain a member of an organization that they respect. Likewise, most managers have two primary goals for their employees: to maximize their job performance and to ensure that they stay with the firm for a significant length of time. As described in Chapter 2, there are several specific behaviors that, when taken together, constitute good job performance. Similarly, as described in Chapter 3, there are a number of beliefs, attitudes, and emotions that cause an employee to remain committed to an employer.

This book starts by covering job performance and organizational commitment so that you can better understand the two primary organizational behavior goals. Our hope is that by using performance and commitment as starting points, we can highlight the practical importance of OB topics. After all, what could be more important than having employees who perform well and want to stay with the company? This structure also enables us to conclude the other chapters in the book with sections that describe the relationships between each chapter's topic and performance and commitment. For example, the chapter on motivation concludes by describing the relationships between motivation and performance and motivation and commitment. In this way, you'll learn which of the topics in the model are most useful for understanding your own attitudes and behaviors.

1.3

What factors affect the two primary OB outcomes?

INDIVIDUAL MECHANISMS. Our integrative model also illustrates a number of individual mechanisms that directly affect job performance and organizational commitment. These include *job satisfaction,* which captures what employees feel when

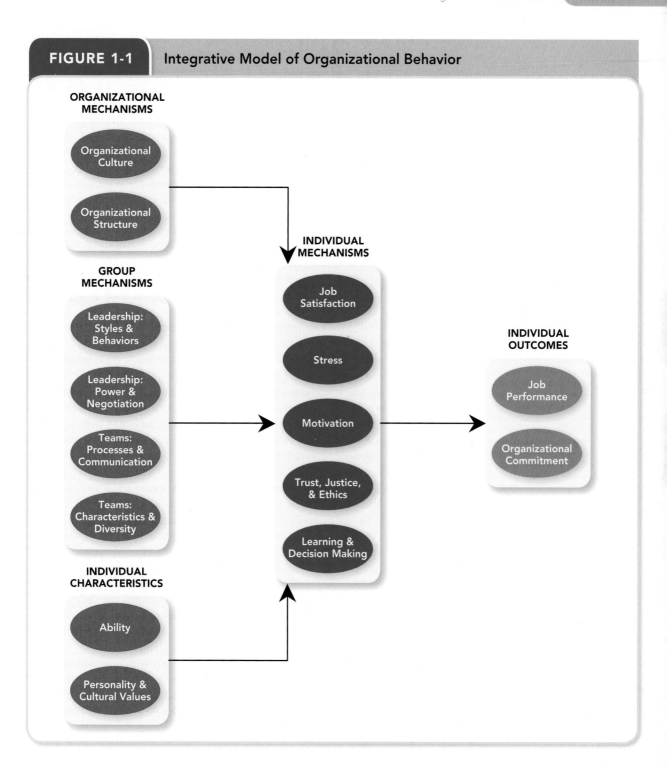

FIGURE 1-1   Integrative Model of Organizational Behavior

thinking about their jobs and doing their day-to-day work (Chapter 4). Another individual mechanism is *stress,* which reflects employees' psychological responses to job demands that tax or exceed their capacities (Chapter 5). The model also includes *motivation,* which captures the energetic forces that drive employees' work effort (Chapter 6). *Trust, justice, and ethics* reflect the degree to which employees feel that their company does business with fairness, honesty, and integrity (Chapter 7). The final individual mechanism shown in the model is *learning and decision making,* which deals with how employees gain job knowledge and how they use that knowledge to make accurate judgments on the job (Chapter 8).

INDIVIDUAL CHARACTERISTICS. Of course, if satisfaction, stress, motivation, and so forth are key drivers of job performance and organizational commitment, it becomes important to understand what factors improve those individual mechanisms. Two such factors reflect the characteristics of individual employees. *Personality and cultural values* reflect the various traits and tendencies that describe how people act, with commonly studied traits including extraversion, conscientiousness, and collectivism. As described in Chapter 9, personality and cultural values affect the way people behave at work, the kinds of tasks they're interested in, and how they react to events that happen on the job. The model also examines *ability,* which describes the cognitive abilities (verbal, quantitative, etc.), emotional skills (other awareness, emotion regulation, etc.), and physical abilities (strength, endurance, etc.) that employees bring to a job. As described in Chapter 10, ability influences the kinds of tasks an employee is good at (and not so good at).

GROUP MECHANISMS. Our integrative model also acknowledges that employees don't work alone. Instead, they typically work in one or more work teams led by some formal (or sometimes informal) leader. Like the individual characteristics, these group mechanisms shape satisfaction, stress, motivation, trust, and learning. Chapter 11 covers *team characteristics and diversity*—describing how teams are formed, staffed, and composed, and how team members come to rely on one another as they do their work. Chapter 12 then covers *team processes and communication*—how teams behave, including their coordination, conflict, and cohesion. The next two chapters focus on the leaders of those teams. We first describe how individuals become leaders in the first place, covering *leader power and negotiation* to summarize how individuals attain authority over others (Chapter 13). We then describe how leaders behave in their leadership roles, as *leader styles and behaviors* capture the specific actions that leaders take to influence others at work (Chapter 14).

ORGANIZATIONAL MECHANISMS. Finally, our integrative model acknowledges that the teams described in the prior section are grouped into larger organizations that themselves affect satisfaction, stress, motivation, and so forth. For example, every company has an *organizational structure* that dictates how the units within the firm link to (and communicate with) other units (Chapter 15). Sometimes structures are centralized around a decision-making authority, whereas other times, structures are decentralized, affording each unit some autonomy. Every company also has an *organizational culture* that captures "the way things are" in the organization—shared knowledge about the values and beliefs that shape employee attitudes and behaviors (Chapter 16).

SUMMARY. Each of the chapters in this textbook will open with a depiction of this integrative model, with the subject of each chapter highlighted. We hope that this opening will serve as a roadmap for the course—showing you where you are, where you've been, and where you're going. We also hope that the model will give you a feel for the "big picture" of OB—showing you how all the OB topics are connected. The Apple Store is a good example of those connections. Apple's leadership team created a vision for the stores that they reinforce through 40 hours of training.[5] That training reinforces the culture created within the stores while also giving new employees the knowledge and skills needed to succeed. By hiring employees who are enthusiastic about Apple's products, the company encourages some built-in level of job satisfaction among the rank-and-file staff. Motivation then can be fostered by rewarding those salespeople who get customers to purchase "attachments," such as an extended warranty or online storage account (Apple

Store employees are not paid on commission, to preserve the relaxed culture within the stores). Each store also offers a career ladder to give employees advancement opportunities, providing an incentive to stay with the store for a longer period of time. For example, once new employees prove themselves, they may get opportunities to teach in-store classes, offer private lessons, work at the Genius Bar, be in charge of store visuals, or even consult with local businesses about Apple products. With all that attention paid to OB issues, it's not surprising that the Apple Store's retention rate is about four times higher than the retail industry average.[6]

Employees at Apple's Genius Bar provide tips and perform repairs for Apple's customers.

DOES ORGANIZATIONAL BEHAVIOR MATTER?

Having described exactly what OB is, it's time to discuss another fundamental question: Does it really matter? Is there any value in taking a class on this subject, other than fulfilling some requirement of your program? (You might guess that we're biased in our answers to these questions, given that we wrote a book on the subject!) Few would disagree that organizations need to know principles of accounting and finance to be successful; it would be impossible to conduct business without such knowledge. Similarly, few would disagree that organizations need to know principles of marketing, as consumers need to know about the firm's products and what makes those products unique or noteworthy.

However, people sometimes wonder whether a firm's ability to manage OB has any bearing on its bottom-line profitability. After all, if a firm has a good-enough product, won't people buy it regardless of how happy, motivated, or committed its workforce is? Perhaps for a time, but effective OB can help keep a product good over the long term. This same argument can be made in reverse: If a firm has a bad-enough product, isn't it true that people won't buy it, regardless of how happy, motivated, or committed its workforce is? Again, perhaps for a time, but the effective management of OB can help make a product get better, incrementally, over the long term.

Consider this pop quiz about the automotive industry: Which automaker finished behind only Lexus and Porsche in a recent study of initial quality by J.D. Power and Associates?[7] Toyota? Nope. Honda? Uh-uh. The answer is Hyundai (yes, Hyundai). The automaker has come a long way in the decade since comedian Jay Leno likened a Hyundai to a bobsled ("It has no room, you have to push it to get going, and it only goes downhill!").[8] More recent models—including those built in a manufacturing plant in Montgomery, Alabama—are regarded as good looking and well made, with *Consumer Reports* tabbing the Hyundai Elantra SE as the best small sedan in its 2009 rankings.[9] That turnaround can be credited to the company's increased emphasis on quality. Work teams devoted to quality have been expanded eightfold, and almost all employees are enrolled in special training programs devoted to quality issues.[10] Hyundai represents a case in which OB principles are being applied across cultures. Our **OB Internationally** feature spotlights such international and cross-cultural applications of OB topics in each chapter.

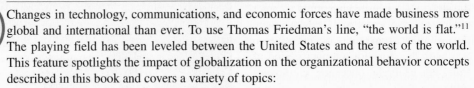

OB INTERNATIONALLY

Changes in technology, communications, and economic forces have made business more global and international than ever. To use Thomas Friedman's line, "the world is flat."[11] The playing field has been leveled between the United States and the rest of the world. This feature spotlights the impact of globalization on the organizational behavior concepts described in this book and covers a variety of topics:

Cross-Cultural Differences. Research in cross-cultural organizational behavior has illustrated that national cultures affect many of the relationships in our integrative model. Put differently, there is little that we know about OB that is "universal" or "culture free."[12]

International Corporations. An increasing number of organizations are international in scope, with both foreign and domestic operations. Applying organizational behavior concepts in these firms represents a special challenge—should policies and practices be consistent across locations or tailored to meet the needs of the culture?

Expatriation. Working as an expatriate—an employee who lives outside his or her native country—can be particularly challenging. What factors influence expatriates' job performance and organizational commitment levels?

Managing Diversity. More and more work groups are composed of members of different cultural backgrounds. What are the special challenges involved in leading and working in such groups?

Hyundai's emphasis on work teams and training has increased the quality of its cars, like these models built in its Montgomery, Alabama, plant.

BUILDING A CONCEPTUAL ARGUMENT

Of course, we shouldn't just accept it on faith that OB matters, nor should we merely look for specific companies that appear to support the premise. What we need instead is a conceptual argument that captures why OB might affect the bottom-line profitability of an organization. One such argument is based on the **resource-based view** of organizations. This perspective describes what exactly makes resources valuable—that is, what makes them capable of creating long-term profits for the firm.[13] A firm's resources include financial (revenue, equity, etc.) and physical (buildings, machines, technology) resources, but they also include resources related to organizational behavior, such as the knowledge, ability, and wisdom of the workforce, as well as the image, culture, and goodwill of the organization.

The resource-based view suggests that the value of resources depends on several factors, shown in Figure 1-2. For example, a resource is more valuable when it is *rare*. Diamonds, oil, Babe Ruth baseball cards, and Action Comics #1 (the debut of Superman) are all expensive precisely because they are rare. Good people are also rare—witness the adage "good people are hard to find." Ask yourself what percentage of the people you've worked with have been talented, motivated, satisfied, and good team players. In many organizations, cities, or job markets, such employees are the exception rather than the rule. If good people really are rare, then the effective management of OB should prove to be a valuable resource.

The resource-based view also suggests that a resource is more valuable when it is **inimitable**, meaning that it cannot be imitated. Many of the firm's resources can be imitated, if competitors have enough money. For example, a new form of technology can help a firm gain an advantage for a short time, but competing firms can switch to the same technology. Manufacturing practices can be copied, equipment and tools can be approximated, and marketing strategies can be mimicked. Good people, in contrast, are much more difficult to imitate. As shown in Figure 1-2, there are three reasons people are inimitable.

HISTORY. People create a **history**—a collective pool of experience, wisdom, and knowledge that benefits the organization. History cannot be bought. Consider an example from the discount airline industry. Southwest and JetBlue are the market leaders in this industry, profiting from more frequent point-to-point daily schedules routed into less expensive airports. Delta launched its own discount brand—Song—to compete in this market, though the brand was ultimately abandoned and folded back into Delta's regular operations.[14] One challenge facing Song was that it was competing, for the first time, in a market in which Southwest had existed for decades. Their respective positions on the "industry learning curve" were quite different.

NUMEROUS SMALL DECISIONS. The concept of **numerous small decisions** captures the idea that people make many small decisions day in and day out, week in and week out. "So what?" you might say, "Why worry about small decisions?" Ask yourself how much time elapsed between the arrival of *Diet Coke with Lime* on grocery store shelves and

FIGURE 1-2 | What Makes a Resource Valuable?

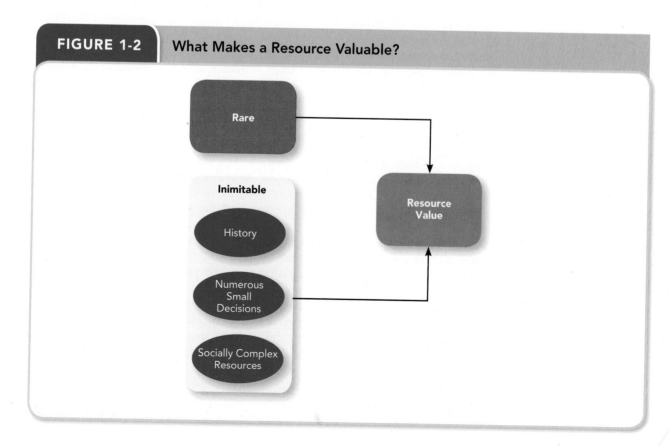

the arrival of *Diet Pepsi Lime.* Answer? About two months.[15] Big decisions can be copied; they are visible to competitors and observable by industry experts and analysts. In the case of Song, the company was able to copy one of JetBlue's signatures—a television for every seat—so that Song passengers were able to watch pay-per-view movies or play video games.[16] However, it would be more difficult to copy one of Southwest's signatures—the playful, whimsical style displayed by flight attendants and service personnel.[17] Officials from Song wouldn't have the opportunity to observe a Southwest flight attendant turning the seatbelt instructions into a comedy routine on a given day or finding a way to make an anxious toddler laugh on a particular flight. Those decisions are invisible to competitors but not to the travelers who make mental notes about their next trip.

SOCIALLY COMPLEX RESOURCES. People also create **socially complex resources**, like culture, teamwork, trust, and reputation. These resources are termed "socially complex" because it's not always clear how they came to develop, though it is clear which organizations do (and do not) possess them. An upper manager at Song could have exited a Southwest flight convinced that the company would benefit from adopting the competitor's playful and fun culture. But how exactly would that be done? A new culture can't just be implemented like a change in software systems. It springs from the social dynamics within a given firm at a given point in time.

In the case of Apple, its decision to open retail stores represents a big decision that can be copied. Microsoft recently announced plans to open its own retail stores to showcase its hardware and software products.[18] The relative success of the two chains will depend largely on the merits of their competing product lines (Mac OS X versus Windows, iPod versus Zune, iPhone versus Windows mobile devices). However, Apple can also bank on its longer history in retailing, the numerous small decisions that go on behind the scenes, and the cool and inviting culture within its stores. There's some evidence that the company understands how people can create an inimitable advantage. A recent article in *Workforce Management* included features on the top human resources executives for 20 of the most admired companies in America.[19] Interestingly, the entry for Apple's executive could only be cryptic, noting that the company "keeps its human resources executive shrouded in secrecy and refuses to respond to any questions about HR's contribution to the company's most admired status."

RESEARCH EVIDENCE

1.4

Why might firms that are good at OB tend to be more profitable?

Thus, we can build a conceptual argument for why OB might affect an organization's profitability: Good people are both rare and inimitable and therefore create a resource that is valuable for creating competitive advantage. Conceptual arguments are helpful, of course, but it would be even better if there were hard data to back them up. Fortunately, it turns out that there is a great deal of research evidence supporting the importance of OB for company performance. Several research studies have been conducted on the topic, each employing a somewhat different approach.

One study began by surveying executives from 968 publicly held firms with 100 or more employees.[20] The survey assessed so-called high performance work practices—OB policies that are widely agreed to be beneficial to firm performance. The survey included 13 questions asking about a combination of hiring, information sharing, training, performance management, and incentive practices, and each question asked what proportion of the company's workforce was involved in the practice. Table 1-2 provides some of the questions used to assess the high performance work practices (and also shows which chapter of the textbook describes each particular practice in more detail). The study also gathered the following information for each firm: average annual rate of turnover, productivity level (defined as sales per employee), market value of the firm, and corporate profitability.

TABLE 1-2	Survey Questions Designed to Assess High Performance Work Practices

SURVEY QUESTION ABOUT OB PRACTICE	COVERED IN CHAPTER:
What is the proportion of the workforce whose jobs have been subjected to a formal job analysis?	2
What is the proportion of the workforce who are administered attitude surveys on a regular basis?	4
What is the proportion of the workforce who have access to company incentive plans, profit-sharing plans, and/or gain-sharing plans?	6
What is the average number of hours of training received by a typical employee over the last 12 months?	8, 10
What is the proportion of the workforce who have access to a formal grievance procedure and/or complaint resolution system?	7
What proportion of the workforce are administered an employment test prior to hiring?	9, 10
What is the proportion of the workforce whose performance appraisals are used to determine compensation?	6

Source: M.A. Huselid, "The Impact of Human Resource Management Practices on Turnover, Productivity, and Corporate Financial Performance," *Academy Of Management Journal* 38 (1995), pp. 635–72. Copyright © 1995 Academy of Management. Reproduced with permission of Academy of Management via Copyright Clearance Center.

The results revealed that a one-unit increase in the proportion of the workforce involved in the practices was associated with an approximately 7 percent decrease in turnover, $27,000 more in sales per employee, $18,000 more in market value, and $3,800 more in profits. Put simply, better OB practices were associated with better firm performance.

Although there is no doubting the importance of turnover, productivity, market value, and profitability, another study examined an outcome that's even more fundamental: firm survival.[21] The study focused on 136 nonfinancial companies that made initial public offerings (IPOs) in 1988. Firms that undergo an IPO typically have shorter histories and need an infusion of cash to grow or introduce some new technology. Rather than conducting a survey, the authors of this study examined the prospectus filed by each firm (the Securities and Exchange Commission requires that prospectuses contain honest information, and firms can be liable for any inaccuracies that might mislead investors). The authors coded each prospectus for information that might suggest OB issues were valued. Examples of valuing OB issues included describing employees as a source of competitive advantage in strategy and mission statements, emphasizing training and continuing education, having a human resources management executive, and emphasizing full-time rather than temporary or contract employees. By 1993, 81 of the 136 firms included in the study had survived (60 percent). The key question is whether the value placed on OB predicted which did (and did not) survive. The results revealed that firms that valued OB had a 19 percent higher survival rate than firms that did not value OB.

A third study focused on *Fortune*'s "100 Best Companies to Work For" list, which has appeared annually since 1998.[22] Table 1-3 provides some highlights from the 2009 version of the list. If the 100 firms on the list really do have good OB practices, and if good OB practices really do influence firm profitability, then it follows that the 100 firms should be more profitable. To explore this premise, the study went back to the original 1998 list and found a "matching firm" for those companies that were included.[23] The matching firm consisted of the most similar company with respect to industry and size in that particular year, with the added requirement that the company had not appeared on the "100 Best" list. This process essentially created two groups of companies that differ only in terms of their inclusion in the "100 Best." The study then compared the profitability of those two groups of companies. The results revealed that the "100 Best" firms were more profitable than their peers. Indeed, the cumulative investment return for a portfolio based on the 1998 "100 Best" companies would have doubled the return for the broader market.

SO WHAT'S SO HARD?

Clearly this research evidence seems to support the conceptual argument that good people constitute a valuable resource for companies. Good OB does seem to matter in terms of company profitability. You may wonder then, "What's so hard?" Why doesn't every company prioritize the effective management of OB, devoting as much attention to it as they do accounting, finance, marketing, technology, physical assets, and so on? Some companies do a bad job when it comes to managing their people. Why is that?

TABLE 1-3	The "100 Best Companies to Work For" in 2009	
1. NetApp	24. Starbucks	65. Texas Instruments
2. Edward Jones	26. Aflac	71. Men's Wearhouse
3. Boston Consulting	32. The Container Store	72. Nordstrom
4. Google	38. Microsoft	78. Marriott
5. Wegmans	47. DreamWorks	83. eBay
6. Cisco Systems	48. Mattel	88. Publix
9. Goldman Sachs	49. Intuit	89. Herman Miller
11. Adobe Systems	51. Ernst & Young	90. FedEx
16. Qualcomm	56. KPMG	92. Four Seasons
20. SAS	58. PricewaterhouseCoopers	96. T-Mobile
22. Whole Foods	60. Scottrade	97. Accenture
23. Zappos.com	61. Deloitte	99. General Mills

Source: R. Levering and M. Moskowitz, "And the Winners Are . . ." *Fortune* (February 2, 2009), pp. 67–78.

One reason is that there is no "magic bullet" OB practice—one thing that, in and of itself, can increase profitability. Instead, the effective management of OB requires a belief that several different practices are important, along with a long-term commitment to improving those practices. This premise can be summarized with what might be called the **Rule of One-Eighth:**

> One must bear in mind that one-half of organizations won't believe the connection between how they manage their people and the profits they earn. One-half of those who do see the connection will do what many organizations have done—try to make a single change to solve their problems, not realizing that the effective management of people requires a more comprehensive and systematic approach. Of the firms that make comprehensive changes, probably only about one-half will persist with their practices long enough to actually derive economic benefits. Since one-half times one-half times one-half equals one-eighth, at best 12 percent of organizations will actually do what is required to build profits by putting people first.[24]

The integrative model of OB used to structure this book was designed with this Rule of One-Eighth in mind. Figure 1-1 suggests that high job performance depends not just on employee motivation but also on fostering high levels of satisfaction, effectively managing stress, creating a trusting climate, and committing to employee learning. Failing to do any one of those things could hinder the effectiveness of the other concepts in the model. Of course, that systemic nature reveals another reality of organizational behavior: It's often difficult to "fix" companies that struggle with OB issues. Such companies often struggle in a number of different areas and on a number of different levels. One such (fictitious) company is spotlighted in our **OB on Screen** feature, which appears in each chapter and uses well-known movies to demonstrate OB concepts.

HOW DO WE "KNOW" WHAT WE KNOW ABOUT ORGANIZATIONAL BEHAVIOR?

Now that we've described what OB is and why it's an important topic of study, we now turn to how we "know" what we know about the topic. In other words, where does the knowledge in this textbook come from? To answer this question, we must first explore how people "know" about anything. Philosophers have argued that there are several different ways of knowing things:[25]

- **Method of Experience:** People hold firmly to some belief because it is consistent with their own experience and observations.
- **Method of Intuition:** People hold firmly to some belief because it "just stands to reason"—it seems obvious or self-evident.
- **Method of Authority:** People hold firmly to some belief because some respected official, agency, or source has said it is so.
- **Method of Science:** People accept some belief because scientific studies have tended to replicate that result using a series of samples, settings, and methods.

Consider the following prediction: Providing social recognition, in the form of public shows of praise and appreciation for good behaviors, will increase the performance and commitment of work units. Perhaps you feel that you "know" this claim to be true because you yourself have always responded well to praise and recognition. Or perhaps you feel that you "know" it to be true because it seems like common sense—who wouldn't work

OB ON SCREEN

This feature is designed to illustrate OB concepts in action on the silver screen. Once you've learned about OB topics, you'll see them playing out all around you, especially in movies. This inaugural edition spotlights (what else?) *Office Space* (Dir: Mike Judge. 20th Century Fox, 1999).

OFFICE SPACE

Since I started working, every single day has been worse than the day before, so that every day you see me is the worst day of my life.

With these words, Peter Gibbons summarizes what it's like to work at Initech, the computer programming firm where he updates bank software. Peter doesn't exhibit particularly good job performance, nor is he very committed to the organization.

Why does Peter feel this way? From the perspective of our integrative model of OB, the problem starts at the top and flows down. The culture of the organization is rigid and emotionless, with management seeming to delight in pointing out mistakes (like Peter's failure to use a cover sheet on his reports). The structure of the organization somehow assigns eight different bosses to Peter (providing eight opportunities to relive the cover sheet conversation). From a leadership perspective, the evil Bill Lumbergh seems to relish the power that comes with his title but does little to improve the functioning of his unit. The result is a workforce that feels little to no motivation, because performance has no impact on the money they earn. All this is worsened by the arrival of "the two Bobs," consultants whose job it is to choose which employees to fire and which to retain.

Clearly it would take a lot of time and effort to turn Initech around. The effort would require several changes to several different practices to address several different components of our OB model. And those changes would need to be in place for a long period of time before the company could turn the corner. An uphill climb, to be sure, but Initech has one thing going for it: The Bobs are on the job!

harder after a few public pats on the back? Maybe you feel that you "know" it to be true because a respected boss from your past always extolled the virtue of public praise and recognition.

However, the methods of experience, intuition, and authority also might have led you to the opposite belief—that providing social recognition has no impact on the performance and commitment of work units. It may be that public praise has always made you uncomfortable or embarrassed, to the point that you've tried to hide especially effective behaviors to avoid being singled out by your boss. Or it may seem logical that social recognition will be viewed as "cheap talk," with employees longing for financial incentives rather than verbal compliments. Or perhaps the best boss you ever worked for never offered a single piece of social recognition in her life, yet her employees always worked their hardest on her behalf.

From a scientist's point of view, it doesn't really matter what a person's experience, intuition, or authority suggests; the prediction must be tested with data. In other words, scientists don't simply assume that their beliefs are accurate; they acknowledge that their beliefs must be tested scientifically. Scientific studies are based on the scientific method, originated by Sir Francis Bacon in the 1600s and adapted in Figure 1-3.[26] The scientific method begins with **theory,** defined as a collection of assertions—both verbal and symbolic—that specify how and why variables are related, as well as the conditions in which they should (and should not) be related.[27] More simply, a theory tells a story and supplies the familiar who, what, where, when, and why elements found in any newspaper or magazine article.[28] Theories are often summarized with theory diagrams, the "boxes and arrows" that graphically depict relationships between variables. Our integrative model of OB in Figure 1-1 represents one such diagram, and there will be many more to come in the remaining chapters of this textbook.

A scientist could build a theory explaining why social recognition might influence the performance and commitment of work units. From what sources would that theory be built?

1.5

What is the role of theory in the scientific method?

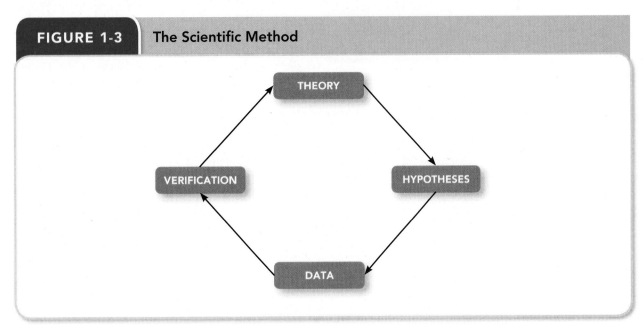

| FIGURE 1-3 | The Scientific Method |

Source: Adapted from F. Bacon, M. Silverthorne, and L. Jardine, *The New Organon* (Cambridge: Cambridge University Press, 2000).

Theories may be built from interviews with employees, or from observations where scientists take notes, keep diaries, and pore over company documents to find all the elements of a theory story.[29] Alternatively, theories may be built from research reviews, which examine findings of previous studies to look for general patterns or themes.[30] To read about a theory that was built in a noted bestseller, see our **OB at the Bookstore** feature, which appears in each chapter to showcase a well-known business book that discusses OB concepts.

OB AT THE BOOKSTORE

This feature is designed to spotlight bestselling OB books that complement the content of each chapter. Drawing a bridge from our chapters to these books lets you see how the titles at the bookstore fit together and complement the content of the course.

GOOD TO GREAT
by Jim Collins (New York: HarperCollins, 2001).

As one of my favorite professors once said, "The best students are those who never quite believe their professors." True enough. But he also said, "One ought not to reject the data merely because one does not like what the data implies."

With those words, Collins lays out the philosophy behind his examination of why some companies go from good to great in terms of their stock market performance. The book was a sequel of sorts to Collins's earlier bestseller, *Built to Last*, which examined the blueprint of a number of great companies.[31] Those companies, however, had always been great, from their founding on. How is it that a merely good company can transform itself into great?

To build a theory that could explain such transformations, Collins's research team first identified companies that had made the leap, defining good performance as 15 years of 1.25 times the market average and great performance as a subsequent 15 years of 3 times the market average. Eleven members of the *Fortune* 500 fit the criteria, including Walgreens, Wells Fargo, Nucor, Kroger, and Philip Morris. The team then identified a set of comparison companies, including 11 that never made the leap (e.g., Eckerd, Bank of America, Bethlehem Steel, A&P, R.J. Reynolds) and 6 that couldn't sustain it. The team then collected all articles published on the 28 companies over the past 50 years, coding anything that could capture what made the "good to great" set different from the rest.

It turned out that the 11 "good to great" transformations were not the product of some big decision. As Collins puts it, "There was no single defining action, no grand program, no one killer innovation, no solitary lucky break, no miracle moment." Instead, the transformations resulted from a commitment to hiring the right people—emphasizing character, work ethic, intelligence, values, and commitment—and refusing to hire when such people were unavailable. The transformations also resulted from leaders who understood their workforce—focusing the company on what it was good at and what it was passionate about. Once the right people were in place, their "numerous small decisions" created the step-by-step, action-by-action movements that eventually resulted in a transformative momentum.

Although many theories are interesting, logical, or thought provoking, many also wind up being completely wrong. After all, scientific theories once predicted that the earth was flat and the sun revolved around it. Closer to home, OB theories once argued that money was not an effective motivator and that the best way to structure jobs was to make them as simple and mundane as possible.[32] Theories must therefore be tested to verify that their predictions are accurate. As shown in Figure 1-3, the scientific method requires that theories be used to inspire **hypotheses**. Hypotheses are written predictions that specify relationships between variables. For example, a theory of social recognition could be used to inspire this hypothesis: "Social recognition behaviors on the part of managers will be positively related to the job performance and organizational commitment of their units." This hypothesis states, in black and white, the expected relationship between social recognition and unit performance.

Assume a family member owned a chain of 21 fast-food restaurants and allowed you to test this hypothesis using the restaurants. Specifically, you decided to train the managers in a subset of the restaurants about how to use social recognition as a tool to reinforce behaviors. Meanwhile, you left another subset of restaurants unchanged to represent a control group. You then tracked the total number of social recognition behaviors exhibited by managers over the next nine months by observing the managers at specific time intervals. You measured job performance by tracking drive-through times for the next nine months and used those times to reflect the minutes it takes for a customer to approach the restaurant, order food, pay, and leave. You also measured the commitment of the work unit by tracking employee retention rates over the next nine months.

So how can you tell whether your hypothesis was supported? You could analyze the data by examining the **correlation** between social recognition behaviors and drive-through times, as well as the correlation between social recognition behaviors and employee turnover. A correlation, abbreviated *r*, describes the statistical relationship between two variables. Correlations can be positive or negative and range from 0 (no statistical relationship) to ±1 (a perfect statistical relationship). Picture a spreadsheet with two columns of numbers. One column contains the total numbers of social recognition behaviors for all 21 restaurants, and the other contains the average drive-through times for those same 21 restaurants. The best way to get a feel for the correlation is to look at a scatterplot—a graph made from those two columns of numbers. Figure 1-4 presents three scatterplots, each depicting different sized correlations. The strength of the correlation can be inferred from the "compactness" of its scatterplot. Panel (a) shows a perfect 1.0 correlation; knowing the score for social recognition allows you to predict the score for drive-through times perfectly. Panel (b) shows a correlation of .50, so the trend in the data is less obvious than in Panel (a) but still easy to see with the naked eye. Finally, Panel (c) shows a correlation of .00—no statistical relationship. Understanding the correlation is important because OB questions are not "yes or no" in nature. That is, the question is not "*Does* social recognition lead to higher job performance?" but rather "*How often* does social recognition lead to higher job performance?" The correlation provides a number that expresses an answer to the "how often" question.

1.6

How are correlations interpreted?

So what is the correlation between social recognition and job performance (and between social recognition and organizational commitment)? It turns out that a study very similar to the one described was actually conducted, using a sample of 21 Burger King restaurants with 525 total employees.[33] The correlation between social recognition and job performance was .28. The restaurants that received training in social recognition averaged 44 seconds of drive-through time nine months later versus 62 seconds for the control group locations. The correlation between social recognition and retention rates was .20. The restaurants that received training in social recognition had a 16

| **FIGURE 1-4** | **Three Different Correlation Sizes** |

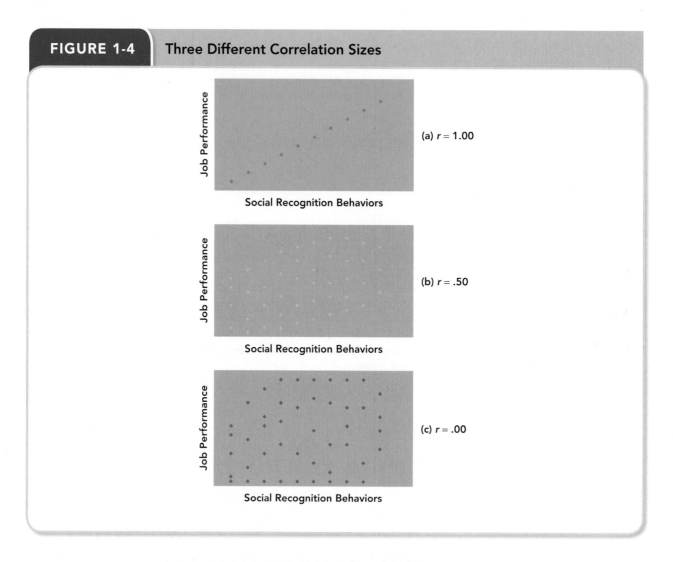

Job Performance — Social Recognition Behaviors — (a) *r* = 1.00

Job Performance — Social Recognition Behaviors — (b) *r* = .50

Job Performance — Social Recognition Behaviors — (c) *r* = .00

A study of Burger King restaurants revealed a correlation between social recognition—praise and appreciation by managers—and employees' performance and commitment. Such studies contribute to the growing body of organizational behavior knowledge.

percent better retention rate than the control group locations nine months later. The study also instituted a financial "pay-for-performance" system in a subset of the locations and found that the social recognition effects were just as strong as the financial effects.

Of course, you might wonder whether correlations of .28 or .20 are impressive or unimpressive. To understand those numbers, let's consider some context for them. Table 1-4 provides some notable correlations from other areas of science. If the correlation between height and weight is only .44, then a correlation of .28 between social recognition and job performance doesn't

TABLE 1-4	Some Notable Correlations		
CORRELATION BETWEEN . . .		*r*	**SAMPLE SIZE**
Height and weight		.44	16,948
Viagra and sexual functioning		.38	779
Ibuprofen and pain reduction		.14	8,488
Antihistamines and reduced sneezing		.11	1,023
Smoking and lung cancer within 25 years		.08	3,956
Coronary bypass surgery and 5-year survival		.08	2,649

Source: R. Hogan, "In Defense of Personality Measurement: New Wine for Old Whiners," *Human Performance* 18 (2005), pp. 331–41. Copyright © 2005 Taylor & Francis Group. Reprinted with permission.

sound too bad! In fact, a correlation of .50 is considered "strong" in organizational behavior research, given the sheer number of things that can affect how employees feel and act.[34] A .30 correlation is considered "moderate," and many studies discussed in this book will have results in this range. Finally, a .10 correlation is considered "weak" in organizational behavior research. It should be noted, however, that even "weak" correlations can be important if they predict costly behaviors such as theft or ethical violations. The .08 correlation between smoking and lung cancer within 25 years is a good example of how important small correlations can be.

Does this one study settle the debate about the value of social recognition for job performance and organizational commitment? Not really, for a variety of reasons. First, it included only 21 restaurants with 525 employees—maybe the results would have turned out differently if the study had included more locations. Second, it focused only on restaurant employees—maybe there's something unique about such employees that makes them particularly responsive to social recognition. Third, it may be that the trained locations differed from the control locations on something *other than* social recognition, and it was that "something" that was responsible for the performance differences. You may have heard the phrase, "correlation does not imply causation." It turns out that making **causal inferences**—establishing that one variable really does cause another—requires establishing three things.[35] First, that the two variables are correlated. Second, that the presumed cause precedes the presumed effect in time. Third, that no alternative explanation exists for the correlation. The third criterion is often fulfilled in experiments, where researchers have more control over the setting in which the study occurs.

The important point is that little can be learned from a single study. The best way to test a theory is to conduct many studies, each of which is as different as possible from the ones that preceded it.[36] So if you really wanted to study the effects of social recognition, you would conduct several studies using different kinds of samples, different kinds of measures, and both experimental and nonexperimental methods. After completing all of those studies, you could look back on the results and create some sort of average correlation across all of the studies. This process is what a technique called **meta-analysis** does. It takes all of the correlations found in studies of a particular relationship and calculates a weighted average (such that correlations based on studies with large samples are weighted more than correlations based on studies with small samples). It turns out that a meta-analysis has been conducted on the effects of social recognition and job performance. That analysis revealed an average correlation of .21 across studies conducted in 96 different organizations in the service industry.[37] That meta-analysis offers more compelling support for the potential benefits of social recognition than the methods of experience, intuition, or authority could have provided. Indeed, meta-analyses can form the foundation for **evidence-based management**—a perspective that argues that scientific findings should form the foundation for management education, much as they do for medical education.[38]

SUMMARY: MOVING FORWARD IN THIS BOOK

The chapters that follow will begin working through the integrative model of OB in Figure 1-1, beginning with the individual outcomes and continuing with the individual, group, and organizational mechanisms that lead to those outcomes. Each chapter begins by spotlighting a company that historically has done a good job of managing a given topic or is currently struggling with a topic. Theories relevant to that topic will be highlighted and discussed. The concepts in those theories will be demonstrated in the **OB on Screen** features to show how OB phenomena have "come to life" in film. The **OB at the Bookstore** feature will then point you to bestsellers that discuss similar concepts. In addition, the **OB Internationally** feature will describe how those concepts operate differently in different cultures and nations.

Each chapter ends with three sections. The first section provides a summarizing theory diagram that explains why some employees exhibit higher levels of a given concept than others. For example, the summarizing theory diagram for Chapter 4 will explain why some employees are more satisfied with their jobs than others. As we noted in the opening of this chapter, knowledge about *why* is critical to any employee who is trying to make sense of his or her working life or any manager who is trying to make his or her unit more effective. How often have you spent time trying to explain your own attitudes and behaviors to yourself? If you consider yourself to be an introspective person, you've probably thought about such questions quite a bit. Our **OB Assessments** feature will help you find out how reflective you really are. This feature also appears in each chapter of the textbook and allows you to gain valuable knowledge about your own personality, abilities, job attitudes, and leadership styles.

The next concluding section will describe the results of meta-analyses that summarize the relationships between that chapter's topic and both job performance and organizational commitment. Over time, you'll gain a feel for which of the topics in Figure 1-1 have strong, moderate, or weak relationships with these outcomes. This knowledge will help you recognize how everything in OB fits together and what the most valuable tools are for improving performance and commitment in the workplace. As you will discover, some of the topics in OB have a greater impact on how well employees perform their jobs, whereas others have a greater impact on how long employees remain with their organizations. Finally, the third concluding section will describe how the content of that chapter can be applied, at a specific level, in an actual organization. For example, the motivation chapter concludes with a section describing how compensation practices can be used to maximize employee effort. If you're currently working, we hope that these concluding sections will help you see how the concepts you're reading about can be used to improve your own organizations. Even if you're not working, these application sections will give you a glimpse into how you will experience OB concepts once you begin your working life.

OB ASSESSMENTS

This feature is designed to illustrate how OB concepts actually get measured in practice. In many cases, these OB assessments will provide you with potentially valuable insights into your own attitudes, skills, and personality. The OB assessments that you'll see in each chapter consist of multiple survey items. Two concepts are critical when evaluating how good the OB assessments are: *reliability* and *validity*. Reliability is defined as the degree to which the survey items are free from random error. If survey items are reliable, then similar items will yield similar answers. Validity is defined as the degree to which the survey items seem to assess what they are meant to assess. If survey items are valid, then experts on the subject will agree that the items seem appropriate.

INTROSPECTION

How introspective are you? This assessment is designed to measure introspection—sometimes termed "private self-consciousness"—which is the tendency to direct attention inward to better understand your attitudes and behaviors. Answer each question using the response scale provided. Then subtract your answers to the boldfaced questions from 4, with the difference being your new answers for those questions. For example, if your original answer for question 5 was "3," your new answer is 1 (4 – 3). Then sum your answers for the ten questions. (For more assessments relevant to this chapter, please visit the Online Learning Center at www.mhhe.com/colquitt).

0	1	2	3	4
EXTREMELY UNCHARACTERISTIC OF ME	SOMEWHAT UNCHARACTERISTIC OF ME	NEUTRAL	SOMEWHAT CHARACTERISTIC OF ME	EXTREMELY CHARACTERISTIC OF ME

1. I'm always trying to figure myself out. _____
2. **Generally, I'm not very aware of myself.** _____
3. I reflect about myself a lot. _____
4. I'm often the subject of my own daydreams. _____
5. **I never scrutinize myself.** _____
6. I'm generally attentive to my inner feelings. _____
7. I'm constantly examining my motives. _____
8. I sometimes have the feeling that I'm off somewhere watching myself. _____
9. I'm alert to changes in my mood. _____
10. I'm aware of the way my mind works when I work through a problem. _____

SCORING AND INTERPRETATION

If your scores sum up to 26 or above, you do a lot of introspection and are highly self-aware. You may find that many of the theories discussed in this textbook will help you better understand your attitudes and feelings about working life.

TAKEAWAYS

1.1 Organizational behavior is a field of study devoted to understanding and explaining the attitudes and behaviors of individuals and groups in organizations. More simply, it focuses on *why* individuals and groups in organizations act the way they do.

1.2 The two primary outcomes in organizational behavior are job performance and organizational commitment.

1.3 A number of factors affect performance and commitment, including individual mechanisms (job satisfaction; stress; motivation; trust, justice, and ethics; learning and decision making), individual characteristics (personality and cultural values; ability), group mechanisms (team characteristics and diversity; team processes and communication; leader power and negotiation; leader styles and behaviors), and organizational mechanisms (organizational structure, organizational culture).

1.4 The effective management of organizational behavior can help a company become more profitable because good people are a valuable resource. Not only are good people rare, but they are also hard to imitate. They create a history that cannot be bought or copied, they make numerous small decisions that cannot be observed by competitors, and they create socially complex resources such as culture, teamwork, trust, and reputation.

1.5 A theory is a collection of assertions, both verbal and symbolic, that specifies how and why variables are related, as well as the conditions in which they should (and should not) be related. Theories about organizational behavior are built from a combination of interviews, observation, research reviews, and reflection. Theories form the beginning point for the scientific method and inspire hypotheses that can be tested with data.

1.6 A correlation is a statistic that expresses the strength of a relationship between two variables (ranging from 0 to ± 1). In OB research, a .50 correlation is considered "strong," a .30 correlation is considered "moderate," and a .10 correlation is considered "weak."

KEY TERMS

- Organizational behavior   *p. 7*
- Human resource management   *p. 7*
- Strategic management   *p. 8*
- Resource-based view   *p. 12*
- Inimitable   *p. 13*
- History   *p. 13*
- Numerous small decisions   *p. 13*
- Socially complex resources   *p. 14*
- Rule of one-eighth   *p. 17*
- Method of experience   *p. 17*
- Method of intuition   *p. 17*
- Method of authority   *p. 17*
- Method of science   *p. 17*
- Theory   *p. 19*
- Hypotheses   *p. 21*
- Correlation   *p. 21*
- Causal inference   *p. 23*
- Meta-analysis   *p. 23*
- Evidence-based management   *p. 24*

DISCUSSION QUESTIONS

1.1 Can you think of other retail businesses that, like the Apple Store, seem to do an effective job with customer service? If you managed a franchise for one of those businesses, which organizational behavior topics would be most important to maintaining that high service level?

1.2 Think again about the worst coworker you've ever had—the one who did some of the things listed in Table 1-1. Think about what that coworker's boss did (or didn't do) to try to improve his or her behavior. What did the boss do well or poorly? What would you have done differently, and which organizational behavior topics would have been most relevant?

1.3 Which of the individual mechanisms in Figure 1-1 (job satisfaction; stress; motivation; trust, justice, and ethics; learning and decision making) seems to drive your performance and commitment the most? Do you think you're unique in that regard, or do you think most people would answer that way?

1.4 Create a list of the most successful companies that you can think of. What do these companies have that others don't? Are the things that those companies possess rare and inimitable (see Figure 1-2)? What makes those things difficult to copy?

1.5 Think of something that you "know" to be true based on the method of experience, the method of intuition, or the method of authority. Could you test your knowledge using the method of science? How would you do it?

CASE: APPLE

Apple's hiring strategy for its retail stores was summarized this way by a journalist who worked part-time at one of the locations: "The company was not looking for great sales-people using sophisticated technology, as one would imagine it easily could; instead it isolates true enthusiasts and true believers in Apple products, of which there are many. . . . As workers all we had to bring to the table was a passion for Apple products; the company supplied the knowledge we needed to teach, share, and sell to customers."[39] Other than that singular focus, the hiring procedures at the Apple Store are fairly typical. Applicants apply online by answering a few questions, pasting in their resume, and selecting the jobs and locations in which they're interested. This process may need to be repeated multiple times before the applicant is contacted by a store. That contact may then lead to one or more face-to-face interviews, perhaps at the store itself or at a local coffee shop.

Two recent decisions, however, signal a departure from Apple's hiring and overall retail philosophies. On the hiring front, Apple recruiters have been spotted handing out black cards to retail employees in other organizations.[40] The front of the card bears the Apple logo and reads, "You're amazing. We should talk." The back of the card reads, "Your customer service just now was exceptional. I work for the Apple Store, and you're exactly the kind of person we'd like to talk to. If you're happy where you are, I'll never ask you to leave. But if you're thinking about a change, give me a call. This could be the start of something great." The card also includes a URL for more information. With respect to its overall retail philosophy, Apple entered into an agreement with Best Buy to create a "store within a store" at select locations.[41] Although it remains a pilot program,

Apple is taking steps to prevent the bad experiences that drove it to launch its own retail stores in the first place. First, Apple is setting up its own space within the Best Buys, mimicking the look and feel of an Apple Store. Second, Apple is sending consultants to the Best Buys to train employees, so that they know almost as much about Macs as they do Hewlett-Packards, Acers, and other PCs.

1.1   Is there something unethical about Apple's "black card strategy," or does it merely represent good, hard-nosed business?

1.2   Should Apple offer different training content for employees recruited through the black card strategy? How might their job satisfaction differ from employees who are recruited in more traditional ways?

1.3   How does the motivation of a Best Buy employee selling a Mac differ from the motivation of an Apple Store employee selling a Mac? Is there anything Apple can do to address such differences?

EXERCISE: IS OB COMMON SENSE?

The purpose of this exercise is to take some of the topics covered in this textbook and examine whether improving them is "just common sense." This exercise uses groups, so your instructor will either assign you to a group or ask you to create your own. The exercise has the following steps:

1.1   Consider the theory diagram shown below. It explains why two "independent variables" (the quality of a movie's script and the fame of its stars) affect a "dependent variable" (how much the movie makes at the box office).

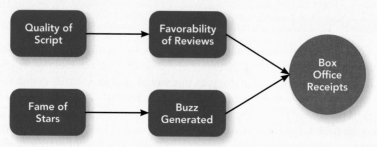

1.2   Now build your own theory diagram about organizational behavior. In your groups, choose one of the following four topics to use as your dependent variable:

- *Job Satisfaction:* The pleasurable emotions felt when performing job tasks.
- *Strain:* The headaches, fatigue, or burnout resulting from workplace stress.
- *Motivation:* The intensity and persistence of job-related effort.
- *Trust in Supervisor:* The willingness to allow a supervisor to have significant influence over key job issues.

Using a transparency, laptop, or chalkboard, build a theory diagram that summarizes the factors that affect your chosen dependent variable. To be as comprehensive as possible, try to include at least four independent variables. Keep your books closed! You should build your diagrams using only your own experience and intuition.

1.3   Each group should present its theory diagram to the class. Do the predicted relationships make sense? Should anything be dropped? Should anything be added?

1.4   Now compare the theory diagram you created with the diagrams in the textbook (Figure 4-7 for Job Satisfaction, Figure 5-3 for Strain, Figure 6-7 for Motivation, and Figure 7-7 for Trust in Supervisor). How does your diagram compare to the textbook's diagrams (search the boldfaced key terms for any jargon that you don't understand)? Did you leave out some important independent variables or suggest some variables that have not been supported by the academic research summarized in the chapters? If so, it shows that OB is more than just common sense.

ENDNOTES

1.1   Edwards, C. "Commentary: Sorry, Steve: Here's Why Apple Stores Won't Work." *Business Week*, May 21, 2001, http://www.businessweek.com/magazine/content/01_21/b3733059.htm (April 20, 2009).

1.2   Useem, J. "Apple: America's Best Retailer." *Fortune*, March 8, 2007, http://money.cnn.com/magazines/fortune/fortune_archive/2007/03/19/8402321 (April 20, 2009).

1.3   Frankel, A. *Punching In*. New York: HarperCollins, 2007.

1.4   Useem, "Apple: American's Best Retailer."

1.5   Frankel, *Punching In*.

1.6   "The Stores." *ifoAppleStore*. http://www.ifoapplestore.com/the_stores.html (April 20, 2009).

1.7   Kiley, D. "Hyundai Still Gets No Respect." *BusinessWeek*, May 21, 2007, pp. 68–70.

1.8   Ihlwan, M., and C. Dawson. "Building a 'Camry Fighter': Can Hyundai Transform Itself into One of the World's Top Auto Makers?" *BusinessWeek*, September 6, 2004, http://www.businessweek.com/magazine/content/04_36/b3898072.htm (April 21, 2009).

1.9   ConsumerReports.org. "Top Picks." http://www.consumerreports.org/cro/cars/new-cars/cr-recommended/top-picks/overview/top-picks-ov.htm (April 21, 2009).

1.10   Ihlwan, M.; L. Armstrong; and M. Eldam. "Kissing Clunkers Goodbye." *BusinessWeek*, May 17, 2004, http://www.businessweek.com/magazine/content/04_20/b3883054.htm (April 21, 2009).

1.11   Friedman, T.L. *The World is Flat*. New York: Farrar, Straus, and Giroux, 2002.

1.12   Aguinis, H., and C.A. Henle. "The Search for Universals in Cross-Cultural Organizational Behavior." In *Organizational Behavior: The State of the Science*, ed. J. Greenberg. Mahwah, NJ: Lawrence Erlbaum Associates, 2003, pp. 373–411.

1.13   Barney, J.B. "Looking Inside for Competitive Advantage." In *Strategic Human Resource Management*, ed. R.S. Schuler and S.E. Jackson. Malden, MA: Blackwell, 1999, pp. 128–41.

1.14   Mokoto, R. "Designing an Identity to Make a Brand Fly." *The New York Times*, November 6, 2003, http://www.nytimes.com/2003/11/06/garden/designing-an-identity-to-make-a-brand-fly.html (April 20, 2009).

1.15   Hu, C. "Lime Coke Dashes to Launch." *The Grocer,* March 5, 2005, http://www.highbeam.com/doc/1G1-130646812.html (April 21, 2009).

1.16   Mokoto, "Designing."

1.17   Serwer, A. "Southwest Airlines: The Hottest Thing in the Sky." *Fortune,* March 8, 2004, http://money.cnn.com/magazines/fortune/fortune_archive/2004/03/08/363700/index.htm (April 20, 2009).

1.18   Romano, B.J. "Microsoft to Open Own Retail Stores." *The Seattle Times,* February 13, 2009, http://seattletimes.nwsource.com/html/microsoft/2008739481_microsoft13.html (April 20, 2009).

1.19   Hansen, F. "Admirable Qualities." *Workforce Management,* June 23, 2008, pp. 25–32.

1.20   Huselid, M.A. "The Impact of Human Resource Management Practice on Turnover, Productivity, and Corporate Financial Performance." *Academy of Management Journal* 38 (1995), pp. 635–72.

1.21   Welbourne, T.M., and A.O. Andrews. "Predicting the Performance of Initial Public Offerings: Should Human Resource Management Be in the Equation?" *Academy of Management Journal* 39 (1996), pp. 891–919.

1.22   Levering, R., and M. Moskowitz. "And the Winners Are . . ." *Fortune,* February 2, 2009, pp. 67–78.

1.23   Fulmer, I.S.; B. Gerhart; and K.S. Scott. "Are the 100 Best Better? An Empirical Investigation of the Relationship Between Being a 'Great Place to Work' and Firm Performance." *Personnel Psychology* 56 (2003), pp. 965–93.

1.24   Pfeffer, J., and J.F. Veiga. "Putting People First for Organizational Success." *Academy of Management Executive* 13 (1999), pp. 37–48.

1.25   Kerlinger, F.N., and H.B. Lee. *Foundations of Behavioral Research.* Fort Worth, TX: Harcourt, 2000.

1.26   Bacon, F.; M. Silverthorne; and L. Jardine. *The New Organon.* Cambridge: Cambridge University Press, 2000.

1.27   Campbell, J.P. "The Role of Theory in Industrial and Organizational Psychology." In *Handbook of Industrial and Organizational Psychology,* Vol. 1, eds. M.D. Dunnette and L.M. Hough. Palo Alto, CA: Consulting Psychologists Press, 1990, pp. 39–74.

1.28   Whetten, D.A. "What Constitutes a Theoretical Contribution?" *Academy of Management Review* 14 (1989), pp. 490–95.

1.29   Locke, K. "The Grounded Theory Approach to Qualitative Research." In *Measuring and Analyzing Behavior in Organizations,* eds. F. Drasgow and N. Schmitt. San Francisco, CA: Jossey-Bass, 2002, pp. 17–43.

1.30   Locke, E.A., and G.P. Latham. "What Should We Do About Motivation Theory? Six Recommendations for the Twenty-First Century." *Academy of Management Review* 29 (2004), 388–403.

1.31   Collins, J., and J.I. Porras. *Built to Last.* New York: HarperCollins, 1994.

1.32   Herzberg, F.; B. Mausner; and B.B. Snyderman. *The Motivation to Work.* New York: John Wiley & Sons, 1959; Taylor, F. W. *The Principles of Scientific Management.* New York: Harper & Row, 1911.

1.33   Peterson, S.J., and F. Luthans. "The Impact of Financial and Nonfinancial Incentives on

Business-Unit Outcomes over Time." *Journal of Applied Psychology* 91 (2006), pp. 156–65.

1.34 Cohen, J.; P. Cohen; S.G. West; and L.S. Aiken (2003). *Applied Multiple Regression/Correlation Analysis for the Behavioral Sciences*. Mahwah, NJ: Erlbaum, 2003.

1.35 Shadish, W.R.; T.D. Cook; and D.T. Campbell. *Experimental and Quasi-Experimental Designs for Generalized Causal Inference*. Boston, MA: Houghton-Mifflin, 2002.

1.36 Ibid.

1.37 Stajkovic, A.D., and F. Luthans. "A Meta-Analysis of the Effects of Organizational Behavior Modification on Task Performance, 1975–1995." *Academy of*

Management Journal 40 (1997), pp. 1122–49.

1.38 Rousseau, D.M. "Is There Such a Thing as Evidence-Based Management?" *Academy of Management Review* 31 (2006), pp. 256–69.

1.39 Frankel, *Punching In*.

1.40 "Apple Recruiters Tempt Exemplary Employees." *ifoAppleStore*, June 5, 2008, http://www.ifoapplestore.com/db/2008/06/05/apple-recruiters-tempt-exemplary-employees/ (April 20, 2009).

1.41 Meyer, J. "Best Buy and Apple Together Again." *Apple Matters*, June 27, 2006, http://www.applematters.com/article/best-buy-and-apple-together-again (April 20, 2009).

chapter 2

Job Performance

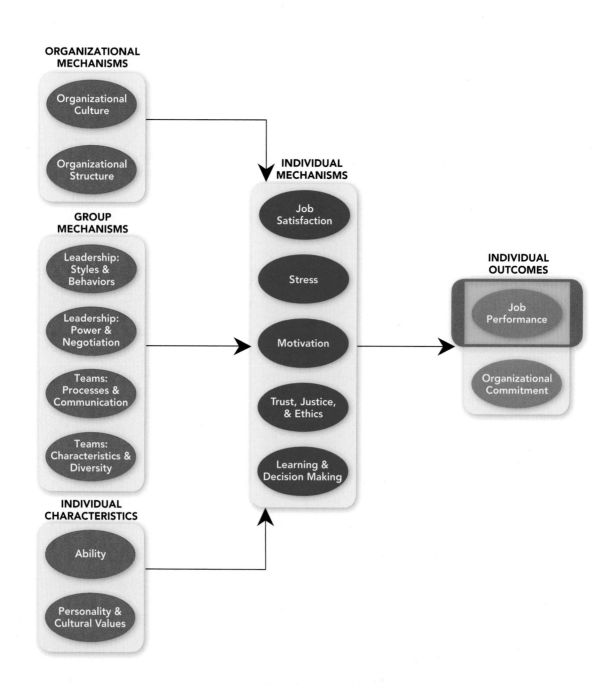

ORGANIZATIONAL MECHANISMS
- Organizational Culture
- Organizational Structure

GROUP MECHANISMS
- Leadership: Styles & Behaviors
- Leadership: Power & Negotiation
- Teams: Processes & Communication
- Teams: Characteristics & Diversity

INDIVIDUAL CHARACTERISTICS
- Ability
- Personality & Cultural Values

INDIVIDUAL MECHANISMS
- Job Satisfaction
- Stress
- Motivation
- Trust, Justice, & Ethics
- Learning & Decision Making

INDIVIDUAL OUTCOMES
- Job Performance
- Organizational Commitment

✓ LEARNING GOALS

After reading this chapter, you should be able to answer the following questions:

2.1 What is job performance?

2.2 What is task performance?

2.3 How do organizations identify the behaviors that underlie task performance?

2.4 What is citizenship behavior?

2.5 What is counterproductive behavior?

2.6 What workplace trends are affecting job performance in today's organizations?

2.7 How can organizations use job performance information to manage employee performance?

BEST BUY

The next time you need to buy something electronic—perhaps a television, computer, cell phone, or GPS, or maybe a Blu-Ray disk or game for your Wii—chances are you'll consider shopping at Best Buy. The store with the blue and yellow logo is the world's largest consumer electronics retailer, with more than 1,400 stores, 150,00 employees, and annual revenues of more than $40 billion. Best Buy continues to grow in the United States and abroad, in both number of stores and market share, and has performed at better than expected levels, even during the economic downturn.[1] How has Best Buy become so successful, and why does it continue to grow in a rough competitive environment?

One potential reason is that Best Buy recognizes that its employees are a key driver of corporate performance. The company has instituted several innovative management practices, the most unique of which focuses on the 4,000 employees at its corporate headquarters in Richfield, Minnesota. This management practice, called the "Results Only Work Environment," or ROWE,[2] places responsibility for managing the performance of work on the employee who's assigned to do that work. Rather than having to spend regular hours at work in an office, employees can come and go as they please without permission. Their job performance is evaluated on the basis of whether the necessary results are achieved, not whether they've put in "face-time" at the office.[3] Best Buy believes that giving employees control over how they manage their work will allow them to work when and where they're most productive.[4]

So far, the employees working under ROWE appear to be more productive and more committed to the firm.[5] Indeed, ROWE has worked so well at corporate headquarters that the company is making plans to expand it to its retail stores.[6] It's not clear how the scheduling flexibility offered by ROWE could apply to an environment where effective performance requires being responsive to customer needs at a given moment. Other questions raised by ROWE apply no matter where it's implemented. For example, let's say you were a manager of two Best Buy employees who achieved the same level of "bottom-line" results. One of those employees regularly helps coworkers with important tasks, makes suggestions that improve working conditions, and refrains from wasting company resources. The other employee ignores coworkers who need help, never volunteers ideas or shares important information, and regularly abuses and wastes the company's property and resources. Clearly you would value the former employee more than the latter, but they would wind up looking similar under the ROWE system. Thus, although there appear to be benefits from ROWE at Best Buy's headquarters, only time will tell if the system works over the long term in a wider variety of work settings.

JOB PERFORMANCE

We begin our journey through the integrative model of organizational behavior with job performance. Why begin with job performance? Because understanding one's own performance is a critical concern for any employee, and understanding the performance of employees in one's unit is a critical concern for any manager. Consider for a moment the job performance of your university's football coach. If you were the university's athletic director, you might gauge the coach's performance by paying attention to various behaviors. How much time does the coach spend on the road during recruiting season? How effective are the coach's practices? Are his offensive and defensive systems well designed, and is his play calling during games appropriate? You might also gauge some other behaviors that fall outside the strict domain of football. Does the coach run a clean program? Do his players graduate on time? Does he represent the university well during interviews with the media?

Of course, as your university's athletic director, you might be tempted to ask a simpler question: Is the coach a winner? After all, fans and boosters may not care how good the coach is at the previously listed behaviors if the team fails to make it to a prestigious bowl game. Moreover, the coach's performance in terms of wins and losses has important implications for the university because it affects ticket sales, bowl revenues, licensing fees, and booster donations. Still, is every unsuccessful season the coach's fault? What if the coach develops a well-conceived game plan but the players repeatedly make mistakes at key times in the game? What if the team experiences a rash of injuries or inherits a schedule that turns out to be much tougher than originally thought? What if one or two games are decided at the last moment and influenced by fluke plays or bad calls by the officials?

This example illustrates one dilemma when examining job performance. Is performance a set of behaviors that a person does (or does not) perform, or is performance the end result of those behaviors? You might be tempted to believe that it's more appropriate to define performance in terms of results rather than behaviors, because results seem more "objective" and are more connected to the central concern of managers—"the bottom line." For example, the job performance of salespeople is often measured by the amount of sales revenue generated by each person over some time span (e.g., a month, a quarter, a year). For the most part, this logic makes perfect sense: Salespeople are hired by organizations to generate sales, and so those who meet or exceed sales goals are worth more to the organization and should be considered high performers. It's very easy to appreciate how the sales revenue from each salesperson might be added up and used as an indicator of a business's financial performance.

However, as sensible as this logic seems, using results to indicate job performance creates potential problems. First, as we mentioned in our overview of Best Buy's management practices, employees contribute to their organization in ways that go beyond bottom-line results, and so evaluating an employee's performance based on results alone might give you an inaccurate picture of which employees are worth more to the organization. Second, results are often influenced by factors that are beyond the employee's control—product quality, competition, equipment, technology, budget constraints, coworkers, and supervision, just to name a few. Third, even if these uncontrollable factors are less relevant in a given situation, there's another problem with a results-based view of job performance: results don't tell you how to reverse a "bad year." That is, performance feedback based on results does not provide people with the information they need to improve their behavior. Given that OB as a field of study aims to understand, predict, and improve behavior, we refer to job performance as behavior. We use the term "results" or "job performance results" to describe the outcomes associated with those behaviors.

So what types of employee behaviors constitute job performance? To understand this question, consider that **job performance** is formally defined as the value of the set of employee behaviors that contribute, either positively or negatively, to organizational goal accomplishment.[7] This definition of job performance includes behaviors that are within the control of employees, but it places a boundary on which behaviors are (and are not) relevant to job performance. For example, going to get a bottle of Orange *Gatorade* (sorry—we

2.1

What is job performance?

meant to say *G)* from a vending machine during a break is not usually relevant (in either a positive or negative sense) to organizational goal accomplishment. That behavior is therefore not relevant to job performance. However, taking that bottle of Orange *G* and pouring it all over one of the company's customers is relevant (in a negative sense) to organizational goal accomplishment. That behavior is therefore relevant to job performance.

WHAT DOES IT MEAN TO BE A "GOOD PERFORMER"?

Our definition of job performance raises a number of important questions. Specifically, you might be wondering which employee behaviors fall under the umbrella heading of "job performance." In other words, what exactly do you have to *do* to be a "good performer"? We could probably spend an entire chapter just listing various behaviors that are relevant to job performance. However, those behaviors generally fit into three broad categories.[8] Two categories are task performance and citizenship behavior, both of which contribute positively to the organization. The third category is counterproductive behavior, which contributes negatively to the organization. The sections that follow describe these broad categories of job performance in greater detail.

TASK PERFORMANCE

Task performance includes employee behaviors that are directly involved in the transformation of organizational resources into the goods or services that the organization produces.[9] If you read a description of a job in an employment ad online, that description will focus on task performance behaviors—the tasks, duties, and responsibilities that are a core part of the job. Put differently, task performance is the set of explicit obligations that an employee must fulfill to receive compensation and continued employment. For a flight attendant, task performance includes announcing and demonstrating safety and emergency procedures and distributing food and beverages to passengers. For a firefighter, task performance includes searching burning buildings to locate fire victims and operating equipment to put out fires. For an accountant, task performance involves preparing, examining, and analyzing accounting records for accuracy and completeness. Finally, for an advertising executive, task performance includes developing advertising campaigns and preparing and delivering presentations to clients.[10]

2.2

What is task performance?

Although the specific activities that constitute task performance differ widely from one job to another, task performance also can be understood in terms of more general categories. One way of categorizing task performance is to consider the extent to which the context of the job is routine, changing, or requires a novel or unique solution. **Routine task performance** involves well-known responses to demands that occur in a normal, routine, or otherwise predictable way. In these cases, employees tend to behave in more or less habitual or programmed ways that vary little from one instance to another.[11] As an example of a routine task activity, you may recall watching an expressionless flight attendant robotically demonstrate how to insert the seatbelt tongue into the seatbelt buckle before your flight takes off. Seatbelts haven't really changed since . . . oh . . . 1920, so the instructions to passengers tend to be conveyed the same way, over and over again.

In contrast, **adaptive task performance**, or more commonly "adaptability," involves employee responses to task demands that are novel, unusual, or, at the very least, unpredictable.[12] For example, on August 2, 2005, Air France Flight 358, carrying 297 passengers and 12 crew members from Paris, France, to Toronto, Canada, skidded off the runway on landing and into a ravine. Amid smoke and flames, the flight attendants quickly responded to the emergency and assisted three-quarters of the 297 passengers safely off the plane within 52 seconds, before the emergency response team arrived. One minute later, the remaining passengers and 12 crew members were out safely.[13] From this example, you can see that flight attendants' task performance shifted from activities such as providing safety demonstrations and handing out beverages to performing emergency procedures to save passengers' lives. Although flight attendants receive training so they can handle emergency situations such as this one, executing these behaviors effectively in the context of an actual emergency differs fundamentally from anything experienced previously. Such adaptive behaviors are becoming increasingly important as globalization, technological advances, and knowledge-based work increase the pace of change in the workplace.[14] Table 2-1 provides a number of examples of adaptability, examples that are relevant to a number of jobs in today's economy.[15]

Finally, **creative task performance** is the degree to which individuals develop ideas or physical outcomes that are both novel and useful.[16] The necessity of including both novelty and usefulness in the definition of creativity can be illustrated with the following example of what effective performance for a swimsuit designer involves. Consider first the case of a swimsuit designer who suggests in a meeting that next season's line of swimsuits should be made entirely out of chrome-plated steel. Although this idea might be very novel, for many reasons it's not likely to be very useful. Indeed, someone who offered an idea like this would likely be considered silly rather than creative. Another swimsuit designer suggests in the meeting that swimsuits for next season should be made out of materials that are attractive and comfortable. Although under some circumstances such an idea might be useful, the idea is not novel because attractiveness and comfort are generally accepted design elements for swimsuits. Someone who offered an idea like this might be appreciated for offering input, but no one would consider this individual's performance to be particularly creative. Finally, a third designer for this swimsuit manufacturer suggests that perhaps a two-piece design would be preferred for women, rather than a more traditional one-piece design. Although such an idea would not be considered creative today, it certainly was in 1946 when, in separate but nearly simultaneous efforts, Jacques Heim and Louis Reard introduced the bikini.[17]

Although you might be tempted to believe that creative task performance is only relevant to jobs such as artist and inventor, its emphasis has been increasing across a wide variety of jobs. Indeed, more than half the total wages and salary in the United States are paid to employees who need to be creative as part of their jobs, and as a consequence, some have argued that we are at the "dawn of the creative age."[18] This increase in the value of creative performance can be explained by the rapid technological change and intense competition that mark today's business landscape. In this context, employee creativity is necessary to spark the types of innovations that enable organizations to stay ahead of their competition.

Now that we've given you a general understanding of task performance behaviors, you might be wondering how organizations identify the sets of behaviors that represent "task performance" for different jobs. Many organizations identify task performance behaviors by conducting a **job analysis**. Although there are many different ways to conduct a job analysis, most boil down to three steps. First, a list of the activities involved in a job is generated. This list generally results from data from several sources, including observations, surveys, and interviews of employees. Second, each activity on this list is rated by "subject matter experts," according to things like the importance and frequency of the activity. Subject matter experts generally have experience performing the job or managing the job and therefore are in a position to judge the importance of specific activities to the organization. Third, the activities that are rated highly in terms of their importance and

2.3

How do organizations identify the behaviors that underlie task performance?

TABLE 2-1	Behaviors Involved in Adaptability

BEHAVIORS	SPECIFIC EXAMPLES
Handling emergencies or crisis situations	Quickly analyzing options for dealing with danger or crises and their implications; making split-second decisions based on clear and focused thinking
Handling work stress	Remaining composed and cool when faced with difficult circumstances or a highly demanding workload or schedule; acting as a calming and settling influence to whom others can look for guidance
Solving problems creatively	Turning problems upside-down and inside-out to find fresh new approaches; integrating seemingly unrelated information and developing creative solutions
Dealing with uncertain and unpredictable work situations	Readily and easily changing gears in response to unpredictable or unexpected events and circumstances; effectively adjusting plans, goals, actions, or priorities to deal with changing situations
Learning work tasks, technologies, and work situations	Quickly and proficiently learning new methods or how to perform previously unlearned tasks; anticipating change in the work demands and searching for and participating in assignments or training to prepare for these changes
Demonstrating interpersonal adaptability	Being flexible and open-minded when dealing with others; listening to and considering others' viewpoints and opinions and altering own opinion when it's appropriate to do so
Demonstrating cultural adaptability	Willingly adjusting behavior or appearance as necessary to comply with or show respect for others' values and customs; understanding the implications of one's actions and adjusting approach to maintain positive relationships with other groups, organizations, or cultures

Source: E.E. Pulakos, S. Arad, M.A. Donovan, and K.E. Plamondon, "Adaptability in the Workplace: Development of a Taxonomy of Adaptive Performance," *Journal of Applied Psychology* 85 (2000), pp. 612–24. Copyright © 2000 by the American Psychological Association. Adapted with permission. No further reproduction or distribution is permitted without permission from the American Psychological Association.

frequency are retained and used to define task performance. Those retained behaviors then find their way into training programs as learning objectives and into performance evaluation systems as measures to evaluate task performance.

As an example, to determine training objectives for production workers, Toyota uses a highly detailed job analysis process to identify important tasks as well as the behaviors necessary to effectively complete those tasks.[19] The core job tasks involved in the job of a bumper-molding operator, for example, include "routine core tasks," "machine tending," and "quality," and each of these tasks further consists of several more detailed steps. For example, routine core tasks include de-molding, trimming, spray-molding, and sanding. Each of these tasks can be broken down further into more detailed steps, and

Toyota production workers assemble vehicles using a highly standardized and efficient set of tasks.

in turn, the specific behaviors involved in each step become the focus of the training. For example, to de-mold the left side of the bumper, the worker must "use left thumb to push along edge of bumper," "place pressure in the crease of thumb," "push toward left side away from mold," and "grasp top edge when bumper is released." Although this level of detail might seem like an awful lot of analysis for what one might imagine to be a relatively straightforward job, Toyota competes on the basis of quality and cost, and its success in selling millions of Camrys, Corollas, and Tacomas each year has been attributed to its ability to train production workers to follow the standardized and efficient procedures.[20]

Men's Wearhouse, the Houston-based retailer, provides another good example of an organization that uses task performance information to manage its employees.[21] The company first gathers information about the employee's on-the-job behaviors, such as those included in Table 2-2 for the job of wardrobe consultant. After the information is gathered, senior managers provide feedback and coaching to the employee about which types of behaviors he or she needs to change to improve. The feedback is framed as constructive criticism meant to improve an employee's behavior. Put yourself in the place of a Men's Wearhouse wardrobe consultant for a moment. Wouldn't you rather have your performance evaluated on the basis of the behaviors in Table 2-2 rather than some overall index of sales? After all, those behaviors are completely within your control, and the feedback you receive from your boss will be more informative than the simple directive to "sell more suits next year than you did this year."

If organizations find it impractical to use job analysis to identify the set of behaviors needed to define task performance, they can turn to a database the government has created to help with that important activity. The **Occupational Information Network** (or O*NET) is an online database that includes, among other things, the characteristics of most jobs in terms of tasks, behaviors, and the required knowledge, skills, and abilities (http://online.onetcenter.org).[22] Figure 2-1 shows the O*NET output for a flight attendant's position, including many of the tasks discussed previously in this chapter. Of course, O*NET represents only a first step in figuring out the important tasks for a given job. Many organizations ask their employees to perform tasks that their competitors do not so their workforce performs in a unique and valuable way. O*NET cannot capture those sorts of unique task requirements—the "numerous small decisions" that separate the most effective organizations from their competitors.

For example, the authors of a book entitled *Nuts* identify "fun" as one of the dominant values of Southwest Airlines.[23] Southwest believes that people are willing to work more productively and creatively in an environment that includes humor and laughter. Consistent with this belief, flight attendant task performance at Southwest includes not only generic flight attendant activities, such as those identified by O*NET, but also activities that reflect

TABLE 2-2	Performance Review Form for a Wardrobe Consultant at Men's Wearhouse

IMPORTANT TASK BEHAVIORS

Greets, interviews, and tapes all customers properly.

Participates in team selling.

Is familiar with merchandise carried at local competitors.

Ensures proper alteration revenue collection.

Treats customers in a warm and caring manner.

Utilizes tailoring staff for fittings whenever possible.

Involves management in all customer problems.

Waits on all customers, without prejudging based on attire, age, or gender.

Contributes to store maintenance and stock work.

Arrives at work at the appointed time and is ready to begin immediately.

Dresses and grooms to the standards set by TMW.

Source: Reprinted by permission of Harvard Business School Publishing. Exhibit from *Hidden Value: How Great Companies Achieve Extraordinary Results with Ordinary People* by C.A. O'Reilly III and J. Pfeffer, 2000. Copyright © 2000 by the Harvard Business School Publishing Corporation; all rights reserved.

a sense of humor and playfulness. Effective flight attendants at Southwest tell jokes over the intercom such as, "We'll be dimming the lights in the cabin . . . pushing the light-bulb button will turn your reading light on. However, pushing the flight attendant button will not turn your flight attendant on."[24] Thus, though O*NET may be a good place to start, the task information from the database should be supplemented with information regarding behaviors that support the organization's values and strategy.

Before concluding our section on task performance, it's important to note that task performance behaviors are not simply performed or not performed. Although poor performers often fail to complete required behaviors, it's just as true that the best performers often exceed all expectations for those behaviors. In fact, you can probably think of examples of

The pilot of Flight 1549 displayed exceptional performance and saved the lives of his passengers and crew.

employees who have engaged in task performance that's truly extraordinary. As an example, consider the case of Chesley B. Sullenberger, the pilot of US Airways Flight 1549, which lost power after hitting a flock of birds shortly after taking off from New York's LaGuardia Airport on January 15, 2009.[25] Sullenberger calmly discussed the

FIGURE 2-1	O*NET Results for Flight Attendants

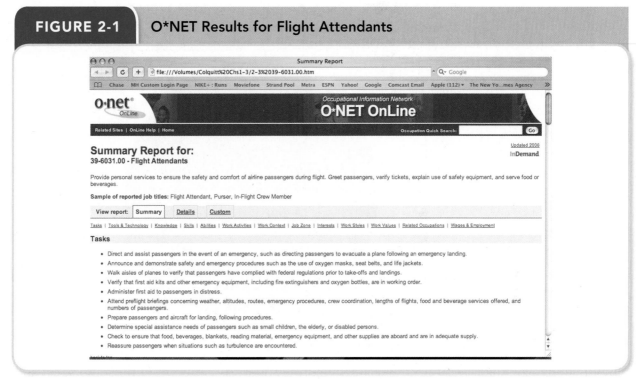

O*NET, or Occupational Information Network, is an online government database that lists the characteristics of most jobs and the knowledge required for each. This sample is for the job of flight attendant.

problem with air traffic control and decided that the only course of action was to land in the Hudson River. Three minutes after the bird strike, he executed a textbook landing on the water, saving the lives of all 150 passengers and crew. Experts agree that Sullenberger's performance that day was remarkable. Not only did Sullenberger accurately assess the situation and make the right decision about where to ditch the aircraft, he also piloted the landing perfectly. If the plane had approached the water going too slow, it would have lost lift and crashed into the water nose first; if the plane had been going too fast when it touched, it would have flipped, cart-wheeled, and disintegrated.[26]

CITIZENSHIP BEHAVIOR

Sometimes employees go the extra mile by actually engaging in behaviors that are not within their job description—and thus that do not fall under the broad heading of task performance. This situation brings us to the second category of job performance, called **citizenship behavior**, which is defined as voluntary employee activities that may or may not be rewarded but that contribute to the organization by improving the overall quality of the setting in which work takes place.[27] Have you ever had a coworker or fellow student who was always willing to help someone who was struggling? Who always attended optional meetings or social functions to support his or her colleagues? Who always maintained a good attitude, even in trying times? We tend to call those people "good citizens" or "good soldiers."[28] High levels of citizenship behavior earn them such titles. Although there are many different types of behaviors that might seem to fit the definition of citizenship behavior, research suggests two main categories that differ according to who benefits from the activity: coworkers or the organization (see Figure 2-2).[29]

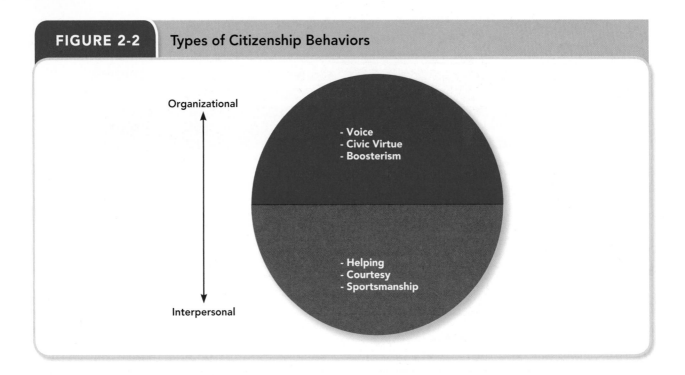

FIGURE 2-2 | **Types of Citizenship Behaviors**

Organizational

- Voice
- Civic Virtue
- Boosterism

- Helping
- Courtesy
- Sportsmanship

Interpersonal

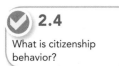

2.4

What is citizenship behavior?

The first category of citizenship behavior is the one with which you're most likely to be familiar: **interpersonal citizenship behavior**. Such behaviors benefit coworkers and colleagues and involve assisting, supporting, and developing other organizational members in a way that goes beyond normal job expectations.[30] For example, **helping** involves assisting coworkers who have heavy workloads, aiding them with personal matters, and showing new employees the ropes when they first arrive on the job. Do you consider yourself a helpful person? Check the **OB Assessments** feature to see how helpful you really are. **Courtesy** refers to keeping coworkers informed about matters that are relevant to them. Some employees have a tendency to keep relevant facts and events secret. Good citizens do the opposite; they keep others in the loop because they never know what information might be useful to someone else. **Sportsmanship** involves maintaining a good attitude with coworkers, even when they've done something annoying or when the unit is going through tough times. Whining and complaining are contagious; good citizens avoid being the squeaky wheel who frequently makes mountains out of molehills.

Although interpersonal citizenship behavior is important in many different job contexts, it may be even more important when employees work in small groups or teams. A team with members who tend to be helpful, respectful, and courteous is also likely to have a positive team atmosphere in which members trust one another. This type of situation is essential to foster the willingness of team members to work toward a common team goal rather than goals that may be more self-serving.[31] In fact, if you think about the behaviors that commonly fall under the "teamwork" heading, you'll probably agree that most are examples of interpersonal citizenship behavior (see Chapter 12 on Team Processes and Communication for more discussion of such issues).[32]

The second category of citizenship behavior is **organizational citizenship behavior**. These behaviors benefit the larger organization by supporting and defending the company, working to improve its operations, and being especially loyal to it.[33] For example, **voice** involves speaking up and offering constructive suggestions for change. Good citizens react

OB ASSESSMENTS

HELPING

How helpful are you? This assessment is designed to measure helping, an interpersonal form of citizenship behavior. Think of the people you work with most frequently, either at school or at work. The questions below refer to these people as your "work group." Answer each question using the scale below, then sum up your answers. (For more assessments relevant to this chapter, please visit the Online Learning Center at www.mhhe.com/colquitt).

1	2	3	4	5	6	7
STRONGLY DISAGREE	MODERATELY DISAGREE	SLIGHTLY DISAGREE	NEITHER DISAGREE NOR AGREE	SLIGHTLY AGREE	MODERATELY AGREE	STRONGLY AGREE

1. I volunteer to do things for my work group. _____

2. I help orient new members of my work group. _____

3. I attend functions that help my work group. _____

4. I assist others in my group with their work for the benefit of the group. _____

5. I get involved to benefit my work group. _____

6. I help others in this group learn about the work. _____

7. I help others in this group with their work responsibilities. _____

SCORING AND INTERPRETATION

If your scores sum up to 40 or higher, you perform a high level of helping behavior, which means you frequently engage in citizenship behaviors directed at your colleagues. This is good, as long as it doesn't distract you from fulfilling your own job duties and responsibilities. If your scores sum up to less than 40, you perform a low level of helping behaviors. You might consider paying more attention to whether your colleagues need assistance while working on their task duties.

Source: L.V. Van Dyne and J.A. LePine, "Helping and Voice Extra-Role Behaviors: Evidence of Construct and Predictive Validity," *Academy of Management Journal* 41 (1998), pp. 108–19. Copyright © 1998 by Academy of Management. Reproduced via permission of Academy of Management via Copyright Clearance Center.

to bad rules or policies by constructively trying to change them as opposed to passively complaining about them (see Chapter 3 on Organizational Commitment for more discussion of such issues).[34] **Civic virtue** refers to participating in the company's operations at a deeper-than-normal level by attending voluntary meetings and functions, reading and keeping up with organizational announcements, and keeping abreast of business news that affects the company. **Boosterism** means representing the organization in a positive way when out in public, away from the office, and away from work. Think of friends you've had who worked for a restaurant. Did they always say good things about the restaurant when talking to you and keep any "kitchen horror stories" to themselves? If so, they were being good citizens by engaging in high levels of boosterism.

Two important points should be emphasized about citizenship behaviors. First, as you've probably realized, citizenship behaviors are relevant in virtually any job, regardless of the particular nature of its tasks,[35] and research suggests that these behaviors can boost organizational effectiveness.[36] As examples, research conducted in a paper mill found that the quantity and quality of crew output was higher in crews that included more workers who engaged in citizenship behavior.[37] Research in 30 restaurants also showed that higher levels of citizenship behavior promoted higher revenue, better operating efficiency, higher customer satisfaction, higher performance quality, less food waste, and fewer customer complaints.[38] Thus, it seems clear that citizenship behaviors have a significant influence on the bottom line.

Second, citizenship behaviors become even more vital during organizational crises, when beneficial suggestions, deep employee involvement, and a positive "public face" are critical. For example, Southwest Airlines relied on high levels of citizenship behaviors after 9/11. Top corporate leaders worked without pay through the end of 2001, while rank-and-file employees voluntarily gave up days or weeks of paid vacation so that the employee profit-sharing plan could remain fully funded. The end result of this organizational citizenship behavior was that Southwest suffered no layoffs after 9/11 and was the only major airline to make a profit that year.[39]

From an employee's perspective, it may be tempting to discount the importance of citizenship behaviors—to just focus on your own job tasks and leave aside any "extra" stuff. After all, citizenship behaviors appear to be voluntary and optional, whereas task performance requirements are not. However, discounting citizenship behaviors is a bad idea because supervisors don't always view such actions as optional. In fact, research on computer salespeople, insurance agents, petrochemical salespeople, pharmaceutical sales managers, office furniture makers, sewing machine operators, U.S. Air Force mechanics, and first-tour U.S. Army soldiers has shown that citizenship behaviors relate strongly to supervisor evaluations of job performance, even when differences in task performance are also considered.[40] As we discuss in our **OB Internationally** feature, the tendency of supervisors to consider citizenship behaviors in evaluating overall job performance appears to hold even across countries with vastly different cultures.[41] Of course, this issue has a lot of relevance to you, given that in most organizations, supervisors' evaluations of employee job performance play significant roles in determining employee pay and promotions. Indeed, employee citizenship behavior has been found to influence the salary and promotion recommendations people receive, over and above their task performance.[42] Put simply, it pays to be a good citizen.

COUNTERPRODUCTIVE BEHAVIOR

2.5

What is counter-productive behavior?

Now we move from the "good soldiers" to the "bad apples." Whereas task performance and citizenship behavior refer to employee activities that help the organization achieve its goals and objectives, other activities in which employees engage do just the opposite. The third broad category of job performance is **counterproductive behavior**, defined as employee behaviors that intentionally hinder organizational goal accomplishment. The word "intentionally" is a key aspect of this definition; these are things that employees mean to do, not things they accidentally do. Although there are many different kinds of counterproductive behaviors, research suggests that—like task performance and citizenship behavior—they can be grouped into more specific categories (see Figure 2-3).[46]

Property deviance refers to behaviors that harm the organization's assets and possessions. For example, **sabotage** represents the purposeful destruction of physical equipment, organizational processes, or company products. Do you know what a laser disc is? Probably not—and the reason you don't is because of sabotage. A company called DiscoVision

OB INTERNATIONALLY

As we've already explained, citizenship behavior tends to be viewed as relatively voluntary because it's not often explicitly outlined in job descriptions or directly rewarded. However, people in organizations vary in their beliefs regarding the degree to which citizenship behavior is truly voluntary, and these differences have important implications.[43] As an example, consider a situation in which an employee engages in citizenship behaviors because of his or her belief that the behaviors are part of the job. However, this employee works for a supervisor who believes that citizenship behaviors are unnecessary. Assuming that the supervisor would not consider the citizenship behaviors on a performance evaluation, the employee would likely react negatively because he or she has not been recognized for putting effort into activities that help other members of the organization.

So what types of factors cause differences in beliefs regarding whether or not citizenship behavior is discretionary? One factor that would appear to be important is national culture. It is widely believed that the culture in countries like the United States, Canada, and the Netherlands encourages behaviors that support competition and individual achievement, whereas the culture in countries like China, Colombia, and Portugal encourages behaviors that promote cooperation and group interests over self-interests.[44] On the basis of these cultural differences, it seems logical to expect that people from the former set of countries would consider citizenship behavior relatively unimportant compared with people from the latter set of countries. In reality, however, the findings from one recent study comparing Canadian and Chinese managers found that this cultural stereotype was simply not true.[45] Managers in both countries not only took citizenship behavior into account when evaluating overall job performance, but the weight they gave to citizenship behavior in their overall evaluation of employees was the same. One explanation for this result is that the realities of running effective business organizations in a global economy have a significantly stronger impact on managerial practices than do cultural norms.

(a subsidiary of MCA) manufactured laser discs in the late 1970s, with popular movie titles like *Smokey and the Bandit* and *Jaws* retailing for $15.95. Although this level matches the price of DVDs today, it was far less than the $50–$100 needed to buy videocassettes (which were of inferior quality) at the time. Unfortunately, laser discs had to be manufactured in "clean rooms," because specs of dust or debris could cause the image on the television to freeze, repeat, skip, or drop out. When MCA merged with IBM in 1979, the morale of the employees fell, and counterproductive behaviors began to occur. Specifically, employees sabotaged the devices that measured the cleanliness of the rooms and began eating in the rooms—even "popping" their potato chip bags to send food particles into the air. This sabotage eventually created a 90 percent disc failure rate that completely alienated customers. As a result, despite its much lower production costs and higher quality picture, the laser disc disappeared, and the organizations that supported the technology suffered incredible losses.[47]

Even if you've never heard of the laser disc, you've certainly eaten in a restaurant. The cost of counterproductive behaviors in the restaurant industry is estimated to be 2–3 percent of revenues per year, but what may be more disturbing is the nature of those counterproductive behaviors.[48] Thirty-one percent of employees who responded to a survey knowingly served improperly prepared food, 13 percent intentionally sabotaged the work of other employees, and 12 percent admitted to intentionally contaminating food they prepared or served to a customer (yuck!). At a minimum, such sabotage of the restaurant's product

| FIGURE 2-3 | Types of Counterproductive Behaviors |

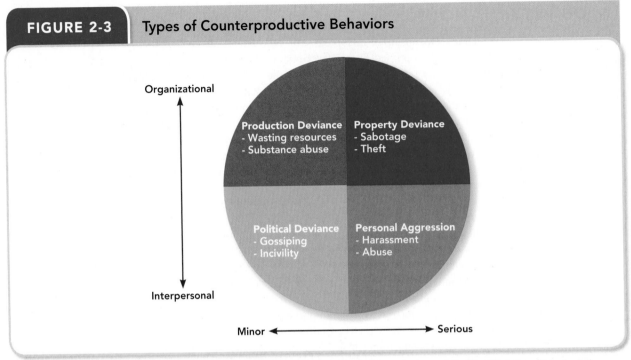

Source: Adapted from S.L. Robinson and R.J. Bennett, "A Typology of Deviant Workplace Behaviors: A Multidimensional Scaling Study," *Academy of Management Journal* 38 (1995), pp. 555–72.

can lead to a bad meal and a customer's promise to never return to that establishment. At a maximum, such behaviors can lead to food poisoning, health code violations, and a damaging lawsuit.

Theft represents another form of property deviance and can be just as expensive as sabotage (if not more). Research has shown that up to three-quarters of all employees have engaged in counterproductive behaviors such as theft, and the cost of these behaviors is staggering.[49] For example, one study estimated that 47 percent of store inventory shrinkage was due to employee theft and that this type of theft costs organizations approximately $14.6 billion per year.[50] Maybe you've had friends who worked at a restaurant or bar and been lucky enough to get discounted (or even free) food and drinks whenever you wanted. Clearly that circumstance is productive for you, but it's quite counterproductive from the perspective of the organization.

Production deviance is also directed against the organization but focuses specifically on reducing the efficiency of work output. **Wasting resources** is the most common form of production deviance,

Counterproductive behavior by employees can be destructive to the organization's goals. In some settings, such as a restaurant, it can even be a problem for customers.

when employees use too many materials or too much time to do too little work. Manufacturing employees who use too much wood or metal are wasting resources, as are restaurant employees who use too many ingredients when preparing the food. Workers who work too slowly or take too many breaks are also wasting resources because "time is money" (see Chapter 3 on Organizational Commitment for more discussion of such issues). **Substance abuse** represents another form of production deviance. If employees abuse drugs or alcohol while on the job or shortly before coming to work, then the efficiency of their production will be compromised because their work will be done more slowly and less accurately.

In contrast to property and production deviance, **political deviance** refers to behaviors that intentionally disadvantage other individuals rather than the larger organization. **Gossiping**—casual conversations about other people in which the facts are not confirmed as true—is one form of political deviance. Everyone has experienced gossip at some point in time and knows the emotions people feel when they discover that other people have been talking about them. Such behaviors undermine the morale of both friendship groups and work groups. **Incivility** represents communication that's rude, impolite, discourteous, and lacking in good manners.[51] The erosion of manners seems like a societywide phenomenon, and the workplace is no exception. Taken one by one, these political forms of counterproductive behavior may not seem particularly serious to most organizations. However, in the aggregate, acts of political deviance can create an organizational climate characterized by distrust and unhealthy competitiveness. Beyond the productivity losses that result from a lack of cooperation among employees, organizations with this type of climate likely cannot retain good employees. Moreover, there's some evidence that gossip and incivility can "spiral"—meaning that they gradually get worse and worse until some tipping point, after which more serious forms of interpersonal actions can occur.[52]

Those more serious interpersonal actions may involve **personal aggression**, defined as hostile verbal and physical actions directed toward other employees. **Harassment** falls under this heading and occurs when employees are subjected to unwanted physical contact or verbal remarks from a colleague. **Abuse** also falls under this heading; it occurs when an employee is assaulted or endangered in such a way that physical and psychological injuries may occur. You might be surprised to know that even the most extreme forms of personal aggression are actually quite prevalent in organizations. For example, one employee is killed by a current or former employee on average each week in the United States.[53] Acts of personal aggression can also be quite costly to organizations. For example, Mitsubishi Motor Manufacturing of America settled a class action sexual harassment lawsuit in 1998 for $34 million after women at a plant in Normal, Illinois, complained of widespread and routine groping, fondling, lewd jokes, lewd behavior, and pornographic graffiti.[54]

Three points should be noted about counterproductive behavior. First, there's evidence that people who engage in one form of counterproductive behavior also engage in others.[55] In other words, such behaviors tend to represent a pattern of behavior rather than isolated incidents. Second, like citizenship behavior, counterproductive behavior is relevant to any job. It doesn't matter what the job entails; there are going to be things to steal, resources to waste, and people to be uncivil toward. Third, it's often surprising which employees engage in counterproductive behavior. You might be tempted to guess that poor task performers will be the ones who do these sorts of things, but there's only a weak negative correlation between task performance and counterproductive behavior.[56] Sometimes the best task performers are the ones who can best get away with counterproductive actions, because they're less likely to be suspected or blamed. Moreover, as our **OB on Screen** feature illustrates, there are circumstances in which counterproductive behaviors might even be tolerated for a while because an employee's task performance contributions are unique or valued highly.

OB ON SCREEN

HANCOCK

Whadda ya want, a cookie? Get out of my face.

With those words, a superhero named John Hancock (Will Smith) tells a little boy (Atticus Shaffer) to stop talking to him about the bad guys who are on the loose in *Hancock* (Dir.: Peter Berg, Columbia Pictures, 2008). You see, Hancock was sleeping off a hangover on a bus stop bench and wasn't thrilled about the prospect of having to perform his superhero duties just then. Nevertheless, Hancock pulled himself together enough to catch the bad guys. In the process of doing so, however, Hancock continued to drink whiskey from a 2-liter bottle as he flew through a freeway sign—a sign that wound up causing a major pile-up of police cars that were in hot pursuit of the same bad guys. Hancock then caused damage to city buildings by unnecessarily tossing the bad guys' car around.

Much of the movie centers on the dichotomy in Hancock's behavior. On the one hand, Hancock does a great job catching criminals and saving the lives of the city's citizens. For example, in one scene, he steps in front of a train to save the life of someone whose car is stuck on the tracks. On the other hand, he's often intoxicated and behaves carelessly, and as a result, he costs the citizens of Los Angeles millions of dollars. For example, Hancock could have easily lifted the car off the tracks to save the driver, without having to stop the train. Instead, he carelessly flips the stuck car over onto another occupied vehicle, and his method of stopping the train ends up destroying it. So though Hancock scores high on superhero task performance, because he engages in behavior that contributes positively to the public's safety, he also scores high on superhero counterproductive behavior, because his irresponsible actions contribute negatively to the welfare of the city because of collateral damage. How does the public attempt to manage the superhero's counterproductive behavior? You'll have to watch the movie to find out.

SUMMARY: WHAT DOES IT MEAN TO BE A "GOOD PERFORMER"?

So what does it mean to be a "good performer"? As shown in Figure 2-4, being a good performer means a lot of different things. It means employees are good at the particular job tasks that fall within their job description, whether those tasks are routine or require

FIGURE 2-4   What Does It Mean to be a "Good Performer"?

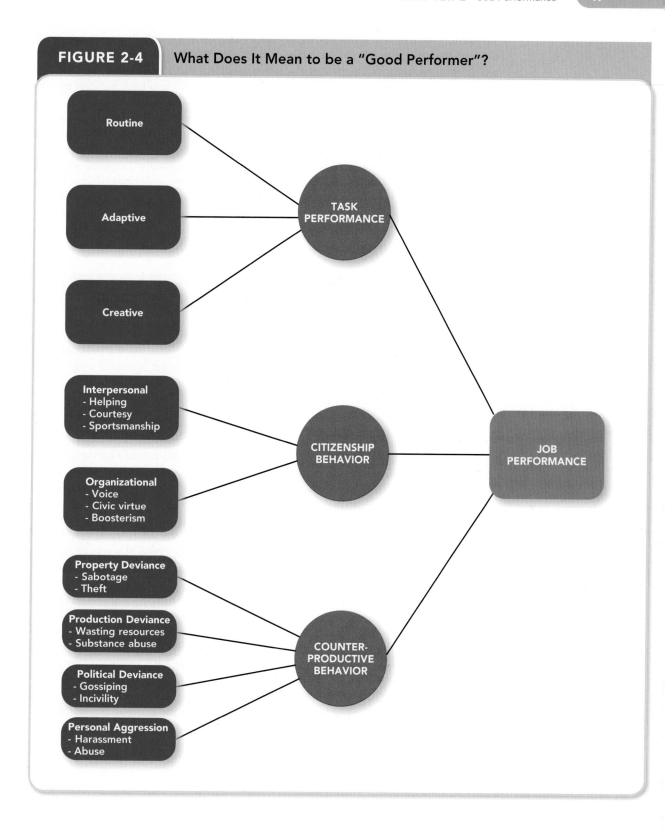

adaptability or creativity. But it also means that employees engage in citizenship behaviors directed at both coworkers and the larger organization. And it also means that employees refrain from engaging in the counterproductive behaviors that can badly damage the climate of an organization. The goal for any manager is therefore to have employees who fulfill all three pieces of this good performer description.

As you move forward in this book, you'll notice that almost every chapter includes a description of how that chapter's topic relates to job performance. For example, Chapter 4 on Job Satisfaction will describe how employees' feelings about their jobs affect their job performance. You'll find that some chapter topics seem more strongly correlated with task performance, whereas other topics are more strongly correlated with citizenship behavior or counterproductive behavior. Such differences will help you understand exactly how and why a given topic, be it satisfaction, stress, motivation, or something else, influences job performance. By the end of the book, you'll have developed a good sense of the most powerful drivers of job performance.

TRENDS AFFECTING PERFORMANCE

Now that we've described exactly what job performance is, it's time to describe some of the trends that affect job performance in the contemporary workplace. Put simply, the kinds of jobs employees do are changing, as is the way workers get organized within companies. These trends put pressure on some elements of job performance while altering the form and function of others.

2.6

What workplace trends are affecting job performance in today's organizations?

KNOWLEDGE WORK

Historically speaking, research on organizational behavior has focused on the physical aspects of job performance. This focus was understandable, given that the U.S. economy was industrial in nature and the productivity of the employees who labored in plants and factories was of great concern. However, by the early 1990s, the majority of new jobs required employees to engage in cognitive work, applying theoretical and analytical knowledge acquired through formal education and continuous learning.[57] Today, statistics from the U.S. Department of Labor confirm that this type of work, also called **knowledge work**, is becoming more prevalent than jobs involving physical activity.[58]

In addition to being more cognitive, knowledge work tends to be more fluid and dynamic in nature. Facts, data, and information are always changing. Moreover, as time goes by, it becomes easier to access more and more of these facts and data, using Google on an iPhone for example. In addition, the tools used to do knowledge work change quickly, with software, databases, and computer systems updated more frequently than ever. As those tools become more powerful, the expectations for completing knowledge work become more ambitious. After all, shouldn't reports and presentations be more comprehensive and finished more quickly when every book used in them is available online 24-7 rather than at some library? In fact, as our **OB at the Bookstore** feature illustrates, expectations regarding knowledge work can become overwhelming for employees, and as a consequence, new ways of performing this work may be necessary.

SERVICE WORK

One of the largest and fastest growing sectors in the economy is not in industries that produce goods but rather in industries that provide services. **Service work**, or work that provides nontangible goods to customers through direct electronic, verbal, or physical

OB AT THE BOOKSTORE

GETTING THINGS DONE
by David Allen (New York: Penguin Books, 2001).

In the old days, work was self-evident. Fields were to be plowed, machines tooled, boxes paced, cows milked, widgets cranked. You knew what work had to be done— you could see it. It was clear when the work was finished. Now, for many of us, there are no edges to most of our projects. Most people I know have at least half a dozen things they're trying to achieve right now, and even if they had the rest of their lives to try, they wouldn't be able to finish these to perfection.

With those words, David Allen describes how knowledge work places demands on people that are quite different from those engaged in more "traditional" work that emphasizes physical tasks that are routine and easy to anticipate and schedule. People involved in knowledge work are often engaged in multiple projects, each with unique requirements and constraints. In addition, the collaboration necessary to complete the projects often involves interactions with different groups of employees, each of whom might be expecting something completely different. The problem for employees who are engaged in this type of work is that the demands often become overwhelming. There's just so much to do that it becomes difficult to prioritize the different tasks (never mind trying to remember them all). As a consequence of not knowing where to begin or how to proceed (and then worrying about it late at night), nothing much gets done.

Allen's main argument is that knowledge workers need to break up larger projects into individual, smaller tasks soon after they're assigned, and then work on the next task that has to be done on each project at the right place and time. He believes that by organizing work this way, people can understand the projects in terms of tasks that are more concrete and certain. If people do this, they spend less time worrying about what has to be done, which frees up their brains to focus more on the performance of the task at hand. The book also describes a fairly elaborate system of lists and scheduling routines that Allen argues should be applied consistently to knowledge work. Of course, to some people, such a system will seem like additional, unnecessary work that actually increases the complexity of their jobs rather than decreasing it. In the end, although the author's system might not work for everyone, there are many specific suggestions that could be applied to improve results in knowledge work contexts.

interaction, accounts for approximately 55 percent of the economic activity in the United States,[59] and projections suggest that almost 20 percent of the new jobs created between now and 2012 will be service jobs, trailing only professional services in terms of growth.[60] Retail salespersons, customer service representatives, and food service workers represent the bulk of that service job growth. By comparison, maintenance, repair, construction, and production jobs are only projected to account for 4–7 percent of new jobs over the next several years.

The increase in service jobs has a number of implications for job performance. For example, the costs of bad task performance are more immediate and more obvious. When customer service representatives do their job duties poorly, the customer is right there to notice. That failure can't be hidden behind the scenes or corrected by other employees chipping in before it's too late. In addition, service work contexts place a greater premium on high levels of citizenship behavior and low levels of counterproductive behavior. If service employees refuse to help one another or maintain good sportsmanship, or if they gossip and insult one another, those negative emotions get transmitted to the customer during the service encounter. Maintaining a positive work environment therefore becomes even more vital.

In fact, some very notable organizations compete successfully by placing special emphasis on the performance of people who do service work. Amazon, for example, believes that

Amazon CEO Jeff Bezos stresses the importance of customer service.

the best way to ensure that customers keep using its Web site to purchase merchandise is to ensure customers are satisfied with their experience, especially when a transaction goes wrong, such as if merchandise arrives broken or an order doesn't ship because the product is back ordered.[61] Amazon customer service employees receive a great deal of training so that they can provide timely and consistent responses to customers who have questions or problems. In fact, customer service is so important to Amazon that each and every employee, including CEO Jeff Bezos, spends two days a year answering customer service calls.[62] Apparently all this training has paid off: Amazon now ranks number one in customer service quality, scoring above companies such as The Ritz-Carlton and Lexus, which are famous for providing world-class customer service.[63]

APPLICATION: PERFORMANCE MANAGEMENT

2.7

How can organizations use job performance information to manage employee performance?

Now that we've described what job performance is, along with some of the workplace trends that affect it, it's time to discuss how organizations use job performance information. As you saw in the Best Buy example, the type of information collected on employee performance can have a significant impact on employee behaviors and, in the end, an organization's ability to achieve its mission. In this section, we describe general ways in which job performance information is used to manage employee performance. We spotlight four of the most representative practices: management by objectives, behaviorally anchored rating scales, 360-degree feedback, and forced ranking. We'll also discuss how social networking software is being used for performance management purposes in organizations.

MANAGEMENT BY OBJECTIVES

Management by objectives (MBO) is a management philosophy that bases an employee's evaluations on whether the employee achieves specific performance goals.[64] How does MBO work? Typically, an employee meets with his or her manager to develop a set of mutually agreed-upon objectives that are measurable and specific (see Chapter 6 on Motivation for more discussion of such issues). In addition, the employee and the manager agree on the time period for achieving those objectives and the methods used to do so. An example of a performance objective for a line manager in a factory might be something like, "Reducing production waste by 35 percent within three months by developing and implementing new production procedures." Employee performance then can be gauged by referring to the degree to which the employee achieves results that are consistent with the objectives. If the line manager cuts production waste by 37 percent within three months, the manager's performance would be deemed effective, whereas if the manager only cuts production waste by 2 percent, his or her performance would be deemed ineffective. MBO is best suited for managing the performance of employees who work in contexts in which objective measures of performance can be quantified.

BEHAVIORALLY ANCHORED RATING SCALES

You might have noticed that MBO emphasizes the results of job performance as much as it does the performance behaviors themselves. In contrast, **behaviorally anchored rating scales** (BARS) assess performance by directly assessing job performance behaviors. The BARS approach uses "critical incidents"—short descriptions of effective and ineffective behaviors—to create a measure that can be used to evaluate employee performance. As an example of a BARS approach, consider the measure of task performance shown in Table 2-3, which focuses on the "planning, organizing, and scheduling" dimension of task performance for a manager.[65] The rater reads the behaviors on the far left column of the measure and matches actual observations of the behavior of the manager being rated to the corresponding level on the measure by placing a check in the blank.[66]

Typically, supervisors rate several performance dimensions using BARS and score an employee's overall job performance by taking the average value across all the dimensions. Because the critical incidents convey the precise kinds of behaviors that are effective and ineffective, feedback from BARS can help an employee develop and improve over time. That is, employees can develop an appreciation of the types of behaviors that would make them effective. Such information provides a nice complement to MBO, which is less capable of providing specific feedback about why an objective might have been missed.

360-DEGREE FEEDBACK

The **360-degree feedback** approach involves collecting performance information not just from the supervisor but from anyone else who might have firsthand knowledge about the employee's performance behaviors. These other sources of performance information typically include the employee's subordinates, peers, and customers. With the exception of the supervisor's ratings, the ratings are combined so that the raters can remain anonymous to the employee. Most 360-degree feedback systems also ask the employee to provide ratings of his or her own performance. The hope is that this 360-degree perspective will provide a more balanced and comprehensive examination of performance. By explicitly comparing self-provided ratings with the ratings obtained from others, employees can develop a better sense of how their performance may be deficient in the eyes of others and exactly where they need to focus their energies to improve.

Although the information from a 360-degree feedback system can be used to evaluate employees for administrative purposes such as raises or promotions, there are problems with that sort of application. First, because ratings vary across sources, there is the question of which source is most "correct." Even if multiple sources are taken into account in generating an overall performance score, it's often unclear how the information from the various sources should be weighted. Second, raters may give biased evaluations if they believe that the information will be used for compensation, as opposed to just skill development. Peers in particular may be unwilling to provide negative information if they believe it will harm the person being rated. As a result, 360-degree feedback is best suited

TABLE 2-3		BARS Example for "Planning Organizing, and Scheduling"
RATING	**RATING**	**BEHAVIORAL ANCHORS**
[7]	Excellent	• Develops a comprehensive project plan, documents it well, obtains required approval, and distributes the plan to all concerned.
[6]	Very Good	• Plans, communicates, and observes milestones; states week by week where the project stands relative to plans. Maintains up-to-date charts of project accomplishment and backlogs and uses these to optimize any schedule modifications required. • Experiences occasional minor operational problems but communicates effectively.
[5]	Good	• Lays out all the parts of a job and schedules each part to beat schedule; will allow for slack. • Satisfies customer's time constraints; time and cost overruns occur infrequently.
[4]	Average	• Makes a list of due dates and revises them as the project progresses, usually adding unforeseen events; investigates frequent customer complaints. • May have a sound plan but does not keep track of milestones; does not report slippages in schedule or other problems as they occur.
[3]	Below Average	• Plans are poorly defined; unrealistic time schedules are common. • Cannot plan more than a day or two ahead; has no concept of a realistic project due date.
[2]	Very Poor	• Has no plan or schedule of work segments to be performed. • Does little or no planning for project assignments.
[1]	Unacceptable	• Seldom, if ever, completes project because of lack of planning and does not seem to care. • Fails consistently due to lack of planning and does not inquire about how to improve.

Source: D.G. Shaw, C.E. Schneier, and R.W. Beatty, "Managing Performance with a Behaviorally Based Appraisal System," in *Applying Psychology in Business: The Handbook for Managers and Human Resource Professionals*, eds. J.W Jones, B.D. Steffy, and D.W. Bray (Lexington, MA: Lexington Books, 2001), pp. 314–25. Reprinted with permission of Lexington Books.

to improving or developing employee talent, especially if the feedback is accompanied by coaching about how to improve the areas identified as points of concern.

FORCED RANKING

One of the most notable strategies that Jack Welch, *Fortune*'s Manager of the 20th Century,[67] used to build a great workforce at General Electric involved evaluations that make clear distinctions among employees in terms of their job performance. Although Welch considered several systems that could differentiate employees, the most effective relied on the "vitality curve," depicted in Figure 2-5, which forces managers to rank all of their people into one of three categories: the top 20 percent (A players), the vital middle 70 percent (B players), or the bottom 10 percent (C players). The A players are thought to possess "the four Es of GE leadership: very high *energy* levels, the ability to *energize* others around common goals, the *edge* to make tough yes-and-no decisions, and finally the ability to consistently *execute* and deliver on their promises."[68] The B players are developed. According to Welch, B players are the backbone of the company but lack the passion of As. The C players are those who

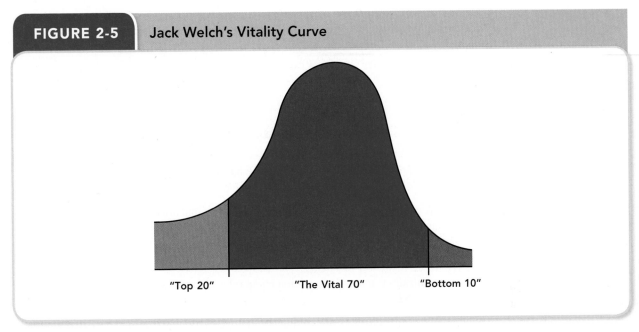

FIGURE 2-5   Jack Welch's Vitality Curve

"Top 20"   "The Vital 70"   "Bottom 10"

Source: Jack Welch and John Byrne, *JACK* (New York: Warner Books, 2001). Copyright © 2001 by the John F. Welch Jr. Foundation. By permission of Grand Central Publishing.

cannot get the job done and are let go. The system was taken so seriously that managers who couldn't differentiate their people tended to find themselves in the C category.[69]

Today, approximately 20 percent of *Fortune* 500 companies use some variant of Welch's **forced ranking** system, which is popularly known as "rank and yank" or the "dead man's curve."[70] (See Figure 2-5.) However, there are some important controversies to consider. For example, some believe the system is inherently unfair because it forces managers to give bad evaluations to employees who may be good performers, just to reach a pre-established percentage. As another example, employees may become hypercompetitive with one another to avoid finding themselves in a lower category. This type of competitiveness is the opposite of what may be needed in today's team-based organizations.

SOCIAL NETWORKING SYSTEMS

Most of you reading this book are familiar with social networking services such as Facebook and Twitter. Well, this technology has recently been applied in organizational contexts for the purposes of developing and evaluating employee job performance.[71] As an example, Accenture uses a Facebook-styled program called "Performance Multiplier," which requires that employees post and update weekly and quarterly goals. Managers then monitor the information and provide feedback.[72] As another example, a company called Rypple uses a Twitter-like program to enable employees to post questions about their own performance so that other employees can give them anonymous feedback.[73] Although the effectiveness of social networking applications for performance evaluation and employee development purposes has not been studied scientifically, there are some advantages that make us believe that they will grow in popularity. For example, these types of systems provide performance information that is much more timely, relative to traditional practices that measure performance quarterly or even yearly. Although it might be unpleasant to learn from your peers that a presentation you gave was boring, it's much better than giving 50 boring presentations over the course of the year and then getting the news from your boss.

TAKEAWAYS

2.1 Job performance is the set of employee behaviors that contribute to organizational goal accomplishment. Job performance has three dimensions: task performance, citizenship behavior, and counterproductive behavior.

2.2 Task performance includes employee behaviors that are directly involved in the transformation of organizational resources into the goods or services that the organization produces. Examples of task performance include routine task performance, adaptive task performance, and creative task performance.

2.3 Organizations gather information about relevant task behaviors using job analysis and O*NET.

2.4 Citizenship behaviors are voluntary employee activities that may or may not be rewarded but that contribute to the organization by improving the overall quality of the setting in which work takes place. Examples of citizenship behavior include helping, courtesy, sportsmanship, voice, civic virtue, and boosterism.

2.5 Counterproductive behaviors are employee behaviors that intentionally hinder organizational goal accomplishment. Examples of counterproductive behavior include sabotage, theft, wasting resources, substance abuse, gossiping, incivility, harassment, and abuse.

2.6 A number of trends have affected job performance in today's organizations, including the rise of knowledge work and the increase in service jobs.

2.7 MBO, BARS, 360-degree feedback, and forced ranking practices are four ways that organizations can use job performance information to manage employee performance.

KEY TERMS

DISCUSSION QUESTIONS

2.1 Describe the job that you currently hold or hope to hold after graduation. Now look up that job in the O*NET database. Does the profile of the job fit your expectations? Are any task behaviors missing from O*NET's profile?

2.2 Describe a job in which citizenship behaviors would be especially critical to an organization's functioning and one in which citizenship behaviors would be less critical. What is it about a job that makes citizenship more important?

2.3 Figure 2-3 classifies production deviance and political deviance as more minor in nature than property deviance and personal aggression. When might those "minor" types of counterproductive behavior prove especially costly?

2.4 Consider how you would react to 360-degree feedback. If you were the one receiving the feedback, whose views would you value most: your manager's or your peer's? If you were asked to assess a peer, would you want your opinion to affect that peer's raises or promotions?

CASE: BEST BUY

As we discussed in the chapter opening, the Results Only Work Environment, or ROWE, gives Best Buy employees at corporate headquarters the freedom to determine where and when they do their work and evaluates their job performance on the basis of whether they achieve work-related productivity goals. Although ROWE has been associated with increases in productivity of up to 35 percent,[74] some people have begun to express concerns about the system's potential drawbacks. Consider the case of Jane Kirshbaum, an attorney who works in the legal department that has not transitioned to ROWE.[75] Kirshbaum recently had her second child and changed her work schedule to four days a week. Although she still struggles with balancing the demands of work and family, she questions whether the transition to ROWE would work well in her department. She realizes that important things sometimes pop up at work that need immediate attention, and she believes that people who are at the office or are easiest to contact will get this work "dumped on" them. She also feels that the effectiveness of the legal department depends on how well it serves other departments, and therefore, it's important that people are willing and able to be present so issues can be dealt with in a timely manner.

Kirshbaum's concerns highlight a problem with evaluating employee performance based on results linked to the achievement of goals. Although such an approach to appraising employees may seem very rational and objective, it may overvalue or undervalue contributions to the organization made by certain employees. For example, an attorney in a legal department might choose to work exclusively away from the office to avoid having to work on issues that arise in the course of a normal day. This attorney might realize that at performance evaluation time, what really matters is whether productivity goals are achieved, and the best way to achieve these goals is to focus exclusively on assigned work tasks. Another attorney in the legal department, with the same amount of assigned work and productivity goals, might realize that the department's overall effectiveness and reputation depend on someone being around to deal with the "extra work" that crops up. So this attorney might choose to work exclusively at the office, even though the interruptions interfere with the ability to accomplish assigned work efficiently. This attorney would be seeing the "big picture" of what allows the legal department to carry out its mission effectively. Unfortunately, under the ROWE system, this employee could be very disappointed at performance evaluation time.

2.1 Consider Best Buy's Results Only Work Environment. What are its major strengths and weaknesses?

2.2 Describe the types of performance that ROWE overlooks. What are the likely consequences of overlooking these aspects of performance in performance evaluations, both to the employee and to the organization? How might these consequences offset some of the strengths of the system?

2.3 Describe the types of jobs for which results-based performance evaluations would work poorly. What are the features of these jobs that make the results-based system inappropriate? Identify modifications that could be made to a system such as ROWE to make it work better in these contexts.

EXERCISE: PERFORMANCE OF A SERVER

The purpose of this exercise is to explore what job performance means for a server in a restaurant. This exercise uses groups of participants, so your instructor will either assign you to a group or ask you to create your own group. The exercise has the following steps:

2.1 Conduct a job analysis for a restaurant server. Begin by drawing a circle like the one below. Use that circle to summarize the major job dimensions of a restaurant server. For example, one job dimension might be "Taking Orders." Divide the circle up with four additional job dimensions. Now get more specific by listing two behaviors per job dimension. For example, two behaviors within the "Taking Orders" dimension might be "Describing the Menu" and "Making Recommendations." At the end of Step 1, you should have a list of eight specific behaviors that summarize the tasks involved in being a restaurant server. Write your group's behaviors down on the board or on a transparency, leaving some space for some additional behaviors down the line.

Taking Orders

2.2 Take a look at the resulting list. Did you come up with any behaviors that would be described as "citizenship behaviors"? If you didn't include any in your list, does that mean that citizenship behavior isn't important in a restaurant setting? If your group includes someone who has worked as a server, ask him or her to describe the importance of citizenship behavior. Come up with two especially important citizenship behaviors and add those to your list.

2.3 Take another look at your list. Did you come up with any behaviors that would be described as "counterproductive behaviors"? If you didn't include any, does that mean that counterproductive behavior isn't an important concern in a restaurant setting? If your group includes someone who has worked as a server, ask him or her to describe the potential costs of counterproductive behavior. Come up with two costly counterproductive behaviors and add (the avoidance of) them to your list.

2.4 Class discussion (whether in groups or as a class) should center on how a restaurant owner or manager might use the resulting list to evaluate the performance of restaurant servers. How could this list be used to assess server performance? Would such an approach be valuable? Why or why not?

ENDNOTES

2.1 Best Buy, Corporate Web Site, http://www.bestbuyinc.com (April 5, 2009).

2.2 Kiger, P. "Throwing Out the Rules of Work." *Workforce Management*, September 26, 2006, http://www.workforce.com/section/09/feature/24/54/28 (June 11, 2008).

2.3 Ressler, C., and J. Thompson. *Why Work Sucks and How to Fix It*. New York: Portfolio, 2008.

2.4 Conlin, M. "Smashing the Clock: No Schedules. No Mandatory Meetings. Inside Best Buy's Radical Reshaping of the Workplace." *BusinessWeek*, December 11, 2006. http://www.businessweek.com/print/magazine/content/06_50/b4013001.htm (June 6, 2008).

2.5 Ibid.

2.6 Barbaro, M. "Service in a Store Stocked with Stress." *Washington Post.com*, December 24, 2004.

http://www.washingtonpost.com/wp-dyn/articles/A23383-2004Dec23.html (June 11, 2008); Brandon, J. "Rethinking the Time Clock: Best Buy is Getting Rid of its Time Clocks—and Wants to Persuade You to Get Rid of Yours Too." *CNNMoney.com*, April 4, 2007. http://money.cnn.com/magazines/business2/business2_archive/2007/03/01/8401022/index.htm (June 10, 2008).

2.7 Campbell, J.P. "Modeling the Performance Prediction Problem in Industrial and Organizational Psychology." In *Handbook of Industrial and Organizational Psychology*, Vol. 1, 2nd ed., eds. M.D. Dunnette and L.M. Hough. Palo Alto, CA: Consulting Psychologists Press, 1990, pp. 687–732; and Motowidlo, S.J.; W.C. Borman; and M.J. Schmit. "A Theory of Individual Differences in Task and Contextual Performance." *Human Performance* 10 (1997), pp. 71–83.

2.8   Borman, W.C., and S.J. Motowidlo. "Expanding the Criterion Domain to Include Elements of Contextual Performance." In *Personnel Selection in Organizations,* eds. N. Schmitt and W.C. Borman. San Francisco: Jossey-Bass, 1993, pp. 71–98.

2.9   Ibid.

2.10 Occupational Information Network (O*Net) Online. http://online. onet-center.org/ (August 17, 2005).

2.11 Weiss, H.M.; and D.R. Ilgen. "Routinized Behavior in Organizations." *Journal of Behavioral Economics* 24 (1985), pp. 57–67.

2.12 LePine, J.A.; J.A. Colquitt; and A. Erez. "Adaptability to Changing Task Contexts: Effects of General Cognitive Ability, Conscientiousness, and Openness to Experience." *Personnel Psychology* 53 (2000), pp. 563–93.

2.13 CBC News, "Plane Fire at Pearson Airport. Flight 358," *Indepth Website,* August 8, 2005, http://www.cbc.ca/news/background/plane_fire/ (August 17, 2005).

2.14 Ilgen, D.R., and E.D. Pulakos. "Employee Performance in Today's Organizations." In *The Changing Nature of Work Performance: Implications for Staffing, Motivation, and Development,* eds. D.R. Ilgen and E.D. Pulakos. San Francisco: Jossey-Bass, 1999, pp. 1–20.

2.15 Pulakos, E.D.; S. Arad; M.A. Donovan; and K.E. Plamondon. "Adaptability in the Workplace: Development of a Taxonomy of Adaptive Performance." *Journal of Applied Psychology* 85 (2000), pp. 612–24.

2.16 Amabile, T.M. "How to Kill Creativity." *Harvard Business Review* 76 (1998), pp. 76–88.

2.17 "Bikini Trivia: History of the Bikini." (n.d.), http://www.everythingbikini.com/bikini-history.html (August 14, 2005).

2.18 Florida, R. "America's Looming Creativity Crisis." *Harvard Business Review* 82 (2004), pp. 122–36.

2.19 Liker, J. K.; and D. P. Meier. *Toyota Talent: Developing Your People the Toyota Way.* Chicago: McGraw Hill, 2007.

2.20 Ibid.

2.21 O'Reilly, III, C.A., and J. Pfeffer. *Hidden Value: How Great Companies Achieve Extraordinary Results with Ordinary People.* Boston: Harvard Business School Press, 2000.

2.22 Occupational Information Network (O*Net) Online.

2.23 Freidberg, K., and J. Freidberg. *Nuts! Southwest Airlines' Crazy Recipe for Business and Personal Success.* Austin, TX: Bard Press, 1996.

2.24 Kaplan, M.D.G. "What Are You, a Comedian?" *USA Weekend. com,* July 13, 2003, http://www.usaweekend.com/03_issues/030713/030713southwest.html (September 15, 2005).

2.25 McFadden, R.D. "Pilot Is Hailed after Jetliner's Icy Plunge." *NYTimes.com,* January 16, 2009, http://www.nytimes.com/2009/01/16/nyregion/16crash.html?_r=1&hp (April 13, 2009).

2.26 Newman, R. "How Sullenberger Really Saved US Airways Flight 1549." *USNews.com,* April 13, 2009, http://www.usnews.com/blogs/flowchart/2009/2/3/how-sullenberger-really-saved-us-airways-flight-1549.html (April 13, 2009).

2.27 Borman and Motowidlo, "Expanding the Criterion Domain."

2.28 Organ, D.W. *Organizational Citizenship Behavior: The Good Soldier Syndrome.* Lexington, MA: Lexington Books, 1988.

2.29 Coleman, V.I., and W.C. Borman. "Investigating the Underlying Structure of the Citizenship Performance Domain." *Human Resource Management Review* 10 (2000), pp. 25–44.

2.30 Ibid.

2.31 MacMillan, P. *The Performance Factor: Unlocking the Secrets of Teamwork.* Nashville, TN: Broadman & Holman Publishers, 2001.

2.32 LePine, J.A.; R.F. Piccolo; C.L. Jackson; J.E. Mathieu; and J.R. Saul. "A Meta-Analysis of Teamwork Process: Towards a Better Understanding of the Dimensional Structure and Relationships with Team Effectiveness Criteria." *Personnel Psychology* 61 (2008), pp. 273–307.

2.33 Coleman and Borman, "Investigating the Underlying Structure."

2.34 Van Dyne, L., and J.A. LePine. "Helping and Voice Extra-Role Behavior: Evidence of Construct and Predictive Validity." *Academy of Management Journal* 41 (1998), pp. 108–19.

2.35 Motowidlo, S.J. "Some Basic Issues Related to Contextual Performance and Organizational Citizenship Behavior in Human Resource Management." *Human Resource Management Review* 10 (2000), pp. 115–26.

2.36 Podsakoff, N.P; S.W. Whiting; P.M. Podsakoff; and B.D. Blume. "Individual- and Organizational-Level Consequences of Organizational Citizenship Behaviors: A Meta-Analysis." *Journal of Applied Psychology* 94 (2009), pp. 122–41;

and Podsakoff, P.M.; S.B. MacKenzie; J.B. Paine; and D.G. Bachrach. "Organizational Citizenship Behaviors: A Critical Review of the Theoretical and Empirical Literature and Suggestions for Future Research." *Journal of Management* 26 (2000), pp. 513–63.

2.37 Podsakoff, P.M.; M. Ahearne; and S.B. MacKenzie. "Organizational Citizenship Behavior and the Quantity and Quality of Work Group Performance." *Journal of Applied Psychology* 82 (1997), pp. 262–70.

2.38 Walz, S.M., and B.P. Neihoff. "Organizational Citizenship Behaviors and Their Effect on Organizational Effectiveness in Limited-Menu Restaurants." In *Academy of Management Best Papers Proceedings,* eds. J.B. Keys and L.N. Dosier. Statesboro, GA: College of Business Administration at Georgia Southern University, 1996, pp. 307–11.

2.39 McGee-Cooper, A.; and G. Looper. "Lessons on Layoffs: Managing in Good Times to Prepare for Bad Times." (n.d.), http://www.amca.com/articles/article-layoffs.html (August 17, 2005).

2.40 Allen, T.D., and M.C. Rush. "The Effects of Organizational Citizenship Behavior on Performance Judgments: A Field Study and a Laboratory Experiment." *Journal of Applied Psychology* 83 (1998), pp. 247–60; Avila, R.A.; E.F. Fern; and O.K. Mann. "Unraveling Criteria for Assessing the Performance of Sales People: A Causal Analysis." *Journal of Personal Selling and Sales Management* 8 (1988), pp. 45–54; Lowery, C.M., and T.J. Krilowicz. "Relationships Among Nontask Behaviors, Rated Performance, and Objective Performance

Measures." *Psychological Reports* 74 (1994), pp. 571–78; MacKenzie, S.B.; P.M. Podsakoff; and R. Fetter. "Organizational Citizenship Behavior and Objective Productivity as Determinants of Managerial Evaluations of Salespersons' Performance." *Organizational Behavior and Human Decision Processes* 50 (1991), pp. 123–50; MacKenzie, S.B.; P.M. Podsakoff; and R. Fetter. "The Impact of Organizational Citizenship Behavior on Evaluation of Sales Performance." *Journal of Marketing* 57 (1993), pp. 70–80; MacKenzie, S.B.; P.M. Podsakoff; and J.B. Paine. "Effects of Organizational Citizenship Behaviors and Productivity on Evaluation of Performance at Different Hierarchical Levels in Sales Organizations." *Journal of the Academy of Marketing Science* 27 (1999), pp. 396–410; Motowidlo, S.J., and J.R. Van Scotter. "Evidence That Task Performance Should Be Distinguished from Contextual Performance." *Journal of Applied Psychology* 79 (1994), pp. 475–80; Podsakoff, P.M., and S.B. MacKenzie. "Organizational Citizenship Behaviors and Sales Unit Effectiveness." *Journal of Marketing Research* 3 (February 1994), pp. 351–63; and Van Scotter, J.R., and S.J. Motowidlo. "Interpersonal Facilitation and Job Dedication as Separate Facets of Contextual Performance." *Journal of Applied Psychology* 81 (1996), pp. 525–31.

2.41   Rotundo, M., and P.R. Sackett. "The Relative Importance of Task, Citizenship, and Counterproductive Performance to Global Ratings of Job Performance: A Policy Capturing Approach." *Journal of Applied Psychology* 87 (2002), pp. 66–80.

2.42   Allen and Rush, "The Effects of Organizational Citizenship Behavior on Performance Judgments"; Kiker, D.S., and S.J. Motowidlo. "Main and Interaction Effects of Task and Contextual Performance on Supervisory Reward Decisions." *Journal of Applied Psychology* 84 (1999), pp. 602–9; and Park, O.S., and H.P Sims Jr. "Beyond Cognition in Leadership: Prosocial Behavior and Affect in Managerial Judgment." Working Paper, Seoul National University and Pennsylvania State University, 1989.

2.43   Morrison, E.W. "Role Definitions and Organizational Citizenship Behavior: The Importance of the Employee's Perspective." *Academy of Management Journal* 37 (1994), pp. 1543–67.

2.44   Hofstede, G. *Cultures and Organizations: Software of the Mind.* New York: McGraw-Hill, 1991.

2.45   Rotundo, M., and J.L. Xie. "Understanding the Domain of Counterproductive Work Behavior in China." Working Paper, University of Toronto, 2007.

2.46   Robinson, S.L., and R.J. Bennett. "A Typology of Deviant Workplace Behaviors: A Multidimensional Scaling Study." *Academy of Management Journal* 38 (1995), pp. 555–72.

2.47   Cellitti, D.R. "MCA DiscoVision: The Record That Plays Pictures." June 25, 2002, http://www.oz.net/blam/DiscoVision/RecordPlays Pictures.htm (August 16, 2005).

2.48   Hollweg, L. *Inside the Four Walls of the Restaurant: The Reality and Risk of Counter-Productive Behaviors.* 2003, http://www.batrushollweg.com/files/Website.Inside_the_Four_Walls_of_the_Restaurant1.Reprint_9.pdf (August 17, 2005).

2.49 Harper, D. "Spotlight Abuse—Save Profits." *Industrial Distribution* 79 (1990), pp. 47–51.

2.50 Hollinger, R.C., and L. Langton. *2004 National Retail Security Survey.* Gainesville, FL: University of Florida, Security Research Project, Department of Criminology, Law and Society, 2005.

2.51 Andersson, L.M., and C.M. Pearson. "Tit for Tat? The Spiraling Effect of Incivility in the Workplace." *Academy of Management Review* 24 (1999), pp. 452–71.

2.52 Ibid.

2.53 Armour, S. "Managers Not Prepared for Workplace Violence." *USA Today,* July 19, 2004, http://www.usatoday.com/money/workplace/2004-07-15-workplace-violence2_x.htm (September 11, 2005).

2.54 PBS. "Isolated Incidents?" *Online Newshour,* April 26, 1996, http://www.pbs.org/newshour/bb/business/april96/mitsubishi_4-26.html (September 11, 2005).

2.55 Sackett, P.R. "The Structure of Counterproductive Work Behaviors: Dimensionality and Performance with Facets of Job Performance." *International Journal of Selection and Assessment* 10 (2002), pp. 5–11.

2.56 Sackett, P.R., and C.J. DeVore. "Counterproductive Behaviors at Work." In *Handbook of Industrial, Work, and Organizational Psychology,* Vol. 1, eds. N. Anderson; D.S. Ones; H.K. Sinangil; and C. Viswesvaran. Thousand Oaks, CA: Sage, 2001, pp. 145–51.

2.57 Drucker, P.F. "The Age of Social Transformation." *The Atlantic Monthly* 274 (1994), pp. 53–80.

2.58 U.S. Department of Labor, Bureau of Labor Statistics. "Tomorrow's Jobs." (n.d.), http://stats.bls.gov/oco/oco2003.htm (August 27, 2005).

2.59 U.S. Census Bureau. "Welcome to the Service Annual Survey." March 30, 2009, http://www.census.gov/econ/www/servmenu.html (April 14, 2009).

2.60 Hecker, D. "Occupational Employment Projections to 2012." *Monthly Labor Review* 127 (2004), pp. 80–105, http://proquest.com (August 27, 2005).

2.61 Green, H. "How Amazon Aims to Keep You Clicking," *BusinessWeek,* March 2, 2009, pp. 34–40.

2.62 Ibid.

2.63 McGregor, J. "Behind the List." *BusinessWeek*, March 2, 2009, p. 32.

2.64 Drucker, P.F. *The Practice of Management.* New York: Harper and Brothers, 1954.

2.65 Shaw, D.G.; C.E. Schneier; and R.W. Beatty. "Managing Performance with a Behaviourally Based Appraisal System." In *Applying Psychology in Business: The Handbook for Managers and Human Resource Professionals*, eds. J.W Jones; B.D. Steffy; and D.W. Bray. Lexington, MA: Lexington Books, 2001, pp. 314–25.

2.66 Pulakos, E.D. "Behavioral Performance Measures." In *Applying Psychology in Business: The Handbook for Managers and Human Resource Professionals*, eds. J.W Jones; B.D. Steffy; and D.W. Bray. Lexington, MA: Lexington Books, 2001, pp. 307–13.

2.67 "*Fortune* Selects Henry Ford Businessman of the Century," November 1, 1999, http://www.timewarner.com/corp/

print/0,20858,667526,00.html (August 27, 2005).

2.68 Welch, J.F. Jr. *Jack: Straight from the Gut*. New York: Warner Books Inc, 2001, p. 158.

2.69 Ibid.

2.70 Johnson, G. "Forced Ranking: The Good, the Bad, and the Alternative." *Training Magazine* 41 (May 2004), pp. 24–34.

2.71 McGregor, J. "Job Review in 140 Keystrokes: Social Networking-style Systems Lighten up the Dreaded Performance Evaluation." *BusinessWeek*, March 29, 2009, p. 58.

2.72 Ibid.

2.73 Ibid.

2.74 Kiger, "Throwing Out the Rules of Work."

2.75 Thottam, J. *"Reworking Work"*. *Time* online edition, July 18, 2005, http://www.time.com/time/ magazine/article/0,9171, 1083900,00.html (accessed June 10, 2008)

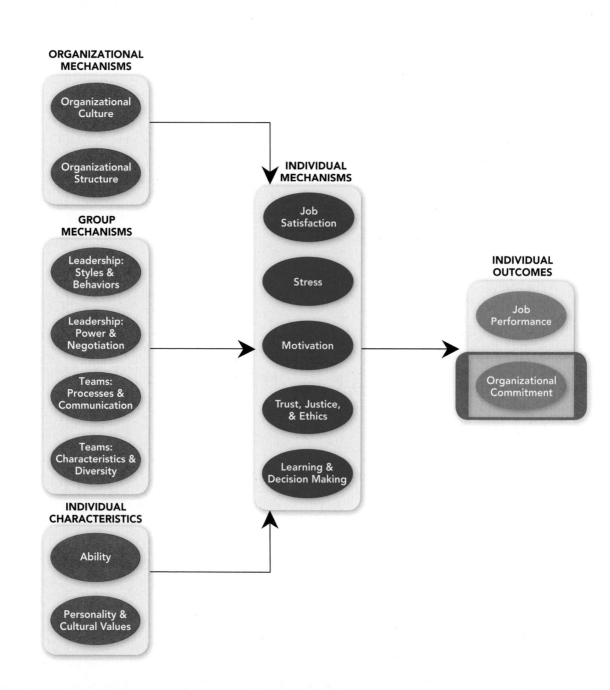

chapter **3**

Organizational Commitment

ORGANIZATIONAL MECHANISMS

Organizational Culture

Organizational Structure

GROUP MECHANISMS

Leadership: Styles & Behaviors

Leadership: Power & Negotiation

Teams: Processes & Communication

Teams: Characteristics & Diversity

INDIVIDUAL CHARACTERISTICS

Ability

Personality & Cultural Values

INDIVIDUAL MECHANISMS

Job Satisfaction

Stress

Motivation

Trust, Justice, & Ethics

Learning & Decision Making

INDIVIDUAL OUTCOMES

Job Performance

Organizational Commitment

✓ LEARNING GOALS

After reading this chapter, you should be able to answer the following questions:

3.1 What is organizational commitment? What is withdrawal behavior? How are the two connected?

3.2 What are the three types of organizational commitment, and how do they differ?

3.3 What are the four primary responses to negative events at work?

3.4 What are some examples of psychological withdrawal? Of physical withdrawal? How do the different forms of withdrawal relate to each other?

3.5 What workplace trends are affecting organizational commitment in today's organizations?

3.6 How can organizations foster a sense of commitment among employees?

ACCENTURE

It's 5:00 in the morning, time to rustle out of bed to catch your flight from Atlanta to San Francisco. You'll be in the City by the Bay for the next four days, helping a major retailing client implement a new information technology system. Then you'll fly back to Atlanta on Thursday, working from home on Friday. You'll need to do it all again next week, and the week after that, and the week after that. That's the schedule for Keyur Patel, a consultant at Accenture[1]—the New York-based consulting firm that stands 97th among *Fortune's* "100 Best Companies to Work For."[2] Accenture's 150 offices can be found in 53 different countries, on six different continents. Although Patel's current assignment is stateside, he works virtually with team members in Manila and Bangalore. This sort of arrangement is typical at Accenture, with the firm's 178,000 employees needing to be able to work from anywhere, depending upon the needs of their clients.

Accenture hires 60,000 employees a year, many of them straight out of college. That may seem like a lot of new hires, given the company's size.[3] The key to understanding that number lies in the turnover rate for the consulting industry. On average, consulting firms lose 15–20 percent of their workforce each year. The career path for consultants is often summarized as "up or out," with employees either being promoted after putting in some time or voluntarily turning over to pursue a job with less travel and more stable hours. The most recent estimates put Accenture's own attrition rate at 15 percent, down from 18 percent two years prior. The challenge for firms like Accenture is keeping employees committed to an organization that they rarely see. After all, consultants like Patel are scattered around the world, rarely coming face-to-face with their manager, and often lacking a true headquarters.

Accenture has pursued several strategies to create a sense of loyalty and attachment among its consultants. It organizes quarterly "community events" where groups of 50–150 employees come together for charity drives, cultural fare, or sports activities. These events are designed to give the consultants some sense of connection, despite the far-flung nature of their work. The company also instituted a sabbatical program, where consultants can arrange to have a portion of their paychecks set aside for a three-month vacation after three years of service. Accenture also invests a great deal in their employees, with consultants spending an average of 75 hours a year in training sessions. For example, consultants can take a training course on leading teams whose members are geographically separated. The hope is that these sorts of investments will instill a sense of value in further years of service, keeping consultants at the firm for a longer time period.

ORGANIZATIONAL COMMITMENT

Organizational commitment sits side by side with job performance in our integrative model of organizational behavior, reflecting one of the starting points for our journey through the concepts covered in this course. Why begin with a discussion of organizational commitment? Because as illustrated in the Accenture example, it's not enough to have talented employees who perform their jobs well. You also need to be able to hang on to those employees for long periods of time so that the organization can benefit from their efforts.

Put yourself in the shoes of a business owner. Let's say you spent a great deal of time recruiting a graduate from the local university, selling her on your business, and making sure that she was as qualified as you initially believed her to be. Now assume that, once hired, you took a personal interest in that employee, showing her the ropes and acting as mentor and instructor. Then, just as the company was set to improve as a result of that employee's presence, she leaves to go to work for a competitor. As an employer, can you think of many things more depressing than that scenario?

Unfortunately, that scenario is not far-fetched. A survey by Manpower revealed that 61 percent of recent college graduates planned to stay at their first job for less than three years.[4] A survey by the Society for Human Resource Management showed that 75 percent of employees were looking for a new job.[5] Of those job seekers, 43 percent were looking for more money, and 35 percent were reacting to a sense of dissatisfaction with their current employer. When employees actually do leave, it can prove quite costly to the organization. Estimates suggest that it costs about .5 times the annual salary + benefits to replace an hourly worker, 1.5 times the annual salary + benefits to replace a salaried employee, and as much as 5 times the annual salary + benefits to replace an executive.[6] Why so expensive? Those estimates include various costs, including the administrative costs involved in the separation, recruitment expenses, screening costs, and training and orientation expenses for the new hire. They also include "hidden costs" due to decreased morale, lost organizational knowledge, and lost productivity. It's no wonder then that 75 percent of employers in one survey described turnover as a "persistent worry."[7]

Organizational commitment is defined as the desire on the part of an employee to remain a member of the organization.[8] Organizational commitment influences whether an employee stays a member of the organization (is retained) or leaves to pursue another job (turns over). It's important to acknowledge that turnover can be both voluntary and involuntary. Voluntary turnover occurs when employees themselves decide to quit; involuntary turnover occurs when employees are fired by the organization for some reason. Our attention in this chapter is focused primarily on reducing voluntary turnover—keeping the employees that the organization wants to keep.

Employees who are not committed to their organizations engage in **withdrawal behavior**, defined as a set of actions that employees perform to avoid the work situation—behaviors that may eventually culminate in quitting the organization.[9] The relationship between commitment and withdrawal is illustrated in Figure 3-1. Some employees may exhibit much more commitment than withdrawal, finding themselves on the green end of

3.1

What is organizational commitment? What is withdrawal behavior? How are the two connected?

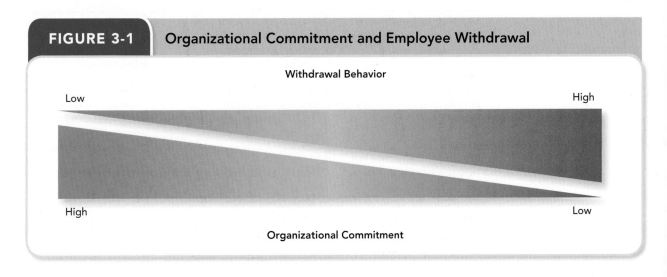

| **FIGURE 3-1** | **Organizational Commitment and Employee Withdrawal** |

Withdrawal Behavior

Low   High

High   Low

Organizational Commitment

the continuum. Leaving aside personal or family issues, these employees are not "retention risks" for the moment. Other employees exhibit much more withdrawal than commitment, finding themselves on the red end of the continuum. These employees are retention risks—teetering on the edge of quitting their jobs. The sections that follow review both commitment and withdrawal in more detail.

WHAT DOES IT MEAN TO BE "COMMITTED"?

One key to understanding organizational commitment is to understand where it comes from. In other words, what creates a desire to remain a member of an organization? To explore this question, consider the following scenario: You've been working full-time for your employer for around five years. The company gave you your start in the business, and you've enjoyed your time there. Your salary is competitive enough that you were able to purchase a home in a good school system, which is important because you have one young child and another on the way. Now assume that a competing firm contacted you while you were attending a conference and offered you a similar position in its company. What kinds of things might you think about? If you created a list to organize your thoughts, what might that list look like?

 3.2

What are the three types of organizational commitment, and how do they differ?

TYPES OF COMMITMENT

One potential list is shown in Table 3-1. The left-hand column reflects some emotional reasons for staying with the current organization, including feelings about friendships, the atmosphere or culture of the company, and a sense of enjoyment when completing job

TABLE 3-1	The Three Types of Organizational Commitment	
What Makes Someone Stay with their Current Organization?		
AFFECTIVE COMMITMENT (EMOTION-BASED)	**CONTINUANCE COMMITMENT (COST-BASED)**	**NORMATIVE COMMITMENT (OBLIGATION-BASED)**
Some of my best friends work in my office . . . I'd miss them if I left.	I'm due for a promotion soon . . . will I advance as quickly at the new company?	My boss has invested so much time in me, mentoring me, training me, showing me the ropes.
I really like the atmosphere at my current job . . . it's fun and relaxed.	My salary and benefits get us a nice house in our town . . . the cost of living is higher in this new area.	My organization gave me my start . . . they hired me when others thought I wasn't qualified.
My current job duties are very rewarding . . . I enjoy coming to work each morning.	The school system is good here, my spouse has a good job . . . we've really put down roots where we are.	My employer has helped me out of a jam on a number of occasions . . . how could I leave now?
Staying because you **want** to.	Staying because you **need** to.	Staying because you **ought** to.

duties. These sorts of emotional reasons create **affective commitment**, defined as a desire to remain a member of an organization due to an emotional attachment to, and involvement with, that organization.[10] Put simply, you stay because you *want* to. The middle column reflects some cost-based reasons for staying, including issues of salary, benefits, and promotions, as well as concerns about uprooting a family. These sorts of reasons create **continuance commitment**, defined as a desire to remain a member of an organization because of an awareness of the costs associated with leaving it.[11] In other words, you stay because you *need* to. The right-hand column reflects some obligation-based reasons for staying with the current organization, including a sense that a debt is owed to a boss, a colleague, or the larger company. These sorts of reasons create **normative commitment**, defined as a desire to remain a member of an organization due to a feeling of obligation.[12] In this case, you stay because you *ought* to.

As shown in Figure 3-2, the three types of organizational commitment combine to create an overall sense of psychological attachment to the company. Of course, different people may weigh the three types differently. Some employees may be very rational and cautious by nature, focusing primarily on continuance commitment when evaluating their overall desire to stay. Other employees may be more emotional and intuitive by nature, going more on "feel" than a calculated assessment of costs and benefits. The importance of the three commitment types also may vary over the course of a career. For example,

FIGURE 3-2 **Drivers of Overall Organizational Commitment**

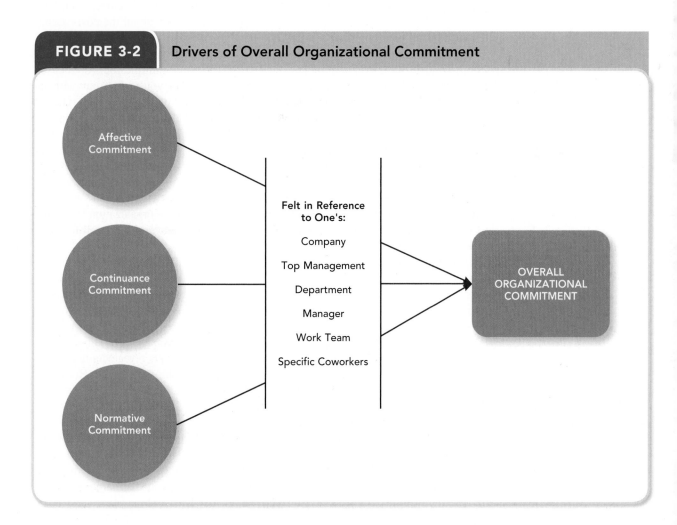

Committed employees often have strong positive feelings about one particular aspect of their job, such as their colleagues, their manager, or the particular work they do.

you might prioritize affective reasons early in your work life before shifting your attention to continuance reasons as you start a family or become more established in a community. Regardless of how the three types are prioritized, however, they offer an important insight into *why* someone might be committed and what an organization can do to make employees feel more committed.

Figure 3-2 also shows that organizational commitment depends on more than just "the organization." That is, people aren't always committed to companies; they're also committed to the top management that leads the firm at a given time, the department in which they work, the manager who directly supervises them, or the specific team or coworkers with whom they work most closely.[13] We use the term **focus of commitment** to refer to the various people, places, and things that can inspire a desire to remain a member of an organization. For example, you might choose to stay with your current employer because you're emotionally attached to your work team, worry about the costs associated with losing your company's salary and benefits package, and feel a sense of obligation to your current manager. If so, your desire to remain cuts across multiple types of commitment (affective, continuance, and normative) and multiple foci (or focuses) of commitment (work team, company, manager). Now that you're familiar with the drivers of commitment in a general sense, let's go into more depth about each type.

AFFECTIVE COMMITMENT. One way to understand the differences among the three types of commitment is to ask yourself what you would feel if you left the organization. Consider the reasons listed in the left-hand column of Table 3-1. What would you feel if, even after taking all those reasons into account, you decided to leave your organization to join another one? Answer: You'd feel a sense of *sadness*. Employees who feel a sense of affective commitment identify with the organization, accept that organization's goals and values, and are more willing to exert extra effort on behalf of the organization.[14] Is affective commitment something that you feel for your current employer or have felt for a past employer? Check the **OB Assessments** feature to find out.

It's safe to say that if managers could choose which type of commitment they'd like to instill in their employees, they'd choose affective commitment. Moreover, when a manager looks at an employee and says "She's committed" or "He's loyal," that manager usually is referring to a behavioral expression of affective commitment.[15] For example, employees who are affectively committed to their employer tend to engage in more interpersonal and organizational citizenship behaviors, such as helping, sportsmanship, and boosterism. One meta-analysis of 22 studies with more than 6,000 participants revealed a moderately strong correlation between affective commitment and citizenship behavior.[16] (Recall that a meta-analysis averages together results from multiple studies investigating the same relationship.) Such results suggest that emotionally committed employees express that commitment by "going the extra mile" whenever they can.

Because affective commitment reflects an emotional bond to the organization, it's only natural that the emotional bonds among coworkers influence it.[17] We can therefore gain a better understanding of affective commitment if we take a closer look at the bonds that tie employees together. Assume you were given a sheet with the names of all the employees in your department or members of your class. Then assume you were asked to

OB ASSESSMENTS

AFFECTIVE COMMITMENT

How emotionally attached are you to your employer? This assessment is designed to measure affective commitment—the feeling that you *want* to stay with your current organization. Think about your current job or the last job that you held (even if it was a part-time or summer job). Answer each question using the response scale provided. Then subtract your answers to the boldfaced questions from 6, with the difference being your new answers for those questions. For example, if your original answer for Question 3 was "4," your new answer is "2" (6 – 4). Then sum your answers for the six questions. (For more assessments relevant to this chapter, please visit the Online Learning Center at www.mhhe.com/colquitt).

1	2	3	4	5
STRONGLY DISAGREE	DISAGREE	NEUTRAL	AGREE	STRONGLY AGREE

1. I would be very happy to spend the rest of my career in this organization. _____

2. I really feel as if this organization's problems are my own. _____

3. **I do not feel like "part of the family" at my organization.** _____

4. **I do not feel "emotionally attached" to this organization.** _____

5. This organization has a great deal of personal meaning for me. _____

6. **I do not feel a strong sense of belonging to my organization.** _____

SCORING AND INTERPRETATION

If your scores sum up to 20 or above, you feel a strong sense of affective commitment to your current or past employer, which means that you feel an emotional attachment to the company, or the people within it, making it less likely that you would leave voluntarily. If your scores sum up to less than 20, you have a weaker sense of affective commitment to your current or past employer. This result is especially likely if you responded to the questions in reference to a part-time or summer job, as there might not have been enough time to develop an emotional bond.

Source: J.P. Meyer and N.J. Allen, 1997, *Commitment in the Workplace: Theory, Research, and Application*, Sage Publications. Copyright © 1997 Sage Publications Inc. Books. Reproduced with permission of Sage Productions Inc Books via Copyright Clearance Center.

rate the frequency with which you communicated with each of those people, as well as the emotional depth of those communications. Those ratings could be used to create a "social network" diagram that summarizes the bonds among employees. Figure 3-3 provides a sample of such a diagram. The lines connecting the 10 members of the work unit represent the communication bonds that tie each of them together, with thicker lines representing more frequent communication with more emotional depth. The diagram illustrates that some employees are "nodes," with several direct connections to other employees, whereas others remain at the fringe of the network.

FIGURE 3-3 | A Social Network Diagram

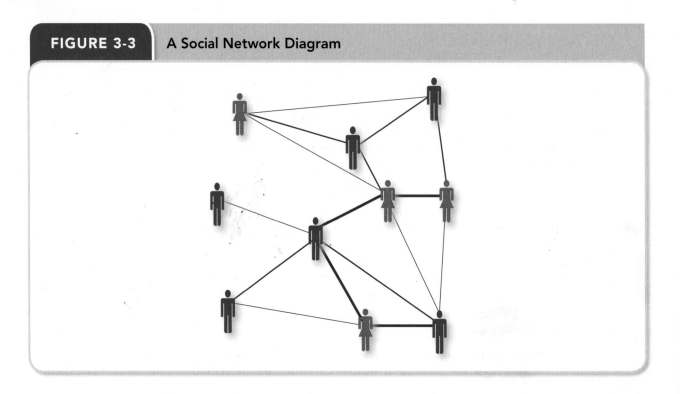

The **erosion model** suggests that employees with fewer bonds will be most likely to quit the organization.[18] If you look at Figure 3-3, who's most at risk for turning over? That's right—the employee who only has one bond with someone else (and a relatively weak bond at that). From an affective commitment perspective, that employee is likely to feel less emotional attachment to work colleagues, which makes it easier to decide to leave the organization. Social network diagrams can also help us understand another explanation for turnover. The **social influence model** suggests that employees who have direct linkages with "leavers" will themselves become more likely to leave.[19] In this way, reductions in affective commitment become contagious, spreading like a disease across the work unit. Think about the damage that would be caused if the central figure in the network (the one who has linkages to five other people) became unhappy with the organization.

Cisco Systems seems to understand the importance of affective commitment. The San Jose, California–based leader in networking hardware and software enjoys one of the lowest voluntary turnover rates in its industry, around 3 percent.[20] Cisco employees point to the fun workplace culture as a key factor, with company cafes offering movie-themed menus at Academy Awards time or "nerd lunches" during which experts discuss important tech topics. Harley-Davidson also appears to understand the importance of fostering an emotional attachment to the organization. The voluntary turnover rate at the motorcycle manufacturer is less than 2 percent, and employee surveys reveal that workers strongly identify with the culture of motorcycle riding. In fact, Harley-Davidson pays some employees to work at biker rallies.[21] These sorts of activities reinforce the emotional bonds between the company and its employees, fostering affective commitment.

CONTINUANCE COMMITMENT. Now consider the reasons for staying listed in the middle column of Table 3-1. What would you feel if, even after taking all those reasons into account, you decided to leave your organization to join another one? Answer: You'd feel a sense of *anxiety*. Continuance commitment exists when there is a profit associated with staying and a cost associated with leaving,[22] with high continuance commitment

Not only are Harley riders loyal to their bikes, but employees are also dedicated to the company and identify with the culture of motorcycle riding. Some even get to work at biker rallies like this one.

making it very difficult to change organizations because of the steep penalties associated with the switch.[23] One factor that increases continuance commitment is the total amount of investment (in terms of time, effort, energy, etc.) employees have made in mastering their work roles or fulfilling their organizational duties.[24] Picture a scenario in which you've worked extremely hard for a number of years to finally master the "ins and outs" of working at a particular organization, and now you're beginning to enjoy the fruits of that labor in terms of financial rewards and better work assignments. That effort might be wasted if you moved to another organization (and had to start over on the learning curve).

Another factor that increases continuance commitment is a lack of employment alternatives.[25] If an employee has nowhere else to go, the need to stay will be higher. Employment alternatives themselves depend on several factors, including economic conditions, the unemployment rate, and the marketability of a person's skills and abilities.[26] Of course, no one likes to feel "stuck" in a situation, so it may not be surprising that the behavioral benefits associated with affective commitment don't really occur with continuance commitment. There's no statistical relationship between continuance commitment and citizenship behavior, for example, or any other aspects of job performance.[27] Continuance commitment therefore tends to create more of a passive form of loyalty.

It's important to note that some of the reasons in the middle column of Table 3-1 center on personal or family issues. Continuance commitment focuses on personal and family issues more than the other two commitment types, because employees often need to stay for both work and nonwork reasons. One concept that demonstrates the work and nonwork forces that can bind us to our current employer is **embeddedness**, which summarizes employees' links to their organization and community, their sense of fit with their organization and community, and what they would have to sacrifice for a job change.[28] As demonstrated in Table 3-2, embeddedness strengthens continuance commitment by providing more reasons employees need to stay in their current positions (and more sources of anxiety if they were to leave).[29]

TABLE 3-2	Embeddedness and Continuance Commitment

	"Embedded" People Feel:	
FACET	**FOR THE ORGANIZATION:**	**FOR THE COMMUNITY:**
Links	• I've worked here for such a long time. • I'm serving on so many teams and committees.	• Several close friends and family live nearby. • My family's roots are in this community.
Fit	• My job utilizes my skills and talents well. • I like the authority and responsibility I have at this company.	• The weather where I live is suitable for me. • I think of the community where I live as home.
Sacrifice	• The retirement benefits provided by the organization are excellent. • I would sacrifice a lot if I left this job.	• People respect me a lot in my community. • Leaving this community would be very hard.

Source: Adapted from T.R. Mitchell, B.C. Holtom, T.W. Lee, C.J. Sablynski, and M. Erez, "Why People Stay: Using Job Embeddedness to Predict Voluntary Turnover," *Academy of Management Journal* 44 (2001), pp. 1102–21.

Think about your current situation. If you're a college student who is working part-time, you likely don't feel very embedded. Your links to your job are probably only short term, and you may feel that the job is more routine than you'd like from a fit perspective. You probably also wouldn't feel you were sacrificing much if you left the job. From a community perspective, you may be going to school in a different city or state than where you grew up, again resulting in few links, low perceived fit, or a lack of felt sacrifice. However, if you're a full-time employee who is relatively established in your job and community, you may feel quite embedded in your current situation. To see how a one-time hero grapples with embeddedness and continuance commitment, see our **OB on Screen** feature.

Alcon Labs seems to understand the value of continuance commitment. The Fort Worth, Texas–based leader in eye care products enjoys a voluntary turnover rate of less than 2 percent.[30] One likely reason for that low rate is the benefits package Alcon offers its employees. For example, Alcon offers a 401(k) retirement plan in which it matches 240 percent of what employees contribute, up to a total of 5 percent of total compensation. So, for example, if an employee invests $500 toward retirement in a given month, Alcon contributes $1,200. That policy more than doubles the most generous rates of other companies, allowing employees to build a comfortable "nest egg" for retirement more quickly. Clearly, employees would feel a bit anxious about giving up that benefit if a competitor came calling.

NORMATIVE COMMITMENT. Now consider the reasons for staying listed in the right-hand column of Table 3-1. What would you feel if, even after taking all those reasons into account, you decided to leave your organization to join another one? Answer: You'd feel a sense of *guilt*. Normative commitment exists when there is a sense that staying is the "right" or "moral" thing to do.[31] The sense that people *should* stay with their current employers may result from personal work philosophies or more general codes of right and wrong developed over the course of their lives. They may also be dictated by early experiences within the company, if employees are socialized to believe that long-term loyalty is the norm rather than the exception.[32]

OB ON SCREEN

THE INCREDIBLES

I can't do that to my family again, everyone just got settled.

With those words, Bob Parr summarizes his plight to his government handler in *The Incredibles* (Dir: Brad Bird. Pixar, 2004). You see, Bob was once a superhero named Mr. Incredible. Like other costumed "supers," Mr. Incredible saved lives every day. All that changed when Mr. Incredible rescued someone who didn't want to be saved. The resulting lawsuit triggered a barrage of legal action against supers. In response, the government passed the Superhero Relocation Program, granting heroes amnesty from legal action so long as they agreed to live anonymously as average citizens.

That's what brought Bob to Insuracare—the mind-numbingly generic insurance company where he toils away as a claims agent. Bob doesn't feel any emotional attachment to Insuracare. We don't see any coworkers to speak of, and Bob certainly isn't attached to his boss. He also lacks a sense of obligation to the company. In fact, he's begun "bending the rules" to help clients—teaching them how to exploit loopholes to get the money they need. As his boss points out, such actions harm Insuracare's bottom line. For Bob, however, they help him recapture a small piece of his past heroic life.

Why doesn't Bob quit? Because he needs to stay. The government has already paid to relocate him several times, and he feels like this is his last chance to make it work. His kids are in a good school, and his wife has finally unpacked the last box. The Parrs are now officially embedded, giving Bob a sense of continuance commitment. Still, he is getting restless. In fact, he's begun spending his "bowling nights" listening to police scanners. When Bob witnesses a mugging outside his boss's window, he just might reach a breaking point that will put his Insuracare days behind him forever.

Aside from personal work philosophies or organizational socialization, there seem to be two ways to build a sense of obligation-based commitment among employees. One way is to create a feeling that employees are in the organization's debt—that they owe something to the organization. For example, an organization may spend a great deal of money training and developing an employee. In recognition of that investment, the employee may feel obligated to "repay" the organization with several more years of loyal service.[33] Picture a scenario in which your employer paid your tuition, allowing you to further your education, while also providing you with training and developmental job assignments that increased your skills. Wouldn't you feel a bit guilty if you took the first job opportunity that came your way?

Another possible way to build an obligation-based sense of commitment is by becoming a particularly charitable organization. Did you ever wonder why organizations spend time and money on charitable things—for example, building playgrounds in the local community? Don't those kinds of projects take away from research and development, product improvements, or profits for shareholders? Well, charitable efforts have several potential advantages. First, they can provide good public relations for the organization, potentially generating goodwill for its products and services and helping attract new recruits.[34] Second, they can help existing employees feel better about the organization, creating a deeper sense of normative commitment. Those benefits may be particularly relevant with younger employees. Some evidence indicates that members of Generation Y (those born between 1977 and 1994) are somewhat more charitably minded than other generations. In support of that view, a growing number of MBA graduates are joining socially conscious online networks, such as Netimpact.org (see Chapter 7 on Trust, Justice, and Ethics for more discussion of such issues).[35]

Qualcomm recognizes the value of normative commitment. The San Diego, California–based firm, specializing in wireless technologies, has a voluntary turnover rate of just over 3 percent. After six Qualcomm employees lost their homes in a forest fire, other Qualcomm employees collected donations and contributed $60,000 to the Red Cross disaster relief fund.[36] Qualcomm matched that contribution and gives 1–2 percent of its pretax profits to charitable causes each year.[37] Charitable actions are also an important element of Microsoft's culture. Not only does Bill Gates himself donate a large percentage of his wealth to philanthropic efforts,[38] but his organization matches any charitable contribution made by its employees.[39] These sorts of activities create a sense that employees ought to remain with their current organization.

WITHDRAWAL BEHAVIOR

A recent survey revealed that only 25 percent of the largest 500 companies are confident that their current talent pool is sufficient.[40] Organizational commitment is therefore a vital concern, because the loss of even one talented employee can only worsen that situation. However, there are times when organizational commitment becomes even more critical, namely, in the face of some negative work event. To paraphrase the old saying, "When the going gets tough, the organization doesn't want you to get going." In tough times, organizations need their employees to demonstrate loyalty, not "get going" right out the door. Of course, it's those same tough times that put an employee's loyalty and allegiance to the test.

Consider the following scenario: You've been working at your company for three years and served on a key product development team for the past several months. Unfortunately, the team has been struggling of late. In an effort to enhance the team's performance, the organization has added a new member to the group. This member has a solid history of product development but is, by all accounts, a horrible person to work with. You can easily see the employee's talent but find yourself hating every moment spent in the employee's presence. This situation is particularly distressing because the team won't finish its work for another nine months, at the earliest. What would you do in this situation?

 3.3

What are the four primary responses to negative events at work?

Research on reactions to negative work events suggests that you might respond in one of four general ways.[41] First, you might attempt to remove yourself from the situation, either by being absent from work more frequently or by voluntarily leaving the organization. This removal is termed **exit**, defined as an active, destructive response by which an individual either ends or restricts organizational membership.[42] Second, you might attempt to change the circumstances by meeting with the new team member to attempt to work out the situation. This action is termed **voice**, defined as an active, constructive response in which individuals attempt to improve the situation (see Chapter 2 on Job Performance for more discussion of such issues).[43] Third, you might just "grin and bear it," maintaining your effort level despite your unhappiness. This response is termed **loyalty**, defined as a passive, constructive response that maintains public support for the situation while the individual privately hopes for improvement.[44] Fourth, you might just go through the motions, allowing your performance to deteriorate slowly as you mentally "check out." This reaction is termed **neglect**, defined as a passive, destructive response in which interest and effort in the job declines.[45] Sometimes neglect can be even more costly than exit because it's not as readily noticed. Employees may neglect their duties for months (or even years) before their bosses catch on to their poor behaviors.

Taken together, the exit–voice–loyalty–neglect framework captures most of the possible responses to a negative work event, like the addition of a new colleague who makes work more difficult. Where does organizational commitment fit in? Organizational commitment should decrease the likelihood that an individual will respond to a negative work event with exit or neglect (the two destructive responses). At the same time, organizational commitment should increase the likelihood that the negative work event will prompt voice or loyalty (the two constructive responses). Consistent with that logic, research indeed suggests that organizational commitment increases the likelihood of voice and loyalty while decreasing the likelihood of exit and neglect.[46]

If we consider employees' task performance levels, together with their organizational commitment levels, we can gain an even clearer picture of how people might respond to negative work events. Consider Table 3-3, which depicts combinations of high and low levels of organizational commitment and task performance. **Stars** possess high commitment and high performance and are held up as role models for other employees. Stars likely respond to negative events with voice because they have the desire to improve the status quo and the credibility needed to inspire change.[47] It's pretty easy to spot the stars in a given unit, and you can probably think about your current or past job experiences and identify the employees who would fit that description. **Citizens** possess high commitment and low task performance but perform many of the voluntary "extra-role" activities that are needed to make the organization function smoothly.[48] Citizens are likely to respond to negative events with loyalty because they may lack the credibility needed to inspire change but do possess the desire to remain a member of the organization. You can spot citizens by looking for the people who do the little things—showing around new employees, picking up birthday cakes, ordering new supplies when needed, and so forth.

Lone wolves possess low levels of organizational commitment but high levels of task performance and are motivated to achieve work goals for themselves, not necessarily for their company.[49] They are likely to respond to negative events with exit. Although their performance would give them the credibility needed to inspire change, their lack of attachment prevents them from using that credibility constructively. Instead, they rely on their

TABLE 3-3	Four Types of Employees		
		Task Performance	
		HIGH	**LOW**
Organizational Commitment	**HIGH**	Stars	Citizens
	LOW	Lone wolves	Apathetics

Source: Adapted from R.W. Griffeth, S. Gaertner, and J.K. Sager, "Taxonomic Model of Withdrawal Behaviors: The Adaptive Response Model," *Human Resource Management Review* 9 (1999), pp. 577–90.

performance levels to make them marketable to their next employer. To spot lone wolves, look for the talented employees who never seem to want to get involved in important decisions about the future of the company. Finally, **apathetics** possess low levels of both organizational commitment and task performance and merely exert the minimum level of effort needed to keep their jobs.[50] Apathetics should respond to negative events with neglect, because they lack the performance needed to be marketable and the commitment needed to engage in acts of citizenship.

It's clear from this discussion that exit and neglect represent the flip side of organizational commitment: withdrawal behavior. How common is withdrawal behavior within organizations? Quite common, it turns out. One study clocked employees' on-the-job behaviors over a two-year period and found that only about 51 percent of their time was actually spent working! The other 49 percent was lost to late starts, early departures, long coffee breaks, personal matters, and other forms of withdrawal.[51] As a manager, wouldn't you like to feel like there was more than a coin-flip's chance that your employees were actually working during the course of a given day?

As shown in Figure 3-4, withdrawal comes in two forms: psychological (or neglect) and physical (or exit). **Psychological withdrawal** consists of actions that provide a

3.4

What are some examples of psychological withdrawal? Of physical withdrawal? How do the different forms of withdrawal relate to each other?

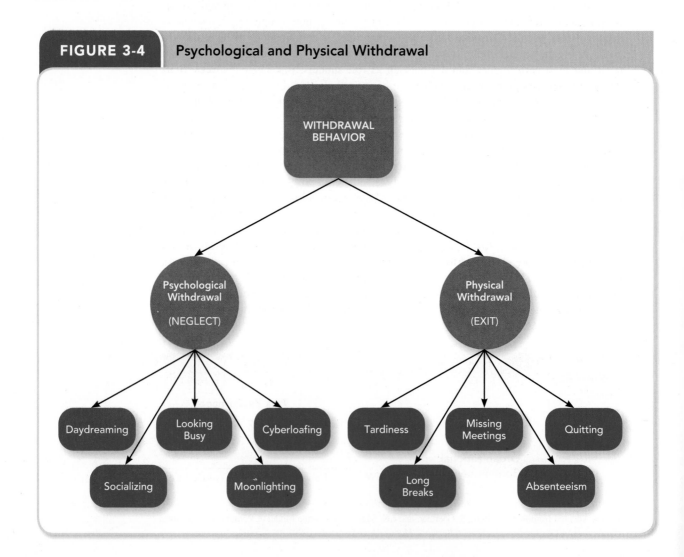

| FIGURE 3-4 | Psychological and Physical Withdrawal |

WITHDRAWAL BEHAVIOR

Psychological Withdrawal (NEGLECT)

- Daydreaming
- Looking Busy
- Cyberloafing
- Socializing
- Moonlighting

Physical Withdrawal (EXIT)

- Tardiness
- Missing Meetings
- Quitting
- Long Breaks
- Absenteeism

mental escape from the work environment.[52] Some business articles refer to psychological withdrawal as "warm-chair attrition," meaning that employees have essentially been lost even though their chairs remain occupied.[53] This withdrawal form comes in a number of shapes and sizes.[54] The least serious is **daydreaming**, when employees appear to be working but are actually distracted by random thoughts or concerns. **Socializing** refers to the verbal chatting about nonwork topics that goes on in cubicles and offices or at the mailbox or vending machines. **Looking busy** indicates an intentional desire on the part of employees to look like they're working, even when not performing work tasks. Sometimes employees decide to reorganize their desks or go for a stroll around the building, even though they have nowhere to go. (Those who are very good at managing impressions do such things very briskly and with a focused look on their faces!) When employees engage in **moonlighting**, they use work time and resources to complete something other than their job duties, such as assignments for another job.

"Hewes, it's come to my attention that you've been using our internet access to troll for babes."

Source: Copyright © The New Yorker Collection 1994 Robert Mankoff from cartoonbank.com. All rights reserved.

Perhaps the most widespread form of psychological withdrawal among white collar employees is **cyberloafing**—using Internet, e-mail, and instant messaging access for their personal enjoyment rather than work duties.[55] Some estimates suggest that typical cubicle dwellers stop what they're doing about once every three minutes to send e-mail, check Facebook or Twitter, surf over to YouTube, and so forth.[56] Such distractions consume as much as 28 percent of employees' workdays and cost some $650 billion a year in lost productivity. Cyberloafing tends to peak every March during the NCAA tournament, with estimates suggesting that employers lose $1.2 billion in lost productivity as employees watch or follow the games online.[57] Some employees view cyberloafing as a way of "balancing the scales" when it comes to personal versus work time. For example, one participant in a cyberloafing study noted, "It is alright for me to use the Internet for personal reasons at work. After all, I do work overtime without receiving extra pay from my employer."[58] Although such views may seem quite reasonable, other employees view cyberloafing as a means to retaliate for negative work events. One participant in the same study noted, "My boss is not the appreciative kind; I take what I can whenever I can. Surfing the net is my way of hitting back."

Physical withdrawal consists of actions that provide a physical escape, whether short term or long term, from the work environment.[59] Physical withdrawal also comes in a number of shapes and sizes. **Tardiness** reflects the tendency to arrive at work late (or leave work early).[60] Of course, tardiness can sometimes be unavoidable, as when employees have car trouble or must fight through bad weather, but it often represents a calculated desire to spend less time at work.[61] **Long breaks** involve longer-than-normal lunches, soda breaks, coffee breaks, and so forth that provide a physical escape from work. Ben Hamper's classic book *Rivethead: Tales of the Assembly Line*[62] is filled with examples of General Motors manufacturing employees taking excessively long breaks. For example, employees would routinely take turns covering for one another on the assembly line for half a shift so that they could spend several hours sleeping in their cars or at home, running errands, or even drinking beer at local bars. Sometimes long breaks stretch into **missing meetings**, which means employees neglect important work functions while away from the office. As a manager, you'd like to be sure that employees who leave for lunch are actually going to come back, but sometimes that's not a safe bet!

Absenteeism occurs when employees miss an entire day of work.[63] Of course, people stay home from work for a variety of reasons, including illness and family emergencies. There's also a rhythm to absenteeism. For example, employees are more likely to be absent on Mondays or Fridays. Moreover, streaks of good attendance create a sort of pressure to be absent, as personal responsibilities build until a day at home becomes irresistible.[64] That type of absence can sometimes be functional, because people may return to work with their "batteries recharged."[65] Group and departmental norms also affect absenteeism by signaling whether an employee can get away with missing a day here or there without being noticed.[66] These issues aside, a consistent pattern of absenteeism, month in and month out, is a symptom of the kind of low commitment that concerns most managers.

Finally, the most serious form of physical withdrawal is **quitting**—voluntarily leaving the organization. As with the other forms of withdrawal, employees can choose to "turn over" for a variety of reasons. The most frequent reasons include leaving for more money or a better career opportunity; dissatisfaction with supervision, working conditions, or working schedule; family factors; and health.[67] Note that many of those reasons reflect avoidable turnover, meaning that the organization could have done something to keep the employee, perhaps by offering more money, more frequent promotions, or a better work situation. Family factors and health, in contrast, usually reflect unavoidable turnover that doesn't necessarily signal a lack of commitment on the part of employees.

Regardless of their reasons, some employees choose to quit after engaging in a very thorough, careful, and reasoned analysis. Typically some sort of "shock," whether it be a critical job change, a negative work experience, or an unsolicited job offer, jars employees enough that it triggers the thought of quitting in them.[68] Once the idea of quitting has occurred to them, employees begin searching for other places to work, compare those alternatives to their current job, and—if the comparisons seem favorable—quit.[69] This process may take days, weeks, or even months as employees grapple with the decision. In other cases, though, a shock may result in an impulsive, knee-jerk decision to quit, with little or no thought given to alternative jobs (or how those jobs compare to the current one).[70] Of course, sometimes a shock never occurs. Instead, an employee decides to quit as a result of a slow but steady decrease in happiness until a "straw breaks the camel's back" and voluntary turnover results.

Figure 3-4 shows 10 different behaviors that employees can perform to psychologically or physically escape from a negative work environment. A key question remains though: "How do all those behaviors relate to one another?" Consider the following testimonials from uncommitted (and admittedly fictional) employees:

- "I can't stand my job, so I do what I can to get by. Sometimes I'm absent, sometimes I socialize, sometimes I come in late. There's no real rhyme or reason to it; I just do whatever seems practical at the time."
- "I can't handle being around my boss. I hate to miss work, so I do what's needed to avoid being absent. I figure if I socialize a bit and spend some time surfing the Web, I don't need to ever be absent. But if I couldn't do those things, I'd definitely have to stay home . . . a lot."
- "I just don't have any respect for my employer anymore. In the beginning, I'd daydream a bit during work or socialize with my colleagues. As time went on, I began coming in late or taking a long lunch. Lately I've been staying home altogether, and I'm starting to think I should just quit my job and go somewhere else."

Each of these statements sounds like something that an uncommitted employee might say. However, each statement makes a different prediction about the relationships among the withdrawal behaviors in Figure 3-4. The first statement summarizes the **independent forms model** of withdrawal, which argues that the various withdrawal behaviors are uncorrelated with one another, occur for different reasons, and fulfill different needs on the part of employees.[71] From this perspective, knowing that an employee cyberloafs tells you nothing about whether that employee is likely to be absent. The second statement summarizes the **compensatory forms model** of withdrawal, which argues that the various withdrawal behaviors negatively correlate with one another—that doing one means you're less likely to do another. The idea is that any form of withdrawal can compensate for, or neutralize, a sense of dissatisfaction, which makes the other forms unnecessary. From this perspective, knowing that an employee cyberloafs tells you that the same employee probably isn't going to be absent. The third statement summarizes the **progression model** of withdrawal, which argues that the various withdrawal behaviors are positively correlated: The tendency to daydream or socialize leads to the tendency to come in late or take long breaks, which leads to the tendency to be absent or quit. From this perspective, knowing that an employee cyberloafs tells you that the same employee is probably going to be absent in the near future.

Which of the three models seems most logical to you? Although all three make some sense, the progression model has received the most scientific support.[72] Studies tend to show that the withdrawal behaviors in Figure 3-4 are positively correlated with one another.[73] Moreover, if you view the behaviors as a causal sequence moving from left (daydreaming) to right (quitting), the behaviors that are closest to each other in the sequence tend to be more highly correlated.[74] For example, quitting is more closely related to absenteeism than to tardiness, because absenteeism is right next to it in the withdrawal progression. These results illustrate that withdrawal behaviors may begin with very minor actions but eventually can escalate to more serious actions that may harm the organization.

SUMMARY: WHAT DOES IT MEAN TO BE "COMMITTED"?

So what does it mean to be a "committed" employee? As shown in Figure 3-5, it means a lot of different things. It means that employees have a strong desire to remain a member of the organization, maybe because they want to stay, need to stay, or feel they ought to stay. Regardless of the reasons for their attachment though, retaining these employees means stopping the progression of withdrawal that begins with psychological forms and then escalates to behavioral forms. Note that the negative sign (−) in Figure 3-5 illustrates that high levels of overall organizational commitment reduce the frequency of psychological and physical withdrawal. Note also that psychological withdrawal goes on to affect physical withdrawal, which represents the progressive nature of such behaviors.

As you move forward in this book, you'll notice that every chapter includes a description of how that chapter's topic relates to organizational commitment. For example, Chapter 4 on Job Satisfaction describes how employees' satisfaction levels influence their organizational commitment. Chapter 7 on Trust, Justice, and Ethics explains how employees' trust in management influences their organizational commitment. Sometimes you'll notice that a given chapter's topic relates more strongly to organizational commitment than to job performance. Other times, however, the topic may relate similarly to commitment and performance, or even relate more strongly to performance. Regardless, such differences will help you see exactly why the various topics in this book are so important to managers.

FIGURE 3-5   What Does It Mean to Be "Committed"?

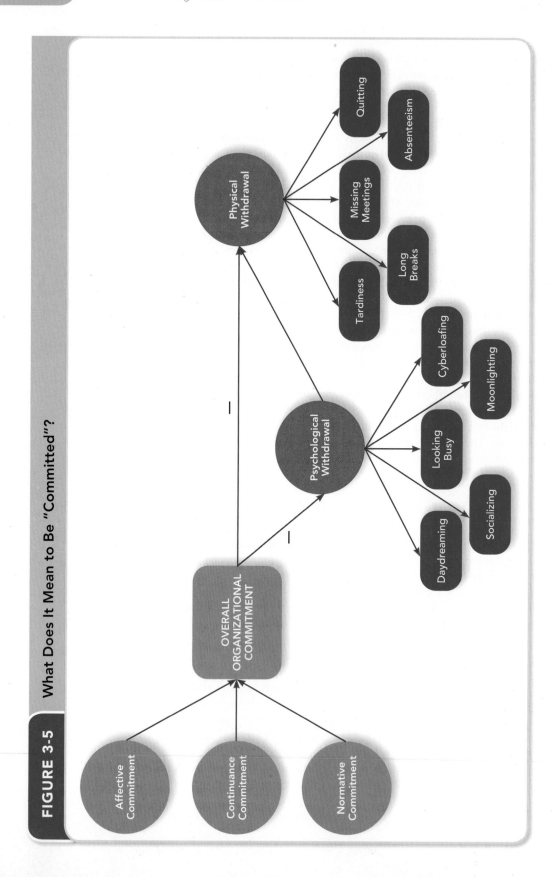

TRENDS THAT AFFECT COMMITMENT

Now that we've described exactly what organizational commitment represents, it's time to describe some of the trends that affect it in the contemporary workplace. Put simply, the composition of the workforce is changing, as is the traditional relationship between employees and employers. These trends put pressure on some types of commitment and alter the kinds of withdrawal seen in the workplace.

DIVERSITY OF THE WORKFORCE

One of the most visible trends affecting the workplace is the increased diversity of the United States' labor force. Demographically speaking, the percentage of the workforce that is white is expected to drop to around 65 percent by 2012.[75] Meanwhile, the percentage of minorities in the workforce is expected to rise to the following levels: African Americans (12 percent), Hispanics (15 percent), and Asians (6 percent). Thus, by 2012, minority groups will make up one-third of the workforce. Meanwhile, women have virtually matched men in terms of workforce percentages, with 53 percent of jobs filled by men and 47 percent by women. These statistics show that the "white, male-dominated" workforce is becoming a thing of the past.

3.5

What workplace trends are affecting organizational commitment in today's organizations?

The workforce is becoming diverse in other ways as well. The percentage of members of the workforce who are 60 years or older is expected to grow to 10 percent in 2012.[76] As the 78 million Baby Boomers near retirement, they're expected to remain in the workforce significantly longer than previous generations.[77] Research suggests that remaining a member of the workforce is actually beneficial to older people's health, keeping them more mentally and physically fit. Moreover, medical advances are helping older employees stay vital longer, just as the physical labor component of most jobs keeps shrinking. The Baby Boomers are also one of the most educated generations, and research suggests that their continued participation in the workforce could add $3 trillion a year to the country's economic output. That, combined with the uncertainty surrounding Social Security and stock market–based retirement plans, makes staying in the workforce a logical call.

As the economy continues to become more global, U.S. businesses face another important form of diversity: More and more employees are foreign-born. Although stereotypes view immigrants as staffing blue collar or service jobs, many of the most educated employees come from abroad. Consider that half of the PhDs working in the United States are foreign-born, as are 45 percent of the physicists, computer scientists, and mathematicians.[78] At the same time, more and more American employees are working as expatriates who staff offices in foreign countries for long periods of time. Serving as an expatriate can be a very stressful assignment for employees as they adjust to a new country, a new style of working, and increased distance from family and friends. See our **OB Internationally** feature for more discussion of organizational commitment in multinational corporations.

These forms of diversity make it more challenging to retain valued employees. Consider the social network diagram in Figure 3-3. As work groups become more diverse with respect to race, gender, age, and national origin, there's a danger that minorities or older employees will find themselves on the fringe of such networks, which potentially reduces their affective commitment. At the same time, foreign-born employees are likely to feel less embedded in their current jobs and perceive fewer links to their community and less fit with their geographic area. This feeling may reduce their sense of continuance

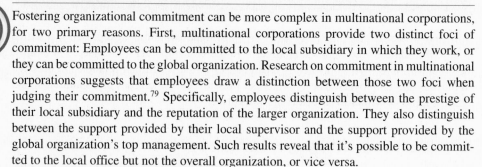

OB INTERNATIONALLY

Fostering organizational commitment can be more complex in multinational corporations, for two primary reasons. First, multinational corporations provide two distinct foci of commitment: Employees can be committed to the local subsidiary in which they work, or they can be committed to the global organization. Research on commitment in multinational corporations suggests that employees draw a distinction between those two foci when judging their commitment.[79] Specifically, employees distinguish between the prestige of their local subsidiary and the reputation of the larger organization. They also distinguish between the support provided by their local supervisor and the support provided by the global organization's top management. Such results reveal that it's possible to be committed to the local office but not the overall organization, or vice versa.

Second, multinational corporations require many employees to serve as expatriates for significant periods of time. Research suggests that the organizational commitment of expatriates depends, in part, on how well they adjust to their foreign assignments.[80] Research further suggests that expatriates' adjustment comes in three distinct forms:[81]

- *Work adjustment.* The degree of comfort with specific job responsibilities and performance expectations.
- *Cultural adjustment.* The degree of comfort with the general living conditions, climate, cost of living, transportation, and housing offered by the host culture.
- *Interaction adjustment.* The degree of comfort when socializing and interacting with members of the host culture.

A study of American multinational corporations in the transportation, service, manufacturing, chemical, and pharmaceutical industries showed that all three forms of adjustment relate significantly to affective commitment.[82] If expatriates cannot feel comfortable in their assignment, it's difficult for them to develop an emotional bond to their organization. Instead, they're likely to withdraw from the assignment, both psychologically and physically.

What factors contribute to an expatriate's adjustment levels? It turns out that work adjustment depends on many of the same things that drive domestic employees' job satisfaction and motivation.[83] Cultural and interaction adjustment, in contrast, are very dependent on spousal and family comfort. If an expatriate's spouse or children are unhappy in their new environment, it becomes very difficult for the expatriate to remain committed. Fortunately, research suggests that cultural and interaction adjustment can increase with time, as experiences in the host nation gradually increase expatriates' sense of comfort and, ultimately, their commitment to the work assignment.

commitment. Recent trends suggest that the most educated and skilled immigrants are leaving the U.S. workforce at a rate of about 1,000 a day, particularly when their home country's economy begins to boom.[84]

THE CHANGING EMPLOYEE–EMPLOYER RELATIONSHIP

A few generations ago, many employees assumed that they would work for a single organization for their entire career. The assumption was that they would exchange a lifetime of loyalty and good work for a lifetime of job security. That perception changed in the 1980s and 1990s as downsizing became a more common part of working life. In 1992, downsizing statistics peaked as 3.4 million jobs were lost, and annual job losses have remained that high ever since.[85] Downsizing represents a form of involuntary turnover, when employees are forced to leave the organization regardless of their previous levels of commitment. The increase in downsizing has gone hand-in-hand with increases in temporary workers and outsourcing, fundamentally altering the way employees view their relationships with their employers.

Companies usually downsize to cut costs, particularly during a recession or economic downturn. Does downsizing work? Does it make the company more profitable? One study suggests that the answer is "not usually." This study examined 3,628 companies between 1980 and 1994, of which 59 percent downsized 5 percent or more of their workforce at least once and 33 percent fired 15 percent or more of their workforce at least once.[86] The most important result was that downsizing actually harmed company profitability and stock price. In fact, it typically took firms two years to return to the performance levels that prompted the downsizing in the first place. The exception to this rule was companies that downsized in the context of some larger change in assets (e.g., the sale of a line of business, a merger, an acquisition). However, such firms were relatively rare; only one-eighth of the downsizers were involved in some sort of asset change at the time the layoffs occurred.

Why doesn't downsizing tend to work? One reason revolves around the organizational commitment levels of the so-called "survivors." The employees who remain in the organization after a downsizing are often stricken with "survivor syndrome," characterized by anger, depression, fear, distrust, and guilt.[87] One study found that downsizing survivors actually experienced more work-related stress than did the downsizing victims who went on to find new employment.[88] Survivor syndrome tends to reduce organizational commitment levels at the worst possible time, as downsizing survivors are often asked to work extra hard to compensate for their lost colleagues.

The change in employee–employer relationships brought about by a generation of downsizing makes it more challenging to retain valued employees. The most obvious challenge is finding a way to maintain affective commitment. The negative emotions aroused by survivor syndrome likely reduce emotional attachment to the organization. Moreover, if the downsizing has caused the loss of key figures in employees' social networks, then their desire to stay will be harmed. However, a second challenge is to find some way to maintain normative commitment. The sense that people *should* stay with their employer may have been eroded by downsizing, with personal work philosophies now focusing on maximizing marketability for the next opportunity that comes along. Even if employees felt obligated to remain at a firm in the past, seeing colleagues get dismissed in a downsizing effort could change that belief rather quickly.

One way of quantifying the change in employee–employer relationships is to assess how employees view those relationships psychologically. Research suggests that employees tend to view their employment relationships in quasi-contractual terms. Specifically, **psychological contracts** reflect employees' beliefs about what they owe the organization and what the organization owes them.[89] These contracts are shaped by the recruitment and socialization activities that employees experience, which often convey promises and expectations that shape beliefs about reciprocal obligations. Some employees develop **transactional contracts** that are based on a narrow set of specific monetary obligations (e.g., the employee owes attendance and protection of proprietary information; the organization owes pay and advancement opportunities).[90] Other employees develop **relational contracts** that are based on a broader set of open-ended and subjective obligations (e.g., the employee owes loyalty and the willingness to go above and beyond; the organization owes job security, development, and support).[91] Seeing one's coworkers downsized can constitute a "breach" of an employee's psychological contract, and research

OB AT THE BOOKSTORE

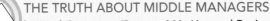

THE TRUTH ABOUT MIDDLE MANAGERS
by Paul Osterman (Boston, MA: Harvard Business Press, 2008).

My interviews strongly suggest that managers are akin to craft workers, both enjoy-ing what they do and committed to a high quality of work. A not-so-optimistic picture emerges, however, when I examine their relationships to their employers.

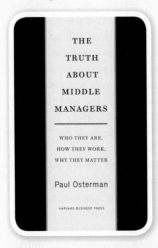

With those words, Osterman hints at the principal finding of his research on middle managers—a group that consti-tutes roughly one-fifth of the working population. Oster-man spent two years interviewing and observing 50 middle managers at two organizations: Fleet Bank (which was in the process of being acquired by Bank of America) and an unnamed high-tech firm. He focused on middle managers specifically because they're often blamed for the inefficien-cies within organizations and viewed as the "fat" that gets "trimmed" during restructuring efforts. The fact remains, however, that middle managers make many important deci-sions within organizations, even if they themselves have little impact on the strategic direction of the firm.

Osterman begins his analysis by examining census and employment data to determine the impact of downsizing and restructuring on the ranks of middle managers. On the one hand, middle managers represent a disproportionately high percentage of "displaced workers"—employees with three or more years of tenure who have lost their jobs due to job changes. On the other hand, the raw number of middle managers continues to grow, and they earn an average of $57 an hour (versus $27 an hour for all employees). If the economic data on middle managers seem a bit of a mixed bag, Osterman's interview data yielded a clearer picture. Almost to a person, middle managers lacked a sense of loyalty and enthusiasm for top management. As Osterman summarized: "The ties of mutual commitment between firms and managers seem to have frayed substantially." Rather than being committed to the organization, the managers were committed only to their craft. They still worked hard and took pride in their work, but they no longer viewed themselves as "of the corporation."

suggests that psychological contract breach leads to psychological and physical with-drawal.[92] However, trends such as downsizing, use of temporary workers, and outsourcing may also cause employees to define their contracts in more transactional (as opposed to relational) terms. See our **OB at the Bookstore** feature to see how these workplace trends have shaped the way middle managers view their organizational relationship.

APPLICATION: COMMITMENT INITIATIVES

Now that you've gained a good understanding of organizational commitment, as well as some of the workforce trends that affect it, we close with a discussion of strategies and initiatives that can be used to maximize commitment. As the Accenture example illustrates, almost every company could benefit from improving its commitment levels. What can they do to increase loyalty? At a general level, organizations can be supportive. **Perceived organizational support** reflects the degree to which employees believe that the organization values their contributions and cares about their well-being.[93] Organizations can do a number of things to be supportive, including providing adequate rewards, protecting job security, improving work conditions, and minimizing the impact of politics.[94] In a sense, such support represents the organization's commitment to its employees. A meta-analysis of 42 research studies with almost 12,000 participants revealed that perceptions of support are strongly related to organizational commitment.[95] That same review showed that perceptions of support are associated with lower levels of psychological and physical withdrawal.

Beyond being supportive, organizations can engage in specific practices that target the three forms of commitment. For example, organizations could foster affective commitment by increasing the bonds that link employees together. Ben & Jerry's holds monthly "joy events" during which all production stops for a few hours, to be replaced by Cajun-themed parties, table tennis contests, and employee appreciation celebrations.[96] Monsanto, the St. Louis, Missouri–based provider of agricultural products, groups staffers into "people teams" charged with designing employee-bonding activities like "snowshoe softball."[97] Such tight bonding among employees may explain why Monsanto's voluntary turnover rate is only 3 percent. Companies like PepsiCo and Procter & Gamble pay particular attention to mentoring and team-building programs for female and minority employees to create a sense of solidarity among employees who might otherwise remain on the fringe of social networks.[98]

From a continuance commitment perspective, the priority should be to create a salary and benefits package that creates a financial need to stay. One study compared the impact of a variety of human resource management practices on voluntary turnover and found that two of the most significant predictors were average pay level and quality of the benefits package.[99] Of course, one factor that goes hand-in-hand with salaries and benefits is advancements and promotions, because salaries cannot remain competitive if employees get stuck in neutral when climbing the career ladder.[100] Perhaps that's why companies that are well-known for their commitment to promotion-from-within policies, like A.G. Edwards and the Principal Financial Group, also enjoy especially low voluntary turnover rates.[101] Paying attention to career paths is especially important for star employees and foreign-born employees, both of whom have many options for employment elsewhere.[102]

3.6

How can organizations foster a sense of commitment among employees?

Ben & Jerry's, founded by Ben Cohen and Jerry Greenfield, goes to great lengths to encourage employees to hang out together and have fun during their workweek. Such bonding activities lower turnover and encourage valued employees to remain.

From a normative commitment perspective, the employer can provide various training and development opportunities for employees, which means investing in them to create the sense that they owe further service to the organization. As the nature of the employee–employer relationship has changed, opportunities for development have overtaken secure employment on the list of employee priorities.[103] IBM is one company with a reputation for prioritizing development. Its "workforce management initiative" keeps a database of 33,000 resumes to develop a snapshot of employee skills.[104] IBM uses that snapshot to plan its future training and development activities, with $400 million of the company's $750 million training budget devoted to giving employees the skills they may need in the future. If employees find developmental activities beneficial and rewarding, they may be tempted to repay those efforts with additional years of service.

A final practical suggestion centers on what to do if withdrawal begins to occur. Managers are usually tempted to look the other way when employees engage in minor forms of withdrawal. After all, sometimes such behaviors simply represent a break in an otherwise busy day. However, the progression model of withdrawal shows that even minor forms of psychological withdrawal often escalate, eventually to the point of absenteeism and turnover. The implication is therefore to stop the progression in its early stages by trying to root out the source of the reduced commitment. Many of the most effective companies take great strides to investigate the causes of low commitment, whether at the psychological withdrawal stage or during exit interviews. As one senior oil executive acknowledged, the loss of a talented employee warrants the same sort of investigation as a technical malfunction that causes significant downtime on an oil rig.[105]

TAKEAWAYS

3.1 Organizational commitment is the desire on the part of an employee to remain a member of the organization. Withdrawal behavior is a set of actions that employees perform to avoid the work situation. Commitment and withdrawal are negatively related to each other—the more committed employees are, the less likely they are to engage in withdrawal.

3.2 There are three types of organizational commitment. Affective commitment occurs when employees *want* to stay and is influenced by the emotional bonds between employees. Continuance commitment occurs when employees *need* to stay and is influenced by salary and benefits and the degree to which they are embedded in the community. Normative commitment occurs when employees feel that they *ought* to stay and is influenced by an organization investing in its employees or engaging in charitable efforts.

3.3 Employees can respond to negative work events in four ways: exit, voice, loyalty, and neglect. Exit is a form of physical withdrawal in which the employee either ends or restricts organizational membership. Voice is an active and constructive response by which employees attempt to improve the situation. Loyalty is passive and constructive; employees remain supportive while hoping the situation improves on its own. Neglect is a form of psychological withdrawal in which interest and effort in the job decrease.

3.4 Examples of psychological withdrawal include daydreaming, socializing, looking busy, moonlighting, and cyberloafing. Examples of physical withdrawal include tardiness, long breaks, missing meetings, absenteeism, and quitting. Consistent with the progression model, withdrawal behaviors tend to start with minor psychological forms before escalating to more major physical varieties.

3.5 The increased diversity of the workforce can reduce commitment if employees feel lower levels of affective commitment or become less embedded in their current jobs. The employee–employer relationship, which has changed due to decades of downsizing, can reduce affective and normative commitment, making it more of a challenge to retain talented employees.

3.6 Organizations can foster commitment among employees by fostering perceived organizational support, which reflects the degree to which the organization cares about employees' well-being. Commitment can also be fostered by specific initiatives directed at the three commitment types.

KEY TERMS

- Organizational commitment   *p. 69*
- Withdrawal behavior   *p. 69*
- Affective commitment   *p. 71*
- Continuance commitment   *p. 71*
- Normative commitment   *p. 71*
- Focus of commitment   *p. 72*
- Erosion model   *p. 74*
- Social influence model   *p. 74*
- Embeddedness   *p. 75*
- Exit   *p. 78*
- Voice   *p. 78*
- Loyalty   *p. 79*
- Neglect   *p. 79*
- Stars   *p. 79*
- Citizens   *p. 79*
- Lone wolves   *p. 79*
- Apathetics   *p. 80*
- Psychological withdrawal   *p. 80*
- Daydreaming   *p. 81*
- Socializing   *p. 81*
- Looking busy   *p. 81*
- Moonlighting   *p. 81*
- Cyberloafing   *p. 81*
- Physical withdrawal   *p. 81*
- Tardiness   *p. 81*
- Long breaks   *p. 81*
- Missing meetings   *p. 81*
- Absenteeism   *p. 82*
- Quitting   *p. 82*
- Independent forms model   *p. 83*
- Compensatory forms model   *p. 83*
- Progression model   *p. 83*
- Psychological contracts   *p. 87*
- Transactional contracts   *p. 87*
- Relational contracts   *p. 87*
- Perceived organizational support   *p. 89*

DISCUSSION QUESTIONS

3.1 Which type of organizational commitment (affective, continuance, or normative) do you think is most important to the majority of employees? Which do you think is most important to you?

3.2 Describe other ways that organizations can improve affective, continuance, and normative commitment, other than the strategies suggested in this chapter. How expensive are those strategies?

3.3 Consider times when you've reacted to a negative event with exit, voice, loyalty, or neglect. What was it about the situation that caused you to respond the way you did? Do you usually respond to negative events in the same way, or does your response vary across the four options?

3.4 Can organizations use a combination of monitoring and punishment procedures to reduce psychological and physical withdrawal? How might such programs work from a practical perspective? Do you think they would be effective?

3.5 Can you think of reasons the increased diversity of the workforce might actually increase organizational commitment? Why? Which of the three types of commitment might explain that sort of result?

3.6 Studies suggest that decades of downsizing have lowered organizational commitment levels. Can you think of a way that an organization can conduct layoffs without harming the commitment of the survivors? How?

CASE: ACCENTURE

You might think that Accenture's primary concern is losing its people to other top consulting firms. In fact, Accenture actually loses most of its consultants to its very own clients.[106] A consultant at another firm explains the appeal of client firms this way: "The coolest thing about being a consultant is that I know exactly where I would go work if I left, because I already have assessed the workplace of the company." As Accenture consultants work with more and more clients, they develop a broader network of contacts that become potential employers. Those moves typically bring more stability and the sense of moving into a "smaller pond." Jill Smart, the chief human resources officer at Accenture, understands the unique difficulties in retaining consultants. In reflecting on the company's commitment efforts, she notes, "We saw that we had people leaving to go do work that they could do here, and when we asked them about it, they said, 'We didn't know that we could do that'."

Smart's observation explains the rationale for Accenture's "Career Counselor" program. Each new hire is assigned a career counselor—an employee a few levels up, chosen by the human resources groups, who works in the same functional area.[107] The counselors know all the career options within the company, so they can explain all the options to good employees before they're even tempted to go elsewhere. Consultants such as Keyur Patel have monthly conversations with their counselors, who typically mentor four or five consultants. "He will talk to me about how I am doing and what opportunities he sees for me," Patel says of his counselor. "He advised me to use my Fridays to really connect with the local office and make sure I always feel a sense of belonging." Although around half of the companies on the *Fortune* 500 list offer some sort of formalized mentoring program, many prove ineffective.[108] In Accenture's case, the company takes the time to evaluate the "people-development skills" of its counselors, and those ratings have a direct impact on counselor paychecks. "If you are not a good career counselor, there are consequences," Smart explains.

3.1 What could Accenture do to reduce the number of consultants who leave to work for client firms? Would those strategies have any unintended drawbacks?

3.2 Can you think of any "silver lining" for Accenture when consultants leave to work for clients? Can such situations benefit the firm in some way?

3.3 Some companies are reluctant to institute formal programs like Accenture's career counselors, assuming instead that advice can be passed down informally by supervisors. What are some arguments for formalizing the process the way Accenture has?

EXERCISE: REACTING TO NEGATIVE EVENTS

The purpose of this exercise is to explore how individuals react to three all-too-common scenarios that represent negative workplace events. This exercise uses groups, so your instructor will either assign you to a group or ask you to create your own group. The exercise has the following steps:

3.1 Individually read the following three scenarios: the annoying boss, the boring job, and pay and seniority. For each scenario, write down two specific behaviors in which you would likely engage in response to that scenario. Write down what you would actually do, as opposed to what you wish you would do. For example, you may wish that you would march into your boss's office and demand a change, but if you would actually do nothing, write down "nothing."

Annoying Boss	You've been working at your current company for about a year. Over time, your boss has become more and more annoying to you. It's not that your boss is a bad person, or even necessarily a bad boss. It's more a personality conflict—the way your boss talks, the way your boss manages every little thing, even the facial expressions your boss uses. The more time passes, the more you just can't stand to be around your boss.	Two likely behaviors:
Boring Job	You've been working at your current company for about a year. You've come to realize that your job is pretty boring. It's the first real job you've ever had, and at first it was nice to have some money and something to do every day. But the "new job" excitement has worn off, and things are actually quite monotonous. Same thing every day. It's to the point that you check your watch every hour, and Wednesdays feel like they should be Fridays.	Two likely behaviors:
Pay and Seniority	You've been working at your current company for about a year. The consensus is that you're doing a great job—you've gotten excellent performance evaluations and have emerged as a leader on many projects. As you've achieved this high status, however, you've come to feel that you're underpaid. Your company's pay procedures emphasize seniority much more than job performance. As a result, you look at other members of your project teams and see poor performers making much more than you, just because they've been with the company longer.	Two likely behaviors:

3.2   In groups, compare and contrast your likely responses to the three scenarios. Come to a consensus on the two most likely responses for the group as a whole. Elect one group member to write the two likely responses to each of the three scenarios on the board or on a transparency.

3.3   Class discussion (whether in groups or as a class) should center on where the likely responses fit into the exit–voice–loyalty–neglect framework. What personal and situational factors would lead someone to one category of responses over another? Are there any responses that do not fit into the exit–voice–loyalty–neglect framework?

ENDNOTES

3.1   Marquez, J. "Accentuating the Positive." *Workforce Management*, September 22, 2008, pp. 18–25.

3.2   Levering, R., and M. Moskowitz. "And the Winners Are. . ." *Fortune*, February 2, 2009, pp. 67–78.

3.3   Marquez, "Accentuating the Positive."

3.4   Ruiz, G. "Study: Keeping Young Talent Won't Be Easy." *Workforce Management*, October 22, 2007, p. 14.

3.5   "By the Numbers." *Fortune*, December 27, 2005, p. 32.

3.6   "Estimating Turnover Costs." http://www.keepemployees.com/turnovercost.htm (October 20, 2005).

3.7   Fisher, A. "Playing for Keeps." *Fortune*, January 22, 2007, p. 85.

3.8   Meyer, J.P., and N.J. Allen. *Commitment in the Workplace.* Thousand Oaks, CA: Sage, 1997; and Mowday, R.T.; R.M. Steers; and L.W. Porter. "The Measurement of Organizational Commitment." *Journal of Vocational Behavior* 14 (1979), pp. 224–47.

3.9   Hulin, C.L. "Adaptation, Persistence, and Commitment in Organizations." In *Handbook of Industrial and Organizational Psychology,* Vol. 2, ed. M.D. Dunnette and L.M. Hough. Palo Alto, CA: Consulting Psychologists Press, Inc., 1991, pp. 445–506.

3.10   Allen, N.J., and J.P. Meyer. "The Measurement and Antecedents of Affective, Continuance and Normative Commitment to the Organization." *Journal of Occupational Psychology* 63 (1990), pp. 1-18; Meyer, J.P., and N.J. Allen. "A Three-Component Conceptualization of Organizational Commitment." *Human Resource Management Review* 1 (1991), pp. 61–89; and Meyer and Allen, *Commitment in the Workplace.*

3.11   Ibid.

3.12   Ibid.

3.13   Meyer and Allen, *Commitment in the Workplace.*

3.14   Mowday et al., "The Measurement of Organizational Commitment."

3.15   Ibid.

3.16   Meyer, J.P.; D.J. Stanley; L. Herscovitch; and L. Topolnytsky. "Affective, Continuance, and Normative Commitment to the Organization: A Meta-Analysis of Antecedents, Correlates, and Consequences." *Journal of Vocational Behavior* 61 (2002), pp. 20–52.

3.17 Mathieu, J.E., and D.M. Zajac. "A Review and Meta-Analysis of the Antecedents, Correlates, and Consequences of Organizational Commitment." *Psychological Bulletin* 108 (1990), pp. 171–94.

3.18 Johns, G. "The Psychology of Lateness, Absenteeism, and Turnover." In *Handbook of Industrial, Work, and Organizational Psychology,* eds. N. Anderson; D.S. Ones; H.K. Sinangil; and C. Viswesvaran. Thousand Oaks, CA: Sage, 2001, pp. 232–52.

3.19 Ibid.

3.20 Levering, R., and M. Moskowitz. "The 100 Best Companies to Work For." *Fortune,* January 24, 2005, pp. 64–94.

3.21 Ibid.

3.22 Kanter, R.M. "Commitment and Social Organization: A Study of Commitment Mechanisms in Utopian Communities." *American Sociological Review* 33 (1968), pp. 499–517.

3.23 Stebbins, R.A. *Commitment to Deviance: The Nonprofessional Criminal in the Community.* Westport, CT: Greenwood Press, 1970.

3.24 Becker, H.S. "Notes on the Concept of Commitment." *American Journal of Sociology* 66 (1960), pp. 32–42.

3.25 Rusbult, C.E., and D. Farrell. "A Longitudinal Test of the Investment Model: The Impact of Job Satisfaction, Job Commitment, and Turnover of Variations in Rewards, Costs, Alternatives, and Investments." *Journal of Applied Psychology* 68 (1983), pp. 429–38.

3.26 Meyer and Allen, *Commitment in the Workplace.*

3.27 Meyer et al., "Affective, Continuance, and Normative Commitment."

3.28 Mitchell, T.R.; B.C. Holtom; T.W. Lee; C.J. Sablynski; and M. Erez. "Why People Stay: Using Job Embeddedness to Predict Voluntary Turnover." *Academy of Management Journal* 44 (2001), pp. 1102–21.

3.29 Felps, W.; T.R. Mitchell; D.R. Hekman; T.W. Lee; B.C. Holtom; and W.S. Harman. "Turnover Contagion: How Coworkers' Job Embeddedness and Job Search Behaviors Influence Quitting." *Academy of Management Journal* 52 (2009), pp. 545–61; Hom, P.W.; A.S. Tsui; J.B. Wu; T.W. Lee; A.Y. Zhang; P.P. Fu; and L. Li. "Explaining Employment Relationships with Social Exchange and Job Embeddedness." *Journal of Applied Psychology* 94 (2009), pp. 277–97.

3.30 Levering and Moskowitz, "The 100 Best Companies to Work For."

3.31 Allen and Meyer, "The Measurement and Antecedents of Affective, Continuance and Normative Commitment to the Organization"; Meyer and Allen, "A Three-Component Conceptualization"; and Meyer and Allen, *Commitment in the Workplace.*

3.32 Wiener, Y. "Commitment in Organizations: A Normative View." *Academy of Management Review* 7 (1982), pp. 418–28.

3.33 Meyer and Allen, "A Three-Component Conceptualization."

3.34 Grow, B. "The Debate over Doing Good." *BusinessWeek,* August 15, 2005, pp. 76–78.

3.35 Ibid.

3.36 Levering and Moskowitz, "The 100 Best Companies to Work For."

3.37   "Qualcomm Community Involvement–Corporate Giving." 2005, http://www.qualcomm.com/community/corporate_giving.html (October 23, 2005).

3.38   Roth, D. "The $91 Billion Conversation." *Fortune,* October 31, 2005. http://money.cnn.com/magazines/fortune/fortune_archive/2005/10/31/8359156/ (May 18, 2007).

3.39   Levering, R., and M. Moskowitz. "In Good Company." *Fortune,* January 22, 2007, pp. 94–114.

3.40   Barrett, A. "Star Search: How to Recruit, Train, and Hold on to Great People. What Works, What Doesn't." *BusinessWeek,* October 10, 2005, pp. 68–78.

3.41   Hirschman, A.O. *Exit, Voice, and Loyalty: Responses to Decline in Firms, Organizations, and States.* Cambridge, MA: Harvard University Press, 1970; and Farrell, D. "Exit, Voice, Loyalty, and Neglect as Responses to Job Dissatisfaction: A Multidimensional Scaling Study." *Academy of Management Journal* 26 (1983), pp. 596–607.

3.42   Hirschman, *Exit, Voice, and Loyalty;* Farrell, "Exit, Voice, Loyalty, and Neglect"; and Rusbult, C.E.; D. Farrell; C. Rogers; and A.G. Mainous III. "Impact of Exchange Variables on Exit, Voice, Loyalty, and Neglect: An Integrating Model of Responses to Declining Job Satisfaction." *Academy of Management Journal* 31 (1988), pp. 599–627.

3.43   Ibid.

3.44   Ibid.

3.45   Farrell, "Exit, Voice, Loyalty, and Neglect"; and Rusbult et al., "Impact of Exchange Variables."

3.46   Withey, M.J., and W.H. Cooper. "Predicting Exit, Voice, Loyalty, and Neglect." *Administrative Science Quarterly* 34 (1989), pp. 521–39; and Burris, E.R.; J.R. Detert; and D.S. Chiaburu. "Quitting Before Leaving: The Mediating Effects of Psychological Attachment and Detachment on Voice." *Journal of Applied Psychology* 93 (2008), pp. 912–22.

3.47   Griffeth, R.W.; S. Gaertner; and J.K. Sager. "Taxonomic Model of Withdrawal Behaviors: The Adaptive Response Model." *Human Resource Management Review* 9 (1999), pp. 577–90.

3.48   Ibid.

3.49   Ibid.

3.50   Ibid.

3.51   Cherrington, D. *The Work Ethic.* New York: AMACOM, 1980.

3.52   Hulin, C.L.; M. Roznowski; and D. Hachiya. "Alternative Opportunities and Withdrawal Decisions: Empirical and Theoretical Discrepancies and an Integration." *Psychological Bulletin* 97 (1985), pp. 233–50.

3.53   Fisher, A. "Turning Clock-Watchers into Stars." *Fortune,* March 22, 2004, p. 60.

3.54   Hulin et al., "Alternative Opportunities and Withdrawal Decisions."

3.55   Lim, V.K.G. "The IT Way of Loafing on the Job: Cyberloafing, Neutralizing, and Organizational Justice." *Journal of Organizational Behavior* 23 (2002), pp. 675–94.

3.56   Jackson, M. "May We Have Your Attention, Please?" *BusinessWeek,* June 23, 2008, p. 55.

3.57   Gerdes, L. "Nothin' But Net." *BusinessWeek,* March 26, 2007, p. 16.

3.58   Lim, "The IT Way of Loafing on the Job."

3.59 Hulin et al., "Alternative Opportunities and Withdrawal Decisions."

3.60 Koslowsky, M.; A. Sagie; M. Krausz; and A.D. Singer. "Correlates of Employee Lateness: Some Theoretical Considerations." *Journal of Applied Psychology* 82 (1997), pp. 79–88.

3.61 Blau, G. "Developing and Testing a Taxonomy of Lateness Behavior." *Journal of Applied Psychology* 79 (1994), pp. 959–70.

3.62 Hamper, B. *Rivethead: Tales from the Assembly Line.* New York: Warner Books, 1991.

3.63 Muchinsky, P.M. "Employee Absenteeism: A Review of the Literature." *Journal of Vocational Behavior* 10 (1977), pp. 316–40; and Harrison, D.A. "Time for Absenteeism: A 20-Year Review of Origins, Offshoots, and Outcomes." *Journal of Management* 24 (1998), pp. 305-50.

3.64 Fichman, M. "Motivational Consequences of Absence and Attendance: Proportional Hazard Estimation of a Dynamic Motivation Model." *Journal of Applied Psychology* 73 (1988), pp. 119–34.

3.65 Martocchio, J.J., and D.I. Jimeno. "Employee Absenteeism as an Affective Event." *Human Resource Management Review* 13 (2003), pp. 227–41.

3.66 Nicholson, N., and G. Johns. "The Absence Climate and the Psychological Contract: Who's in Control of Absence?" *Academy of Management Review* 10 (1985), pp. 397–407.

3.67 Campion, M.A. "Meaning and Measurement of Turnover: Comparison of Alternative Measures and Recommendations for Research." *Journal of*

Applied Psychology 76 (1991), pp. 199–212.

3.68 Lee, T.W., and T.R. Mitchell. "An Alternative Approach: The Unfolding Model of Voluntary Employee Turnover." *Academy of Management Review* 19 (1994), pp. 51–89; Lee, T.W., and T.R. Mitchell. "An Unfolding Model of Voluntary Employee Turnover." *Academy of Management Journal* 39 (1996), pp. 5–36; Lee, T.W.; T.R. Mitchell; B.C. Holtom; L.S. McDaniel; and J.W. Hill. "The Unfolding Model of Voluntary Turnover: A Replication and Extension." *Academy of Management Journal* 42 (1999), pp. 450–62; and Lee, T.H.; B. Gerhart; I. Weller; and C.O. Trevor. "Understanding Voluntary Turnover: Path-Specific Job Satisfaction Effects and the Importance of Unsolicited Job Offers." *Academy of Management Journal* 51 (2008), pp. 651–71.

3.69 Mobley, W. "Intermediate Linkages in the Relationship Between Job Satisfaction and Employee Turnover." *Journal of Applied Psychology* 62 (1977), pp. 237–40; and Hom, P.W.; R. Griffeth; and C.L. Sellaro. "The Validity of Mobley's (1977) Model of Employee Turnover." *Organizational Behavior and Human Performance* 34 (1984), pp. 141–74.

3.70 Lee and Mitchell, "An Alternative Approach"; Lee and Mitchell, "An Unfolding Model of Voluntary Employee Turnover"; Lee and Mitchell, "The Unfolding Model of Voluntary Turnover"; and Porter, L.W., and R.M. Steers. "Organizational, Work, and Personal Factors in Employee Turnover and Absenteeism." *Psychological Bulletin* 80 (1973), pp. 151–76.

3.71 Johns, "The Psychology of Lateness, Absenteeism, and Turnover."

3.72   Rosse, J.G. "Relations among Lateness, Absence, and Turnover: Is There a Progression of Withdrawal?" *Human Relations* 41 (1988), pp. 517–31.

3.73   Mitra, A.; G.D. Jenkins, Jr.; and N. Gupta. "A Meta-Analytic Review of the Relationship Between Absence and Turnover." *Journal of Applied Psychology* 77 (1992), p. 879–89; Koslowsky et al., "Correlates of Employee Lateness"; and Griffeth, R.W.; P.W. Hom; and S. Gaertner. "A Meta-Analysis of Antecedents and Correlates of Employee Turnover: Update, Moderator Tests, and Research Implications for the Next Millennium." *Journal of Management* 26 (2000), pp. 463–88.

3.74   Koslowsky et al., "Correlates of Employee Lateness."

3.75   U.S. Bureau of Labor Statistics, 2005, http://www.wnjpin.net/OneStopCareerCenter/LaborMarketInformation/lmi03/uslfproj.htm (October 26, 2005).

3.76   Ibid.

3.77   Coy, P. "Old. Smart. Productive." *BusinessWeek,* June 27, 2005, pp. 78–86.

3.78   Fisher, A. "Holding on to Global Talent." *BusinessWeek,* October 31, 2005, p. 202.

3.79   Reade, C. "Antecedents of Organizational Identification in Multinational Corporations: Fostering Psychological Attachment to the Local Subsidiary and the Global Organization." *International Journal of Human Resource Management* 12 (2001), pp. 1269–91.

3.80   Shaffer, M.A., and D.A. Harrison. "Expatriates' Psychological Withdrawal from International Assignments: Work, Nonwork,

and Family Influences." *Personnel Psychology* 51 (1998), pp. 87–118; and Hechanova, R.; T.A. Beehr; and N.D. Christiansen. "Antecedents and Consequences of Employees' Adjustment to Overseas Assignment: A Meta-Analytic Review." *Applied Psychology: An International Review* 52 (2003), pp. 213–36.

3.81   Black, J.S.; M. Mendenhall; and G. Oddou. "Toward a Comprehensive Model of International Adjustment: An Integration of Multiple Theoretical Perspectives." *Academy of Management Review* 16 (1991), pp. 291–317.

3.82   Shaffer and Harrison, "Expatriates' Psychological Withdrawal."

3.83   Hechanova et al., "Antecedents and Consequences of Employees' Adjustment."

3.84   Fisher, A. "Holding on to Global Talent." *BusinessWeek,* October 31, 2005, p. 202.

3.85   Morris, J.R.; W.F. Cascio; and C.E. Young. "Downsizing after All These Years: Questions and Answers about Who Did It, How Many Did It, and Who Benefited from It." *Organizational Dynamics* 27 (1999), pp. 78–87.

3.86   Ibid.

3.87   Devine, K.; T. Reay; L. Stainton; and R. Collins-Nakai. "Downsizing Outcomes: Better a Victim than a Survivor?" *Human Resource Management* 42 (2003), pp. 109–24.

3.88   Ibid.

3.89   Rousseau, D.M. "Psychological and Implied Contracts in Organizations." *Employee Responsibilities and Rights Journal* 2 (1989), pp. 121–39.

3.90   Rousseau, D.M. "New Hire Perceptions of their Own and their

Employer's Obligations: A Study of Psychological Contracts." *Journal of Organizational Behavior* 11 (1990), pp. 389–400; Robinson, S.L.; M.S. Kraatz; and D.M. Rousseau. "Changing Obligations and the Psychological Contract: A Longitudinal Study." *Academy of Management Journal* 37 (1994), pp. 137–52; Robinson, S.L., and E.W. Morrison. "Psychological Contracts and OCB: The Effect of Unfulfilled Obligations on Civic Virtue Behavior." *Journal of Organizational Behavior* 16 (1995), pp. 289–98.

3.91 Ibid.

3.92 Robinson, S.L. "Violating the Psychological Contract: Not the Exception but the Norm." *Journal of Organizational Behavior* 15 (1994), pp. 245–59; Robinson, S.L. "Trust and Breach of the Psychological Contract." *Administrative Science Quarterly* 41 (1996), pp. 574–99; and Zhao, H.; S.J. Wayne; B.C. Glibkowski; and J. Bravo. "The Impact of Psychological Contract Breach on Work-Related Outcomes: A Meta-Analysis." *Personnel Psychology* 60 (2007), pp. 647–80.

3.93 Eisenberger, R.; R. Huntington; S. Hutchison; and D. Sowa. "Perceived Organizational Support." *Journal of Applied Psychology* 71 (1986), pp. 500–507.

3.94 Rhoades, L., and R. Eisenberger. "Perceived Organizational Support." *Journal of Applied Psychology* 87 (2002), pp. 698–714; and Allen, D.G.; L.M. Shore; and R.W. Griffeth. "The Role of Perceived Organizational Support and Supportive Human Resources Practices in the Turnover Process." *Journal of Management* 29 (2003), pp. 99–118.

3.95 Rhoades and Eisenberger, "Perceived Organizational Support."

3.96 Dessler, G. "How to Earn your Employees' Commitment." *Academy of Management Executive* 13 (1999), pp. 58–67.

3.97 Levering and Moskowitz, "In Good Company."

3.98 Fisher, A. "How You Can Do Better on Diversity." *BusinessWeek,* November 15, 2005, p. 60; and Fisher, "Holding on to Global Talent."

3.99 Shaw, J.D.; J.E. Delery; G.D. Jenkins Jr.; and N. Gupta. "An Organization-Level Analysis of Voluntary and Involuntary Turnover." *Academy of Management Journal* 41 (1998), pp. 511–25.

3.100 Dessler, "How to Earn your Employees' Commitment."

3.101 Levering and Moskowitz, "In Good Company."

3.102 Fisher, "Holding on to Global Talent"; and Fisher, A. "How to Keep your Stars from Leaving." *BusinessWeek,* July 26, 2005, p. 44.

3.103 Cappelli, P. "Managing without Commitment." *Organizational Dynamics* 28 (2000), pp. 11–24.

3.104 Byrnes, N. "Star Search." *BusinessWeek*, October 10, 2005, pp. 68–78.

3.105 Ibid.

3.106 Marquez, "Accentuating the Positive."

3.107 Ibid.

3.108 Berfield, S. "Mentoring Can Be Messy." *BusinessWeek*, January 29, 2007, pp. 80–81.

PART

2

INDIVIDUAL MECHANISMS

chapter 4

Job Satisfaction

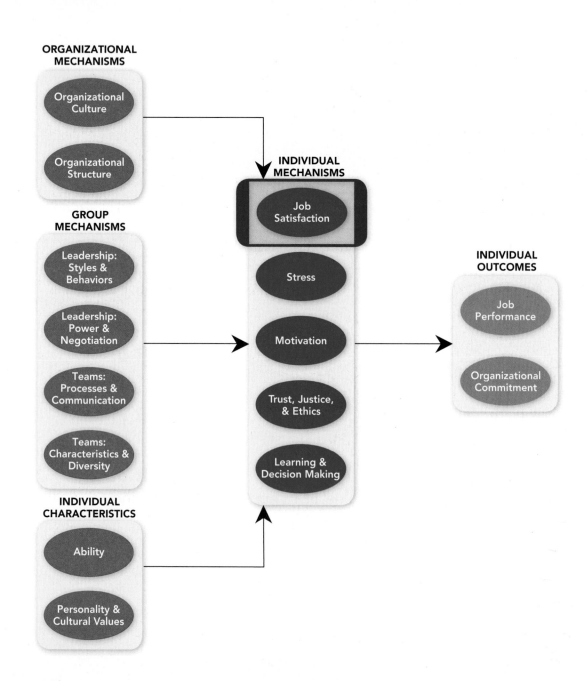

After reading this chapter, you should be able to answer the following questions:

4.1 What is job satisfaction?

4.2 What are values, and how do they affect job satisfaction?

4.3 What specific facets do employees consider when evaluating their job satisfaction?

4.4 Which job characteristics can create a sense of satisfaction with the work itself?

4.5 How is job satisfaction affected by day-to-day events?

4.6 What are mood and emotions, and what specific forms do they take?

4.7 How does job satisfaction affect job performance and organizational commitment? How does it affect life satisfaction?

4.8 What steps can organizations take to assess and manage job satisfaction?

ZAPPOS

"Create fun and a little weirdness." That's one of the core values of Zappos, the Las Vegas–based e-commerce site that specializes in shoes, apparel, and electronics.[1] The site was recently acquired by e-commerce giant Amazon, but continues to operate as an independent brand. What's weird at Zappos? Well, for starters, the CEO, Tony Hsieh, hosts company pajama parties and obsessively blogs about a variety of subjects,[2] from how Twitter can make you a happier person to whether eggnog tastes good on mashed potatoes.[3] The company also employs a full-time life coach.[4] Employees can talk about personal issues, chat off-the-record about their workgroup, or get advice on advancing at the company. The one requirement is that they sit on a red velvet throne during their session. Even the hiring process is a little weird, including some nontraditional interview questions such as, "What's your theme song?," "If you could be a superhero, which one would you be?," and "How weird are you?"[5] Those who get through that process don't just read about fireable offenses in some employment manual; instead, they watch human resources employees act out the "no-no's" in *Saturday Night Live*–style skits.[6]

The company also lives up to the "fun" part of its core value by taking steps to keep employees satisfied with their jobs. Everybody gets a free lunch and access to a nap room and concierge service.[7] Zappos also covers 100 percent of employees' health insurance premiums.[8] Employees can even give another employee a $50 bonus for a job well done.[9] Zappos also creates a family-style feel by encouraging managers to spend 10–20 percent of their time with employees outside the office. And the company closely guards the fun culture that it's created, placing an emphasis on positive thinkers during its hiring process. These sorts of practices explain how Zappos finished 23rd on *Fortune*'s "100 Best Companies to Work For" list,[10] the highest ranking ever for a newcomer to the list.[11]

Zappos also believes that satisfied employees will ultimately result in satisfied customers. The company finished seventh in *BusinessWeek*'s annual ranking of customer service quality with around 70 percent of surveyed customers reporting they would "definitely recommend" Zappos to others.[12] One likely reason for these high marks is that Zappos doesn't outsource its call center duties.[13] Employees understand that their job is to delight customers, and they're encouraged to use their imaginations—rather than some predetermined script—during calls. They might encourage customers to order two sizes of shoes, because Zappos offers free shipping for both purchases and returns, or recommend a competitor for items that are out of stock. Zappos employees even have been known to send handwritten notes or flowers in cases in which customers complained about a tough workday. Such gestures can have a significant impact because three-quarters of the company's purchases are made by repeat customers.

JOB SATISFACTION

This chapter takes us to a new portion of our integrative model of organizational behavior. Job satisfaction is one of several individual mechanisms that directly affects job performance and organizational commitment. As shown in the Zappos example, if employees are very satisfied with their jobs and experience positive emotions while

"You'll enjoy rationalizing working for this company."

Source: Copyright © Peter Vey. Reprinted with permission.

working, they may perform their jobs better and choose to remain with the company for a longer period of time. Think about the worst job that you've held in your life, even if it was just a summer job or a short-term work assignment. What did you feel during the course of the day? How did those feelings influence the way you behaved, in terms of your time spent on task and citizenship behaviors rather than counterproductive or withdrawal behaviors?

Job satisfaction is a pleasurable emotional state resulting from the appraisal of one's job or job experiences.[14] In other words, it represents how you *feel* about your job and what you *think* about your job. Employees with high job satisfaction experience positive feelings when they think about their duties or take part in task activities. Employees with low job satisfaction experience negative feelings when they think about their duties or take part in their task activities. Unfortunately, workplace surveys suggest that satisfied employees are becoming more and more rare. For example, one survey showed that just 49 percent of Americans are satisfied with their jobs, down from 58 percent a decade ago.[15] The survey also revealed that only 20 percent are satisfied with their employer's promotion and reward policies whereas 33 percent are satisfied with their pay. Reversing such trends requires a deeper understanding of exactly what drives job satisfaction levels.

4.1

What is job satisfaction?

WHY ARE SOME EMPLOYEES MORE SATISFIED THAN OTHERS?

So what explains why some employees are more satisfied than others? At a general level, employees are satisfied when their job provides the things that they value. **Values** are those things that people consciously or subconsciously want to seek or attain.[16] Think about this question for a few moments: What do you want to attain from your job, that is, what things do you want your job to give you? A good wage? A sense of achievement? Colleagues who are fun to be around? If you had to make a list of the things you value with respect to your job, most or all of them would likely be shown in Table 4-1. This table summarizes the content of popular surveys of work values, broken down into more general categories.[17]

4.2

What are values, and how do they affect job satisfaction?

TABLE 4-1	Commonly Assessed Work Values
CATEGORIES	**SPECIFIC VALUES**
Pay	High salary Secure salary
Promotions	Frequent promotions Promotions based on ability
Supervision	Good supervisory relations Praise for good work
Coworkers	Enjoyable coworkers Responsible coworkers
Work Itself	Utilization of ability Freedom and independence Intellectual stimulation Creative expression Sense of achievement
Altruism	Helping others Moral causes
Status	Prestige Power over others Fame
Environment	Comfort Safety

Key Question:
Which of these things are *most important* to you?

Source: Adapted from R.V. Dawis, "Vocational Interests, Values, and Preferences," in *Handbook of Industrial and Organizational Psychology,* Vol. 2, Eds. M.D. Dunnette and L.M. Hough (Palo Alto, CA: Consulting Psychologists Press, 1991), pp. 834–71. D.M. Cable and J.R. Edwards. "Complementary and Supplementary Fit: A Theoretical and Empirical Investigation." *Journal of Applied Psychology* 89 (2004), pp. 822-34.

Many of those values deal with the things that your work can give you, such as good pay or the chance for frequent promotions. Other values pertain to the context that surrounds your work, including whether you have a good boss or good coworkers. Still other values deal with the work itself, like whether your job tasks provide you with freedom or a sense of achievement.

Consider the list of values in Table 4-1. Which would make your "top five" in terms of importance right now, at this stage of your life? Maybe you have a part-time job during college and you value enjoyable coworkers or a comfortable work environment above everything else. Or maybe you're getting established in your career and starting a family, which makes a high salary and frequent promotions especially critical. Or perhaps you're at a point in your career that you feel a need to help others or find an outlet for your creative expression. (In our case, we value fame, which is what led us to write this textbook. We're still waiting for Conan's call . . . or at least Kimmel's.) Regardless of your "top five," you can see that different people value different things and that your values may change during the course of your working life.

VALUE FULFILLMENT

Values play a key role in explaining job satisfaction. **Value-percept theory** argues that job satisfaction depends on whether you *perceive* that your job supplies the things that you *value.*[18] This theory can be summarized with the following equation:

$$\text{Dissatisfaction} = (V_{want} - V_{have})(V_{importance})$$

In this equation, V_{want} reflects how much of a value an employee wants, V_{have} indicates how much of that value the job supplies, and $V_{importance}$ reflects how important the value is to the employee. Big differences between wants and haves create a sense of dissatisfaction, especially when the value in question is important. Note that the difference between V_{want} and V_{have} gets multiplied by importance, so existing discrepancies get magnified for important values and minimized for trivial values. As an example, say that you were evaluating your pay satisfaction. You want to be earning around $70,000 a year but are currently earning $50,000 a year, so there's a $20,000 discrepancy. Does that mean you feel a great deal of pay dissatisfaction? Only if pay is one of the most important values to you from Table 4-1. If pay isn't that important, you probably don't feel much dissatisfaction.

Value-percept theory also suggests that people evaluate job satisfaction according to specific "facets" of the job.[19] After all, a "job" isn't one thing—it's a collection of tasks, relationships, and rewards.[20] The most common facets that employees consider in judging their job satisfaction appear in Figure 4-1. The figure includes the "want vs. have" calculations that drive satisfaction with pay, promotions, supervision, coworkers, and the work itself. The figure also shows how satisfaction with those five facets adds together to create "overall job satisfaction." Figure 4-1 shows that employees might be satisfied for all kinds of reasons. One person may be satisfied because she's in a high-paying job and working for a good boss. Another person may be satisfied because he has good coworkers and enjoyable work tasks. You may have noticed that a few of the values in Table 4-1, such as working for moral causes and gaining fame and prestige, are not represented in Figure 4-1. Those values are missing because they're not as relevant in all jobs, unlike pay, promotions, and so forth.

The first facet in Figure 4-1, **pay satisfaction**, refers to employees' feelings about their pay, including whether it's as much as they deserve, secure, and adequate for both normal expenses and luxury items.[21] Similar to the other facets, pay satisfaction is based on a comparison of the pay that employees want and the pay they receive.[22] Although more money is almost always better, most employees base their desired pay on a careful examination of their job duties and the pay given to comparable colleagues.[23] As a result, even nonmillionaires can be quite satisfied with their pay (thankfully for most of us!). Take the employees at Bright Horizons, for example. The Watertown, Massachusetts-based provider of child care and early education programs provides its employees with an average salary of around $50,000 in an industry known for significantly lower wages.[24] Bright Horizons employees experience high pay satisfaction because they make more than comparable colleagues working in the child care area.

The next facet in Figure 4-1, **promotion satisfaction**, refers to employees' feelings about the company's promotion policies and their execution, including whether promotions are frequent, fair, and based on ability.[25] Unlike pay, some employees may not want frequent promotions because promotions bring more responsibility and increased work hours.[26] However, many employees value promotions because they provide opportunities for more personal growth, a better wage, and more prestige. QuikTrip, the Tulsa, Oklahoma–based chain of gas and convenience stores, does a good job fostering promotion

4.3

What specific facets do employees consider when evaluating their job satisfaction?

FIGURE 4-1	The Value-Percept Theory of Job Satisfaction

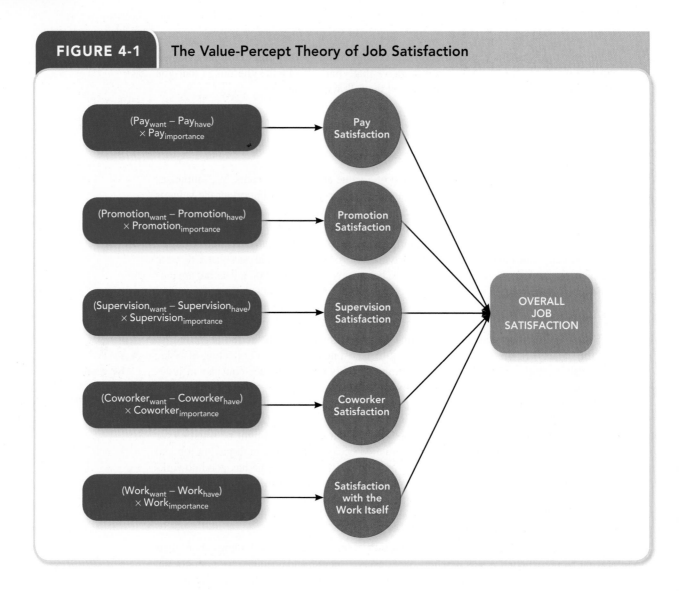

satisfaction on the part of its employees. "Promote from within" is a key motto in the company, and all 400-plus of its managers worked their way up from entry-level positions.[27]

Supervision satisfaction reflects employees' feelings about their boss, including whether the boss is competent, polite, and a good communicator (rather than lazy, annoying, and too distant).[28] Most employees ask two questions about their supervisors: (1) "Can they help me attain the things that I value?" and (2) "Are they generally likable?"[29] The first question depends on whether supervisors provide rewards for good performance, help employees obtain necessary resources, and protect employees from unnecessary distractions. The second question depends on whether supervisors have good personalities, as well as values and beliefs similar to the employees' philosophies. Valero Energy, the San Antonio–based oil refiner and gas retailer, works hard to foster a sense of supervision satisfaction. When it comes to receiving bonuses, executives only get theirs when everyone else in the organization has received one.[30] As a result, supervisors work harder to make sure that employees can get their jobs done.

QuikTrip, a chain of gas and convenience stores, excels at providing promotion satisfaction to its employees. Virtually all its managers—over 400 people—were promoted from entry-level jobs.

Coworker satisfaction refers to employees' feelings about their fellow employees, including whether coworkers are smart, responsible, helpful, fun, and interesting as opposed to lazy, gossipy, unpleasant, and boring.[31] Employees ask the same kinds of questions about their coworkers that they do about their supervisors: (1) "Can they help me do my job?" and (2) "Do I enjoy being around them?" The first question is critical because most of us rely, to some extent, on our coworkers when performing job tasks. The second question also is important because we spend just as much time with coworkers as we do members of our own family. Coworkers who are pleasant and fun can make the workweek go much faster, whereas coworkers who are disrespectful and annoying can make even one day seem like an eternity. Arbitron, the Columbia, Maryland–based radio market research firm, takes an unusual step to increase coworker satisfaction. Employees can choose to recognize their coworkers' achievements with a $100 American Express gift card, with no restrictions on how many they can give out.[32] Last year, 300 of its 1,400-plus employees received rewards totaling $50,000.

The last facet in Figure 4-1, **satisfaction with the work itself**, reflects employees' feelings about their actual work tasks, including whether those tasks are challenging, interesting, respected, and make use of key skills rather than being dull, repetitive, and uncomfortable.[33] Whereas the previous four facets described the outcomes that result from work (pay, promotions) and the people who surround work (supervisors, coworkers), this facet focuses on what employees actually *do*. After all, even the best boss or most interesting coworkers can't compensate for 40 or 50 hours of complete boredom each week! How can employers instill a sense of satisfaction with the work itself? Valassis, the Livonia, Michigan–based publisher of newspaper inserts and coupons, gives employees annual skill assessments to get a better feel for what they're good at.[34] It then provides employees with growth opportunities, sometimes even creating new positions to employ special talents.

In summary, value-percept theory suggests that employees will be satisfied when they perceive that their job offers the pay, promotions, supervision, coworkers, and work tasks that they value. Of course, this theory begs the question: Which of those ingredients is most important? In other words, which of the five facets in Figure 4-1 has the strongest influence on overall job satisfaction? Several research studies have examined these issues and come up with the results shown in Figure 4-2. The figure depicts the correlation between each of the five satisfaction facets and an overall index of job satisfaction. (Recall that correlations of .10, .30, and .50 indicate weak, moderate, and strong relationships, respectively.)

FIGURE 4-2	Correlations Between Satisfaction Facets and Overall Job Satisfaction

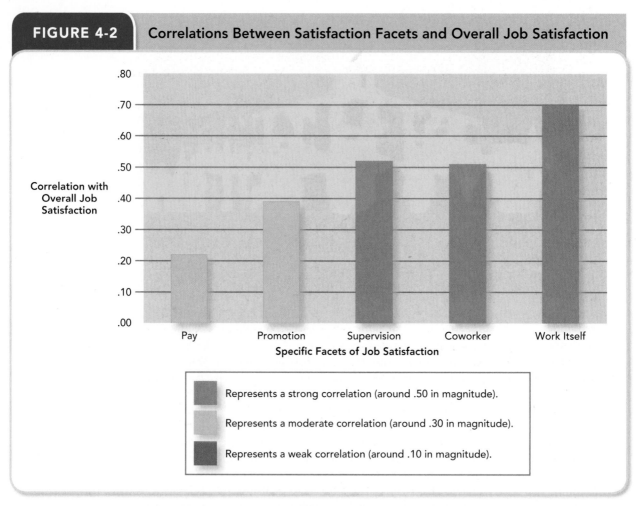

Sources: G.H. Ironson, P.C. Smith, M.T. Brannick, W.M. Gibson, and K.B. Paul, "Construction of a Job in General Scale: A Comparison of Global, Composite, and Specific Measures," *Journal of Applied Psychology* 74 (1989), pp. 193–200; S.S. Russell, C. Spitzmuller, L.F. Lin, J.M. Stanton, P.C. Smith, and G.H. Ironson, "Shorter Can Also Be Better: The Abridged Job in General Scale," *Educational and Psychological Measurement* 64 (2004), pp. 878–93.

Figure 4-2 suggests that satisfaction with the work itself is the single strongest driver of overall job satisfaction.[35] Supervision and coworker satisfaction are also strong drivers, and promotion and pay satisfaction have moderately strong effects. Why is satisfaction with the work itself so critical? Well, consider that a typical workweek contains around 2,400 minutes. How much of that time is spent thinking about how much money you make? 10 minutes? Maybe 20? The same is true for promotions—we may want them, but we don't necessarily spend hours a day thinking about them. We do spend a significant chunk of that time with other people though. Between lunches, meetings, hallway chats, and other conversations, we might easily spend 600 minutes a week with supervisors and coworkers. That leaves almost 1,800 minutes for just us and our work. As a result, it's hard to be satisfied with your job if you don't like what you actually do.

SATISFACTION WITH THE WORK ITSELF

Given how important enjoyable work tasks are to overall job satisfaction, it's worth spending more time describing the kinds of tasks that most people find enjoyable. Researchers began focusing on this question in the 1950s and 1960s, partly in reaction to practices based in the "scientific management" perspective. Scientific management focuses on increasing the efficiency of job tasks by making them more simplified and specialized and using time and motion studies to plan task movements and sequences carefully.[36] The hope was that such steps would increase worker productivity and reduce the breadth of skills required to complete a job, ultimately improving organizational profitability. Instead, the simplified and routine jobs tended to lower job satisfaction while increasing absenteeism and turnover.[37] Put simply: Boring jobs may be easier, but they're not necessarily better.

So what kinds of work tasks are especially satisfying? Research suggests that three "critical psychological states" make work satisfying. The first psychological state is believing in the **meaningfulness of work**, which reflects the degree to which work tasks are viewed as something that "counts" in the employee's system of philosophies and beliefs (see Chapter 6 on Motivation for more discussion of such issues).[38] Trivial tasks tend to be less satisfying than tasks that make employees feel like they're aiding the organization or society in some meaningful way. The second psychological state is perceiving **responsibility for outcomes**, which captures the degree to which employees feel that they're key drivers of the quality of the unit's work.[39] Sometimes employees feel like their efforts don't really matter, because work outcomes are dictated by effective procedures, efficient technologies, or more influential colleagues. Finally, the third psychological state is **knowledge of results**, which reflects the extent to which employees know how well (or how poorly) they're doing.[40] Many employees work in jobs in which they never find out about their mistakes or notice times when they did particularly well. See our **OB at the Bookstore** feature for a discussion of three psychological states that create job misery, rather than job satisfaction.

Think about times when you felt especially proud of a job well done. At that moment, you were probably experiencing all three psychological states. You were aware of the result (after all, some job had been done well). You felt you were somehow responsible for that result (otherwise, why would you feel proud?). Finally, you felt that the result of the work was somehow meaningful (otherwise, why would you have remembered it just now?). The next obvious question then becomes, "What kinds of tasks create these psychological states?" **Job characteristics theory**, which describes the central characteristics of intrinsically satisfying jobs, attempts to answer this question. As shown in Figure 4-3, job characteristics theory argues that five core job characteristics (variety, identity, significance, autonomy, and feedback, which you can remember with the acronym "VISAF") result in high levels of the three psychological states, making work tasks more satisfying.[41]

The first core job characteristic in Figure 4-3, **variety**, is the degree to which the job requires a number of different activities that involve a number of different skills and talents.[42] When variety is high, almost every workday is different in some way, and job holders rarely feel a sense of monotony or repetition.[43] Of course, we could picture jobs that have a variety of boring tasks, such as screwing different sized nuts onto different colored bolts, but such jobs do not involve a number of different skills and talents.[44] To provide some examples of low and high job variety, we offer excerpts from Studs Terkel's classic book *Working: People Talk About What They Do All Day and How They Feel About What They Do.*

4.4

Which job characteristics can create a sense of satisfaction with the work itself?

OB AT THE BOOKSTORE

THE THREE SIGNS OF A MISERABLE JOB
by Patrick Lencioni (San Francisco, CA: Jossey-Bass, 2007).

As long as you think you've hired a bunch of misfits who don't want to be here and will only do what they're required to do, then that's what you'll get. . . . And that's all you've been getting for years. And now you have a chance to change things, to be something real to these people, and wake up a business that's been asleep for years. It's up to you Joe. It really is.

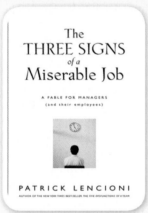

With those words, Brian challenges Joe, the owner of Gene and Joe's pizzeria, to take ownership of his employees' job satisfaction. In Lencioni's fictional tale, Brian is a semiretired former CEO who has bought into a local pizzeria in Lake Tahoe, to pass the time and to tinker with his theory about job satisfaction. Over the course of the tale, Brian becomes convinced that "miserable jobs" have three telltale signs:

- *Irrelevance*. Employees need to feel that their work matters to someone, anyone.
- *Immeasurement*. Employees need to be able to gauge their own performance and their own progress.
- *Anonymity*. Employees need to feel that they're part of something—that they're known and that they count.

To some extent, the three signs of miserable jobs represent the flip sides of the critical psychological states that foster job satisfaction. Brian's true challenge in the book is not identifying the three signs though. Instead, the difficulty comes in getting Joe, the grizzled, long-time owner of the restaurant, to buy into the importance of the concepts. Joe comes to symbolize all the reasons managers might resist insights from OB theories. Maybe they think positive job attitudes are the result of business success rather than the cause of it; maybe they find the concepts too corny; or maybe they view them as too obvious to be valuable. Lencioni sets his sights on the last possibility in his conclusion, noting: "Obvious? Perhaps. But if so, then why in the world do so many managers—dare I say, most managers—fail to provide their people with these basics of a meaningful job? Maybe because it is too obvious. Well-educated people often have a hard time getting their hands around simple solutions."

▼ Low Variety: Phil Stallings, Spot-Welder

I stand in one spot, about two- or three-feet area, all night. The only time a person stops is when the line stops. We do about thirty-two jobs per car, per unit. Forty-eight units an hour, eight hours a day. Thirty-two times forty-eight times eight. Figure it out. That's how many times I push that button. . . . It don't stop. It just goes and goes and goes. I bet there's men who have lived and died out there, never seen the end of that line. And they never will—because it's endless. It's like the serpent. It's just all body, no tail. It can do things to you . . . (Laughs).[45]

▲ High Variety: Eugene Russell, Piano Tuner
Every day is different. I work Saturdays and Sundays sometimes. Monday I'm tuning a piano for a record company that had to be done before nine o'clock. When I finish that, I go to another company and do at least four pianos. During that day there's a couple of harpsichords mixed in. . . . I get a big kick out of it, because there are so many facets. Other people go through a routine. At a certain time they punch a clock. . . . Then they're through with it and *then* their life begins. With us the piano business is an integral part of our life. I had a discussion with another tuner, who is a great guitar man. He said "Why are we tuners?" I said, "Because we want to hear good sounds."[46]

FIGURE 4-3   **Job Characteristics Theory**

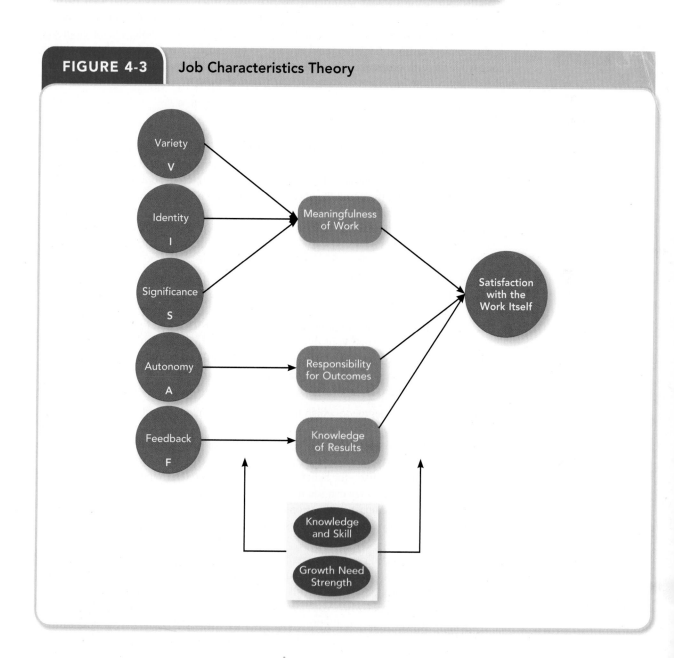

Evidence indicates that our preference for variety is hardwired into our brains. Research in psychiatry and neuroscience shows that the brain releases a chemical called dopamine whenever a novel stimulus (a new painting, a new meal, a new work challenge) is experienced, and we tend to find this dopamine release quite pleasurable. Unfortunately, the amount of dopamine present in our brains declines over our life spans. One neuroscientist therefore suggests that the best way to protect our dopamine system is through novel, challenging experiences, writing, "The sense of satisfaction after you've successfully handled unexpected tasks or sought out unfamiliar, physically and emotionally demanding activities is your brain's signal that you're doing what nature designed you to do."[47] Something to think about the next time you plan to order the same old thing at your favorite restaurant!

The second core job characteristic in Figure 4-3, **identity**, is the degree to which the job requires completing a whole, identifiable, piece of work from beginning to end with a visible outcome.[48] When a job has high identity, employees can point to something and say, "There, I did that." The transformation from inputs to finished product is very visible, and the employee feels a distinct sense of beginning and closure.[49] Think about how you feel when you work for a while on some project but don't quite get it finished—does that lack of closure bug you? If so, identity is an important concern for you. Consider these excerpts from *Working:*

▼ Low Identity: Mike Lefevre, Steelworker
It's not just the work. Somebody built the pyramids. Somebody's going to build something. Pyramids, Empire State Building—these things don't just happen. There's hard work behind it. I would like to see a building, say the Empire State, I would like to see on one side of it a foot-wide strip from top to bottom with the name of every bricklayer, the name of every electrician, with all the names. So when a guy walked by, he could take his son and say, "See, that's me over there on the forty-fifth floor. I put the steel beam in." Picasso can point to a painting. What can I point to? A writer can point to a book. Everybody should have something to point to.[50]

▲ High Identity: Frank Decker, Interstate Truckdriver
Every load is a challenge and when you finally off-load it, you have a feeling of having completed a job—which I don't think you get in a production line. I pick up a load at the mill, going to Hotpoint in Milwaukee. I take a job and I go through all the process. . . . You feel like your day's work is well done when you're coming back. I used to have problems in the morning, a lot of heartburn, I couldn't eat. But once I off-loaded, the pressure was off. Then I could eat anything.[51]

Significance is the degree to which the job has a substantial impact on the lives of other people, particularly people in the world at large.[52] Virtually any job can be important if it helps put food on the table for a family, send kids to college, or make employees feel like they're doing their part for the working world. That said, significance as a core job characteristic captures something beyond that—the belief that this job *really matters*. When employees feel that their jobs are significant, they can see that others value what they do and they're aware that their job has a positive impact on the people around them.[53] There's the sense that, if their job was taken away, society would be the worse for it. Consider these excerpts from *Working:*

▼ Low Significance: Louis Hayward, Washroom Attendant
They come in. They wash their hands after using the service—you hope. (A soft chuckle.) I go through the old brush routine, stand back, expecting a tip. A quarter is what you expect when you hand the guy a towel and a couple of licks of the broom. . . . I'm not particularly proud of what I'm doing. The shine man and I discuss

it quite freely. In my own habitat I don't go around saying I'm a washroom attendant at the Palmer House. Outside of my immediate family, very few people know what I do. They do know I work at the Palmer House and let that suffice. You say Palmer House, they automatically assume you're a waiter. . . . The whole thing is obsolete. It's on its way out. This work isn't necessary in the first place. It's so superfluous. It was *never* necessary. (Laughs.)[54]

▲ High Significance: Tom Patrick, Fireman

Last month there was a second alarm. I was off duty. I ran over there. I'm a bystander. I see these firemen on the roof, with the smoke pouring out around them, and the flames, and they go in. . . . You could see the pride that they were seein'. The ***** world's so ***** up, the country's ***** up. But the firemen, you actually see them produce. You see them put out a fire. You see them come out with babies in their hands. You see them give mouth-to-mouth when a guy's dying. You can't get around that ****. That's real. To me, that's what I want to be.[55]

Autonomy is the degree to which the job provides freedom, independence, and discretion to the individual performing the work.[56] When your job provides autonomy, you view the outcomes of it as the product of your efforts rather than the result of careful instructions from your boss or a well-written manual of procedures.[57] Autonomy comes in multiple forms, including the freedom to control the timing, scheduling, and sequencing of work activities, as well as the procedures and methods used to complete work tasks.[58] To many of us, high levels of autonomy are the difference between "having a long leash" and being "micromanaged." Consider these excerpts from *Working:*

▼ Low Autonomy: Beryl Simpson, Airline Reservationist

They brought in a computer called Sabre. . . . It has a memory drum and you can retrieve that information forever. . . . With Sabre being so valuable, you were allowed no more than three minutes on the telephone. You had twenty seconds, busy-out time it was called, to put the information into Sabre. Then you had to be available for another phone call. It was almost like a production line. We adjusted to the machine. The casualness, the informality that had been there previously was no longer there. . . . You took thirty minutes for lunch, not thirty-one. If you got a break, you took ten minutes, not eleven. . . . With the airline I had no free will. I was just part of that stupid computer.[59]

▲ High Autonomy: Bud Freeman, Jazz Musician

I live in absolute freedom. I do what I do because I want to do it. What's wrong with making a living doing something interesting. . . ? The jazz man is expressing freedom in every note he plays. We can only please the audience doing what *we* do. We have to please ourselves first. I want to play for the rest of my life. I don't see any sense in stopping. Were I to live another thirty years—that would make me ninety-five—why not try to play? I can just hear the critics: "Did you hear that wonderful note old man Freeman played last night?" (Laughs.) As Ben Webster says, "I'm going to play this **** saxophone until they put it on top of me."

The last core job characteristic in Figure 4-3, **feedback**, is the degree to which carrying out the activities required by the job provides employees with clear information about how well they're performing.[60] A critical distinction must be noted: This core characteristic reflects feedback obtained *directly from the job* as opposed to feedback from coworkers or supervisors. Most employees receive formal performance appraisals from their bosses, but that feedback occurs once or maybe twice a year. When the job provides its

Despite the need for discipline and practice, the job of a jazz musician is one with a high degree of autonomy.

own feedback, that feedback can be experienced almost every day. Consider these excerpts from *Working:*

> ▼ Low Feedback: Lilith Reynolds, Government Project Coordinator
> I'm very discouraged about my job right now. . . . I'm to come up with some kind of paper on economic development. It won't be very hard because there's little that can be done. At the end of sixty days I'll present the paper. But because of the reorganization that's come up I'll probably never be asked about the paper.[61]

> ▲ High Feedback: Dolores Dante, Waitress
> When somebody says to me, "You're great, how come you're *just* a waitress?" *Just* a waitress. I'd say, "Why, don't you think you deserve to be served by me?" . . . Tips? I feel like Carmen. It's like a gypsy holding out a tambourine and they throw the coin. (Laughs.) . . . People would ask for me. . . . I would like to say to the customer, "Go to so-and-so." But you can't do that, because you feel a sense of loyalty. So you would rush, get to your customers quickly. Some don't care to drink and still they wait for you. That's a compliment.[62]

The passages in this section illustrate the potential importance of each of the five core characteristics. But how important are the core characteristics to satisfaction with the work itself? Meta-analyses of around 200 different research studies employing around 90,000 total participants showed that the five core job characteristics are moderately to strongly related to work satisfaction.[63] However, those results don't mean that *every* employee wants more variety, more autonomy, and so forth. The bottom of Figure 4-3 includes two other variables: **knowledge and skill** and **growth need strength** (which captures whether employees have strong needs for personal accomplishment or developing themselves beyond where they currently are).[64] In the jargon of theory diagrams, these variables are called "moderators." Rather than directly affecting other variables in the diagram, moderators influence the strength of the relationships between variables. If employees lack the required knowledge and skill or lack a desire for growth and development, more variety and autonomy should *not* increase their satisfaction very much.[65] However, when employees are very talented and feel a strong need for growth, the core job characteristics become even more powerful. A graphical depiction of this moderator effect appears in Figure 4-4, where you can see that the relationship between the core job characteristics and satisfaction becomes stronger when growth need strength increases.

| FIGURE 4-4 | Growth Need Strength as a Moderator of Job Characteristic Effects |

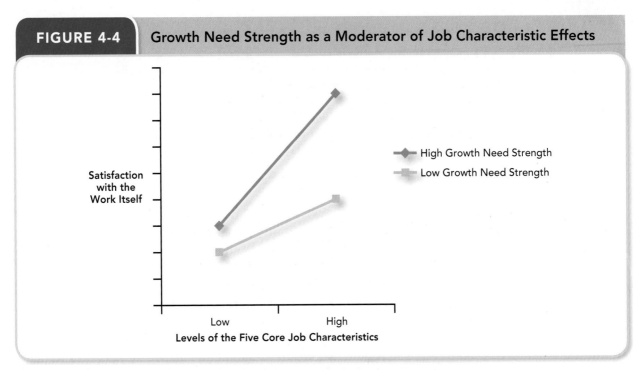

Source: Adapted from B.T. Loher, R.A. Noe, N.L. Moeller, and M.P. Fitzgerald, "A Meta-Analysis of the Relation of Job Characteristics to Job Satisfaction," *Journal of Applied Psychology* 70 (1985), pp. 280–89.

Given how critical the five core job characteristics are to job satisfaction, many organizations have employed job characteristics theory to help improve satisfaction among their employees. The first step in this process is assessing the current level of the characteristics to arrive at a "satisfaction potential score." See our **OB Assessments** feature for more about that step. The organization, together with job design consultants, then attempts to redesign aspects of the job to increase the core job characteristic levels. Often this step results in **job enrichment,** such that the duties and responsibilities associated with a job are expanded to provide more variety, identity, autonomy, and so forth. Research suggests that such enrichment efforts can indeed boost job satisfaction levels.[66] Moreover, enrichment efforts can heighten work accuracy and customer satisfaction, though training and labor costs tend to rise as a result of such changes.[67]

MOOD AND EMOTIONS

Let's say you're a satisfied employee, maybe because you get paid well and work for a good boss or because your work tasks provide you with variety and autonomy. Does this mean you'll definitely be satisfied at 11:00 a.m. next Tuesday? Or 2:30 p.m. the following Thursday? Obviously it doesn't. Each employee's satisfaction levels fluctuate over time, rising and falling like some sort of emotional stock market. This fluctuation might seem strange, given that people's pay, supervisors, coworkers, and work tasks don't change from one hour to the next. The key lies in remembering that job satisfaction reflects what you think and feel about your job. So part of it is rational, based on a careful appraisal of the job and the things it supplies. But another part of it is emotional, based on what you feel "in your gut" while you're at work or thinking about work. So satisfied employees feel good about their job *on average,* but things happen during the course of the day to make them feel better at some times (and worse at others).

 4.5

How is job satisfaction affected by day-to-day events?

OB ASSESSMENTS

CORE JOB CHARACTERISTICS

How satisfying are your work tasks? This assessment is designed to measure the five core job characteristics. Think of your current job or the last job that you held (even if it was a part-time or summer job). Answer each question using the response scale provided. Then subtract your answers to the boldfaced question from 8, with the difference being your new answer for that question. For example, if your original answer for Question 2 was "5," your new answer is "3" (8 – 5). Then use the formula to compute a satisfaction potential score (SPS).

1	2	3	4	5	6	7
VERY INACCURATE	MOSTLY INACCURATE	SLIGHTLY INACCURATE	UNCERTAIN	SLIGHTLY ACCURATE	MOSTLY ACCURATE	VERY ACCURATE

V1. The job requires me to use a number of complex or high-level skills. _____

V2. The job is quite simple and repetitive. _____

I1. The job is arranged so that I can do an entire piece of work from beginning to end. _____

I2. The job provides me the chance to completely finish the pieces of work I begin. _____

S1. This job is one where a lot of other people can be affected by how well the work gets done. _____

S2. The job itself is very significant and important in the broader scheme of things. _____

A1. The job gives me a chance to use my personal initiative and judgment in carrying out the work. _____

A2. The job gives me considerable opportunity for independence and freedom in how I do the work. _____

F1. Just doing the work required by the job provides many chances for me to figure out how well I am doing. _____

F2. After I finish a job, I know whether I performed well. _____

$$SPS = \left| \frac{V1+V2+I1+I2+S1+S2}{6} \right| \times \left| \frac{A1+A2}{2} \right| \times \left| \frac{F1+F2}{2} \right|$$

$$SPS = \left| \frac{}{6} \right| \times \left| \frac{}{2} \right| \times \left| \frac{}{2} \right|$$

$$SPS = \boxed{} \times \boxed{} \times \boxed{} = \boxed{}$$

SCORING AND INTERPRETATION

If your score is 150 or above, your work tasks tend to be satisfying and enjoyable. If your score is less than 150, you might benefit from trying to "enrich" your job by asking your supervisor for more challenging assignments.

Sources: J.R. Hackman and G.R. Oldham, *The Job Diagnostic Survey: An Instrument for the Diagnosis of Jobs and the Evaluation of Job Redesign Projects* (New Haven, CT: Yale University, 1974); J.R. Idaszak and F. Drasgow, "A Revision of the Job Diagnostic Survey: Elimination of a Measurement Artifact," *Journal of Applied Psychology* 72 (1987), pp. 69–74.

Figure 4-5 illustrates the satisfaction levels for one employee during the course of a workday, from around 9:00 a.m. to 5:00 p.m. You can see that this employee did a number of different things during the day, from answering e-mails to eating lunch with friends to participating in a brainstorming meeting regarding a new project. You can also see that the employee came into the day feeling relatively satisfied, though satisfaction levels had several ebbs and flows during the next eight hours. What's responsible for those ebbs and flows in satisfaction levels? Two related concepts: mood and emotions.

What kind of mood are you in right now? Good? Bad? Somewhere in between? Why are you in that kind of mood? Do you really even know? (If it's a bad mood, we hope it has nothing to do with this book!) **Moods** are states of feeling that are often mild in intensity, last for an extended period of time, and are not explicitly directed at or caused by anything.[68] When people are in a good or bad mood, they don't always know who (or what) deserves the credit or blame; they just happen to be feeling that way for a stretch of their day. Of course, it would be oversimplifying things to call all moods either good or

4.6

What are mood and emotions, and what specific forms do they take?

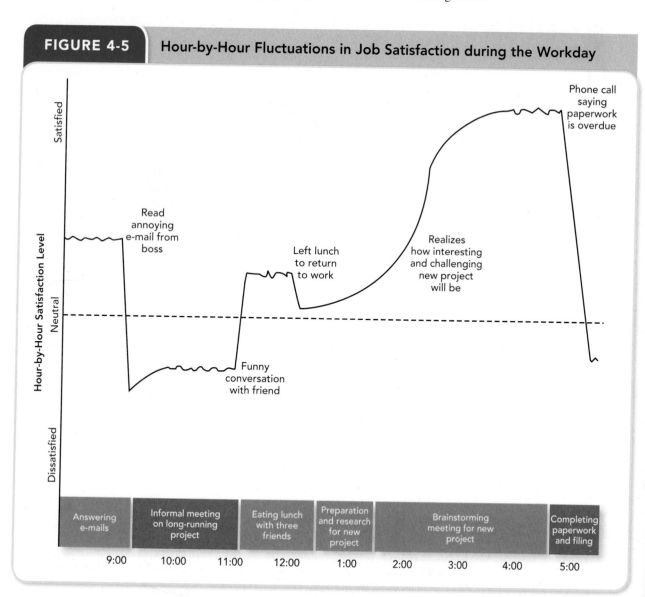

| FIGURE 4-5 | Hour-by-Hour Fluctuations in Job Satisfaction during the Workday |

bad. Sometimes we're in a serene mood; sometimes we're in an enthusiastic mood. Both are "good" but obviously feel quite different. Similarly, sometimes we're in a bored mood; sometimes we're in a hostile mood. Both are "bad" but, again, feel quite different.

It turns out that there are a number of different moods that we might experience during the workday. Figure 4-6 summarizes the different moods in which people sometimes find themselves. The figure illustrates that moods can be categorized in two ways: **pleasantness** and **activation**. First, the horizontal axis of the figure reflects whether you feel pleasant (in a "good mood") or unpleasant (in a "bad mood").[69] The figure uses green colors to illustrate pleasant moods and red colors to illustrate unpleasant moods. Second, the vertical axis of the figure reflects whether you feel activated and aroused or deactivated and unaroused.[70] The figure uses darker colors to convey higher levels of activation and lighter colors to convey lower levels. Note that some moods are neither good nor bad. For example, being surprised or astonished (high activation) and quiet or still (low activation) are neither pleasant nor unpleasant. As a result, those latter moods are left colorless in Figure 4-6.

FIGURE 4-6	Different Kinds of Mood

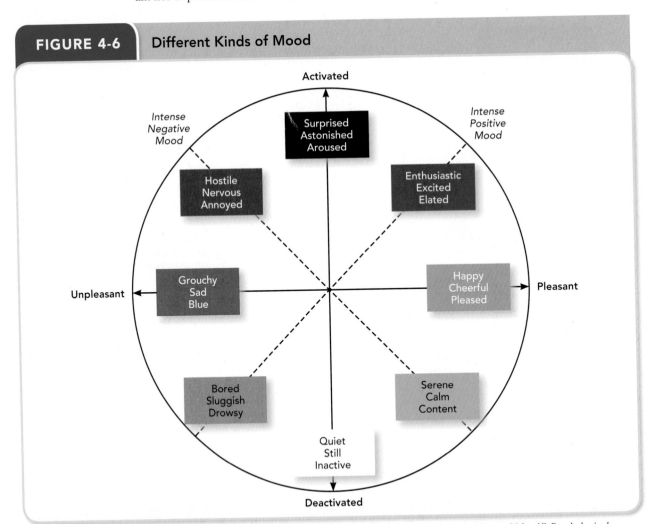

Sources: Adapted from D. Watson and A. Tellegen, "Toward a Consensual Structure of Mood," *Psychological Bulletin* 98 (1985), pp. 219–35; J.A. Russell, "A Circumplex Model of Affect," *Journal of Personality and Social Psychology* 39 (1980), pp. 1161–78; R.J. Larsen and E. Diener, "Promises and Problems with the Circumplex Model of Emotion," in *Review of Personality and Social Psychology: Emotion*, Vol. 13, ed. M.S. Clark (Newbury Park, CA: Sage, 1992), pp. 25–59.

Figure 4-6 illustrates that the most intense positive mood is characterized by feeling enthusiastic, excited, and elated. When employees feel this way, coworkers are likely to remark, "Wow, you're sure in a good mood!" In contrast, the most intense negative mood is characterized by feeling hostile, nervous, and annoyed. This kind of mood often triggers the question, "Wow, what's gotten you in such a bad mood?" If we return to our chart of hour-by-hour job satisfaction in Figure 4-5, what kind of mood do you think the employee was in while answering e-mails? Probably a happy, cheerful, and pleased mood. What kind of mood was the employee in during the informal meeting on the long-running project? Probably a grouchy, sad, and blue mood. Finally, what kind of mood do you think the employee was in during the brainstorming meeting for the new project? Clearly, an enthusiastic, excited, and elated mood. This employee would report especially high levels of job satisfaction at this point in time.

Some organizations take creative steps to foster positive moods among their employees. For example, the SAS Institute, the Cary, North Carolina–based maker of statistical software packages, has an on-site gym with a pool, billiards, volleyball courts, soccer fields, tennis courts, Ping-Pong tables, and a putting green.[71] Sometimes a good game of Ping-Pong is all it takes to make a grouchy mood turn cheerful! Griffin Hospital, based in Derby, Connecticut, offers its employees (and patients) family-style kitchens, strolling musicians, nonfluorescent lighting, and chair massages.[72] Such perks may not rival the importance of pay, promotions, supervision, coworkers, and the work itself as far as job satisfaction is concerned, but they can help boost employees' moods during a particular workday.

Although the strategies used by SAS and Griffin Hospital are valuable, the most intense forms of positive mood often come directly from work activities, like the brainstorming project in Figure 4-5. Research suggests that two conditions are critical to triggering intense positive mood. First, the activity in question has to be challenging. Second, the employee must possess the unique skills needed to meet that challenge. That high challenge–high skill combination can result in **flow**—a state in which employees feel a total immersion in the task at hand, sometimes losing track of how much time has passed.[73] People often describe flow as being "in the zone" and report heightened states of clarity, control, and concentration, along with a sense of enjoyment, interest, and loss of self-consciousness.[74] Although you may have experienced flow during leisure activities, such as playing sports or making music, research suggests that we experience flow more often in our working lives. Much of our leisure time is spent in passive recreation, such as watching TV or chatting with friends, that lacks the challenge needed to trigger flow states. Work tasks, in contrast, may supply the sorts of challenges that require concentration and immersion— particularly when those tasks contain high levels of variety, significance, autonomy, and so forth (see Chapter 6 on Motivation for more discussion of such issues).

Returning to Figure 4-5, it's clear that specific events triggered variations in satisfaction levels. According to **affective events theory**, workplace events can generate affective reactions—reactions that then can go on to influence work attitudes and behaviors.[75] Workplace events include happenings, like an annoying e-mail from a boss or a funny conversation with a friend, that are relevant to an employee's general desires and concerns. These events can trigger **emotions**, which are states of feeling that are often intense, last for only a few minutes, and are clearly directed at (and caused by) someone or some circumstance. The difference between moods and emotions becomes clear in the way we describe them to others. We describe moods by saying, "I'm feeling grouchy," but we describe emotions by saying, "I'm feeling angry *at my boss*."[76] According to affective events theory, these emotions can create the ebb and flow in satisfaction levels in Figure 4-5 and can also trigger spontaneous behaviors.[77] For example, positive emotions may trigger spontaneous instances of citizenship behavior, whereas negative emotions may trigger spontaneous instances of counterproductive behavior.

As with mood, it's possible to differentiate between specific examples of positive and negative emotions. Table 4-2 provides a summary of many of the most important.[78] **Positive emotions** include joy, pride, relief, hope, love, and compassion. **Negative emotions** include anger, anxiety, fear, guilt, shame, sadness, envy, and disgust. What emotion do you think the employee experienced in Figure 4-5 when reading a disrespectful e-mail from the boss? Probably anger. What emotion do you think that same employee enjoyed during a funny conversation with a friend? Possibly joy, or maybe relief that lunch had arrived and a somewhat bad day was halfway over. Leaving lunch to return to work might have triggered either anxiety (because the bad day might resume) or sadness (because the fun time with friends had ended). Luckily, the employee's sense of joy at taking on a new project that was interesting and challenging was right around the corner. The day did end on a down note, however, as the phone call signaling overdue paperwork was likely met with some mix of anger, fear, guilt, or even disgust (no one likes paperwork!).

Of course, just because employees *feel* many of the emotions in Table 4-2 during the workday doesn't mean they're supposed to *show* those emotions. Some jobs demand that employees live up to the adage "never let 'em see you sweat." In particular, service jobs in which employees make direct contact with customers often require those employees to

| TABLE 4-2 | Different Kinds of Emotions |

POSITIVE EMOTIONS	DESCRIPTION
Joy	A feeling of great pleasure
Pride	Enhancement of identity by taking credit for achievement
Relief	A distressing condition has changed for the better
Hope	Fearing the worst but wanting better
Love	Desiring or participating in affection
Compassion	Being moved by another's situation
NEGATIVE EMOTIONS	
Anger	A demeaning offense against me and mine
Anxiety	Facing an uncertain or vague threat
Fear	Facing an immediate and concrete danger
Guilt	Having broken a moral code
Shame	Failing to live up to your ideal self
Sadness	Having experienced an irreversible loss
Envy	Wanting what someone else has
Disgust	Revulsion aroused by something offensive

Source: Adapted from R.S. Lazarus, *Emotion and Adaptation* (New York: Oxford University, 1991).

hide any anger, anxiety, sadness, or disgust that they may feel, suppressing the urge to spontaneously engage in some negative behavior. Such jobs are high in what's called **emotional labor**, or the need to manage emotions to complete job duties success-fully.[79] Flight attendants are trained to "put on a happy face" in front of passengers, retail salespeople are trained to suppress any annoyance with customers, and restaurant servers are trained to act like they're having fun on their job even when they're not.

Is it a good idea to require emotional labor on the part of employees? Research on **emotional contagion** shows that one person can "catch" or "be infected by" the emotions of another person.[80] If a customer service representative is angry or sad, those negative emotions can be transferred to a customer (like a cold or disease). If that transfer occurs, it becomes less likely that customers will view the experience favorably and spend money, which poten-tially harms the bottom line. From this perspective, emotional labor seems like a vital part of good customer service. Unfortunately, other evidence suggests that emotional labor places great strain on employees and that their "bottled up" emotions may end up bubbling over, sometimes resulting in angry outbursts against customers or emotional exhaustion and burn-out on the part of employees (see Chapter 5 on Stress for more discussion of such issues).[81]

SUMMARY: WHY ARE SOME EMPLOYEES MORE SATISFIED THAN OTHERS?

So what explains why some employees are more satisfied than others? As we show in Fig-ure 4-7, answering that question requires paying attention to the more rational appraisals people make about their job and the things it supplies for them, such as pay, promotions, supervision, coworkers, and the work itself. Satisfaction with the work itself, in turn, is affected by the five core job characteristics: variety, identity, significance, autonomy, and feedback. However, answering that question also requires paying attention to daily fluctuations in how people feel, in terms of their positive and negative moods and positive and negative emotions. In this way, a generally satisfied employee may act unhappy at a given moment, just as a generally dissatisfied employee may act happy at a given moment. Understanding those sorts of fluctuations can help managers separate long-term problems (boring tasks, incompetent coworkers) from more short-lived issues (a bad meeting, an annoying interaction).

HOW IMPORTANT IS JOB SATISFACTION?

Several factors influence an employee's job satisfaction, from pay to coworkers to job tasks to day-to-day moods and emotions. Of course, the most obvious remaining question is, "Does job satisfaction really matter?" More precisely, does job satisfaction have a significant impact on job performance and organizational commitment—the two primary outcomes in our integrative model of OB? Figure 4-8 summarizes the research evidence linking job satisfaction to job performance and organizational commitment. This same sort of figure will appear in each of the remaining chapters of this book, so that you can get a better feel for which of the concepts in our integrative model has the strongest impact on performance and commitment.

Figure 4-8 reveals that job satisfaction does predict job performance. Why? One reason is that job satisfaction is moderately correlated with task performance. Satisfied employees do a better job of fulfilling the duties described in their job descriptions,[82] and evidence suggests that positive feelings foster creativity,[83] improve problem solving and decision making,[84] and enhance memory and recall of certain kinds of information.[85] Positive

4.7

How does job satisfaction affect job performance and organizational com-mitment? How does it affect life satisfaction?

FIGURE 4-7   Why Are Some Employees More Satisfied than Others?

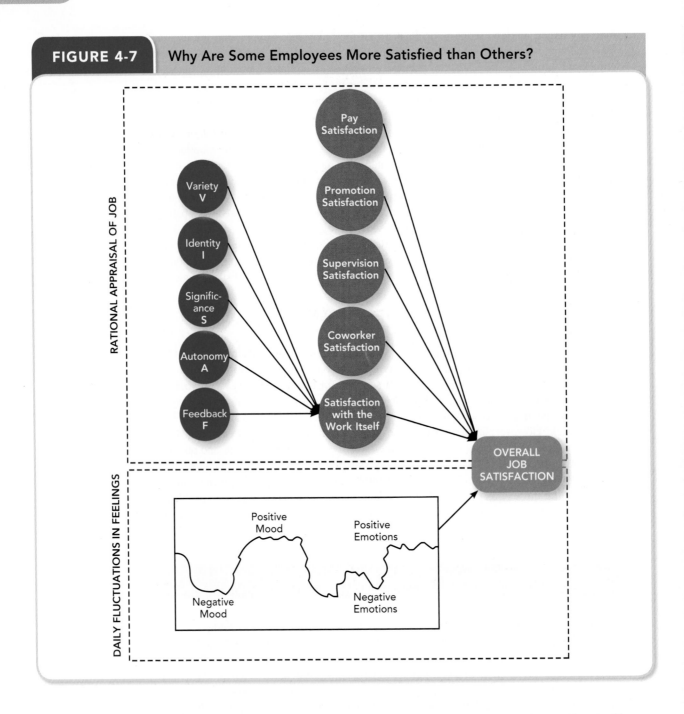

feelings also improve task persistence and attract more help and support from colleagues.[86] Apart from these sorts of findings, the benefits of job satisfaction for task performance might best be explained on an hour-by-hour basis. At any given moment, employees wage a war between paying attention to a given work task and attending to "off-task" things, such as stray thoughts, distractions, interruptions, and so forth. Positive feelings when working on job tasks can pull attention away from those distractions and channel people's attention to task accomplishment.[87] When such concentration occurs, an employee is more focused on work at a given point in time. Of course, the relationship between satisfaction

FIGURE 4-8   Effects of Job Satisfaction on Performance and Commitment

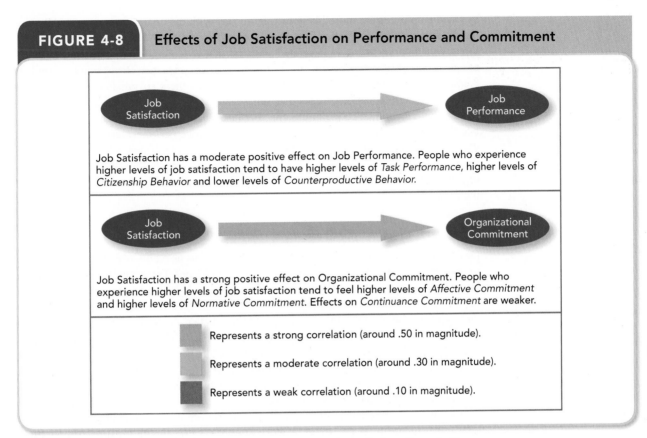

Job Satisfaction has a moderate positive effect on Job Performance. People who experience higher levels of job satisfaction tend to have higher levels of *Task Performance*, higher levels of *Citizenship Behavior* and lower levels of *Counterproductive Behavior*.

Job Satisfaction has a strong positive effect on Organizational Commitment. People who experience higher levels of job satisfaction tend to feel higher levels of *Affective Commitment* and higher levels of *Normative Commitment*. Effects on *Continuance Commitment* are weaker.

Represents a strong correlation (around .50 in magnitude).

Represents a moderate correlation (around .30 in magnitude).

Represents a weak correlation (around .10 in magnitude).

Sources: A. Cooper-Hakim and C. Viswesvaran, "The Construct of Work Commitment: Testing an Integrative Framework," *Psychological Bulletin* 131 (2005), pp. 241–59; R.S. Dalal, "A Meta-Analysis of the Relationship Between Organizational Citizenship Behavior and Counterproductive Work Behavior," *Journal of Applied Psychology* 90 (2005), pp. 1241–55; D.A. Harrison, D.A. Newman, and P.L. Roth, "How Important Are Job Attitudes? Meta-Analytic Comparisons of Integrative Behavioral Outcomes and Time Sequences," *Academy of Management Journal* 49 (2006), pp. 305–25; T.A. Judge, C.J. Thoreson, J.E. Bono, and G.K. Patton, "The Job Satisfaction–Job Performance Relationship: A Qualitative and Quantitative Review," *Psychological Bulletin* 127 (2001), pp. 376–407; J.A. LePine, A. Erez, and D.E. Johnson, "The Nature and Dimensionality of Organizational Citizenship Behavior: A Critical Review and Meta-Analysis," *Journal of Applied Psychology* 87 (2002), pp. 52–65; J.P. Meyer, D.J. Stanley, L. Herscovitch, and L. Topolnytsky, "Affective, Continuance, and Normative Commitment to the Organization: A Meta-Analysis of Antecedents, Correlates, and Consequences," *Journal of Vocational Behavior* 61 (2002), pp. 20–52.

and task performance can work in reverse to some extent, such that people tend to enjoy jobs that they can perform more successfully.[88] Meta-analyses tend to be less supportive of this causal direction, however.[89]

Job satisfaction also is correlated moderately with citizenship behavior. Satisfied employees engage in more frequent "extra mile" behaviors to help their coworkers and their organization.[90] Positive feelings increase their desire to interact with others and often result in spontaneous acts of helping and other instances of good citizenship.[91] In addition, job satisfaction has a moderate negative correlation with counterproductive behavior. Satisfied employees engage in fewer intentionally destructive actions that could harm their workplace.[92] Events that trigger negative emotions can prompts employees to "lash out" against the organization by engaging in rule breaking, theft, sabotage, or other retaliatory behaviors.[93] The more satisfied employees are, the less likely they'll feel those sorts of temptations.

Figure 4-8 also reveals that job satisfaction influences organizational commitment. Why? Job satisfaction is strongly correlated with affective commitment, so satisfied employees are more likely to want to stay with the organization.[94] After all, why would employees want to leave a place where they're happy? Another reason is that job satisfaction is strongly correlated with normative commitment. Satisfied employees are more likely to feel an obligation to remain with their firm[95] and a need to "repay" the organization for whatever it is that makes them so satisfied, whether good pay, interesting job tasks, or effective supervision. However, job satisfaction is uncorrelated with continuance commitment, because satisfaction does not create a cost-based need to remain with the organization. Taken together, these commitment effects become more apparent when you consider the kinds of employees who withdraw from the organization. In many cases, dissatisfied employees are the ones who sit daydreaming at their desks, come in late, are frequently absent, and eventually decide to quit their jobs.

LIFE SATISFACTION

Of course, job satisfaction is important for other reasons as well—reasons that have little to do with job performance or organizational commitment. For example, job satisfaction is strongly related to **life satisfaction**, or the degree to which employees feel a sense of happiness with their lives. Research shows that job satisfaction is one of the strongest predictors of life satisfaction. Put simply, people feel better about their lives when they feel better about their jobs.[96] This link makes sense when you realize how much of our identity is wrapped up in our jobs. What's the first question that people ask one another after being introduced? That's right—"What do you do?" If you feel bad about your answer to that question, it's hard to feel good about your life. As our **OB on Screen** feature illustrates, that adage is even true for George Clooney!

The connection between job satisfaction and life satisfaction also makes sense given how much of our lives are spent at work. Table 4-3 presents the results of one study that examines time spent on daily activities, along with reported levels of positive and negative feelings during the course of those activities.[97] The participants in the study spent most of their day at work. Unfortunately, that time resulted in the highest levels of negative feelings and the second-lowest levels of positive feelings (behind only commuting). Home and leisure activities (e.g., socializing, relaxing, exercising, intimate relations) were deemed much more satisfying but took up a much smaller portion of the day. The implication is clear: If we want to feel better about our days, we need to find a way to be more satisfied with our jobs.

Indeed, increases in job satisfaction have a stronger impact on life satisfaction than do increases in salary or income. As the old adage goes, "money can't buy happiness." This finding may seem surprising, given that pay

"Researchers say I'm not happier for being richer, but do you know how much researchers make?"

OB ON SCREEN

MICHAEL CLAYTON

There's no play here . . . there's no angle . . . I'm not a miracle worker, I'm a janitor.

With those words, Michael Clayton (George Clooney) reveals what he thinks of his job (Dir.: Tony Gilroy, Warner Brothers, 2007). He's an attorney working for one of the largest firms in the world—Kenner, Bach, and Ledeen. His job gets him a nice car and a nice suit but unfortunately not a nice life. You see, Clayton is the firm's "fixer"—the guy who uses his contacts and street smarts to solve messy situations. One night he's flying to Milwaukee to babysit an attorney who's had a breakdown. The next night he's driving to upstate New York to help a client who has committed a hit and run.

It's difficult to find much significance in Clayton's job. Fixing the situations that demand his attention may help his firm, but they have no benefit for society in general. He also lacks autonomy, constantly waiting for his cell phone to ring to send him on his next excursion. Moreover, those excursions don't tend to provide positive affective events. Listening to a client weasel out of a hit-and-run situation triggers feelings of shame and disgust, not joy or pride. It's not even clear that Kenner, Bach appreciates his efforts, because he's still not a partner, even after 17 years. Why not? Because as one of his colleagues points out, "Michael . . . you're a bag man, not an attorney."

All of this perspective hits home for Clayton as he's driving back from the hit-and-run meeting. He sees three horses, standing still on a misty hill, next to the road at sunrise. He stops his car, gets out, and slowly walks toward them, entranced—as if the horses represent all the honor and childhood innocence that he's lost in his life. The moment is surreal and haunting—made all the more so when his car explodes in a ball of flame.

satisfaction is one facet of overall job satisfaction (see Figure 4-1). However, you might recall that pay satisfaction is a weaker driver of overall job satisfaction than other facets, such as the work itself, supervision, or coworkers (see Figure 4-2). We should also note that pay satisfaction depends less on absolute salary levels and more on relative salary levels (i.e., how your salary compares to your circle of peers). As the writer H.L. Mencken once remarked, "A wealthy man is one who earns $100 a year more than his wife's sister's husband."[98] For more on the relationship between money and happiness, see our **OB Internationally** feature.

TABLE 4-3	How We Spend Our Days		
ACTIVITY	AVERAGE HOURS PER DAY	POSITIVE FEELINGS	NEGATIVE FEELINGS
Working	6.9	3.62	0.97
On the phone	2.5	3.92	0.85
Socializing	2.3	4.59	0.57
Eating	2.2	4.34	0.59
Relaxing	2.2	4.42	0.51
Watching TV	2.2	4.19	0.58
Computer/e-mail/Internet	1.9	3.81	0.80
Commuting	1.6	3.45	0.89
Housework	1.1	3.73	0.77
Interacting with kids	1.1	3.86	0.91
Napping	0.9	3.87	0.60
Praying/meditating	0.4	4.35	0.59
Exercising	0.2	4.31	0.50
Intimate relations	0.2	5.10	0.36

Notes: Positive and negative feelings measured using a scale of 0 (not at all) to 6 (very much).
Source: D. Kahneman, A.B. Krueger, D.A. Schkade, N. Schwarz, and A.A. Stone, "A Survey Method for Characterizing Daily Life Experience: The Day Reconstruction Method," *Science* 306 (2004), pp. 1776–80. Copyright © 2004 The American Association for the Advancement of Science. Reprinted with permission.

APPLICATION: TRACKING SATISFACTION

Because job satisfaction seems to be a key driver of job performance, organizational commitment, and life satisfaction, it's important for managers to understand just how satisfied their employees are. Gauging satisfaction is vital for organizations like Zappos, whose employees have direct customer contact, but it can be important in other organizations as well. Several methods assess the job satisfaction of rank-and-file employees, including focus groups, interviews, and attitude surveys. Of those three choices, attitude surveys are often the most accurate and most effective.[99] Attitude surveys can provide a "snapshot" of how satisfied the workforce is and, if repeated over time, reveal trends in satisfaction levels. They also can explore the effectiveness of major job changes by comparing attitude survey results before and after a change.

Although organizations are often tempted to design their own attitude surveys, there are benefits to using existing surveys that are already in wide use. One of the most widely administered job satisfaction surveys is the Job Descriptive Index (JDI). The JDI assesses all five satisfaction facets in Figure 4-1: pay satisfaction, promotion satisfaction, supervisor

4.8

What steps can organizations take to assess and manage job satisfaction?

OB INTERNATIONALLY

The "money can't buy happiness" adage can even be supported using nation-level data. For example, survey data in the United States, Britain, and Japan show that people are no happier today than they were 50 years ago, even though average incomes have more than doubled during that span.[100] Another way of examining this issue explores the connection between national wealth and average happiness: Do wealthier nations have citizens with higher levels of life satisfaction? The figure below provides a representation of the relationship between average income per citizen for a nation and the percentage of respondents who describe themselves as happy, according to population surveys.[101]

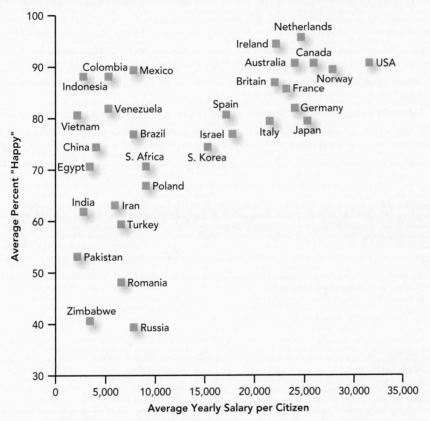

Comparing countries reveals that nations above the poverty line are indeed happier than nations below the poverty line. However, for countries with an average income of $20,000 or more, additional income is not associated with higher levels of life satisfaction.[102] For example, the United States is the richest country on Earth, but it trails nations like the Netherlands and Ireland in life satisfaction. Understanding differences in life satisfaction across nations is important to organizations for two reasons. First, such differences may influence how receptive a given nation is to the company's products. Second, such differences may affect the kinds of policies and practices an organization needs to use when employing individuals in that nation.

satisfaction, coworker satisfaction, and satisfaction with the work itself. The JDI also has been subjected to a great deal of research attention that, by and large, supports its accuracy.[103] Furthermore, the JDI includes a companion survey—the Job in General (JIG) scale—that assesses overall job satisfaction.[104] Excerpts from the JDI and JIG appear in Table 4-4.[105] One strength of the JDI is that the questions are written in a very simple and straightforward fashion so that they can be easily understood by most employees.

The developers of the JDI offer several suggestions regarding its administration.[106] For example, they recommend surveying as much of the company as possible because any unsurveyed employees might feel that their feelings are less important. They also recommend that surveys be anonymous so that employees can be as honest as possible without worrying about being punished for any critical comments about the organization. Therefore, companies must be careful in collecting demographic information on the surveys. Some demographic information is vital for comparing satisfaction levels across relevant groups, but too much information will make employees feel like they could be identified. Finally, the developers suggest that the survey should be administered by the firm's human resources group or an outside consulting agency. This structure will help employees feel that their anonymity is more protected.

Once JDI data have been collected, a number of interesting questions can be explored.[107] First, the data can indicate whether the organization is satisfied or dissatisfied by comparing average scores for each facet with the JDI's "neutral levels" for those facets (the "neutral levels" are available in the JDI manual). Second, it becomes possible to compare the

TABLE 4-4	Excerpts from the Job Descriptive Index and the Job in General Scale

Think of the work you do at present. How well does each of the following words or phrases describe your work? In the blank beside each word or phrase below, write
Y_ for "Yes" if it describes your work
N_ for "No" if it does NOT describe it
?_ for "?" if you cannot decide

Pay Satisfaction[a]	**Coworker Satisfaction**[a]
____ Well paid	____ Stimulating
____ Bad	____ Smart
____ Barely live on income	____ Unpleasant
Promotion Satisfaction[a]	**Satisfaction with Work Itself**[a]
____ Regular promotions	____ Fascinating
____ Promotion on ability	____ Pleasant
____ Opportunities somewhat limited	____ Can see my results
Supervision Satisfaction[a]	**OVERALL JOB SATISFACTION**[b]
____ Knows job well	____ Better than most
____ Around when needed	____ Worthwhile
____ Doesn't supervise enough	____ Worse than most

[a]The Job Descriptive Index, © Bowling Green State University (1975, 1985, 1997).
[b]The Job in General Scale, © Bowling Green State University (1982, 1985).
Source: W.K. Balzer, J.A. Kihn, P.C. Smith, J.L. Irwin, P.D. Bachiochi, C. Robie, E.F. Sinar, and L.F. Parra, "Users' Manual for the Job Descriptive Index (JDI; 1997 version) and the Job in General Scales," in *Electronic Resources for the JDI and JIG,* eds. J.M. Stanton and C.D. Crossley (Bowling Green, OH: Bowling Green State University, 2000). Reprinted with permission.

organization's scores with national norms to provide some context for the firm's satisfaction levels. The JDI manual also provides national norms for all facets and breaks down those norms according to relevant demographic groups (e.g., managers vs. nonmanagers, new vs. senior employees, gender, education). Third, the JDI allows for within-organization comparisons to determine which departments have the highest satisfaction levels and which have the lowest.

The results of attitude survey efforts should then be fed back to employees so that they feel involved in the process. Of course, attitude surveys ideally should be a catalyst for some kind of improvement effort.[108] Surveys that never lead to any kind of on-the-job change eventually may be viewed as a waste of time. As a result, the organization should be prepared to react to the survey results with specific goals and action steps. For example, an organization with low pay satisfaction may react by conducting additional benchmarking to see whether compensation levels are trailing those of competitors. An organization with low promotion satisfaction might react by revising its system for assessing performance. Finally, an organization that struggles with satisfaction with the work itself could attempt to redesign key job tasks or, if that proves too costly, train supervisors in strategies for increasing the five core job characteristics on a more informal basis.

TAKEAWAYS

4.1 Job satisfaction is a pleasurable emotional state resulting from the appraisal of one's job or job experiences. It represents how you feel about your job and what you think about your job.

4.2 Values are things that people consciously or subconsciously want to seek or attain. According to value-percept theory, job satisfaction depends on whether you perceive that your job supplies those things that you value.

4.3 Employees consider a number of specific facets when evaluating their job satisfaction. These facets include pay satisfaction, promotion satisfaction, supervision satisfaction, coworker satisfaction, and satisfaction with the work itself.

4.4 Job characteristics theory suggests that five "core characteristics"—variety, identity, significance, autonomy, and feedback—combine to result in particularly high levels of satisfaction with the work itself.

4.5 Apart from the influence of supervision, coworkers, pay, and the work itself, job satisfaction levels fluctuate during the course of the day. Rises and falls in job satisfaction are triggered by positive and negative events that are experienced. Those events trigger changes in emotions that eventually give way to changes in mood.

4.6 Moods are states of feeling that are often mild in intensity, last for an extended period of time, and are not explicitly directed at anything. Intense positive moods include being enthusiastic, excited, and elated. Intense negative moods include being hostile, nervous, and annoyed. Emotions are states of feeling that are often intense, last only for a few minutes, and are clearly directed at someone or some circumstance. Positive emotions include joy, pride, relief, hope, love, and compassion. Negative emotions include anger, anxiety, fear, guilt, shame, sadness, envy, and disgust.

4.7 Job satisfaction has a moderately positive relationship with job performance and a strong positive relationship with organizational commitment. It also has a strong positive relationship with life satisfaction.

4.8 Organizations can assess and manage job satisfaction using attitude surveys such as the Job Descriptive Index (JDI), which assesses pay satisfaction, promotion satisfaction, supervisor satisfaction, coworker satisfaction, and satisfaction with the work itself. It can be used to assess the levels of job satisfaction experienced by employees, and its specific facet scores can identify interventions that could be helpful.

KEY TERMS

- Job satisfaction   p. 105
- Values   p. 105
- Value-percept theory   p. 107
- Pay satisfaction   p. 107
- Promotion satisfaction   p. 107
- Supervision satisfaction   p. 108
- Coworker satisfaction   p. 109
- Satisfaction with the work itself   p. 109
- Meaningfulness of work   p. 111
- Responsibility for outcomes   p. 111
- Knowledge of results   p. 111
- Job characteristics theory   p. 111
- Variety   p. 111
- Identity   p. 114
- Significance   p. 114
- Autonomy   p. 115
- Feedback   p. 115
- Knowledge and skill   p. 116
- Growth need strength   p. 116
- Job enrichment   p. 117
- Moods   p. 119
- Pleasantness   p. 120
- Activation   p. 120
- Flow   p. 121
- Affective events theory   p. 121
- Emotions   p. 121
- Positive emotions   p. 122
- Negative emotions   p. 122
- Emotional labor   p. 123
- Emotional contagion   p. 123
- Life satisfaction   p. 126

DISCUSSION QUESTIONS

4.1 Which of the values in Table 4-1 do you think are the most important to employees in general? Are there times when the values in the last three categories (altruism, status, and environment) become more important than the values in the first five categories (pay, promotions, supervision, coworkers, and the work itself)?

4.2 What steps can organizations take to improve promotion satisfaction, supervision satisfaction, and coworker satisfaction?

4.3 Consider the five core job characteristics (variety, identity, significance, autonomy, and feedback). Do you think that any one of those characteristics is more important than the other four? Is it possible to have too much of some job characteristics?

4.4 We sometimes describe colleagues or friends as "moody." What do you think it means to be "moody" from the perspective of Figure 4-6?

4.5 Consider the list of positive and negative emotions in Table 4-2. Which of these emotions are most frequently experienced at work? What causes them?

CASE: ZAPPOS

When a company promotes "a little weirdness,"[109] it becomes important to hire people who will be satisfied in that sort of environment. Zappos does so by focusing on positive people during its hiring process. But what happens if new hires realize that they're not satisfied with their job, their coworkers, or the organization? That's where "The Offer" comes in: New hires begin their Zappos employment with a four-week training period that acquaints them with the company's strategy and its approach to customer service, receiving their full salary along the way.[110] One week in, the new hires are offered a $2,000 bonus . . . to quit.[111] That's right—new hires can walk away with one week's salary and an extra $2,000 in their pocket. Zappos uses "The Offer" to give employees who may not enjoy working at Zappos an easy out.

Zappos' CEO Tony Hsieh justifies "The Offer" this way: "It's best to know early on if an employee doesn't buy into the vision or the culture. It just makes economic sense."[112] Indeed, Zappos has actually upped "The Offer" over the years, from $100 to $500, then to $1,000, and then to its current level.[113] Hsieh reports that around 3 percent of employees take the money and run, but 97 percent evidently view Zappos as a place where they will be happy to work.[114] There's no telling how the job satisfaction within a unit would be altered had those 3 percent stuck around, despite their lack of enthusiasm for the company's practices. At the very least, the 97 percent number is a testament to all the things Zappos does to maximize job satisfaction, as well as the diligence it shows during the hiring process.

4.1   What do you think of "The Offer" as a strategy for maximizing job satisfaction?

4.2   Could that strategy be used at other organizations, or does it require the sort of "quirky environment" that Zappos emphasizes?

4.3   As the profile of Zappos increases, and as the notoriety of "The Offer" rises, do you think the policy will need to evolve? In what way?

EXERCISE: JOB SATISFACTION ACROSS JOBS

The purpose of this exercise is to examine satisfaction with the work itself across jobs. This exercise uses groups, so your instructor will either assign you to a group or ask you to create your own group. The exercise has the following steps:

4.1   Use the OB Assessments for Chapter 4 to calculate the Satisfaction Potential Score (SPS) for the following four jobs:

   a. A third-grade public school teacher.

   b. A standup comedian.

   c. A computer programmer whose job is to replace "98" with "1998" in thousands of lines of computer code.

   d. A president of the United States.

4.2   Which job has the highest SPS? Which core job characteristics best explain why some jobs have high scores and other jobs have low scores? Write down the scores for the four jobs in an Excel file on the classroom computer or on the board.

4.3   Class discussion (whether in groups or as a class) should center on two questions. First, is the job that scored the highest really the one that would be the most enjoyable on a day-in, day-out basis? Second, does that mean it would be the job that you would pick if you could snap your fingers and magically attain one of the jobs on the list? Why or why not? What other job satisfaction theory is relevant to this issue?

ENDNOTES

4.1 O'Brien, J.M. "The 10 Commandments of Zappos." *Fortune,* January 22, 2009, http://money.cnn.com/2009/01/21/news/companies/obrien_zappos10.fortune/index.htm (June 3, 2009).

4.2 O'Brien, J.M. "Zappos Knows How to Kick It." *Fortune,* February 2, 2009; pp. 55–60.

4.3 "Zappos Blogs: CEO and COO Blog." January 25, 2009, http://blogs.zappos.com/blogs/ceo-and-coo-blog (June 12, 2009).

4.4 O'Brien, "Zappos Know How to Kick It."

4.5 Ibid.; O'Brien, "The 10 Commandments of Zappos."

4.6 O'Brien, "The 10 Commandments of Zappos."

4.7 Levering, R., and M. Moskowitz. "And the Winners Are . . ." *Fortune,* February 2, 2009, pp. 67–78; and O'Brien, "Zappos Knows How to Kick It."

4.8 Ibid.

4.9 O'Brien, "Zappos Knows How to Kick It."

4.10 Levering and Moskowitz, "And the Winners Are . . ."

4.11 O'Brien, "Zappos Knows How to Kick It."

4.12 "The Customer Service Champs." *BusinessWeek,* February 19, 2009, http://bwnt.businessweek.com/interactive_reports/customer_service_2009/index.asp (June 12, 2009).

4.13 O'Brien, "Zappos Knows How to Kick It."

4.14 Locke, E.A. "The Nature and Causes of Job Satisfaction." In *Handbook of Industrial and Organizational Psychology,* ed. M. Dunnette. Chicago, IL: Rand McNally, 1976, pp. 1297–1350.

4.15 Koretz, G. "Hate Your Job? Join the Club." *BusinessWeek,* October 6, 2003, p. 40.

4.16 Locke, "The Nature and Causes"; Rokeach, M. *The Nature of Human Values.* New York: Free Press, 1973; Schwartz, S.H. "Universals in the Content and Structure of Values: Theoretical Advances and Empirical Tests in 20 Countries. In *Advances in Experimental Social Psychology,* ed. M. Zanna. New York: Academic Press, 1992, vol. 25, pp. 1-65; and Edwards, J.R., and D.M. Cable. "The Value of Value Congruence." *Journal of Applied Psychology* 94 (2009), pp. 654-77.

4.17 Dawis, R.V. "Vocational Interests, Values, and Preferences." In *Handbook of Industrial and Organizational Psychology,* Vol. 2, eds. M.D. Dunnette and L.M. Hough Palo Alto, CA: Consulting Psychologists Press, 1991, pp. 834–71; and Cable, D.M., and J.R. Edwards. "Complementary and Supplementary Fit: A Theoretical and Empirical Integration." *Journal of Applied Psychology* 89 (2004), pp. 822-34.

4.18 Locke, "The Nature and Causes."

4.19 Judge, T.A., and A.H. Church. "Job Satisfaction: Research and Practice." In *Industrial and Organizational Psychology: Linking Theory with Practice,* eds. C.L. Cooper and E.A. Locke. Oxford, UK: Blackwell, 2000, pp. 166–98.

4.20 Locke, "The Nature and Causes."

4.21 Smith, P.C.; L.M. Kendall; and C.L. Hulin. *The Measurement of Satisfaction in Work and Retirement.* Chicago: Rand McNally, 1969.

4.22 Lawler, E.E. *Pay and Organizational Effectiveness: A Psychological View.* New York: McGraw-Hill, 1971.

4.23 Locke, "The Nature and Causes."

4.24 Levering, R., and M. Moskowitz. "In Good Company." *Fortune,* January 22, 2007, pp. 94–114.

4.25 Smith, Kendall, and Hulin, "The Measurement of Satisfaction."

4.26 Locke, "The Nature and Causes."

4.27 Levering, R., and M. Moskowitz. "The 100 Best Companies to Work For." *Fortune,* January 24, 2005, pp. 64–68.

4.28 Smith, Kendall, and Hulin, "The Measurement of Satisfaction."

4.29 Locke, "The Nature and Causes."

4.30 Levering and Moskowitz, "The 100 Best."

4.31 Smith, Kendall, and Hulin, "The Measurement of Satisfaction."

4.32 Levering and Moskowitz, "The 100 Best."

4.33 Smith, Kendall, and Hulin, "The Measurement of Satisfaction."

4.34 Levering and Moskowitz, "The 100 Best."

4.35 Ironson, G.H.; P.C. Smith; M.T. Brannick; W.M. Gibson; and K.B. Paul. "Construction of a Job in General Scale: A Comparison of Global, Composite, and Specific Measures." *Journal of Applied Psychology* 74 (1989), pp. 193–200; and Russell, S.S.; C. Spitzmuller; L.F. Lin; J.M. Stanton; P.C. Smith; and G.H. Ironson. "Shorter Can Also Be Better: The Abridged Job in General Scale." *Educational and Psychological Measurement* 64 (2004), pp. 878–93.

4.36 Taylor, F.W. *The Principles of Scientific Management.* New York: Wiley, 1911; and Gilbreth, F.B. *Motion Study: A Method for Increasing the Efficiency of the Workman.* New York: Van Nostrand, 1911.

4.37 Hackman, J.R., and E.E. Lawler III. "Employee Reactions to Job Characteristics." *Journal of Applied Psychology* 55 (1971), pp. 259–86.

4.38 Hackman, J.R., and G.R. Oldham. *Work Redesign.* Reading, MA: Addison-Wesley, 1980.

4.39 Ibid.

4.40 Ibid.

4.41 Hackman, J.R., and G.R. Oldham. "Motivation through the Design of Work: Test of a Theory." *Organizational Behavior and Human Decision Processes* 16 (1976), pp. 250–79.

4.42 Hackman and Oldham, *Work Redesign.*

4.43 Turner, A.N., and P.R. Lawrence. *Industrial Jobs and the Worker.* Boston: Harvard University Graduate School of Business Administration, 1965.

4.44 Hackman and Lawler, "Employee Reactions."

4.45 Terkel, S. *Working: People Talk About What They Do All Day and How They Feel About What They Do.* New York: Pantheon Books, 1974, pp. 159–60.

4.46 Ibid., pp. 318–21.

4.47 Berns, G. *Satisfaction: The Science of Finding True Fulfillment*. New York: Henry Holt and Company, 2005, p. xiv.

4.48 Hackman and Oldham, *Work Redesign*.

4.49 Turner and Lawrence, *Industrial Jobs*.

4.50 Terkel, *Working*, p. xxxii.

4.51 Ibid., pp. 213–14.

4.52 Hackman and Oldham, *Work Redesign*.

4.53 Grant, A.M. "The Significance of Task Significance: Job Performance Effects, Relational Mechanisms, and Boundary Conditions." *Journal of Applied Psychology* 93 (2008), pp. 108-24.

4.54 Terkel, *Working*, pp. 107–09.

4.55 Ibid., p. 589.

4.56 Hackman and Oldham, *Work Redesign*.

4.57 Turner and Lawrence, *Industrial Jobs*.

4.58 Breaugh, J.A. "The Measurement of Work Autonomy." *Human Relations* 38 (1985), pp. 551–70.

4.59 Terkel, *Working*, pp. 49–50.

4.60 Hackman and Oldham, *Work Redesign*.

4.61 Terkel, *Working*, p. 346.

4.62 Ibid., pp. 295–96.

4.63 Humphrey, S.E.; J.D. Nahrgang; and F.P. Morgeson. "Integrating Motivational, Social, and Contextual Work Design Features: A Meta-Analytic Summary and Theoretical Extension of the Work Design Literature. *Journal of Applied Psychology* 92 (2007), pp. 1332-56. and Fried, Y., and G.R. Ferris. "The Validity of the Job Characteristics Model: A Review and Meta-Analysis." *Personnel Psychology* 40 (1987), pp. 287–322.

4.64 Hackman and Oldham, *Work Redesign*.

4.65 Loher, B.T.; R.A. Noe; N.L. Moeller; and M.P. Fitzgerald. "A Meta-Analysis of the Relation of Job Characteristics to Job Satisfaction." *Journal of Applied Psychology* 70 (1985), pp. 280–89.

4.66 Campion, M.A.; and C.L. McClelland. "Interdisciplinary Examination of the Costs and Benefits of Enlarged Jobs: A Job Design Quasi-Experiment." *Journal of Applied Psychology* 76 (1991), pp. 186–98.

4.67 Ibid.

4.68 Morris, W.N. *Mood: The Frame of Mind*. New York: Springer-Verlag, 1989.

4.69 Watson, D., and A. Tellegen. "Toward a Consensual Structure of Mood." *Psychological Bulletin* 98 (1985), pp. 219–35; Russell, J.A. "A Circumplex Model of Affect." *Journal of Personality and Social Psychology* 39 (1980), pp. 1161–78; and Larsen, R.J., and E. Diener. "Promises and Problems with the Circumplex Model of Emotion." In *Review of Personality and Social Psychology: Emotion*, Vol. 13, ed. M.S. Clark. Newbury Park, CA: Sage, 1992, pp. 25–59.

4.70 Ibid.

4.71 Levering and Moskowitz, "The 100 Best."

4.72 Ibid.

4.73 Csikszentmihalyi, M. *Finding Flow: The Psychology of Engagement with Everyday Life*. New York: Basic Books, 1997;

Csikszentmihalyi, M. *Flow: The Psychology of Optimal Experience.* New York: HarperPerennial, 1990; and Csikszentmihalyi, M. *Beyond Boredom and Anxiety.* San Francisco: Jossey-Bass, 1975.

4.74 Quinn, R.W. "Flow in Knowledge Work: High Performance Experience in the Design of National Security Technology." *Administrative Science Quarterly* 50 (2005), pp. 610–41; and Jackson, S.A., and H.W. Marsh. "Development and Validation of a Scale to Measure Optimal Experience: The Flow State Scale." *Journal of Sport and Exercise Psychology* 18 (1996), pp. 17–35.

4.75 Weiss, H.M., and R. Cropanzano. "Affective Events Theory: A Theoretical Discussion of the Structure, Causes, and Consequences of Affective Experiences at Work." In *Research in Organizational Behavior*, Vol. 18, eds. B.M. Staw and L.L. Cummings. Greenwich, CT: JAI Press, 1996, pp. 1–74

4.76 Weiss, H.M.; and K.E. Kurek. "Dispositional Influences on Affective Experiences at Work." In *Personality and Work: Reconsidering the Role of Personality in Organizations,* eds. M.R. Barrick and A.M. Ryan. San Francisco: Jossey-Bass, 2003, pp. 121–49.

4.77 Weiss and Cropanzano, "Affective Events Theory."

4.78 Lazarus, R.S. *Emotion and Adaptation.* New York: Oxford University, 1991.

4.79 Hochschild, A.R. *The Managed Heart: Commercialization of Human Feeling.* Berkeley, CA: University of California Press, 1983; and Rafaeli, A., and R.I. Sutton. "The Expression of Emotion in Organizational Life." *Research in Organizational Behavior* 11 (1989), pp. 1–42.

4.80 Hatfield, E.; J.T. Cacioppo; and R.L. Rapson. *Emotional Contagion.* New York: Cambridge University Press, 1994.

4.81 Ashkanasy, N.M.; C.E.J. Hartel; and C.S. Daus. "Diversity and Emotion: The New Frontiers in Organizational Behavior Research." *Journal of Management* 28 (2002), pp. 307–38.

4.82 Judge, T.A.; C.J. Thoreson; J.E. Bono; and G.K Patton. "The Job Satisfaction–Job Performance Relationship: A Qualitative and Quantitative Review." *Psychological Bulletin* 127 (2001), pp. 376–407.

4.83 Baas, M.; C.K.W. De Dreu; and B.A. Nijstad. "A Meta-Analysis of 25 Years of Mood-Creativity Research: Hedonic Tone, Activation, or Regulatory Focus." *Psychological Bulletin* 134 (2008), pp. 779-806; and Lyubomirsky, S.; L. King; and E. Diener. "The Benefits of Frequent Positive Affect: Does Happiness Lead to Success?" *Psychological Bulletin* 131 (2005), pp. 803-55.

4.84 Brief, A.P., and H.M. Weiss. "Organizational Behavior: Affect in the Workplace." *Annual Review of Psychology* 53 (2002), pp. 279–307.

4.85 Isen, A.M., and R.A. Baron. "Positive Affect as a Factor in Organizational Behavior." *Research in Organizational Behavior* 13 (1991), pp. 1–53.

4.86 Tsai, W.C.; C.C. Chen; and H.L. Liu. "Test of a Model Linking Employee Positive Moods and Task Performance." *Journal of Applied Psychology* 92 (2007), pp. 1570-83.

4.87 Beal, D.J.; H.M. Weiss; E. Barros; and S.M. MacDermid. "An Episodic Process Model of Affective Influences on Performance." *Journal of Applied Psychology* 90 (2005), pp. 1054–68.

4.88 Locke, "The Nature and Causes."

4.89 Riketta, M. "The Causal Relation Between Job Attitudes and Job Performance: A Meta-Analysis of Panel Studies." *Journal of Applied Psychology* 93 (2008), pp. 472-81.

4.90 LePine, J.A.; A. Erez; and D.E. Johnson. "The Nature and Dimensionality of Organizational Citizenship Behavior: A Critical Review and Meta-Analysis." *Journal of Applied Psychology* 87 (2002), pp. 52–65.

4.91 Lyubomirsky, King, and Diener, "The Benefits of Frequent Positive Affect."

4.92 Dalal, R.S. "A Meta-Analysis of the Relationship Between Organizational Citizenship Behavior and Counterproductive Work Behavior." *Journal of Applied Psychology* 90 (2005), pp. 1241–55.

4.93 Yang, J.; and J.M. Diefendorff. "The Relations of Daily Counterproductive Workplace Behavior with Emotions, Situational Antecedents, and Personality Moderators: A Diary Study in Hong Kong." *Personnel Psychology* 62 (2009), pp. 259-95.

4.94 Cooper-Hakim, A., and C. Viswesvaran. "The Construct of Work Commitment: Testing an Integrative Framework." *Psychological Bulletin* 131 (2005), pp. 241–59; Harrison, D.A.; D. Newman; and P.L. Roth. "How Important Are Job Attitudes? Meta-Analytic Comparisons of Integrative Behavioral Outcomes and Time Sequences." *Academy of Management Journal* 49 (2006), pp. 305–25; and Meyer, J.P.; D.J. Stanley; L. Herscovitch; and L. Topolnytsky. "Affective, Continuance, and Normative Commitment to the Organization: A Meta-Analysis of Antecedents, Correlates, and Consequences." *Journal of Vocational Behavior* 61 (2002), pp. 20–52.

4.95 Ibid.

4.96 Tait, M.; M.Y. Padgett; and T.T. Baldwin. "Job and Life Satisfaction: A Reexamination of the Strength of the Relationship and Gender Effects as a Function of the Date of the Study." *Journal of Applied Psychology* 74 (1989), pp. 502–507; and Judge, T.A., and S. Watanabe. "Another Look at the Job Satisfaction–Life Satisfaction Relationship." *Journal of Applied Psychology* 78 (1993), pp. 939–48.

4.97 Kahneman, D.; A.B. Krueger; D.A. Schkade; N. Schwarz; and A.A. Stone. "A Survey Method for Characterizing Daily Life Experience: The Day Reconstruction Method." *Science* 306 (2004), pp. 1776–80.

4.98 Layard, R. *Happiness.* New York: Penguin Press, 2005, p. 41.

4.99 Saari, L.M., and T.A. Judge. "Employee Attitudes and Job Satisfaction." *Human Resource Management* 43 (2004), pp. 395–407.

4.100 Layard, *Happiness.*

4.101 R. Layard, qtd. in Diener, E., and E. Suh. "National Differences in Subjective Well-Being." In *Well-Being: The Foundations of Hedonic Psychology,* eds. D. Kahneman, E. Diener, and N. Schwarz. New York: Russell Sage Foundation, 1999, pp. 434-450.

4.102 Layard, *Happiness.*

4.103 Kinicki, A.J.; F.M. McKee-Ryan; C.A. Schriesheim; and K.P. Carson. "Assessing the Construct Validity of the Job Descriptive Index: A Review and Meta-Analysis." *Journal of Applied Psychology* 87 (2002), pp. 14–32; Hanisch, K.A. "The Job Descriptive Index Revisited: Questions about the Question Mark." *Journal of Applied Psychology* 77 (1992), pp. 377–82; and Jung, K.G.; A. Dalessio; and S.M. Johnson. "Stability of the Factor Structure of the Job Descriptive Index." *Academy of Management Journal* 29 (1986), pp. 609–16.

4.104 Ironson et al., "Construction"; and Russell et al., "Shorter Can also Be Better."

4.105 Balzer, W.K.; J.A. Kihn; P.C. Smith; J.L. Irwin; P.D. Bachiochi; C. Robie; E.F. Sinar; and LF. Parra. "Users' Manual for the Job Descriptive Index (JDI; 1997 version) and the Job in General Scales." In *Electronic Resources for the JDI and JIG,* eds. J.M. Stanton and C.D. Crossley. Bowling Green, OH: Bowling Green State University, 2000.

4.106 Ibid.

4.107 Ibid.

4.108 Saari and Judge, "Employee Attitudes."

4.109 O'Brien, "Zappos Knows How to Kick It."

4.110 Taylor, B. "Why Zappos Pays New Employees to Quit—and You Should Too." *Harvard Business Review,* May 19, 2008, http://blogs. harvardbusiness.org/taylor/2008/05/ why_zappos_pays_new_employees. html (June 12, 2009).

4.111 Ibid.; and McFarland, K. "Why Zappos Offers New Hires $2000 to Quit." *BusinessWeek,* September 16, 2008, http://www.businessweek. com/smallbiz/content/sep2008/ sb20080916_288698.htm (June 12, 2009).

4.112 Borden, M. "#20 Zappos." *Fast Company,* February 11, 2009, http://www.fastcompany.com/ fast50_09/profile/list/zappos (June 12, 2009).

4.113 Taylor, "Why Zappos Pays New Employees to Quit."

4.114 McFarland, "Why Zappos Offers New Hires $2000 to Quit."

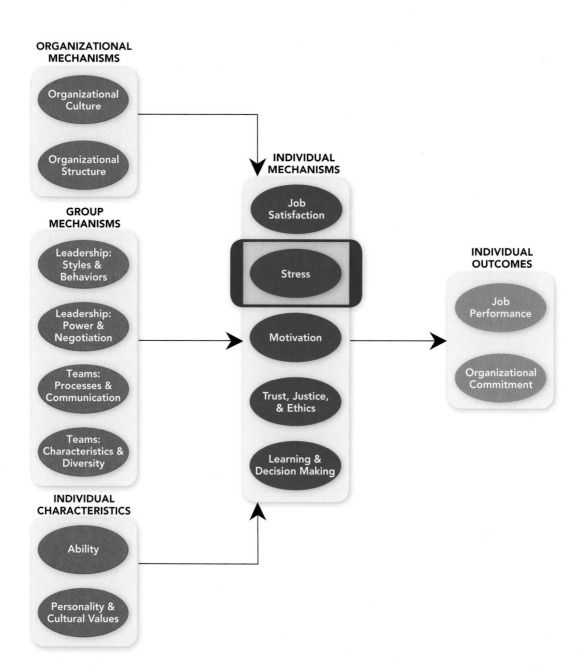

ORGANIZATIONAL
MECHANISMS

Organizational
Culture

Organizational
Structure

GROUP
MECHANISMS

Leadership:
Styles &
Behaviors

Leadership:
Power &
Negotiation

Teams:
Processes &
Communication

Teams:
Characteristics &
Diversity

INDIVIDUAL
CHARACTERISTICS

Ability

Personality &
Cultural Values

INDIVIDUAL
MECHANISMS

Job
Satisfaction

Stress

Motivation

Trust, Justice,
& Ethics

Learning &
Decision Making

INDIVIDUAL
OUTCOMES

Job
Performance

Organizational
Commitment

✓ LEARNING GOALS

After reading this chapter, you should be able to answer the following questions:

5.1 What is stress, and how is it different than stressors and strains?

5.2 What are the four main types of stressors?

5.3 How do individuals cope with stress?

5.4 How does the Type A Behavior Pattern influence the stress process?

5.5 How does stress affect job performance and organizational commitment?

5.6 What steps can organizations take to manage employee stress?

HUMANA

At this point in life, you probably realize that there's an important connection between your health and your effectiveness in just about every aspect of life. After all, if you feel healthy, you have more energy, you're more enthusiastic and confident, and you can better cope with all the stressful demands that come your way. In fact, if you're like most people, at some point you've told yourself that you want to be healthier, and you may have even promised yourself to cut down on junk food and to exercise more. The problem is that most of us are really busy, and trying to fit in time for healthy activities can be a major inconvenience. So just imagine how great it would be if your employer made it easier for you to be healthy.

Humana, a *Fortune* 100 company that administers health care benefits for organizations in the public and private sectors, is doing just that with its "Freewheelin'" program.[1] Introduced in 2007, the Freewheelin' program gives Humana employees who work at the corporate offices in Louisville, Kentucky, the opportunity to borrow bikes for free from stations located throughout the city. An employee who wishes to check out one of the bikes simply swipes an ID card at one of the stations, puts on a helmet, and goes. The employee is then free to ride the bike to meetings at another office, go to lunch, or just take a spin around the city to burn off steam. It's not unusual for large organizations such as Humana to offer programs that encourage employees to engage in healthy behaviors. In fact, it's estimated that more than two-thirds of all businesses offer benefits related to health promotion.[2] However, Humana went a step further than most companies by offering employees something fun to do during the workday at a time when it's hard to get fresh air. How popular has the program become? About half of the 8,500 employees at the corporate offices have signed up for the program, and because demand for the bikes has been so high, Humana is taking steps to expand the program even further.[3]

Providing employees with a program like Freewheelin' is consistent with Humana's mission as a business in the health care industry. The program therefore benefits the company by reinforcing its corporate image. However, providing such a program makes sense for reasons that go beyond marketing. Participation in fitness activities reduces participants' stress levels, risk of coronary heart disease, and memory loss,[4] and in turn, these benefits translate to increases in employee productivity and reductions in absenteeism and health care costs.[5] Estimates suggest potential reductions of $1.65 in health care expenses for every dollar an organization invests in programs that promote its employees' health and wellness.[6] Of course, the return on the investment from the Freewheelin' program is not likely to be on the minds of Humana employees as they zip around the city on the program's lime green Trek bikes.

STRESS

Stress is an OB topic that's probably quite familiar to you. Even if you don't have a lot of work experience, consider how you feel toward the end of a semester when you have to cram for several final exams and finish a couple of term projects. At the same time, you might have also been looking for a job or planning a trip with friends or family. Although some people might be able to deal with all of these demands without becoming too frazzled, most people would say that this type of scenario causes them to feel "stressed out." This stressed-out feeling might even be accompanied by headaches, stomach upsets, backaches, or sleeping difficulties. Although you might believe your stress will diminish once you graduate and settle down, high stress on the job is more prevalent than it's ever been before.[7] The federal government's National Institute for Occupational Safety and Health (NIOSH) summarized findings from several sources that indicated that up to 40 percent of U.S. workers feel their jobs are "very stressful" or "extremely stressful."[8] Unfortunately, high stress is even more prevalent in the types of jobs that most of you are likely to have after you graduate. This is because managers are approximately 21 percent more likely than the average worker to describe their jobs as stressful.[9] Table 5-1 provides a listing of how several jobs rank on the list of least to most stressful.

TABLE 5-1	Jobs Rated from Least Stressful (1) to Most Stressful (250)		
LEAST STRESSFUL JOBS	STRESS LEVEL	MOST STRESSFUL JOBS	STRESS LEVEL
1. Musical instrument repairer	18.77	212. Registered nurse	62.14
2. Florist	18.80	220. Attorney	64.33
4. Actuary	20.18	223. Newspaper reporter	65.26
6. Appliance repairer	21.12	226. Architect	66.92
8. Librarian	21.40	228. Lumberjack	67.60
10. File clerk	21.71	229. Fisherman	69.82
11. Piano tuner	22.29	230. Stockbroker	71.65
12. Janitor	22.44	231. U.S. Congressperson	72.05
16. Vending machine repairer	23.47	233. Real estate agent	73.06
18. Barber	23.62	234. Advertising account exec	74.55
24. Mathematician	24.67	238. Public relations exec	78.52
29. Cashier	25.11	240. Air traffic controller	83.13
30. Dishwasher	25.32	241. Airline pilot	85.35
32. Pharmacist	25.87	243. Police officer	93.89
40. Biologist	26.94	244. Astronaut	99.34
44. Computer programmer	27.00	245. Surgeon	99.46
50. Astronomer	28.06	246. Taxi driver	100.49
56. Historian	28.41	248. Senior corporate exec	108.62
67. Bank teller	30.12	249. Firefighter	110.93
78. Accountant	31.13	250. U.S. President	176.55

Source: Adapted from L. Krantz, *Jobs Rated Almanac,* 6th ed. (Fort Lee, NJ: Barricade Books, Inc., 2002). The stress level score is calculated by summing points in 21 categories, including deadlines, competitiveness, environmental conditions, speed required, precision required, initiative required, physical demands, and hazards encountered.

5.1

What is stress, and how is it different than stressors and strains?

Stress is defined as a psychological response to demands that possess certain stakes and that tax or exceed a person's capacity or resources.[10] The demands that cause people to experience stress are called **stressors**. The negative consequences that occur when demands tax or exceed a person's capacity or resources are called **strains**. This definition of stress illustrates that it depends on both the nature of the demand and the person who confronts it. People differ in terms of how they evaluate stressors and the way they cope with them. As a result, different people may experience different levels of stress even when confronted with the exact same situation.

WHY ARE SOME EMPLOYEES MORE "STRESSED" THAN OTHERS?

To fully understand what it means to feel "stressed," it's helpful to consider the **transactional theory of stress**. This theory explains how stressors are perceived and appraised, as well as how people respond to those perceptions and appraisals.[11] When people first encounter stressors, the process of **primary appraisal** is triggered.[12] As shown in Figure 5-1, primary appraisal occurs as people evaluate the significance and the meaning of the stressors they are confronting. Here, people first consider whether a demand causes them to feel stressed, and if it does, they consider the implications of the stressor in terms of their personal goals and overall well-being.

As an example of a primary appraisal, consider the job of a cashier at a well-run convenience store. In this store, cashiers engage in routine sales transactions with customers. Customers walk in the store and select merchandise, and the cashiers on duty ring up the sale and collect the money. Under normal day-to-day circumstances at this store, well-trained cashiers would not likely feel that these transactions are overly taxing or exceeding their capacity, so those cashiers would not likely appraise these job demands as stressful. Job demands that tend not to be appraised as stressful are called **benign job demands.**

However, consider how convenience store cashiers would react in a different store in which the cash register and credit card machine break down often and without warning. The cashiers who work at this store would likely view their job as more stressful, because they have to diagnose and fix problems with equipment while dealing with customers who are growing more and more impatient. Furthermore, the cashiers in this store might appraise the stressful situation as one that unnecessarily prevents them from achieving their goal of being viewed as an effective employee in the eyes of the customers and the store manager.

Finally, consider a third convenience store in which the cashiers' workload is higher due to additional responsibilities that include receiving merchandise from vendors, taking physical inventory, and training new employees. In this store, the cashiers may appraise their jobs as stressful because of the higher workload and the need to balance different priorities. However, in contrast to the cashiers in the previous example, cashiers in this store might appraise these demands as providing an opportunity to learn and demonstrate the type of competence that often is rewarded with satisfying promotions and pay raises.

TYPES OF STRESSORS

5.2

What are the four main types of stressors?

In the previous two examples, the cashiers were confronted with demands that a primary appraisal would label as "stressful." However, the specific demands in the two examples have an important difference. Dealing with equipment breakdowns or unhappy customers has little to no benefit to the employee in the long term. These kinds of stressors are called

FIGURE 5-1 Transactional Theory of Stress

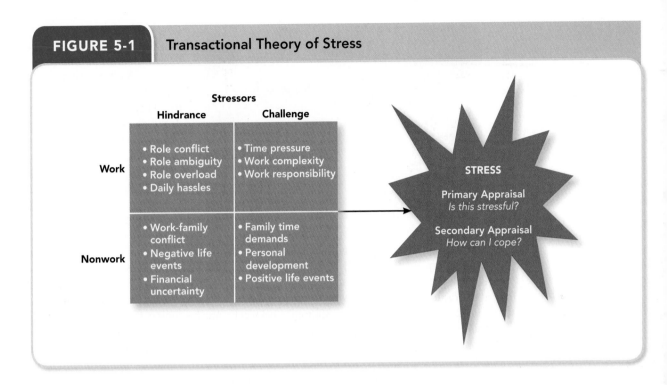

hindrance stressors—stressful demands that are perceived as hindering progress toward personal accomplishments or goal attainment.[13] Hindrance stressors tend to trigger negative emotions such as anger and anxiety. In contrast, managing additional responsibilities or higher workloads has a long-term benefit, in that it helps build the employee's skills. These kinds of stressors are called **challenge stressors**—stressful demands that are perceived as opportunities for learning, growth, and achievement. Although challenge stressors can be exhausting, they often trigger positive emotions such as pride and enthusiasm. Figure 5-1 lists a number of hindrance and challenge stressors, some of which are experienced at work and some of which are experienced outside work.[14]

WORK HINDRANCE STRESSORS. The various roles we fill at work are the source of different types of work-related hindrance stressors.[15] One type of work-related hindrance stressor is **role conflict**, which refers to conflicting expectations that other people may have of us. As an example of role conflict that occurs from incompatible demands within a single role that a person may hold, consider the job of a call center operator. People holding these jobs are generally expected to contact as many people as possible over a given time period, which means spending as little time as possible with each person who is contacted. At the same time however, call center operators are also expected to be responsive to the questions and concerns raised by the people they contact. Because effectiveness in this aspect of the job may require a great deal of time, call center operators are put in a position in which they simply cannot meet both types of expectations.

Role ambiguity refers to a lack of information about what needs to be done in a role, as well as unpredictability regarding the consequences of performance in that role. Employees are sometimes asked to work on projects for which they are given very few instructions or guidelines about how things are supposed to be done. In these cases, employees may not know how much money they can spend on the project, how long it's supposed to take, or what exactly the finished product is supposed to look like. Role ambiguity is often experienced among new employees who haven't been around long enough to receive

Call center operators experience role conflict. On the one hand, they need to be polite and responsive to the people they contact. On the other hand, they need to spend as little time as possible on each call.

instructions from supervisors or observe and model the role behaviors of more senior colleagues. Students sometimes experience role ambiguity when professors remain vague about particular course requirements or how grading is going to be performed. In such cases, the class becomes stressful because it's not quite clear what it takes to get a good grade.

Role overload occurs when the number of demanding roles a person holds is so high that the person simply cannot perform some or all of the roles effectively. Role overload as a source of stress is becoming very prevalent for employees in many different industries. For example, the workload for executives and managers who work in investment banking, consulting, and law is so high that 80-hour workweeks are becoming the norm.[16] Although this trend may not be surprising to some of you, people holding these jobs also indicate that they would not be able to complete most of the work that's required of them, even if they worked twice as many hours. If employees actually put in enough time to meet those sorts of role demands, they might forget what life was like outside of their offices or cubicles!

One final type of work-related hindrance stressor, **daily hassles**, reflects the relatively minor day-to-day demands that get in the way of accomplishing the things that we really want to accomplish. Examples of hassles include having to deal with unnecessary paperwork, office equipment malfunctions, conflict with abrasive coworkers, and useless communications. Although these examples of daily hassles may seem relatively minor, taken together, they can be extremely time consuming and stressful. Indeed, according to one survey, 40 percent of executives spend somewhere between a half-day and a full day each week on communications that are not useful or necessary.[17] For a clear example of a job filled with hassles and other types of hindrance stressors, see our **OB on Screen** feature.

WORK CHALLENGE STRESSORS. One type of work-related challenge stressor is **time pressure**—a strong sense that the amount of time you have to do a task is just not quite enough. Although most people appraise situations with high time pressure as rather stressful, they also tend to appraise these situations as more challenging than hindering. Time pressure demands tend to be viewed as something to strive for because success in meeting such demands can be satisfying. As an example of this positive effect of high time pressure, consider Michael Jones, an architect at a top New York firm. His job involves overseeing multiple projects

"Some of the poor wretches eventually become unable to leave the safety of their cubicles."

OB ON SCREEN

THE DEVIL WEARS PRADA

Please bore someone else with your questions.

With those words, fashion magazine editor Miranda Priestly (Meryl Streep) foreshadows the stress she imposes on her new "second assistant," Andy Sachs (Anne Hathaway) in *The Devil Wears Prada* (Dir.: David Frankel, Fox 2000 Pictures, 2006). You see, immediately after walking into the office on her first day on the job, Andy receives an order from Miranda to get 10 or 15 skirts from Calvin Klein. When Andy asks, "What kind of skirts do you need?", Miranda responds with the line quoted above.

Unfortunately, Miranda's reply creates role ambiguity for Andy. She has no one at the magazine to turn to for help, and to make matters worse, she has no clue about fashion. Later in the same conversation, Miranda gives Andy a dose of role overload, giving her several unrelated tasks that are difficult to understand and impossible to accomplish. Andy's new job is filled with role conflict and daily hassles as well. Not only does Andy have to run time-consuming personal errands for Miranda while ensuring the completion of important magazine-related tasks, but she's also subjected to constant insults from Miranda and her first assistant Emily (Emily Blunt). Andy seems to understand that the demands of working for Miranda are preventing her from reaching her goal of being a journalist, but she can't quit because she needs the money.

Later in the movie, things begin to change for Andy. She begins to believe that if she works harder to please Miranda, she'll be able to make connections with important people in the magazine industry, which in turn, will open doors for her successful future in journalism. In essence, Andy begins to appraise her job demands as consisting of challenge stressors rather than hindrance stressors. So what are the consequences of Andy's reappraisal of her job demands? You'll have to watch the movie to find out.

with tight deadlines, and as a result, he has to work at a hectic pace. Although Jones readily acknowledges that his job is stressful, he also believes that the outcome of having all the stress is satisfying. Jones is able to see the product of his labor over the Manhattan skyline, which makes him feel like he's a part of something.[18]

Work complexity refers to the degree to which the requirements of the work, in terms of knowledge, skills, and abilities, tax or exceed the capabilities of the person who is responsible for performing the work. As an example of work complexity, consider the nature of employee development practices that organizations use to train future executives and organizational leaders. In many cases, these practices involve giving people jobs that require skills and knowledge that the people do not yet possess. A successful marketing manager who is being groomed for an executive-level position may, for example, be asked to manage a poorly performing production facility with poor labor relations in a country halfway around the world. Although these types of developmental experiences tend to be quite stressful, managers report that being stretched beyond their capacity is well worth the associated discomfort.[19]

Work responsibility refers to the nature of the obligations that a person has toward others. Generally speaking, the level of responsibility in a job is higher when the number, scope, and importance of the obligations in that job are higher. As an example, the level of work responsibility for an air traffic controller, who may be accountable for the lives of tens of thousands of people every day, is very high. Controllers understand that if they make an error while directing an aircraft—for example, saying "turn left" instead of "turn right"—hundreds of people can die in an instant. Although controller errors that result in midair collisions and crashes are extremely rare, the possibility weighs heavily on the minds of controllers, especially after they lose "the picture" (controller jargon for the mental representation of an assigned airspace and all the aircraft within it) due to extreme workloads, a loss of concentration, or equipment malfunctions. As with people's reactions to time pressure and work complexity, people tend to evaluate demands associated with high responsibility as both stressful and potentially positive.

NONWORK HINDRANCE STRESSORS. Although the majority of people in the U.S. spend more time at the office than anywhere else,[20] there are a number of stressful demands outside of work that have implications for managing behavior in organizations. In essence, stressors experienced outside of work may have effects that "spill over" to affect the employee at work.[21] One example of nonwork hindrance stressors is **work–family conflict**, a special form of role conflict in which the demands of a work role hinder the fulfillment of the demands of a family role (or vice versa). We most often think of cases in which work demands hinder effectiveness in the family context, termed "work to family conflict." For example, employees who have to deal with lots of hindrances at work may have trouble switching off their frustration after they get home, and as a consequence, they may become irritable and impatient with family and friends. However, work–family conflict can occur in the other direction as well. For example, "family to work conflict" would occur if a salesperson who is experiencing the stress of marital conflict comes to work harboring emotional pain and negative feelings, which makes it difficult to interact with customers effectively.

Nonwork hindrance stressors also come in the form of **negative life events**. Research has revealed that a number of life events are perceived as quite stressful, particularly when they result in significant changes to a person's life.[22] Table 5-2 provides a listing of some commonly experienced life events, along with a score that estimates how stressful each event is perceived to be. As the table reveals, many of the most stressful life events do not occur at work. Rather, they include family events such as the death of a spouse or close family member, a divorce or marital separation, a jail term, or a personal illness. These events would be classified as hindrance stressors because they hinder the ability to achieve life goals and are associated with negative emotions.

A third type of nonwork hindrance stressor is **financial uncertainty**. This type of stressor refers to conditions that create uncertainties with regard to the loss of livelihood, savings, or the ability to pay expenses. This type of stressor is highly relevant during recessions or economic downturns. When people have concerns about losing their jobs, homes, and life savings because of economic factors that are beyond their control, it's understandable why nearly half of the respondents to a recent survey indicated that stress was making it hard for them to do their jobs.[23]

NONWORK CHALLENGE STRESSORS. Of course, the nonwork domain can be a source of challenge stressors as well. **Family time demands** refer to the time that a person commits to participate in an array of family activities and responsibilities. Specific examples of family time demands include time spent involved in family pursuits such as traveling, attending social events and organized activities, hosting parties, and planning and making home improvements. Examples of **personal development** activities include participation in formal education programs, music lessons, sports-related training, hobby-related self-education, participation in local government, or volunteer work. Finally, Table 5-2 includes some **positive life events** that are sources of nonwork challenge stressors. For example, marriage, pregnancy, the addition of a new family member, and ending school are all stressful in their own way. However, each is associated with some positive, rather than negative, emotions.

TABLE 5-2	Stressful Life Events		
LIFE EVENT	**STRESS SCORE**	**LIFE EVENT**	**STRESS SCORE**
Death of a spouse	100	Trouble with in-laws	29
Divorce	73	Outstanding achievement	28
Marital separation	65	Begin or end school	26
Jail term	63	Change in living conditions	25
Death of close family member	63	Trouble with boss	23
Personal illness	53	Change in work hours	20
Marriage	50	Change in residence	20
Fired at work	47	Change in schools	20
Marital reconciliation	45	Change in social activities	18
Retirement	45	Change in sleeping habits	16
Pregnancy	40	Change in family get-togethers	15
Gain of new family member	39	Change in eating habits	15
Death of close friend	37	Vacations	13
Change in occupation	36	The holiday season	12
Child leaving home	29	Minor violations of the law	11

Source: Adapted from T.H. Holmes and R.H. Rahe, "The Social Re-Adjustment Rating Scale," *Journal of Psychosomatic Research* 11 (1967), pp. 213–18.

HOW DO PEOPLE COPE WITH STRESSORS?

5.3

How do individuals cope with stress?

According to the transactional theory of stress, after people appraise a stressful demand, they ask themselves, "What *should* I do" and "What *can* I do" to deal with this situation? These questions, which refer to the **secondary appraisal** shown in Figure 5-1, center on the issue of how people cope with the various stressors they face.[24] **Coping** refers to the behaviors and thoughts that people use to manage both the stressful demands they face and the emotions associated with those stressful demands.[25] As Table 5-3 illustrates, coping can involve many different types of activities, and these activities can be grouped into four broad categories based on two dimensions.[26] The first dimension refers to the method of coping (behavioral versus cognitive), and the second dimension refers to the focus of coping (problem solving versus regulation of emotions).

The first part of our coping definition highlights the idea that methods of coping can be categorized on the basis of whether they involve behaviors or cognitions. **Behavioral coping** involves the set of physical activities that are used to deal with a stressful situation.[27] In one example of behavioral coping, a person who is confronted with a lot of time pressure at work might choose to cope by working faster. In another example, an employee who has several daily hassles might cope by avoiding work—coming in late, leaving early, or even staying home. As a final example, employees often cope with the stress of an international assignment by returning home from the assignment prematurely. As our **OB Internationally**

OB INTERNATIONALLY

The number of expatriates, or employees who are sent abroad to work for their organization, has increased recently. In one recent survey, for example, 47 percent of the companies reported an increase in the number of expatriate assignments over the previous year, and 54 percent projected increases in these assignments in the following year. This survey also indicated that more than half of all employees sent abroad expected their assignment to last between one and three years.[28] Unfortunately, a significant number of expatriate assignments do not succeed because the employee returns home earlier than planned. In fact, up to 40 percent of all American expatriates return home early, and it has been estimated that each early return costs the host organization approximately $100,000.[29] Of course, a second way that international assignments fail is when the expatriates fails to perform their roles effectively.

One key factor that influences the commitment and effectiveness of expatriates is how they handle the stress of being abroad.[30] Expatriates who experience more stress as a result of cultural, interpersonal, or job factors tend to be less satisfied with their assignment, more likely to think about leaving their assignment early, and more likely to perform at subpar levels. One practice that could prove useful in managing expatriate stress is cross-cultural training, which focuses on helping people appreciate cultural differences and interacting more comfortably with the host country nationals. Unfortunately, this type of training isn't offered as frequently as you might think.[31] Surveys suggest that many U.S. companies offer no formal cross-cultural training at all. Even when training is offered, it tends to focus more on language skills than on cultural understanding and interaction skills. Given that the number of expatriate assignments is on the rise, organizations might be well served if they increased emphasis on training in these types of skills so that their expratriates are better able to cope with the stress from being abroad.

TABLE 5-3	Examples of Coping Strategies	
	PROBLEM-FOCUSED	**EMOTION-FOCUSED**
Behavioral Methods	• Working harder • Seeking assistance • Acquiring additional resources	• Engaging in alternative activities • Seeking support • Venting anger
Cognitive Methods	• Strategizing • Self-motivation • Changing priorities	• Avoiding, distancing, and ignoring • Looking for the positive in the negative • Reappraising

Source: Adapted from J.C. Latack and S.J. Havlovic, "Coping with Job Stress: A Conceptual Evaluation Framework for Coping Measures," *Journal of Organizational Behavior* 13 (1992), pp. 479–508.

feature illustrates, international assignments are becoming increasingly prevalent, and the costs of these early returns to organizations can be significant.

In contrast to behavioral coping, **cognitive coping** refers to the thoughts that are involved in trying to deal with a stressful situation.[32] For example, the person who is confronted with an increase in time pressure might cope by thinking about different ways of accomplishing the work more efficiently. As another example of cognitive coping, employees who are confronted with daily hassles might try to convince themselves that the hassles are not that bad after all, perhaps by dwelling on less annoying aspects of the daily events.

Whereas the first part of our coping definition refers to the method of coping, the second part refers to the focus of coping—that is, does the coping attempt to address the stressful demand or the emotions triggered by the demand?[33] **Problem-focused coping** refers to behaviors and cognitions intended to manage the stressful situation itself.[34] To understand problem-focused coping, consider how the people in the previous two paragraphs coped with time pressure. In the first example, the person attempted to address the time pressure by working harder, whereas in the second example, the person focused on how to accomplish the work more efficiently. Although the specific coping methods differed, both of these people reacted to the time pressure similarly, in that they focused their effort on meeting the demand rather than trying to avoid it.

In contrast to problem-focused coping, **emotion-focused coping** refers to the various ways in which people manage their own emotional reactions to stressful demands.[35] The reactions to the daily hassles that we described previously illustrate two types of emotion-focused coping. In the first example, the employee used avoidance and distancing behaviors to reduce the emotional distress caused by the stressful situation. In the second example, the employee reappraised the demand to make it seem less stressful and threatening. Although people may be successful at changing the way different situations are construed to avoid feeling unpleasant emotions, the demand or problem that initially triggered the appraisal process remains.

Of course, the coping strategy that is ultimately used has important implications for how effectively people can meet or adapt to the different stressors that they face. In the work context, for example, a manager would most likely want subordinates to cope with the stress of a heavy workload by using a problem-focused strategy—working harder—rather

Although avoidance and distancing behaviors may reduce the emotional distress one feels, these strategies do not help to manage the demand that is causing the stress.

than an emotion-focused strategy—drinking two beers at lunch to create distance from the stressor. Of course, there are some situations in which emotion-focused coping may be functional for the person. As an example, consider people who repeatedly fail to make it through the auditions for *American Idol,* despite years of voice lessons and countless hours of practice. At some point, if these people did not have the capability to cope emotionally—perhaps by lowering their aspirations, or at least ignoring Simon Cowell's sarcastic barbs—their self-esteem could be damaged, which could translate into reduced effectiveness in other roles that they fill.

How do people choose a particular coping strategy? One factor that influences this choice is the set of beliefs that people have about how well different coping strategies can address different demands. In essence, people are likely to choose the coping strategy they believe has the highest likelihood of meeting the demand they face. For example, successful students may come to understand that the likelihood of effectively coping with demanding final exams is higher if they study hard rather than trying to escape from the situation by going out until 3:00 a.m. The choice also depends on the degree to which people believe that they have what it takes to execute the coping strategy effectively. Returning to the previous example, if students have already failed the first two exams in the course, despite trying hard, they may come to believe that a problem-focused coping strategy won't work. In this situation, because students may feel helpless to address the demand directly, an emotion-focused coping strategy would be most likely.

One critical factor that determines coping strategy choice is the degree to which people believe that a particular strategy gives them some degree of control over the stressor. If people believe that a demand can be addressed with a problem-focused coping strategy and have confidence that they can use that problem-focused strategy effectively, then they will feel some control over the situation and will likely use a problem-focused strategy. If people believe that a demand cannot be addressed with a problem-focused strategy or do not believe they can effectively execute that strategy, then they'll feel a lack of control over the situation and will tend to use an emotion-focused coping strategy.

So what determines how people develop a sense of control? It appears that one important factor is the nature of the stressful demand itself. In particular, people are likely to feel less control over a stressor when they appraise it as a hindrance rather than a challenge. Consider one of the life events in Table 5-2: "Trouble with boss." This event would be categorized as a hindrance stressor because it hinders goal achievement and triggers negative emotions. If you're like most people, you would want to change the behavior of your boss so that the trouble would stop and you could get on with your work. However, it's also likely that you would feel like you have little control over this situation because bosses are in a position of power, and complaining to your boss's boss might not be an option for you. The anxiety and hopelessness triggered by the situation would further erode any sense of control over the situation, likely leading to emotion-focused coping.[36]

THE EXPERIENCE OF STRAIN

Earlier in this chapter, we defined strain as the negative consequences associated with stress. How exactly does stress cause strain? Consider the case of Naomi Henderson, the CEO of RIVA, a Rockville, Maryland–based market research firm. The job of CEO is quite demanding, and Henderson found herself working 120 hours a week to cope with the heavy workload. One night she woke up to go to the bathroom and found that she literally could not move—she was paralyzed. After she was rushed to the emergency room, the doctor told Henderson and her husband that her diagnosis was stress. The doctor recommended rest in bed for 14 hours a day for six weeks.[37] Although this example may seem extreme to you, the demands of many managerial and executive-level jobs are often excessive,[38] and the negative health consequences that result are fairly predictable. In fact, if you've ever been in a situation in which you've experienced heavy stress for more than a couple of days, you can probably appreciate the toll that stress can take on you. Although people react to stress differently, you may have felt unusually exhausted, irritable, and achy. What might be surprising to you is that the mechanism within your body that gives you the ability to function effectively in the face of stressful demands is the same mechanism that ends up causing you these problems. So what is this mechanism?

Essentially, the body has a set of responses that allow it to adapt and function effectively in the face of stressful demands, but if the stressful demands do not ramp down or the demands occur too frequently, the body's adaptive responses become toxic.[39] More specifically, when people are confronted with a stressor, their bodies secrete chemical compounds that increase their heart rate and blood pressure as blood is redirected away from vital organs, such as the spleen, to the brain and skeletal muscles.[40] Unfortunately, if the chemicals in the blood remain elevated because of prolonged or repeated exposure to the stressor, the body begins to break down, and several negative consequences are set into motion. As shown in Figure 5-2, those negative consequences come in three varieties: physiological strains, psychological strains, and behavioral strains.[41]

Physiological strains that result from stressors occur in at least four systems of the human body. First, stressors can reduce the effectiveness of the body's immune system, which makes it more difficult for the body to ward off illness and infection. Have you ever noticed that you're more likely to catch a cold during or immediately after final exam week? Second, stressors can harm the body's cardiovascular system, cause the heart to race, increase blood pressure, and create coronary artery disease. Third, stressors can cause problems in the body's musculoskeletal system. Tension headaches, tight shoulders, and back pain have all been linked to a variety of stressors. Fourth, stressors cause gastrointestinal system problems. Symptoms of this type of strain include stomachaches, indigestion, diarrhea, and constipation.[42]

Although you might be tempted to dismiss the importance of physiological strains because the likelihood of serious illness and disease is low for people in their 20s and 30s, research shows that dismissal may be a mistake. For example, high-pressure work deadlines increase the chance of heart attack within the next 24 hours by a factor of six.[43] So even though your likelihood of suffering a heart attack may be low, who would want to increase their risk by 600 percent? Perhaps more important, the negative physiological effects of stress persist over time and may not show up until far into the future. One study showed that eye problems, allergic complaints, and chronic diseases could be attributed to stress measured eight years earlier.[44]

Psychological strains that result from stressors include depression, anxiety, anger, hostility, reduced self-confidence, irritability, inability to think clearly, forgetfulness, lack of creativity, memory loss, and (not surprising, given the rest of this list) a loss of sense of humor.[45] You might be tempted to think of these problems as isolated incidents; however, they may reflect a more general psychological condition known as **burnout**, which we define as the emotional, mental, and physical exhaustion that results from having to cope with stressful demands on an ongoing basis.[46] There are many familiar examples of people

| FIGURE 5-2 | Examples of Strain |

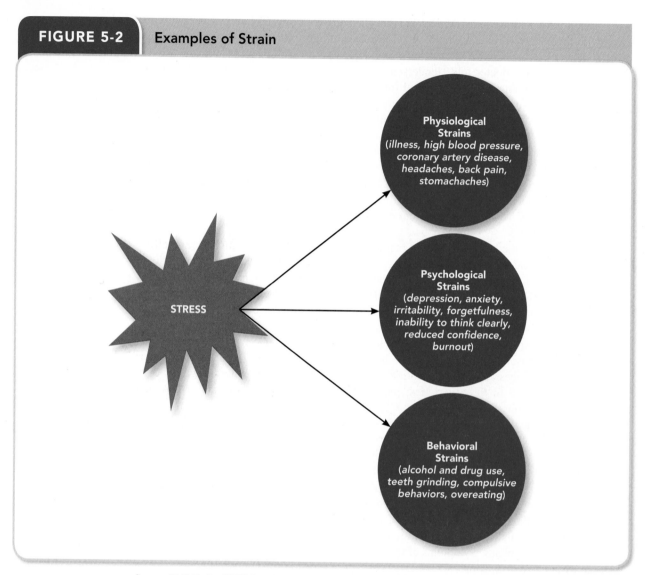

Source: M.E. Burke, "2005 Benefits Survey Report," *Society of Human Resource Management.* Reprinted with permission.

who have experienced burnout, and the majority of them illustrate how burnout can lead to a decision to quit a job or even change careers. As an example, after playing for 17 seasons for the Green Bay Packers, Brett Favre decided to retire from professional football after leading his team to the NFC championship game in 2008.[47] Favre explained to reporters that he was just tired of all the stress.[48] The pressure of the challenge of winning compelled him to spend an ever-increasing amount of time preparing for the next game, and over time, this pressure built up and resulted in exhaustion and reduced commitment. Of course, over the next few seasons Favre would unretire (to join the New York Jets), re-retire, then unretire again (to join the Minnesota Vikings). Such changes of heart are not unusual after someone retires from an exciting job due to burnout. A break from stressors associated with the work not only gives the person a chance to rest and recharge, but it also provides a lot of free time to think about the excitement and challenge of performing again.

Finally, in addition to physiological and psychological strains, the stress process can result in *behavioral strains.* Behavioral strains are unhealthy behaviors such as grinding one's teeth at night, being overly critical and bossy, excessive smoking, compulsive gum chewing, overuse of alcohol, and compulsive eating.[49] Although it is unknown why exposure to stressors results in these specific behaviors, it's easy to see why these behaviors are undesirable both from personal and organizational standpoints.

ACCOUNTING FOR INDIVIDUALS IN THE STRESS PROCESS

So far in this chapter, we've discussed how the typical or average person reacts to different sorts of stressors. However, we've yet to discuss how people differ in terms of how they react to demands. One way that people differ in their reactions to stress depends on whether they exhibit the **Type A Behavior Pattern**. "Type A" people have a strong sense of time urgency and tend to be impatient, hard-driving, competitive, controlling, aggressive, and even hostile.[50] If you walk, talk, and eat at a quick pace, and if you find yourself constantly annoyed with people who do things too slowly, chances are that you're a Type A person. With that said, one way to tell for sure is to fill out the Type A questionnaire in our **OB Assessments** feature.

In the context of this chapter, the Type A Behavior Pattern is important because it can influence stressors, stress, and strains. First, the Type A Behavior Pattern may have a direct influence on the level of stressors that a person confronts. To understand why this connection might be true, consider that Type A persons tend to be hard-driving and have a strong desire to achieve. Because the behaviors that reflect these tendencies are valued by the organization, Type A individuals receive "rewards" in the form of increases in the amount and level of work required. In addition, because Type A people tend to be aggressive and competitive, they may be more prone to interpersonal conflict. We're sure that most of you would agree that conflict with peers and coworkers is an important stressor.

Second, in addition to the effect on stressors, the Type A Behavior Pattern is important because it influences the stress process itself.[51] This effect of the Type A Behavior Pattern is easy to understand if you consider that hard-driving competitiveness makes people hypersensitive to demands that could potentially affect their progress toward their goal attainment. In essence, Type A individuals are simply more likely to appraise demands as being stressful rather than being benign.

Third, and perhaps most important, the Type A Behavior Pattern has been directly linked to coronary heart disease[52] and other physiological, psychological, and behavioral strains.[53] The size of the relationship between the Type A Behavior Pattern and these strains is not so strong as to suggest that if you're a Type A person, you should immediately call 911. However, the linkage is strong enough to suggest that the risk of these problems is significantly higher for people who typically engage in Type A behaviors.

Another individual factor that affects the way people manage stress is the degree of **social support** that they receive. Social support refers to the help that people receive when they're confronted with stressful demands, and there are at least two major types.[54] One type of social support is called **instrumental support,** which refers to the help people receive that

> **✓ 5.4**
>
> How does the Type A Behavior Pattern influence the stress process?

An emotional Brett Favre announces his (first) retirement from the Green Bay Packers due to stress. Of course, Favre later unretired (twice!) after an off-season's worth of rest to recharge.

OB ASSESSMENTS

TYPE A BEHAVIOR PATTERN

Do you think that you're especially sensitive to stress? This assessment is designed to measure the extent to which you're a Type A person—someone who typically engages in hard-driving, competitive, and aggressive behavior. Answer each question using the response scale provided. Then subtract your answers to the boldfaced questions from 8, with the difference being your new answers for those questions. For example, if your original answer for Question 3 was "2," your new answer is "6" (8 – 2). Then sum your answers for the twelve questions. (For more assessments relevant to this chapter, please visit the Online Learning Center at www.mhhe.com/colquitt).

1 STRONGLY DISAGREE	2 DISAGREE	3 SLIGHTLY DISAGREE	4 NEUTRAL	5 SLIGHTLY AGREE	6 AGREE	7 STRONGLY AGREE

1. Having work to complete "stirs me into action" more than other people. _____

2. When a person is talking and takes too long to come to the point, I frequently feel like hurrying the person along. _____

3. **Nowadays, I consider myself to be relaxed and easygoing.** _____

4. Typically, I get irritated extremely easily. _____

5. My best friends would rate my general activity level as very high. _____

6. I definitely tend to do most things in a hurry. _____

7. I take my work much more seriously than most. _____

8. **I seldom get angry.** _____

9. I often set deadlines for myself work-wise. _____

10. I feel very impatient when I have to wait in line. _____

11. I put much more effort into my work than other people do. _____

12. **Compared with others, I approach life much less seriously.** _____

SCORING AND INTERPRETATION

If your scores sum up to 53 or above, you would be considered a Type A person, which means that you may perceive higher stress levels in your life and be more sensitive to that stress. If your scores sum up to 52 or below, you would be considered a Type B person. This means that you sense less stress in your life and are less sensitive to the stress that is experienced.

Source: C. D. Jenkins, S. J. Zyzanski, and R. H. Rosenman. "Progress Toward Validation of a Computer Scored Test for the Type A Coronary Prone Behavior Pattern," *Psychosomatic Medicine* 33, 193, 202 (1971). Reprinted with permission of Lippincott, Williams & Wilkins.

Social support from friends, coworkers, and family can be a big help in managing stress, even though it often occurs outside the stress-causing environment.

can be used to address the stressful demand directly. For example, if a person is overloaded with work, a coworker could provide instrumental support by taking over some of the work or offering suggestions about how to do the work more efficiently. A second type of social support is called **emotional support**. This type of support refers to the help people receive in addressing the emotional distress that accompanies stressful demands. As an example, the supervisor of the individual who is overloaded with work might provide emotional support by showing interest in the employee's situation and appearing to be understanding and sympathetic. As alluded to in these examples, social support may come from coworkers as well as from supervisors. However, social support also may be provided by family members and friends outside the context of the stressful demand.[55]

Similar to the Type A Behavior Pattern, social support has the potential to influence the stress process in several different ways. However, most research on social support focuses on the ways that social support buffers the relationship between stressors and strains. According to this research, high levels of social support provide a person with instrumental or emotional resources that are useful for coping with the stressor, which tends to reduce the harmful consequences of the stressor to that individual. With low levels of social support, the person does not have extra coping resources available, so the stressor tends to have effects that are more harmful. In essence, this perspective casts social support as a "moderator" of the relationship between stressors and strains (recall that moderators are variables that affect the strength of the relationship between two other variables). In this particular case, the relationship between stress and strain tends to be weaker at higher levels of social support and stronger at lower levels of social support. Although not every research study has found support for the buffering effect of social support,[56] the majority of research evidence has been supportive.[57]

SUMMARY: WHY ARE SOME EMPLOYEES MORE "STRESSED" THAN OTHERS?

So what explains why some employees are more stressed than others? As shown in Figure 5-3, answering that question requires paying attention to the particular stressors the employee is experiencing, including hindrance and challenge stressors originating in both the work and nonwork domains. However, it also depends on how those stressors are appraised and coped with, which determines whether physiological, psychological, and

FIGURE 5-3

FIGURE 5-3 **Why Are Some Employees More "Stressed" Than Others?**

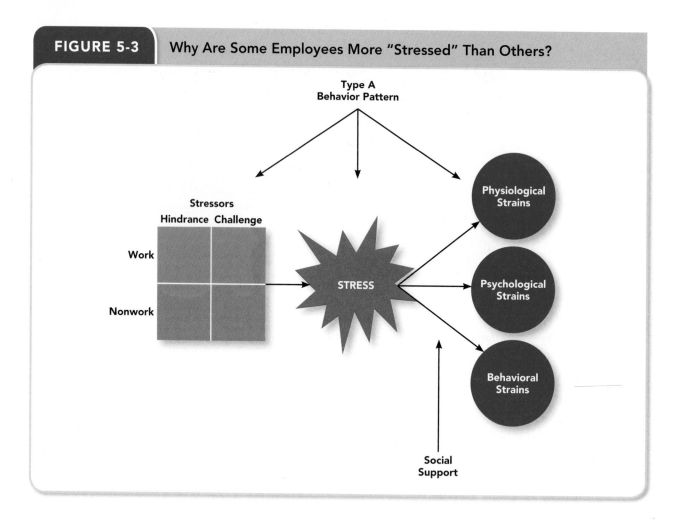

behavioral strains are experienced. Finally, answering the question depends on whether the employee is "Type A" or "Type B" and whether the employee has a high or low amount of social support. Understanding all of these factors can help explain why some people can shoulder stressful circumstances for weeks at a time, whereas others seem to be "at the end of their rope" when faced with even relatively minor job demands.

HOW IMPORTANT IS STRESS?

In the previous sections, we described how stressors and the stress process influence strains and, ultimately, people's health and well-being. Although these relationships are important to understand, you're probably more curious about the impact that stressors have on job performance and organizational commitment, the two outcomes in our integrative model of OB. Figure 5-4 summarizes the research evidence linking hindrance stressors to performance and commitment, and Figure 5-5 summarizes the research evidence linking challenge stressors to performance and commitment. We limit our discussion to relationships with work stressors rather than nonwork stressors, because this is where researchers have focused the most attention.

Figure 5-4 reveals that hindrance stressors have a weak negative relationship with job performance.[58] A general explanation for this negative relationship is that hindrance stressors result in strains and negative emotions that reduce the overall level of energy and attention that people could otherwise bring to their job duties.[59] The detrimental effect that strains have on job performance becomes quite easy to understand when you consider the nature of the individual strains that we mentioned in the previous section. Certainly, you would agree that physiological, psychological, and behavioral strains in the form of illnesses, exhaustion, and drunkenness would detract from employee effectiveness in almost any job context.

Figure 5-4 also reveals that hindrance stressors have a strong negative relationship with organizational commitment.[60] Why might this be? Well, hindrance stressors evoke strains, which are generally dissatisfying to people, and as we discussed in the previous chapter, satisfaction has a strong impact on the degree to which people feel committed to their organization.[61] People who work at jobs that they know are causing them to feel constantly sick and exhausted will likely be dissatisfied with their jobs and feel less desire to stay with the organization and more desire to consider alternatives.

5.5

How does stress affect job performance and organizational commitment?

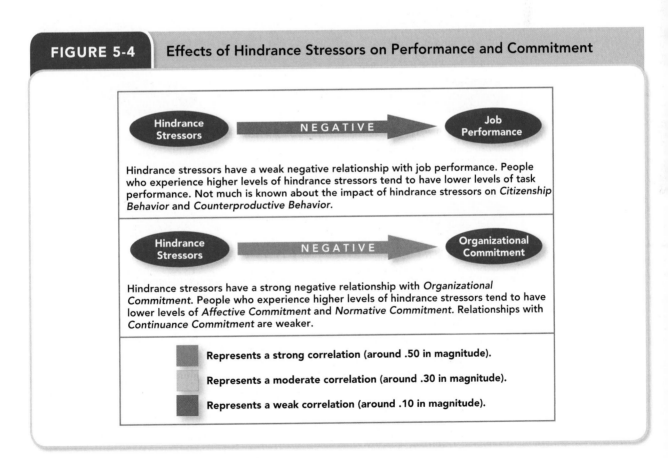

| **FIGURE 5-4** | **Effects of Hindrance Stressors on Performance and Commitment** |

Hindrance Stressors → NEGATIVE → Job Performance

Hindrance stressors have a weak negative relationship with job performance. People who experience higher levels of hindrance stressors tend to have lower levels of task performance. Not much is known about the impact of hindrance stressors on *Citizenship Behavior* and *Counterproductive Behavior*.

Hindrance Stressors → NEGATIVE → Organizational Commitment

Hindrance stressors have a strong negative relationship with *Organizational Commitment*. People who experience higher levels of hindrance stressors tend to have lower levels of *Affective Commitment* and *Normative Commitment*. Relationships with *Continuance Commitment* are weaker.

Represents a strong correlation (around .50 in magnitude).

Represents a moderate correlation (around .30 in magnitude).

Represents a weak correlation (around .10 in magnitude).

Sources: J.A. LePine, N.P. Podsakoff, and M.A. LePine, "A Meta-Analytic Test of the Challenge Stressor–Hindrance Stressor Framework: An Explanation for Inconsistent Relationships Among Stressors and Performance," *Academy of Management Journal* 48 (2005), pp. 764–75; N.P. Podsakoff, J.A. LePine, and M.A. LePine, "Differential Challenge Stressor–Hindrance Stressor Relationships with Job Attitudes, Turnover Intentions, Turnover, and Withdrawal Behavior: A Meta-Analysis," *Journal of Applied Psychology* 92 (2007), pp. 438–454.

Turning now to challenge stressors, the story becomes somewhat different. As shown in Figure 5-5, challenge stressors have a weak relationship with job performance and a moderate relationship with organizational commitment. However, in contrast to the results for hindrance stressors, the relationships are positive rather than negative.[62] In other words, employees who experience higher levels of challenge stressors also tend to have higher levels of job performance and organizational commitment. These relationships stand in sharp contrast with the lower levels of job performance and organizational commitment that result when employees confront higher levels of hindrance stressors. So what explains this difference? Although challenge stressors create strain, which detracts from performance and commitment, they also tend to trigger positive emotions and problem-focused coping strategies. The net benefits of those positive emotions and coping strategies outweigh the costs of the added strain, meaning that challenge stressors tend to be beneficial to employees in the long run.[63] These positive effects of challenge stressors have been demonstrated for executives,[64] employees in lower-level jobs,[65] and even students.[66]

FIGURE 5-5   Effects of Challenge Stressors on Performance and Commitment

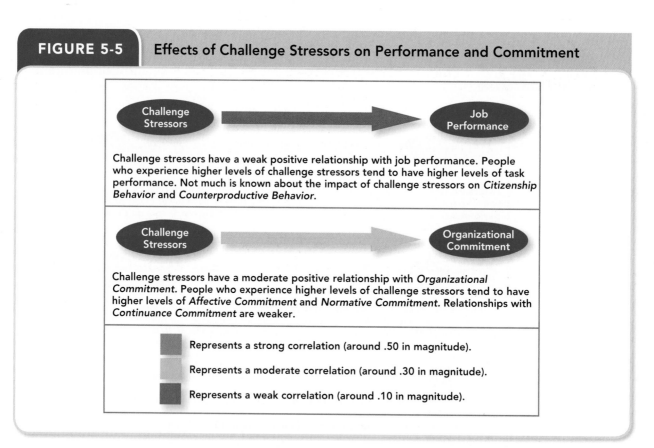

Challenge stressors have a weak positive relationship with job performance. People who experience higher levels of challenge stressors tend to have higher levels of task performance. Not much is known about the impact of challenge stressors on *Citizenship Behavior* and *Counterproductive Behavior*.

Challenge stressors have a moderate positive relationship with *Organizational Commitment*. People who experience higher levels of challenge stressors tend to have higher levels of *Affective Commitment* and *Normative Commitment*. Relationships with *Continuance Commitment* are weaker.

Represents a strong correlation (around .50 in magnitude).

Represents a moderate correlation (around .30 in magnitude).

Represents a weak correlation (around .10 in magnitude).

Sources: J.A. LePine, N.P. Podsakoff, and M.A. LePine, "A Meta-Analytic Test of the Challenge Stressor–Hindrance Stressor Framework: An Explanation for Inconsistent Relationships Among Stressors and Performance," *Academy of Management Journal* 48 (2005), pp. 764–75; N.P. Podsakoff, J.A. LePine, and M.A. LePine, "Differential Challenge Stressor–Hindrance Stressor Relationships with Job Attitudes, Turnover Intentions, Turnover, and Withdrawal Behavior: A Meta-Analysis," *Journal of Applied Psychology* 92 (2007), pp. 438–454.

APPLICATION: STRESS MANAGEMENT

Previously, we described how employee stress results in strains that cost organizations in terms of reduced employee performance and commitment. However, there are other important costs to consider that relate to employee health. Most organizations provide some sort of health care benefits for their employees,[67] and all but the smallest organizations pay worker's compensation insurance, the rates for which are determined, in part, by the nature of the job and the organization's history of work-related injuries and illnesses. So what role does stress play in these costs?

Well, it turns out that these health-related costs are driven to a great extent by employee stress. Estimates are that between 60 percent and 90 percent of all doctor visits can be attributed to stress-related causes,[68] and the cost of providing health care to people who experience high levels of stress appears to be approximately 50 percent higher than that for those who experience lower levels of stress.[69] Statistics from jobs in different industries indicate that the frequency of worker's compensation claims is dramatically higher when the level of stress on the job is high. As one example, the frequency of claims was more than 800 percent higher for a copy machine distributor when the level of stress at the job site was high.[70] So what do all these costs mean to you as a student of organizational behavior or as a manager?

For one thing, the relationship between stress and health care costs means that there may be huge dividends for organizations that learn how to manage stress more effectively. As the opening of this chapter illustrated, companies such as Humana recognize the potential for a positive return on their investments in practices aimed at reducing employee stress. In fact, surveys indicate that the vast majority of companies in the United States provide benefits, in one form or another, that are intended to help employees cope with stressful demands and reduce the associated strains.[71] Next, we describe some approaches that organizations use to manage employee stress.

 5.6

What steps can organizations take to manage employee stress?

ASSESSMENT

The first step in managing stress is to assess the level and sources of stress in the workplace. Although there are many ways to accomplish this type of evaluation, often referred to as a *stress audit*, managers can begin by asking themselves questions about the nature of the jobs in their organization to estimate whether high stress levels may be a problem.[72] The first category of questions might involve the degree to which the organization is going through changes that would likely increase uncertainty among employees. As an example, a merger between two companies might increase employees' uncertainty about their job security and possible career paths. As another example, employees in an organization that has transitioned to team-based work might be concerned about how their individual performance contributions will be recognized and rewarded. A second category of questions might center on the work itself. These questions typically focus on the level and types of stressors experienced by the employees. The third category of questions could involve the quality of relationships between not only employees but also employees and the organization. Here, an important question to consider is whether organizational politics play a large role in administrative decisions.

REDUCING STRESSORS

Once a stress audit reveals that stress may be a problem, the next step is to consider alternative courses of action. One general course of action involves managing stressors, which may be accomplished in one of two ways. First, organizations could try to eliminate or significantly reduce stressful demands. As an example of this approach, 19 percent of organizations in one recent survey used *job sharing* to reduce role overload and work–family conflict.[73] Job sharing doesn't mean splitting one job into two but rather indicates that two people share the responsibilities of a single job, as if the two people were a single performing unit. The assumption underlying the practice is that "although businesses are becoming 24/7, people don't."[74] You might be tempted to believe that job sharing would be most appropriate in lower-level jobs, where responsibilities and tasks are limited in number and relatively easy to divide. In actuality, job sharing is being used even at the highest levels in organizations. At Boston–based Fleet Bank, for example, two women shared the position of vice president for global markets and foreign exchange for six years until their department was dissolved when Fleet was acquired by Bank of America. During this time, they had one desk, one chair, one computer, one telephone, one voicemail account, one set of goals, and one performance review. They each worked 20–25 hours a week and performed the role effectively and seamlessly.[75]

Another example of how companies reduce stressors is employee sabbaticals. A *sabbatical* gives employees the opportunity to take time off from work to engage in an alternative activity. Estimates indicate that approximately 11 percent of large companies offer paid sabbaticals, and almost one-third offer unpaid sabbaticals.[76] American Express, for example, allows employees who have 10 years' tenure to apply for a paid sabbatical for up to six months. These employees are encouraged to work for a nonprofit organization or school, but the institution cannot have religious or political affiliations.[77] Pricewater-houseCoopers also offers paid sabbaticals for up to six months for personal growth reasons or for work in social services; this program is available to employees with as little as two years' experience.[78] Relative to job sharing, sabbaticals allow for a cleaner break from the stressful routine for a fairly lengthy period of time, so for the period of the sabbatical, the employee's stress may be quite low. However, because the level of stressors never changes in the job itself, the employee is likely to experience the same level of stress upon returning from the sabbatical. See our **OB at the Bookstore** feature for an additional perspective about ways to reduce the number and level of stressors in one's job.

PROVIDING RESOURCES

Although reducing stressors may reduce the overall level of stress that a person experiences, this approach is likely to be most beneficial when the focus of the effort is on hindrance stressors rather than challenge stressors.[79] Hindrance stressors such as role ambiguity, conflict, and overload not only cause strain but also decrease commitment and job performance. In contrast, though challenge stressors such as time pressure and responsibility cause strain, they also tend to be motivating and satisfying, and as a consequence, they generally are positively related to commitment and performance.

So as a supplement to reducing stressors, organizations can provide resources that help employees cope with stressful demands.[80] One way that organizations provide resources to employees is through *training interventions* aimed at increasing job-related competencies and skills. Employees who possess more competencies and skills can handle more demands rather than appraise the demands as overly taxing or exceeding their capacity. Training that increases employee competencies and skills is also beneficial to the extent that it promotes a sense that the demands are more controllable, and as we discussed in a previous section, a sense of control promotes problem-focused coping strategies.

A second way that organizations provide resources to employees so that they can cope more effectively is through *supportive practices* that help employees manage and balance the demands that exist in the different roles they have. Although we only have room in this chapter to describe a few of these practices, Table 5-4 lists many examples, as well as the

OB AT THE BOOKSTORE

THE 4-HOUR WORKWEEK
by Timothy Ferriss (New York: Crown Publishing, 2007).

Most people, my past self included, have spent too much time convincing themselves that life has to be hard, a resignation to 9-to-5 drudgery in exchange for (sometimes) relaxing weekends and the occasional keep-it-short-or-get-fired vacation.

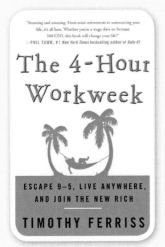

With those words, Timothy Ferriss suggests that we can reduce the level of stress in our lives by changing the way we approach our work. According to Ferris, we should approach work by focusing on only the most important tasks and doing them well, then not bothering much with the rest. Although this suggestion seems like common sense, most of us try to accomplish everything that's asked of us, and because only 20 percent of these tasks are important, the majority of our time is spent on minutiae that mean very little in the grand scheme of things.

Ferriss also argues that people should schedule time for work for only as long as it takes to accomplish the most important aspects of the most important tasks. This suggestion is based on *Parkinson's Law*, which asserts that the perceived importance and complexity of tasks will grow in relation to the time we have to do them. In other words, if we give ourselves longer to do something than is absolutely necessary, we'll find ways to fill that time. If we instead give ourselves tight deadlines, we're forced to focus on the most important priorities, and we think of the creative ways to accomplish them.

Although the book presents some interesting ideas about ways of reducing stress, there are important questions about the practicality of applying them in jobs that involve collaboration. For example, certain tasks might seem like a "time waster" to you, and according to Ferris, they should be given very low priority. But to your colleague, your work on the task may mean the difference between success and failure on an important project, and what do you think will happen if you should need help from this colleague in the future? In summary, though it may be possible to implement many of the lessons of *The 4-Hour Workweek* to reduce your stress, there may be some unintended consequences as well.

percentage of organizations that were found to use them in a recent survey of almost 400 organizations.[81]

The first supportive practice example is flextime, which was used by 56 percent of the organizations in the survey. Organizations that use flextime give employees some degree of latitude in terms of which hours they need to be present at the workplace. Flexible working hours give employees the ability to cope with demands away from work, so they don't have to worry about these demands while they're at work. As another example, 37 percent of the organizations in the survey allowed telecommuting on a part-time basis. By providing the opportunity to work at home or some other location with computer access, employees are put in a better position to cope with demands that might be impossible to cope with otherwise. Compressed workweeks, which is used

TABLE 5-4	Supportive Practices Used by Organizations		
PRACTICE	% OF SMALL ORGANIZATIONS	% OF MEDIUM ORGANIZATIONS	% OF LARGE ORGANIZATIONS
Flextime	57%	56%	56%
Part-time telecommuting	36%	33%	43%
Compressed workweek	27%	30%	41%
Bring child to work if needed	43%	25%	18%
Full-time telecommuting	14%	18%	24%
Lactation program	8%	20%	28%
On-site child care	1%	3%	13%
Company-supported child care center	0%	1%	11%

Source: M.E. Burke, "2005 Benefits Survey Report," *Society of Human Resource Management*. Reprinted with permission.

by approximately one-third of all companies in the survey, allows full-time employees to work additional hours on some days and have shorter days or time off on others. As with flextime and telecommuting, compressed workweeks give employees the ability to manage both work and nonwork role demands. We should also note that practices such as flextime, telecommuting, and compressed work weeks not only facilitate stress management but also appear to have other benefits. At companies such as Xerox, Corning, and United Parcel Service, implementing these types of practices resulted in improvements in productivity, innovation, absenteeism, and turnover.[82] As we discussed in Chapter 2 on Job Performance, Best Buy has implemented a program called the Results Only Work Environment for employees who work at the corporate headquarters. This program takes flexibility to the extreme, in that it allows employees to work wherever and whenever they please as long as they achieve the results required by their assigned work.[83]

REDUCING STRAINS

As an alternative to managing stressors, many organizations use practices that reduce strains.[84] One type of strain-reducing practice involves training in *relaxation techniques*, such as progressive muscle relaxation, meditation, and miscellaneous calming activities like taking walks, writing in a journal, and deep breathing.[85] Although these relaxation techniques differ, the basic idea is the same—they teach people how to counteract the effects of stressors by engaging in activities that slow the heart rate, breathing rate, and blood pressure.[86] As an example of a relatively simple relaxation technique, consider the recommendation of Herbert Benson, a physician and president of the Mind/Body Medical Institute in Boston. He suggests that people under stress should repeat a word, sound, prayer, phrase, or motion for 10–20 minutes once or twice a day and, during that time, try to completely ignore other thoughts that may come to mind.[87] As another example, recall the case of Naomi Henderson, the market research firm CEO who literally became paralyzed by all the stress in her job. Well, we're happy to say that Henderson got better, but she was able to do so only after being treated by a physician who helped her learn how to reduce her own strains by doing "mental aerobics." Those exercises involved taking breaks every hour to stretch and do deep breathing, taking short naps to replenish energy, and learning how to say no politely to unreasonable demands.[88] As a final example, BlueCross BlueShield of Tennessee has trained approximately one-fifth of its 4,500 employees in the use of biofeedback technology to reduce the stress associated with financial uncertainties stemming from the economic downturn.[89] The training uses a heart monitor and software to help people learn how to change their heart rhythms from an irregular pattern to a regular pattern by shifting from an anxious emotional state to a more positive one. Apparently, the training worked: A preliminary evaluation of the program revealed that those employees who received biofeedback training reported being less exhausted and anxious than they were before the training.

A second general category of strain-reducing practices involves *cognitive–behavioral techniques*. In general, these techniques attempt to help people appraise and cope with stressors in a more rational manner.[90] To understand what these techniques involve, think of someone you know who not only exaggerates the level and importance of stressful demands but also predicts doom and disaster after quickly concluding that the demands simply cannot be met. If you know someone

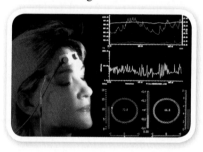

People can learn how to reduce strain using biofeedback technology.

like this, you might recommend cognitive–behavioral training that involves "self-talk," a technique in which people learn to say things about stressful demands that reflect rationality and optimism. So, when confronted with a stressful demand, this person might be trained to say, "This demand isn't so tough; if I work hard I can accomplish it." In addition, cognitive–behavioral training typically involves instruction about tools that foster effective coping. So, in addition to the self-talk, the person might be trained on how to prioritize demands, manage time, communicate needs, and seek support.[91]

A third category of strain-reducing practices involves *health and wellness programs*. For example, almost three-quarters of the organizations in one survey reported having employee assistance programs intended to help people with personal problems such as alcoholism and other addictions. More than 60 percent of organizations in this survey provided employees with wellness programs and resources. The nature of these programs and resources varies a great deal from organization to organization, but in general, they are comprehensive efforts that include health screening (blood pressure, cholesterol levels, pulmonary functioning) and health-related courses and information. Other examples of health and wellness programs intended to reduce strain include smoking cessation programs, on-site fitness centers or fitness center memberships, and weight loss and nutrition programs.[92] Today, health and wellness programs that encourage and support exercise are a growing trend. Humana's Freewheelin' program is an example of such an effort; however, there are many others. For example, consider how Grant Thornton, the Chicago–based tax, audit, and advisory firm, encourages exercise: It spent more than $200,000 helping 230 of its employees train and compete in a marathon. It also reimburses employees for participation in up to three races or walks per year, and it even set up running clubs in each of its 50 offices.[93]

TAKEAWAYS

5.1   Stress refers to the psychological response to demands when there is something at stake for the individual and coping with these demands would tax or exceed the individual's capacity or resources. Stressors are the demands that cause the stress response, and strains are the negative consequences of the stress response.

5.2   Stressors come in two general forms: challenge stressors, which are perceived as opportunities for growth and achievement, and hindrance stressors, which are perceived as hurdles to goal achievement. These two stressors can be found in both work and nonwork domains.

5.3   Coping with stress involves thoughts and behaviors that address one of two goals: addressing the stressful demand or decreasing the emotional discomfort associated with the demand.

5.4   Individual differences in the Type A Behavior Pattern affect how people experience stress in three ways. Type A people tend to experience more stressors, appraise more demands as stressful, and be prone to experiencing more strains.

5.5   The effects of stress depend on the type of stressor. Hindrance stressors have a weak negative relationship with job performance and a strong negative relationship with organizational commitment. In contrast, challenge stressors have a weak positive relationship with job performance and a moderate positive relationship with organizational commitment.

5.6   Because of the high costs associated with employee stress, organizations assess and manage stress using a number of different practices. In general, these practices focus on reducing or eliminating stressors, providing resources that employees can use to cope with stressors, or trying to reduce the strains.

KEY TERMS

DISCUSSION QUESTIONS

5.1 Prior to reading this chapter, how did you define stress? Did your definition of stress reflect stressors, the stress process, strains, or some combination?

5.2 Describe your dream job and then provide a list of the types of stressors that you would expect to be present. Is the list dominated by challenge stressors or hindrance stressors? Why do you think that is?

5.3 Think about the dream job that you described in the previous question. How much of your salary, if any at all, would you give up to eliminate the most important hindrance stressors? Why?

5.4 If you had several job offers after graduating, to what degree would the level of challenge stressors in the different jobs influence your choice of which job to take? Why?

5.5 How would you assess your ability to handle stress? Given the information provided in this chapter, what could you do to improve your effectiveness in this area?

5.6 If you managed people in an organization in which there were lots of hindrance stressors, what actions would you take to help ensure that your employees coped with the stressors using a problem-focused (as opposed to emotion-focused) strategy?

CASE: HUMANA

Companies spend significant resources on practices that help their employees cope with stress so that they can be healthy and productive. In fact, approximately 40 percent of all large companies in the United States spend more than $200,000 on programs that promote employee health and wellness, and nearly one-quarter of these companies spend a million dollars or more.[94] Humana has made significant investments in the health of its employees. Its Freewheelin' program, which allows employees to check out bicycles for free from stations located throughout the city, is intended to encourage employees to engage in healthier behaviors on a day-to-day basis.[95] The assumption is that once employees experience the joy and freedom of pedaling to a midday meeting across town, they'll be less likely to use their cars, making biking a normal part of their daily routine. This new healthy habit should then result in a reduction of the illnesses associated with stress and physical inactivity. As described on the Freewheelin' Web site, 10 minutes of biking a day can reduce depression and improve mood, and 30 minutes per day can cut the risk of heart disease and strokes by 50 percent.[96]

Humana's Freewheelin' program seems to make a lot of sense, but are programs like this the perfect solution to help employees stay healthy and cope with the stress they face at work and at home? One potential issue is the cost of setting up and maintaining the program, which may be prohibitive for smaller companies. Beyond the cost of the bike stations, bikes, and helmets, there's a surprising amount of costly technology involved.[97] For example, the program uses ID cards and computers to track each user's distance traveled, calories burned, and carbon footprint. Users also have Freewheelin' Web pages where they can post their favorite routes and connect with other users. Another potential drawback is the reactions of employees who do not, or cannot, ride bicycles. Although about half of the eligible employees signed up for the program when it was first offered, only 28 percent ever checked out a bike. How might the other 72 percent feel knowing that Humana has invested so much money in a program that has no direct value to them? Might there be backlash among employees who feel the resources could have been spent on programs that would benefit employees more equally?

5.1   In what ways does Humana's Freewheelin' program influence the various parts of the stress process?

5.2   Describe how employees might use the Freewheelin' program in the coping process. How might using this program as a coping mechanism have both positive and negative consequences?

5.3   Do you believe that backlash among employees who do not use the program is a serious issue? Why or why not? What could be done to mitigate this issue?

EXERCISE: MANAGING STRESS

The purpose of this exercise is to explore ways of managing stress to reduce strain. This exercise uses groups, so your instructor will either assign you to a group or ask you to create your own group. The exercise has the following steps:

5.1   One method of managing stress is finding a way to reduce the hindrance stressors encountered on the job. In your group, describe the hindrance stressors that you currently are experiencing. Each student should describe the two to three most important stressors following the chart below. Other students should then offer strategies for reducing or alleviating the stressors.

HINDRANCE STRESSORS EXPERIENCED	STRATEGIES FOR MANAGING STRESSORS
Role Conflict:	
Role Ambiguity:	
Role Overload:	
Daily Hassles:	

5.2   Another method of managing stress is to improve work–life balance. The circle below represents how "waking hours" are divided among five types of activities: school, work, personal relaxation, time with friends, and time with family. Draw two versions of your own circle: your waking hours as they currently are, and your waking hours as you wish them to be. Other students should then offer strategies for making the necessary life changes.

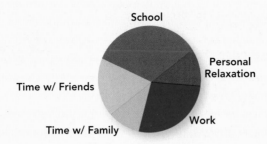

5.3 A third method of managing stress is improving *hardiness*—a sort of mental and physical health that can act as a buffer, preventing stress from resulting in strain. The table below lists a number of questions that can help diagnose your hardiness. Discuss your answers for each question, then with the help of other students, brainstorm ways to increase that hardiness factor.

HARDINESS FACTOR	STRATEGIES FOR IMPROVING FACTOR
Relaxation: Do you spend enough time reading, listening to music, meditating, or pursuing your hobbies?	
Exercise: Do you spend enough time doing cardiovascular, strength, and flexibility sorts of exercises?	
Diet: Do you manage your diet adequately by eating healthily and avoiding foods high in fat?	

5.4 Class discussion (whether in groups or as a class) should center on two issues. First, many of the stress-managing factors, especially in Steps 2 and 3, take up precious time. Does this make them an ineffective strategy for managing stress? Why or why not? Second, consider your Type A score in the OB Assessments for this chapter. If you are high on Type A, does that make these strategies more or less important?

Source: Adapted from D. Marcic, J. Seltzer, and P. Vail, *Organizational Behavior: Experiences and Cases.* Cincinnati, OH : South-Western, 2001.

ENDNOTES

5.1 Kvamme, N. "Humana's Freewheelin' Program Proves to Be Good for Business." *Workspan*, August 2008, pp. 75–77.

5.2 Wells, S. "Finding Wellness's Return on Investment: Calculating Wellness Programs' ROI Is Sometimes Complex, but It Can Be Done." *HR Magazine*, June 2008, pp. 75–84.

5.3   Kvamme, "Humana's Freewheelin' Program."

5.4   "Workplace Wellbeing: A Positive Touch," *Employee Benefits Magazine*, June 2004, www. ProQuest.com (March 27, 2007); Gebhardt, D.L., and C.E. Crump. "Employee Fitness and Wellness Programs in the Workplace." *American Psychologist* 45 (1990), pp. 262–72; Jacobson, B.H., and S.G. Aldana. "Relationship between Frequency of Aerobic Activity and Illness-Related Absenteeism in a Large Employee Sample." *Journal of Occupational and Environmental Medicine* 43 (2001), pp. 1019–25; Parker-Pope, T. "Personal Health (Special Report); The Secrets of Successful Aging: What Science Tells Us about Growing Older—and Staying Healthy." *The Wall Street Journal,* June 20, 2005, p. R1, www.ProQuest.com (March 27, 2007).

5.5   Kozlowski, D. "The Facility Factor: Can Buildings Boost Productivity?" *Building Operating Management*, August 2004, pp. 24–30, www.ProQuest.com (March 27, 2007).

5.6   Kvamme, "Humana's Freewheelin' Program."

5.7   Miller, J., and M. Miller. "Get a Life!" *Fortune*, November 28, 2005, pp. 109–124, www.ProQuest.com (March 27, 2007).

5.8   Sauter, S.; L. Murphy; M. Colligan; N. Swanson; J. Hurrell Jr.; F. Scharf Jr.; R. Sinclair; P. Grubb; L. Goldenhar; T. Alterman; J. Johnston; A. Hamilton; and J. Tisdale. *Stress at Work,* DHHS (NIOSH) Publication No. 99-101. Cincinnati, OH: U.S. Department of Health and Human Services, Public Health Service, Centers for Disease Control and Prevention, National Institute for Occupational Safety and Health, 1999.

5.9   Johnson, S.R., and L.D. Eldridge. *Employee-Related Stress on the Job: Sources, Consequences, and What's Next,* Technical Report #003. Rochester, NY: Genesee Survey Services, Inc., 2004.

5.10   Lazarus, R.S., and S. Folkman. *Stress, Appraisal, and Coping.* New York: Springer Publishing Company, Inc., 1984.

5.11   Ibid.

5.12   Ibid.

5.13   LePine, J.A.; M.A. LePine; and C.L. Jackson. "Challenge and Hindrance Stress: Relationships with Exhaustion, Motivation to Learn, and Learning Performance." *Journal of Applied Psychology* 89 (2004), pp. 883–91; LePine, J.A.; N.P. Podsakoff; and M.A. LePine. "A Meta-Analytic Test of the Challenge Stressor–Hindrance Stressor Framework: An Explanation for Inconsistent Relationships among Stressors and Performance." *Academy of Management Journal* 48 (2005), pp. 764–75; and Podsakoff, N.P.; J.A. LePine; and M.A. LePine. "Differential Challenge Stressor–Hindrance Stressor Relationships with Job Attitudes, Turnover Intentions, Turnover, and Withdrawal Behavior: A Meta-Analysis." *Journal of Applied Psychology* 92 (2007), pp. 438–54.

5.14   LePine, J.A.; M.A. LePine; and J.R. Saul. "Relationships among Work and Non-Work Challenge and Hindrance Stressors and Non-Work and Work Criteria: A Theory of Cross-Domain Stressor Effects." In *Research in Occupational Stress and Well Being,* ed. P.L. Perrewé and D.C. Ganster. San Diego: JAI Press/ Elsevier, 2006, pp. 35–72.

5.15   Kahn, R.; D. Wolfe; R. Quinn; J. Snoek; and R.A. Rosenthal. *Organizational Stress: Studies in Role*

Conflict and Ambiguity. New York: John Wiley, 1964; and Pearce, J. "Bringing Some Clarity to Role Ambiguity Research." *Academy of Management Review* 6 (1981), pp. 665–74.

5.16 Miller and Miller, "Get a Life!"

5.17 Mandel, M. "The Real Reasons You're Working So Hard . . . and What You Can Do about It." *BusinessWeek*, October 3, 2005, pp. 60–67, www.ProQuest.com (March 27, 2007).

5.18 O'Connor, A. "Cracking under Pressure? It's Just the Opposite for Some; Sick of Work—Last of Three Articles: Thriving under Stress." *The New York Times,* Section A, Column 5, September 10, 2004, p. 1, www. ProQuest.com (March 27, 2007).

5.19 McCall, M.W.; M.M. Lombardo; and A.M. Morrison. *The Lessons of Experience: How Successful Executives Develop on the Job.* Lexington, MA: Lexington Books, 1988.

5.20 Neufeld, S. *Work-Related Stress: What You Need to Know* (n.d.) http:// healthyplace.healthology.com/focus_ article.asp?f=mentalhealth&c=work_ related_stress (October 27, 2005); http://www.breastcancerfocus.com/ focus_article.asp?b=healthology& f=mentalhealth&c=work_related_ stress&pg=1 (March 27, 2007).

5.21 Crouter, A. "Spillover from Family to Work: The Neglected Side of the Work–Family Interface." *Human Relations* 37 (1984), pp. 425–42; and Rice, R.W.; M.R. Frone; and D.B. McFarlin. "Work and Nonwork Conflict and the Perceived Quality of Life." *Journal of Organizational Behavior* 13 (1992), pp. 155–68.

5.22 Holmes, T.H., and R.H. Rahe. "The Social Readjustment Rating Scale." *Journal of Psychosomatic Research* 11 (1967), pp. 213–18; and U.S.

Department of Health and Human Services. *Mental Health: A Report of the Surgeon General.* Rockville, MD: U.S. Department of Health and Human Services, Substance Abuse and Mental Health Services, National Institutes of Health Services Administration, Center for Health, National Institute of Mental Health, 1999, Ch. 4.

5.23 Frauenheim, E., and J. Marquez. "Reducing the Fear Factor." *Workforce Management,* November 18, 2008, pp. 17–22.

5.24 Lazarus and Folkman, *Stress, Appraisal, and Coping.*

5.25 Folkman, S.; R.S. Lazarus; C. Dunkel-Schetter; A. Delongis; and R.J. Gruen. "Dynamics of a Stressful Encounter: Cognitive Appraisal, Coping, and Encounter Outcomes." *Journal of Personality and Social Psychology* 50 (1986), pp. 992–1003.

5.26 Latack, J.C., and S.J. Havlovic. "Coping with Job Stress: A Conceptual Evaluation Framework for Coping Measures." *Journal of Organizational Behavior* 13 (1992), pp. 479–508.

5.27 Ibid.

5.28 *Global Relocation Trends, 2005 Survey Report.* Woodridge, IL: GMAC Global Relocation Services, 2006, http://www. gmacglobalrelocation.com/insight_ support/global_ relocation.asp (March 27, 2007).

5.29 Black, J.S.; M. Mendenhall; and G. Oddou. "Toward a Comprehensive Model of International Adjustment: An Integration of Multiple Theoretical Perspectives." *Academy of Management Review* 16 (1991), pp. 291–317.

5.30 Bhaskar-Shrinivas, P.; D.A. Harrison; M.A. Shaffer; and D.M.

Luk. "Input-Based and Time-Based Models of International Adjustment: Meta-Analytic Evidence and Theoretical Extensions." *Academy of Management Journal* 48 (2005), pp. 257–81.

5.31 Mendenhall, M.E.; T.M. Kulmann; G.K. Stahl; and J.S. Osland. "Employee Development and Expatriate Assignments." In *Blackwell Handbook of Cross-Cultural Management,* eds. M.J. Gannon and K.L. Newman. Malden, MA: Blackwell, 2002, pp. 155–84.

5.32 Latack, J.C., and S.J. Havlovic. "Coping with Job Stress."

5.33 Kahn et al., *Organizational Stress;* and Lazarus and Folkman, *Stress, Appraisal, and Coping.*

5.34 Latack and Havlovic, "Coping with Job Stress."

5.35 Ibid.

5.36 Lazarus, R.S. "Progress on a Cognitive–Motivational–Relational Theory of Emotion." *American Psychologist* 46 (1991), pp. 819–34.

5.37 Daniels, C. "The Last Taboo: It's Not Sex. It's Not Drinking. It's Stress—and It's Soaring." *Fortune,* October 28, 2002, pp. 136–44, www.ProQuest.com (March 27, 2007).

5.38 Miller and Miller, "Get a Life!"

5.39 Selye, H. *The Stress of Life.* New York: McGraw-Hill, 1976.

5.40 Cannon, W.B. "Stresses and Strains of Homeostasis." *American Journal of Medical Science* 189 (1935), pp. 1–14; and Goldstein, D.L. *Stress, Catecholamines, & Cardiovascular Disease.* New York: Oxford University Press, 1995.

5.41 Kahn, R.L., and P. Byosiere. "Stress in Organizations." In *Handbook of Industrial and Organizational Psychology,* Vol. 4, ed. M.D.

Dunette, J.M.R. Hough, and H.C. Triandis. Palo Alto, CA: Consulting Psychologists Press, 1992, pp. 517–650.

5.42 Defrank, R.S., and J.M. Ivancevich. "Stress on the Job: An Executive Update." *Academy of Management Executive* 12 (1998), pp. 55–66; and Haran, C. "Do You Know Your Early Warning Stress Signals?" 2005, http://abcnews.go.com/Health/Healthology/story?id=421825 (October 27, 2005).

5.43 Stöppler, M.C. "High Pressure Work Deadlines Raise Heart Attack Risk," http://stress.about.com/od/ heartdissease/a/deadline.htm (October 1, 2005).

5.44 Leitner, K., and M.G. Resch. "Do the Effects of Job Stressors on Health Persist over Time? A Longitudinal Study with Observational Stress Measures." *Journal of Occupational Health Psychology* 10 (2005), pp. 18–30.

5.45 Defrank and Ivancevich, "Stress on the Job"; and Haran, *"Do You Know?"*

5.46 Pines, A., and D. Kafry. "Occupational Tedium in the Social Services." *Social Work* 23 (1978), pp. 499–507.

5.47 ESPN.com. "Mentally Tired Favre Tells Packers his Playing Career Is Over," March 4, 2008, http://sports.espn.go.com/nfl/news/story?id=3276034 (June 5, 2008).

5.48 Packers.com. "Brett Favre Retirement Press Conference Transcript—March 6," March 6, 2008, http://packers.com (June 5, 2008).

5.49 Defrank and Ivancevich, "Stress on the Job."

5.50 Friedman, M., and R.H. Rosenman. *Type A Behavior and Your Heart.* New York: Knopf, 1974.

5.51 Ganster, D.C. "Type A Behavior and Occupational Stress. Job Stress: From Theory to Suggestion." *Journal of Organizational Behavior Management* 8 (1987), pp. 61–84.

5.52 Friedman and Rosenman, *Type A Behavior;* and Yarnold, P.R., and F.B. Bryant. "A Note on Measurement Issues in Type A Research: Let's Not Throw Out the Baby with the Bath Water." *Journal of Personality Assessment* 52 (1988), pp. 410–19.

5.53 Abush, R., and E.J. Burkhead. "Job Stress in Midlife Working Women: Relationships among Personality Type, Job Characteristics, and Job Tension." *Journal of Counseling Psychology* 31 (1984), pp. 36–44; Dearborn, M.J., and J.E. Hastings. "Type A Personality as a Mediator of Stress and Strain in Employed Women." *Journal of Human Stress* 13 (1987), pp. 53–60; and Howard, J.H.; D.A. Cunningham; and P.A. Rechnitzer. "Role Ambiguity, Type A Behavior, and Job Satisfaction: Moderating Effects on Cardiovascular and Biochemical Responses Associated with Coronary Risk." *Journal of Applied Psychology* 71 (1986), pp. 95–101.

5.54 Cooper, C.L.; P.J. Dewe; and M.P. O'Driscoll. *Organizational Stress.* Thousand Oaks, CA: Sage Publications, 2001.

5.55 Fusilier, M.R.; D.C. Ganster; and B.T. Mayes. "Effects of Social Support, Role Stress, and Locus of Control on Health." *Journal of Management* 13 (1987), pp. 517–28.

5.56 Jayaratne, S.; T. Tripodi; and W.A. Chess. "Perceptions of Emotional Support, Stress, and Strain by Male and Female Social Workers." *Social Work Research and Abstracts* 19 (1983), pp. 19–27; Kobasa, S. "Commitment and Coping in Stress among Lawyers." *Journal of*

Personality and Social Psychology 42 (1982), pp. 707–17; and LaRocco, J.M., and A.P. Jones. "Co-Worker and Leader Support as Moderators of Stress–Strain Relationships in Work Situations." *Journal of Applied Psychology* 63 (1978), pp. 629–34.

5.57 Kahn and Byosiere, "Stress in Organizations."

5.58 LePine et al., "A Meta-Analytic Test."

5.59 Cohen, S. "After Effects of Stress on Human Performance and Social Behavior: A Review of Research and Theory." *Psychological Bulletin* 88 (1980), pp. 82–108.

5.60 Podsakoff et al., "Differential Challenge Stressor–Hindrance Stressor Relationships."

5.61 Bedeian, A.G., and A. Armenakis. "A Path-Analytic Study of the Consequences of Role Conflict and Ambiguity." *Academy of Management Journal* 24 (1981), pp. 417–24; and Schaubroeck, J.; J.L. Cotton; and K.R. Jennings. "Antecedents and Consequences of Role Stress: A Covariance Structure Analysis." *Journal of Organizational Behavior* 10 (1989), pp. 35–58.

5.62 LePine et al., "A Meta-Analytic Test"; Podsakoff et al., "Differential Challenge Stressor–Hindrance Stressor Relationships."

5.63 Ibid.

5.64 Cavanaugh, M.A.; W.R. Boswell; M.V. Roehling; and J.W. Boudreau. "An Empirical Examination of Self-Reported Work Stress among U.S. Managers." *Journal of Applied Psychology* 85 (2000), pp. 65–74.

5.65 Boswell, W.R.; J.B. Olson-Buchanan; and M.A. LePine. "The Relationship between Work-Related Stress and Work Outcomes: The Role of Felt-Challenge and

Psychological Strain." *Journal of Vocational Behavior* 64 (2004), pp. 165–81.

5.66   LePine et al., "Challenge and Hindrance Stress."

5.67   Burke, M.E. "2005 Benefits Survey Report." Alexandria, VA: Society of Human Resource Management Research Department, 2005.

5.68   Perkins, A. "Medical Costs: Saving Money by Reducing Stress." *Harvard Business Review* 72 (1994), p. 12.

5.69   Sauter, S.; L. Murphy; M. Colligan; N. Swanson; J. Hurrell Jr.; F. Scharf Jr.; R. Sinclair; P. Grubb; L. Goldenhar; T. Alterman; J. Johnston; A. Hamilton; and J. Tisdale. *Is Your Boss Making You Sick?* http://abcnews.go.com/GMA/Careers/story?id=1251346&gma=true (October 27, 2005).

5.70   Defrank and Ivancevich, "Stress on the Job."

5.71   Noyce, J. "Help Employees Manage Stress to Prevent Absenteeism, Errors. *Minneapolis/St. Paul The Business Journal.* August 22, 2003. http://twincities.bizjournals.com/twincities/stories/2003/08/25/smallb2.html (March 27, 2007); and Burke, "2005 Benefits Survey Report."

5.72   Defrank and Ivancevich, "Stress on the Job"; Cooper, C.L. "The Costs of Stress at Work." *The Safety & Health Practitioner* 19 (2001), pp. 24–26.

5.73   Burke, "2005 Benefits Survey Report."

5.74   Miller and Miller, "Get a Life!"

5.75   Ibid.; Cunningham, C.R., and S.S. Murray. "Two Executives, One Career." *Harvard Business Review* 83 (February 2005), pp. 125–31.

5.76   Sahadi, J. "The World's Best Perk." *CNNMoney.com*, June 13, 2006, http://money.cnn.com/2006/06/13/commentary/everyday/sahadi/index.htm (May 8, 2009).

5.77   Ibid.

5.78   Ibid.

5.79   LePine et al., "A Meta-Analytic Test"; and Podsakoff et al., "Differential Challenge Stressor–Hindrance Stress Relationships."

5.80   Sonnentag, S., and M. Frese. "Stress in Organizations." In *Comprehensive Handbook of Psychology: Vol. 12, Industrial and Organizational Psychology,* eds. W.C. Borman, D.R. Ilgen, and R.J. Klimoski. New York: Wiley, 2003, pp. 453–91.

5.81   Burke, "2005 Benefits Survey Report."

5.82   Defrank and Ivancevich, "Stress on the Job"; and Austin, N.K. "Work–Life Paradox." *Incentive* 178 (2004), p. 18.

5.83   Ressler, C., and J. Thompson. *Why Work Sucks and How to Fix it.* New York: Portfolio, 2008.

5.84   Murphy, L.R. "Stress Management in Work Settings: A Critical Review of Health Effects." *American Journal of Health Promotion* 11 (1996), pp. 112–35.

5.85   Neufeld, *Work-Related Stress.*

5.86   Haran, *"Do You Know?"*

5.87   Ibid.

5.88   Daniels, "The Last Taboo."

5.89   Frauenheim and Marquez, "Reducing the Fear Factor."

5.90   Sonnentag and Frese, "Stress in Organizations."

5.91   Neufeld, *Work-Related Stress.*

5.92 Ibid.; Burke, "2005 Benefits Survey Report."

5.93 Doheny, K. "Going the Extra Mile." *Workforce Management*, January 19, 2009, pp. 27–28.

5.94 Wells, "Finding Wellness's Return on Investment."

5.95 Kvamme, "Humana's Freewheelin' Program."

5.96 Humana, Freewheelin' Web site, http://freewheelinwaytogo.com/anyquestion.aspx (May 5, 2009).

5.97 Ibid.

chapter 6

Motivation

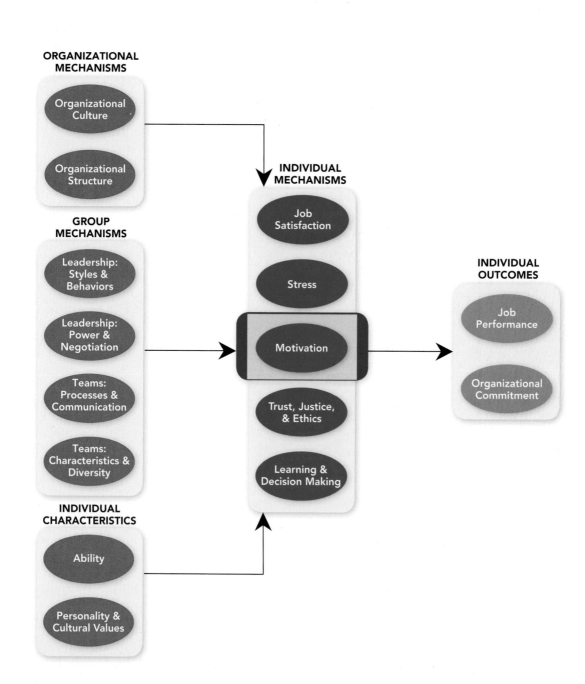

ORGANIZATIONAL MECHANISMS

Organizational Culture

Organizational Structure

GROUP MECHANISMS

Leadership: Styles & Behaviors

Leadership: Power & Negotiation

Teams: Processes & Communication

Teams: Characteristics & Diversity

INDIVIDUAL CHARACTERISTICS

Ability

Personality & Cultural Values

INDIVIDUAL MECHANISMS

Job Satisfaction

Stress

Motivation

Trust, Justice, & Ethics

Learning & Decision Making

INDIVIDUAL OUTCOMES

Job Performance

Organizational Commitment

✓ LEARNING GOALS

After reading this chapter, you should be able to answer the following questions:

6.1 What is motivation?

6.2 What three beliefs help determine work effort, according to expectancy theory?

6.3 What two qualities make goals strong predictors of task performance, according to goal setting theory?

6.4 What does it mean to be equitably treated according to equity theory, and how do employees respond to inequity?

6.5 What is psychological empowerment, and what four beliefs determine empowerment levels?

6.6 How does motivation affect job performance and organizational commitment?

6.7 What steps can organizations take to increase employee motivation?

ENTERPRISE RENT-A-CAR

What do you think of when you hear "Enterprise Rent-A-Car"? Do you think of "We'll pick you up"—the catchphrase that reflects the company's willingness to come to your door when your car's in the shop or you're ready to take a trip? You probably don't think "largest rental car company in the United States" or "hires more college grads than any other company." Both of those descriptions are true, however.[1] The company started in St. Louis when Jack Taylor opened a tiny auto-leasing business and named it after the aircraft carrier on which he'd served. When the company transitioned to car rentals, it retained its downtown locations, focusing on leisure rentals and auto insurer referrals rather than the airport business travelers. This unique business model allowed it to grow beyond the notice of competitors like Hertz, which paid little attention to Enterprise until it began advertising nationally in 1989 with images of that car wrapped in brown paper, on its way to a customer pick up.

Enterprise hires 7,000 college graduates a year as management trainees, recruiting from 220 different college campuses.[2] *BusinessWeek* has included Enterprise in its listing of the 50 best places to launch a career for three years running.[3] One college recruiter sums up what Enterprise looks for in its new hires this way: "The students that fit are highly motivated, positive, energetic, and enthusiastic."[4] Motivation is key, because the hours are long, and the work isn't always glamorous. The company describes the standard work week as no more than 49.5 hours,[5] but some employees report a norm that's closer to 60 hours.[6] And much of that time is spent behind a counter, picking up customers, or washing cars—all while wearing professional business attire.[7] Estimates suggest that about half of the new hires don't last a year at the company.

But those who stick it out do so for two major reasons: a clear career ladder for promotions and an impressive array of incentives. Management training can last 8 to 12 months, giving employees a chance to learn every aspect of the business. Promotions often follow after a year, first to management assistant and then to assistant manager.[8] From there, the best become branch managers, in charge of hiring and firing, the rental car fleet, and finances. The best of those can look forward to positions at corporate headquarters or the chance to be in charge of a whole region of branches. As Enterprise's vice president for corporate communications points out, "100% of our operations personnel started as management trainees." Although base pay is low—less than $35,000 a year— performance-based bonuses can add almost $10,000 more to that total.[9] Bonuses can be earned in a variety of ways, from signing customers up for supplemental liability protection to stopping to help a customer who needs roadside assistance.[10] And once employees reach the assistant manager stage, a profit-sharing system kicks in, with rewards linked to the performance of their branch.[11] That structure then extends up the ladder, with regional managers benefitting from the profitability of all of their branches. All these motivational strategies seem to be paying off for Enterprise's customers; the company usually occupies the top spot in rental car customer satisfaction rankings published by J.D. Power and Associates.[12]

MOTIVATION

Few OB topics matter more to employees and managers than motivation. How many times have you wondered to yourself, "Why can't I get myself going today?" Or how many times have you looked at a friend or coworker and wondered, "Why are they working so slowly right now?" Both of these questions are asking about "motivation," which is a derivation of the Latin word for movement, *movere*.[13] Those Latin roots nicely capture the meaning of motivation, as motivated employees simply move faster and longer than unmotivated employees. More formally, **motivation** is defined as a set of energetic forces that originates both within and outside an employee, initiates work-related effort, and determines its direction, intensity, and persistence.[14] Motivation is a critical consideration because effective job performance often requires high levels of both ability and motivation (see Chapter 10 on Ability for more discussion of such issues).[15] Our **OB at the Bookstore** feature offers a deeper look at the interplay of ability and motivation.

6.1

What is motivation?

OB AT THE BOOKSTORE

TALENT IS OVERRATED
by Geoff Colvin (New York: Penguin Group, 2008).

The conventional wisdom about "the natural" is a myth. The real path to great performance is a matter of choice. The question is, how bad do you want it?

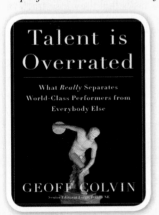

With those words, Geoff Colvin challenges our views about why some people achieve unusually high levels of performance. We often assume that professional athletes and musicians were prodigies with innate talent. Certainly Tiger Woods has that sort of talent—after all, he shot a 48 for nine holes at the age of 3.[16] However, that focus on talent ignores a critical piece of the puzzle for world-class performers: practice. But not the kind of practice that most of us engage in.

Colvin's book describes *deliberate practice*, which focuses on a remarkably specific set of activities that an individual has not yet mastered. Those of us who are casual musicians consider it "practice" when we play the same scales that we learned long ago. Deliberate practice would demand a razor-sharp focus on a note we can't hit, a speed we can't maintain, or a technique that seems beyond us. Admittedly, that sort of practice is a lot less fun. Woods has been seen dropping golf balls into sand traps, stepping on them, then hitting shots from those seemingly impossible lies. Although it would be more fun to hit approach shots from the fairway, doing so wouldn't make him a better golfer.

In organizational settings, deliberate practice might involve using some different piece of software, performing presentations in some different way, or relating to customers using some different strategy. The problem, of course, is that the short-term performance demands of the workplace discourage the struggles that deliberate practice requires. The most motivated employees therefore will engage in deliberate practice inside and outside of work. On the bright side, Colvin points out, "The reality that deliberate practice is hard can even be seen as good news. It means that most people won't do it. So your willingness to do it will distinguish you all the more."

The first part of our motivation definition illustrates that motivation is not one thing but rather a set of distinct forces. Some of those forces are internal to the employee, such as a sense of self-confidence, whereas others are external to the employee, such as the goals an employee is given. The next part of that definition illustrates that motivation determines a number of facets of an employee's work effort. These facets are summarized in Figure 6-1, which depicts a scenario in which your boss has given you an assignment to work on. Motivation determines *what* employees do at a given moment—the direction in which their effort is channeled. Every moment of the workday offers choices between task and citizenship sorts of actions or withdrawal and counterproductive sorts of actions. When it's 3:00 p.m. on a Thursday, do you keep working on the assignment your boss gave you, or do you send e-mails or surf the Web for a while? Once the direction of effort has been decided, motivation goes on to determine *how hard* an employee works—the intensity of effort—and *for how long*—the persistence of effort. We all have friends or coworkers who work extremely hard for . . . say . . . 5 minutes. We also have friends or coworkers who work extremely long hours but always seem to be functioning at half-speed. Neither of those groups of people would be described as extremely motivated.

As the Enterprise Rent-A-Car example illustrates, organizations are always on the lookout for new and better ways to motivate their employees. These days, however, those discussions are more likely to focus on a concept called **engagement**. You can think of engagement as a contemporary synonym, more or less, for high levels of intensity and persistence in work effort. Employees who are "engaged" completely invest themselves and their energies into their jobs.[17] Outwardly, engaged employees devote a lot of energy to their jobs, striving as hard as they can to take initiative and get the job done.[18] Inwardly, engaged employees focus a great deal of attention and concentration on their work, sometimes becoming so absorbed, involved, and interested in their tasks that they lose track of

FIGURE 6-1   Motivation and Effort

MOTIVATION DETERMINES THE . . .

DIRECTION of Effort:	INTENSITY of Effort:	PERSISTENCE of Effort:
What are you going to do right now?	*How hard are you going to work on it?*	*How long are you going to work on it?*
☑ The assignment your boss gave you yesterday	As hard as you can, or only at half-speed?	For five hours or five minutes?
☐ Send e-mails to your friends		
☐ Surf the Web for a while		

time (see Chapter 4 on Job Satisfaction for more discussion of such issues).[19] It's easy to see from those descriptions why organizations want engaged employees, which makes it important to understand the drivers of effort levels.

WHY ARE SOME EMPLOYEES MORE MOTIVATED THAN OTHERS?

There are a number of theories and concepts that attempt to explain why some employees are more motivated than others. The sections that follow review those theories and concepts in some detail. Most of them are relevant to each of the effort facets described in Figure 6-1. However, some of them are uniquely suited to explaining the direction of effort, whereas others do a better job of explaining the intensity and persistence of effort.

EXPECTANCY THEORY

What makes you decide to direct your effort to work assignments rather than taking a break or wasting time? Or what makes you decide to be a "good citizen" by helping out a colleague or attending some optional company function? **Expectancy theory** describes the cognitive process that employees go through to make choices among different voluntary responses.[20] Drawing on earlier models from psychology, expectancy theory argues that employee behavior is directed toward pleasure and away from pain or, more generally, toward certain outcomes and away from others.[21] How do employees make the choices that take them in the "right direction"? The theory suggests that our choices depend on three specific beliefs that are based in our past learning and experience: expectancy, instrumentality, and valence. These three beliefs are summarized in Figure 6-2, and we review each of them in turn.

6.2

What three beliefs help determine work effort, according to expectancy theory?

EXPECTANCY. **Expectancy** represents the belief that exerting a high level of effort will result in the successful performance of some task. More technically, expectancy is a subjective probability, ranging from 0 (no chance!) to 1 (a mortal lock!) that a specific amount of effort will result in a specific level of performance (abbreviated $E \longrightarrow P$). Think of a task at which you're not particularly good, such as writing romantic poetry. You may not be very motivated to write romantic poetry because you don't believe that your effort, no matter how hard you try, will result in a poem that "moves" your significant other. As another example, you'll be more motivated to work on the assignment described in Figure 6-1 if you're confident that trying hard will allow you to complete it successfully.

What factors shape our expectancy for a particular task? One of the most critical factors is **self-efficacy**, defined as the belief that a person has the capabilities needed to execute the behaviors required for task success.[22] Think of self-efficacy as a kind of self-confidence or a task-specific version of self-esteem.[23] Employees who feel more "efficacious" (that is, self-confident) for a particular task will tend to perceive higher levels of expectancy—and therefore be more likely to choose to exert high levels of effort. Why do some employees have higher self-efficacy for a given task than other employees? Figure 6-3 can help explain such differences.

When employees consider efficacy levels for a given task, they first consider their **past accomplishments**—the degree to which they have succeeded or failed in similar sorts of tasks in the past.[24] They also consider **vicarious experiences** by taking into account their observations and discussions with others who have performed such tasks.[25] Self-efficacy is also dictated by **verbal persuasion**, because friends, coworkers, and leaders

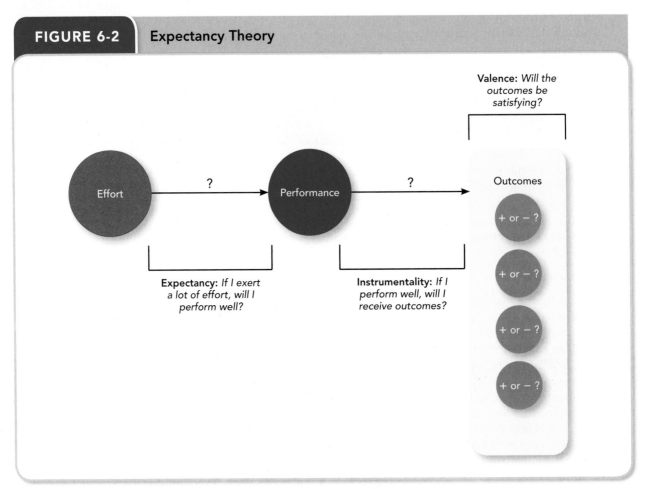

FIGURE 6-2 | **Expectancy Theory**

Source: Adapted from V.H. Vroom, *Work and Motivation* (New York: Wiley, 1964).

can persuade employees that they can "get the job done." Finally, efficacy is dictated by **emotional cues**, in that feelings of fear or anxiety can create doubts about task accomplishment, whereas pride and enthusiasm can bolster confidence levels.[26] Taken together, these efficacy sources shape analyses of how difficult the task requirements are and how adequate an employee's personal and situational resources will prove to be.[27] They also explain the content of most "halftime speeches" offered by coaches during sporting events; such speeches commonly include references to past comebacks or victories (past accomplishments), pep talks about how good the team is (verbal persuasion), and cheers to rally the troops (emotional cues).

INSTRUMENTALITY. **Instrumentality** represents the belief that successful performance will result in some outcome(s).[28] More technically, instrumentality is a set of subjective probabilities, each ranging from 0 (no chance!) to 1 (a mortal lock!) that successful performance will bring a set of outcomes (abbreviated P $\rightarrow$ O). The term "instrumentality" makes sense when you consider the meaning of the adjective "instrumental." We say something is "instrumental" when it helps attain something else—for example, reading this chapter is instrumental for getting a good grade in an OB class (at least, we hope so!).[29] Unfortunately, evidence indicates that many employees don't perceive high levels of instrumentality in their workplace. One survey of more than 10,000

FIGURE 6-3	Sources of Self-Efficacy

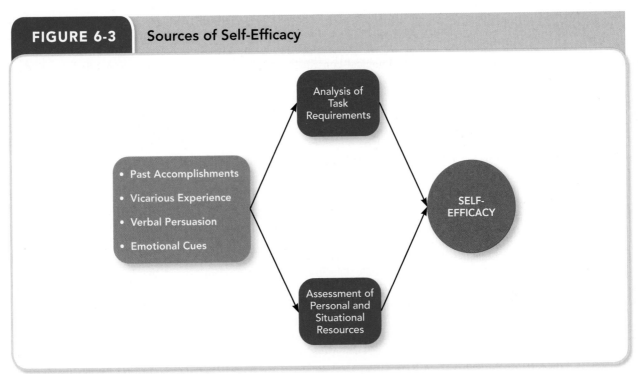

Source: Adapted from A. Bandura, "Self-Efficacy: Toward a Unifying Theory of Behavioral Change," *Psychological Review* 84 (1977), pp. 191–215; M.E. Gist and T.R. Mitchell, "Self-Efficacy: A Theoretical Analysis of its Determinants and Malleability," *Academy of Management Review* 17 (1992), pp. 183–211.

employees revealed that only 35 percent viewed performance as the key driver of their pay.[30] By comparison, 60 percent viewed seniority as the key driver.

Although organizations often struggle to foster instrumentality in the best of times, linking performance to outcomes is even more difficult during an economic downturn. One employment consulting firm reported that 60–70 percent of organizations froze the pay for their salaried employees in 2009.[31] Other companies, from FedEx to Saks Fifth Avenue to Hewlett-Packard, have actually cut the base pay for their salaried employees as a means of controlling labor costs.[32] Organizations may decide to cut salaries as a means of avoiding widespread layoffs that could take away critical knowledge, skills, and wisdom. Still, some compensation experts point to the risk of losing star performers whose efforts have gone unrewarded.[33] For example, the head of compensation at Hewitt Associates, a human resources consulting firm, argues that pay cuts "fly in the face of all the theory and philosophy that companies have been talking about for decades around pay for performance."[34] Indeed, some organizations are offering key employees retention bonuses even as they announce wider pay freezes or cuts.[35]

VALENCE. **Valence** reflects the anticipated value of the outcomes associated with performance (abbreviated V).[36] Valences can be positive ("I would prefer *having* outcome X to not having it"), negative ("I would prefer *not having* outcome X to having it"), or zero ("I'm bored . . . are we still talking about outcome X?"). Salary increases, bonuses, and more informal rewards are typical examples of "positively valenced" outcomes, whereas disciplinary actions, demotions, and terminations are typical examples of "negatively valenced" outcomes.[37] In this way, employees are more motivated when successful performance helps them attain attractive outcomes, such as bonuses, while helping them avoid unattractive outcomes, such as disciplinary actions.

What exactly makes some outcomes more "positively valenced" than others? In general, outcomes are deemed more attractive when they help satisfy needs. **Needs** can be defined as cognitive groupings or clusters of outcomes that are viewed as having critical psychological or physiological consequences.[38] Although scholars once suggested that certain needs are "universal" across people,[39] it's likely that different people have different "need hierarchies" that they use to evaluate potential outcomes. Table 6-1 describes many of the needs that are commonly studied in OB.[40] The terms and labels assigned to those needs often vary, so the table includes our labels as well as alternative labels that might sometimes be encountered.

Table 6-2 lists some of the most commonly considered outcomes in studies of motivation. Outcomes that are deemed particularly attractive are likely to satisfy a number of different needs. For example, praise can signal that interpersonal bonds are strong (satisfying relatedness needs) while also signaling competence (satisfying esteem needs). Note also that some of the outcomes in Table 6-2, such as bonuses, promotions, and praise, result from other people acknowledging successful performance. These outcomes foster **extrinsic motivation**—motivation that is controlled by some contingency that depends on task performance.[41] Other outcomes in the table, such as enjoyment, interestingness, and personal expression, are self-generated, originating in the mere act of performing the task. These outcomes foster **intrinsic motivation**—motivation that is felt when task performance serves as its own reward.[42] Taken together, extrinsic and intrinsic motivation represent an employee's "total motivation" level. For more on the distinction between extrinsic and intrinsic motivation, see our **OB on Screen** feature.

TABLE 6-1	Commonly Studied Needs in OB	
NEED LABEL	**ALTERNATIVE LABELS**	**DESCRIPTION**
Existence	Physiological, Safety	The need for the food, shelter, safety, and protection required for human existence.
Relatedness	Love, Belongingness	The need to create and maintain lasting, positive, interpersonal relationships.
Control	Autonomy, Responsibility	The need to be able to predict and control one's future.
Esteem	Self-regard, Growth	The need to hold a high evaluation of oneself and to feel effective and respected by others.
Meaning	Self-actualization	The need to perform tasks that one cares about and that appeal to one's ideals and sense of purpose.

Sources: Adapted from E.L. Deci and R.M Ryan, "The 'What' and 'Why' of Goal Pursuits: Human Needs and the Self-Determination of Behavior," *Psychological Inquiry* 11 (2000), pp. 227–68; R. Cropanzano, Z.S. Byrne, D.R. Bobocel, and D.R. Rupp, "Moral Virtues, Fairness Heuristics, Social Entities, and Other Denizens of Organizational Justice," *Journal of Vocational Behavior* 58 (2001), pp. 164–209; A.H. Maslow, "A Theory of Human Motivation," *Psychological Review* 50 (1943), pp. 370–96; and C.P. Alderfer, "An Empirical Test of a New Theory of Human Needs," *Organizational Behavior and Human Performance* 4 (1969), pp. 142–75.

You might wonder which of the outcomes in the table are most attractive to employees. That's a difficult question to answer, given that different employees emphasize different needs. However, two things are clear. First, the attractiveness of many rewards varies across cultures. One expert on cross-cultural recognition programs notes, "Different cultures have different motivators. In fact, giving a gift card could be extremely insulting because it could be saying that you are bribing them to do what they already do."[43] Good performance on a project in an American company might earn a trip to Las Vegas. However, trips to alcohol- and gambling-intensive areas are taboo in parts of Asia or the Middle East.[44] A better award in India would be tickets to a newly released movie or a moped for navigating in congested areas.[45]

Second, research suggests that employees underestimate how powerful a motivator pay is to them.[46] When employees rank the importance of extrinsic and intrinsic outcomes, they often put pay in fifth or sixth place. However, research studies show that financial incentives often have a stronger impact on motivation than other sorts of outcomes.[47] One reason is that money is relevant to many of the needs in Table 6-1. For example, money can help satisfy existence needs by helping employees buy food, afford a house, and save for retirement. However, money also conveys a sense of esteem, as it signals that employees are competent and well-regarded.[48] In fact, research suggests that people differ in how

TABLE 6-2	Extrinsic and Intrinsic Outcomes

EXTRINSIC OUTCOMES	INTRINSIC OUTCOMES
Pay	Enjoyment
Bonuses	Interestingness
Promotions	Accomplishment
Benefits and perks	Knowledge gain
Spot awards	Skill development
Praise	Personal expression
Job security	(Lack of) Boredom
Support	(Lack of) Anxiety
Free time	(Lack of) Frustration
(Lack of) Disciplinary actions	
(Lack of) Demotions	
(Lack of) Terminations	

Sources: Adapted from E.E. Lawler III and J.L. Suttle, "Expectancy Theory and Job Behavior," *Organizational Behavior and Human Performance* 9 (1973), pp. 482–503; J. Galbraith and L.L. Cummings, "An Empirical Investigation of the Motivational Determinants of Task Performance: Interactive Effects between Instrumentality–Valence and Motivation–Ability," *Organizational Behavior and Human Performance* 2 (1967), pp. 237–57; E. McAuley, S. Wraith, and T.E. Duncan, "Self-Efficacy, Perceptions of Success, and Intrinsic Motivation for Exercise," *Journal of Applied Social Psychology* 21 (1991), pp. 139–55; and A.S. Waterman, S.J. Schwartz, E. Goldbacher, H. Green, C. Miller, and S. Philip, "Predicting the Subjective Experience of Intrinsic Motivation: The Roles of Self-Determination, the Balance of Challenges and Skills, and Self-Realization Values," *Personality and Social Psychology Bulletin* 29 (2003), pp. 1447–58.

OB ON SCREEN

THE DARK KNIGHT

Bruce: *Criminals aren't complicated Alfred, we just need to figure out what he's after.*

Alfred: *With respect Mr. Wayne, perhaps this is a man you don't fully understand either . . . . Some men aren't looking for anything logical like money . . . some men just want to watch the world burn.*

With those words, Alfred (Michael Caine) explains why the Joker (Heath Ledger) is the perfect foil for the Batman (Christian Bale) in *The Dark Knight* (Dir.: Christopher Nolan, Warner Brothers, 2008). In donning the Batman persona, Bruce Wayne has dedicated his life to understanding the behavior of criminals. As the world's greatest detective, his job is to understand what motivates criminals so that he can predict what they'll do next. Fortunately, that's usually an easy task, because most criminals are motivated by money.

The Joker is cut from a different cloth, however. When he first arrived in Gotham, he told the reigning mob bosses that he would solve their "Batman problem" in exchange for half of their cash. Then, when the problem appeared to be solved, the Joker piled his money 30 feet high and lit it on fire. As one of the mob bosses looked on in shock, the Joker explained, "I'm a guy of simple tastes. I enjoy dynamite, gunpowder, and gasoline. . . . And you know the thing that they all have in common? They're cheap. . . . All you care about is money. This town deserves a better class of criminal."

The Joker's motivation is intrinsic in nature, which is exactly what Alfred was conveying to Bruce. The Joker recognizes this, noting "You know what I am? I'm a dog chasing cars . . . I just *do* things." The Joker's schemes and plots wind up being murals for his self-expression and creativity. In fact, he comes to view Batman as a vital ingredient in the enjoyment he derives from his exploits. As he explains during their climactic battle, "You won't kill me out of some misplaced sense of self-righteousness. And I won't kill you because you're just too much fun. I think you and I are destined to do this forever."

they view the **meaning of money**—the degree to which they view money as having symbolic, not just economic, value.[49] The symbolic value of money can be summarized in at least three dimensions: achievement (i.e., money symbolizes success), respect (i.e., money brings respect in one's community), and freedom (i.e., money provides opportunity).[50]

Who's more likely to view money from these more symbolic perspectives? Some research suggests that men are more likely to view money as representing achievement, respect, and freedom than are women.[51] Research also suggests that employees with higher salaries are more likely to view money in achievement-related terms.[52] Younger employees are less likely to view money in a positive light, relative to older employees.[53] Differences in education do not appear to impact the meaning of money, however.[54] How do you view the meaning of money? See our **OB Assessments** feature to find out.

MOTIVATIONAL FORCE. According to expectancy theory, the direction of effort is dictated by three beliefs: expectancy ($E \rightarrow P$), instrumentality ($P \rightarrow O$), and valence (V). More specifically, the theory suggests that the total "motivational force" to perform a given action can be described using the following formula:[55]

$$\text{Motivational Force} = \boxed{E \rightarrow P} \times \boxed{\Sigma[(P \rightarrow O) \times V]}$$

The Σ symbol in the equation signifies that instrumentalities and valences are judged with various outcomes in mind, and motivation increases as successful performance is linked to more and more attractive outcomes. Note the significance of the multiplication signs in the formula: Motivational force equals zero if any one of the three beliefs is zero. In other words, it doesn't matter how confident you are if performance doesn't result in any outcomes. Similarly, it doesn't matter how well performance is evaluated and rewarded if you don't believe you can perform well.

GOAL SETTING THEORY

So, returning to the choice shown in Figure 6-1, let's say that you feel confident you can perform well on the assignment your boss gave you and that you also believe successful performance will bring valued outcomes. Now that you've chosen to direct your effort to that assignment, two critical questions remain: How hard will you work, and for how long? To shed some more light on these questions, you stop by your boss's office and ask her, "So, when exactly do you need this done?" After thinking about it for a while, she concludes, "Just do your best." After returning to your desk, you realize that you're still not sure how much to focus on the assignment, or how long you should work on it before turning to something else.

Goal setting theory views goals as the primary drivers of the intensity and persistence of effort.[56] Goals are defined as the objective or aim of an action and typically refer to attaining a specific standard of proficiency, often within a specified time limit.[57] More specifically, the theory argues that assigning employees **specific and difficult goals** will result in higher levels of performance than assigning no goals, easy goals, or "do-your-best" goals.[58] Why are specific and difficult goals more effective than do-your-best ones? After all, doesn't "your best" imply the highest possible levels of effort? The reason is that few people know what their "best" is (and even fewer managers can tell whether employees are truly doing their "best"). Assigning specific and difficult goals gives people a number to shoot for—a "measuring stick" that can be used to tell them how hard they need to work and for how long. So if your boss had said, "Have the assignment on my desk by 10:30 a.m. on Tuesday, with no more than two mistakes," you would have known exactly how hard to work and for how long.

6.3

What two qualities make goals strong predictors of task performance, according to goal setting theory?

OB ASSESSMENTS

THE MEANING OF MONEY

How do you view money—what meaning do you attach to it? This assessment will tell you where you stand on the three facets of the meaning of money—money as achievement, money as respect, and money as freedom. Answer each question using the response scale provided. Then follow the instructions below to score yourself. (For more assessments relevant to this chapter, please visit the Online Learning Center at www.mhhe.com/colquitt).

1 STRONGLY DISAGREE	2 DISAGREE	3 SLIGHTLY DISAGREE	4 NEUTRAL	5 SLIGHTLY AGREE	6 AGREE	7 STRONGLY AGREE

1. Money represents one's achievement. _____

2. Money is a symbol of success. _____

3. Money is the most important goal in my life. _____

4. Money can buy everything. _____

5. Money makes people respect you in the community. _____

6. Money will help you express your competence and abilities. _____

7. Money can bring you many friends. _____

8. Money is honorable. _____

9. Money gives you autonomy and freedom. _____

10. Money can give you the opportunity to be what you want to be. _____

11. Money in the bank is a sign of security. _____

12. Money means power. _____

SCORING AND INTERPRETATION

Money as Achievement: Sum up items 1–4. _____
Money as Respect: Sum up items 5–8. _____
Money as Freedom: Sum up items 9–12. _____

Money as Achievement:	High = 13 or above. Low = 12 or below.
Money as Respect:	High = 15 or above. Low = 14 or below.
Money as Freedom:	High = 20 or above. Low = 19 or below.

If you scored high on all three dimensions, then you view money as having multiple, noneconomic meanings. This result means that money is likely to be a powerful motivator for you.

Source: Adapted from T.L. Tang, "The Meaning of Money Revisited," *Journal of Organizational Behavior* 13 (1992), pp. 197–202.

Of course, a key question then becomes, "What's a difficult goal?" Figure 6-4 illustrates the predicted relationship between goal difficulty and task performance. When goals are easy, there's no reason to work your hardest or your longest, so task effort is lower. As goals move from moderate to difficult, the intensity and persistence of effort become maximized. At some point, however, the limits of a person's ability get reached, and self-efficacy begins to diminish. Also at that point, goals move from difficult to impossible, and employees feel somewhat helpless when attempting to achieve them. In turn, effort and performance inevitably decline. So a difficult goal is one that stretches employees to perform at their maximum level while still staying within the boundaries of their ability.

The effects of specific and difficult goals on task performance have been tested in several hundred studies using many kinds of settings and tasks. A sampling of those settings and tasks is shown in Table 6-3.[59] Overall, around 90 percent of the goal setting studies support the beneficial effects of specific and difficult goals on task performance.[60] Although some of the settings and tasks shown in the table are unlikely to be major parts of your career (archery, handball, LEGO construction), others should be very relevant to the readers (and authors!) of this book (managing and supervision, studying, faculty research). Then again, who wouldn't want a career in LEGO construction?

Why exactly do specific and difficult goals have such positive effects? Figure 6-5 presents goal setting theory in more detail to understand that question better.[61] First, the assignment of a specific and difficult goal shapes people's own **self-set goals**—the internalized goals that people use to monitor their own task progress.[62] In the absence of an assigned goal, employees may not even consider what their own goals are, or they may self-set relatively easy goals that they're certain to meet. As a self-set goal becomes more difficult, the intensity of effort increases, and the persistence of effort gets extended. However, goals have another effect; they trigger the creation of **task strategies**, defined as learning plans

FIGURE 6-4 Goal Difficulty and Task Performance

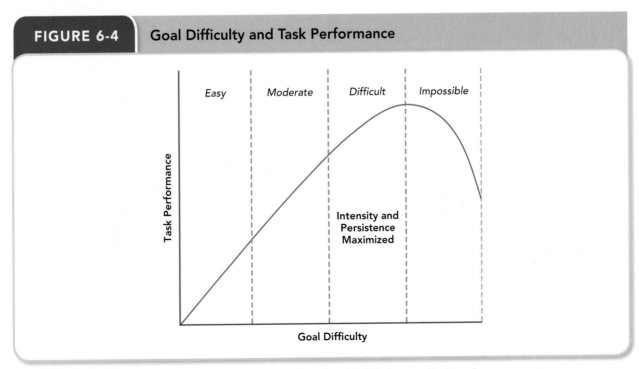

Source: Adapted from E.A. Locke and G.P. Latham, *A Theory of Goal Setting and Task Performance* (Englewood Cliffs, NJ: Prentice Hall, 1990).

TABLE 6-3	Settings and Tasks Used in Goal Setting Research

SETTINGS AND TASKS

Air traffic control	Management training
Archery	Marine recruit performance
Arithmetic	Maze learning
Beverage consumption	Mining
Chess	Proofreading
Computer games	Production and manufacturing
Course work	Puzzles
Energy conservation	Safety behaviors
Exercise	Sales
Faculty research	Scientific and R&D work
Juggling	Sit-ups
LEGO construction	Studying
Logging	Weight lifting
Managing and supervision	Weight loss

Source: Adapted from E.A. Locke and G.P. Latham, *A Theory of Goal Setting and Task Performance* (Englewood Cliffs, NJ: Prentice Hall, 1990).

and problem-solving approaches used to achieve successful performance.[63] In the absence of a goal, it's easy to rely on trial and error to figure out how best to do a task. Under the pressure of a measuring stick, however, it becomes more effective to plan out the next move. Put differently, goals can motivate employees to work both harder and smarter.

Figure 6-5 also includes three variables that specify when assigned goals will have stronger or weaker effects on task performance. In the jargon of theory diagrams, these variables are called "moderators." Rather than directly affecting other variables in the diagram, moderators affect the strength of the relationships between variables. One moderator is **feedback**, which consists of updates on employee progress toward goal attainment.[64] Imagine being challenged to beat a friend's score on the *Halo 3* video game but having your own score hidden as you played. How would you know how hard to try? Another moderator is **task complexity**, which reflects how complicated the information and actions involved in a task are, as well as how much the task changes.[65] In general, the effects of specific and difficult goals are almost twice as strong on simple tasks as on complex tasks, though the effects of goals remain beneficial even in complex cases.[66] Goal setting at Wyeth, the Madison, New Jersey–based pharmaceuticals company, illustrates the value of goals for complex tasks (after all, what's more complicated than chemistry?).[67] When Robert Ruffolo was appointed the new chief of R&D several years ago, he was concerned about the low number of new drug compounds being generated by Wyeth's

FIGURE 6-5	Goal Setting Theory

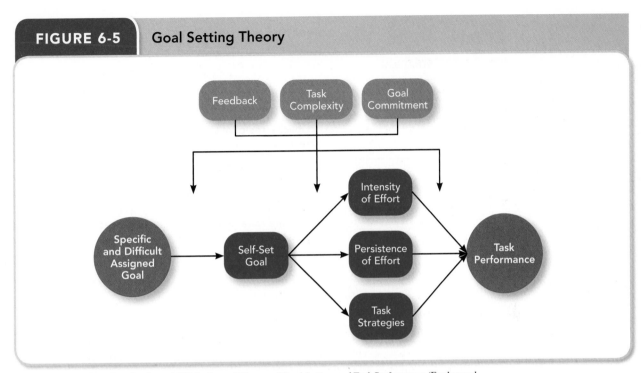

Sources: Adapted from E.A. Locke and G.P. Latham, *A Theory of Goal Setting and Task Performance* (Englewood Cliffs, NJ: Prentice Hall, 1990); E.A. Locke and G.P. Latham, "Building a Practically Useful Theory of Goal Setting and Task Motivation: A 35-Year Odyssey," *American Psychologist* 57 (2002), pp. 705–17; and G.P. Latham, "Motivate Employee Performance through Goal-Setting," in *Blackwell Handbook of Principles of Organizational Behavior,* ed. E.A. Locke (Malden, MA: Blackwell, 2000), pp. 107–19.

labs. His solution? He gave scientists a goal of discovering 12 new drug compounds every year, up from the 4 compounds they were previously averaging, with bonuses contingent on reaching the goals. Wyeth's scientists have reached the goal every year since, and the goal was eventually upped to 15 compounds per year.

The final moderator shown in Figure 6-5 is **goal commitment**, defined as the degree to which a person accepts a goal and is determined to try to reach it.[68] When goal commitment is high, assigning specific and difficult goals will have significant benefits for task performance. However, when goal commitment is low, those effects become much weaker.[69]

The importance of goal commitment raises the question of how best to foster commitment when assigning goals to employees. Table 6-4 summarizes some of the most powerful strategies for fostering goal commitment, which range from rewards to supervisory support to employee participation.[70]

Microsoft recently revised its use of goal setting principles in an effort to boost goal commitment and task performance.[71] The company had become concerned that employees

As the new chief of research and development at Wyeth, Inc., a pharmaceutical company, Robert Ruffolo offered company scientists a bonus for discovering 12 new drug compounds every year. They've done it every year and are now reaching for a new goal of 15.

TABLE 6-4	Strategies for Fostering Goal Commitment

STRATEGY	DESCRIPTION
Rewards	Tie goal achievement to the receipt of monetary or nonmonetary rewards.
Publicity	Publicize the goal to significant others and coworkers to create some social pressure to attain it.
Support	Provide supportive supervision to aid employees if they struggle to attain the goal.
Participation	Collaborate on setting the specific proficiency level and due date for a goal, so that the employee feels a sense of ownership over the goal.
Resources	Provide the resources needed to attain the goal and remove any constraints that could hold back task efforts.

Sources: Adapted from J.R. Hollenbeck and H.J. Klein, "Goal Commitment and the Goal-Setting Process: Problems, Prospects, and Proposals for Future Research," *Journal of Applied Psychology* 72 (1987), pp. 212–20; H.J. Klein, M.J. Wesson, J.R. Hollenbeck, and B.J. Alge, "Goal Commitment and the Goal-Setting Process: Conceptual Clarification and Empirical Synthesis," *Journal of Applied Psychology* 84 (1999), pp. 885–96; E.A. Locke, G.P. Latham, and M. Erez, "The Determinants of Goal Commitment," *Academy of Management Review* 13 (1988), pp. 23–29; and G.P. Latham, "The Motivational Benefits of Goal-Setting," *Academy of Management Executive* 18 (2004), pp. 126–29.

viewed their goals as objectives they *hoped* to meet rather than objectives they were *committed* to meeting. Moreover, approximately 25–40 percent of employees were working under goals that were either not specific enough or not measurable enough to offer feedback. To combat these trends, managers are now trained to identify five to seven **S.M.A.R.T. goals** for each employee and to link rewards directly to goal achievement. The S.M.A.R.T. acronym summarizes many beneficial goal characteristics, standing for **S**pecific, **M**easurable, **A**chievable, **R**esults-Based, and **T**ime-Sensitive. (Although that acronym is a useful reminder, note that it omits the all-important "Difficult" characteristic). Managers and employees at Microsoft participate jointly in the goal setting process, and managers offer support by suggesting task strategies that employees can use to achieve the goals. In this way, managers and employees come to understand the "how" of achievement, not just the "what."[72] For insights into how goal setting operates across cultures, see our **OB Internationally** feature.

EQUITY THEORY

Returning to our running example in Figure 6-1, imagine that at this point, you've decided to work on the assignment your boss gave you, and you've been told that it's due by Tuesday at 10:30 a.m. and can't have more than two mistakes in it. That's a specific and difficult goal, so Internet Explorer hasn't been launched in a while, and you haven't even thought about checking your e-mail. In short, you've been working very hard for a few hours, until the guy from across the hall pops his head in. You tell him what you're working on, and he nods sympathetically, saying, "Yeah, the boss gave me a similar assignment that sounds just as tough. I think she realized how tough it was though, because she said I could use the

OB INTERNATIONALLY

Research in cross-cultural OB suggests that there are some "universals" when it comes to motivation. For example, interesting work, pay, achievement, and growth are billed as motivating forces whose importance does not vary across cultures.[73] Of course, some motivation principles do vary in their effectiveness across cultures, including some of the strategies for fostering goal commitment.

Types of Goals. Should goals be given on an individual or a groupwide basis? Employees in the United States usually prefer to be given individual goals. In contrast, employees in other countries, including China and Japan, prefer to receive team goals.[74] This difference likely reflects the stronger emphasis on collective responsibility and cooperation in those cultures.

Rewards. Rewards tend to increase goal commitment across cultures, but cultures vary in the types of rewards that they value. Employees in the United States prefer to have rewards allocated according to merit. In contrast, employees in other countries, including China, Japan, and Sweden, prefer that rewards be allocated equally across members of the work unit.[75] Employees in India prefer a third allocation strategy—doling out rewards according to need. These cultural differences show that nations differ in how they prioritize individual achievement, collective solidarity, and the welfare of others.

Participation. National culture also affects the importance of participation in setting goals. Research suggests that employees in the United States are likely to accept assigned goals because the culture emphasizes hierarchical authority. In contrast, employees in Israel, which lacks a cultural emphasis on hierarchy, do not respond as well to assigned goals.[76] Instead, employees in Israel place a premium on participation in goal setting.

Feedback. Culture also influences how individuals respond when they receive feedback regarding goal progress. As with participation, research suggests that employees in the United States are more likely to accept feedback because they are comfortable with hierarchical authority relationships and have a strong desire to reduce uncertainty.[77] Other cultures, like England, place less value on reducing uncertainty, making feedback less critical to them.

---

company's playoff tickets if I finish it on time." Playoff tickets? Playoff tickets?? Looks like it's time to check that e-mail after all. . . .

Unlike the first two theories, **equity theory** acknowledges that motivation doesn't just depend on your own beliefs and circumstances but also on what happens to *other people.*[78] More specifically, equity theory suggests that employees create a "mental ledger" of the outcomes (or rewards) they get from their job duties.[79] What outcomes might be part of your mental ledger? That's completely up to you and depends on what you find valuable, though Table 6-5 provides a listing of some commonly considered outcomes. Equity theory further suggests that employees create a mental ledger of the inputs (or contributions and investments) they put into their job duties.[80] Again, the composition of your mental ledger is completely specific to you, but Table 6-5 provides a listing of some inputs that seem to matter to most employees.

So what exactly do you do with these mental tallies of outcomes and inputs? Equity theory argues that you compare your ratio of outcomes and inputs to the ratio of some

 6.4

What does it mean to be equitably treated according to equity theory, and how do employees respond to inequity?

| TABLE 6-5 | Some Outcomes and Inputs Considered by Equity Theory |

OUTCOMES	INPUTS
Pay	Effort
Seniority benefits	Performance
Fringe benefits	Skills and abilities
Status symbols	Education
Satisfying supervision	Experience
Workplace perks	Training
Intrinsic rewards	Seniority

Sources: Adapted from J.S. Adams, "Inequity in Social Exchange," in *Advances in Experimental Social Psychology,* Vol. 2, ed. L. Berkowitz (New York: Academic Press, 1965), pp. 267–99.

comparison other—some person who seems to provide an intuitive frame of reference for judging equity.[81] There are three general possibilities that can result from this "cognitive calculus," as shown in Figure 6-6. The first possibility is that the ratio of outcomes to inputs is balanced between you and your comparison other. In this case, you feel a sense of equity, and you're likely to maintain the intensity and persistence of your effort. This situation would have occurred if you had been offered playoff tickets, just like your colleague.

The second possibility is that your ratio of outcomes to inputs is less than your comparison other's ratio. According to equity theory, any imbalance in ratios triggers **equity distress**—an internal tension that can only be alleviated by restoring balance to the ratios.[82] In an underreward case, the equity distress likely takes the form of negative emotions such as anger or envy. One way to stop feeling those emotions is to try to restore the balance in some way, and Figure 6-6 reveals two methods for doing so. You could be constructive and proactive by talking to your boss and explaining why you deserve better outcomes. Such actions would result in the growth of your outcomes, restoring balance to the ratio. Of course, anger often results in actions that are destructive rather than constructive, and research shows that feelings of underreward inequity are among the strongest predictors of counterproductive behaviors, such as employee theft (see Chapter 7 on Trust, Justice, and Ethics for more on such issues).[83] More relevant to this chapter, another means of restoring balance is to shrink your inputs by lowering the intensity and persistence of effort. Remember, it's not the total outcomes or inputs that matter in equity theory—it's only the ratio.

The third possibility is that your ratio of outcomes to inputs is greater than your comparison other's ratio. Equity distress again gets experienced, and the tension likely creates negative emotions such as guilt or anxiety. Balance could be restored by shrinking your outcomes (taking less money, giving something back to the comparison other), but the theory acknowledges that such actions are unlikely in most cases.[84] Instead, the more likely solution is to increase your inputs in some way. You could increase the intensity and persistence of your task effort or decide to engage in more "extra mile" citizenship behaviors. At some point though, there may not be enough hours in the day to increase your inputs any further. An alternative (and less labor-intensive) means of increasing your inputs is to simply rethink them—to reexamine your mental ledger to see if you may have "undersold" your true contributions. On second thought, maybe your education or seniority is more

FIGURE 6-6 Three Possible Outcomes of Equity Theory Comparisons

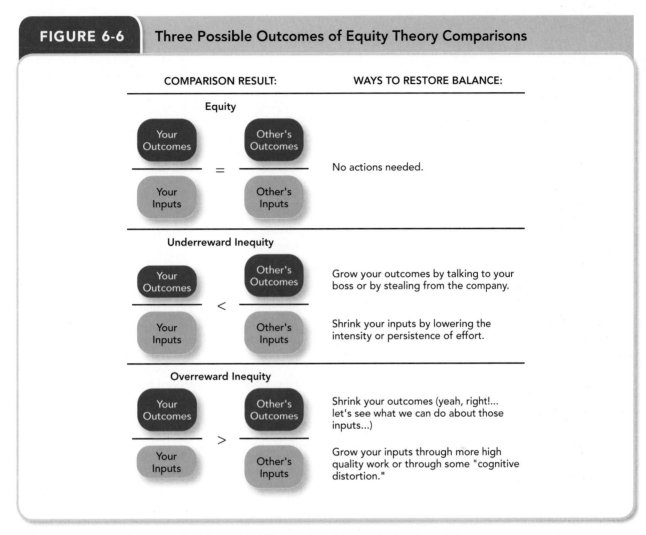

COMPARISON RESULT: WAYS TO RESTORE BALANCE:

Equity

$$\frac{\text{Your Outcomes}}{\text{Your Inputs}} = \frac{\text{Other's Outcomes}}{\text{Other's Inputs}}$$

No actions needed.

Underreward Inequity

$$\frac{\text{Your Outcomes}}{\text{Your Inputs}} < \frac{\text{Other's Outcomes}}{\text{Other's Inputs}}$$

Grow your outcomes by talking to your boss or by stealing from the company.

Shrink your inputs by lowering the intensity or persistence of effort.

Overreward Inequity

$$\frac{\text{Your Outcomes}}{\text{Your Inputs}} > \frac{\text{Other's Outcomes}}{\text{Other's Inputs}}$$

Shrink your outcomes (yeah, right!... let's see what we can do about those inputs...)

Grow your inputs through more high quality work or through some "cognitive distortion."

Sources: Adapted from J.S. Adams, "Inequity in Social Exchange," in *Advances in Experimental Social Psychology*, Vol. 2, ed. L. Berkowitz (New York: Academic Press, 1965), pp. 267–99.

critical than you realized, or maybe your skills and abilities are more vital to the organization. This **cognitive distortion** allows you to restore balance mentally, without altering your behavior in any way.

There is one other way of restoring balance, regardless of underreward or overreward circumstances, that's not depicted in Figure 6-6: Change your comparison other. After all, we compare our "lots in life" to a variety of other individuals. Table 6-6 summarizes the different kinds of comparison others that can be used.[85] Some of those comparisons are **internal comparisons**, meaning they refer to someone in the same company.[86] Others are **external comparisons**, meaning that they refer to someone in a different company. If a given comparison results in high levels of anger and envy or high levels of guilt and anxiety, the frame of reference may be shifted. In fact, research suggests that employees don't just compare themselves to one other person; instead, they make multiple comparisons to a variety of different others.[87] Although it may be possible to create a sort of "overall equity" judgment, research shows that people draw distinctions between the various equity comparisons shown in the table. For example, one study showed that job equity was the most

TABLE 6-6	Judging Equity with Different Comparison Others

COMPARISON TYPE	DESCRIPTION AND SAMPLE SURVEY ITEM
Job Equity	Compare with others doing the same job in the same organization. Sample survey item: *Compared with others doing the same job as me in my company with similar education, seniority, and effort, I earn about:*
Company Equity	Compare with others in the same organization doing substantially different jobs. Sample survey item: *Compared with others in my company on other jobs doing work that is similar in responsibility, skill, effort, education, and working condition required, I earn about:*
Occupational Equity	Compare with others doing essentially the same job in other organizations. Sample survey item: *Compared with others doing my job in other companies in the area with similar education, seniority, and effort, I earn about:*
Educational Equity	Compare with others who have attained the same education level. Sample survey item: *Compared with people I know with similar education and responsibility as me, I earn about:*
Age Equity	Compare with others of the same age. Sample survey item: *Compared with those of my age, I earn about:*

40% less	30% less	20% less	10% less	About the same	10% more	20% more	30% more	40% more

Source: R.W. Scholl, E.A. Cooper, and J.F. McKenna, "Referent Selection in Determining Equity Perceptions: Differential Effects on Behavioral and Attitudinal Outcomes," *Personnel Psychology* 40 (1987), pp. 113–24. Reprinted with permission of Wiley-Blackwell.

powerful driver of citizenship behaviors, whereas occupational equity was the most powerful driver of employee withdrawal.[88]

These mechanisms make it clear that judging equity is a very subjective process. Recent data from a Salary.com report highlight that very subjectivity. A survey of 1,500 employees revealed that 65 percent of the respondents planned to look for a new job in the next three months, with 57 percent doing so because they felt underpaid. However, Salary.com estimated that only 19 percent of those workers really were underpaid, taking into account their relevant inputs and the current market conditions. In fact, it was estimated that 17 percent were actually being overpaid by their companies! On the one hand, that subjectivity is likely to be frustrating to most managers in charge of compensation. On the other hand, it's important to realize that the intensity and persistence of employees' effort is driven by their own equity perceptions, not anyone else's.

Perhaps many employees feel they're underpaid because they compare their earnings with their CEO's. Just consider some of the names on *Forbes*'s listing of the 25 top-paid CEOs in 2008: Lawrence Ellison of Oracle ($193 million), Angelo Mozilo of

Countrywide Financial ($103 million), Howard Schultz of Starbucks ($99 million), Daniel Amos of Aflac ($75 million), Lloyd Blankfein of Goldman Sachs ($74 million), Richard Fairbank of Capital One ($73 million), Richard Fuld Jr. of Lehman Bros. ($72 million), John Chambers of Cisco Systems ($55 million), and Bradbury Anderson of Best Buy ($49 million).[89] Those numbers include salary and cash bonuses, vested stock grants, stock gains, and the value of exercised stock options.

Although CEO pay fell 15 percent from 2007 to 2008, those numbers reflect the disconnect between what CEOs make and what the typical employee makes.[90] In 1980, the median compensation for CEOs was 33 times that of the average worker. Three decades later, that ratio is more than 100 times the average worker's compensation. Why do boards of directors grant such large compensation packages to CEOs? Although there are many reasons, some have speculated that the pay packages represent status symbols, with many CEOs viewing themselves in celebrity terms, along the lines of professional athletes.[91] Alternatively, CEO pay packages may represent rewards for years of climbing the corporate ladder or insurance policies against the low job security for most CEOs.

Can such high pay totals ever be viewed as equitable in an equity theory sense? Well, CEOs likely have unusually high levels of many inputs, including effort, skills and abilities, education, experience, training, and seniority. CEOs may also use other CEOs as their comparison others—as opposed to rank-and-file employees—making them less likely to feel a sense of overreward inequity. Ultimately, however, the equity of their pay depends on how the company performs under them. For example, few would view Angelo Mozilo's $103 million as equitable given Countrywide's –6 percent annual return during his 10 years at the top,[92] not to mention its role in the subprime mortgage crisis, which contributed to the economic downturn. On the other end of the spectrum, *Forbes* named Amazon.com's Jeffrey Bezos as the most valuable boss in 2008.[93] Bezos earned an average of $1 million over the past six years while delivering a 32 percent annual return to Amazon shareholders.

Some organizations grapple with concerns about equity by emphasizing pay secrecy (though that doesn't help with CEO comparisons, given that the Securities and Exchange Commission demands the disclosure of CEO pay for all publicly traded companies).

"This is sloth—greed is on the top floor."

One survey indicated that 36 percent of companies explicitly discourage employees from discussing pay with their colleagues, and surveys also indicate that most employees approve of pay secrecy.[94] Is pay secrecy a good idea? Although it has not been the subject of much research, there appear to be pluses and minuses associated with pay secrecy. On the plus side, such policies may reduce conflict between employees while appealing to concerns about personal privacy. On the minus side, employees may respond to a lack of accurate information by guessing at equity levels, possibly perceiving more underpayment inequity than truly exists. In addition, the insistence on secrecy might cause employees to view the company with a sense of distrust (see Chapter 7 on Trust, Justice, and Ethics for more on this issue).[95]

PSYCHOLOGICAL EMPOWERMENT

Now we return, for one last time, to our running example in Figure 6-1. When last we checked in, your motivation levels had suffered because you learned your coworker was offered the company's playoff tickets for successfully completing a similar assignment. As you browse the Web in total "time-wasting mode," you begin thinking about all the reasons you hate working on this assignment. Even aside from the issue of goals and rewards, you keep coming back to this issue: You would never have taken on this project *by choice.* More specifically, the project itself doesn't seem very meaningful, and you doubt that it will have any real impact on the functioning of the organization.

Those sentiments signal a low level of **psychological empowerment**, which reflects an energy rooted in the belief that work tasks contribute to some larger purpose.[96] Psychological empowerment represents a form of intrinsic motivation, in that merely performing the work tasks serves as its own reward and supplies many of the intrinsic outcomes shown in Table 6-2. The concept of psychological empowerment has much in common with our discussion of "satisfaction with the work itself" in Chapter 4 on Job Satisfaction. That discussion illustrated that jobs with high levels of variety, significance, and autonomy can be intrinsically satisfying.[97] Models of psychological empowerment argue that a similar set of concepts can make work tasks intrinsically motivating. Four concepts are particularly important: meaningfulness, self-determination, competence, and impact.

Meaningfulness captures the value of a work goal or purpose, relative to a person's own ideals and passions.[98] When a task is relevant to a meaningful purpose, it becomes easier to concentrate on the task and get excited about it. You might even find yourself cutting other tasks short so you can devote more time to the meaningful one or thinking about the task outside of work hours.[99] In contrast, working on tasks that are not meaningful brings a sense of emptiness and detachment. As a result, you might need to mentally force yourself to keep working on the task. Managers can instill a sense of meaningfulness by articulating an exciting vision or purpose and fostering a noncynical climate in which employees are free to express idealism and passion without criticism.[100] For their part, employees can build their own sense of meaningfulness by identifying and clarifying their own passions. Employees who are fortunate enough to be extremely passionate about their work sometimes describe it as "a calling"—something they were born to do.[101]

6.5

What is psychological empowerment, and what four beliefs determine empowerment levels?

"Really, I'm fine. It was just a fleeting sense of purpose—I'm sure it will pass."

Self-determination reflects a sense of choice in the initiation and continuation of work tasks. Employees with high levels of self-determination can choose what tasks to work on, how to structure those tasks, and how long to pursue those tasks. That sense of self-determination is a strong driver of intrinsic motivation, because it allows employees to pursue activities that they themselves find meaningful and interesting.[102] Managers can instill a sense of self-determination in their employees by delegating work tasks, rather than micromanaging them, and by trusting employees to come up with their own approach to certain tasks.[103] For their part, employees can gain more self-determination by earning the trust of their bosses and negotiating for the latitude that comes with that increased trust.

Competence captures a person's belief in his or her capability to perform work tasks successfully.[104] Competence is identical to the self-efficacy concept reviewed previously in this chapter; employees with a strong sense of competence (or self-efficacy) believe they can execute the particular behaviors needed to achieve success at work. Competence brings with it a sense of pride and mastery that is itself intrinsically motivating. Managers can instill a sense of competence in their employees by providing opportunities for training and knowledge gain, expressing positive feedback, and providing challenges that are an appropriate match for employees' skill levels.[105] Employees can build their own competence by engaging in self-directed learning, seeking out feedback from their managers, and managing their own workloads.

Impact reflects the sense that a person's actions "make a difference"—that progress is being made toward fulfilling some important purpose.[106] Phrases such as "moving forward," "being on track," and "getting there" convey a sense of impact.[107] The polar opposite of impact is "learned helplessness"—the sense that it doesn't matter what a person does, nothing will make a difference. Here, phrases such as "stuck in a rut," "at a standstill," or "going nowhere" become more relevant. Managers can instill a sense of impact by celebrating milestones along the journey to task accomplishment, particularly for tasks that span a long time frame.[108] Employees can attain a deeper sense of impact by building the collaborative relationships needed to speed task progress and initiating their own celebrations of "small wins" along the way.

Studies of generational trends point to the increasing interest of psychological empowerment as a motivating force. For example, one survey of 3,332 teens worldwide revealed that 78 percent viewed personal fulfillment as a key motivator.[109] There is also a sense that younger employees enter the workplace with higher expectations for the importance of their roles, the autonomy they'll be given, and the progress they'll make in their organizational careers. That trend is especially apparent in India, where the younger generation is coming of age in a time of unprecedented job opportunities due to the tech-services boom. MindTree, an IT consulting firm headquartered in New Jersey and Bangalore, India, takes steps to prevent young employees from feeling "lost in a sea of people."[110] The company places new hires into "houses" with their own assembly space and work areas, providing opportunities for more personal attention and mentoring. Infosys,

Young employees at MindTree, an information technology consulting firm, are given mentoring and personal attention to build a sense of empowerment.

another IT consulting firm based in Bangalore, established a "Voice of Youth Council" that places a dozen under-30 employees on its executive management committee. The committee gives younger employees the chance to impact the company's operations. Bela Gupta, the council's youngest member at 24 years of age, describes the experience as "very empowering."

SUMMARY: WHY ARE SOME EMPLOYEES MORE MOTIVATED THAN OTHERS?

So what explains why some employees are more motivated than others? As shown in Figure 6-7, answering that question requires considering all the energetic forces that initiate work-related effort, including expectancy theory concepts (expectancy, instrumentality, valence), the existence (or absence) of specific and difficult goals, perceptions of equity, and feelings of psychological empowerment. Unmotivated employees may simply lack confidence due to a lack of expectancy or competence or the assignment of an unachievable goal. Alternatively, such employees may feel their performance is not properly rewarded due to a lack of instrumentality, a lack of valence, or feelings of inequity. Finally, it may be that their work simply isn't challenging or intrinsically rewarding due to the assignment of easy or abstract goals or the absence of meaningfulness, self-determination, and impact.

HOW IMPORTANT IS MOTIVATION?

Does motivation have a significant impact on the two primary outcomes in our integrative model of OB—does it correlate with job performance and organizational commitment? Answering that question is somewhat complicated, because motivation is not just one thing but rather a set of energetic forces. Figure 6-8 summarizes the research evidence linking motivation to job performance and organizational commitment. The figure expresses the likely combined impact of those energetic forces on the two outcomes in our OB model.

6.6

How does motivation affect job performance and organizational commitment?

Turning first to job performance, literally thousands of studies support the relationships between the various motivating forces and task performance. The motivating force with the strongest performance effect is self-efficacy/competence, because people who feel a sense of internal self-confidence tend to outperform those who doubt their capabilities.[111] Difficult goals are the second most powerful motivating force; people who receive such goals outperform the recipients of easy goals.[112] The motivational force created by high levels of valence, instrumentality, and expectancy is the next most powerful motivational variable for task performance.[113] Finally, perceptions of equity have a somewhat weaker effect on task performance.[114]

Less attention has been devoted to the linkages between motivation variables and citizenship and counterproductive behavior. With respect to the former, employees who engage in more work-related effort would seem more likely to perform "extra-mile" sorts of actions, because those actions themselves require extra effort. The best evidence in support of that claim comes from research on equity. Specifically, employees who feel a sense of equity on the job are more likely to engage in citizenship behaviors, particularly when those behaviors aid the organization.[115] The same employees are less likely to engage in counterproductive behaviors, because such behaviors often serve as a retaliation against perceived inequities.[116]

FIGURE 6-7   Why Are Some Employees More Motivated Than Others?

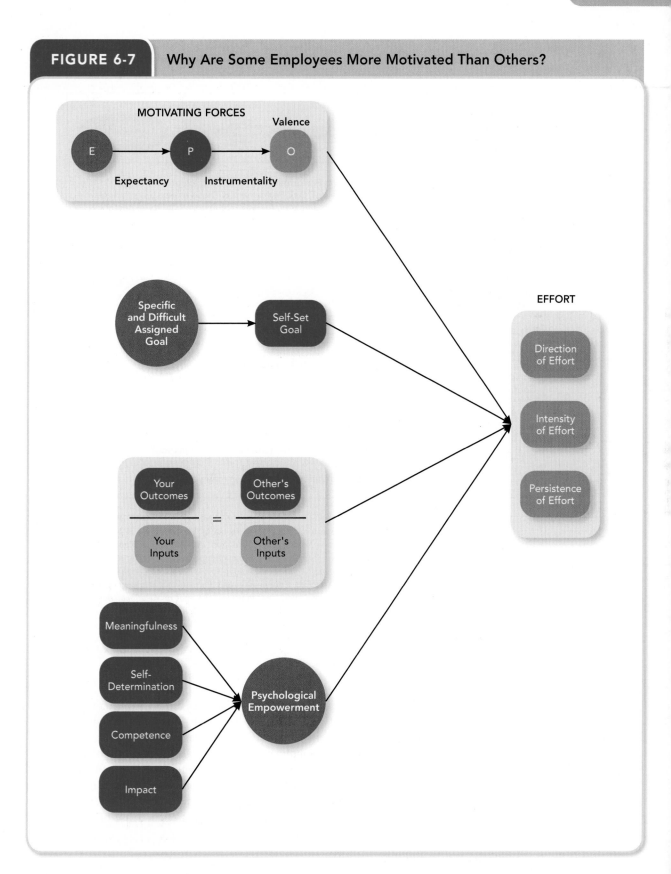

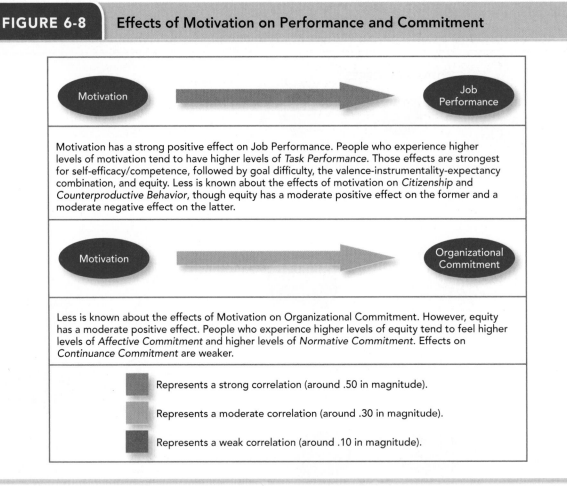

FIGURE 6-8   Effects of Motivation on Performance and Commitment

Motivation → Job Performance

Motivation has a strong positive effect on Job Performance. People who experience higher levels of motivation tend to have higher levels of *Task Performance*. Those effects are strongest for self-efficacy/competence, followed by goal difficulty, the valence-instrumentality-expectancy combination, and equity. Less is known about the effects of motivation on *Citizenship* and *Counterproductive Behavior*, though equity has a moderate positive effect on the former and a moderate negative effect on the latter.

Motivation → Organizational Commitment

Less is known about the effects of Motivation on Organizational Commitment. However, equity has a moderate positive effect. People who experience higher levels of equity tend to feel higher levels of *Affective Commitment* and higher levels of *Normative Commitment*. Effects on *Continuance Commitment* are weaker.

Represents a strong correlation (around .50 in magnitude).

Represents a moderate correlation (around .30 in magnitude).

Represents a weak correlation (around .10 in magnitude).

Sources: Y. Cohen-Charash and P.E. Spector, "The Role of Justice in Organizations: A Meta-Analysis," *Organizational Behavior and Human Decision Processes* 86 (2001), pp. 287–321; J.A. Colquitt, D.E. Conlon, M.J. Wesson, C.O.L.H. Porter, and K.Y. Ng, "Justice at the Millennium: A Meta-Analytic Review of 25 Years of Organizational Justice Research," *Journal of Applied Psychology* 86 (2001), pp. 425–45; J.P. Meyer, D.J. Stanley, L. Herscovitch, and L. Topolnytsky, "Affective, Continuance, and Normative Commitment to the Organization: A Meta-Analysis of Antecedents, Correlates, and Consequences," *Journal of Vocational Behavior* 61 (2002), pp. 20–52; A.D. Stajkovic and F. Luthans, "Self-Efficacy and Work-Related Performance: A Meta-Analysis," *Psychological Bulletin* 124 (1998), pp. 240–61; W. Van Eerde and H. Thierry, "Vroom's Expectancy Models and Work-Related Criteria: A Meta-Analysis," *Journal of Applied Psychology* 81 (1996), pp. 575–86; and R.E. Wood, A.J. Mento, and E.A. Locke, "Task Complexity as a Moderator of Goal Effects: A Meta-Analysis," *Journal of Applied Psychology* 72 (1987), pp. 416–25.

As with citizenship behaviors, the relationship between motivation and organizational commitment seems straightforward. After all, the psychological and physical forms of withdrawal that characterize less committed employees are themselves evidence of low levels of motivation. Clearly employees who are daydreaming, coming in late, and taking longer breaks are struggling to put forth consistently high levels of work effort. Research on equity and organizational commitment offers the clearest insights into the motivation–commitment relationship. Specifically, employees who feel a sense of equity are more emotionally attached to their firms and feel a stronger sense of obligation to remain.[117]

APPLICATION: COMPENSATION SYSTEMS

The most important area in which motivation concepts are applied in organizations is in the design of compensation systems. Table 6-7 provides an overview of many of the elements used in typical compensation systems. We use the term "element" in the table to acknowledge that most organizations use a combination of multiple approaches to compensate their employees. Two points must be noted about Table 6-7. First, the descriptions of the elements are simplistic; the reality is that each of the elements can be implemented and executed in a variety of ways.[118] Second, the elements are designed to do more than just motivate. For example, plans that put pay "at risk" rather than creating increases in base salary are geared toward control of labor costs. As another example, plans that reward unit or organizational performance are designed to reinforce collaboration, information sharing, and monitoring among employees, regardless of their impact on motivation levels.

TABLE 6-7	Compensation Plan Elements
ELEMENT	**DESCRIPTION**
Individual-Focused	
Piece-Rate	A specified rate is paid for each unit produced, each unit sold, or each service provided.
Merit Pay	An increase to base salary is made in accordance with performance evaluation ratings.
Lump-Sum Bonuses	A bonus is received for meeting individual goals but no change is made to base salary. The potential bonus represents "at risk" pay that must be re-earned each year. Base salary may be lower in cases in which potential bonuses may be large.
Recognition Awards	Tangible awards (gift cards, merchandise, trips, special events, time off, plaques) or intangible awards (praise) are given on an impromptu basis to recognize achievement.
Unit-Focused	
Gainsharing	A bonus is received for meeting unit goals (department goals, plant goals, business unit goals) for criteria controllable by employees (labor costs, use of materials, quality). No change is made to base salary. The potential bonus represents "at risk" pay that must be re-earned each year. Base salary may be lower in cases in which potential bonuses may be large.
Organization-Focused	
Profit Sharing	A bonus is received when the publicly reported earnings of a company exceed some minimum level, with the magnitude of the bonus contingent on the magnitude of the profits. No change is made to base salary. The potential bonus represents "at risk" pay that must be re-earned each year. Base salary may be lower in cases in which potential bonuses may be large.

6.7

What steps can organizations take to increase employee motivation?

One way of judging the motivational impact of compensation plan elements is to consider whether the elements provide difficult and specific goals for channeling work effort. Merit pay and profit sharing offer little in the way of difficult and specific goals, because both essentially challenge employees to make next year as good (or better) than this year. In contrast, lump-sum bonuses and gainsharing provide a forum for assigning difficult and specific goals; the former does so at the individual level and the latter at the unit level. Partly for this reason, both types of plans have been credited with improvements in employee productivity.[119]

Another way of judging the motivational impact of the compensation plan elements is to consider the correspondence between individual performance levels and individual monetary outcomes. After all, that correspondence influences perceptions of both instrumentality and equity. Profit sharing, for example, is unlikely to have strong motivational consequences because an individual employee can do little to improve the profitability of the company, regardless of his or her job performance.[120] Instrumentality and equity are more achievable with gainsharing, because the relevant unit is smaller and the relevant outcomes are more controllable. Still, the highest instrumentality and equity levels will typically be achieved through individual-focused compensation elements. Piece-rate plans can create stronger performance–outcome contingencies but are difficult to apply outside of manufacturing, sales, and service contexts. Merit pay represents the most common element of organizational compensation plans, yet the pay increase for top performers (5.6 percent on average) is only modestly greater than the pay increase for average performers (3.3 percent on average).[121] Moreover, the effects of merit pay raises depends largely on what employees expect to get,[122] and it can be difficult for managers to effectively manage those expectations.

Perhaps the most critical factor in merit pay is the accuracy of the performance evaluations that feed into the compensation decision. Think of all the times you've been evaluated by someone else, whether in school or in the workplace. How many times have you reacted by thinking, "Where did that rating come from?" or "I think I'm being evaluated on the wrong things!" Performance evaluation experts suggest that employees should be evaluated on behaviors that are controllable by the employees (see Chapter 2 on Job Performance for more discussion of such issues), observable by managers, and critical to the implementation of the firm's strategy.[123] The managers who conduct evaluations also need to be trained in how to conduct them, which typically involves gaining knowledge of the relevant behaviors ahead of time and being taught to keep records of employee behavior between evaluation sessions.[124]

Even if employees are evaluated on the right things by a boss who has a good handle on their performance, it's important to understand the context in which performance ratings occur. Some managers might knowingly give inaccurate evaluations due to workplace politics or a desire to not "make waves." One survey showed that 70 percent of managers have trouble giving poor ratings to underachieving employees.[125] Unfortunately, such practices only serve to damage instrumentality and equity, because they fail to separate star employees from struggling employees. To ensure that such separation occurs, Yahoo has instituted a "stacked ranking" system to determine compensation, in which managers rank all the employees within their unit from top to bottom.[126] Employees at the top end of those rankings then receive higher bonuses than employees at the bottom end. Although such practices raise concerns about employee morale and excessive competitiveness, research suggests that such forced distribution systems can boost the performance of a company's workforce, especially for the first few years after their implementation.[127]

TAKEAWAYS

6.1 Motivation is defined as a set of energetic forces that originates both within and outside an employee, initiates work-related effort, and determines its direction, intensity, and persistence.

6.2 According to expectancy theory, effort is directed toward behaviors when effort is believed to result in performance (expectancy), performance is believed to result in outcomes (instrumentality), and those outcomes are anticipated to be valuable (valence).

6.3 According to goal setting theory, goals become strong drivers of motivation and performance when they are difficult and specific. Specific and difficult goals affect performance by increasing self-set goals and task strategies. Those effects occur more frequently when employees are given feedback, tasks are not too complex, and goal commitment is high.

6.4 According to equity theory, rewards are equitable when a person's ratio of outcomes to inputs matches those of some relevant comparison other. A sense of inequity triggers equity distress. Underreward inequity typically results in lower levels of motivation or higher levels of counterproductive behavior. Overreward inequity typically results in cognitive distortion, in which inputs are reevaluated in a more positive light.

6.5 Psychological empowerment reflects an energy rooted in the belief that tasks are contributing to some larger purpose. Psychological empowerment is fostered when work goals appeal to employees' passions (meaningfulness), employees have a sense of choice regarding work tasks (self-determination), employees feel capable of performing successfully (competence), and employees feel they are making progress toward fulfilling their purpose (impact).

6.6 Motivation has a strong positive relationship with job performance and a moderate positive relationship with organizational commitment. Of all the energetic forces subsumed by motivation, self-efficacy/competence has the strongest relationship with performance.

6.7 Organizations use compensation practices to increase motivation. Those practices may include individual-focused elements (piece-rate, merit pay, lump-sum bonuses, recognition awards), unit-focused elements (gainsharing), or organization-focused elements (profit sharing).

KEY TERMS

DISCUSSION QUESTIONS

6.1 Which of the outcomes in Table 6-2 are most appealing to you? Are you more attracted to extrinsic outcomes or intrinsic outcomes? Do you think that your preferences will change as you get older?

6.2 Assume that you were working on a group project and that one of your teammates was nervous about speaking in front of the class during the presentation. Drawing on Figure 6-3, what exactly could you do to make your classmate feel more confident?

6.3 Consider the five strategies for fostering goal commitment (rewards, publicity, support, participation, and resources). Which of those strategies do you think is most effective? Can you picture any of them having potential drawbacks?

6.4 How do you tend to respond when you experience overreward and underreward inequity? Why do you respond that way rather than with some other combination in Figure 6-6?

6.5 Think about a job that you've held in which you felt very low levels of psychological empowerment. What could the organization have done to increase empowerment levels?

CASE: ENTERPRISE RENT-A-CAR

The opportunity for promotion is one of the primary motivators at Enterprise. Stephen Cullen, an assistant manager in Fort Pierce, Florida, notes, "Everyone here looks at you as future management potential. Your goal is to get everyone under you promoted."[128] That promotability, however, depends on both individual and branch-level factors. On an individual basis, employees are often judged on their ability to sign up customers for supplemental liability protection.[129] The company offers three choices for coverage: a basic damage waiver, a supplemental protection package, and personal accident insurance. The goal is to have customers sign up for all three packages, or "trips," thereby adding around $25 a day to the customer's purchase. Management trainees are taught how to sell these packages to customers using role plays and are encouraged to experiment with different methods of persuasion. Those efforts continue until a customer says "no" three times. Employees in a given region compete for bonuses of $50 or $100 based on their "protection stats," and excelling in this task adds to an employee's perceived potential.

On a branch-wide basis, promotions depend on scores on the Enterprise Service Quality Index, or ESQi.[130] The ESQi is calculated by an independent survey group each month, based on follow-up phone calls to one out of every 15 Enterprise customers. The customers are asked how satisfied they were with their rental experience, on a scale ranging from "completely satisfied" to "completely dissatisfied." If 50 percent of the respondents for a given branch answer "completely satisfied," that branch earns an ESQi score of 50. The ESQi average across Enterprise branches typically hovers around 80, signaling that most customers are indeed quite satisfied. If a branch falls below that average, however, its employees are no longer eligible for promotions or transfers. Employees therefore understand that their careers depend on making their branches above average—and keeping them there.

6.1 As an Enterprise employee, would you be motivated by bonuses for signing up customers for supplemental liability protection? Why or why not?

6.2 Would you be motivated by making promotions contingent on your branch's ESQi score? Why or why not?

6.3 Consider these two practices in the context of the theories reviewed in this chapter (expectancy theory, goal setting theory, equity theory, psychological empowerment). Which theories would support the effectiveness of these strategies and which theories might raise doubts about their effectiveness?

EXERCISE: EXPLAINING PAY DIFFERENCES

The purpose of this exercise is to demonstrate how compensation can be used to influence motivation. This exercise uses groups, so your instructor will either assign you to a group or ask you to create your own group. The exercise has the following steps:

6.1 Read the following scenario:

Chris Clements and Pat Palmer are both computer programmers working for the same *Fortune* 500 company. One day they found out that Chris earns $50,820 per year, while Pat earns $62,890. Chris was surprised and said, "I can't think of any reason why we should be paid so differently." "I can think of at least 10 reasons," Pat responded. Can you, like Pat, think of at least 10 reasons that could cause this difference in salary between two people? These reasons can be legal or illegal, wise or unwise.

6.2 Going around the group from member to member, generate a list of 10 conceivable reasons why Pat may be earning more than Chris. Remember, the reasons can be legal or illegal, wise or unwise.

6.3 Consider whether the theories discussed in the chapter—expectancy theory, goal setting theory, equity theory, and psychological empowerment—are relevant to the list of reasons you've generated. Maybe one of the theories supports the wisdom of a given reason. For example, maybe Pat's job is more difficult than Chris's job. Equity theory would support the wisdom of that reason because job difficulty is a relevant input. Maybe one of the theories questions the wisdom of a given reason. For example, maybe Chris's boss believes that salary increases are a poor use of limited financial resources. Expectancy theory would question the wisdom of that reason because that philosophy harms instrumentality.

6.4   Elect a group member to write the group's 10 reasons on the board. Then indicate which theories are relevant to the various reasons by writing one or more of the following abbreviations next to a given reason: EX for expectancy theory, GS for goal setting theory, EQ for equity theory, and PE for psychological empowerment.

6.5   Class discussion (whether in groups or as a class) should center on which theories seem most relevant to the potential reasons for the pay differences between Chris and Pat. Are there some potential reasons that don't seem relevant to any of the four theories? Do those reasons tend to be legal or illegal, wise or unwise?

Source: Adapted from M.K. Renard, "It's All About the Money: Chris and Pat Compare Salaries," *Journal of Management Education* 32 (2008), pp. 248–61.

ENDNOTES

6.1   Loomis, C.J. "The Big Surprise Is Enterprise." *Fortune*, July 14, 2006, http://money.cnn.com/magazines/fortune/fortune_archive/2006/07/24/8381691/index.htm (June 24, 2009).

6.2   Ibid.

6.3   Gerdes, L. "The Best Places to Launch a Career." *BusinessWeek*, September 18, 2006, http://www.businessweek.com/magazine/content/06_38/b4001601.htm (June 24, 2009); Gerdes, L. "The Best Places to Launch a Career." *BusinessWeek*, September 24, 2007, pp. 48–60; Gerdes, L. "The Best Places to Launch a Career." *BusinessWeek*, September 15, 2008, pp. 36–44.

6.4   Loomis, "The Big Surprise Is Enterprise."

6.5   Ibid.

6.6   Frankel, A. *Punching In*. New York: HarperCollins, 2007.

6.7   Loomis, "The Big Surprise Is Enterprise."

6.8   Lehman, P. "No. 5 Enterprise: A Clear Road to the Top." *BusinessWeek*, September 18, 2006, http://www.businessweek.com/magazine/content/06_38/b4001609.htm?chan=careers_first+jobs_employers (June 24, 2009).

6.9   Gerdes, "The Best Place to Launch a Career." 2008.

6.10 Frankel, *Punching In*.

6.11 Loomis, "The Big Surprise Is Enterprise."

6.12 "Enterprise Rent-A-Car Ranks Highest on J.D. Power Survey." *St. Louis Business Journal*, November 15, 2005, http://stlouis.bizjournals.com/stlouis/stories/2005/11/14/daily34.html (June 24, 2009).

6.13 Steers, R.M.; R.T. Mowday; and D. Shapiro. "The Future of Work Motivation." *Academy of Management Review* 29 (2004), pp. 379–87; and Latham, G.P. *Work Motivation: History, Theory, Research, and Practice*. Thousand Oaks, CA: Sage, 2006.

6.14 Latham, G.P., and C.C. Pinder. "Work Motivation Theory and Research at the Dawn of the Twenty-First Century." *Annual Review of Psychology* 56 (2005), pp. 485–516.

6.15 Maier, N.R.F. *Psychology in Industry.* 2nd ed. Boston: Houghton- Mifflin, 1955.

6.16 Morrison, M., and C. Frantz. "Tiger Woods Timeline." http://www.infoplease.com/spot/tigertime1.html (June 29, 2009).

6.17 Kahn, W.A. "Psychological Conditions of Personal Engagement and Disengagement at Work." *Academy of Management Journal* 33 (1990), pp. 692–724.

6.18 Rich, B.L.; J.A. LePine; and E.R. Crawford. "Job Engagement: Antecedents and Effects on Job Performance." *Academy of Management Journal* 52 (2009); Schaufeli, W.B.; M. Salanova; V. Gonzalez-Roma; and A.B. Bakker. "The Measurement of Engagement and Burnout: A Two Sample Confirmatory Factor Analytic Approach." *Journal of Happiness Studies* 3 (2002), pp. 71–92; and Macy, W.H., and B. Schneider. "The Meaning of Employee Engagement." *Industrial and Organizational Psychology* 1 (2008), pp. 3–30.

6.19 Ibid.; and Rothbard, N.P. "Enriching or Depleting? The Dynamics of Engagement in Work and Family Roles." *Administrative Science Quarterly* 46 (2001), pp. 655–84.

6.20 Vroom, V.H. *Work and Motivation.* New York: Wiley, 1964.

6.21 Ibid.; see also Thorndike, E.L. "The Law of Effect." *American Journal of Psychology* 39 (1964), pp. 212–22; Hull, C.L. *Essentials of Behavior.* New Haven: Yale University Press, 1951; and Postman, L. "The History and Present Status of the Law of Effect." *Psychological Bulletin* 44 (1947), pp. 489–563.

6.22 Bandura, A. "Self-Efficacy: Toward a Unifying Theory of Behavioral Change." *Psychological Review* 84 (1977), pp. 191–215.

6.23 Brockner, J. *Self-Esteem at Work.* Lexington, MA: Lexington Books, 1988.

6.24 Bandura, "Self-Efficacy."

6.25 Ibid.

6.26 Ibid.

6.27 Gist, M.E., and T.R. Mitchell. "Self-Efficacy: A Theoretical Analysis of its Determinants and Malleability." *Academy of Management Review* 17 (1992), pp. 183–211.

6.28 Vroom, *Work and Motivation.*

6.29 Pinder, C.C. *Work Motivation.* Glenview, IL: Scott, Foresman, 1984.

6.30 Stillings, J., and L. Snyder. "Up Front: The Stat." *BusinessWeek,* July 4, 2005, p. 12.

6.31 Hansen, F. "The Great Pay Freeze." *Workforce Management*, March 16, 2009, pp. 24–25.

6.32 McGregor, J. "Cutting Salaries Instead of Jobs." *BusinessWeek*, June 8, 2009, pp. 46–48; and Conlin, M. "Pay Cuts Made Palatable." *BusinessWeek*, May 4, 2009, p. 67.

6.33 Conlin, "Pay Cuts Made Palatable"; and Conlin, M. "The Case for Unequal Perks." *BusinessWeek*, March 23 and 30, 2009, pp. 54–55.

6.34 McGregor. "Cutting Salaries Instead of Jobs."

6.35 Hansen. "The Great Pay Freeze."

6.36 Vroom, *Work and Motivation.*

6.37 Pinder, *Work Motivation.*

6.38 Landy, F.J., and W.S. Becker. "Motivation Theory Reconsidered." In *Research in Organizational Behavior,* Vol. 9, ed. B.M. Staw and L.L. Cummings. Greenwich, CT: JAI Press, 1987, pp. 1–38; and Naylor, J.C.; D.R. Pritchard; and D.R. Ilgen. *A Theory of Behavior in Organizations.* New York: Academic Press, 1980.

6.39   Maslow, A.H. "A Theory of Human Motivation." *Psychological Review* 50 (1943), pp. 370–96; and Alderfer, C.P. "An Empirical Test of a New Theory of Human Needs." *Organizational Behavior and Human Performance* 4 (1969), pp. 142–75.

6.40   Ibid.; see also Deci, E.L., and R.M. Ryan. "The 'What' and 'Why' of Goal Pursuits: Human Needs and the Self-Determination of Behavior." *Psychological Inquiry* 11 (2000), pp. 227–68; Cropanzano, R.; Z.S. Byrne; D.R. Bobocel; and D.R. Rupp. "Moral Virtues, Fairness Heuristics, Social Entities, and Other Denizens of Organizational Justice." *Journal of Vocational Behavior* 58 (2001), pp. 164–209; Williams, K.D. "Social Ostracism." In *Aversive Interpersonal Behaviors,* ed. R.M. Kowalski. New York: Plenum Press, 1997, pp. 133–70; and Thomas, K.W., and B.A. Velthouse. "Cognitive Elements of Empowerment: An 'Interpretive' Model of Intrinsic Task Motivation." *Academy of Management Review* 15 (1990), pp. 666–81.

6.41   Deci and Ryan, "The 'What' and 'Why'"; and Naylor, Pritchard, and Ilgen, *A Theory of Behavior in Organizations.*

6.42   Ibid.

6.43   Huff, C. "Motivating the World." *Workforce Management,* September 24, 2007, pp. 25–31.

6.44   Speizer, I. "Incentives Catch on Overseas, but Value of Awards Can Too Easily Get Lost in Translation." *Workforce,* November 21, 2005, pp. 46–49.

6.45   Huff, "Motivating the World"; and Speizer, "Incentives Catch on Overseas."

6.46   Rynes, S.L.; B. Gerhart; and K.A. Minette. "The Importance of Pay in Employee Motivation: Discrepancies between What People Say and What They Do." *Human Resource Management* 43 (2004), pp. 381–94; and Rynes, S.L.; K.G. Brown; and A.E. Colbert. "Seven Common Misconceptions about Human Resource Practices: Research Findings Versus Practitioner Beliefs." *Academy of Management Executive* 16 (2002), pp. 92–102.

6.47   Rynes, Gerhart, and Minette, "The Importance of Pay."

6.48   Ibid.

6.49   Mitchell, T.R., and A.E. Mickel. "The Meaning of Money: An Individual Differences Perspective." *Academy of Management Review* 24 (1999), pp. 568–78.

6.50   Tang, T.L. "The Meaning of Money Revisited." *Journal of Organizational Behavior* 13 (1992), pp. 197–202; and Mickel, A.E., and L.A. Barron. "Getting 'More Bang for the Buck'." *Journal of Management Inquiry* 17 (2008), pp. 329–38.

6.51   Tang, T.L. "The Development of a Short Money Ethic Scale: Attitudes Toward Money and Pay Satisfaction Revisited." *Personality and Individual Differences* 19 (1995), pp. 809–16.

6.52   Tang, "The Meaning of Money Revisited."

6.53   Ibid.; and Tang, "The Development of a Short Money Ethic Scale."

6.54   Tang, "The Development of a Short Money Ethic Scale."

6.55   Vroom, *Work and Motivation;* and Lawler E.E. III, and J.L. Suttle. "Expectancy Theory and Job Behavior." *Organizational Behavior and Human Performance* 9 (1973), pp. 482–503.

6.56   Locke, E.A. "Toward a Theory of Task Motivation and Incentives." *Organizational Behavior and Human Performance* 3 (1968), pp. 157–89.

6.57   Locke, E.A.; K.N. Shaw; L.M. Saari; and G.P. Latham. "Goal Setting and Task Performance: 1969–1980." *Psychological Bulletin* 90 (1981), pp. 125–52.

6.58   Locke, E.A.; and G.P. Latham. *A Theory of Goal Setting and Task Performance.* Englewood Cliffs, NJ: Prentice Hall, 1990.

6.59   Ibid.

6.60   Ibid.

6.61   Ibid.; see also Locke, E.A.; and G.P. Latham. "Building a Practically Useful Theory of Goal Setting and Task Motivation: A 35-Year Odyssey." *American Psychologist* 57 (2002), pp. 705–17; and Latham, G.P. "Motivate Employee Performance through Goal-Setting." In *Blackwell Handbook of Principles of Organizational Behavior,* ed. E.A. Locke. Malden, MA: Blackwell, 2000, pp. 107–19.

6.62   Locke and Latham, *A Theory of Goal Setting.*

6.63   Locke et al., "Goal Setting and Task Performance."

6.64   Ibid.; Locke and Latham, *A Theory of Goal Setting*; and Locke and Latham, "Building a Practically Useful Theory."

6.65   Wood, R.E.; A.J. Mento; and E.A. Locke. "Task Complexity as a Moderator of Goal Effects: A Meta-Analysis." *Journal of Applied Psychology* 72 (1987), pp. 416–25.

6.66   Ibid.

6.67   Barrett, A. "Cracking the Whip at Wyeth." *BusinessWeek,* February 6, 2006, pp. 70–71.

6.68   Hollenbeck, J.R., and H.J. Klein. "Goal Commitment and the Goal-Setting Process: Problems, Prospects, and Proposal for Future Research." *Journal of Applied Psychology* 72 (1987), pp. 212–20; see also Locke et al., "Goal Setting and Task Performance."

6.69   Klein, H.J.; M.J. Wesson; J.R. Hollenbeck; and B.J. Alge. "Goal Commitment and the Goal-Setting Process: Conceptual Clarification and Empirical Synthesis." *Journal of Applied Psychology* 84 (1999), pp. 885–96; and Donovan, J.J., and D.J. Radosevich. "The Moderating Role of Goal Commitment on the Goal Difficulty–Performance Relationship. A Meta-Analytic Review and Critical Reanalysis." *Journal of Applied Psychology* 83 (1998), pp. 308–15.

6.70   Hollenbeck and Klein, "Goal Commitment and the Goal-Setting Process"; Klein et al., "Goal Commitment"; Locke, E.A.; G.P Latham; and M. Erez. "The Determinants of Goal Commitment." *Academy of Management Review* 13 (1988), pp. 23–29; and Latham, G.P. "The Motivational Benefits of Goal-Setting." *Academy of Management Executive* 18 (2004), pp. 126–29.

6.71   Shaw, K.N. "Changing the Goal Setting Process at Microsoft." *Academy of Management Executive* 18 (2004), pp. 139–42.

6.72   Ibid.

6.73   Aguinis, H., and C.A. Henle. "The Search for Universals in Cross-Cultural Organizational Behavior." In *Organizational Behavior: The State of the Science,* ed. J. Greenberg. Mahwah, NJ: Erlbaum, 2003, pp. 373–411.

6.74   Earley, P.C., and C.B Gibson. "Taking Stock in our Progress on

Individualism–Collectivism: 100 Years of Solidarity and Community." *Journal of Management* 24 (1998), pp. 265–304.

6.75   Erez, M. "A Culture-Based Model of Work Motivation." In *New Perspectives on International Industrial/Organizational Psychology,* ed. P.C. Earley and M. Erez. San Francisco: New Lexington Press, 1997, pp. 193–242.

6.76   Erez, M., and P.C. Earley. "Comparative Analysis of Goal-Setting Strategies Across Cultures." *Journal of Applied Psychology* 72 (1987), pp. 658–65.

6.77   Audia, P.G., and S. Tams. "Goal Setting, Performance Appraisal, and Feedback Across Cultures." In *Blackwell Handbook of Cross-Cultural Management,* ed. M.J. Gannon and K.L. Newman. Malden, MA: Blackwell, 2002, pp. 142–54.

6.78   Adams, J.S., and W.B. Rosenbaum. "The Relationship of Worker Productivity to Cognitive Dissonance about Wage Inequities." *Journal of Applied Psychology* 46 (1962), pp. 161–64.

6.79   Adams, J.S. "Inequity in Social Exchange." In *Advances in Experimental Social Psychology,* Vol. 2, ed. L. Berkowitz. New York: Academic Press, 1965, pp. 267–99; and Homans, G.C. *Social Behaviour: Its Elementary Forms.* London: Routledge & Kegan Paul, 1961.

6.80   Ibid.

6.81   Adams, "Inequality in Social Exchange."

6.82   Ibid.

6.83   Greenberg, J. "Employee Theft as a Reaction to Underpayment Inequity: The Hidden Cost of Paycuts." *Journal of Applied Psychology* 75 (1990), pp. 561–68; and Greenberg,

J. "Stealing in the Name of Justice: Informational and Interpersonal Moderators of Theft Reactions to Underpayment Inequity." *Organizational Behavior and Human Decision Processes* 54 (1993), pp. 81–103.

6.84   Adams, "Inequality in Social Exchange."

6.85   Scholl, R.W.; E.A. Cooper; and J.F. McKenna. "Referent Selection in Determining Equity Perceptions: Differential Effects on Behavioral and Attitudinal Outcomes." *Personnel Psychology* 40 (1987), pp. 113–24.

6.86   Ibid.

6.87   Ibid.; see also Finn, R.H., and S.M. Lee. "Salary Equity: Its Determination, Analysis, and Correlates." *Journal of Applied Psychology* 56 (1972), pp. 283–92.

6.88   Scholl, Cooper, and McKenna, "Referent Selection."

6.89   DeCarlo, S. "Top Paid CEO's." *Forbes,* April 30, 2008, http://www.forbes.com/2008/04/30/ceo-pay-compensation-lead-best-bosses08-cx-sd_0430ceo_intro.html?boxes=custom (June 26, 2009).

6.90   Kirkland, R. "The Real CEO." *Fortune,* July 10, 2006, pp. 78–92.

6.91   Sulkowicz, K. "CEO Pay: The Prestige, the Peril." *BusinessWeek,* November 20, 2006, p. 18.

6.92   DeCarlo, S. "By the Numbers: Overpaid Bosses." *Forbes,* April 30, 2008, http://www.forbes.com/2008/04/30/overpaid-bosses-ceos-lead-bestbosses08-cz_sd_0430overpaidceo_slide_2.html?thisSpeed=20000 (June 26, 2009).

6.93   DeCarlo, "Top Paid CEO's."

6.94 Colella, A.; R.L. Paetzold; A. Zard-koohi; and M. Wesson. "Exposing Pay Secrecy." *Academy of Management Review 32* (2007), pp. 55–71.

6.95 Ibid.

6.96 Thomas, K.W., and B.A. Velthouse. "Cognitive Elements of Empowerment: An 'Interpretive' Model of Intrinsic Task Motivation." *Academy of Management Review* 15 (1990), pp. 666–81.

6.97 Hackman, J.R., and G.R. Oldham. *Work Redesign.* Reading, MA: Addison-Wesley, 1980.

6.98 Thomas and Velthouse, "Cognitive Elements of Empowerment"; Spreitzer, G.M. "Psychological Empowerment in the Workplace: Dimensions, Measurement, and Validation." *Academy of Management Journal* 38 (1995), pp. 1442–65; Deci, E.L., and R.M. Ryan. *Intrinsic Motivation and Self-Determination in Human Behavior.* New York: Plenum, 1985; and Hackman and Oldham, *Work Redesign.*

6.99 Thomas, K.W. *Intrinsic Motivation at Work: Building Energy and Commitment.* San Francisco, CA: Berrett-Koehler Publishers, 2000.

6.100 Ibid.

6.101 Bunderson, J.S., and J.A. Thompson. "The Call of the Wild: Zookeepers, Callings, and the Double-Edged Sword of Deeply Meaningful Work." *Administrative Science Quarterly* 54 (2009), pp. 32–57; and Duffy, R.D., and W.E. Sedlacek. "The Presence of and Search for a Calling: Connections to Career Development." *Journal of Vocational Behavior* 70 (2007), pp. 590–601.

6.102 Thomas and Velthouse, "Cognitive Elements of Empowerment";

and Spreitzer, "Psychological Empowerment."

6.103 Thomas, *Intrinsic Motivation at Work.*

6.104 Thomas and Velthouse, "Cognitive Elements of Empowerment"; and Spreitzer, "Psychological Empowerment."

6.105 Thomas, *Intrinsic Motivation at Work.*

6.106 Thomas and Velthouse, "Cognitive Elements of Empowerment."

6.107 Thomas, *Intrinsic Motivation at Work.*

6.108 Ibid.

6.109 Gerdes, L. "Get Ready for a Pickier Workforce." *BusinessWeek*, September 18, 2006, p. 82.

6.110 Hamm, S. "Young and Impatient in India." *BusinessWeek*, January 28, 2008, pp. 45–48.

6.111 Stajkovic, A.D., and F. Luthans. "Self-Efficacy and Work-Related Performance: A Meta-Analysis." *Psychological Bulletin* 124 (1998), pp. 240–61.

6.112 Wood, Mento, and Locke, "Task Complexity as a Moderator."

6.113 Van Eerde, W., and H. Thierry. "Vroom's Expectancy Models and Work-Related Criteria: A Meta-Analysis." *Journal of Applied Psychology* 81 (1996), pp. 575–86.

6.114 Cohen-Charash, Y., and P.E. Spector. "The Role of Justice in Organizations: A Meta-Analysis." *Organizational Behavior and Human Decision Processes* 86 (2001), pp. 287–321; and Colquitt, J.A.; D.E. Conlon; M.J. Wesson; C.O.L.H. Porter; and K.Y. Ng. "Justice at the Millennium: A Meta-Analytic Review of 25 Years of Organizational Justice Research."

Journal of Applied Psychology 86 (2001), pp. 425–45.

6.115   Ibid.

6.116   Ibid.

6.117   Ibid.

6.118   Lawler, E.E., III. *Rewarding Excellence: Pay Strategies for the New Economy.* San Francisco, CA: Jossey-Bass, 2000.

6.119   Ibid.; see also Durham, C.C., and K.M. Bartol. "Pay for Performance." In *Handbook of Principles of Organizational Behavior,* ed. E.A. Locke. Malden, MA: Blackwell, 2000, pp. 150–65; and Gerhart, B.; H.B. Minkoff; and R.N. Olsen. "Employee Compensation: Theory, Practice, and Evidence." In *Handbook of Human Resource Management,* ed. G.R. Ferris, S.D. Rosen, and D.T. Barnum. Malden, MA: Blackwell, 1995, pp. 528–47

6.120   Ibid.

6.121   Hansen, F. "Pushing Performance Management." *Workforce Management,* November 3, 2008, pp. 33–39.

6.122   Schaubroeck, J.; J.D. Shaw; M.K. Duffy; and A. Mitra. "An Under-Met and Over-Met Expectations Model of Employee Reactions to Merit Raises." *Journal of Applied Psychology* 93 (2008), pp. 424–34.

6.123   Latham, G., and S. Latham. "Overlooking Theory and Research in Performance Appraisal at One's Peril: Much Done, More to Do." In *Industrial and Organizational Psychology: Linking Theory with Practice,* ed. C.L. Cooper and E.A. Locke. Oxford, UK: Blackwell, 2000, pp. 199–215.

6.124   Ibid.

6.125   Sulkowicz, K. "Straight Talk at Review Time." *BusinessWeek*, September 10, 2007, p. 16.

6.126   McGregor, J. "The Struggle to Measure Performance." *BusinessWeek,* January 9, 2006, pp. 26–28.

6.127   Scullen, S.E.; P.K. Bergey; and L. Aiman-Smith. "Forced Distribution Rating Systems and the Improvement of Workforce Potential: A Baseline Simulation." *Personnel Psychology* 58 (2005), pp. 1–32.

6.128   Lehman, "No. 5 Enterprise: A Clear Road to the Top."

6.129   Frankel, *Punching In*.

6.130   Loomis, "The Big Surprise Is Enterprise"; and Frankel, *Punching In*.

chapter 7

Trust, Justice, and Ethics

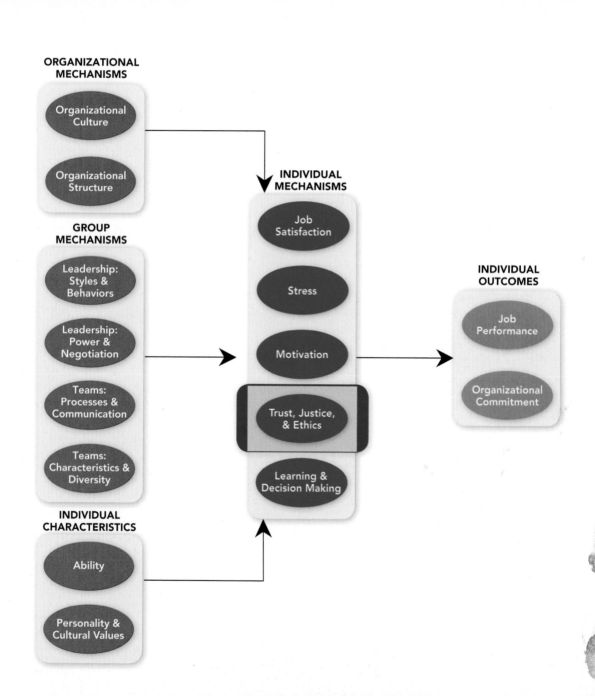

ORGANIZATIONAL MECHANISMS

- Organizational Culture
- Organizational Structure

GROUP MECHANISMS

- Leadership: Styles & Behaviors
- Leadership: Power & Negotiation
- Teams: Processes & Communication
- Teams: Characteristics & Diversity

INDIVIDUAL CHARACTERISTICS

- Ability
- Personality & Cultural Values

INDIVIDUAL MECHANISMS

- Job Satisfaction
- Stress
- Motivation
- Trust, Justice, & Ethics
- Learning & Decision Making

INDIVIDUAL OUTCOMES

- Job Performance
- Organizational Commitment

✓ LEARNING GOALS

After reading this chapter, you should be able to answer the following questions:

7.1 What is trust, and how does it relate to justice and ethics?

7.2 In what three sources can trust be rooted?

7.3 What dimensions can be used to describe the trustworthiness of an authority?

7.4 What dimensions can be used to describe the fairness of an authority's decision making?

7.5 What is the four-component model of ethical decision making?

7.6 How does trust affect job performance and organizational commitment?

7.7 What steps can organizations take to become more trustworthy?

NIKE

The columns of running shoes stretch 8 feet high and 20 feet wide. How do you decide which ones to try on? Price? Color? Nike hopes you narrow down your choices by focusing on brand. The shoe giant, headquartered in Beaverton, Oregon, has been a dominant force in the shoe and athletic apparel markets for decades. Scores of weekend warriors have looked to the Nike Air—that lightweight air pocket in the heels of many Nike shoes—to give them that extra step or that added bit of comfort.[1] In the 1990s, however, many of those same weekend warriors were confronted with the reality of how those shoes were made. That's when disclosures of sweatshop conditions and labor abuses sparked protests outside Nike stores and boycotts on many college campuses. In 1998, founder and then-CEO Phil Knight was forced to admit that the "Nike product has become synonymous with slave wages, forced overtime, and arbitrary abuse."[2]

Nike has worked hard to rebuild trust in its brand over the past decade. Nike became the first company in the industry to post the names and locations of its 700 factories—most located in China, Vietnam, Indonesia, and Thailand—on the Web (see www.nikeresponsibility.com).[3] It created a code of conduct that sets standards for wages, the number of hours in a standard workweek, and the rules for overtime pay. It also paid a network of auditors to perform inspections of factories, giving each a grade between A and D. Unfortunately, it's not clear that those efforts are paying off. A recent analysis of the inspection data by a professor at MIT noted that despite "significant efforts and investments by Nike . . . workplace conditions in almost 80% of its suppliers have either remained the same or worsened over time."[4] Almost one-third of the factories in one audit earned D grades because of multiple violations, including failing to pay the minimum wage and forcing employees to work more than 14 days in a row.

Why has it been so difficult for Nike to improve the working conditions in its factories? One reason is that government regulations are weak in emerging economies, placing more pressure on companies to police their factories.[5] And many of the facilities compete for Nike's business, with higher employee salaries making their pricing less competitive.[6] Those factories often find themselves working under tight deadlines, with power outages or design adjustments triggering work shift abuses. Other factories have learned to fool the audits by keeping fake records, distributing scripts for employees to read if they're questioned, or shifting work to secret subcontractors that violate standards. And dropping a troubled facility can raise its own ethical issues for Nike, as it results in the loss of jobs that may be vital to that local economy. For its part, Nike has reacted to the limitations of its auditing strategy by helping convert factories to more modern manufacturing techniques and seeking to limit its own last-minute design adjustments.[7] Those sorts of steps will reduce the pressures on the facilities, eliminating some of the need for overtime and excessively long work schedules. Nike's current CEO, Mark Parker, summarizes this state of affairs by noting, "I'm proud of what we've accomplished, but we're still not where we need to be. This is a never-ending challenge."[8]

TRUST, JUSTICE, AND ETHICS

One reason Nike's CEO cares so deeply about the problems in the company's factories is that they can damage the company's reputation. An organization's **reputation** reflects the prominence of its brand in the minds of the public and the perceived quality of its goods and services.[9] Reputation is an intangible asset that can take a long time to build but, as Ben Franklin once noted, can be cracked as easily as glass or china.[10] An organization's reputation matters not just to potential consumers but also to potential employees. Recruitment experts maintain that top performers want to work at organizations with clean reputations, in part because they want to protect their own personal image. Indeed, one survey found that 78 percent of adults would rather work at a company with an excellent reputation and an average salary than at a company with a high salary and a poor reputation.[11] Who are some companies with excellent reputations? Table 7-1 provides the top 25 from *Fortune*'s list of "Most Admired Companies" (with Nike placing 23rd).

Reputations depend on many things, but one of the most important factors is trust. **Trust** is defined as the willingness to be vulnerable to a trustee based on positive expectations about the trustee's actions and intentions.[12] If a customer in a shoe store trusts the quality of Nike's products, that customer is willing to accept the consequences of paying money for Nike shoes. If a potential recruit trusts the words of Nike management, that recruit is willing to accept the consequences of becoming a member of the organization. Both examples illustrate that trusting reflects a willingness to "put yourself out there," even though doing so could be met with disappointment. The examples also highlight the difference between "trust" and "risk." Actually making yourself vulnerable—by buying shoes or accepting a job—constitutes risk. Trust reflects the willingness to take that risk. Unfortunately, trust in many companies has declined sharply due to corporate scandals and

7.1

What is trust, and how does it relate to justice and ethics?

TABLE 7-1	The World's Most Admired Companies	
1. Apple		14. Wells Fargo
2. Berkshire Hathaway		15. Goldman Sachs
3. Toyota Motor		16. McDonald's
4. Google		17. IBM
5. Johnson & Johnson		18. 3M
6. Proctor & Gamble		19. Target
7. FedEx		20. J.P. Morgan Chase
8. Southwest Airlines		21. PepsiCo
9. General Electric		22. Costco Wholesale
10. Microsoft		23. Nike
11. Wal-Mart		24. Nordstrom
12. Coca-Cola		25. ExxonMobil
13. Walt Disney		

Source: G. Colvin, "All-Stars: The World's Most Admired Companies," *Fortune*, March 16, 2009, pp. 75–78.

the economic downturn. Indeed, the same *Fortune* article that introduced the most admired companies noted that trust in U.S. businesses is lower than it was after the Enron collapse and the dot-com bust.[13]

This chapter focuses on trust in organizational authorities, a group that could include the CEO of an organization, its top management team, or supervisors and managers within the firm. These authorities "put a face on a company," giving employees and customers a means of judging a company's reputation. These authorities are also capable of having a significant influence on the performance and commitment of employees. As you'll see in the chapter, trust in these authorities depends on two related concepts. **Justice** reflects the perceived fairness of an authority's decision making.[14] When employees perceive high levels of justice, they believe that decision outcomes are fair and that decision-making processes are designed and implemented in a fair manner. Justice concepts can be used to explain why employees judge some authorities to be more trustworthy than others.[15] **Ethics** reflects the degree to which the behaviors of an authority are in accordance with generally accepted moral norms.[16] When employees perceive high levels of ethics, they believe that things are being done the way they "should be" or "ought to be" done. Ethics concepts can be used to explain why authorities decide to act in a trustworthy or untrustworthy manner.

WHY ARE SOME AUTHORITIES MORE TRUSTED THAN OTHERS?

Think about a particular boss or instructor—someone you've spent a significant amount of time around. Do you trust that person? Would you be willing to let that person have significant influence over your professional or educational future? For example, would you be willing to let that person serve as a reference for you or write you a letter of recommendation, even though you'd have no way of monitoring what he or she said about you? When you think about the level of trust you feel for that particular authority, what exactly makes you feel that way? This question speaks to the factors that drive trust—the factors that help inspire a willingness to be vulnerable.

TRUST

7.2

In what three sources can trust be rooted?

As shown in Figure 7-1, trust is rooted in three different kinds of factors. Sometimes trust is **disposition-based**, meaning that your personality traits include a general propensity to trust others. Sometimes trust is **cognition-based**, meaning that it's rooted in a rational assessment of the authority's trustworthiness.[17] Sometimes trust is **affect-based**, meaning that it depends on feelings toward the authority that go beyond any rational assessment.[18] The sections that follow describe each of these trust forms in more detail.

DISPOSITION-BASED TRUST. Disposition-based trust has less to do with a particular authority and more to do with the trustor. Some trustors are high in **trust propensity**—a general expectation that the words, promises, and statements of individuals and groups can be relied upon.[19] Some have argued that trust propensity represents a sort of "faith in human nature," in that trusting people view others in more favorable terms than do suspicious people.[20] The importance of trust propensity is most obvious in interactions with strangers, in which any acceptance of vulnerability would amount to "blind trust."[21] On the one hand, people who are high in trust propensity may be fooled into trusting others who are not worthy of it.[22] On the other hand, those who are low in trust propensity may be penalized by not trusting someone who is actually deserving of it. Both situations can

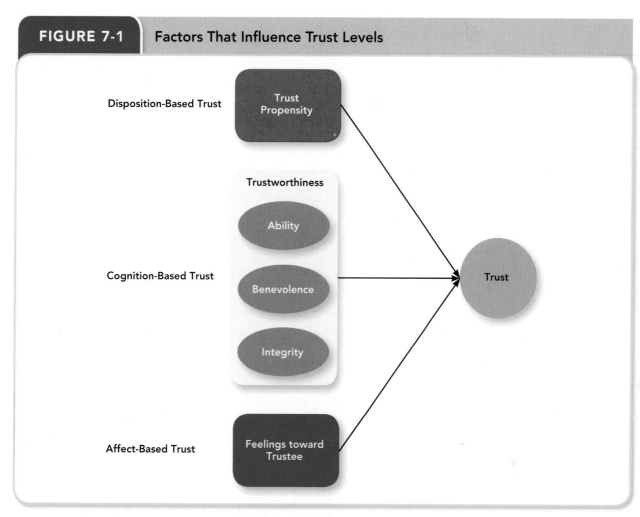

FIGURE 7-1   Factors That Influence Trust Levels

Sources: Adapted from R.C. Mayer, J.H. Davis, and F.D. Schoorman, "An Integrative Model of Organizational Trust," *Academy of Management Review* 20 (1995), pp. 709–34; and D.J. McAllister, "Affect- and Cognition-Based Trust as Foundations for Interpersonal Cooperation in Organizations," *Academy of Management Journal* 38 (1995), pp. 24–59.

be damaging; as one scholar noted, "We are doomed if we trust all and equally doomed if we trust none."[23] Where do you stack up on trust propensity? See our **OB Assessments** feature to find out.

Where does our trust propensity come from? As with all traits, trust propensity is a product of both nature and nurture (see Chapter 9 on Personality and Cultural Values for more discussion of such issues). If our parents are dispositionally suspicious, we may either inherit that tendency genetically or model it as we watch them exhibit distrust in their day-to-day lives. Research also suggests that trust propensity is shaped by early childhood experiences.[24] In fact, trust propensity may be one of the first personality traits to develop, because infants must immediately learn to trust their parents to meet their needs. The more our needs are met as children, the more trusting we become; the more we are disappointed as children, the less trusting we become. Our propensities continue to be shaped later in life as we gain experiences with friends, schools, churches, local government authorities, and other relevant groups.[25]

OB ASSESSMENTS

TRUST PROPENSITY

Are you a trusting person or a suspicious person by nature? This assessment is designed to measure trust propensity—a dispositional willingness to trust other people. Answer each question using the response scale provided. Then subtract your answers to the boldfaced questions from 6, with the difference being your new answers for those questions. For example, if your original answer for question 4 was "4," your new answer is "2" (6 – 4). Then sum up your answers for the eight questions. (For more assessments relevant to this chapter, please visit the Online Learning Center at www.mhhe.com/colquitt).

1 STRONGLY DISAGREE	2 DISAGREE	3 NEUTRAL	4 AGREE	5 STRONGLY AGREE

1. **One should be very cautious with strangers.** _____

2. Most experts tell the truth about the limits of their knowledge. _____

3. Most people can be counted on to do what they say they will do. _____

4. **These days, you must be alert or someone is likely to take advantage of you.** _____

5. Most salespeople are honest in describing their products. _____

6. Most repair people will not overcharge people who are ignorant of their specialty. _____

7. Most people answer public opinion polls honestly. _____

8. Most adults are competent at their jobs. _____

SCORING AND INTERPRETATION

If your scores sum up to 21 or above, you tend to be trusting of other people, which means you're often willing to accept some vulnerability to others under conditions of risk. If your scores sum up to 20 or below, you tend to be suspicious of other people, which means you're rarely willing to accept such vulnerability.

Sources: R.C. Mayer and J.H. Davis, "The Effect of the Performance Appraisal System on Trust for Management: A Field Quasi-Experiment," *Journal of Applied Psychology* 84 (1999), pp. 123–36. Copyright © 1999 by the American Psychological Association. Adapted with permission. No further reproduction or distribution is permitted without written permission from the American Psychological Association. See also F.D. Schoorman, R.C. Mayer, C. Roger, and J.H. Davis. "Empowerment in Veterinary Clinics: The Role of Trust in Delegation." Presented in a Symposium on Trust at the 11th Annual Conference, Society for Industrial and Organizational Psychology (SIOP), (April 1996), San Diego.

The nation in which we live also affects our trust propensity. Research by the World Values Study Group examines differences between nations on various attitudes and perceptions. The study group collects interview data from 45 different societies with a total sample size of more than 90,000 participants. One of the questions asked by the study group measures trust propensity. Specifically, participants are asked, "Generally speaking, would you say that most people can be trusted or that you can't be too careful in dealing with people?" Figure 7-2 shows the percentage of participants who answered "Most people

FIGURE 7-2   Trust Propensities by Nation

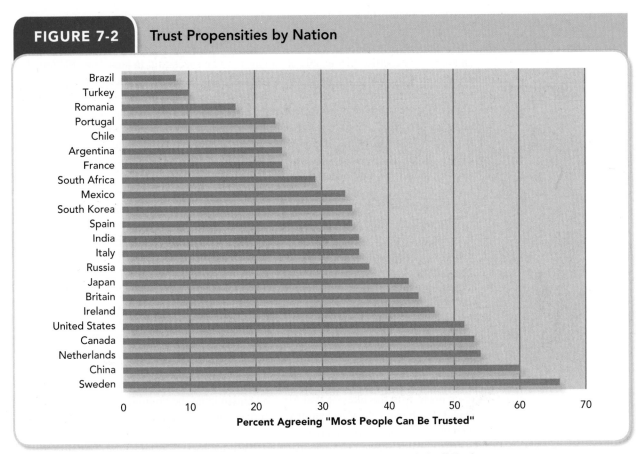

Percent Agreeing "Most People Can Be Trusted"

Source: Adapted from J.J. Johnson and J.B. Cullen, "Trust in Cross-Cultural Relationships," in *Blackwell Handbook of Cross-Cultural Management*, eds. M.J. Gannon and K.L. Newman (Malden, MA: Blackwell, 2002), pp. 335–60.

can be trusted" for this question, as opposed to "Can't be too careful," for several of the nations included in the study. The results reveal that trust propensity levels are actually relatively high in the United States, especially in relation to countries in Europe and South America.

COGNITION-BASED TRUST. Disposition-based trust guides us in cases when we don't yet have data about a particular authority. However, eventually we gain enough knowledge to gauge the authority's **trustworthiness**, defined as the characteristics or attributes of a trustee that inspire trust.[26] At that point, our trust begins to be based on cognitions we've developed about the authority, as opposed to our own personality or disposition. In this way, cognition-based trust is driven by the authority's "track record."[27] If that track record has shown the authority to be trustworthy, then vulnerability to the authority can be accepted. If that track record is spotty however, then trust may not be warranted.

7.3

What dimensions can be used to describe the trustworthiness of an authority?

Children whose needs are generally met tend to grow into trusting adults.

Research suggests that we gauge the track record of an authority along three dimensions: ability, benevolence, and integrity.[28]

The first dimension of trustworthiness is **ability**, defined as the skills, competencies, and areas of expertise that enable an authority to be successful in some specific area (see Chapter 10 on Ability for more discussion of such issues).[29] Think about the decision-making process that you go through when choosing a doctor, lawyer, or mechanic. Clearly one of the first things you consider is ability, because you're not going to trust them if they don't know a scalpel from a retractor, a tort from a writ, or a camshaft from a crankshaft. Of course, listing a specific area is a key component of the ability definition; you wouldn't trust a mechanic to perform surgery, nor would you trust a doctor to fix your car! The ability of business authorities may be considered on a number of levels. For example, managers may be judged according to their functional expertise in a particular vocation but also according to their leadership skills and their general business sense.

The second dimension of trustworthiness is **benevolence**, defined as the belief that the authority wants to do good for the trustor, apart from any selfish or profit-centered motives.[30] When authorities are perceived as benevolent, it means that they care for employees, are concerned about their well-being, and feel a sense of loyalty to them. The mentor–protégé relationship provides a good example of benevolence at work, in that the best mentors go out of their way to be helpful apart from concerns about financial rewards.[31] The management at Meijer, the Grand Rapids, Michigan–based supermarket chain, seems to understand the importance of benevolence.[32] Meijer recently added a five-day course on "positive organizational scholarship" to its leadership training program. The training stresses the importance of positive communication and a culture of kindness in the organization. The chain, which operates 180 stores with 60,000 employees, is attempting to compete with the likes of Wal-Mart by maximizing the commitment of its workforce. David Beach, the vice president of workforce planning and development, noted, "We realized that we need our company to be a place where people want to work."[33]

The third dimension of trustworthiness is **integrity**, defined as the perception that the authority adheres to a set of values and principles that the trustor finds acceptable.[34] When authorities have integrity, they are of sound character—they have good intentions and strong moral discipline.[35] Integrity also conveys an alignment between words and deeds—a sense that authorities keep their promises, "walk the talk," and "do what they say they will do."[36] Unfortunately, one survey indicated that only around 20 percent of American workers view senior managers as acting in accordance with their words.[37] Questions about integrity extend beyond senior management, however. For example, studies suggest that rank-and-file employees lie more frequently when communicating by e-mail because there are no "shifty eyes" or nervous ticks to give them away. Sometimes the lies begin even before employees are hired, as one survey of hiring managers by CareerBuilder.com revealed that 49 percent had caught an applicant lying on a resume.[38] Among the more colorful "exaggerations" were claims of membership in Mensa, listing a degree from a fictitious university, and pretending to be a Kennedy. For more discussion of lying and trustworthiness, see our **OB on Screen** feature.

AFFECT-BASED TRUST. Although ability, benevolence, and integrity provide three good reasons to trust an authority, the third form of trust isn't actually rooted in reason. Affect-based trust is more emotional than rational. With affect-based trust, we trust because we have feelings for the person in question; we really like them and have a fondness for them. Those feelings are what prompt us to accept vulnerability to another person. Put simply, we trust them because we like them.

Affect-based trust acts as a supplement to the types of trust discussed previously.[39] Figure 7-3 describes how the various forms of trust can build on one another over time. In new relationships, trust depends solely on our own trust propensity. In most relationships,

OB ON SCREEN

SLUMDOG MILLIONAIRE

You can't take the money and run now. . . . You're gonna win this. Trust me Jamal. You're gonna win.

With those words, Prem Kumar (Anil Kapoor) tries to help Jamal Malik (Dev Patel) out of a tough spot in *Slumdog Millionaire* (Dir. Danny Boyle and Loveleen Tandan, Fox Searchlight, 2008). Prem is the host of India's version of *Who Wants to Be a Millionaire?* He's been watching as Jamal—an uneducated "slumdog" from the streets of Mumbai— improbably answers question after question on the show, until Jamal is just two answers away from the 20 million rupee prize. The problem? Jamal doesn't know which "cricketer" has scored the most "first class centuries" in history. Two options remain: either B (Ricky Ponting) or D (Jack Hobbs).

When a commercial affords a chance to go to the restroom, Jamal tells Prem that he doesn't know the answer—that he'll stop and take the money he's earned so far. That's when Prem gives his pep talk, before silently writing a letter "B" in the mirror, fogged over from the steam of the hot water. When Jamal emerges to see the B, one question arises: Should he trust Prem? Is he willing to accept the vulnerability that comes with risking the money to answer "B"? On the one hand, Prem talked to Jamal in a benevolent way, though he was less polite several questions back. On the other hand, how can Prem have integrity if he's willing to help someone cheat on his own show?

Without giving too much away, Jamal gets the question right, bringing him one answer away from the grand prize when the show ends for the night. As he leaves the studio to rest up for the next day, a hood is thrown over his head and he's shoved into a police car. Now it's his integrity on the line: How did he get all those questions correct? As Jamal reveals the life experiences that gave him the answers, can he convince the police inspector to trust him?

that propensity eventually gets supplemented by knowledge about ability, benevolence, or integrity, at which point cognition-based trust develops. In a select few of those relationships, an emotional bond develops, and our feelings for the trustee further increase our willingness to accept vulnerability. These relationships are characterized by a mutual

FIGURE 7-3   Types of Trust Over Time

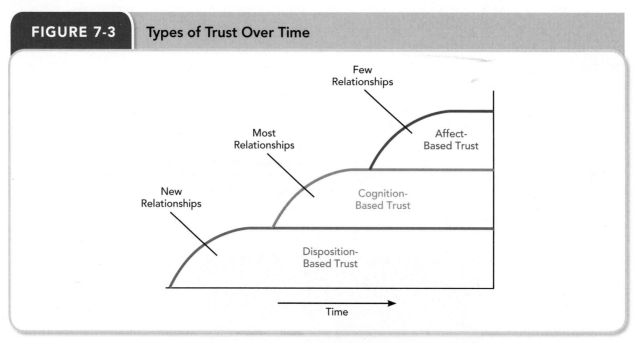

Sources: Adapted from R.J. Lewicki and B.B. Bunker, "Developing and Maintaining Trust in Work Relationships," in *Trust in Organizations: Frontiers of Theory and Research,* eds. R.M. Kramer and T.R. Tyler (Thousand Oaks, CA: Sage, 1996), pp. 114–39; and R.C. Mayer, J.H. Davis, and F.D. Schoorman, "An Integrative Model of Organizational Trust," *Academy of Management Review* 20 (1995), pp. 709–34.

investment of time and energy, a sense of deep attachment, and the realization that both parties would feel a sense of loss if the relationship were dissolved.[40]

SUMMARY. Taken together, disposition-based trust, cognition-based trust, and affect-based trust provide three completely different sources of trust in a particular authority. In the case of disposition-based trust, our willingness to be vulnerable has little to do with the authority and more to do with our genes and our early life experiences. In the case of affect-based trust, our willingness to be vulnerable has little to do with a rational assessment of the authority's merits and more to do with our emotional fondness for the authority. Only in the case of cognition-based trust do we rationally evaluate the pluses and minuses of an authority, in terms of its ability, benevolence, and integrity. But how exactly do we gauge those trustworthiness forms? One way is to consider whether authorities adhere to rules of justice.

JUSTICE

 7.4

What dimensions can be used to describe the fairness of an authority's decision making?

It's often difficult to assess the ability, benevolence, and integrity of authorities accurately, particularly early in a working relationship. What employees need in such circumstances is some sort of observable behavioral evidence that an authority might be trustworthy. Justice provides that sort of behavioral evidence, because authorities who treat employees more fairly are usually judged to be more trustworthy.[41] As shown in Table 7-2, employees can judge the fairness of an authority's decision making along four dimensions: distributive justice, procedural justice, interpersonal justice, and informational justice.

DISTRIBUTIVE JUSTICE. **Distributive justice** reflects the perceived fairness of decision-making outcomes.[42] Employees gauge distributive justice by asking whether decision outcomes, such as pay, rewards, evaluations, promotions, and work assignments,

TABLE 7-2	The Four Dimensions of Justice
Distributive Justice Rules	**Description**
Equity vs. equality vs. need	Are rewards allocated according to the proper norm?
Procedural Justice Rules	
Voice	Do employees get to provide input into procedures?
Correctability	Do procedures build in mechanisms for appeals?
Consistency	Are procedures consistent across people and time?
Bias Suppression	Are procedures neutral and unbiased?
Representativeness	Do procedures consider the needs of all groups?
Accuracy	Are procedures based on accurate information?
Interpersonal Justice Rules	
Respect	Do authorities treat employees with sincerity?
Propriety	Do authorities refrain from improper remarks?
Informational Justice Rules	
Justification	Do authorities explain procedures thoroughly?
Truthfulness	Are those explanations honest?

Sources: J.S. Adams, "Inequity in Social Exchange," in *Advances in Experimental Social Psychology,* Vol. 2, ed. L. Berkowitz (New York: Academic Press, 1965), pp. 267–99; R.J. Bies and J.F. Moag, "Interactional Justice: Communication Criteria of Fairness," in *Research on Negotiations in Organizations,* Vol. 1, eds. R.J. Lewicki, B.H. Sheppard, and M.H. Bazerman (Greenwich, CT: JAI Press, 1986), pp. 43–55; G.S. Leventhal, "The Distribution of Rewards and Resources in Groups and Organizations," in *Advances in Experimental Social Psychology,* Vol. 9, eds. L. Berkowitz and W. Walster (New York: Academic Press, 1976), pp. 91–131; G.S. Leventhal, "What Should Be Done with Equity Theory? New Approaches to the Study of Fairness in Social Relationships," in *Social Exchange: Advances in Theory and Research,* eds. K. Gergen, M. Greenberg, and R. Willis (New York: Plenum Press, 1980), pp. 27–55; and J. Thibaut and L. Walker, *Procedural Justice: A Psychological Analysis* (Hillsdale, NJ: Erlbaum, 1975).

are allocated using proper norms. In most business situations, the proper norm is equity, with more outcomes allocated to those who contribute more inputs (see Chapter 6 on Motivation for more discussion of such issues). The equity norm is typically judged to be the fairest choice in situations in which the goal is to maximize the productivity of individual employees.[43]

However, other allocation norms become appropriate in situations in which other goals are critical. In team-based work, building harmony and solidarity in work groups can become just as important as individual productivity. In such cases, an equality norm may be judged more fair, such that all team members receive the same amount of relevant rewards.[44] The equality norm is typically used in student project groups, in which all group members receive exactly the same grade on a project, regardless of their individual productivity levels. In cases in which the welfare of a particular employee is the critical concern, a need norm may be judged more fair. For example, some organizations protect new employees from committee assignments and other extra activities, so that they can get their careers off to a productive start.

PROCEDURAL JUSTICE. In addition to judging the fairness of a decision outcome, employees may consider the process that led to that outcome. **Procedural justice** reflects the perceived fairness of decision-making processes.[45] Procedural justice is fostered when authorities adhere to rules of fair process. One of those rules is voice, or giving employees a chance to express their opinions and views during the course of decision making.[46] A related rule is correctability, which provides employees with a chance to request an appeal when a procedure seems to have worked ineffectively. Research suggests that these rules improve employees reactions to decisions,[47] largely because they give employees a sense of ownership over the decisions. Employees tend to value voice and appeals even when they don't result in the desired outcome,[48] because they like to be heard. That is, the expression of opinions is a valued end, in and of itself, when employees believe that their opinions have been truly considered.

Aside from voice and correctability, procedural justice is fostered when authorities adhere to four rules that serve to create equal employment opportunity.[49] The consistency, bias suppression, representativeness, and accuracy rules help ensure that procedures are neutral and objective, as opposed to biased and discriminatory. These sorts of procedural rules are relevant in many areas of working life. As one example, the rules can be used to make hiring practices more fair by ensuring that interview questions are unbiased and asked in the same manner across applications. As another example, the rules can be used to make compensation practices more fair by ensuring that accurate measures of job performance are used to provide input for merit raises.

These sorts of procedural justice rules are critical because employment data suggest that gender and race continue to have significant influences on organizational decision making. Compensation data suggest that women often earn less than men for doing the same job. More specifically, women and men earn roughly the same in jobs that pay $25,000–$30,000 a year, but the gap widens as the salary increases.[50] Female psychologists earn 83 percent of what males earn, female college professors earn 75 percent of what males earn, and female lawyers and judges earn 69 percent of what males earn. As a result, sex discrimination cases have risen dramatically in recent years, with each victory adding weight to existing concerns about justice. As one employment lawyer put it, "Employees already mistrust employers. So each time a case reveals a secret that was never told, employees think, 'Aha! They really are paying men more than women.'"[51]

Compensation data also suggest that African American men only earn 76 percent of what Caucasian men earn.[52] Education differences don't explain the gap, because Caucasian high school dropouts are twice as likely to find jobs as African American dropouts. Such differences are likely due to procedural injustice in some form, with procedures functioning in an inconsistent, biased, and inaccurate manner across Caucasian and African American applicants. Indeed, one study of almost 9,000 personnel files in an information technology firm found that Caucasian men received bigger merit raises than minority and female employees, even when their performance evaluation ratings were identical.[53] The study's author noted, "The disparities are small but very real. And any difference is evidence of bias." Of course, some companies seem to excel at treating employees fairly. Table 7-3 provides excerpts from *Fortune*'s "50 Best Companies for Minorities," a list that is based on hiring, promotion, and retention rates for minority employees. Now you have two reasons to eat at McDonald's: tasty fries and procedural justice!

Consumer Reports serves as a good example of procedural justice in action. The magazine conducts the tests for its influential automotive ratings on its own 327-acre test site.[54] The ratings are performed by both experienced engineers and more typical drivers, while also taking into account surveys of the magazine's print and online subscribers. *Consumer Reports* helps ensure bias suppression by refusing to include advertisements in its magazine. It also buys all its test cars anonymously from regular dealerships, as opposed to using the vehicles offered by automakers. It helps ensure accuracy by putting 5,000–6,000 miles on a car for as long as 10 months and taking the car through approximately 50 different tests. Indeed, to measure fuel efficiency, it installs a fuel meter directly on the gas line, rather than relying on the accuracy of the vehicle's own gauges. Finally, *Consumer Reports*

TABLE 7-3	Some of the 50 Best Companies for Minorities	
1. McDonald's	26. Coca-Cola
5. Denny's	27. Nordstrom
6. U.S. Postal Service	28. Avon Products
7. PepsiCo	33. Darden Restaurants
13. Hilton Hotels	36. Levi Strauss
14. Verizon Communications	41. American Express
17. Xerox	45. Procter & Gamble
18. Hyatt	46. General Motors
20. TIAA-CREF	47. Eastman Kodak
23. United Parcel Service	49. AT&T
25. BellSouth	50. Bank of America

Source: C. Daniels, "50 Best Companies for Minorities," *Fortune*, June 28, 2004, Volume 149, No. 13/U.S. Edition. Copyright © 2004 Time Inc. All rights reserved.

helps ensure consistency by putting each vehicle through the exact same set of examinations. Although automakers have occasionally sued *Consumer Reports* to protest negative ratings, the magazine has never lost a case and has never paid a dime in settlements.

You might be wondering, "Does procedural justice really matter—don't people just care about the outcomes that they receive?" In the case of *Consumer Reports*, doesn't Ford just care how its cars score, not how those scores are actually calculated? Research suggests that distributive justice and procedural justice combine to influence employee reactions, as shown in Figure 7-4.[55] It's true that when outcomes are good, people don't spend as much time worrying about how fair the process was, as illustrated by the green line in the figure, which shows that procedural justice has little impact on reactions when outcome favorability is high. However, when outcomes are bad, procedural justice becomes enormously important, as illustrated by the red line in the figure. Research shows that negative or unexpected events trigger a thorough examination of process issues, making adherence to rules like consistency, bias suppression, and accuracy much more vital.[56] It's a good bet that Toyota studied *Consumer Reports*' procedures thoroughly when its Lexus GS450h received an uncharacteristically scathing critique in a recent set of ratings.[57]

In fact, research shows that procedural justice tends to be a stronger driver of reactions to authorities than distributive justice. For example, a meta-analysis of 183 studies showed that procedural justice was a stronger predictor of satisfaction with supervision, overall job satisfaction, and organizational commitment than distributive justice.[58] Why does the decision-making process sometimes matter more than the decision-making outcome? Likely because employees understand that outcomes come and go—some may be in your favor while others may be a bit disappointing. Procedures, however, are more long-lasting and stay in place until the organization redesigns them or a new authority arrives to revise them.

INTERPERSONAL JUSTICE. In addition to judging the fairness of decision outcomes and processes, employees might consider how authorities treat them as the procedures are implemented. **Interpersonal justice** reflects the perceived fairness of the treatment

FIGURE 7-4   **Combined Effects of Distributive and Procedural Justice**

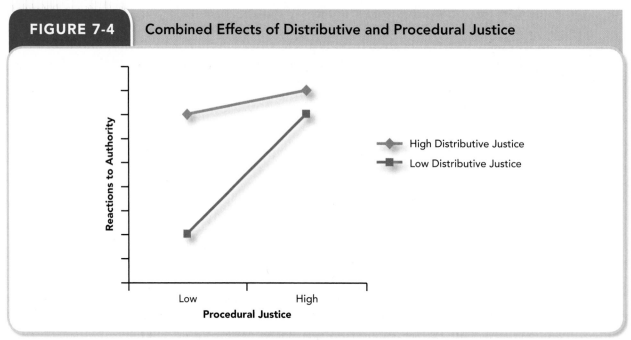

Source: Adapted from J. Brockner and B.M. Wiesenfeld, "An Integrative Framework for Explaining Reactions to Decisions: Interactive Effects of Outcomes and Procedures," *Psychological Bulletin* 120 (1996), pp. 189–208.

received by employees from authorities.[59] Interpersonal justice is fostered when authorities adhere to two particular rules. The respect rule pertains to whether authorities treat employees in a dignified and sincere manner, and the propriety rule reflects whether authorities refrain from making improper or offensive remarks. From this perspective, interpersonal *injustice* occurs when authorities are rude or disrespectful to employees, or when they refer to them with inappropriate labels.[60]

When taken to the extremes, interpersonally unjust actions create **abusive supervision**, defined as the sustained display of hostile verbal and nonverbal behaviors, excluding physical contact.[61] A national study suggests that approximately 15 percent of employees are victims of abusive behaviors, ranging from angry outbursts to public ridiculing to being used as scapegoats for negative events.[62] Estimates also indicate that such actions cost U.S. businesses around $24 billion annually due to absenteeism, health care costs, and lost productivity.[63] Employees who are abused by their supervisors report more anxiety, burnout, and strain, as well as less satisfaction with their lives in general.[64] They are also more likely to strike back at their supervisors with counterproductive behaviors—a response that may even spill over to their coworkers and the larger organization.[65]

Why are interpersonally unjust actions so damaging? One reason may be that people remember unfair acts more vividly than fair ones. A recent study asked 41 employees to complete a survey on interactions with authorities and coworkers four times a day for 2 to 3 weeks using a palmtop computer.[66] Two kinds of interactions were coded—positive experiences and negative experiences—and participants also reported on their current mood (e.g., happy, pleased, sad, blue, unhappy). The results of the study showed that positive interactions were more common than negative interactions, but the effects of negative interactions on mood were five times stronger than the effects of positive interactions. Such findings suggest that a violation of the respect and propriety rules looms much larger than adherence to those rules.[67]

INFORMATIONAL JUSTICE. Finally, employees may consider the kind of information that authorities provide during the course of organizational decision making. **Informational justice** reflects the perceived fairness of the communications provided to employees from authorities.[68] Informational justice is fostered when authorities adhere to two particular rules. The justification rule mandates that authorities explain decision-making procedures and outcomes in a comprehensive and reasonable manner, and the truthfulness rule requires that those communications be honest and candid. Although it seems like common sense that organizations would explain decisions in a comprehensive and adequate manner, that's often not the case. For example, RadioShack, the Fort Worth, Texas–based home electronics retailer, was recently criticized for firing 400 employees via e-mail.[69] Employees at corporate headquarters received messages on a Tuesday morning saying: "The work force reduction notification is currently in progress. Unfortunately your position is one that has been eliminated." After receiving the 18-word message, employees had 30 minutes to make phone calls and say goodbye to fellow employees, before packing up their belongings in boxes and plastic bags.

These sorts of informational injustices are all too common, for a variety of reasons. One factor is that sharing bad news is the worst part of the job for most managers, leading them to distance themselves when it's time to play messenger.[70] A survey of 372 human resources professionals revealed that almost 75 percent felt stress, anxiety, and depression when they had to conduct layoffs during the economic downturn.[71] Another factor may be that managers worry about triggering a lawsuit if they comprehensively and honestly explain the reasons for a layoff, a poor evaluation, or a missed promotion. Ironically, that defense mechanism is typically counterproductive, because research suggests that honest and adequate explanations are actually a powerful strategy for reducing retaliation responses against the organization.[72] In fact, low levels of informational justice can come back to haunt the organization if a wrongful termination claim is actually filed. How? Because the organization typically needs to provide performance evaluations for the terminated employee over the past few years, to show that the employee was fired for poor performance.[73] If managers refrained from offering candid and honest explanations on those evaluations, then the organization can't offer anything to justify the termination.

One study provides a particularly effective demonstration of the power of informational justice (and interpersonal justice). The study occurred in three plants of a Midwestern manufacturing company that specialized in small mechanical parts for the aerospace and automotive industries.[74] The company had recently lost two of its largest contracts and was forced to cut wages by 15 percent in two of the three plants. The company was planning to offer a short, impersonal explanation for the pay cut to both of the affected plants. However, as part of a research study, the company was convinced to offer a longer, more sincere explanation at one of the plants. Theft levels were then tracked before, during, and after the 10-week pay cut using the company's standard accounting formulas for inventory "shrinkage."

The results of the study are shown in Figure 7-5. In the plant without the pay cut, no change in theft levels occurred over the 10-week period. In the plant with the

RadioShack violated the norms of informational justice by laying off 400 employees in Fort Worth via a curt e-mail of 18 words.

| FIGURE 7-5 | The Effects of Justice on Theft During a Pay Cut |

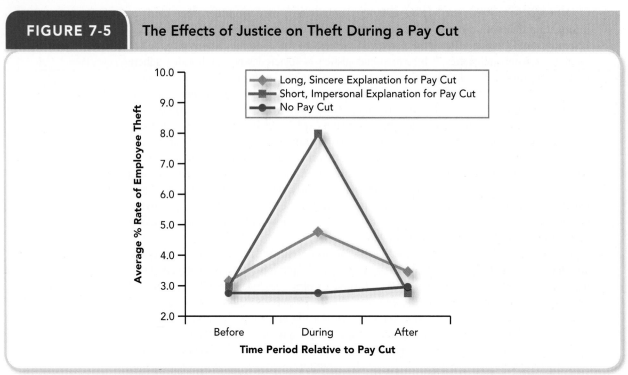

Source: Adapted from J. Greenberg, "Employee Theft as a Reaction to Underpayment Inequity: The Hidden Cost of Paycuts," *Journal of Applied Psychology* 75 (1990), pp. 561–68.

short, impersonal explanation, theft rose dramatically during the pay cut, likely as a means of retaliating for perceived inequity, before falling to previous levels once the cut had passed. Importantly, in the plant with the long, sincere explanation, the rise in theft was much less significant during the pay cut, with theft levels again falling back to normal levels once the cut had ended. Clearly, the higher levels of informational and interpersonal justice were worth it from a cost-savings perspective. The difference in theft across the two plants is remarkable, given that the long, sincere explanation was only a few minutes longer than the short, impersonal explanation. What's a few extra minutes if it can save a few thousand dollars?

SUMMARY. Taken together, distributive, procedural, interpersonal, and informational justice can be used to describe how fairly employees are treated by authorities. When an authority adheres to the justice rules in Table 7-2, those actions provide behavioral data that the authority might be trustworthy. Indeed, studies show that all four justice forms have strong correlations with employee trust levels.[75] All else being equal, employees trust authorities who allocate outcomes fairly; make decisions in a consistent, unbiased, and accurate way; and communicate decision-making details in a respectful, comprehensive, and honest manner. Which authorities are most likely to adhere to these sorts of rules? Research on ethics can provide some answers.

ETHICS

Research on ethics seeks to explain why people behave in a manner consistent with generally accepted norms of morality, and why they sometimes violate those norms.[76] The study of business ethics has two primary threads to it. One thread is *prescriptive* in nature, with scholars in philosophy debating how people *ought* to act using various codes and principles.[77] The prescriptive model is the dominant lens in discussions of legal ethics, medical ethics, and much of economics. The second thread is *descriptive* in nature, with scholars relying on scientific studies to observe how people *tend* to act based on certain individual and situational characteristics. The descriptive model is the dominant lens in psychology. Although the differences between these two threads gives the study of business ethics a certain complexity, the philosophical and empirical approaches can be integrated to develop a more complete understanding of ethical behavior.

Some studies of business ethics focus on unethical behavior—behavior that clearly violates accepted norms of morality.[78] Unethical behaviors in organizations can be directed at employees (e.g., discrimination, harassment, health and safety violations, ignoring labor laws), customers (e.g., invading privacy, violating contract terms, using false advertising, fabricating test results), financiers (e.g., falsifying financial information, misusing confidential information, trading securities based on inside information), or society as a whole (e.g., violating environmental regulations, exposing the public to safety risks, doing business with third parties who are themselves unethical).[79] How prevalent are such behaviors? Recent surveys suggest that 76 percent of employees have observed illegal or unethical conduct in their organizations within the past 12 months.[80] Those base rates may be even higher in some countries, as described in our **OB Internationally** feature.

Other studies focus on what might be termed "merely ethical" behavior—behavior that adheres to some minimally accepted standard of morality.[81] Merely ethical behaviors might include obeying labor laws and complying with formal rules and contracts. Still other studies focus on what could be called "especially ethical" behaviors—behaviors that exceed some minimally accepted standard of morality. Especially ethical behaviors might include charitable giving or **whistle-blowing**, which occurs when former or current employees expose illegal or immoral actions by their organization.[82] Whistle-blowing can be viewed as especially ethical because whistle-blowers risk potential retaliation by other members of the organization, especially when whistle-blowers lack status and power.[83] Ironically, the company often winds up benefitting from that risk taking, as whistle-blowing can bring significant improvements to the ethical culture in an organization over the long term.[84]

Why do some authorities behave unethically while others engage in ethical (or especially ethical) behaviors? One set of answers can be derived from research in social psychology. The **four-component model** of ethical decision making argues that ethical behaviors result from a multistage sequence beginning with moral awareness, continuing on to moral judgment, then to moral intent, and ultimately to ethical behavior.[85] Figure 7-6 presents an adaptation of this model. In addition to depicting the four components, the figure illustrates that unethical behavior can be triggered by characteristics of a person or the situation.[86] Put differently, and drawing on the adage "one bad apple can spoil the barrel," ethical behavior can be driven by both good versus bad apples and good versus bad barrels.[87] The sections that follow review the components of this model in more detail.

MORAL AWARENESS. The first step needed to explain why an authority acts ethically is **moral awareness**, which occurs when an authority recognizes that a moral issue exists in a situation or that an ethical code or principle is relevant to the circumstance.[88] Ethical issues rarely come equipped with "red flags" that mark them as morally sensitive.[89] Sometimes authorities act unethically simply because they don't perceive that moral issues are relevant in a given situation, so the ethical merits of certain actions are never debated. For example, assume you worked for a videogame company whose most popular game involves assuming the role of a criminal in a big city and taking part in multiple storylines involving a variety of illegal activities, such as carjacking, bank robbery, assassination, and the killing of law enforcement personnel and innocent bystanders. A member of this game's development team has suggested embedding hidden sex scenes

7.5

What is the four-component model of ethical decision making?

OB INTERNATIONALLY

If unethical actions are defined as behaviors that fall below minimum standards of morality, the key question becomes "Whose standards of morality?" Research on business ethics across cultures reveals that different countries have different baseline levels of unethical actions. Transparency International is an organization that monitors unethical practices in countries around the world. Using data from businesspeople, risk analysts, investigative journalists, country experts, and public citizens, the organization rates countries on a scale of 1 (unethical) to 10 (ethical).[90] Here are some of the scores from the 1999 version of the rankings:

SCORE	COUNTRY	SCORE	COUNTRY
10.0	Denmark	3.8	South Korea
9.8	Finland	3.6	Turkey
9.4	Sweden	3.4	China
9.2	Canada	3.4	Mexico
8.7	Australia	3.2	Thailand
8.6	Germany	3.0	Argentina
7.7	Hong Kong	2.9	Colombia
7.7	Ireland	2.9	India
7.5	United States	2.6	Ukraine
6.8	Israel	2.6	Venezuela
6.6	France	2.6	Vietnam
6.0	Japan	2.4	Russia
4.9	Greece	1.6	Nigeria
4.7	Italy	1.5	Cameroon

These rankings reveal the challenges involved for any multinational corporation that does business in areas at the top and bottom of the rankings. Should the company have the same ethical expectations for employees in all countries, regardless of ethical norms? For now, that seems to be the most common position. For example, the Coca-Cola Company's Code of Business Conduct "applies to all the Company's business worldwide and to all Company employees."[91] The code is given to all employees and covers topics such as conflicts of interest, dealing with government officials, customer and supplier interactions, and political contributions. The code also describes the disciplinary actions associated with any violations of the code.

into the game, which is currently rated "mature" by the Entertainment Software Rating Board.

Is there an ethical issue at play here? On the one hand, you might be tempted to say that the game is already rated "mature" and that such hidden scenes are only extending the

FIGURE 7-6	The Four-Component Model of Ethical Decision Making

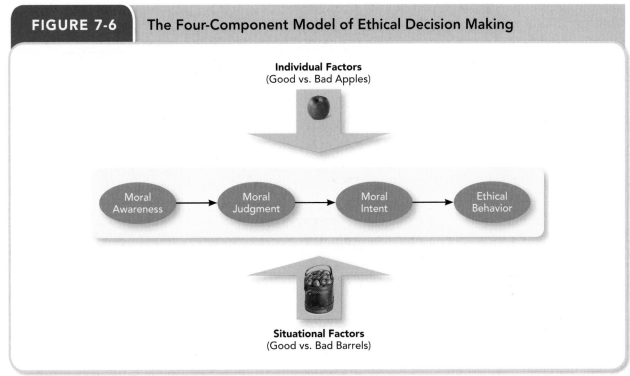

Source: Adapted from J.R. Rest, *Moral Development: Advances in Research and Theory* (New York: Praeger, 1986).

already less-than-wholesome nature of the game. Besides, "Easter eggs"—hidden objects in movies, DVDs, or computer and video games—have a long history in the entertainment industry. On the other hand, the hidden scenes constitute deception of the rating board, the customer, and potentially the customer's parents. And that deception issue stands apart from any moral issues raised by the actual content of the hidden scenes. If this story sounds familiar to you, it's because it actually happened with *Grand Theft Auto: San Andreas,* a game manufactured by a division of Take Two Interactive Software.[92] The hidden scenes, which began with the invitation, "How 'bout some coffee?" could be accessed using software available on the Internet. Take Two contends that the code for the scenes was put into early drafts of the game but was supposed to be removed before the game went to market.

Moral awareness depends in part on characteristics of the issue itself, as some issues have more built-in ethical salience than others. A concept called **moral intensity** captures the degree to which an issue has ethical urgency.[93] As described in Table 7-4, moral intensity is driven by two general concerns, both of which have more specific facets.[94] First and foremost, a particular issue is high in moral intensity if the potential for harm is perceived to be high. An act that could injure 1,000 people is more morally intense than an act that could injure 10 people, and an act that could result in death is more morally intense than an act that could result in illness.[95] Second, a particular issue is high in moral intensity if there is social pressure surrounding it. An act that violates a clear social norm is more morally intense than an act that seems similar to what everyone else is doing. In the case of *Grand Theft Auto,* it may be that Take Two never considered the ethicality of the hidden scenes because the potential for harm would be minor, or because the customers drawn to the game would probably not view the act as unethical.

Moral awareness also depends on the way authorities observe and perceive the events that happen around them. A concept called **moral attentiveness** captures the degree to which

TABLE 7-4	The Dimensions of Moral Intensity	
GENERAL DIMENSION	**SPECIFIC FACET**	**DESCRIPTION**
Potential for harm	Magnitude of consequences	How much harm would be done to other people?
	Probability of effect	How likely is it that the act will actually occur and that the assumed consequences will match predictions?
	Temporal immediacy	How much time will pass between the act and the onset of its consequences?
	Concentration of effect	Will the consequences be concentrated on a limited set of people, or will they be more far reaching?
Social pressure	Social consensus	How much agreement is there that the proposed act would be unethical?
	Proximity	How near (in a psychological or physical sense) is the authority to those who will be affected?

Source: Adapted from T.M. Jones, "Ethical Decision Making by Individuals in Organizations: An Issue-Contingent Model." *Academy of Management Review* 16 (1991), pp. 366–95. A. Singhapakdi, S.J. Vitell, and K.L. Kraft, "Moral Intensity and Ethical Decision-Making of Marketing Professionals." *Journal of Business Research* 36 (1996), pp. 245–55.

people chronically perceive and consider issues of morality during their experiences.[96] Research in cognitive psychology shows that people pay more attention to stimuli that are significant, vivid, and recognizable. Authorities who are morally attentive tend to view the world through a lens of morality, giving ethical issues a particular significance, vividness, and recognizability. That lens colors the way they identify and interpret information and also shapes the way they analyze and reflect on it. Morally attentive people are likely to report that they face several ethical dilemmas in a typical day, that many of the decisions they face have ethical consequences, that they regularly think about issues of morality, and that they enjoy pondering moral issues. In the Take Two example, it may be that the employees in charge of the *Grand Theft Auto* game weren't morally attentive enough to recognize that the hidden scenes represented an ethical issue. That premise makes some sense, given that

The programmers of *Grand Theft Auto* appeared to lack moral awareness when it was discovered that a hidden portion of the popular computer game, which could be easily accessed with free software, contained sex scenes.

Take Two has had other ethical struggles, including having to settle charges of fraudulent accounting with the Securities and Exchange Commission.

Some business schools are taking an unusual approach to increasing moral awareness on the part of their students. New York University, University of California at Berkeley, Purdue, and Penn State have invited convicted white-collar criminals to speak to students about their unethical actions, as well as the consequences of those actions.[97] For example, Walter Pavlo Jr. earns up to $2,500 a visit to detail the $6 million money-laundering scheme he perpetrated at MCI. The 40-year-old served two years in federal prison and is now divorced, unemployed, and living with his parents. Such testimonials can highlight the potential harm involved in unethical actions while also making students a bit more attentive to ethical issues. Although some professors consider the payment of convicted felons to be an ethical issue in its own right, part of what Pavlo earns goes to make restitution for his crimes. One professor at Penn State summarizes, "Here's a real person telling students what happened to his life. I don't think there's any substitute for that."[98]

MORAL JUDGMENT. Some authorities may recognize that a moral issue exists in a given situation but then be unable to determine whether a given course of action is right or wrong. The second step needed to explain why an authority acts ethically is therefore **moral judgment**, which reflects the process people use to determine whether a particular course of action is ethical or unethical.[99] One of the most important factors influencing moral judgment is described in Kohlberg's theory of **cognitive moral development**.[100] This theory argues that as people age and mature, they move through various stages of moral development—each more mature and sophisticated than the prior one. All else equal, authorities who operate at more mature stages of moral development should demonstrate better moral judgment. You might wonder how the moral development of a person can be measured. One approach is to give people a series of ethical dilemmas like the one in Table 7-5, then ask questions to gain insights into their decision-making process.[101]

TABLE 7-5	Ethical Dilemma Used to Assess Moral Development

Pat is responsible for providing expenditure estimates for his unit to the controller in his company who then determines the budget for all units in the company. Upper management has always emphasized the importance of providing timely and accurate financial estimates, and they have backed up this policy by disciplining managers for inaccurate or late estimates. Pat recently realized that the figures that he supplied contained a mistake. The mistake was that an expense was projected to be larger than it should have been. It will not affect the ability of the company to stay within the budget. However, the money could be used to cover other company expenditures. Up to this point, no one else has identified the mistake and it is unlikely that they will. Should Pat report the mistake?

On a scale from 1 = *No Importance* to 5 = *Great Importance*, rate how important each of the following questions are to your decision:

1. Could Pat receive a more harsh punishment if the company finds the mistake without his/her help?
2. Whether Pat's subordinates and peers would lose faith in Pat if Pat is caught instead of reporting the mistake him/herself.
3. Whether or not company policy ought to be respected by all employees.
4. Would reporting the mistake do any good for Pat or society?
5. What values Pat has set for himself in his personal code of behavior.

Source: Reprinted with kind permission from Springer Science+Business Media: *Journal of Business Ethics*, *"Assessing Managers' Ethical Decision-Making: An Objective Measure of Managerial Moral Judgment,"* 73 (2007), by Greg Loviscky.

According to Kohlberg, people begin their moral development at the *preconventional* stage.[102] At this stage, right versus wrong is viewed in terms of the consequences of various actions for the individual. For example, children seek to avoid punishment for its own sake, regardless of any concern about moral order. Similarly, children obey adults for its own sake, regardless of the respect or wisdom shown by those adults. Over time, the desire to obtain pleasure and avoid pain expands to the formation of "you scratch my back, I'll scratch yours" sort of exchanges. Such relationships remain self-interested however, with little concern for loyalty, gratitude, or fairness. In the case of the ethical dilemma in Table 7-5, viewing Question 1 as one of the most important issues would signal preconventional thinking.

As people mature, their moral judgment reaches the *conventional* stage.[103] At this stage, right versus wrong is referenced to the expectations of one's family and one's society. At first, people seek the approval of friends and family members, conforming to stereotypes about what's right. Question 2 in Table 7-5 reflects this sort of priority. Over time, people come to emphasize the laws, rules, and orders that govern society. Concepts such as doing one's duty and maintaining the social order come to be valued for their own sakes. Question 3 reflects this level of moral sophistication. Research suggests that most adults find themselves at the conventional stage.[104] That positioning is relevant to organizations because it shows that moral judgment can be influenced by organizational policies, practices, and norms.

The most sophisticated moral thinkers reach the *principled* (or postconventional) stage.[105] At this stage, right versus wrong is referenced to a set of defined, established moral principles. Research suggests that fewer than 20 percent of Americans reach this principled stage.[106] Philosophers have identified a number of **moral principles** that serve as prescriptive guides for making moral judgments, with some of the most influential shown in Table 7-6. Rather than viewing a given principle as the single, best lens for making decisions, it's better to view the principles as a prism for shedding light on a given situation from a number of different angles.[107] The consequentialist principles in Table 7-6 judge the morality of an action according to its goals, aims, or outcomes (these principles are sometimes termed "teleological," after the Greek word for "goal").[108] Question 4 in Table 7-5 reflects these sorts of concerns. The nonconsequentialist principles judge the morality of an action solely on its intrinsic desirability (these principles are sometimes termed "deontological," after the Greek word for "duty," or "formalist," due to their emphasis on formalized codes and standards). Viewing Question 5 as one of the most important issues in the dilemma would signal nonconsequentialist thinking.

Returning to the Take Two example, a utilitarian analysis would focus on whether the scenes maximized the happiness of Take Two's customers. Would more customers derive pleasure from the scenes, or would more customers be upset about the hidden content? An egoistic analysis of the morality of the hidden scenes would focus on whether the scenes boosted the short-term and long-term interests of the company. Would the scenes add to the appeal of *Grand Theft Auto*, or would consumers who felt misled decide to take their business elsewhere? Although the takeaways from those analyses may be debatable, the judgment of the three remaining principles seems clear. From the perspective of the

"*Miss Dugan, will you send someone in here who can distinguish right from wrong?*"

TABLE 7-6	Moral Principles Used in the Principled Stage	
TYPE OF PRINCIPLE	**SPECIFIC PRINCIPLE**	**DESCRIPTION (AND CONTRIBUTORS)**
Consequentialist	Utilitarianism	An act is morally right if it results in the greatest amount of good for the greatest number of people—sometimes termed the "greatest happiness principle" (Jeremy Bentham, John Stuart Mill)
	Egoism	An act is morally right if the decision maker freely decides to pursue either short-term or long-term interests. Markets are purported to limit the degree to which one egoist's interests harm the interests of another (Adam Smith).
Nonconsequentialist	Ethics of Duties	An act is morally right if it fulfills the "categorical imperative"—an unambiguously explicit set of three crucial maxims: (a) the act should be performable by everyone with no harm to society; (b) the act should respect human dignity; (c) the act should be endorsable by others (Immanuel Kant)
	Ethics of Rights	An act is morally right if it respects the natural rights of others, such as the right to life, liberty, justice, expression, association, consent, privacy, and education (John Locke, John Rawls)
	Virtue ethics	An act is morally right if it allows the decision maker to lead a "good life" by adhering to virtues like wisdom, honesty, courage, friendship, mercy, loyalty, modesty, and patience (Aristotle)

Source: Adapted from A. Crane and D. Matten, *Business Ethics* (New York: Oxford University Press, 2007).

ethics of duties, society would clearly be harmed if all companies kept product details hidden from their customers, and few people would have endorsed Take Two's actions if they had been made public from the beginning. From an ethics of rights viewpoint, the hidden scenes violated the right of consent, as customers didn't choose to buy a game with those specific scenes in it. Finally, an analysis using virtue ethics would reveal that Take Two's actions lacked, at a minimum, the virtue of honesty.

MORAL INTENT. Assuming that an authority recognizes that a moral issue exists in a situation and possesses the cognitive moral development to choose the right course of action, one step remains: The authority has to *want* to act ethically. **Moral intent** reflects an authority's degree of commitment to the moral course of action.[109] The distinction between awareness or judgment on the one hand and intent on the other is important, because many unethical people know and understand that what they're doing is wrong—they just choose to do it anyway. Why? Sometimes situational factors encourage people to go against their moral convictions. For example, organizations may possess unethical cultures, where violations of moral codes become the rule rather than the exception (see Chapter 16 on Organizational Culture for more discussion of such issues).[110] This seems particularly possible in the Take Two example, given the company's other ethical missteps. As another example, economic pressures from assigned goals or specific incentives can encourage people to set aside their moral judgment, at least for a time.[111]

What explains the ability of some people to resist situational pressures and stay true to their moral judgment? One factor is **moral identity**—the degree to which a person self-identifies as a moral person.[112] Our self-concepts have a number of components to them: We may define ourselves by what we do, where we come from, what our family status is, or what cultural or ethnic groups we belong to. People with strong moral identities define themselves as compassionate, generous, honest, kind, fair, and hardworking. Their emotional well-being and sense of self is wrapped up in living up to those virtues. Moreover, the actions they take in their daily life, from the things they buy to the hobbies they have to the groups they join, are viewed as symbols of those virtues. Research suggests that people with strong moral identities volunteer more for charitable work and donate more to charity drives.[113] Research also suggests that moral identity "moderates" the effects of moral judgment on ethical behavior. Recall that, in the language of theory diagrams, moderators affect the strength of the relationship between two variables. For example, one study shows that managers who emphasize specific ethics principles are less likely to engage in unethical behaviors (e.g., calling in sick to take a day off, ignoring others' unethical actions), but only when they define themselves as a moral person.[114] When morality is not an important piece of their identity, their moral principles have no relationship with their actual behavior.

SUMMARY. Taken together, the stages of the four-component model can be used to explain why authorities act in an ethical or unethical manner. When authorities are morally aware, when they have sophisticated moral judgment, and when they possess strong moral intent, chances are their actions will tend to be ethical. By extension, those authorities should attend more to the rules of distributive, procedural, interpersonal, and informational justice, because treating employees fairly is itself an ethical act.[115] Those authorities should also be viewed as trustworthy, in that moral awareness, judgment, and intent should result in higher levels of both benevolence and integrity.

SUMMARY: WHY ARE SOME AUTHORITIES MORE TRUSTED THAN OTHERS?

So what explains why some authorities are more trusted than others? As shown in Figure 7-7, answering that question requires understanding the different sources in which trust can be rooted, including dispositions, cognitions, and affect. Disposition-based trust is rooted in an individual's trust propensity, whereas affect-based trust is rooted in a fondness for the authority. Cognition-based trust is driven by perceptions of trustworthiness, as employees attempt to assess the ability, benevolence, and integrity of authorities. Unfortunately, it's often difficult to gauge trustworthiness accurately, so employees instead look to more observable behaviors that can be used as indirect evidence of trustworthiness. Those behaviors may center on the justice of authorities, with employees considering the distributive, procedural, interpersonal, and informational justice they have experienced at work. The justice and general trustworthiness of authorities in turn can be explained by authorities' own moral awareness, moral judgment, and moral intent.

 7.6

How does trust affect job performance and organizational commitment?

HOW IMPORTANT IS TRUST?

Does trust have a significant impact on the two primary outcomes in our integrative model of OB—does it correlate with job performance and organizational commitment? Figure 7-8 summarizes the research evidence linking trust to job performance and organizational

FIGURE 7-7 Why Are Some Authorities More Trusted Than Others?

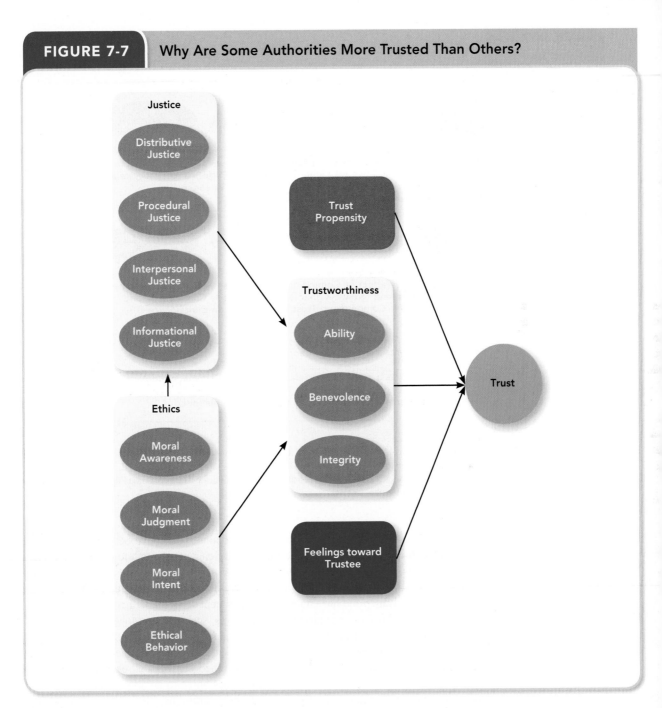

commitment. The figure reveals that trust does affect job performance. Why? One reason is that trust is moderately correlated with task performance. A study of employees in eight plants of a tool manufacturing company sheds some light on why trust benefits task performance.[116] The study gave employees survey measures of their trust in two different authorities: their plant's manager and the company's top management team. Both trust measures were significant predictors of employees' **ability to focus**, which reflects the degree to which employees can devote their attention to work, as opposed to "covering their backside," "playing politics," and "keeping an eye on the boss." The ability to focus is clearly vital to task performance in many jobs, particularly when job duties become more complex.

FIGURE 7-8	Effects of Trust on Performance and Commitment

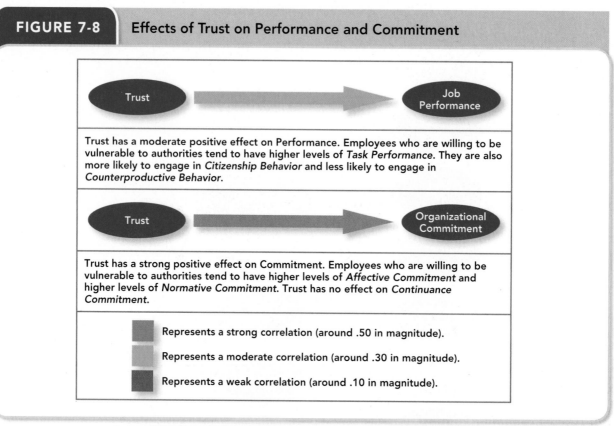

Trust has a moderate positive effect on Performance. Employees who are willing to be vulnerable to authorities tend to have higher levels of *Task Performance*. They are also more likely to engage in *Citizenship Behavior* and less likely to engage in *Counterproductive Behavior*.

Trust has a strong positive effect on Commitment. Employees who are willing to be vulnerable to authorities tend to have higher levels of *Affective Commitment* and higher levels of *Normative Commitment*. Trust has no effect on *Continuance Commitment*.

Represents a strong correlation (around .50 in magnitude).

Represents a moderate correlation (around .30 in magnitude).

Represents a weak correlation (around .10 in magnitude).

Sources: K.T. Dirks and D.L. Ferrin, "Trust in Leadership: Meta-Analytic Findings and Implications for Research and Practice," *Journal of Applied Psychology* 87 (2002), pp. 611–28; and J.A. Colquitt, B.A. Scott, and J.A. LePine, "Trust, Trustworthiness, and Trust Propensity: A Meta-Analytic Test of their Unique Relationships with Risk Taking and Job Performance," *Journal of Applied Psychology* 92 (2007), pp. 909–27.

Trust also influences citizenship behavior and counterproductive behavior. Why? One reason is that the willingness to accept vulnerability changes the nature of the employee–employer relationship. Employees who don't trust their authorities have **economic exchange** relationships that are based on narrowly defined, quid pro quo obligations that are specified in advance and have an explicit repayment schedule.[117] Economic exchanges are impersonal and resemble contractual agreements, such that employees agree to fulfill the duties in their job description in exchange for financial compensation. As trust increases, **social exchange** relationships develop that are based on vaguely defined obligations that are open-ended and long term in their repayment schedule.[118] Social exchanges are characterized by mutual investment, such that employees agree to go above and beyond their duties in exchange for fair and proper treatment by authorities. In social exchange contexts, employees are willing to engage in beneficial behaviors because they trust that those efforts will eventually be rewarded (see Chapter 3 on Organizational Commitment for more discussion of such issues).

Figure 7-8 also reveals that trust affects organizational commitment. Why? One reason is that trusting an authority increases the likelihood that an emotional bond will develop,[119] particularly if that trust is rooted in positive feelings for the authority. Trusting an authority also makes it more likely that a sense of obligation will develop, because employees feel more confident that the authority deserves that obligation. When negative events occur, employees who trust the authority are willing to accept the vulnerability that comes with continued employment,[120] remaining confident in their belief that the situation will eventually improve. For more discussion of the importance of trust in the workplace, see our **OB at the Bookstore** feature.

OB AT THE BOOKSTORE

THE SPEED OF TRUST
by Stephen M. R. Covey (New York: The Free Press, 2006).

There is one thing that is common to every individual, relationship, team, family, organization, nation, economy, and civilization throughout the world—one thing which, if removed, will destroy the most powerful government, the most successful business, the most thriving economy. . . . That one thing is trust.

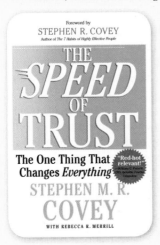

With these words, Covey summarizes the central premise of his book: Trust is vital within and outside organizations. Covey summarizes the importance of trust with one simple formula:

$$\downarrow \text{Trust} = \downarrow \text{Speed} \uparrow \text{Cost}$$

He uses an example to illustrate the formula: The Sarbanes-Oxley Act was passed in response to the accounting scandals at Enron, WorldCom, and others. The Act's many regulations represent an expression of distrust. Chief financial officers report that compliance with the Act requires an enormous amount of time, reducing the speed of company operations. Costs in turn increase; one study suggests that compliance with the Sarbanes-Oxley Act costs $35 billion annually.

Covey conveys the same sort of premise in another way by describing what could be called a *distrust tax*. Every time you work with someone whom you distrust, you spend some portion of your time monitoring and checking up on them. That distrust mimics a tax, reducing your productivity by 10 percent, 20 percent, or even 30 percent. Similarly, every time you work with people who distrust you, they spend time performing the same sorts of behaviors. That distrust tax can be contrasted with what Covey terms the *trust dividend*, where high trust amplifies the gains derived from employee skills and effort. As Covey describes it, "High trust is like the leaven in bread, which lifts everything around it."

APPLICATION: SOCIAL RESPONSIBILITY

Now that you understand the factors that drive trust in authorities and the importance of trust levels to performance and commitment, we turn our attention to a very practical question: "How can organizations become more trustworthy?" In the case of Nike, how can it continue to improve its reputation as an organization worthy of trust? Certainly that's a

7.7

What steps can organizations take to become more trustworthy?

big question with no single answer. However, one strategy is to focus the organization's attention on **corporate social responsibility**, a perspective that acknowledges that the responsibilities of a business encompass the economic, legal, ethical, and citizenship expectations of society.[121] This perspective maintains the belief that the foundation of any business is profitability, because organizations must fulfill their economic responsibilities to their employees and their shareholders. However, the social responsibility lens supplements that belief by arguing that the company's obligations do not end with profit maximization.

The legal component of corporate social responsibility argues that the law represents society's codification of right and wrong and must therefore be followed.[122] Fulfilling this component speaks to the integrity of the organization and suggests that it has reached the conventional level of moral development. Further violations of labor laws on Nike's part would signal a breach of this component, so protecting its reputation will likely require a continuing emphasis on monitoring and inspections. Many organizations turn to compliance officers to police the legality of their operations. For example, Computer Associates International, a New York–based maker of computer security software, recently installed a new compliance officer.[123] As part of a series of reforms to avoid a trial over accounting fraud, the company gave its new officer, who was a former chief trial attorney for the U.S. Navy, unprecedented power. The officer has direct access to the CEO, can go over the CEO's head if need be, and has the authority to fire managers and employees who violate company guidelines.

The ethical component of corporate social responsibility argues that organizations have an obligation to do what is right, just, and fair and to avoid harm.[124] Fulfilling this component is relevant to the benevolence and integrity of the organization and suggests that it has reached the principled level of moral development.[125] Regardless of its legal implications, the way Nike manages the employees who work in its factories speaks to the ethical makeup of its culture. What can organizations do to improve that ethical makeup? J.M. Smuckers, the Orrville, Ohio–based food and beverage maker, requires all of its 3,500 employees to attend training sessions on moral awareness and moral judgment. Employees go through programs every 3–5 years and sign a nine-page ethics statement annually. That statement, which the company treats as a living document, spells out the codes and principles that Smuckers employees can use to navigate moral dilemmas.

The citizenship component of corporate social responsibility argues that organizations should contribute resources to improve the quality of life in the communities in which they work.[126] Sometimes this component involves philanthropic efforts, in which donations of time or cash are given to charitable groups. At Home Depot, for example, 50,000 of its 325,000 employees donated a total of 2 million hours to community groups in a single year.[127] The citizenship component may also involve efforts geared toward environmental sustainability. On that front, Nike has joined a number of notable companies, including Wal-Mart and General Electric, in adopting "green" manufacturing processes.[128] Wal-Mart has taken steps to reduce waste and inefficiency, an important goal given that the company is the nation's largest private user of electricity.[129] General Electric issues an annual "citizenship report" to highlight several aspects of its corporate social responsibility, from increases in volunteer hours to efforts to reduce air pollution.[130]

TAKEAWAYS

7.1 Trust is the willingness to be vulnerable to an authority based on positive expectations about the authority's actions and intentions. Justice reflects the perceived fairness of an authority's decision making and can be used to explain why employees judge some authorities as more trustworthy than others. Ethics reflects the degree to which the behaviors of an authority are in accordance with generally accepted moral norms and can be used to explain why authorities choose to act in a trustworthy manner.

7.2 Trust can be disposition-based, meaning that one's personality includes a general propensity to trust others. Trust can also be cognition-based, meaning that it's rooted in a rational assessment of the authority's trustworthiness. Finally, trust can be affect-based, meaning that it's rooted in feelings toward the authority that go beyond any rational assessment of trustworthiness.

7.3 Trustworthiness is judged along three dimensions. Ability reflects the skills, competencies, and areas of expertise that an authority possesses. Benevolence is the degree to which an authority wants to do good for the trustor, apart from any selfish or profit-centered motives. Integrity is the degree to which an authority adheres to a set of values and principles that the trustor finds acceptable.

7.4 The fairness of an authority's decision making can be judged along four dimensions. Distributive justice reflects the perceived fairness of decision-making outcomes. Procedural justice reflects the perceived fairness of decision-making processes. Interpersonal justice reflects the perceived fairness of the treatment received by employees from authorities. Informational justice reflects the perceived fairness of the communications provided to employees from authorities.

7.5 The four-component model of ethical decision making argues that ethical behavior depends on three concepts. Moral awareness reflects whether an authority recognizes that a moral issue exists in a situation. Moral judgment reflects whether the authority can accurately identify the "right" course of action. Moral intent reflects an authority's degree of commitment to the moral course of action.

7.6 Trust has a moderate positive relationship with job performance and a strong positive relationship with organizational commitment.

7.7 Organizations can become more trustworthy by emphasizing corporate social responsibility, a perspective that acknowledges that the responsibilities of a business encompass the economic, legal, ethical, and citizenship expectations of society.

KEY TERMS

- Reputation   *p. 219*
- Trust   *p. 219*
- Justice   *p. 220*
- Ethics   *p. 220*
- Disposition-based trust   *p. 220*
- Cognition-based trust   *p. 220*
- Affect-based trust   *p. 220*
- Trust propensity   *p. 220*
- Trustworthiness   *p. 223*
- Ability   *p. 224*
- Benevolence   *p. 224*
- Integrity   *p. 224*

DISCUSSION QUESTIONS

7.1 Which would be more damaging in organizational life—being too trusting or not being trusting enough? Why do you feel that way?

7.2 Consider the three dimensions of trustworthiness (ability, benevolence, and integrity). Which of those dimensions would be most important when deciding whether to trust your boss? What about when deciding whether to trust a friend? If your two answers differ, why do they?

7.3 Putting yourself in the shoes of a manager, which of the four justice dimensions (distributive, procedural, interpersonal, informational) would you find most difficult to maximize? Which would be the easiest to maximize?

7.4 Which component of ethical decision making do you believe best explains student cheating: moral awareness, moral judgment, or moral intent? Why do you feel that way?

7.5 Assume you were applying for a job at a company known for its corporate social responsibility. How important would that be to you when deciding whether to accept a job offer?

CASE: NIKE

Hannah Jones serves as Nike's vice president of corporate social responsibility, overseeing a 135-person team and reporting directly to CEO Mark Parker.[131] Jones's team is charged with weaving issues of corporate social responsibility throughout Nike's operations. That mission includes auditing and managing Nike's factories around the world. However, it also includes issues of environmental sustainability. In 1992, a German magazine pointed out that the signature Nike Air pocket included more than just air—it also contained sulfur hexafluoride, or SF6—a potent greenhouse gas more commonly linked to older refrigerators and air conditioners.[132] SF6 breaks up slowly in the atmosphere, which means that even very small amounts have a significant environmental impact. Estimates suggest that at the peak of SF6 production in 1997, Nike Air footwear carried a greenhouse effect equivalent to the tailpipes of 1 million automobiles.

It took Nike almost 14 years to devise a new air pocket that was as light, durable, and shock-absorbing as the SF6 version.[133] The breakthrough wound up utilizing nitrogen, held in by a redesigned sole that includes 65 wafer-thin layers of plastic film. The new approach, which debuted with Nike's Air Max 360, allows the air pocket to stretch throughout the sole, giving even more comfort at even less weight. The company has also devised a program that calculates an environmental impact rating for each shoe, based on use of toxic adhesives, curbing of waste, and use of recycled materials.[134] Even the Air Jordan—arguably Nike's flagship shoe—was designed with environmental impact in mind, such that the shoe's sole consists of ground-up bits of old Nike sneakers.[135] You won't see these issues discussed in television or print ads for Nike shoes, however. Unlike Wal-Mart or General Electric, which aggressively trumpet their "green" initiatives, Nike prefers to deemphasize sustainability in its marketing efforts. One independent branding consultant explains that strategy by noting, "Nike has always been about winning. How is sustainability relevant to its brand?"[136]

7.1   Do you agree with Nike's decision to downplay "green" issues when marketing its shoes? Why or why not?

7.2   Assuming price and quality are both acceptable, to what degree do you consider the ethical reputation of a company when buying a product or service?

7.3   Does it seem like Nike is doing enough to build and maintain the trust in its brand? If not, what else would you like to see the company pursue?

EXERCISE: UNETHICAL BEHAVIOR

The purpose of this exercise is to explore how authorities can prevent unethical behaviors on the part of their employees. This exercise uses groups, so your instructor will either assign you to a group or ask you to create your own group. The exercise has the following steps:

7.1   Read the following scenario:

Alex Grant recently graduated from college and is excited to be starting his first job as a store manager for The Grocery Cart, a large supermarket chain. The company has a very good management training program, and it is one of the fastest growing chains in the nation. If Alex does well managing his first store, there are a number of promising advancement opportunities in the company. After completing the store management training program, Alex met with Regina Hill, his area supervisor. She informed Alex that he would be taking charge of a medium-volume store ($250,000 in sales/week) in an upper-class neighborhood. This store had been operating without a store manager for the past 6 months. The store had also not made a profit in any of the monthly financial reports for the last year.

Hill also shared the following information with Alex: Because the store has been without a store manager for the last six months, the assistant manager (Drew Smith) has been in charge. Drew is known for being highly competent and a solid performer. However, there have been complaints that he is frequently rude to employees and insults and ridicules them whenever they make mistakes. Turnover among sales clerks and cashiers at this store has been somewhat higher than in other stores in the area. The average pay of clerks and cashiers is $6.44/hour. The last two semiannual inventories at this store showed significant losses. There has been a large amount of theft from the store stockroom (an area where only employees are allowed). Given that the store has generally done well in sales (compared with others in the area) and that most expenses seem well under control, Hill believes that the profitability problem for this store is primarily due to theft. Therefore, she suggested that Alex's plans for the store should focus on this priority over any others.

7.2 As a manager, what steps should Alex take to reduce employee theft? Come up with a list of three ideas. Elect a group member to write the group's three ideas on the board or on a transparency.

7.3 Now read the following scenario:

When Alex arrived for his first day of work in his new store, he saw that Drew was in the process of terminating an employee (Rudy Johnson) who had been caught stealing. Alex immediately went to the break room of the store where the termination interview was being conducted to learn more about the situation. Drew informed Alex that Rudy had been a grocery clerk for the past six weeks and that he had apparently figured out how to tell if the alarms to the stockroom doors were off. Rudy would then open the back stockroom doors and stack cases of beer outside the store to pick up after his shift. After Drew caught Rudy doing this, Drew had a conversation with one of his friends who works as a restaurant manager down the street. Drew's friend noted that he had hired Rudy a few months ago and that he'd been caught stealing there too.

Turning to Rudy, Drew asked, "So, Rudy, what do you have to say for yourself?" Rudy quickly replied: "Look here, [expletive], you don't pay me enough to work here and put up with this garbage. In fact, you're always riding everyone like they're your personal servant or something. So I was trying to get some beer. I've seen you let stockers take home damaged merchandise a dozen times. So just because they cut open a box of cookies, which we all know they do on purpose, they get to take stuff home for free. For that matter, we've all seen you do the same thing! I've never seen you make a big deal about this stuff before. Why can't I get a few cases of beer? What's the big deal?"

7.4 Do these events give you any additional insights into how to decrease employee theft in this store? If so, elect a group member to write an additional one or two reasons in your spot on the board or on your transparency.

7.5 Class discussion (whether in groups or as a class) should center on whether the theft that's occurring at The Grocery Cart reveals a problem of moral awareness, moral judgment, or moral intent. In addition, does the theft point to a problem with "bad apples," a "bad barrel," or both?

Source: Adapted from E.C. Tomlinson, "Teaching the Interactionist Model of Ethics," *Journal of Management Education* 33 (2009), pp. 142–65.

ENDNOTES

7.1 Holmes, S. "Nike Goes for the Green." *BusinessWeek*, September 25, 2006, pp. 106–108.

7.2 Levenson, E. "Citizen Nike." *Fortune,* November 24, 2008, pp. 165–70.

7.3 Ibid.

7.4 Ibid.

7.5 Ibid.

7.6 Roberts, D.; and P. Engardio. "Secrets, Lies, and Sweatshops." *BusinessWeek,* November 27, 2006, pp. 50–58.

7.7 Ibid.; and Levenson, "Citizen Nike."

7.8 Levenson, "Citizen Nike."

7.9 Rindova, V.P.; I.O. Williamson; A.P. Petkova; and J.M. Sever. "Being Good or Being Known: An Empirical Examination of the Dimensions, Antecedents, and Consequences of Organizational Reputation." *Academy of Management Journal* 48 (2005), pp. 1033–49.

7.10 Frauenheim, E. "Does Reputation Matter?" *Workforce Management,* November 20, 2006, pp. 22–26.

7.11 Ibid.

7.12 Mayer, R.C.; J.H. Davis; and F.D. Schoorman. "An Integrative Model of Organizational Trust." *Academy of Management Review* 20 (1995), pp. 709–34; and Rousseau, D.M.; S.B. Sitkin; R.S. Burt; and C. Camerer. "Not So Different After All: A Cross-Discipline View of Trust." *Academy of Management Review* 23 (1998), pp. 393–404.

7.13 Colvin, G. "The World's Most Admired Companies." *Fortune,* March 16, 2009, pp. 75–78.

7.14 Greenberg, J. "A Taxonomy of Organizational Justice Theories." *Academy of Management Review* 12 (1987), pp. 9–22.

7.15 Lind, E.A. "Fairness Heuristic Theory: Justice Judgments as Pivotal Cognitions in Organizational Relations." In *Advances in Organizational Justice,* eds. J. Greenberg and R. Cropanzano. Stanford, CA: Stanford University Press, 2001, pp. 56–88; Van den Bos, K. "Fairness Heuristic Theory: Assessing the Information to Which People Are Reacting Has a Pivotal Role in Understanding Organizational Justice." In *Theoretical and Cultural Perspectives on Organizational Justice,* eds. S. Gilliland, D. Steiner, and D. Skarlicki. Greenwich, CT: Information Age Publishing, 2001, pp. 63–84; and Van den Bos, K.; E.A. Lind; and H.A.M. Wilke. "The Psychology of Procedural and Distributive Justice Viewed from the Perspective of Fairness Heuristic Theory." In *Justice in the Workplace,* Vol. 2, ed. R. Cropanzano. Mahwah, NJ: Erlbaum, 2001, pp. 49–66.

7.16 Treviño, L.K.; G.R. Weaver; and S.J. Reynolds. "Behavioral Ethics in Organizations: A Review." *Journal of Management* 32 (2006), pp. 951–90.

7.17 McAllister, D.J. "Affect- and Cognition-Based Trust as Foundations for Interpersonal Cooperation in Organizations." *Academy of Management Journal* 38 (1995), pp. 24–59.

7.18 Ibid.

7.19 Mayer et al., "An Integrative Model"; Rotter, J.B. "A New Scale for the Measurement of Interpersonal Trust." *Journal of Personality* 35 (1967), pp. 651–65; Rotter, J.B. "Generalized Expectancies for Interpersonal Trust." *American Psychologist* 26 (1971), pp. 443–52; and Rotter, J.B. "Interpersonal Trust, Trustworthiness, and Gullibility." *American Psychologist* 35 (1980), pp. 1–7.

7.20 Rosenberg, M. "Misanthropy and Political Ideology." *American Sociological Review* 21 (1956), pp. 690–95; and Wrightsman, L.S. Jr. "Measurement of Philosophies of Human Nature." *Psychological Reports* 14 (1964), pp. 743–51.

7.56   Ibid.

7.57   Taylor, "No Test Dummies."

7.58   Colquitt et al., "Justice at the Millennium"; and Cohen-Charash, Y., and P.E. Spector. "The Role of Justice in Organizations: A Meta-Analysis." *Organizational Behavior and Human Decision Processes* 86 (2001), pp. 278–321.

7.59   Bies, R.J., and J.F. Moag. "Interactional Justice: Communication Criteria of Fairness." In *Research on Negotiations in Organizations,* Vol. 1, eds. R.J. Lewicki, B.H. Sheppard, and M.H. Bazerman. Greenwich, CT: JAI Press, 1986, pp. 43–55; and Greenberg, J. "The Social Side of Fairness: Interpersonal and Informational Classes of Organizational Justice." In *Justice in the Workplace: Approaching Fairness in Human Resource Management,* ed. R. Cropanzano. Hillsdale, NJ: Erlbaum, 1993, pp. 79–103.

7.60   Bies, R.J. "Interactional (In)justice: The Sacred and the Profane." In *Advances in Organizational Justice,* eds. J. Greenberg and R. Cropanzano. Stanford, CA: Stanford University Press, 2001, pp. 85–108.

7.61   Tepper, B.J. "Consequences of Abusive Supervision." *Academy of Management Journal* 43 (2000), pp. 178–90.

7.62   Schat, A.C.H.; M.R. Frone; and E.K. Kelloway. "Prevalence of Workplace Aggression in the U.S. Workforce: Findings from a National Study." In *Handbook of Workplace Violence,* eds. E.K. Kelloway, J. Barling, and J.J. Hurrell. Thousand Oaks, CA: Sage, 2006, pp. 47–89.

7.63   Tepper, B.J.; M.K. Duffy; C.A. Henle; and L.S. Lambert. "Procedural Injustice, Victim Precipitation, and Abusive Supervision."

Personnel Psychology 28 (2006), pp. 101–23.

7.64   Tepper, B.J. "Abusive Supervision in Work Organizations: Review, Synthesis, and Research Agenda." *Journal of Management* 33 (2007), pp. 261–89.

7.65   Mitchell, M.S., and M.L. Ambrose. "Abusive Supervision and Workplace Deviance and the Moderating Effects of Negative Reciprocity Beliefs." *Journal of Applied Psychology* 92 (2007), pp. 1159–68; Tepper, B.J.; C.A. Henle; L.S. Lambert; R.A. Giacalone; and M.K. Duffy. "Abusive Supervision and Subordinates' Organizational Deviance." *Journal of Applied Psychology* 93 (2008), pp. 721–32; and Tepper, B.J.; J.C. Carr; D.M. Breaux; S. Geider; C. Hu; and W. Hua. "Abusive Supervision, Intentions to Quit, and Employees' Workplace Deviance: A Power/Dependence Analysis." *Organizational Behavior and Human Decision Processes* 109 (2009), pp. 156–67.

7.66   Miner, A.G.; T.M. Glomb; and C. Hulin. "Experience Sampling Mode and Its Correlates at Work." *Journal of Occupational and Organizational Psychology* 78 (2005), pp. 171–93.

7.67   Gilliland, S.W.; L. Benson; and D.H. Schepers. "A Rejection Threshold in Justice Evaluations: Effects on Judgment and Decision-Making." *Organizational Behavior and Human Decision Processes* 76 (1998), pp. 113–31.

7.68   Bies and Moag, "Interactional Justice"; and Greenberg, "The Social Side of Fairness."

7.69   "RadioShack Fires 400 Employees by Email," http://abcnews.go.com/Technology/

wireStory?id52374917&CMPOTC-RSSFeeds0312 (May 28, 2007).

7.70   Folger, R., and D.P. Skarlicki. "Fairness as a Dependent Variable: Why Tough Times Can Lead to Bad Management." In *Justice in the Workplace: From Theory to Practice,* ed. R. Cropanzano. Mahwah, NJ: Erlbaum, 2001, pp. 97–118.

7.71   Marquez, J.; E. Frauenheim; and M. Schoeff, Jr. "Harsh Reality." *Workforce Management,* June 22, 2009, pp. 18-23.

7.72   Shaw, J.C.; R.E. Wild; and J.A. Colquitt. "To Justify or Excuse?: A Meta-Analysis of the Effects of Explanations." *Journal of Applied Psychology* 88 (2003), pp. 444–58.

7.73   Orey, M. "Fear of Firing." *BusinessWeek,* April 23, 2007, pp. 52–62.

7.74   Greenberg, J. "Employee Theft as a Reaction to Underpayment Inequity: The Hidden Cost of Paycuts." *Journal of Applied Psychology* 75 (1990), pp. 561–68.

7.75   Colquitt et al., "Justice at the Millennium"; and Cohen-Charash and Spector, "The Role of Justice."

7.76   Treviño et al., "Behavioral Ethics."

7.77   Donaldson, T., and T.W. Dunfee. "Toward a Unified Conception of Business Ethics: Integrative Social Contracts Theory." *Academy of Management Review* 19 (1994), pp. 252–84.

7.78   Treviño et al., "Behavioral Ethics."

7.79   Kaptein, M. "Developing a Measure of Unethical Behavior in the Workplace: A Stakeholder Perspective." *Journal of Management* 34 (2008), pp. 978–1008.

7.80   Covey, S.M.R. *The Speed of Trust: The One Thing that Changes Everything.* New York: The Free Press, 2006.

7.81   Treviño et al., "Behavioral Ethics."

7.82   Near, J.P., and M.P. Miceli. "Organizational Dissidence: The Case of Whistle-Blowing." *Journal of Business Ethics* 4 (1985), pp. 1–16.

7.83   Rehg, M.T.; M.P. Miceli; J.P. Near; and J.R. Van Scotter. "Antecedents and Outcomes of Retaliation Against Whistleblowers: Gender Differences and Power Relationships." *Organization Science* 19 (2008), pp. 221-40.

7.84   Miceli, M.P.; J.P. Near; and T.M. Dworkin. "A Word to the Wise: How Managers and Policy-Makers Can Encourage Employees to Report Wrongdoing." *Journal of Business Ethics* 86 (2009), pp. 379–96.

7.85   Rest, J.R. *Moral Development: Advances in Research and Theory.* New York: Praeger, 2006.

7.86   Treviño, L.K. "Ethical Decision Making in Organizations: A Person-Situation Interactionist Model." *Academy of Management Review* 11 (1996), pp. 601–17.

7.87   Tomlinson, E.C. "Teaching the Interactionist Model of Ethics." *Journal of Management Education* 33 (2009), pp. 142–65; and Treviño, L.K., and M.E. Brown. "Managing to be Ethical: Debunking Five Business Ethics Myths." *Academy of Management Executive* 18 (2004), pp. 69–83.

7.88   Rest, *Moral Development.*

7.89   Butterfield, K.D.; L.K. Treviño; and G.R. Weaver. "Moral Awareness in Business Organizations: Influence of Issue-Related and Social Context Factors." *Human Relations* 53 (2000), pp. 981–1017.

7.90   Robertson, D.C. "Business Ethics Across Cultures." In *The Blackwell Handbook of Cross-Cultural Management,* eds. M.J. Gannon and K.L. Newman. Malden, MA: Blackwell, 2002, pp. 361–92.

7.91 Ibid.

7.92 McLean, B. "Sex, Lies, and Videogames." *Fortune,* August 22, 2005, pp. 66–70.

7.93 Jones, T.M. "Ethical Decision Making by Individuals in Organizations: An Issue-Contingent Model." *Academy of Management Review* 16 (1991), pp. 366–95.

7.94 Singhapakdi, A.; S.J. Vitell; and K.L. Kraft. "Moral Intensity and Ethical Decision-Making of Marketing Professionals." *Journal of Business Research* 36 (1996), pp. 245–55.

7.95 Jones, "Ethical Decision Making by Individuals in Organizations."

7.96 Reynolds, S.J. "Moral Attentiveness: Who Pays Attention to the Moral Aspects of Life?" *Journal of Applied Psychology* 93 (2008), pp. 1027–41.

7.97 Porter, J. "Using Ex-Cons to Scare MBAs Straight." *BusinessWeek,* May 5, 2008, p. 58.

7.98 Ibid.

7.99 Rest, *Moral Development.*

7.100 Kohlberg, L. "Stage and Sequence: The Cognitive Developmental Approach to Socialization." In *Handbook of Socialization Theory,* ed. D.A. Goslin. Chicago: Rand McNally, 1969, pp. 347–480; and Kohlberg, L. "The Claim to Moral Adequacy of a Highest Stage of Moral Judgment." *Journal of Philosophy* 70 (1973), pp. 630–46.

7.101 Rest, J. *Manual for the Defining Issues Test.* Minneapolis, MN: Center for the Study of Ethical Development, 1986; and Loviscky, G.E.; L.K. Treviño; and R.R.

Jacobs. *Journal of Business Ethics* 73 (2007), pp. 263–85.

7.102 Kohlberg, "Stage and Sequence"; and Kohlberg, "The Claim to Moral Adequacy."

7.103 Ibid.

7.104 Treviño et al., "Behavioral Ethics"

7.105 Kohlberg, "Stage and Sequence"; and Kohlberg, "The Claim to Moral Adequacy."

7.106 Treviño et al., "Behavioral Ethics;" and Rest, J.; D. Narvaez; M.J. Bebeau; and S.J. Thoma. *Postconventional Moral Thinking: A Neo-Kohlbergian Approach. Mahwah,* NJ: Lawrence Erlbaum, 1999.

7.107 Crane and Matten, *Business Ethics.* New York: Oxford University Press, 2007.

7.108 Ibid.

7.109 Rest, *Moral Development.*

7.110 Kaptein, M. "Developing and Testing a Measure for the Ethical Culture of Organizations: The Corporate Ethics Virtues Model." *Journal of Organizational Behavior* 29 (2008), pp. 923–47; Schminke, M.; M.L. Ambrose; and D.O. Neubaum. "The Effect of Leader Moral Development on Ethical Climate and Employee Attitudes." *Organizational Behavior and Human Decision Processes* 97 (2005), pp. 135–51; and Treviño, "Ethical Decision Making in Organizations"

7.111 Schweitzer, M.E.; L. Ordòñez; and B. Douma. "Goal Setting as a Motivator of Unethical Behavior." *Academy of Management Journal* 47 (2004), pp. 422–32.

7.112 Aquino, K., and A. Reed II. "The Self-Importance of Moral Identity." *Journal of Personality and Social Psychology* 83 (2002), pp. 1423–40.

7.113 Ibid.

7.114 Reynolds, S.J., and T.L. Ceranic. "The Effects of Moral Judgment and Moral Identity on Moral Behavior: An Empirical Examination of the Moral Individual." *Journal of Applied Psychology* 92 (2007), pp. 1610–24.

7.115 Schminke, M.; M.L. Ambrose; and T.W. Noel. "The Effects of Ethical Frameworks on Perceptions of Organizational Justice." *Academy of Management Journal* 40 (1997), pp. 1190–1207; and Wendorf, C.A.; S. Alexander; and I.J. Firestone. "Social Justice and Moral Reasoning: An Empirical Integration of Two Paradigms in Psychological Research." *Social Justice Research* 15 (2002), pp. 19–39.

7.116 Mayer, R.C.; and M.B. Gavin. "Trust in Management and Performance: Who Minds the Shop While the Employees Watch the Boss?" *Academy of Management Journal* 48 (2005), pp. 874–88.

7.117 Blau, P. *Exchange and Power in Social Life*. New York: Wiley, 1964; and Shore, L.M.; L.E. Tetrick; P. Lynch; and K. Barksdale. "Social and Economic Exchange: Construct Development and Validation." *Journal of Applied Social Psychology* 36 (2006), pp. 837–67.

7.118 Ibid.

7.119 Dirks, K.T., and D.L. Ferrin. "Trust in Leadership: Meta-Analytic Findings and Implications for Research and Practice." *Journal of Applied Psychology* 87 (2002), pp. 611–28.

7.120 Ibid.

7.121 Carroll, A.B. "A Three-Dimensional Model of Corporate Social Performance." *Academy of Management Review* 4 (1979), pp. 497–505; Carroll, A.B. "The Pyramid of Corporate Social Responsibility: Toward the Moral Management of Organizational Stakeholders." *Business Horizons* 34 (1991), pp. 39–48; Carroll, A.B. "The Four Faces of Corporate Citizenship." *Business and Society Review* 100 (1998), pp. 1–7; and Carroll, A.B. "Corporate Social Responsibility— Evolution of a Definitional Construct." *Business and Society* 38 (1999), pp. 268–95.

7.122 Carroll, "The Pyramid."

7.123 Weber, J. "The New Ethics Enforcers." *BusinessWeek,* February 13, 2006, pp. 76–77.

7.124 Carroll, "The Pyramid."

7.125 Schoeff, M. Jr. "J. M. Smuckers Co." *Workforce Management,* March 13, 2006, p. 19.

7.126 Carroll, "The Pyramid."

7.127 Grow, B.; S. Hamm; and L. Lee. "The Debate Over Doing Good." *BusinessWeek,* August 15, 2005, pp. 76–78.

7.128 Holmes, "Nike Goes for the Green."

7.129 Gunther, M. "The Green Machine." *Fortune,* August 7, 2006, pp. 42–57.

7.130 Grow et al., "The Debate Over Doing Good."

7.131 Levenson, "Citizen Nike."

7.132 Holmes, "Nike Goes for the Green."

7.133 Ibid.

7.134 Levenson, "Citizen Nike."

7.135 Jana, R. "Nike Goes Green. Very Quietly." *BusinessWeek,* June 22, 2009.

7.136 Ibid.

chapter 8

Learning and Decision Making

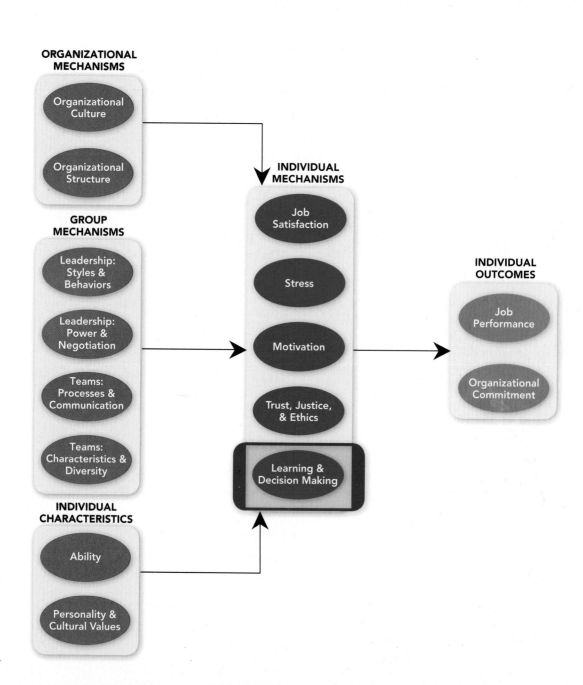

✅ LEARNING GOALS

After reading this chapter, you should be able to answer the following questions:

8.1 What is learning, and how does it affect decision making?

8.2 What types of knowledge can employees gain as they learn and build expertise?

8.3 What are the methods by which employees learn in organizations?

8.4 What two methods can employees use to make decisions?

8.5 What decision-making problems can prevent employees from translating their learning into accurate decisions?

8.6 How does learning affect job performance and organizational commitment?

8.7 What steps can organizations take to foster learning?

XEROX

If you were a manager in Xerox's global services division with a question about how to best get something done, you'd have a couple of options at your disposal. You could run up and down the hall asking colleagues for an answer (they *might* have one for you), or you could try to look it up in a product manual or a written guide of some sort (which probably does not exist). If you could though, wouldn't it be nice to tap into the knowledge of many people at once who have an expertise in the area of your question? Luckily, many Xerox employees have access to online learning communities that allow them to do just that. Xerox, like many other organizations, including Caterpillar, Raytheon, World Bank, and hundreds more, have developed online "communities of practice" that are designed as workplace learning tools.[1] These online communities of practice attempt to put employees with similar jobs, interests, or problems together through social networking, allowing them to take advantage of the collective wisdom of the group or the tacit knowledge of a highly experienced member. Xerox is in the middle of a three-year process of developing and implementing various online learning communities for employees in vital positions.[2]

These online communities give employees a means to share the types of information that they couldn't find in a book or procedural manual, and would instead have to learn from experience on the job. In essence, they take the unwritten knowledge (or human capital) that Xerox employees possess and provide a conduit to other employees who need that information to perform their jobs effectively. These types of online social networking tools are perhaps most useful in passing information between employees who might be geographically dispersed.[3] Their value doesn't end with the sharing of job information, however. Gary Vastola, Xerox's vice president of learning and development, states that "The communities also provide a clear roadway to career growth by mapping out expectations."[4] Communities of practice can take many shapes, including face-to-face meetings, online bulletin boards, blogs, or even wikis (i.e., software that allows users to edit or create Web pages). The cutting edge for Xerox at the moment is an experiment with virtual worlds in which coworkers can do everything from holding brainstorming sessions to practicing presentations online.[5] These virtual worlds allow employees to create representations of themselves (see this chapter's opening picture) and interact with one another remotely. These sorts of tools have allowed the managing principals at Xerox to communicate with one another across areas of the company, which helps take them out of the silos created by their own business lines.[6]

Although many of these online communities are geared toward managerial-level employees, Xerox's "Eureka" system, which operates among the community of repair technicians, saves the company perhaps millions of dollars a year in repair costs by allowing them to pass along information.[7] Putting these communities of practice together is not as easy as throwing together a bulletin board though. The planning process usually evolves over a three-month timeframe, beginning with meetings between learning leaders and executives.[8] They key to success is determining what types of information employees might need and how they search for that information. Xerox realizes that as its workforce comes and goes, the information these workers possess becomes an increasingly valuable commodity that can be retained only through knowledge sharing and management. Many other companies believe the same thing; nearly two-thirds of large organizations rely on knowledge sharing between employees and employ various forms of communities of practice.[9]

LEARNING AND DECISION MAKING

Xerox and many other companies are focused on promoting knowledge sharing between their employees because learning and decision making are so important in organizations. **Learning** reflects relatively permanent changes in an employee's knowledge or skill that result from experience.[10] The more employees learn, the more they bring to the table when they come to work. Why is learning so important? Because it has a significant impact on **decision making**, which refers to the process of generating and choosing from a set of alternatives to solve a problem. The more knowledge and skills employees possess, the more likely they are to make accurate and sound decisions. The risk, at Xerox and other organizations, is that less experienced employees will lack the knowledge base needed to make the right decisions when performing their jobs or stepping into new roles.

One reason inexperience can be so problematic is that learning is not necessarily easy. Have you ever watched "experts" perform their jobs? How is it that someone becomes an expert? It takes a significant amount of time to become proficient at most complex jobs. It takes most employees anywhere from three months to a year to perform their job at a satisfactory level.[11] To develop high levels of expertise takes significantly longer. This difficulty makes it even more important for companies to find a way to improve learning and decision making by their employees.

8.1

What is learning, and how does it affect decision making?

WHY DO SOME EMPLOYEES LEARN TO MAKE DECISIONS BETTER THAN OTHERS?

Bill Buford, a journalist interested in becoming a chef, was hired by Mario Batali's world-renowned restaurant Babbo in New York. At some point early in his tenure in the kitchen, he realized he was in over his head while he stood and watched other, more experienced cooks work at an unbelievably frantic pace. He knew right then that he had a decision to make:

> It was at a go-forward-or-backward moment. If I went backward, I'd be saying, 'Thanks for the visit, very interesting, that's sure not me.' But how to go forward? There was no place for me. These people were at a higher level of labor. They didn't think. Their skills were so deeply inculcated they were available to them as instincts. I didn't have skills of that kind and couldn't imagine how you'd learn them. I was aware of being poised on the verge of something: a long, arduous, confidence-bashing, profoundly humiliating experience.[12]

In this situation, Buford realized that his coworkers had more expertise than he did. **Expertise** refers to the knowledge and skills that distinguish experts from novices and less experienced people.[13] Research shows that the differences between experts and novices is almost always a function of learning as opposed to the more popular view that intelligence or other innate differences make the difference.[14] Although learning cannot be directly seen or observed, we can tell when people have learned by observing their behaviors. It is those behaviors that can be used to tell experts from novices, and it is changes in those behaviors that can be used to show that learners are gaining knowledge. Although it's sometimes easy for employees to mimic a behavior once or twice, or get lucky with a few key decisions, true learning only occurs when changes in behavior become relatively permanent and are repeated over time. Understanding why some employees prove better at this than others requires understanding what exactly employees learn and how they do it.

Expertise is the accumulation of superior knowledge and skills in a field that separates experts from everyone else.

8.2

What types of knowledge can employees gain as they learn and build expertise?

TYPES OF KNOWLEDGE

Employees learn two basic types of knowledge, both of which have important implications for organizations. **Explicit knowledge** is the kind of information you're likely to think about when you picture someone sitting down at a desk to learn. It's information that's relatively easily communicated and a large part of what companies teach during training sessions. Think about it this way: If you can put the information or knowledge in a manual or write it down for someone else, chances are good you're talking about explicit knowledge. As you read this textbook, we're doing our best to communicate explicit knowledge to you that will be useful to you in your future job. Although such information is necessary to perform well, it winds up being a relatively minor portion of all that you need to know.

Tacit knowledge, in contrast, is what employees can typically learn only through experience.[15] It's not easily communicated but could very well be the most important aspect of what we learn in organizations.[16] In fact, it's been argued that up to 90 percent of the knowledge contained in organizations occurs in tacit form.[17] Did you ever get to be so good at something that you had the ability to do it but couldn't really explain it to someone else? That's a common way to explain tacit knowledge. It's been described as the "know-how," "know-what," and "know who" acquired solely through experience.[18] Others have used terms such as intuition, skills, insight, beliefs, mental models, and practical intelligence.[19] Table 8-1 lists the qualities that help explain the differences between explicit and tacit knowledge. Some would say that explicit knowledge is what everyone can find and use, but tacit knowledge is what separates experts from common people.[20]

TABLE 8-1	Characteristics of Explicit and Tacit Knowledge
EXPLICIT KNOWLEDGE	**TACIT KNOWLEDGE**
Easily transferred through written or verbal communication	Very difficult, if not impossible, to articulate to others
Readily available to most	Highly personal in nature
Can be learned through books	Based on experience
Always conscious and accessible information	Sometimes holders don't even recognize that they possess it
General information	Typically job- or situation-specific

Source: Adapted from R. McAdam, B. Mason, and J. McCrory, "Exploring the Dichotomies within the Tacit Knowledge Literature: Towards a Process of Tacit Knowing in Organizations," *Journal of Knowledge Management* 11 (2007), pp. 43–59.

METHODS OF LEARNING

Tacit and explicit knowledge are extremely important to employees and organizations. As an employee, it's hard to build a high level of tacit knowledge without some level of explicit knowledge to build from. From an organization's perspective, the tacit knowledge its employees accumulate may be the single most important strategic asset a company possesses.[21] The question then becomes: How do employees learn these types of knowledge? The short answer is that we learn through reinforcement (i.e., rewards and punishment), observation, and experience.

8.3

What are the methods by which employees learn in organizations?

REINFORCEMENT. We've long known that managers use various methods of reinforcement to induce desirable or reduce undesirable behaviors by their employees. Originally known as operant conditioning, B.F. Skinner was the first to pioneer the notion that we learn by observing the link between our voluntary behavior and the consequences that follow it. Research has continually demonstrated that people will exhibit specific behaviors if they're rewarded for doing so. Not surprisingly, we have a tendency to repeat behaviors that result in consequences that we like and to reduce behaviors that result in consequences we don't like. Figure 8-1 shows this operant conditioning process.

In the model in Figure 8-1, you can see that there are antecedents or events that precede or signal certain behaviors, which are then followed by consequences. Antecedents in organizations are typically goals, rules, instructions, or other types of information that help show employees what is expected of them. Although antecedents are useful for motivational reasons, it's primarily the consequences of actions that drive behavior. This entire process of reinforcement is a continuous cycle, and the repetition of behaviors is strengthened to the degree that reinforcement continues to occur. There are four specific consequences typically used by organizations to modify employee behavior, known as the **contingencies of reinforcement**.[22] Figure 8-2 summarizes these contingencies. It's important to separate them according to what they're designed to do, namely, increase desired behaviors or decrease unwanted behaviors.

Two contingencies of reinforcement are used to increase desired behaviors. **Positive reinforcement** occurs when a positive outcome follows a desired behavior. It's perhaps the most common type of reinforcement and the type we think of when an employee receives some type of "reward." Increased pay, promotions, praise from a manager or coworkers, and public recognition would all be considered positive reinforcement when given as a result of an employee exhibiting desired behaviors. For positive reinforcement to be successful, employees need to see a direct link between their behaviors and desired outcomes (see Chapter 6 on Motivation for more discussion of such issues). If the consequences

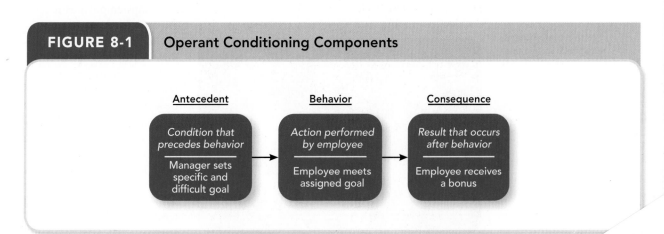

| **FIGURE 8-1** | **Operant Conditioning Components** |

Antecedent → **Behavior** → **Consequence**

Antecedent	Behavior	Consequence
Condition that precedes behavior	*Action performed by employee*	*Result that occurs after behavior*
Manager sets specific and difficult goal	Employee meets assigned goal	Employee receives a bonus

FIGURE 8-2 | Contingencies of Reinforcement

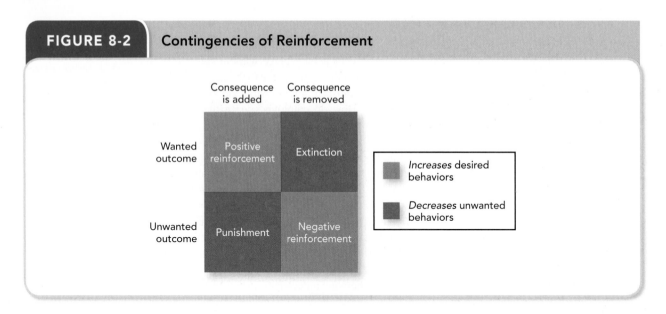

	Consequence is added	Consequence is removed
Wanted outcome	Positive reinforcement	Extinction
Unwanted outcome	Punishment	Negative reinforcement

Increases desired behaviors

Decreases unwanted behaviors

aren't realized until long after the specific behaviors, then the odds that employees will link the two are minimized. **Negative reinforcement** occurs when an unwanted outcome is removed following a desired behavior. Have you ever performed a task for the specific reason of not getting yelled at? If so, you learned to perform certain behaviors through the use of negative reinforcement. Perhaps there are some tasks your job requires that you don't enjoy. If your manager removes these responsibilities specifically because you perform well at another aspect of your job, then this could also be seen as negative reinforcement. It's important to remember that even though the word "negative" has a sour connotation to it, it's designed to *increase* desired behaviors.

The next two contingencies of reinforcement are designed to decrease undesired behaviors. **Punishment** occurs when an unwanted outcome follows an unwanted behavior. Punishment is exactly what it sounds like. In other words, employees are given something they don't like as a result of performing behaviors that the organization doesn't like. Suspending an employee for showing up to work late, assigning job tasks generally seen as demeaning for not following safety procedures, or even firing an employee for gross misconduct are all examples of punishment. **Extinction** occurs when there is the removal of a consequence following an unwanted behavior. The use of extinction to reinforce behavior can be purposeful or accidental. Perhaps employees receive attention from coworkers when they act in ways that are somewhat childish at work. Finding a way to remove the attention would be a purposeful act of extinction. Similarly though, perhaps employees work late every now and then to finish up job tasks when work gets busy, but their manager stops acknowledging that hard work. Desired behavior that's not reinforced will

Positive reinforcement, like public recognition, both encourages employees and helps ensure that desirable behaviors will be imitated and repeated.

diminish over time. In this way, a manager who does nothing to reinforce good behavior is actually decreasing the odds that it will be repeated!

In general, positive reinforcement and extinction should be the most common forms of reinforcement used by managers to create learning among their employees. Positive reinforcement doesn't have to be in the form of material rewards to be effective. There are many ways for managers to encourage wanted behaviors. Offering praise, providing feedback, public recognition, and small celebrations are all ways to encourage employees and increase the chances they will continue to exhibit desired behaviors. At the same time, extinction is an effective way to stop unwanted behaviors. Both of these contingencies deliver their intended results, but perhaps more importantly, they do so without creating feelings of animosity and conflict. Although punishment and negative reinforcement will work, they tend to bring other, detrimental consequences along with them.

Whereas the type of reinforcement used to modify behavior is important, research also shows that the timing of reinforcement is equally important.[23] Therefore, it's important to examine the timing of when the contingencies are applied, referred to as **schedules of reinforcement**. Table 8-2 provides a summary of the five schedules of reinforcement. **Continuous reinforcement** is the simplest schedule and happens when a specific consequence follows each and every occurrence of a desired behavior. For most jobs, continuous reinforcement is impractical. As a manager, can you imagine providing positive reinforcement every time someone exhibits a desired behavior? It's a good thing that research also shows that under many circumstances, continuous reinforcement might be considered the least long-lasting, because as soon as the consequence stops, the desired behavior stops along with it.[24]

The other four schedules differ in terms of their variability and the basis of the consequences. Two schedules are interval based; that is, they distribute reinforcement based on the amount of time that passes. A **fixed interval schedule** is probably the single most common form of reinforcement schedule. With this schedule, workers are rewarded after a certain amount of time, and the length of time between reinforcement periods stays the same. Every time employees get a paycheck after a predetermined period of time, they're being reinforced on a fixed interval schedule. **Variable interval schedules** are designed to reinforce behavior at more random points in time. A supervisor walking around at different points of time every day is a good example of a variable interval schedule. If that supervisor walked around at the same exact time every day, do you think workers would be more or less prone to exhibit good behaviors throughout the day?

TABLE 8-2	**Schedules of Reinforcement**		
REINFORCEMENT SCHEDULE	**REWARD GIVEN FOLLOWING**	**POTENTIAL LEVEL OF PERFORMANCE**	**EXAMPLE**
Continuous	Every desired behavior	High, but difficult to maintain	Praise
Fixed Interval	Fixed time periods	Average	Paycheck
Variable Interval	Variable time periods	Moderately high	Supervisor walk-by
Fixed Ratio	Fixed number of desired behaviors	High	Piece-rate pay
Variable Ratio	Variable number of desired behaviors	Very high	Commission pay

The other two reinforcement schedules are based on actual behaviors. **Fixed ratio schedules** reinforce behaviors after a certain number of them have been exhibited. Some manufacturing plants have created piece-rate pay systems in which workers are paid according to the number of items they produce. Employees know ahead of time how many items they have to produce to be reinforced. **Variable ratio schedules** reward people after a varying number of exhibited behaviors. Salespeople, for example, are often compensated based on commission because they receive extra pay every time they sell an item. However, a car salesperson doesn't make a sale every time someone walks in the door of the dealership. Sometimes it takes exhibiting good sales behaviors to 8 or 9 customers to make a sale. Take a slot machine as an example. The machine doesn't reward you for every lever pull or even every 10 lever pulls—you never know when the next winning pull will be. Would you say that slot machines do a good job of reinforcing the behavior that casinos would like you to have? You bet!

On the whole, research has consistently shown that variable schedules lead to higher levels of performance than fixed schedules. Think about it this way: Do you study more consistently in a class that gives pop quizzes or one that simply tests you three set times a semester? Research also shows that desired behaviors tend to disappear much more quickly when reinforcement is discontinued under fixed plans. However, variable schedules are not always appropriate for some types of reinforcement. How would you like it if your employer decided to give you your paychecks on a variable schedule? Sorry, you're not getting a paycheck this week—maybe next week! Moreover, studies suggest that continuous or fixed schedules can be better for reinforcing new behaviors or behaviors that don't occur on a frequent basis.

OBSERVATION. In addition to learning through reinforcement, **social learning theory** argues that people in organizations have the ability to learn through the observation of others.[25] In fact, many would argue that social learning is the primary way by which employees gain knowledge in organizations.[26] Think about where you're most likely to get your cues while working in an organization. When possible, chances are good you'll look around at other employees to figure out the appropriate behaviors on your job. Not only do employees have the ability to see the link between their own behaviors and their consequences, they can also observe the behaviors and consequences of others.[27] When employees observe the actions of others, learn from what they observe, and then repeat

"Oh, not bad. The light comes on, I press the bar, they write me a check. How about you?"

OB ON SCREEN

HARRY POTTER AND THE ORDER OF THE PHOENIX

I can't imagine why you would need to USE spells in my classroom. You will be learning about defensive spells in a secure, risk-free way . . .

With those words, Dolores Jane Umbridge (Imelda Staunton), a new teacher at Hogwart's School of Witchcraft and Wizardry, lays out her plan for teaching her fifth-year "Defense against the Dark Arts" class—out of a book, with no actual casting of spells—in *Harry Potter and the Order of the Phoenix* (Dir.: David Yates, Warner Bros., 2007). As we soon find out in the movie, casting spells is not as easy as it seems, and it doesn't come naturally for most students after merely reading about it in a book.

Undaunted, the students decide to meet outside of class by forming a secret society taught and led by Harry Potter (Daniel Radcliffe). Harry had the experience to know what they might encounter in the real world and had actually cast some spells a time or two. Behind Ms. Umbridge's back, Harry attempts to show the students how to perform the spells by brandishing their wands in just the right way and emphasizing certain words over others. After students learn the material (explicit knowledge), Harry shares information that they cannot read in a book (tacit knowledge), models the behavior for them (observation), and offers encouragement when students perform well (reinforcement). After a lot of practice (sometimes with close to disastrous consequences!), the students are able to cast spells effectively. Learning for them required understanding both types of knowledge, and it took multiple methods of instruction to impart that understanding.

the observed behavior, they're engaging in **behavioral modeling**. See our **OB on Screen** feature for behavioral modeling in action.

For behavior modeling to occur successfully, a number of processes have to take place. These steps are shown in Figure 8-3. First, the learner must focus attention on an appropriate model and accurately perceive the critical behavior the model exhibits. That model might be a supervisor, a coworker, or even a subordinate. Some organizations go out of their way to supply role models for newcomers or inexperienced workers to watch and learn from. Many companies, such as the Tennessee Valley Authority (the largest public power company in the country) assign younger workers to follow and model older workers in the hopes of

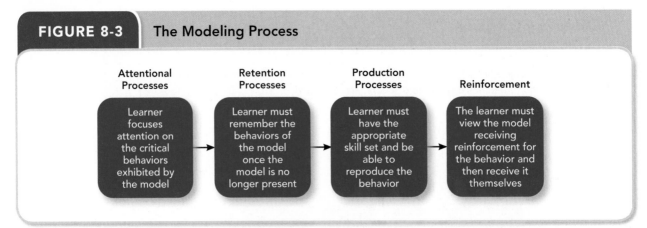

FIGURE 8-3   The Modeling Process

Attentional Processes	Retention Processes	Production Processes	Reinforcement
Learner focuses attention on the critical behaviors exhibited by the model	Learner must remember the behaviors of the model once the model is no longer present	Learner must have the appropriate skill set and be able to reproduce the behavior	The learner must view the model receiving reinforcement for the behavior and then receive it themselves

Source: Adapted from H.M. Weiss, "Learning Theory and Industrial and Organizational Psychology," in *Handbook of Industrial and Organizational Psychology,* eds. M.D. Dunnette and L.M. Hough. (Consulting Psychologists Press: Palo Alto, CA, 1990), pp. 75–169.

capturing the tacit knowledge they've acquired.[28] In fact, because tacit knowledge is so difficult to communicate, modeling might be the single best way to acquire it. For that reason, modeling is a continual process that is used at all levels of many organizations. Kellogg's, the Battle Creek, Michigan–based cereal company, groomed current CEO David Mackay for two years by allowing him to observe and model an interim, experienced CEO prior to taking over the helm. Mackay shadowed the CEO and observed boardroom proceedings to gain the insider experience that the Kellogg's board felt he was lacking.[29] Needless to say, choosing a good model is important, and not all models are good ones. Salomon Brothers, the New York–based investment bank, learned this lesson the hard way when employees began to model the unethical behaviors of their managers and leaders.[30]

Second, the learner needs to remember exactly what the model's behavior was and how they did it. This step is easier said than done when watching experts perform their job, because so much of what they do remains unspoken and can occur at a rapid pace. Third, the learner must undertake production processes, or actually be able to reproduce what the model did. Not only must the learner have the requisite knowledge and physical skills to be able to perform the task; now he or she must translate what's been observed into action. Do you remember the first time you drove a car? Chances are good you'd been watching other drivers for many years, picking up bits and pieces of how to do it through observation. However, things became different when you were behind the wheel for the first time. All of the sudden, there was a lot of information to process, and years and years of observation had to be put into action.

Fourth, the last step of behavior modeling is reinforcement. This reinforcement can come from observation, direct experience, or both. The learner can observe the

David Mackay was provided an unusual opportunity to learn by observation and behavioral modeling before becoming CEO of Kellogg's. He "shadowed" his predecessor for two years to gain insider experience before taking the helm.

consequences of the model having exhibited the behavior (positive reinforcement or punishment), which in itself will help ingrain the desirability of performing the behavior. In addition, it's important for the learner to receive reinforcement after replicating the behavior. If the newly acquired behaviors are positively reinforced, the likelihood of continued behavior increases.

GOAL ORIENTATION. Before we leave this section, it's important to recognize that people learn somewhat differently according to their predispositions or attitudes toward learning and performance. These differences are reflected in different "goal orientations" that capture the kinds of activities and goals that people prioritize. Some people have what's known as a **learning orientation**, where building competence is deemed more important than demonstrating competence. "Learning-oriented" persons enjoy working on new kinds of tasks, even if they fail during their early experiences. Such people view failure in positive terms—as a means of increasing knowledge and skills in the long run.[31]

For others, the demonstration of competence is deemed a more important goal than the building of competence. That demonstration of competence can be motivated by two different thought processes. Those with a **performance-prove orientation** focus on demonstrating their competence so that others think favorably of them. Those with a **performance-avoid orientation** focus on demonstrating their competence so that others will not think poorly of them. In either case, "performance-oriented" people tend to work mainly on tasks at which they're already good, preventing them from failing in front of others. Such individuals view failure in negative terms—as an indictment of their ability and competence.

Research has shown that a learning goal orientation improves self-confidence, feedback-seeking behavior, learning strategy development, and learning performance.[32] Research on the two performance orientations is more mixed. Although it would seem that focusing on performance should improve performance-based outcomes, research shows that isn't necessarily the case. On the whole, a performance-prove orientation tends to be a mixed bag, producing varying levels of performance and outcomes. What's more clear are the detrimental effects of having a performance-avoid orientation. Employees who enter learning situations with a fear of looking bad in front of others tend to learn less and have substantially higher levels of anxiety.[33] What kind of orientation do you tend to exhibit? See our **OB Assessments** feature to find out.

METHODS OF DECISION MAKING

How do employees take explicit and tacit knowledge, however it's gained, and turn that knowledge into effective decision making? Sometimes that process is very straightforward. **Programmed decisions** are decisions that become somewhat automatic because people's knowledge allows them to recognize and identify a situation and the course of action that needs to be taken. As shown in Figure 8-4, experts often respond to an identified problem by realizing that they've dealt with it before. That realization triggers a programmed decision that's implemented and then evaluated according to its ability to deliver the expected outcome. For experts who possess high levels of explicit and tacit knowledge, many decisions they face are of this programmed variety. That's not to say that the decisions are necessarily easy. It simply means that their experience and knowledge allows them to see the problems more easily and recognize and implement solutions more quickly.

To experts, this kind of decision making sometimes comes across as intuition or a "gut feeling." **Intuition** can be described as emotionally charged judgments that arise through quick, nonconscious, and holistic associations.[34] Because of their tacit knowledge, experts sometimes cannot put into words why they know that a problem exists, why a solution will work, or how they accomplished a task. They just "know." Of course, the difficulty arises in knowing when to trust that "gut instinct" and when not to.[35] As a general rule of thumb,

8.4

What two methods can employees use to make decisions?

OB ASSESSMENTS

GOAL ORIENTATION

What does your goal orientation look like? This assessment is designed to measure all three dimensions of goal orientation. Please write a number next to each statement that indicates the extent to which it accurately describes your attitude toward work while you are on the job. Answer each question using the response scale provided. Then sum up your answers for each of the three dimensions. (For more assessments relevant to this chapter, please visit the Online Learning Center at www.mhhe.com/colquitt).

1 STRONGLY DISAGREE	2 DISAGREE	3 NEUTRAL	4 AGREE	5 STRONGLY AGREE

1. I am willing to select challenging assignments that I can learn a lot from. _____

2. I often look for opportunities to develop new skills and knowledge. _____

3. I enjoy challenging and difficult tasks where I'll learn new skills. _____

4. For me, development of my ability is important enough to take risks. _____

5. I prefer to work in situations that require a high level of ability and talent. _____

6. I like to show that I can perform better than my coworkers. _____

7. I try to figure out what it takes to prove my ability to others at work. _____

8. I enjoy it when others at work are aware of how well I am doing. _____

9. I prefer to work on projects where I can prove my ability to others. _____

10. I would avoid taking on a new task if there was a chance that I would appear incompetent to others. _____

11. Avoiding a show of low ability is more important to me than learning a new skill. _____

12. I'm concerned about taking on a task at work if my performance would reveal that I had low ability. _____

13. I prefer to avoid situations at work where I might perform poorly. _____

SCORING AND INTERPRETATION

Learning Orientation: Sum up items 1–5. _____
Performance-Prove Orientation: Sum up items 6–9. _____
Performance-Avoid Orientation: Sum up items 10–13. _____

For learning orientation, scores of 20 or more are above average, and scores of 19 or less are below average. For the two performance orientations, scores of 15 or more are above average, and scores of 14 or less are below average.

FIGURE 8-4   Programmed and Nonprogrammed Decisions

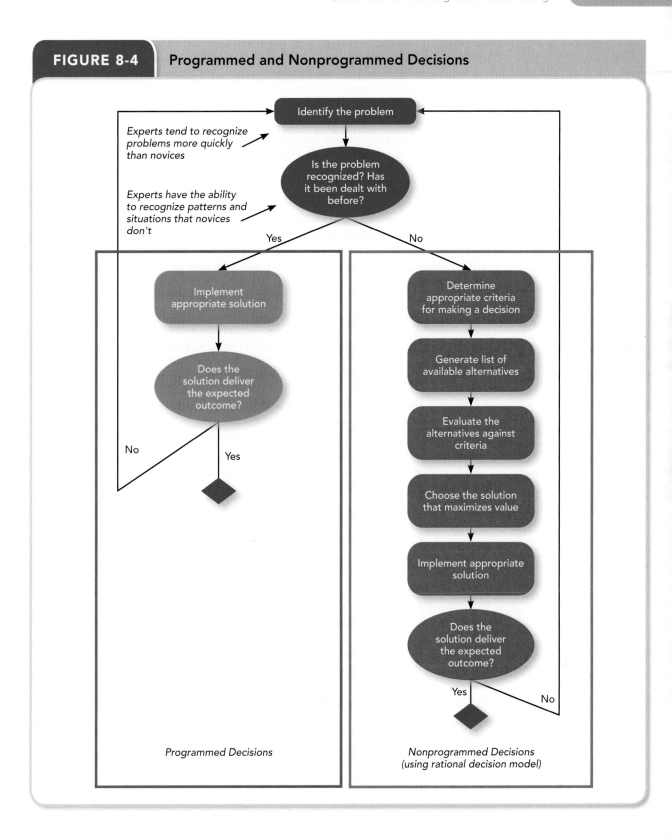

Programmed Decisions

*Nonprogrammed Decisions
(using rational decision model)*

you should probably ask yourself how much expertise you have about the subject of the judgment. In other words, don't go laying down your life savings on a spin of the roulette wheel in Vegas because your intuition tells you "red"! Effective intuition results when people have a large amount of tacit knowledge. For more discussion of such issues, see our **OB at the Bookstore** feature.

Intuitive decision making is perhaps never more important than during a crisis. A **crisis situation** is a change—whether sudden or evolving—that results in an urgent problem that must be addressed immediately. For businesses, a crisis is anything with the potential to cause sudden and serious damage to its employees, reputation, or bottom line. One of the key factors in almost all crises is that decisions must be made quickly.[36] Unless there has been some form of specific preplanning for that crisis, managers (who should have the most tacit knowledge to support their decisions) must use their intuition rather than take a lengthy period of time to think through all of their options.[37] When a manager uses intuition to make a decision in a crisis situation, followers often misinterpret the manager's intent, because the managers can't put the reasons for their decisions into words (or don't have the time to do so).[38] In turn, the implementation of their plan often suffers. Therefore, managers who make decisions face two major questions: How can they ensure that others follow their lead when the path is unclear, and how can they confirm that their intuition is not faulty? Karl Weick, a preeminent scholar on crisis management at the University of Michigan, suggests five steps for communicating intent when using intuition:

1. *Here's what I think we face* (How does the manager perceive the situation?).
2. *Here's what I think we should do* (A task-focused statement of what the manager wants to happen).
3. *Here's why* (The reasoning behind the decision).
4. *Here's what we should keep our eye on* (What things should the staff look for to ensure the intuition is correct or that the situation hasn't changed?).
5. *Now, talk to me.* (Confirm that everyone understands their roles and that there is no other information to consider).[39]

These communications steps are important for a manager making intuitive decisions, because they help others follow directives more easily, while also providing a check on the manager to ensure he or she observes the crisis environment correctly.

When a situation arises that is new, complex, and not recognized, it calls for a **nonprogrammed decision** on the part of the employee. Organizations are complex and changing environments, and many workers face uncertainty on a daily basis. In these instances, employees have to make sense of their environment, understand the problems they're faced with, and come up with solutions to overcome them. As a general rule of thumb, as employees move up the corporate ladder, a larger percentage of their decisions become less and less programmed. How should decision making proceed in such contexts? The **rational decision-making model** offers a step-by-step approach to making decisions that maximize outcomes by examining all available alternatives. As shown in Figure 8-4, this model becomes relevant when people don't recognize a problem as one they've dealt with before.

The first step in the rational decision-making model is to identify the criteria that are important in making the decision, taking into account all involved parties. The second step is to generate a list of all available alternatives that might be potential solutions to the problem. At this point, evaluating the alternatives is not necessary. The responsibility simply lies in coming up with as many potential solutions as possible. The third step in the model is the evaluation of those alternatives against the criteria laid out in step one. Does it matter how much the alternative costs? What exactly will happen as a result of various

OB AT THE BOOKSTORE

BLINK

by Malcolm Gladwell (New York: Little, Brown & Co., 2005).

Decisions made very quickly can be every bit as good as decisions made cautiously and deliberately.

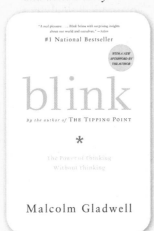

With those words, Malcolm Gladwell summarizes his book's take on decision making. The book opens with a story about a rare, ancient, Greek statue under consideration for purchase by the J. Paul Getty Museum in California. Due diligence had been performed on the statue, its papers seemed to be in order, and numerous, detailed scientific analyses had been performed by a geologist to confirm its authenticity. After purchasing this extraordinary statue and publicizing its purchase to the outside world, the museum began to show it to numerous art experts. Expert after expert told the museum that there was something wrong with the piece. They couldn't put their finger on why they knew it was a fake; they just knew. The fingernails weren't right, the statue was too fresh, it just felt wrong. These experts were able to come to a conclusion simply on the basis of their quick first impressions. When the experts turned out to be right, the statue was uncovered as a fraud, creating considerable expense and embarrassment for the museum.

Clearly, some people have the ability to make immediate and accurate decisions based on their snap judgments. Gladwell details numerous examples of such cases, but also describes other examples of people making faulty judgments. Observant readers will notice that the people who have the ability to make accurate snap judgments are invariably an *expert* on the topic at hand. These experts have spent years and years developing knowledge and skill through practice, repetition, and experience. To the nonexpert, these decisions may seem like "intuition" or "snap judgments," but in reality, the processing time for these experts to gather pertinent information has become so automatic that it only seems that way. They actually bring a great deal of tacit knowledge into specific situations, and many times, as Gladwell notes, they are unable to verbalize exactly why it is that they make the decisions they do.

choices? What will the side effects of the alternative be? The fourth step is to select the alternative that results in the best outcome. That is, given the costs and benefits of each alternative, which alternative provides us with the most value? The fifth step is to implement the alternative.

The rational decision-making model assumes that people are, of course, perfectly rational. However, problems immediately arise when we start to examine some of the assumptions the model makes about human decision makers.[40] The model assumes there is a clear and definite problem to solve and that people have the ability to identify what that exact problem is. It also assumes that decision makers have perfect information—that they know and are able to identify the available alternatives and the outcomes that would be associated with those alternatives. The model further assumes that time and money are generally not issues when it comes to making a decision, that decision makers always choose the solution that maximizes value, and that they will act in the best interests of the organization. Given all these assumptions, perhaps we shouldn't label the model as "rational" after all!

DECISION-MAKING PROBLEMS

8.5

What decision-making problems can prevent employees from translating their learning into accurate decisions?

Because employees don't always make rational decisions, it's easy to second-guess decisions after the fact. Many decisions made inside organizations look good at the time and were made with perfectly good justifications to support them but turn out to have what are perceived as "bad results." The reality, however, is that it's a lot easier to question decisions in hindsight. As Warren Buffet, CEO of Berkshire Hathaway, is often quoted as saying, "In the business world, the rearview mirror is always clearer than the windshield."[41] Our responsibility here is not to rehash all the poor decisions employees and managers have made (and there are many of them!) but rather to detail some of the most common reasons for bad decision making—in other words, when are people most likely to falter in terms of the rational decision-making model and why?

LIMITED INFORMATION. Although most employees perceive themselves as rational decision makers, the reality is that they are all subject to **bounded rationality**. Bounded rationality is the notion that decision makers simply do not have the ability or resources to process all available information and alternatives to make an optimal decision.[42] A comparison of bounded rationality and rational decision making is presented in Table 8-3. This limit results in two major problems for making decisions. First, people have to filter and simplify information to make sense of their complex environment and the myriad of potential choices they face.[43] This simplification leads them to miss information when perceiving problems, generating and evaluating alternatives, or judging the results. Second, because people cannot possibly consider every single alternative when making a decision, they satisfice. **Satisficing** results when decision makers select the first acceptable alternative considered.[44]

TABLE 8-3	Rational Decision Making vs. Bounded Rationality
TO BE RATIONAL DECISION MAKERS, WE *SHOULD*. . .	**BOUNDED RATIONALITY SAYS WE *ARE LIKELY TO*. . .**
Identify the problem by thoroughly examining the situation and considering all interested parties.	Boil the problem down to something that is easily understood.
Develop an exhaustive list of alternatives to consider as solutions.	Come up with a few solutions that tend to be straightforward, familiar, and similar to what is currently being done.
Evaluate all the alternatives simultaneously.	Evaluate each alternative as soon as we think of it.
Use accurate information to evaluate alternatives.	Use distorted and inaccurate information during the evaluation process.
Pick the alternative that maximizes value.	Pick the first acceptable alternative (satisfice).

Sources: Adapted from H.A. Simon, "Rational Decision Making in Organizations," *American Economic Review* 69 (1979), pp. 493–513; D. Kahneman, "Maps of Bounded Rationality: Psychology for Behavioral Economics," *The American Economic Review* 93 (2003), pp. 1449–75; and S.W. Williams, *Making Better Business Decisions* (Thousand Oaks, CA: Sage Publications, 2002).

In addition to choosing the first acceptable alternative, decision makers tend to come up with alternatives that are straightforward and not that different from what they're already doing. When you and another person are deciding where to go out for dinner tonight, will you sit down and list every restaurant available to you within a certain mile limit? Of course not. You'll start listing off alternatives, generally starting with the closest and most familiar, until both parties arrive at a restaurant that's acceptable to them. Making decisions this way is no big deal when it comes to deciding where to go for dinner, because the consequences of a poor decision are minimal. However, many managers make decisions that have critical consequences for their employees and their customers. In those cases, making a decision without thoroughly looking into the alternatives becomes a problem!

FAULTY PERCEPTIONS. As decision makers, employees are forced to rely on their perceptions to make decisions. Perception is the process of selecting, organizing, storing, and retrieving information about the environment. Although perceptions can be very useful, because they help us to make sense of the environment around us, they can often become distorted versions of reality. Perceptions can be dangerous in decision making, because we tend to make assumptions or evaluations on the basis of them. **Selective perception** is the tendency for people to see their environment only as it affects them and as it is consistent with their expectations. Has someone ever told you, "You only see what you want to see"? If a relative, spouse, or significant other said that to you, chances are good it probably wasn't the best experience. That person was likely upset that you didn't perceive the environment (or what was important to them) the same way they did. Selective perception affects our ability to identify problems, generate and evaluate alternatives, and judge outcomes. In other words, we take "shortcuts" when we process information. In the following paragraphs, we'll discuss some of the ways in which we take shortcuts when dealing with people and situations.

One false assumption people tend to make when it comes to other people is the belief that others think, feel, and act the same way they do. This assumption is known as a **projection bias**. That is, people project their own thoughts, attitudes, and motives onto other people. "I would never do that—that's unethical" equates to "They would never do that—that's unethical." Projection bias causes problems in decision making because it limits our ability to develop appropriate criteria for a decision and evaluate decisions carefully. The bias causes people to assume that everyone's criteria will be just like theirs and that everyone will react to the decision just as they did.

Another example of faulty perceptions is caused by the way we cognitively organize people into groups. **Social identity theory** holds that people identify themselves by the groups to which they belong and perceive and judge others by their group memberships.[45] There is a substantial amount of research that shows that we like to categorize people on the basis of the groups to which they belong.[46] These groups could be based on demographic information (gender, race, religion, hair color), occupational information (scientists, engineers, accountants), where they work (GE, Halliburton, Microsoft), what country they're from (Americans, French, Chinese), or any other subgroup that makes sense to the perceiver. You might categorize students on campus by whether they're a member of a fraternity or sorority. Those inside the Greek system categorize people by which fraternity or sorority they belong to. And people within a certain fraternity might group their own members on the basis of whom they hang out with the most. There is practically no end to the number of subgroups that people can come up with.

A **stereotype** occurs when assumptions are made about others on the basis of their membership in a social group.[47] Although not all stereotypes are bad per se, our decision-making process becomes faulty when we make inaccurate generalizations. Many companies work hard to help their employees avoid stereotyping, because doing so can lead to illegal discrimination in the workplace. Ortho-McNeil Pharmaceutical, Wells Fargo,

Kaiser Permanente, and Microsoft (just to name a few) have developed extensive diversity training programs to help their employees overcome specific cultural, racial, and gender stereotypes in the workplace.[48]

When confronted with situations of uncertainty that require a decision on our part, we often use **heuristics**—simple, efficient, rules of thumb that allow us to make decisions more easily. In general, heuristics are not bad. In fact, they lead to correct decisions more often than not.[49] However, heuristics can also bias us toward inaccurate decisions at times. Consider this example from one of the earliest studies on decision-making heuristics: "Consider the letter R. Is R more likely to appear in the first position of a word or the third position of a word?"[50] If your answer was the first position of a word, you answered incorrectly and fell victim to one of the most frequently talked about heuristics. The **availability bias** is the tendency for people to base their judgments on information that is easier to recall. It is significantly easier for almost everyone to remember words in which R is the first letter as opposed to the third. The availability bias is why more people are afraid to fly than statistics would support. Every single plane crash is plastered all over the news, making plane crashes more available in memory than successful plane landings.

Aside from the availability bias, there are many other biases that affect the way we make decisions. Table 8-4 describes five more of the most well-researched decision-making biases. After reading them, you might wonder how we ever make accurate decisions at all! The answer is that we do our best to think rationally through our most important decisions prior to making them and tend to use heuristics for decisions that are less important or that need to be made more quickly. Regardless of how often we fall victim to the biases, being aware of potential decision errors can help us make them less frequently.

FAULTY ATTRIBUTIONS. Another category of decision-making problems centers on how we explain the actions and events that occur around us. Research on attributions suggests that when people witness a behavior or outcome, they make a judgment about whether it was internally or externally caused. For example, when a coworker of yours named Joe shows up late to work and misses an important group presentation, you'll almost certainly make a judgment about why that happened. You might attribute Joe's outcome to internal factors—for example, suggesting that he is lazy or has a poor work ethic. Or you might attribute Joe's outcome to external factors—for example, suggesting that there was unusually bad traffic that day or that other factors prevented him from arriving on time.

The **fundamental attribution error** argues that people have a tendency to judge others' behaviors as due to internal factors.[51] This error suggests that you would likely judge Joe as having low motivation, poor organizational skills, or some other negative internal attribute. What if you yourself had showed up late? It turns out that we're less harsh when judging ourselves. The **self-serving bias** occurs when we attribute our own failures to external factors and our own successes to internal factors. Interestingly, evidence suggests that attributions across cultures don't always work the same way; see our **OB Internationally** feature for more discussion of this issue.

One model of attribution processes suggests that when people have a level of familiarity with the person being judged, they'll use a more detailed decision framework. This model is illustrated in Figure 8–5.[52] To return to our previous example, if we want to explore why Joe arrived late to work, we can ask three kinds of questions:

Consensus: Did others act the same way under similar situations? In other words, did others arrive late on the same day?

Distinctiveness: Does this person tend to act differently in other circumstances? In other words, is Joe responsible when it comes to personal appointments, not just work appointments?

TABLE 8-4	Decision-Making Biases

NAME OF BIAS	DESCRIPTION
Anchoring	The tendency to rely too heavily, or "anchor," on one trait or piece of information when making decisions even when the anchor might be unreliable or irrelevant.
	Example: One recent study showed that initial bids for a bottle of wine in an auction could be heavily influenced by simply having subjects write down the last two digits of their Social Security number prior to putting a value on the bottle. Those with higher two digit numbers tended to bid 60–120 percent more for a bottle of wine than those with low numbers.
Framing	The tendency to make different decisions based on how the question or situation is phrased.
	Example: Why do gas stations (or any retailer) give out discounts for paying cash as opposed to adding a surcharge for using a credit card? The discount is seen as a gain while the surcharge is seen as a loss. Because humans are loss averse, we are more likely to give up the discount (the gain) than accept the surcharge (the loss).
Representativeness	The tendency to assess the likelihood of an event by comparing it to a similar event and assuming it will be similar.
	Example: Assuming because a flipped coin has come up heads 10 times in a row, the likelihood that it will come up tails is greater than 50/50. Sometimes referred to as the "gambler's fallacy".
Contrast	The tendency to judge things erroneously based on a reference that is near to them.
	Example: If you were to take your hand out of a bowl of hot water and place it in a bowl of lukewarm water, you would describe that water as "cold". If someone else were to take their hand out of a bowl of extremely cold water and place it in the same bowl of lukewarm water, they would describe that water as "hot".
Recency	The tendency to weigh recent events more than earlier events.
	Example: A manager's tendency to weight ratings in performance evaluations based on an employee's behavior during the prior month as opposed to his or her behavior over the entire evaluation period.

Sources: J. Baron, *Thinking and Deciding*, 3rd ed. (Cambridge, UK: Cambridge University Press, 2000); R.E. Nisbett and L. Ross, *Human Inference: Strategies and Shortcomings of Social Judgment* (Englewood Cliffs, NJ: Prentice Hall, 1980); D.G. Meyers, *Social Psychology* (Boston, MA: McGraw-Hill, 2005); G. Gigerenzer, P.M. Todd, and ABC Research Group, *Simple Heuristics that Make Us Smart* (New York: Oxford University Press, 1999); D. Kahneman, A. Tversky, and P. Slovic, *Judgment under Uncertainty: Heuristics & Biases* (Cambridge, UK: Cambridge University Press, 1982); and D. Kahneman and A. Tversky "Choices, Values and Frames," *American Psychologist* 39 (1984), pp. 341–50.

Consistency: Does this person always do this when performing this task? In other words, has Joe arrived late for work before?

The way in which these questions are answered will determine if an internal or external attribution is made. An internal attribution, such as laziness or low motivation for Joe, will occur if there is low consensus (others arrived on time), low distinctiveness (Joe is

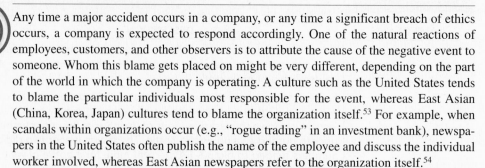

OB INTERNATIONALLY

Any time a major accident occurs in a company, or any time a significant breach of ethics occurs, a company is expected to respond accordingly. One of the natural reactions of employees, customers, and other observers is to attribute the cause of the negative event to someone. Whom this blame gets placed on might be very different, depending on the part of the world in which the company is operating. A culture such as the United States tends to blame the particular individuals most responsible for the event, whereas East Asian (China, Korea, Japan) cultures tend to blame the organization itself.[53] For example, when scandals within organizations occur (e.g., "rogue trading" in an investment bank), newspapers in the United States often publish the name of the employee and discuss the individual worker involved, whereas East Asian newspapers refer to the organization itself.[54]

Interestingly, these biases place different responsibilities on the leaders of organizations in these countries. In East Asian cultures, it's typical for the leader of an organization to take the blame for accidents, regardless of whether he or she had direct responsibility for them.[55] For example, in 2002, the director of a hospital in Tokyo was forced to resign when the cover-up of a medical accident was discovered, even though the director didn't start his job until after the cover-up took place! Similar events are common, such as the resignation of the CEO of Japan Airlines after a jet crashed, killing 500 people. In the United States, in contrast, CEOs rarely take the same level of blame. When Joseph Hazelwood crashed the Exxon Valdez into the Alaskan coastline, there were no calls for the Exxon CEO to resign. It was simply assumed by the American public that he had nothing to do with the accident.

Much of the reasoning for such differences has to do with the way the cultures view individuals and groups. East Asian cultures tend to treat groups as entities and not as individuals, whereas the culture in the United States tends to see individuals acting of their own accord.[56] This difference means that organizational leaders should be very cognizant of how to handle crises, depending on the country in which the negative event occurs. An apology offered by a senior leader is likely to be seen by East Asians as the company taking responsibility, whereas in the United States, it's more likely to be taken as an admission of personal guilt.[57]

---

irresponsible with other commitments as well), and high consistency (Joe has arrived late before). An external attribution, such as bad traffic or a power outage, will occur if there is high consensus (others arrived late), high distinctiveness (Joe is responsible with other commitments), and low consistency (Joe has never come late to work before).

ESCALATION OF COMMITMENT. Our last category of decision-making problems centers on what happens as a decision begins to go wrong. **Escalation of commitment** refers to the decision to continue to follow a failing course of action.[58] The expression "throwing good money after bad" captures this common decision-making error. An enormous amount of research shows that people have a tendency, when presented with a series of decisions, to escalate their commitment to previous decisions, even in the face of obvious failures.[59] Why do decision makers fall victim to this sort of error? They may feel an obligation to stick with their decision to avoid looking incompetent. They may also want to avoid admitting that they made a mistake. Those escalation tendencies become particularly strong when decision makers have invested a lot of money into the decision and when the project in question seems quite close to completion.[60]

One recent example of escalation of commitment is United Airlines' abandonment of the automated baggage handling system at the Denver International Airport. When it opened in 1995 (after a two-year delay), the baggage handling system with 26 miles of

FIGURE 8-5   Consensus, Distinctiveness, and Consistency

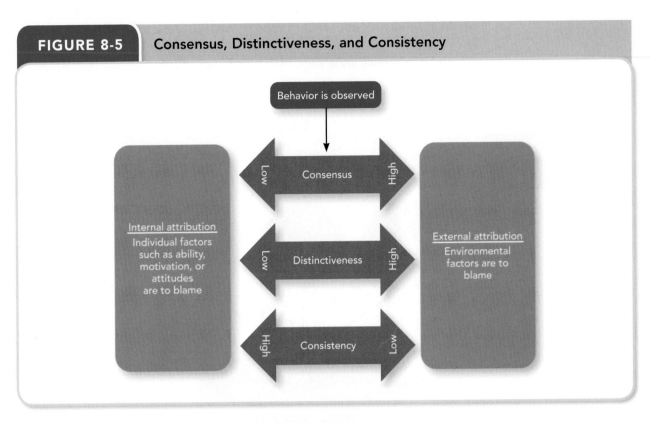

track designed to haul baggage across three terminals was supposed to be the single most advanced baggage handling system in the world. However, originally scheduled to cost $186 million dollars, a series of delays and technological problems caused the cost of the system to skyrocket by $1 million per day. Because of a series of technological issues, the system never really worked very well. In fact, United was the only airline in the airport willing to use it. It took 10 years and many mangled and lost suitcases before United finally "cut its losses," saving itself $1 million a month in maintenance fees.[61]

United Airlines took 10 years to finally abandon an expensive but faulty baggage handling system at Denver International Airport, illustrating the power of escalation of commitment.

SUMMARY: WHY DO SOME EMPLOYEES LEARN TO MAKE DECISIONS BETTER THAN OTHERS?

So what explains why some employees learn to make better decisions than others? As shown in Figure 8-6, answering that question requires understanding how employees learn, what kind of knowledge they gain, and how they use that knowledge to make

---

FIGURE 8-6   Why Do Some Employees Learn to Make Decisions Better Than Others?

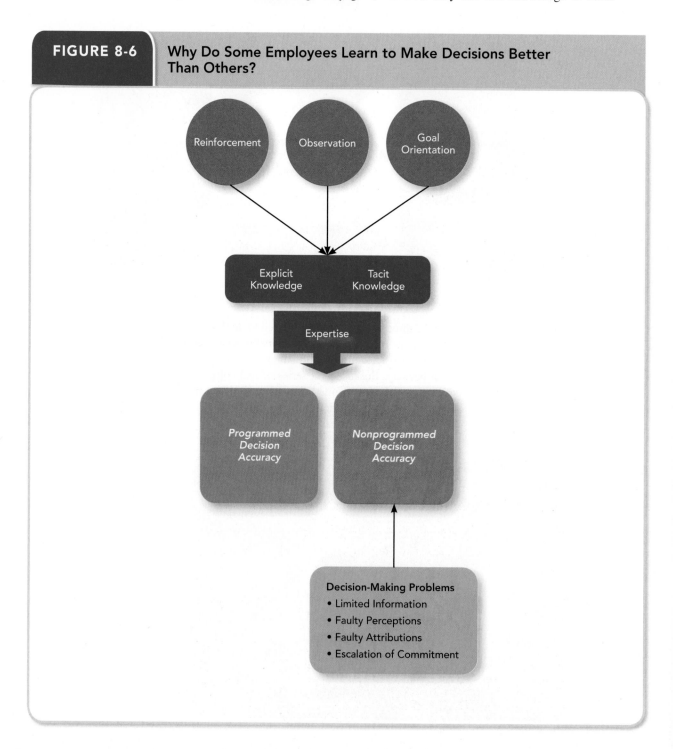

decisions. Employees learn from a combination of reinforcement and observation, and that learning depends in part on whether they are learning-oriented or performance-oriented. Some of that learning results in increases in explicit knowledge, and some of that learning results in increases in tacit knowledge. Those two forms of knowledge, which combine to form an employee's expertise, are then used in decision making. If a given problem has been encountered before, decision making occurs in a more automatic, programmed fashion. If the problem is new or unfamiliar, nonprogrammed decision making occurs and, in the best-case scenario, follows the rational decision-making model. Unfortunately, a number of decision-making problems can hinder the effectiveness of such decisions, including limited information, faulty perceptions, faulty attributions, and escalation of commitment.

HOW IMPORTANT IS LEARNING?

Does learning have a significant impact on the two primary outcomes in our integrative model of OB—does it correlate with job performance and organizational commitment? Figure 8-7 summarizes the research evidence linking learning to job performance and

FIGURE 8-7   Effects of Learning on Performance and Commitment

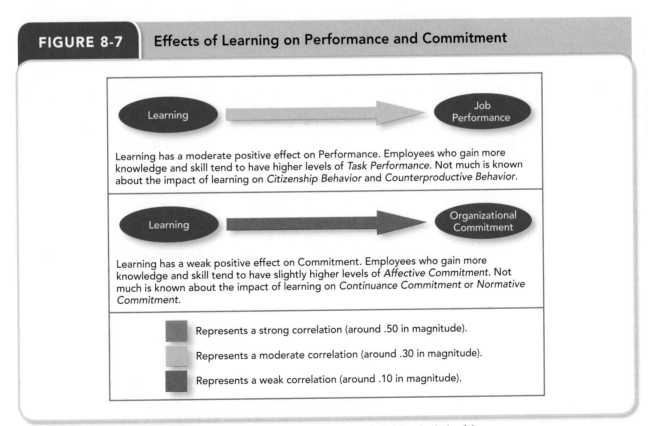

Learning has a moderate positive effect on Performance. Employees who gain more knowledge and skill tend to have higher levels of *Task Performance*. Not much is known about the impact of learning on *Citizenship Behavior* and *Counterproductive Behavior*.

Learning has a weak positive effect on Commitment. Employees who gain more knowledge and skill tend to have slightly higher levels of *Affective Commitment*. Not much is known about the impact of learning on *Continuance Commitment* or *Normative Commitment*.

Represents a strong correlation (around .50 in magnitude).

Represents a moderate correlation (around .30 in magnitude).

Represents a weak correlation (around .10 in magnitude).

Sources: G.M. Alliger, S.I. Tannenbaum, W. Bennett Jr., H. Traver, and A. Shotland, "A Meta-Analysis of the Relations among Training Criteria," *Personnel Psychology* 50 (1997), pp. 341–58; J.A. Colquitt, J.A. LePine, and R.A. Noe, "Toward an Integrative Theory of Training Motivation: A Meta-Analytic Path Analysis of 20 Years of Research," *Journal of Applied Psychology* 85 (2000), pp. 678–707; and J.P. Meyer, D.J. Stanley, L. Herscovitch, and L. Topolnytsky, "Affective, Continuance, and Normative Commitment to the Organization: A Meta-Analysis of Antecedents, Correlates, and Consequences," *Journal of Vocational Behavior* 61 (2002), pp. 20–52.

8.6

How does learning affect job performance and organizational commitment?

organizational commitment. The figure reveals that learning does influence job performance. Why? The primary reason is that learning is moderately correlated with task performance. It's difficult to fulfill one's job duties if the employee doesn't possess adequate levels of job knowledge. In fact, there are reasons to suggest that the moderate correlation depicted in the figure is actually an underestimate of learning's importance. That's because most of the research linking learning to task performance focuses on explicit knowledge, which is more practical to measure. It's difficult to measure tacit knowledge because of its unspoken nature, but clearly such knowledge is relevant to task performance. Learning seems less relevant to citizenship behavior and counterproductive behavior however, given that those behaviors are often less dependent on knowledge and expertise.

Figure 8-7 also reveals that learning is only weakly related to organizational commitment.[62] In general, having higher levels of job knowledge is associated with slight increases in emotional attachment to the firm. It's true that companies that have a reputation as organizations that value learning tend to receive higher-quality applicants for jobs.[63] However, there's an important distinction between organizations that offer learning opportunities and employees who take advantage of those opportunities to actually gain knowledge. Moreover, it may be that employees with higher levels of expertise become more highly valued commodities on the job market, thereby reducing their levels of continuance commitment.

APPLICATION: TRAINING

8.7

What steps can organizations take to foster learning?

How can organizations improve learning in an effort to boost employee expertise and, ultimately, improve decision making? One approach is to rely on **training**, which represents a systematic effort by organizations to facilitate the learning of job-related knowledge and behavior. Organizations spent $134.39 billion on employee learning and development in 2007, or $1,103 per employee (an increase of 6 percent over 2006).[64] A full discussion of all the types of training companies offer is beyond the scope of this section, but suffice it to say that companies are using many different methods to help their employees acquire explicit and tacit knowledge. Technological changes are altering the way those methods are delivered, as instructor-led classroom training has declined while online self-study programs have increased.[65]

In addition to traditional training experiences, companies are also heavily focused on **knowledge transfer** from their older, experienced workers to their younger employees. Some companies are using variations of **behavior modeling training** to ensure that employees have the ability to observe and learn from those in the company with significant amounts of tacit knowledge. For example, Raytheon, the Waltham, Massachusetts–based defense and aerospace supplier, has created a training program called "Leave-a-Legacy" that pairs employees holding vital knowledge with high-potential subordinates. Raytheon's program is not one of those "have lunch once a month" mentor programs; it's a relatively regimented program in which younger workers follow older workers around for extended periods of time, ensuring adequate opportunities for observation. Each pair of employees is also assigned a third-party coach that helps the knowledge transfer take place.[66]

Another form of knowledge transfer that's being used by companies more frequently, as described in our opening example, is communities of practice. **Communities of practice** are groups of employees who work together and learn from one another by collaborating over an extended period of time.[67] Many companies are adopting this newer form of informal social learning. John Deere, the Moline, Illinois–based manufacturer of agricultural equipment, implemented an informal training process in 2002 and now has a network of more than 300 communities dealing with issues such as mergers and acquisitions and its Deere Production System.[68] Communities of practice introduce their own unique complications, but their potential for transferring knowledge through employees is significant.[69]

The success of these programs, as well as more traditional types of training, hinges on transfer of training. **Transfer of training** occurs when the knowledge, skills, and behaviors used on the job are maintained by the learner once training ends and generalized to the workplace once the learner returns to the job.[70] Transfer of training can be fostered if organizations create a **climate for transfer**—an environment that can support the use of new skills. There are a variety of factors that can help organizations foster such a climate. The degree to which the trainee's manager supports the importance of the newly acquired knowledge and skills and stresses their application to the job is perhaps the most important factor. Peer support is helpful, because having multiple trainees learning the same material reduces anxiety and allows the trainees to share concerns and work through problems. Opportunities to use the learned knowledge are also crucial, because practice and repetition are key components of learning. Because companies have a huge stake in increasing and transferring knowledge within their employee base, creating a climate for the transfer of that knowledge is imperative to the success of formal learning systems.

TAKEAWAYS

8.1 Learning is a relatively permanent change in an employee's knowledge or skill that results from experience. Decision making refers to the process of generating and choosing from a set of alternatives to solve a problem. Learning allows employees to make better decisions by making those decisions more quickly and by being able to generate a better set of alternatives.

8.2 Employees gain both explicit and tacit knowledge as they build expertise. Explicit knowledge is easily communicated and available to everyone. Tacit knowledge, however, is something employees can only learn through experience.

8.3 Employees learn new knowledge through reinforcement and observation of others. That learning also depends on whether the employees are learning-oriented or performance-oriented.

8.4 Programmed decisions are decisions that become somewhat automatic because a person's knowledge allows him or her to recognize and identify a situation and the course of action that needs to be taken. Many task-related decisions made by experts are programmed decisions. Nonprogrammed decisions are made when a problem is new, complex, or not recognized. Ideally, such decisions are made by following the steps in the rational decision-making model.

8.5 Employees are less able to translate their learning into accurate decisions when they struggle with limited information, faulty perceptions, faulty attributions, and escalation of commitment.

8.6 Learning has a moderate positive relationship with job performance and a weak positive relationship with organizational commitment.

8.7 Through various forms of training, companies can give employees more knowledge and a wider array of experiences that they can use to make decisions.

KEY TERMS

- Learning   *p. 259*
- Decision making   *p. 259*
- Expertise   *p. 259*
- Explicit knowledge   *p. 260*
- Tacit knowledge   *p. 260*
- Contingencies of reinforcement *p. 261*
- Positive reinforcement   *p. 261*
- Negative reinforcement   *p. 262*
- Punishment   *p. 262*
- Extinction   *p. 262*
- Schedules of reinforcement   *p. 263*
- Continuous reinforcement   *p. 263*
- Fixed interval schedule   *p. 263*
- Variable interval schedule   *p. 263*
- Fixed ratio schedule   *p. 264*
- Variable ratio schedule   *p. 264*
- Social learning theory   *p. 264*
- Behavioral modeling   *p. 265*
- Learning orientation   *p. 267*
- Performance-prove orientation   *p. 267*
- Performance-avoid orientation   *p. 267*
- Programmed decision   *p. 267*
- Intuition   *p. 267*

- Crisis situation   *p. 270*
- Nonprogrammed decision   *p. 270*
- Rational decision-making model *p. 270*
- Bounded rationality   *p. 272*
- Satisficing   *p. 272*
- Selective perception   *p. 273*
- Projection bias   *p. 273*
- Social identity theory   *p. 273*
- Stereotype   *p. 273*
- Heuristics   *p. 274*
- Availability bias   *p. 274*
- Fundamental attribution error   *p. 274*
- Self-serving bias   *p. 274*
- Consensus   *p. 274*
- Distinctiveness   *p. 274*
- Consistency   *p. 275*
- Escalation of commitment   *p. 276*
- Training   *p. 280*
- Knowledge transfer   *p. 280*
- Behavior modeling training   *p. 280*
- Communities of practice   *p. 280*
- Transfer of training   *p. 281*
- Climate for transfer   *p. 281*

DISCUSSION QUESTIONS

8.1 In your current or past workplaces, what types of tacit knowledge did experienced workers possess? What did this knowledge allow them to do?

8.2 Companies rely on employees with substantial amounts of tacit knowledge. Why do companies struggle when these employees leave the organization unexpectedly? What can companies do to help ensure that they retain tacit knowledge?

8.3 What does the term "expert" mean to you? What exactly do experts do that novices don't?

8.4 Given your occupational choice, how do you expect to learn what you need to know when you start working? Do you expect the company to provide you with these opportunities, or will you have to seek them out on your own?

8.5 Do you consider yourself to be a "rational" decision maker? For what types of decisions are you determined to be the most rational? What types of decisions are likely to cause you to behave irrationally?

8.6 Given your background, with which of the decision-making biases listed in the chapter do you most struggle? What could you do to overcome those biases to make more accurate decisions?

CASE: XEROX

One of the major factors behind the push for knowledge sharing in companies is the large group of older workers in the baby boom generation who will soon be retiring and taking their tacit knowledge with them. Companies want these older workers to mentor and interact with younger workers so they don't lose that knowledge. However, a recent annual World of Work survey reveals that the four generations that currently appear in the U.S. workforce actually interact very little.[71] Much of the reason has to do with faulty perceptions. Eric Buntin, managing director of marketing and operations for Atlanta–based Randstad USA, finds that "Stereotyping is real. If Gen X'ers think their baby boomer colleagues are less flexible—even if they're not—they believe it."[72]

Xerox and other companies are banking on knowledge sharing practices, such as communities of practice, to help bridge this gap between generations. Such knowledge sharing becomes even more important as the type of work life that Xerox employees can expect to see evolves. Xerox has hired ethnographers to follow workers as they go about their daily work lives. Although not complete, this research likely will show that Xerox workers live in a strongly project-based environment in which they interact and have relationships with their coworkers for short periods of time and then must move on to the next project.[73] This environment clearly makes natural mentoring relationships between employees extremely difficult, and it doesn't help with traditional forms of knowledge sharing. However, Xerox has launched a mentoring program, run by an employee caucus group known as The Women's Alliance, that has developed an online mentor–mentee matching program to help women find more experienced, effective mentors.[74] Anne Mulcahey, the outgoing CEO, was one of the founders of the group.

8.1 Are communities of practice, which tend to be technology-based, likely to bridge the generation gap and allow knowledge sharing between the generations of employees at Xerox? Explain.

8.2 Given these generational issues and the type of work life that Xerox employees tend to have, can you think of another possible way to encourage knowledge sharing within the organization?

8.3 How might Xerox attempt to break down the perceptions and stereotypes that exist between generations in order to help the knowledge sharing process?

EXERCISE: DECISION-MAKING BIAS

The purpose of this exercise is to illustrate how decision making can be influenced by decision heuristics, availability bias, and escalation of commitment. This exercise uses groups, so your instructor will either assign you to a group or ask you to create your own group. The exercise has the following steps:

8.1 In your groups, come to consensus on an answer to each of the problems below.

A. A certain town is served by two hospitals. In the larger hospital, about 45 babies are born each day, and in the smaller hospital, about 15 babies are born each day. Although the overall proportion of boys is about 50 percent, the actual proportion at either hospital may be greater or less than 50 percent on any given day. At the end of a year, which hospital will have the greater number of days on which more than 60 percent of the babies born were boys?

   a. The large hospital.

   b. The small hospital.

   c. Neither—the number of days will be about the same (within 5 percent of each other).

B. Linda is 31 years of age, single, outspoken, and very bright. She majored in philosophy in college. As a student, she was deeply concerned with discrimination and other social issues and participated in antinuclear demonstrations. Which statement is more likely:

   a. Linda is a bank teller.

   b. Linda is a bank teller and active in the feminist movement.

C. A cab was involved in a hit-and-run accident. Two cab companies serve the city: the Green, which operates 85 percent of the cabs, and the Blue, which operates the remaining 15 percent. A witness identifies the hit-and-run cab as Blue. When the court tests the reliability of the witness under circumstances similar to those on the night of the accident, he correctly identifies the color of the cab 80 percent of the time and misidentifies it the other 20 percent. What's the probability that the cab involved in the accident was Blue, as the witness stated?

D. Imagine that you face this pair of concurrent decisions. Examine these decisions, then indicate which choices you prefer.

Decision I: Choose between:

   a. A sure gain of $240 and

   b. A 25 percent chance of winning $1,000 and a 75 percent chance of winning nothing.

Decision II: Choose between:

   a. A sure loss of $750 and

   b. A 75 percent chance of losing $1,000 and a 25 percent chance of losing nothing.

Decision III: Choose between:

   a. A sure loss of $3,000 and

   b. An 80 percent chance of losing $4,000 and a 20 percent chance of losing nothing.

E. You've decided to see a Broadway play and have bought a $40 ticket. As you enter the theater, you realize you've lost your ticket. You can't remember the seat number, so you can't prove to the management that you bought a ticket. Would you spend $40 for a new ticket?

F. You've reserved a seat for a Broadway play, for which the ticket price is $40. As you enter the theater to buy your ticket, you discover you've lost $40 from your pocket. Would you still buy the ticket? (Assume you have enough cash left to do so.)

G. Imagine you have operable lung cancer and must choose between two treatments: surgery and radiation. Of 100 people having surgery, 10 die during the operation, 32 (including those original 10) are dead after 1 year, and 66 are dead after 5 years. Of 100 people having radiation therapy, none dies during treatment, 23 are dead after one year, and 78 after 5 years. Which treatment would you prefer?

Your instructor will give you the correct answer to each problem. Class discussion, whether in groups or as a class, should focus on the following questions: How accurate were the decisions you reached? What decision-making problems were evident in the decisions you reached? Consider especially where decision heuristics, availability, and escalation of commitment may have influenced your decisions. How could you improve your decision making to make it more accurate?

Source: This exercise originally appeared in Ivancevich, J., R. Konopaske, and M. Matteson. *Organizational Behavior and Management.* 7th ed. New York: McGraw-Hill, 2005. Reprinted with permission of The McGraw-Hill Companies. The original exercises are based on the following sources: (1) Tversky, A., and D. Kahneman. "Rational Choice and the Framing of Decisions," *Journal of Business* 59 (1986), pp. 251–78; (2) Tversky, A., and D. Kahneman. "The Framing of Decisions and the Psychology of Choice," *Science* 211 (1981), pp. 453–58; (3) Tversky, A., and D. Kahneman. "Extensional vs. Intuitive Reasoning: The Conjunction Fallacy in Probability Judgment," *Psychological Review* 90 (1983), pp. 293–315; and (4) McKean, K. "Decisions, Decisions," *Discovery Magazine,* June 1985.

ENDNOTES

8.1 Salopek, J.J. "Knowledge in Numbers." *T+D*, July, 2008, pp. 24–26.

8.2 Kranz, G. "At Xerox, Learning Is a Community Activity." *Workforce Management*, December, 2008, http://www.workforce.com/archive/feature/26/05/23/index.php?ht (accessed May 25, 2009).

8.3 Ibid.

8.4 Ibid.

8.5 Agnvall, E. "Hitchhiker's Guide to Developing Leaders." *HR Magazine*, September, 2008, pp. 121–24.

8.6 Kranz, "At Xerox."

8.7 Thurm, S. "Companies Struggle to Pass on Knowledge that Workers Acquire." *The Wall Street Journal*, January 23, 2006, p. B1.

8.8 Kranz, "At Xerox."

8.9 Ibid.

8.10 Weiss, H.M. "Learning Theory and Industrial and Organizational Psychology." In *Handbook of Industrial and Organizational Psychology,* eds. M.D. Dunnette and L.M. Hough. Palo Alto, CA: Consulting Psychologists Press, 1990, pp. 75–169.

8.11 Tai, B., and N.R. Lockwood. "Organizational Entry: Onboarding, Orientation, and Socialization." *SHRM Research Paper,* http://www.shrm.org (accessed June 4, 2007).

8.12 Buford, B. *Heat.* New York: Knopf, 2006, pp. 49–50.

8.13 Ericsson, K.A. "An Introduction to *Cambridge Handbook of Expertise and Expert Performance:* Its Development, Organization, and Content." In *The Cambridge Handbook of Expertise and Expert Performance,* eds. K.A. Ericsson, N. Charness, P.J. Feltovich, and R.R. Hoffman. New York: Cambridge University Press, 2006, pp. 3–19.

8.14 Ericsson, K.A., and A.C. Lehmann. "Experts and Exceptional Performance: Evidence of Maximal Adaptation to Task Constraints." *Annual Review of Psychology* 47 (1996), pp. 273–305.

8.15 Brockmann, E.N., and W.P. Anthony. "Tacit Knowledge and Strategic Decision Making." *Group & Organizational Management* 27 (December 2002), pp. 436–55.

8.16 Wagner, R.K., and R.J. Sternberg. "Practical Intelligence in Real-World Pursuits: The Role of Tacit Knowledge." *Journal of Personality and Social Psychology* 4 (1985), pp. 436–58.

8.17 Wah, L. "Making Knowledge Stick." *Management Review* 88 (1999), pp. 24–33.

8.18 Eucker, T.R. "Understanding the Impact of Tacit Knowledge Loss." *Knowledge Management Review,* March, 2007, pp. 10–13.

8.19 McAdam, R.; B. Mason; and J. McCrory. "Exploring the Dichotomies Within the Tacit Knowledge Literature: Towards a Process of Tacit Knowing in Organizations." *Journal of Knowledge Management* 11 (2007), pp. 43–59.

8.20 Lawson, C., and E. Lorenzi. "Collective Learning, Tacit Knowledge, and Regional Innovative Capacity." *Regional Studies* 21 (1999), pp. 487–513.

8.21 Nonaka, I. "The Knowledge-Creating Company." *Harvard Business Review* 69 (1991), pp. 96–104; and Nonaka, I. "A Dynamic Theory of Organizational Knowledge Creation." *Organizational Science* 5 (1994), pp. 14–37.

8.22 Luthans, F., and R. Kreitner. *Organizational Behavior Modification and Beyond.* Glenview, IL: Scott, Foresman, 1985.

8.23 Latham, G.P., and V.L. Huber. "Schedules of Reinforcement: Lessons from the Past and Issues for Future." *Journal of Organizational Behavior Management* 13 (1992), pp. 125–49.

8.24 Luthans and Kreitner, *Organizational Behavior Modification.*

8.25 Bandura, A. *Social Foundations of Thought and Action: A Social Cognitive Theory.* Englewood Cliffs, NJ: Prentice Hall, 1986.

8.26 Weiss, "Learning Theory."

8.27 Pescuric, A., and W.C. Byham. "The New Look of Behavior Modeling." *Training & Development,* July, 1996, pp. 24–30.

8.28 De Long, D.W., and T. Davenport. "Better Practices for Retaining Organizational Knowledge: Lessons from the Leading Edge." *Employment Relations Today* 30 (2003), pp. 51–63; and Fisher, A. "Retain Your Brains." *Fortune,* July 24, 2006, pp. 49–50.

8.29 Weber, J. "The Accidental CEO." *BusinessWeek,* April 23, 2007, pp. 64–72.

8.30 Sims, R.R., and J. Brinkmann. "Leaders as Moral Role Models: The Case of John Gutfreund at Salomon Brothers." *Journal of Business Ethics* 35 (2002), pp. 327–40.

8.31 VandeWalle, D. "Development and Validation of a Work Domain Goal Orientation Instrument." *Educational and Psychological Measurement* 8 (1997), pp. 995–1015.

8.32 Payne, S.C.; S. Youngcourt; and J.M. Beaubien. "A Meta-Analytic Examination of the Goal Orientation Nomological Net." *Journal of Applied Psychology* 92 (2007), pp. 128–50.

8.33 Ibid.

8.34 Dane, E., and M.G. Pratt. "Exploring Intuition and Its Role in Managerial Decision Making." *Academy of Management Review,* 32 (2007), pp. 33–54; and Hayashi, A.M. "When to Trust Your Gut."

Harvard Business Review, February, 2001, pp. 59–65.

8.35 March, J.G. *A Primer on Decision Making.* New York: The Free Press, 1994.

8.36 Seeger, M.W.; T.L. Sellnow; and R.R. Ulmer. "Communication, Organization and Crisis." *Communication Yearbook* 21 (1998), pp. 231–75.

8.37 Weick, K.E., and K.M. Sutcliffe *Managing the Unexpected: Resilient Performance in an Age of Uncertainty.* 2nd ed. San Francisco: Jossey Bass, 2007.

8.38 Klein, G. *Sources of Power.* Cambridge, MA: MIT Press, 1999.

8.39 Weick, K.E. "Managerial Thought in the Context of Action." In *The Executive Mind*, ed. S. Srivasta. San Francisco, CA: Jossey Bass, 1983, pp. 221–42; Weick and Sutcliffe, *Managing the Unexpected*; and Klein, G. *The Power of Intuition.* New York: Currency Doubleday, 2003.

8.40 http://www.quotationspage.com/quote/25953.html (April 2007).

8.41 Simon, H.A. "A Behavioral Model of Rational Choice." *Quarterly Journal of Economics* 69 (1955), pp. 99–118.

8.42 Simon, H.A. "Rational Decision Making in Organizations." *American Economic Review* 69 (1979), pp. 493–513.

8.43 March, J.G., and H.A. Simon. *Organizations.* New York: Wiley, 1958.

8.44 Hogg, M.A., and D.J. Terry. "Social Identity and Self-Categorization Process in Organizational Contexts." *Academy of Management Review* 25 (January 2000), pp. 121–40.

8.45 Judd, C.M., and B. Park. "Definition and Assessment of Accuracy in Social Stereotypes." *Psychological Review* 100 (January 1993), pp. 109–28.

8.46 Ashforth, B.E., and F. Mael. "Social Identity Theory and the Organization." *Academy of Management Review* 14 (1989), pp. 20–39; and Howard, J.A. "Social Psychology of Identities." *Annual Review of Sociology* 26 (2000), pp. 367–93.

8.47 Society for Human Resource Management. "Diversity Training." 2006, http://www.shrm.org/diversity (accessed June 1, 2007).

8.48 Kahneman, D.; P. Slovic; and A. Tversky, eds. *Judgment under Uncertainty: Heuristics and Biases.* Cambridge, UK: Cambridge University Press, 1982.

8.49 Kahneman, D., and A. Tversky. "On the Psychology of Prediction." *Psychological Review* 80 (1973), pp. 237–51.

8.50 Ross, L. "The Intuitive Psychologist and His Shortcomings: Distortions in the Attribution Process." In *Advances in Experimental Social Psychology,* ed. L. Berkowitz. New York: Academic Press, 1977, pp. 173–220. See also Jones, E.E., and V.A. Harris. "The Attribution of Attitudes." *Journal of Experimental Social Psychology* 3 (1967), pp. 1–24.

8.51 Zemba, Y.; M.I. Young; and M.W. Morris. "Blaming Leaders for Organizational Accidents: Proxy Logic in Collective versus Individual-Agency Cultures." *Organizational Behavior and Human Decision Processes* 101 (2006), pp. 36–51.

8.52 Staw, B.M., and J. Ross. "Behavior in Escalation Situations: Antecedents, Prototypes, and Solutions." In *Research in Organizational Behavior,* Vol. 9, eds. L.L. Cummings and B.M. Staw. Greenwich, CT: JAI

Press, 1987, pp. 39–78; and Staw, B.M. "Knee-Deep in the Big Muddy: A Study of Escalating Commitment to a Chosen Course of Action." *Organizational Behavior and Human Performance* 16 (1976), pp. 27–44.

8.53 Menon, T.; M.W. Morris; C. Chiu; and Y. Hong. "Culture and the Construal of Agency: Attribution to Individual Versus Group Dispositions." *Journal of Personality and Social Psychology* 76 (1999), pp. 701–17.

8.54 Zemba et al., "Blaming Leaders."

8.55 Chiu, C.; M.W. Morris; Y. Hong; and T. Menon. "Motivated Cultural Cognition: The Impact of Implicit Cultural Theories on Dispositional Attribution Varies as a Function of Need for Closure." *Journal of Personality and Social Psychology* 78 (2000), pp. 247–59.

8.56 Zemba et al., "Blaming Leaders."

8.57 Kelley, H.H. "The Processes of Casual Attribution." *American Psychologist* 28 (1973), pp. 107–28; and Kelley, H.H. "Attribution in Social Interaction." In *Attribution: Perceiving the Causes of Behavior,* ed. E. Jones. Morristown, NJ: General Learning Press, 1972.

8.58 Brockner, J. "The Escalation of Commitment to a Failing Course of Action: Toward Theoretical Progress." *Academy of Management Review* 17 (1992), pp. 39–61; and Staw, B.M. "The Escalation of Commitment: An Update and Appraisal." In *Organizational Decision Making,* ed. Z. Shapira. New York: Cambridge University Press, 1997.

8.59 Conlon, D.E., and H. Garland. "The Role of Project Completion Information in Resource Allocation Decisions." *Academy of Management Journal* 36 (1993), pp. 402–13; and Moon, H. "Looking Forward and Looking Back: Integrating

Completion and Sunk-Cost Effects within an Escalation of Commitment Progress Decision." *Journal of Applied Psychology* 86 (2001), pp. 104–13.

8.60 Johnson, K. "Denver Airport to Mangle Last Bag." *The New York Times,* August 27, 2005.

8.61 Alliger, G.M.; S.I. Tannenbaum; W. Bennett Jr.; H. Traver; and A. Shotland. "A Meta-Analysis of the Relations among Training Criteria." *Personnel Psychology* 50 (1997), pp. 341–58; Colquitt, J.A.; J.A. LePine; and R..A. Noe. "Toward an Integrative Theory of Training Motivation: A Meta-Analytic Path Analysis of 20 Years of Research." *Journal of Applied Psychology* 85 (2000), pp. 678–707; and Meyer, J.P.; D.J. Stanley; L. Herscovitch, and L. Topolnytsky. "Affective, Continuance, and Normative Commitment to the Organization: A Meta-Analysis of Antecedents, Correlates, and Consequences." *Journal of Vocational Behavior* 61 (2002), pp. 20–52.

8.62 Averbrook, J. "Connecting CLO's with the Recruiting Process." *Chief Learning Officer* 4 (2005), pp. 24–27.

8.63 "Spending on Learning and Training Is Increasing: ASTD Report." *HR Focus* 83 (2006), p. 9.

8.64 Paradise, A. "Investment in Learning Remains Strong." *T+D,* November, 2008, pp. 44–51.

8.65 Folkers, D. "Competing in the Marketspace: Incorporating Online Education into Higher Education–An Organizational Perspective." *Information Resources Management Journal* 18 (2005), pp. 61–77.

8.66 Stamps, D. "Communities of Practice." *Training,* February, 1997, pp. 35–42.

8.67   Sauve, E. "Informal Knowledge Transfer." *T+D* 61 (2007), pp. 22–24.

8.68   Allan, B., and D. Lewis. "Virtual Learning Communities as a Vehicle for Workforce Development: A Case Study." *Journal of Workplace Learning* 18 (2006), pp. 367–83.

8.69   Noe, R.A. *Employee Training and Development.* Burr Ridge, IL: Irwin/McGrawHill, 1999.

8.70   Tracey, J.B.; S.I. Tannenbaum; and M.J. Kavanaugh. "Applying Trained Skills on the Job: The Importance of the Work Environment." *Journal of Applied Psychology* 80 (1995), pp. 239–52.

8.71   Randstad USA. "2008 World at Work," http://www.us.randstad.com/2008WorldofWork.pdf (accessed May 15, 2009).

8.72   Lawson, M. "Survey Reveals Alarming Lack of Generational Workplace Interaction." *Workforce Management*, July, 2008, http://www.workforce.com/archive/feature/25/68/23/index.php?ht (accessed May 15, 2009).

8.73   Menro, J. "Field Study: The Evolution of Work." *Fortune* 158 (September 2008), p. 223.

8.74   Carvin, B.N. "The Great Mentor Match." *T + D* 63 (January 2009), pp. 46–50.

chapter 9

Personality and Cultural Values

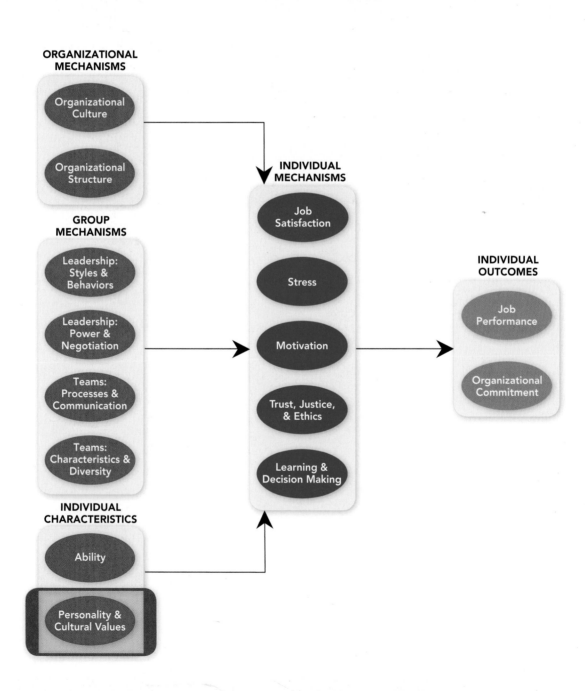

ORGANIZATIONAL MECHANISMS

- Organizational Culture
- Organizational Structure

GROUP MECHANISMS

- Leadership: Styles & Behaviors
- Leadership: Power & Negotiation
- Teams: Processes & Communication
- Teams: Characteristics & Diversity

INDIVIDUAL CHARACTERISTICS

- Ability
- Personality & Cultural Values

INDIVIDUAL MECHANISMS

- Job Satisfaction
- Stress
- Motivation
- Trust, Justice, & Ethics
- Learning & Decision Making

INDIVIDUAL OUTCOMES

- Job Performance
- Organizational Commitment

KRONOS

Have you ever heard of a company called Kronos? No? Well, surely you've heard of the following companies: Best Buy, Blockbuster, Target, Toys "R" Us, Marriott, Bennigan's, Universal Studios, Sports Authority, CVS Pharmacy, and The Fresh Market. All of those companies have one thing in common: They use the personality tests offered by Kronos, a workforce management software and services provider headquartered in Chelmsford, Massachusetts.[1] Applicants who apply for hourly positions at those companies are asked to fill out a personality test at a computer kiosk as part of their application. During the test, they indicate their degree of agreement with statements like:

- You do things carefully so you don't make mistakes.[2]
- You can easily cheer up and forget a problem.[3]
- You don't act polite when you don't want to.[4]
- You'd rather blend into the crowd than stand out.[5]

The test includes 50 such statements, designed to assess personality traits relevant to job performance. Ten minutes after the applicant completes the test at the kiosk, the hiring manager receives an e-mailed or faxed report from Kronos. That report identifies the applicant with a "green light," "yellow light," or "red light."[6] Green lights earn an automatic follow-up interview, yellow lights require some managerial discretion about granting that follow-up, and red lights get politely excused from the hiring process. Kronos' report even includes some recommended interview questions that managers can use to delve more deeply into any potential question marks.

Kronos' test was originally designed by another company you've probably never heard of: Unicru, based in Beaverton, Oregon. Kronos acquired Unicru in 2006, giving it the biggest piece of the burgeoning personality testing industry. To give you some idea of the size of that industry, a recent survey of *Fortune* 1000 firms suggests that around one-third of the firms rely on or plan to implement personality testing.[7] Such tests are controversial, of course, especially for applicants (and hiring managers) who are used to the traditional half-hour employment interview. To find out how controversial, type "Unicru personality test" into Google (we got over 15,000 hits, which no doubt include a fair number of post-ings from applicants rejected at the companies that use it). For its part, Kronos encourages organizations to save the data from its personality test for several years. That way, organizations can make up their own minds about whether the scores seem to relate to performance and commitment on the job.

PERSONALITY AND CULTURAL VALUES

Companies that use tests from vendors like Kronos believe that the personality of employees influences their performance and commitment. **Personality** refers to the structures and propensities inside people that explain their characteristic patterns of thought, emotion, and behavior.[8] Personality creates people's social reputations—the way they are perceived by friends, family, coworkers, and supervisors.[9] In this way, personality captures *what people are like*. That's in contrast to ability, the subject of Chapter 10, which captures *what people* *can do.* Although we sometimes describe people as having "a good personality," personality is actually a collection of multiple traits. **Traits** are defined as recurring regularities or trends in people's responses to their environment.[10] Adjectives such as responsible, easygoing, polite, and reserved are examples of traits that can be used to summarize someone's personality.

As we'll describe later, personality traits are a function of both your genes and your environment. One important piece of the environmental part of that equation is the culture in which you were raised. **Cultural values** are defined as shared beliefs about desirable end states or modes of conduct in a given culture.[11] You can think of cultural values as capturing *what cultures are like.* Adjectives such as traditional, informal, risk averse, or assertive are all examples of values that can be used to summarize a nation's culture. Cultural values can influence the development of people's personality traits, as well as how those traits are expressed in daily life. In this way, a responsible person in the United States may act somewhat differently than a responsible person in China, just as an easy-going person in France may act somewhat differently than an easy-going person in Indonesia.

9.1

What is personality? What are cultural values?

HOW CAN WE DESCRIBE WHAT EMPLOYEES ARE LIKE?

We can use personality traits and cultural values to describe what employees are like. For example, how would you describe your first college roommate to one of your classmates? You'd start off using certain adjectives—maybe the roommate was funny and outgoing, or maybe frugal and organized. Of course, it would take more than a few adjectives to describe your roommate fully. You could probably go on listing traits for several minutes, maybe even coming up with 100 traits or more. Although 100 traits may sound like a lot, personality researchers note that the third edition of Webster's Unabridged Dictionary contained 1,710 adjectives that can be used to describe someone's traits![12] Was your roommate abrasive, adulterous, agitable, alarmable, antisocial, arbitrative, arrogant, asocial, audacious, aweless, and awkward? We hope not!

THE BIG FIVE TAXONOMY

With 1,710 adjectives, you might be worrying about the length of this chapter (or the difficulty of your next exam!). Fortunately, it turns out that most adjectives are variations of five broad dimensions or "factors" that can be used to summarize our personalities.[13] Those five personality dimensions include **conscientiousness**, **agreeableness**, **neuroticism**, **openness to experience**, and **extraversion**. Collectively, these dimensions have been dubbed the **Big Five**.[14] Figure 9-1 lists the traits that can be found within each of the Big Five dimensions. We acknowledge that it can be hard to remember the particular labels for the Big Five dimensions, and we only wish there was some acronym that could make the process easier. . . .

9.2

What are the "Big Five"?

Would you like to see what your Big Five profile looks like? Our **OB Assessments** feature will show you where you stand on each of the five dimensions. After you've gotten a feel for your personality profile, you might be wondering about some of the following questions: How does personality develop? Why do people have the traits that they possess? Will those traits change over time? All of these questions are variations on the "nature vs. nurture" debate: Is personality a function of our genes, or is it something that we develop as a function of our experiences and environment? As you might guess, it's sometimes

FIGURE 9-1	Trait Adjectives Associated with the Big Five

C	A	N	O	E
Conscientiousness	**Agreeableness**	**Neuroticism**	**Openness**	**Extraversion**
• Dependable • Organized • Reliable • Ambitious • Hardworking • Persevering	• Kind • Cooperative • Sympathetic • Helpful • Courteous • Warm	• Nervous • Moody • Emotional • Insecure • Jealous • Unstable	• Curious • Imaginative • Creative • Complex • Refined • Sophisticated	• Talkative • Sociable • Passionate • Assertive • Bold • Dominant
NOT	NOT	NOT	NOT	NOT
• Careless • Sloppy • Inefficient • Negligent • Lazy • Irresponsible	• Critical • Antagonistic • Callous • Selfish • Rude • Cold	• Calm • Steady • Relaxed • At ease • Secure • Contented	• Uninquisitive • Conventional • Conforming • Simple • Unartistic • Traditional	• Quiet • Shy • Inhibited • Bashful • Reserved • Submissive

Sources: G. Saucier, "Mini-Markers: A Brief Version of Goldberg's Unipolar Big-Five Markers," *Journal of Personality Assessment* 63 (1994), pp. 506–516; L.R. Goldberg, "The Development of Markers for the Big-Five Factor Structure," *Psychological Assessment* 4 (1992), pp. 26–42; R.R. McCrae and P.T. Costa Jr., "Validation of the Five-Factor Model of Personality across Instruments and Observers," *Journal of Personality and Social Psychology* 52 (1987), pp. 81–90; and C.M. Gill and G.P. Hodgkinson, "Development and Validation of the Five-Factor Model Questionnaire (FFMQ): An Adjectival-Based Personality Inventory for Use in Occupational Settings," *Personnel Psychology* 60 (2007), pp. 731–766.

difficult to tease apart the impact of nature and nurture on personality. Let's assume for a moment that you're especially extraverted and so are your parents. Does this mean you've inherited their "extraversion gene"? Or does it mean that you observed and copied their extraverted behavior during your childhood (and were rewarded with praise for doing so)? It's impossible to know, because the effects of nature and nurture are acting in combination in this example.

9.3

Is personality driven by nature or by nurture?

One method of separating nature and nurture effects is to study identical twins who've been adopted by different sets of parents at birth. For example, the University of Minnesota has been conducting studies of pairs of identical twins reared apart for several decades.[15] Such studies find, for example, that extraversion scores tend to be significantly correlated across pairs of identical twins.[16] Such findings can clearly be attributed to "nature," because identical twins share 100 percent of their genetic material, but cannot be explained by "nurture," because the twins were raised in different environments. A review of several different twin studies concludes that genes have a significant impact on people's Big Five profile. More specifically, 49 percent of the variation in extraversion is accounted for by genetic differences.[17] The genetic impact is somewhat smaller for the rest of the Big Five: 45 percent for openness, 41 percent for neuroticism, 38 percent for conscientiousness, and 35 percent for agreeableness.

OB ASSESSMENTS

THE BIG FIVE

What does your personality profile look like? This assessment is designed to measure the five major dimensions of personality: conscientiousness (C), agreeableness (A), neuroticism (N), openness to experience (O), and extraversion (E). Listed below are phrases describing people's behaviors. Please write a number next to each statement that indicates the extent to which it accurately describes you. Answer each question using the response scale provided. Then subtract your answers to the boldfaced questions from 6, with the difference being your new answer for those questions. For example, if your original answer for question 6 was "2," your new answer is "4" (6 – 2). (For more assessments relevant to this chapter, please visit the Online Learning Center at www.mhhe.com/colquitt).

1	2	3	4	5
VERY INACCURATE	MODERATELY INACCURATE	NEITHER INACCURATE NOR ACCURATE	MODERATELY ACCURATE	VERY ACCURATE

1. I am the life of the party.

2. I sympathize with others' feelings.

3. I get chores done right away.

4. I have frequent mood swings.

5. I have a vivid imagination.

6. I don't talk a lot.

7. I am not interested in other people's problems.

8. I often forget to put things back in their proper place.

9. I am relaxed most of the time.

10. I am not interested in abstract ideas.

11. I talk to a lot of different people at parties.

12. I feel others' emotions.

13. I like order.

14. I get upset easily.

15. I have difficulty understanding abstract ideas.

16. I keep in the background.

17. I am not really interested in others.

18. I make a mess of things.

19. I seldom feel blue.

20. I do not have a good imagination.

SCORING AND INTERPRETATION

Conscientiousness: Sum up items 3, 8, 13, and 18. _____

Agreeableness: Sum up items 2, 7, 12, and 17. _____

react to conflict by walking away, adopting a "wait-and-see" attitude, or giving in to the other person.

One study provides unique insights into the effects of agreeableness. The study used a variation of "lived day analysis," where a portion of a participant's daily routine is recorded and analyzed.[36] Ninety-six undergraduates completed assessments of the Big Five personality dimensions before being fitted with a digital recorder and an electronic microphone that could be clipped to their shirt collar. The microphone recorded 30 seconds of footage at 12-minute intervals over the course of two weekdays, with participants unable to track when footage was actually being recorded. Trained coders then rated the sounds and conversations recorded on the microphone. The results of the study revealed a number of interesting expressions of agreeableness. Agreeable participants were significantly less likely to be at home in their apartment during recordings; instead, they spent more time in public places. They were also less likely to use swear words and more likely to use words that conveyed personal rapport during conversations.

EXTRAVERSION. Extraverted people are talkative, sociable, passionate, assertive, bold, and dominant (in contrast to introverts, who are quiet, shy, and reserved). Of the Big Five, extraversion is the easiest to judge in **zero acquaintance** situations—situations in which two people have only just met. Consider times when you've been around a stranger in a doctor's office, in line at a grocery store, or in an airport terminal. It only takes about 5 minutes to figure out whether that stranger is extraverted or introverted.[37] Extraversion is also the Big Five dimension that you knew your standing on, even before taking our self-assessment. People rarely consider how open they are to new experiences or how agreeable they are, but almost everyone already self-identifies as an "extravert" or "introvert."

Like agreeableness, extraversion is not necessarily related to performance across all jobs or occupations. However, extraverted people prioritize **status striving**, which reflects a strong desire to obtain power and influence within a social structure as a means of expressing personality.[38] Extraverts care a lot about being successful and influential and direct their work efforts toward "moving up" and developing a strong reputation. Indeed, research suggests that extraverts are more likely to emerge as leaders in social and task-related groups.[39] They also tend to be rated as more effective in a leadership role by the people who are following them.[40] One potential reason for these findings is that people tend to view extraverts, who are more energetic and outgoing, as more "leaderlike" than introverts.

In addition to being related to leadership emergence and effectiveness, research suggests that extraverts tend to be happier with their jobs. You may recall from Chapter 4 on Job Satisfaction that people's day-to-day moods can be categorized along two dimensions: pleasantness and activation. As illustrated in Figure 9-3, extraverted employees tend to be high in what's called **positive affectivity**—a dispositional tendency to experience pleasant, engaging moods such as enthusiasm, excitement, and elation.[41] That tendency to experience positive moods across situations explains why extraverts tend to be more satisfied with their jobs.[42] Research now acknowledges that employees' genes have a significant impact on their job satisfaction and that much of that genetic influence is due to extraversion (and neuroticism, as discussed next). For example, one study of identical twins reared apart showed that twins' job satisfaction levels were significantly correlated, even when the

"I could cry when I think of the years I wasted accumulating money, only to learn that my cheerful disposition is genetic."

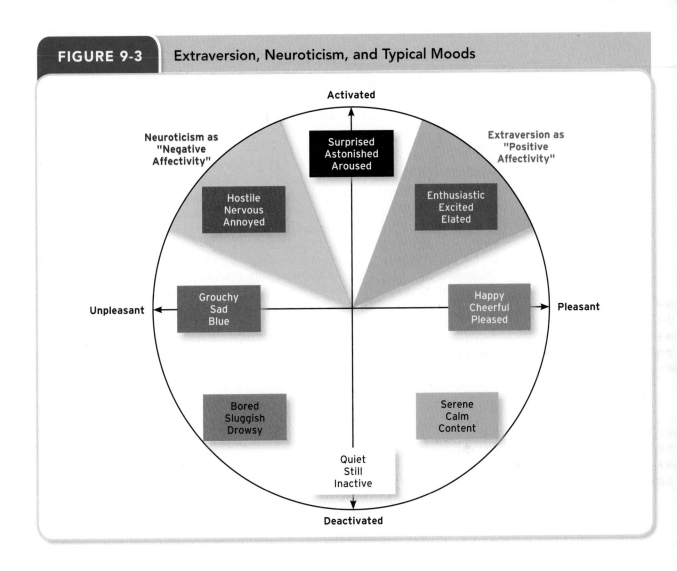

FIGURE 9-3 Extraversion, Neuroticism, and Typical Moods

twins held jobs that were quite different in terms of their duties, their complexity, and their working conditions.[43] In fact, this study suggested that around 30 percent of the variation in job satisfaction is due to genetic factors such as personality.

Other research suggests that extraverts have more to be happy about than just their jobs. Specifically, research suggests that extraversion is positively related to more general life satisfaction.[44] To shed light on that finding, one study asked students to complete a "life event checklist" by indicating whether various events had happened to them in the preceding four years.[45] The results showed that extraversion was associated with more positive events, such as joining a club or athletic team, going on vacation with friends, getting a raise at work, receiving an award for nonacademic reasons, and getting married or engaged. Other studies have linked extraversion to the number of same-sex peers, number of dating partners, frequency of alcohol consumption, and frequency of attending parties.[46] However, extraverts spend so much time doing those things that they wind up having less frequent interactions with their family.[47] Even parents of extraverts enjoy a phone call home now and again!

NEUROTICISM. Neurotic people are nervous, moody, emotional, insecure, and jealous. Occasionally you may see this Big Five dimension called by its flip side: "Emotional Stability" or "Emotional Adjustment." If conscientiousness is the most important of the Big Five from the perspective of job performance, neuroticism is the second most important.[48] There are few jobs for which the traits associated with neuroticism are beneficial to on-the-job behaviors. Instead, most jobs benefit from employees who are calm, steady, and secure.

Whereas extraversion is synonymous with positive affectivity, neuroticism is synonymous with **negative affectivity**—a dispositional tendency to experience unpleasant moods such as hostility, nervousness, and annoyance (see Figure 9-3).[49] That tendency to experience negative moods explains why neurotic employees often experience lower levels of job satisfaction than their less neurotic counterparts.[50] Along with extraversion, neuroticism explains much of the impact of genetic factors on job satisfaction. Research suggests that the negative affectivity associated with neuroticism also influences life satisfaction, with neurotic people tending to be less happy with their lives in general.[51] In fact, one method of assessing neuroticism (or negative affectivity) is to determine how unhappy people are with everyday objects and things. This "gripe index" is shown in Table 9-1. If you find yourself dissatisfied with several of the objects in that table, then you probably experience negative moods quite frequently.

Neuroticism also influences the way that people deal with stressful situations. Specifically, neuroticism is associated with a **differential exposure** to stressors, meaning that neurotic people are more likely to appraise day-to-day situations as stressful (and therefore feel like they are exposed to stressors more frequently).[52] Neuroticism is also associated with a **differential reactivity** to stressors, meaning that neurotic people are less likely to believe they can cope with the stressors that they experience.[53] Neuroticism is largely responsible for the Type A Behavior Pattern that has been shown to affect employees' health and ability to manage stressful environments.[54] That is, neurotic people are much more likely to be "Type As," whereas less neurotic individuals are much more likely to be "Type Bs" (see Chapter 5 on Stress for more discussion of such issues).

Neuroticism is also strongly related to **locus of control**, which reflects whether people attribute the causes of events to themselves or to the external environment.[55] Neurotic people tend to hold an *external* locus of control, meaning that they often believe that the events that occur around them are driven by luck, chance, or fate. Less neurotic people tend to hold an *internal* locus of control, meaning that they believe that their own behavior dictates events. Table 9-2 provides more detail about the external versus internal distinction. The table includes a number of beliefs that are representative of an external or internal viewpoint, including beliefs about life in general, work, school, politics, and relationships. If you tend to agree more strongly with the beliefs in the left column, then you have a more external locus of control. If you tend to agree more with the right column, your locus is more internal.

How important is locus of control? One meta-analysis of 135 different research studies showed that an internal locus of control was associated with higher levels of job satisfaction and job performance.[56] A second meta-analysis of 222 different research studies showed that people with an internal locus of control enjoyed better health, including higher self-reported mental well-being, fewer self-reported physical symptoms, lower blood pressure, and lower stress hormone secretion.[57] Internals also enjoyed more social support at work than externals and sensed that they had a stronger relationship with their supervisors. They viewed their jobs as having more beneficial characteristics, such as autonomy and significance, and fewer negative characteristics, such as conflict and ambiguity. In addition, those with an internal locus of control earned a higher salary than those with an external locus.

TABLE 9-1	The Neutral Objects Questionnaire (a.k.a. The "Gripe Index")

Instructions: The following questions ask about your degree of satisfaction with several items. Consider each item carefully. Circle the numbered response that best represents your feelings about the corresponding item. Then sum up your score.

	DISSATISFIED	NEUTRAL	SATISFIED
Your telephone number	1	2	3
8½ × 11 paper	1	2	3
Popular music	1	2	3
Modern art	1	2	3
Your first name	1	2	3
Restaurant food	1	2	3
Public transportation	1	2	3
Telephone service	1	2	3
The way you were raised	1	2	3
Advertising	1	2	3
The way people drive	1	2	3
Local speed limits	1	2	3
Television programs	1	2	3
The people you know	1	2	3
Yourself	1	2	3
Your relaxation time	1	2	3
Local newspapers	1	2	3
Today's cars	1	2	3
The quality of food you buy	1	2	3
The movies being produced today	1	2	3
The climate where you live	1	2	3
The high school you attended	1	2	3
The neighbors you have	1	2	3
The residence where you live	1	2	3
The city in which you live	1	2	3

Interpretation: If you scored below a 50, you tend to be less satisfied with everyday objects than the typical respondent. Such a score may indicate negative affectivity, a tendency to feel negative emotional states frequently. (Or perhaps you should change your phone number!)

Sources: Adapted from T.A. Judge, "Does Affective Disposition Moderate the Relationship Between Job Satisfaction and Voluntary Turnover?" *Journal of Applied Psychology* 78 (1993), pp. 395–401; and J. Weitz, "A Neglected Concept in the Study of Job Satisfaction," *Personnel Psychology* 5 (1952), pp. 201–205.

TABLE 9-2	External and Internal Locus of Control

PEOPLE WITH AN EXTERNAL LOCUS OF CONTROL TEND TO BELIEVE:	PEOPLE WITH AN INTERNAL LOCUS OF CONTROL TEND TO BELIEVE:
Many of the unhappy things in people's lives are partly due to bad luck.	People's misfortunes result from the mistakes they make.
Getting a good job depends mainly on being in the right place at the right time.	Becoming a success is a matter of hard work; luck has little or nothing to do with it.
Many times exam questions tend to be so unrelated to course work that studying is really useless.	In the case of the well-prepared student, there is rarely if ever such a thing as an unfair test.
This world is run by the few people in power, and there is not much the little guy can do about it.	The average citizen can have an influence in government decisions.
There's not much use in trying too hard to please people; if they like you, they like you.	People are lonely because they don't try to be friendly.

Source: Adapted from J.B. Rotter, "Generalized Expectancies for Internal versus External Control of Reinforcement," *Psychological Monographs* 80 (1966), pp. 1–28.

OPENNESS TO EXPERIENCE. The final dimension of the Big Five is openness to experience. Open people are curious, imaginative, creative, complex, refined, and sophisticated. Of all the Big Five, openness to experience has the most alternative labels. Sometimes it's called "Inquisitiveness" or "Intellectualness" or even "Culture" (not in the national culture sense—rather, in the "high culture" sense of knowing fine wine, art, and classical music). Much like agreeableness and extraversion, the traits associated with openness are beneficial in some jobs but not others. As a result, openness is not related to job performance across all occupations.

What jobs benefit from high levels of openness? Generally speaking, jobs that are

very fluid and dynamic, with rapid changes in job demands. Research shows that open employees excel in learning and training environments, because their curiosity gives them a built-in desire to learn new things.[58] They also tend to be more adaptable and quick to identify when the "old way of doing things" is no longer effective, excelling at the search for a new and better approach.[59] In fact, conscientious employees are sometimes less effective than open employees in such environments, because their persevering nature sometimes prevents them from abandoning "tried-and-true" task strategies.

Openness to experience is also more likely to be valuable in jobs that require high levels of creative performance, where job holders need to be able to generate novel and useful ideas and solutions.[60] The relationship between openness and creative performance can be seen in Figure 9-4. Together

People who are open to new experiences tend to do well in situations that offer frequent opportunities to learn new things, such as teaching.

FIGURE 9-4 | Openness to Experience and Creativity

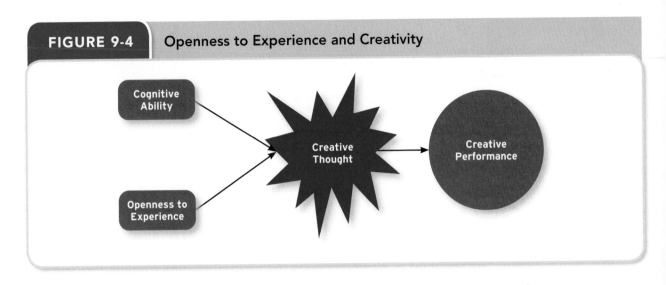

with cognitive ability, openness to experience is a key driver of creative thought, as smart and open people excel at the style of thinking demanded by creativity (see Chapter 10 on Ability for more discussion of such issues). How good are you at creative thinking? See Figure 9-5 to find out. Creative thought results in creative performance when people come up with new ideas, create fresh approaches to problems, or suggest new innovations that can help improve the workplace.[61] The creativity benefits of openness likely explain why highly open individuals are more likely to migrate into artistic and scientific fields, in which novel and original products are so critical.[62] Dragonfly, a New York–based Web video–networking company, goes to unusual lengths to foster creative thought.[63] The company pays $10,000 to $20,000 to put employees through six hours of hypnotism. The idea is that the relaxation, meditation, and visualization used in hypnosis can unlock the imagination of employees, even if they're lower in openness.

BMW, the German automaker, seems to understand the importance of the Big Five dimensions of personality. BMW has worked hard to create a culture of innovation in which there is never a penalty for proposing new and outlandish ways of improving its cars.[64] Those proposed improvements include a "smart card" that can be taken out of your own BMW and plugged into a rented one, passing along your music, podcast, and comfort settings

The cafeteria at BMW's Leipzig facility, where the assembly line moves above to give employees a feel for the rhythm of the plant.

FIGURE 9-5   Tests of Creative Thinking

Instructions: Do you consider yourself to be a creative thinker? See if you can solve the problems below. If you need help, the answers can be found in the Takeaways section of this chapter.

1. What gets wetter as it dries?

2. A woman had two sons who were born on the same hour of the same day of the same year. But they were not twins. How could this be so?

3. What occurs once in June, once in July, and twice in August?

4. Make this mathematical expression true by drawing only a single noncurving line:

5. Join all nine of the dots below using only four (or fewer) noncurving lines, without lifting your pen from the paper and without retracing the lines.

Source: http://home.swipnet.se/~w-19502/puzzles.htm; http://www.mycoted.com/Category:Puzzles

to the new vehicle. Openness is needed to foster such creative thought, but agreeableness is also key to BMW's culture. Stefan Krause, BMW's chief financial officer, summarizes how to push a creative idea successfully: "You can go into fighting mode or you can ask permission and get everyone to support you. If you do it without building ties, you will be blocked."

BMW employees also draw on their conscientiousness in those critical times when a new technology is introduced or production volume is expanded. During those time periods, employees from other factories may move into temporary housing far from home to put in extra hours on another plant's line. Why are employees so devoted? For one thing, no one at BMW can remember a layoff—something that is incredibly unique in the auto industry. That's part of the reason BMW's human resources group receives more than 200,000 applications annually. Those fortunate enough to make it to the interview stage participate in elaborate, day-long drills in teams to make sure that their personalities provide a good match for the company.

OTHER TAXONOMIES OF PERSONALITY

Although the Big Five is the dominant lens for examining personality, it's not the only framework with which you might be familiar. One of the most widely administered personality measures in organizations is the **Myers-Briggs Type Indicator** (or MBTI).[65] This instrument was originally created to test a theory of psychological types advanced by the noted psychologist Carl Jung.[66] The MBTI evaluates individuals on the basis of four types of preferences:[67]

9.4

What taxonomies can be used to describe personality, other than the Big Five?

- *Extraversion* (being energized by people and social interactions) versus *Introversion* (being energized by private time and reflection).
- *Sensing* (preferring clear and concrete facts and data) versus *Intuition* (preferring hunches and speculations based on theory and imagination).
- *Thinking* (approaching decisions with logic and critical analysis) versus *Feeling* (approaching decisions with an emphasis on others' needs and feelings).
- *Judging* (approaching tasks by planning and setting goals) versus *Perceiving* (preferring to have flexibility and spontaneity when performing tasks).

The MBTI categorizes people into one of 16 different types on the basis of their preferences. For example, an "ISTJ" has a preference for Introversion, Sensing, Thinking, and Judging. Research on the MBTI suggests that managers are more likely to be "TJs" than the general population.[68] Moreover, the different personality types seem to approach decision-making tasks with differing emphases on facts, logic, and plans. That said, there is little evidence that the MBTI is a useful tool for predicting the job satisfaction, motivation, performance, or commitment of employees across jobs.[69] Indeed, one of the reasons the MBTI is so widely used is that there really isn't a "bad type"—no one who gets their profile is receiving negative news. As a result, the most appropriate use of the MBTI is in a team-building context, to help different members understand their varying approaches to accomplishing tasks. Using the MBTI as any kind of hiring or selection tool does not appear to be warranted, based on existing research.

A second alternative to the Big Five is offered by research on vocational interests.[70] **Interests** are expressions of personality that influence behavior through preferences for certain environments and activities.[71] Interests reflect stable and enduring likes and dislikes that can explain why people are drawn toward some careers and away from others.[72] Holland's **RIASEC model** suggests that interests can be summarized by six different personality types:[73]

- *Realistic*: Enjoys practical, hands-on, real-world tasks. Tends to be frank, practical, determined, and rugged.
- *Investigative*: Enjoys abstract, analytical, theory-oriented tasks. Tends to be analytical, intellectual, reserved, and scholarly.
- *Artistic*: Enjoys entertaining and fascinating others using imagination. Tends to be original, independent, impulsive, and creative.
- *Social*: Enjoys helping, serving, or assisting others. Tends to be helpful, inspiring, informative, and empathic.
- *Enterprising*: Enjoys persuading, leading, or outperforming others. Tends to be energetic, sociable, ambitious, and risk-taking.
- *Conventional*: Enjoys organizing, counting, or regulating people or things. Tends to be careful, conservative, self-controlled, and structured.

As shown in Figure 9-6, the RIASEC model further suggests that the personality types can be classified along two dimensions: the degree to which employees prefer to work with

FIGURE 9-6 | Holland's RIASEC Model

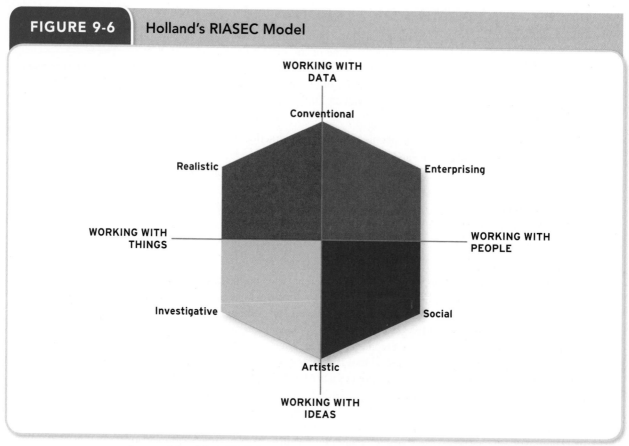

Sources: Adapted from J.L. Holland, *Making Vocational Choices: A Theory of Careers* (Englewood Cliffs, NJ: Prentice-Hall, 1973).

data versus ideas and the degree to which they prefer to work with people versus things. For example, those with a Realistic personality prefer to work with things and data more than people and ideas. The model arranges the personality types in a hexagonal fashion, with types adjacent to one another being more similar than types that are more distant. The central premise of the RIASEC model is that employees have more career satisfaction and longevity in occupations that match their personality type.[74] For example, Realistic people should be happier as craftspeople than as counselors because a craftsperson's duties provide a good match to their personality. One of the most common applications of the RIASEC model is interest inventories, which provide people their scores on relevant personality dimensions, along with a list of occupations that could provide a good match for that profile.[75]

CULTURAL VALUES

As noted previously, our personalities are influenced by both our genes and our environment. One significant aspect of that environment is the society in which we were raised. Societies can be described in a number of ways, including their climate and habitat, their sovereignty and political system, their language and religion, their education and technology levels, and their economic development.[76] However, one of the most important aspects of societies is culture. **Culture** is defined as the shared values, beliefs, motives, identities, and interpretations that result from common experiences of members of a society and are transmitted across generations.[77] Culture has been described as patterns resulting from societal traditions and as the collective programming of the mind that separates one society from another.[78] The shared values, societal traditions, and collective programming that underlies culture influences the development of our personalities while also shaping the way our traits are expressed. In this way, explaining "what we're like" requires an awareness of "where we're from."

To some extent, cultures provide societies with their own distinct personalities.[79] One study on the Big Five profiles of 51 different cultures showed that some societies tend to value certain personality traits more than other societies.[80] For example, people from India tend to be more conscientious than people from Belgium. People from the Czech Republic tend to be more agreeable than people from Hong Kong. People from Brazil tend to be more neurotic than people from China. People from Australia tend to be more extraverted than people from Russia. People from Denmark tend to be more open than people from Argentina. For their part, people in the United States trend toward the high end of the 51 culture sample on extraversion and openness, staying near the middle for the other Big Five dimensions. Of course, that doesn't mean that all of the members of these societies have exactly the same personality. Instead, those results merely convey that certain cultures tend to place a higher value on certain traits.

Although it's possible to contrast nations using the Big Five, as we just did, cross-cultural research focuses more attention on the shared values aspect of culture. The values that are salient in a given culture influence how people select and justify courses of action and how they evaluate themselves and other people.[81] To some extent, cultural values come to reflect the way things *should be done* in a given society.[82] Acting in a manner that's consistent with those values helps people to fit in, and going against those values causes people to stand out. Just as there are a number of traits that can be used to describe personality, there are a number of values that can be used to describe cultures. Given the sheer complexity of culture, it's not surprising that different studies have arrived at different taxonomies that can be used to summarize cultural values.

 9.5

What taxonomies can be used to describe cultural values?

The most well-known taxonomy of cultural values was derived from a landmark study in the late 1960s and early 1970s by Geert Hofstede, who analyzed data from 88,000 IBM employees from 72 countries in 20 languages.[83] His research showed that employees working in different countries tended to prioritize different values, and those values clustered into several distinct dimensions. Those dimensions are summarized in Table 9-3 and include **individualism–collectivism**, **power distance**, **uncertainty avoidance**, and **masculinity–femininity**. A subsequent study added a fifth dimension to the taxonomy: **short-term vs. long-term orientation**.[84] Hofstede's research introduced scores on each of the dimensions for various cultures, providing researchers with a quantitative tool to summarize and compare and contrast the cultures of different societies. Table 9-3 includes some of the countries that have high or low scores on Hofstede's dimensions.

Although Hofstede's dimensions have formed the foundation for much of the research on cross-cultural management, more recent studies have painted a more nuanced picture of cultural values. **Project GLOBE** (Global Leadership and Organizational Behavior Effectiveness) is a collection of 170 researchers from 62 cultures who have studied 17,300 managers in 951 organizations since 1991.[85] The main purpose of Project GLOBE is to examine the impact of culture on the effectiveness of various leader attributes, behaviors, and practices (see Chapter 14 on Leadership: Styles and Behaviors for more discussion of such issues). In pursing that goal, project researchers asked managers to rate the values

TABLE 9-3	Hofstede's Dimensions of Cultural Values

Individualism-Collectivism

INDIVIDUALISTIC	COLLECTIVISTIC
The culture is a loosely knit social framework in which people take care of themselves and their immediate family.	The culture is a tight social framework in which people take care of the members of a broader ingroup and act loyal to it.
United States, the Netherlands, France	Indonesia, China, West Africa

Power Distance

LOW	HIGH
The culture prefers that power be distributed uniformly where possible, in a more egalitarian fashion.	The culture accepts the fact that power is usually distributed unequally within organizations.
United States, Germany, the Netherlands	Russia, China, Indonesia

Uncertainty Avoidance

LOW	HIGH
The culture tolerates uncertain and ambiguous situations and values unusual ideas and behaviors.	The culture feels threatened by uncertain and ambiguous situations and relies on formal rules to create stability.
United States, Indonesia, the Netherlands	Japan, Russia, France

Masculinity–Femininity

MASCULINE	FEMININE
The culture values stereotypically male traits such as assertiveness and the acquisition of money and things.	The culture values stereotypically female traits such as caring for others and caring about quality of life.
United States, Japan, Germany	The Netherlands, Russia, France

Short-Term vs. Long-Term Orientation

SHORT-TERM ORIENTED	LONG-TERM ORIENTED
The culture stresses values that are more past- and present-oriented, such as respect for tradition and fulfilling obligations.	The culture stresses values that are more future-oriented, such as persistence, prudence, and thrift.
United States, Russia, West Africa	China, Japan, the Netherlands

Sources: G. Hofstede, *Culture's Consequences: Comparing Values, Behaviors, Institutions, and Organizations across Nations* (Thousand Oaks, CA: Sage, 2001). G. Hofstede, "Cultural Constraints in Management Theories," *Academy of Management Executive* 7 (1993), pp. 81–94; and G. Hofstede and M.H. Bond, "The Confucius Connection: From Cultural Roots to Economic Growth," *Organizational Dynamics* 16 (1988), pp. 5–21.

held within their organizations and within their societies. That research identified nine different dimensions that are used to summarize cultures within Project GLOBE. Some of those dimensions can be viewed as replications of Hofstede's work. For example, Project GLOBE identified both *power distance* and *uncertainty avoidance* as key dimensions of cultural values. The project also identified collectivism, though it was differentiated into *institutional collectivism* (where formalized practices encourage collective action and collective distribution of resources) and *in-group collectivism* (where individuals express pride and loyalty to specific in-groups).

Other dimensions bear some similarity to Hofstede's work but are conceptually distinct. Those dimensions are listed below, along with some information on the cultures that score at the higher and lower ends on a given value. Note that Project GLOBE groups cultures into "country clusters." Those clusters include Anglo (United States, Canada, Australia, England), Latin America (Mexico, Brazil, Colombia, Venezuela), Latin Europe (France, Spain, Italy, Israel), Germanic Europe (Germany, Austria, the Netherlands, Switzerland), Nordic Europe (Denmark, Finland, Sweden), Eastern Europe (Poland, Hungary, Russia, Greece), Middle East (Turkey, Egypt, Kuwait, Morocco), Southern Asia (India, Thailand, Indonesia, Malaysia), Confucian Asia (China, South Korea, Japan, Singapore), and Sub-Sahara Africa (Zimbabwe, Namibia, Nigeria). The following descriptions note some of the country clusters that earn high and low scores on a given cultural value. Note that the Anglo group, which includes the United States, scores in the middle on most of the cultural values.

- *Gender Egalitarianism.* The culture promotes gender equality and minimizes role differences between men and women. High: Nordic Europe, Eastern Europe. Low: Middle East.

- *Assertiveness.* The culture values assertiveness, confrontation, and aggressiveness in social relationships. High: Germanic Europe, Eastern Europe. Low: Nordic Europe.

- *Future Orientation.* The culture engages in planning and investment in the future while delaying individual or collective gratification. High: Germanic Europe, Nordic Europe. Low: Middle East, Latin America, Eastern Europe.

- *Performance Orientation.* The culture encourages and rewards members for excellence and performance improvements. High: Anglo, Confucian Asia, Germanic Europe. Low: Latin America, Eastern Europe.

- *Humane Orientation.* The culture encourages and rewards members for being generous, caring, kind, fair, and altruistic. High: Southern Asia, Sub-Saharan Africa. Low: Latin Europe, Germanic Europe.

Taken together, Hofstede's work and the Project GLOBE studies have identified between five and nine cultural value dimensions. However, the lion's share of cross-cultural research focuses on individualism–collectivism, perhaps the most fundamental means of differentiating cultures.[86] The individualism–collectivism distinction is relevant to various topics within organizational behavior.[87] For example, collectivists exhibit higher levels of task performance and citizenship behaviors in work team settings, and also exhibit lower levels of counterproductive and withdrawal behaviors.[88] They are also more likely to feel affectively and normatively committed to their employers than are individualists.[89] Research also suggests that collectivists tend to prefer rewards that are allocated equally on a group-wide basis as opposed to rewards tied solely to individual achievement.[90]

Regardless of the particular value of focus, research on cultural values illustrates the potential differences between the attitudes and beliefs of U.S. employees and the attitudes and beliefs of employees in other societies. Awareness of such cultural variations is critical, given that those differences can influence reactions to change, conflict management styles, negotiation approaches, and reward preferences, just to name a few.[91] Failing to understand those differences can compromise the effectiveness of multinational groups and organizations. Such problems are particularly likely if employees are high in **ethnocentrism**, defined as a propensity to view one's own cultural values as "right" and those of other cultures as "wrong."[92] For more discussion of this issue, see our **OB Internationally** feature.

OB INTERNATIONALLY

Research suggests that ethnocentrism hinders the effectiveness of expatriates, who are employees working full-time in other countries. Ethnocentrism makes expatriates less likely to adjust to a new culture, less likely to fulfill the duties required of their international assignment, and more likely to withdraw from that assignment. How can organizations identify employees with the right personalities to serve as expatriates? One useful tool is the *multicultural personality questionnaire,* which assesses five personality dimensions that can maximize the performance and commitment of expatriates.[93] Those dimensions are listed below, along with some sample items.

Cultural Empathy. A tendency to empathize with the feelings, thoughts, and behaviors of individuals with different cultural values.

- I understand other people's feelings.
- I take other people's habits into consideration.

Open-mindedness. A tendency to have an open and unprejudiced attitude toward other cultural values and norms.

- I get involved in other cultures.
- I find other religions interesting.

Emotional Stability. A tendency to remain calm in the kinds of stressful situations that can be encountered in foreign environments.

- I can put setbacks in perspective.
- I take it for granted that things will turn out right.

Social Initiative. A tendency to be proactive when approaching social situations, which aids in building connections.

- I easily approach other people.
- I am often the driving force behind things.

Flexibility. A tendency to regard new situations as a challenge and to adjust behaviors to meet that challenge.

- I could start a new life easily.
- I feel comfortable in different cultures.

Research has linked these five personality traits to a number of expatriate success factors. For example, individuals with a "multicultural personality" are more likely to aspire to international positions, more likely to gain international experience, more likely to adjust to new assignments, and more likely to be happy with their lives during those assignments.[94]

SUMMARY: HOW CAN WE DESCRIBE WHAT EMPLOYEES ARE LIKE?

So how can we explain what employees are like? As shown in Figure 9-7, many of the thousands of adjectives we use to describe people can be boiled down into the Big Five dimensions of personality. Conscientiousness reflects the reliability, perseverance, and ambition of employees. Agreeableness captures their tendency to cooperate with others in a warm and sympathetic fashion. Neuroticism reflects the tendency to experience negative moods and emotions frequently on a day-to-day basis. Individuals who are high on openness to experience are creative, imaginative, and curious. Finally, extraverts

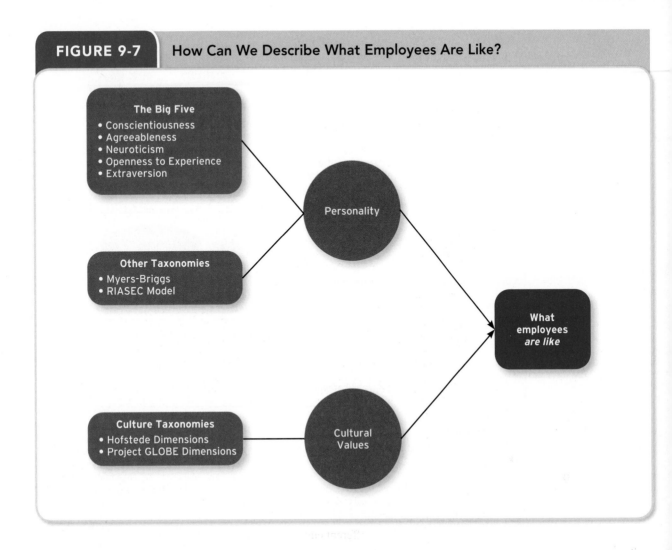

FIGURE 9-7 How Can We Describe What Employees Are Like?

are talkative, sociable, and assertive and typically experience positive moods and emotions. Other personality taxonomies, like the MBTI or the RIASEC model, can also capture many employee traits. Beyond personality, however, what employees are like also depends on the culture in which they were raised. Cultural values like individualism–collectivism, power distance, and so forth also influence employees' thoughts, emotions, and behaviors.

HOW IMPORTANT ARE PERSONALITY AND CULTURAL VALUES?

We've already described a number of reasons why the Big Five should be important considerations, particularly in the case of conscientiousness. What if we focus specifically on the two outcomes in our integrative model of OB, performance and commitment? Figure 9-8 summarizes the research evidence linking conscientiousness to those two outcomes. The figure reveals that conscientiousness affects job performance. Of the Big Five, conscientiousness has the strongest effect on task performance,[95] partly because

| FIGURE 9-8 | Effects of Personality on Performance and Commitment |

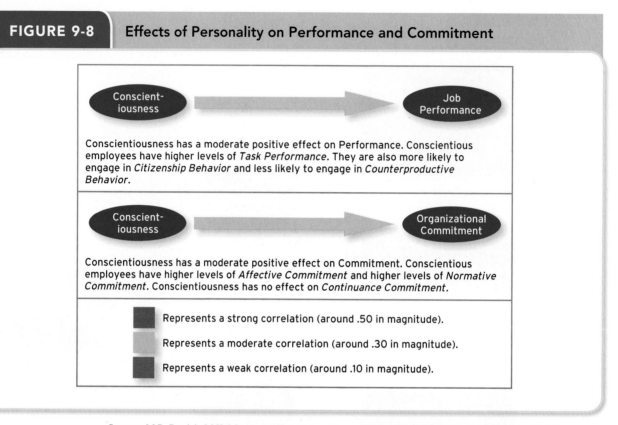

Sources: M.R. Barrick, M.K. Mount, and T.A. Judge, "Personality and Performance at the Beginning of the New Millennium: What Do We Know and Where Do We Go Next?" *International Journal of Selection and Assessment* 9 (2001), pp. 9–30; C.M. Berry, D.S. Ones, and P.R. Sackett, "Interpersonal Deviance, Organizational Deviance, and Their Common Correlates: A Review and Meta-Analysis," *Journal of Applied Psychology* 92 (2007), pp. 410–24; A. Cooper-Hakim and C. Viswesvaran, "The Construct of Work Commitment: Testing an Integrative Framework," *Psychological Bulletin* 131 (2005), pp. 241–59; L.M. Hough and A. Furnham, "Use of Personality Variables in Work Settings," in *Handbook of Psychology,* Vol. 12, eds. W.C. Borman, D.R. Ilgen, and R.J. Klimoski (Hoboken, NJ: Wiley, 2003), pp. 131–69; J.E. Mathieu and D.M. Zajac, "A Review and Meta-Analysis of the Antecedents, Correlates, and Consequences of Organizational Commitment," *Psychological Bulletin* 108 (1990), pp. 171–94; and J.F. Salgado, "The Big Five Personality Dimensions and Counterproductive Behaviors," *International Journal of Selection and Assessment* 10 (2002), pp. 117–25.

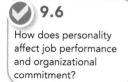

9.6

How does personality affect job performance and organizational commitment?

conscientious employees have higher levels of *motivation* than other employees.[96] They are more self-confident, perceive a clearer linkage between their effort and their performance, and are more likely to set goals and commit to them. For these reasons, conscientiousness is a key driver of what's referred to as **typical performance**, which reflects performance in the routine conditions that surround daily job tasks.[97] An employee's ability, in contrast, is a key driver of **maximum performance**, which reflects performance in brief, special circumstances that demand a person's best effort.

Conscientious employees are also more likely to engage in citizenship behaviors.[98] Why? One reason is that conscientious employees are so punctual and have such good work attendance that they are simply more available to offer "extra mile" sorts of contributions. Another reason is that they engage in so much more work-related effort that they have more energy to devote to citizenship behaviors.[99] A third reason is that they tend to have higher levels of *job satisfaction*,[100] and positive feelings tend to foster spontaneous instances of citizenship. Finally, conscientious employees are less likely to engage in counterproductive behaviors,[101] for two major reasons. First, their higher job satisfaction levels make it less likely that they'll feel a need to retaliate against their organization. Second, even if they do perceive some slight or injustice, their dependable and reliable nature should prevent them from violating organizational norms by engaging in negative actions.[102]

Figure 9-8 also reveals that conscientious employees tend to be more committed to their organization.[103] They're less likely to engage in day-to-day psychological and physical withdrawal behaviors because such actions go against their work habits. They're also significantly less likely to voluntarily leave the organization.[104] Why? One reason is that the persevering nature of conscientious employees prompts them to persist in a given course of action for long periods of time. That persistence can be seen in their daily work effort, but it extends to a sense of commitment to the organization as well.[105] Another reason is that conscientious employees are better at managing *stress*, perceiving lower levels of key stressors, and being less affected by them at work.[106] In some respects, Figure 9-8 understates the importance of conscientiousness (and personality, more generally). Why? Because personality becomes more important in some contexts than in others. The principle of **situational strength** suggests that "strong situations" have clear behavioral expectations, incentives, or instructions that make differences between individuals less important, whereas "weak situations" lack those cues.[107] Personality variables tend to be more significant drivers of behavior in weak situations than in strong situations.[108] Similarly, the principle of **trait activation** suggests that some situations provide cues that trigger the expression of a given trait.[109] For example, a cry for help provides a cue that can trigger the expression of empathy. Personality variables tend to be more significant drivers of behaviors in situations that provide relevant cues than in situations in which those cues are lacking. For more discussion of the importance of the situation, see our **OB at the Bookstore** feature.

APPLICATION: PERSONALITY TESTS

Given how important personality traits can be to job performance and organizational commitment, it's not surprising that many organizations try to gauge the personality of job applicants. What's the best way to do that? Well, many organizations try to gauge personality through interviews by looking for cues that an applicant is conscientious or agreeable or has high levels of some other relevant personality dimension. Can you see a potential problem with this approach? Here's a hint: When was the last time you went into an interview and acted careless, sloppy, moody, or insecure? It's probably been a while. In fact, most interview preparation courses and books train applicants to exhibit the very personality traits that most employers are looking for!

To examine whether interviewers can gauge the Big Five, one study asked 26 interviewers, all of whom were human resources practitioners with more than 12 years of hiring experience, to assess the personalities of undergraduate business students who were on the job market.[110] The interviewers met with an average of three students for 30 minutes and were instructed to follow the interview protocols used in their own organizations. Once the interviews had concluded, the study gathered multiple ratings of the Big Five, including ratings from the interviewer, the student, and a close friend of the student. The results of the study showed that the interviewers' ratings of extraversion, agreeableness, and openness were fairly consistent with the students' own ratings, as well as their friends' ratings. In contrast, interviewers' ratings of conscientiousness and neuroticism were only weakly related to the students' and friends' ratings. This study therefore shows that

OB AT THE BOOKSTORE

STRENGTHSFINDER 2.0
by Tom Rath (Gallup Press: New York, 2007).

Far too many people spend a lifetime headed in the wrong direction. They go not only from the cradle to the cubicle, but then to the casket, without uncovering their greatest talents and potential.

With those words, Tom Rath emphasizes the importance of discovering your talents in a sequel to the best-selling *Now, Discover Your Strengths.*[111] Talents are defined as naturally recurring and relatively enduring patterns of thought, feeling, or behavior. The book provides an overview of 34 different "talent themes" and includes a link to an online assessment for discovering your top five themes. As shown below, the Big Five dimensions of personality seem to underlie many of the 34 talent themes:

- *Conscientiousness:* May underlie talents such as Achiever, Arranger, Deliberative, Focus, and Responsibility.
- *Agreeableness:* May underlie talents such as Empathy, Harmony, Includer, and Relator.
- *Neuroticism:* Low neuroticism may underlie talents such as Connectedness, Maximizer, and Self-Assurance.
- *Openness to Experience:* May underlie talents such as Adaptability, Ideation, Input, Intellection, and Learner.
- *Extraversion:* May underlie talents such as Command, Communication, Positivity, and Woo.

The central thesis of the book is that people will be more successful if they "play to their strengths" as opposed to focusing on improving their weaknesses. Rath notes that The Gallup Organization has asked over 10 million people whether they agree with this statement: "At work, I have the opportunity to do what I do best every day." Research suggests that respondents who agree with that statement are six times more likely to be satisfied with their job and three times more likely to be happy with their lives. Unfortunately, only one-third of respondents strongly agreed that they could focus on their talents every day. The bottom line is this: Don't let yourself be "miscast" into jobs and assignments that don't suit your personality. Instead, figure out what makes you stand out, and place yourself into situations where those talents are valued.

interviewers are unable to gauge the two Big Five dimensions that are most highly related to job performance.

Rather than using interviews to assess personality, more and more companies are relying on paper-and-pencil "personality tests" like the kind shown in our OB Assessments or the kind offered by Kronos. Of course, personality testing is not without controversy, as we have noted. Privacy advocates worry about the security of the personality profiles that are stored in large databases.[112] There's also no guarantee that the personality tests used by a company are actually valid assessments, because few of them have been subject to scientific investigation.[113] For example, we're not aware of any scientific studies in peer-reviewed journals that

9.7

Are personality tests useful tools for organizational hiring?

TABLE 9-4	A Sampling of Well-Validated Measures of the Big Five	
NAME OF INSTRUMENT	**VENDOR**	**TIME REQUIRED**
NEO Five-Factor Inventory (NEO-FFI)	Sigma Assessment Systems	15 minutes
Personal Characteristics Inventory (PCI)	Wonderlic	20 minutes
Personality Research Form (PRF)	Sigma Assessment Systems	45 minutes
Hogan Personality Inventory (HPI)	Hogan Assessment Systems	15 minutes
Big Five Inventory (BFI)	TestMaster	10 minutes

have comprehensively validated Kronos' personality test. Because the personality testing industry is not regulated, the best bet for companies that are thinking about using personality tests is to start with tests that have been validated in scientific journals. Table 9-4 provides a list of some of the most well-validated measures of the Big Five personality dimensions. The vendors that own these measures typically offer software and services for scoring the instruments, interpreting the data against relevant population norms, and creating feedback sheets.

One particular subset of personality tests is particularly controversial. **Integrity tests**, sometimes also called "honesty tests," are personality tests that focus specifically on a predisposition to engage in theft and other counterproductive behaviors.[114] Integrity tests were created, in part, as a reaction to Congress's decision to make polygraph (or "lie detector") tests illegal as a tool for organizational hiring. Integrity tests typically come in two general varieties. **Clear purpose tests** ask applicants about their attitudes toward dishonesty, beliefs about the frequency of dishonesty, endorsements of common rationalizations for dishonesty, desire to punish dishonesty, and confessions of past dishonesty.[115] **Veiled purpose tests** do not reference dishonesty explicitly but instead assess more general personality traits that are associated with dishonest acts. Table 9-5 provides sample items for both types of

TABLE 9-5	Sample Integrity Test Items
TYPE OF TEST	**SAMPLE ITEMS**
Clear Purpose	• Did you ever think about taking money from where you worked, but didn't go through with it? • Have you ever borrowed something from work without telling anyone? • Is it OK to get around the law if you don't break it? • If you were sent an extra item with an order, would you send it back? • Do most employees take small items from work? • What dollar value would a worker have to steal before you would fire them?
Veiled Purpose	• I like to plan things carefully ahead of time. • I often act quickly without stopping to think things through. • I've never hurt anyone's feelings. • I have a feeling someone is out to get me. • I don't feel I've had control over my life.

Source: J.E. Wanek, P.R. Sackett, and D.S. Ones, "Towards an Understanding of Integrity Test Similarities and Differences: An Item-Level Analysis of Seven Tests," *Personnel Psychology* 56 (2003), pp. 873–94. Reprinted with permission of Wiley-Blackwell.

"Remember when I said I was going to be honest with you, Jeff? That was a big, fat lie."

integrity tests. You might notice that the veiled purpose items resemble some of the items in our OB Assessment for the Big Five. Most integrity tests actually assess, in large part, a combination of high conscientiousness, high agreeableness, and low neuroticism,[116] along with an honesty or humility factor that may lay beyond the Big Five.[117]

Do integrity tests actually work? One study examined the effectiveness of integrity tests in a sample of convenience store clerks.[118] The chain had been struggling with inventory "shrinkage" due to theft and began using a clear purpose integrity test to combat that trend. The study compared the integrity test scores for employees who were fired for theft-related reasons (e.g., taking merchandise, mishandling cash, having frequent cash register shortages) with a sample of demographically similar employees who remained in good standing. The results of the study revealed that employees who were terminated for theft had scored significantly lower on the integrity test when they were hired than employees who were not terminated. These sorts of results are not unusual; a meta-analysis of 443 studies including more than 500,000 employees has shown that integrity test scores have a moderately strong, negative correlation with counterproductive behaviors such as theft.[119] In fact, integrity test scores are actually more strongly related to job performance than conscientiousness scores, largely because integrity tests sample a blend of multiple Big Five dimensions.[120]

You might find it surprising that integrity tests (or personality tests in general) can be effective. After all, don't applicants just lie on the test? Before we answer that question, consider what you would do if you applied for a job and had to answer a set of questions on a 1 ("Strongly Disagree") to 5 ("Strongly Agree") scale that were obviously measuring integrity. If a response of 5 indicated high integrity, how would you answer? You probably wouldn't answer all 5s because it would be clear that you were **faking**—exaggerating your responses to a personality test in a socially desirable fashion. You might worry that the computers that score the test have some ability to "flag" faked responses (indeed, the scoring procedures for many personality tests do flag applicants with an unusual pattern of responses).[121]

So how would you answer? Chances are, you'd allow your answers to have "a grain of truth"—you'd just exaggerate that true response a bit to make yourself look better. Figure 9-9 summarizes what this sort of faking might look like, with red circles representing below-average scores on an integrity test and green circles representing above-average scores. Research on personality testing suggests that virtually everyone fakes their responses to some degree, as evidenced in the difference between the faded circles (which represent the "true" responses) and the unfaded circles (which represent the exaggerated responses).[122] Do dishonest people fake more? To some degree. Figure 9-9 reveals that

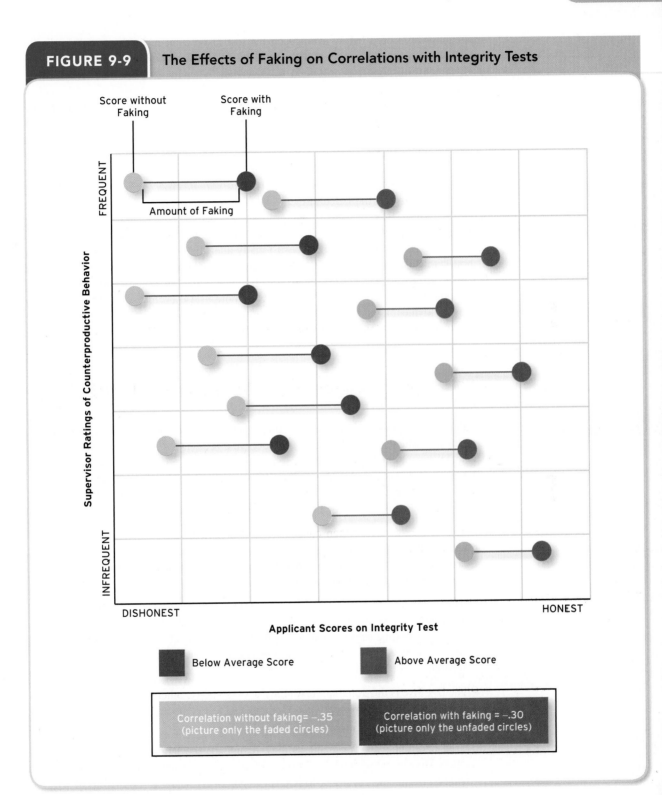

FIGURE 9-9   The Effects of Faking on Correlations with Integrity Tests

applicants who scored below average on the test faked a bit more than applicants who scored above average on the test. But the disparity in the amount of faking is not large, likely because dishonest people tend to view their behavior as perfectly normal—they believe everyone feels and acts just like they do.

The figure reveals that it could be dangerous to set some artificial cutoff score for making hiring decisions, because it's possible for someone to "fake their way" across that cutoff (note that two of the individuals in the figure went from a below-average score to an above-average score by faking). With that caution in mind, here's the critical point illustrated by Figure 9-9: *Because everyone fakes to some degree, correlations with outcomes like theft or other counterproductive behaviors are relatively unaffected.*[123] Picture the scatterplot in the figure with just the faded circles—what does the correlation between integrity test scores and supervisor ratings of counterproductive behavior look like? Now picture the scatterplot with just the unfaded circles—what does that correlation look like? About the same, right? The tendency to fake doesn't really alter the rank order in scores from most dishonest to most honest, so the test is still useful as a tool for predicting counterproductive behavior. In fact, experts on personnel selection agree that personality and integrity tests are among the most useful tools for hiring[124]—more useful even than the typical version of the employment interview.[125] One of the only tools that's more useful than a personality test is an ability test—as noted in our next chapter.[126]

TAKEAWAYS

9.1 Personality refers to the structures and propensities inside people that explain their characteristic patterns of thought, emotion, and behavior. It also refers to people's social reputations—the way they are perceived by others. In this way, personality captures *what people are like* (unlike ability, which reflects *what people can do*). Cultural values are shared beliefs about desirable end states or modes of conduct in a given culture that influence the development and expression of traits.

9.2 The "Big Five" include conscientiousness (e.g., dependable, organized, reliable), agreeableness (e.g., warm, kind, cooperative), neuroticism (e.g., nervous, moody, emotional), openness to experience (e.g., curious, imaginative, creative), and extraversion (e.g., talkative, sociable, passionate).

9.3 Although both nature and nurture are important, personality is affected significantly by genetic factors. Studies of identical twins reared apart and studies of personality stability over time suggest that between 35 and 45 percent of the variation in personality is genetic. Personality can be changed, but such changes are only apparent over the course of several years.

9.4 The Big Five is the dominant taxonomy of personality; other taxonomies include the Myers-Briggs Type Inventory and Holland's RIASEC model.

9.5 Hofstede's taxonomy of cultural values includes individualism–collectivism, power distance, uncertainty avoidance, masculinity–femininity, and short-term vs. long-term orientation. More recent research by Project GLOBE has replicated many of those dimensions and added five other means to distinguish among cultures: gender egalitarianism, assertiveness, future orientation, performance orientation, and humane orientation.

9.6 Conscientiousness has a moderate positive relationship with job performance and a moderate positive relationship with organizational commitment. It has stronger effects on these outcomes than the rest of the Big Five.

9.7 Personality tests are useful tools for organizational hiring. Research suggests that applicants do "fake" to some degree on the tests, but faking does not significantly lower the correlation between test scores and the relevant outcomes.

Here are the answers to the tests of creative thinking in Figure 9-5: (1) A towel. (2) They were triplets. (3) The letter U. (4) Draw a line to turn the + into a 4. (5) Solving this puzzle literally requires you to "think outside the box" (yes, that's where it comes from!) Nowhere in the instructions did it state that you needed to keep the lines inside the square formed by the dots. Connect the dots using the four lines shown below:

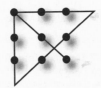

KEY TERMS

DISCUSSION QUESTIONS

9.1 Assume that you applied for a job and were asked to take a personality test, like the one offered by Kronos. How would you react? Would you view the organization with which you were applying in a more or less favorable light? Why?

9.2   Research on genetic influences on personality suggests that more than half of the variation in personality is due to nurture—to life experiences. What life experiences could make someone more conscientious? More agreeable? More neurotic? More extraverted? More open to new experiences?

9.3   Consider the personality dimensions included in the Myers-Briggs Type Inventory and the RIASEC model. If you had to "slot" those dimensions into the Big Five, would you be able to do so? Which dimensions don't seem to fit?

9.4   Consider the profile of the United States on Hofstede's cultural values, as shown in Table 9-3. Do you personally feel like you fit the United States profile, or do your values differ in some respects? If you served as an expatriate, meaning you were working in another country, which cultural value differences would be most difficult for you to deal with?

9.5   If you owned your own business and had a problem with employee theft, would you use an integrity test? Why or why not?

CASE: KRONOS

Before acquiring Unicru, Kronos had specialized in other segments of the human resources technology field, such as time-and-attendance applications and payroll systems.[127] Its other products are relatively uncontroversial, but the Unicru acquisition has thrust Kronos into a vigorous debate about ethics in hiring for the first time. Unicru executives point to the high costs of new-hire turnover as an important reason for using personality tests. Indeed, Unicru's CEO, Chris Marsh, even cites a value of testing for the applicant, noting that matching personality traits to job requirements is "not good just for the company, that's good for the employee." The company acknowledges, however, that the test does result in some "false positives"—applicants who would have turned out to be good employees but got flagged on the test anyway. Of course, "false positives" occur with any hiring method. Traditional employment interviews, often executed by untrained employees with little thought given to the questions, may overlook effective employees because of interviewer bias, applicant nervousness, or random events that alter the complexion of the interview.

Ironically, the economic downturn may wind up boosting Kronos' business. As unemployment rises, the number of applications for open positions goes up, as does the time needed to process all those applications.[128] At the same time, the number of employees available to handle staffing duties is also lower, as organizations downsize to grow as lean as possible. Kronos' personality tests may therefore be seen as a more efficient, not just a more valid, screening option. Mike Roemer, chief operations officer of Blockbuster, points out the efficiency gains that personality testing can offer, noting, "We've taken a two-week hiring process and brought it down to 72 hours. Given that we hire, on average, one employee per store per month—and we have about 4300 company owned stores in the United States—this is a huge improvement."[129] Dennis Hannah, a Blockbuster store manager, also considers the recommended interview questions another benefit of the Kronos system, noting, "Having a guide for the interview phase takes away one-third of the time that I have to spend preparing for an interview."[130]

9.1   Assume you ran a Blockbuster store and you didn't use the Kronos personality test. What kinds of interview questions would you ask potential hires?

9.2 If you did have access to their Big Five scores, what particular profile would you look for when deciding whom to hire at Blockbuster? Would MBTI or RIASEC data seem valuable to you?

9.3 Now assume you were granted access to the Kronos personality test, but you were skeptical of its usefulness. What could you do to "test drive" the system to examine its effectiveness in your own store?

EXERCISE: GUESSING PERSONALITY PROFILES

The purpose of this exercise is to explore how noticeable the Big Five personality dimensions are among classmates. This exercise uses groups, so your instructor will either assign you to a group or ask you to create your own group. The exercise has the following steps:

9.1 Individually, complete the Big Five measure found in the OB Assessments box in the chapter.

9.2 Write your scores on a small white piece of paper, in the following format: C= A = N= O= E= . Try to disguise your handwriting to make it as plain and generic as possible. Fold your piece of paper so that others cannot see your scores.

9.3 In your group, mix up the pieces of paper. Begin by having one group member choose a piece of paper, reading the CANOE scores aloud. The group should then try to come to consensus on which member the scores belong to, given the norms for the various dimensions (C=14, A=16, N=10, O=15, E=13). Keep in mind that group members may wind up reading their own pieces of paper aloud in some cases. Once the group guesses which member the paper belongs to, they should place the paper in front of that member.

9.4 Moving clockwise, the next group member should choose one of the remaining pieces of paper, continuing as before. The process repeats until all the pieces of paper have been assigned to a member. Members can only be assigned one piece of paper, and no switching is permitted once an assignment has been made.

9.5 Group members should then announce whether the piece of paper assigned to them was in fact their set of scores. If the assignment was incorrect, they should find their actual piece of paper and describe the differences in the scores.

9.6 Class discussion (whether in groups or as a class) should center on the following topics: How accurate were the guesses? Were the guesses more accurate in groups that knew one another well than in groups with less familiarity? Which personality dimensions were relied upon most heavily when making assignment decisions? What is it that makes those dimensions more immediately observable?

ENDNOTES

9.1 Frauenheim, E. "The (Would-Be) King of HR Software." *Workforce Management,* August 14, 2006. pp. 34–39; Frauenheim, E. "Unicru Beefs Up Data in Latest Screening Tool." *Workforce Management,*

March 13, 2006, pp. 9–10; Overholt, A. "True or False: You're Hiring the Right People." *Fast Company,* January, 2002, p. 110; and Dixon, P. "Employment Application Kiosks and Sites. Excerpted from the 2003 Job Search Privacy Study: Job Searching in the Networked Environment: Consumer Privacy Benchmarks." *World Privacy Forum,* November 11, 2003, http://www.worldprivacyforum.org (February 24, 2006).

9.2 Overholt, "True or False."

9.3 Ibid.

9.4 Frauenheim, "Unicru Beefs Up Data."

9.5 Gellar, A. "Hiring by Computer." http://jobboomcc.canoe.ca/News/2004/06/09/1225576-sun.html (February 24, 2006).

9.6 Overholt, "True or False."

9.7 Piotrowski, C., and T. Armstrong. "Current Recruitment and Selection Practices: A National Survey of *Fortune* 1000 Firms." *North American Journal of Psychology* 8 (2006), pp. 489–96.

9.8 Funder, D.C. "Personality." *Annual Review of Psychology* 52 (2001), pp. 197–221; and Hogan, R.T. "Personality and Personality Measurement." *Handbook of Industrial and Organizational Psychology,* Vol. 2, eds. M.D. Dunnette and L.M. Hough. Palo Alto, CA: Consulting Psychologists Press, 1991, pp. 873–919.

9.9 Hogan, "Personality and Personality Measurement."

9.10 Ibid.

9.11 Rokeach, M. *The Nature of Human Values.* New York: The Free Press, 1973; and Steers, R.M., and C.J. Sanchez-Runde. "Culture, Motivation, and Work Behavior." In *Blackwell Handbook of Cross-Cultural Management,* eds. M.J. Gannon and K.L. Newman. Malden, MA: Blackwell, 2002, pp. 190–213.

9.12 Goldberg, L.R. "From Ace to Zombie: Some Explorations in the Language of Personality." In *Advances in Personality Assessment,* Vol. 1, eds. C.D. Spielberger and J.N. Butcher. Hillsdale, NJ: Erlbaum, 1982, pp. 203–34; Allport, G.W., and H.S. Odbert. "Trait-Names: A Psycho-Lexical Study." *Psychological Monographs* 47 (1936), Whole No. 211; and Norman, W.T. *2800 Personality Trait Descriptors: Normative Operating Characteristics for a University Population.* Ann Arbor, MI: University of Michigan Department of Psychology, 1967.

9.13 Tupes, E.C., and R.E. Christal. *Recurrent Personality Factors Based on Trait Ratings.* USAF ASD Technical Report No. 61–97, Lackland Air Force Base, TX: United States Air Force, 1961, reprinted in *Journal of Personality* 60, pp. 225–51; Norman, W.T. "Toward an Adequate Taxonomy of Personality Attributes: Replicated Factor Structure in Peer Nomination Personality Ratings." *Journal of Abnormal and Social Psychology* 66 (1963), pp. 574–83; Digman, J.M., and N.K. Takemoto-Chock. "Factors in the Natural Language of Personality: Re-Analysis, Comparison, and Interpretation of Six Major Studies." *Multivariate Behavioral Research* 16 (1981), pp. 149–70; McCrae, R.R., and P.T. Costa Jr. "Updating Norman's 'Adequate Taxonomy': Intelligence and Personality Dimensions in Natural Language and in Questionnaires." *Journal of Personality and Social Psychology* 49 (1985), pp. 710–21; and Goldberg, L.R. "An Alternative 'Description of Personality': The Big-Five Factor Structure."

Journal of Personality and Social Psychology 59 (1990), pp. 1216–29.

9.14 Goldberg, L.R. "Language and Individual Differences: The Search for Universals in Personality Lexicons." In *Review of Personality and Social Psychology,* Vol. 2, ed. L. Wheeler. Beverly Hills, CA: Sage, 1981, pp. 141–65.

9.15 Arvey, R.D., and T.J. Bouchard Jr. "Genetics, Twins, and Organizational Behavior." In *Research in Organizational Behavior,* Vol. 16, eds. B.M. Staw and L.L. Cummings. Greenwich, CT: JAI Press, 1994, pp. 47–82.

9.16 Loehlin, J.C. *Genes and Environment in Personality Development.* Newbury Park, CA: Sage, 1992.

9.17 Ibid.

9.18 Roberts, B.W.; K.E. Walton; and W. Viechtbauer. "Patterns of Mean-Level Change in Personality Traits across the Life Course: A Meta-Analysis of Longitudinal Studies." *Psychological Bulletin* 132 (2006), pp. 1–25.

9.19 Cohen, J. *Statistical Power Analysis for Behavioral Sciences,* 2nd ed. Hillsdale, NJ: Erlbaum, 1988.

9.20 Loehlin, *Genes and Environment.*

9.21 Roberts et al., "Patterns of Mean-Level Change in Personality Traits across the Life Course"; and Jackson, J.J.; T. Bogg; K.E. Walton; D. Wood; P.D. Harms; J. Lodi-Smith; G.W. Edmonds; and B.W. Roberts. "Not all Conscientiousness Scales Change Alike: A Multimethod, Multisample Study of Age Differences in the Facets of Conscientiousness." *Journal of Personality and Social Psychology* 96 (2009), pp. 446–59.

9.22 Saucier, G. "Mini-Markers: A Brief Version of Goldberg's Unipolar Big-Five Markers." *Journal of Personality*

Assessment 63 (1994), pp. 506–16; Goldberg, L.R. "The Development of Markers for the Big-Five Factor Structure." *Psychological Assessment* 4 (1992), pp. 26–42; and McCrae, R.R., and P.T. Costa Jr. "Validation of the Five-Factor Model of Personality Across Instruments and Observers." *Journal of Personality and Social Psychology* 52 (1987), pp. 81–90.

9.23 Barrick, M.R., and M.K. Mount. "The Big Five Personality Dimensions and Job Performance: A Meta-Analysis." *Personnel Psychology* 44 (1991), pp. 1–26.

9.24 Barrick, M.R.; G.L. Stewart; and M. Piotrowski. "Personality and Job Performance: Test of the Mediating Effects of Motivation among Sales Representatives." *Journal of Applied Psychology* 87 (2002), pp. 43–51.

9.25 Barrick, M.R.; M.K. Mount; and J.P. Strauss. "Conscientiousness and Performance of Sales Representatives: Test of the Mediating Effects of Goal Setting." *Journal of Applied Psychology* 78 (1993), pp. 715–22.

9.26 Stewart, G.L. "Trait Bandwidth and Stages of Job Performance: Assessing Differential Effects for Conscientiousness and its Subtraits." *Journal of Applied Psychology* 84 (1999), pp. 959–68.

9.27 Judge, T.A.; C.A. Higgins; C.J. Thoreson; and M.R. Barrick. "The Big Five Personality Traits, General Mental Ability, and Career Success across the Life Span." *Personnel Psychology* 52 (1999), pp. 621–52.

9.28 Friedman, H.S.; J.S. Tucker; J.E. Schwartz; L.R. Martin; C. Tomlinson-Keasey; D.L. Wingard; and M.H. Criqui. "Childhood Conscientiousness and Longevity: Health Behaviors and Cause of Death." *Journal of Personality and Social Psychology* 68 (1995), pp. 696–703.

9.29 Roberts, B.W.; O.S. Chernyshenko; S. Stark; and L.R. Goldberg. "The Structure of Conscientiousness: An Empirical Investigation Based on Seven Major Personality Dimensions." *Personnel Psychology* 58 (2005), pp. 103–39.

9.30 Barrick, Steward, and Piotrowski, "Personality and Job Performance"; and Hogan, J., and B. Holland. "Using Theory to Evaluate Personality and Job-Performance Relations: A Socioanalytic Perspective." *Journal of Applied Psychology* 88 (2003), pp. 100–12.

9.31 Barrick and Mount, "The Big Five Personality Dimensions."

9.32 Frei, R.L., and M.A. McDaniel. "Validity of Customer Service Measures in Personnel Selection: A Review of Criterion and Construct Evidence." *Human Performance* 11 (1998), pp. 1–27.

9.33 Graziano, W.G.; L.A. Jensen-Campbell; and E.C. Hair. "Perceiving Interpersonal Conflict and Reacting to It: The Case for Agreeableness." *Journal of Personality and Social Psychology* 70 (1996), pp. 820–35.

9.34 Palmeri, D. "Dr. Warren's Lonely Hearts Club." *BusinessWeek*, February 20, 2006, pp. 82–84.

9.35 "What Are the 29 Dimensions?" http://www.eharmony.com/singles/servlet/about/dimensions (January 6, 2007).

9.36 Mehl, M.R.; S.D. Gosling; and J.W. Pennebaker. "Personality in Its Natural Habitat: Manifestations and Implicit Folk Theories of Personality in Daily Life." *Journal of Personality and Social Psychology* 90 (2006), pp. 862–77.

9.37 Albright, L.; D.A. Kenny; and T.E. Malloy. "Consensus in Personality Judgments at Zero Acquaintance."

Journal of Personality and Social Psychology 55 (1988), pp. 387–95; and Levesque, M.J., and D.A. Kenny. "Accuracy of Behavioral Predictions at Zero Acquaintance: A Social Relations Analysis." *Journal of Personality and Social Psychology* 65 (1993), pp. 1178–87.

9.38 Barrick, Steward, and Piotrowski, "Personality and Job Performance."

9.39 Judge, T.A.; J.E. Bono; R. Ilies; and M.W. Gerhardt. "Personality and Leadership: A Qualitative and Quantitative Review." *Journal of Applied Psychology* 87 (2002), pp. 765–80.

9.40 Ibid.

9.41 Thoreson, C.J.; S.A. Kaplan; A.P. Barsky; C.R. Warren; and K. de Chermont. "The Affective Underpinnings of Job Perceptions and Attitudes: A Meta-Analytic Review and Integration." *Psychological Bulletin* 129 (2003), pp. 914–45.

9.42 Ibid.; Judge, T.A.; D. Heller; and M.K. Mount. "Five-Factor Model of Personality and Job Satisfaction: A Meta-Analysis." *Journal of Applied Psychology* 87 (2003), pp. 530–41; and Kaplan, S.; J.C. Bradley; J.N. Luchman; and D. Haynes. "On the Role of Positive and Negative Affectivity in Job Performance: A Meta-Analytic Investigation." *Journal of Applied Psychology* 94 (2009), pp. 162–76.

9.43 Arvey, R.D.; T.J. Bouchard; N.L. Segal; and L.M. Abraham. "Job Satisfaction: Environmental and Genetic Components." *Journal of Applied Psychology* 74 (1989), pp. 187–92.

9.44 Steel, P.; J. Schmidt; and J. Shultz. "Refining the Relationship between Personality and Subjective Well-Being." *Psychological Bulletin* 134 (2008), pp. 138-161; and Steel, P., and D.S. Ones. "Personality and Happiness: A National-Level Analysis." *Journal of Personality and Social Psychology* 83 (2002), pp. 767–81.

9.45 Magnus, K.; E. Diener; F. Fujita; and W. Pavot. "Extraversion and Neuroticism as Predictors of Objective Life Events: A Longitudinal Analysis." *Journal of Personality and Social Psychology* 65 (1992), pp. 1046–53.

9.46 Paunonen, S.V. "Big Five Predictors of Personality and Replicated Predictions of Behavior." *Journal of Personality and Social Psychology* 84 (2003), pp. 411–24; and Asendorpf, J.B., and S. Wilpers. "Personality Effects on Social Relationships." *Journal of Personality and Social Psychology* 74 (1998), pp. 1531–44.

9.47 Asendorpf and Wilpers, "Personality Effects on Social Relationships."

9.48 Barrick, M.R., and M.K. Mount. "Select on Conscientiousness and Emotional Stability." In *Blackwell Handbook of Principles of Organizational Behavior,* ed. E.A. Locke. Malden, MA: Blackwell, 2000, pp. 15–28.

9.49 Thoreson et al., "The Affective Underpinnings."

9.50 Ibid.; Kaplan et al., "On the Role of Positive and Negative Affectivity in Job Performance."

9.51 DeNeve, K.M., and H. Cooper. "The Happy Personality: A Meta-Analysis of 137 Personality Traits and Subjective Well-Being." *Psychological Bulletin* 124 (1998), pp. 197–229; Steel et al., "Refining the Relationship between Personality and Subjective Well-Being"; and Steel and Ones, "Personality and Happiness."

9.52 Bolger, N., and A. Zuckerman. "A Framework for Studying Personality in the Stress Process." *Journal of*

Personality and Social Psychology 69 (1995), pp. 890–902.

9.53 Ibid.

9.54 Friedman, M., and R.H. Rosenman. *Type A Behavior and Your Heart.* New York: Knopf, 1974.

9.55 Rotter, J.B. "Generalized Expectancies for Internal versus External Control of Reinforcement." *Psychological Monographs* 80 (1966), pp. 1–28.

9.56 Judge, T.A., and J.E. Bono. "Relationship of Core Self-Evaluations Traits—Self-Esteem, Generalized Self-Efficacy, Locus of Control, and Emotional Stability—with Job Satisfaction and Job Performance: A Meta-Analysis." *Journal of Applied Psychology* 86 (2001), pp. 80–92.

9.57 Ng, T.W.H.; K.L. Sorensen; and L.T. Eby. "Locus of Control at Work: A Meta-Analysis." *Journal of Organizational Behavior* 27 (2006), pp. 1057–87.

9.58 Barrick and Mount, "The Big Five Personality Dimensions"; and Cellar, D.F.; M.L. Miller; D.D. Doverspike; and J.D. Klawsky. "Comparison of Factor Structures and Criterion-Related Validity Coefficients for Two Measures of Personality Based on the Five Factor Model." *Journal of Applied Psychology* 81 (1996), pp. 694–704.

9.59 LePine, J.A.; J.A. Colquitt; and A. Erez. "Adaptability to Changing Task Contexts: Effects of General Cognitive Ability, Conscientiousness, and Openness to Experience." *Personnel Psychology* 53 (2000), pp. 563–93; and Thoreson, C.J.; J.C. Bradley; P.D. Bliese; and J.D. Thoreson. "The Big Five Personality Traits and Individual Job Performance Growth Trajectories in Maintenance and Transitional Job Stages." *Journal of Applied Psychology* 89 (2004), pp. 835–53.

9.60 Shalley, C.E.; J. Zhou; and G.R. Oldham. "The Effects of Personal and Contextual Characteristics on Creativity: Where Should We Go from Here?" *Journal of Management* 30 (2004), pp. 933–58.

9.61 Zhou, J., and J.M. George. "When Job Dissatisfaction Leads to Creativity: Encouraging the Expression of Voice." *Academy of Management Journal* 44 (2001), pp. 682–96.

9.62 Feist, G.J. "A Meta-Analysis of Personality in Scientific and Artistic Creativity." *Personality and Social Psychology Review* 2 (1998), pp. 290–309.

9.63 Stead, D. "You Are Getting Creative . . . Very Creative." *BusinessWeek*, May 12, 2008, p. 18.

9.64 Edmondson, G. "BMW's Dream Factory." *BusinessWeek*, October 16, 2006, pp. 70–80.

9.65 Myers, I.B., and M.H. McCaulley. *Manual: A Guide to the Development and Use of the Myers-Briggs Type Indicator.* Palo Alto, CA: Consulting Psychologists Press, 1985.

9.66 Jung, C.G. *The Collected Works of C. G. Jung*, Vol. 6: Psychological Types, trans. H.G. Baynes, ed. R. F. Hull. Princeton, NJ: Princeton University Press, 1971.

9.67 Gardner, W.L., and M.J. Martinko. "Using the Myers-Briggs Type Indicator to Study Managers: A Literature Review and Research Agenda." *Journal of Management* 22 (1996), pp. 45–83; and "What Is Your Myers Briggs Personality Type?" http://www.personalitypathways .com/type_inventory.html (March 18, 2007).

9.68 Gardner and Martinko, "Using the Myers-Briggs Type Indicator."

9.69 Ibid.

9.70 Holland, J.L. "A Theory of Vocational Choice." *Journal of Counseling Psychology* 6 (1959), pp. 35–45; and Holland, J.L. *Making Vocational Choices: A Theory of Vocational Personalities and Work Environments,* 3rd ed. Odessa, FL: Psychological Assessment Resources, 1997.

9.71 Mount, M.K.; M.R. Barrick; S.M. Scullen; and J. Rounds. "Higher-Order Dimensions of the Big Five Personality Traits and the Big Six Vocational Interests." *Personnel Psychology* 58 (2005), pp. 447–78.

9.72 Strong, E.K. "An 18-Year Longitudinal Report on Interests." In *The Strong Vocational Interest Blank: Research and Uses,* ed. W.L. Layton. Minneapolis, MN: University of Minnesota Press, 1960.

9.73 Holland, *Making Vocational Choices*; "Providing Holland Code Resources Worldwide." Hollandcodes.com, http://www.hollandcodes.com/holland_occupational_codes.html (March 18, 2007); and Armstrong, P.I.; W. Allison; and J. Rounds. "Development and Initial Validation of Brief Public Domain RIASEC Marker Scales." *Journal of Vocational Behavior* 73 (2008), pp. 287–99.

9.74 Muchinsky, P.M. "Applications of Holland's Theory in Industrial and Organizational Settings." *Journal of Vocational Behavior* 55 (1999), pp. 127–35.

9.75 Campbell, D.P., and F.H. Borgen. "Holland's Theory and the Development of Interest Inventories." *Journal of Vocational Behavior* 55 (1999), pp. 86–101; and Rayman, J., and L. Atanasoff. "Holland's Theory of Career Intervention: The Power of the Hexagon." *Journal of Vocational Behavior* 55 (1999), pp. 114–26.

9.76 Tsui, A.S.; S.S. Nifadkar; and A.Y. Ou. "Cross-National, Cross-Cultural Organizational Behavior Research: Advances, Gaps, and Recommendations." *Journal of Management* 33 (2007), pp. 426–78.

9.77 House, R.J.; P.J. Hanges; M. Javidan; P.W. Dorfman; and V. Gupta. *Culture, Leadership, and Organizations: The GLOBE Study of 62 Societies.* Thousand Oaks, CA: Sage, 2004.

9.78 Kroeber, A.L., and C. Kluckhohn. *Culture: A Critical Review of Concepts and Definitions.* Cambridge, MA: Harvard University Press, 1952; and Hofstede, G. *Cultures and Organizations: Software of the Mind.* London: McGraw-Hill, 1991.

9.79 Heine, S.J., and E. E. Buchtel. "Personality: The Universal and the Culturally Specific." *Annual Review of Psychology* 60 (2009), pp. 369–94.

9.80 McCrae, R.R., and A. Terracciano, et al. "Personality Profiles of Cultures: Aggregate Personality Traits." *Journal of Personality and Social Psychology* 89 (2005), pp. 407–25.

9.81 Schwartz, S.H. "Universals in the Content and Structure of Values: Theoretical Advances and Empirical Tests in 20 Countries." *Advances in Experimental Social Psychology,* Vol. 25, ed. M.P. Zanna. San Diego, CA: Academic Press, 1992, pp. 1–65.

9.82 House et al., *Culture, Leadership, and Organizations.*

9.83 Hofstede, G. *Culture's Consequences: Comparing Values, Behaviors, Institutions, and Organizations across Nations.* Thousand Oaks, CA: Sage, 2001; and Kirkman, B.L.; K.B. Lowe; and C.B. Gibson. "A Quarter Century of *Culture's Consequences:* A Review of Empirical Research Incorporating Hofstede's Cultural Values Framework." *Journal of International Business Studies* 37 (2006), pp. 285–320.

9.84 Hofstede, G., and M.H. Bond. "The Confucius Connection: From Cultural Roots to Economic Growth." *Organizational Dynamics* 16 (1988), pp. 5-21.

9.85 House et al., *Culture, Leadership, and Organizations.*

9.86 Chen, Y.; K. Leung; and C. C. Chen. "Bringing National Culture to the Table: Making a Difference with Cross-Cultural Differences and Perspectives." *Academy of Management Annals* 3 (2009), pp. 217–49.

9.87 Oyserman, D.; H.M. Coon; and M. Kemmelmeier. "Rethinking Individualism and Collectivism: Evaluation of Theoretical Assumptions and Meta-Analyses." *Psychological Bulletin* 128 (2002), pp. 3–72; and Earley, P.C., and C.B. Gibson. "Taking Stock in Our Progress on Individualism–Collectivism: 100 Years of Solidarity and Community." *Journal of Management* 24 (1998), pp. 265–304.

9.88 Jackson, C.L.; J.A. Colquitt; M.J. Wesson; and C.P. Zapata-Phelan. "Psychological Collectivism: A Measurement Validation and Linkage to Group Member Performance." *Journal of Applied Psychology* 91 (2006), pp. 884–99.

9.89 Wasti, S.A., and O. Can. "Affective and Normative Commitment to Organization, Supervisor, and Coworker: Do Collectivist Values Matter?" *Journal of Vocational Behavior* 73 (2008), pp. 404–13.

9.90 Earley and Gibson, "Taking Stock in Our Progress."

9.91 Kirkman et al., "A Quarter Century."

9.92 Black, J.S. "The Relationship of Personal Characteristics with the Adjustment of Japanese Expatriate Managers." *Management International Review* 30 (1990), pp. 119–34.

9.93 Van der Zee, K.I., and J.P. Van Oudenhoven. "The Multicultural Personality Questionnaire: Reliability and Validity of Self- and Other Ratings of Multicultural Effectiveness." *Journal of Research in Personality* 35 (2001), pp. 278–88.

9.94 Van der Zee, K.I., and U. Brinkmann. "Construct Validity Evidence for the Intercultural Readiness Check against the Multicultural Personality Questionnaire." *International Journal of Selection and Assessment* 12 (2004), pp. 285–90; Van Oudenhoven, J.P., and K.I. Van der Zee. "Predicting Multicultural Effectiveness of International Students: The Multicultural Personality Questionnaire." *International Journal of Intercultural Relations* 26 (2002), pp. 679–94; and Van Oudenhoven, J.P.; S. Mol; and K.I. Van der Zee. "Study of the Adjustment of Western Expatriates in Taiwan ROC with the Multicultural Personality Questionnaire." *Asian Journal of Social Psychology* 6 (2003), pp. 159–70.

9.95 Barrick, M.R.; M.K. Mount; and T.A. Judge. "Personality and Performance at the Beginning of the New Millennium: What Do We Know and Where Do We Go Next?" *International Journal of Selection and Assessment* 9 (2001), pp. 9–30; and Hough, L.M., and A. Furnham. "Use of Personality Variables in Work Settings." In *Handbook of Psychology,* Vol. 12, eds. W.C. Borman, D.R. Ilgen, and R.J. Klimoski. Hoboken, NJ: Wiley, 2003, pp. 131–69.

9.96 Judge, T. A., and R. Ilies. "Relationship of Personality to Performance Motivation: A Meta-Analysis." *Journal of Applied Psychology* 87 (2002), pp. 797–807.

9.97 Sackett, P.R.; S. Zedeck; and L. Fogli. "Relations Between Measures of Typical and Maximum Job Performance." *Journal of Applied Psychology* 73 (1988), pp. 482–86.

9.98 Hough and Furnham, "Use of Personality Variables in Work Settings"; and Ilies, R.; I.S. Fulmer; M. Spitzmuller; and M.D. Johnson. "Personality and Citizenship Behavior: The Mediating Role of Job Satisfaction." *Journal of Applied Psychology* 94 (2009), pp. 945–59.

9.99 Mount, M.K., and M.R. Barrick. "The Big Five Personality Dimensions: Implications for Research and Practice in Human Resources Management." In *Research in Personnel and Human Resource Management,* ed. G.R. Ferris. Greenwich, CT: JAI Press, 1995, pp. 153–200.

9.100 Ilies et al., "Personality and Citizenship Behavior"; and Judge et al., "Five-Factor Model."

9.101 Salgado, J.F. "The Big Five Personality Dimensions and Counterproductive Behaviors." *International Journal of Selection and Assessment* 10 (2002), pp. 117–25.

9.102 Cullen, M.J., and P. Sackett. "Personality and Counterproductive Work Behavior." In *Personality and Work,* eds. M.A. Barrick and A.M. Ryan. San Francisco: Jossey-Bass, 2003, pp. 150–82.

9.103 Cooper-Hakim, A., and C. Viswesvaran. "The Construct of Work Commitment: Testing an Integrative Framework." *Psychological Bulletin* 131 (2005), pp. 241–59; and Mathieu, J.E., and D.M. Zajac. "A Review and Meta-Analysis of the

Antecedents, Correlates, and Consequences of Organizational Commitment." *Psychological Bulletin* 108 (1990), pp. 171–94.

9.104 Salgado, "The Big Five Personality Dimensions"; and R.D. Zimmerman. "Understanding the Impact of Personality Traits on Individuals' Turnover Decisions: A Meta-Analytic Path Model." *Personnel Psychology* 61 (2008), pp. 309–48.

9.105 Cooper-Hakim and Viswesvaran, "The Construct of Work Commitment."

9.106 Grant, S., and J. Langan-Fox. "Personality and Occupational Stressor–Strain Relationships: The Role of the Big Five." *Journal of Occupational Health Psychology* 12 (2007), pp. 20–33.

9.107 Mischel, W. "The Interaction of Person and Situation." In *Personality at the Crossroads: Current Issues in Interactional Psychology,* eds. D. Magnusson and N.S. Endler. Hillsdale, NJ: Erlbaum, 1977, pp. 333–52; and Weiss, H.M., and S. Adler. "Personality and Organizational Behavior." In *Research in Organizational Behavior,* Vol. 6, eds. B.M. Staw and L.L. Cummings. Greenwich, CT: JAI Press, 1984, pp. 1–50.

9.108 Barrick, M.R., and M.K. Mount. "Autonomy as a Moderator of the Relationship between the Big Five Personality Dimensions and Job Performance." *Journal of Applied Psychology* 78 (1993), pp. 111–18.

9.109 Tett, R.P., and D.D. Burnett. "A Personality Trait-Based Interactionist Model of Job Performance." *Journal of Applied Psychology* 88 (2003), pp. 500–17.

9.110 Barrick, M.R.; G.K. Patton; and S.N. Haugland. "Accuracy of Interviewer Judgments of Job Applicant Personality Traits." *Personnel Psychology* 53 (2000), pp. 925–51.

9.111 Buckingham, M.; and D. Clifton. *Now, Discover Your Strengths.* New York: The Free Press, 2001.

9.112 Dixon, "Employment Application Kiosks and Sites."

9.113 Frauenheim, "The (Would-Be) King."

9.114 Sackett, P.R., and M.M. Harris. "Honesty Testing for Personnel Selection: A Review and Critique." *Personnel Psychology* 37 (1984), pp. 221–45; Sackett, P.R.; L.R. Burris; and C. Callahan. "Integrity Testing for Personnel Selection: An Update." *Personnel Psychology* 42 (1989), pp. 491–528; Sackett, P.R., and J.E. Wanek. "New Developments in the Use of Measures of Honesty, Integrity, Conscientiousness, Dependability, Trustworthiness, and Reliability for Personnel Selection." *Personnel Psychology* 49 (1996), pp. 787–829; Berry, C.M.; P.R. Sackett; and S. Wiemann. "A Review of Recent Developments in Integrity Test Research." *Personnel Psychology* 60 (2007), pp. 271–301; and Miner, J.B., and M.H. Capps. *How Honesty Testing Works.* Westport, CT: Quorum Books, 1996.

9.115 Sackett et al., "Integrity Testing"; and Ones, D.S.; C. Viswesvaran; and F.L. Schmidt. "Comprehensive Meta-Analysis of Integrity Test Validities: Findings and Implications for Personnel Selection and Theories of Job Performance." *Journal of Applied Psychology* 78 (1993), pp. 679–703.

9.116 Wanek, J.E.; P.R. Sackett; and D.S. Ones. "Towards an Understanding of Integrity Test Similarities and Differences: An Item-Level Analysis of Seven Tests." *Personnel Psychology* 56 (2003), pp. 873–94;

and Marcus, B.; S. Hoft; and M. Riediger. "Integrity Tests and the Five-Factor Model of Personality: A Review and Empirical Test of Two Alternative Positions." *International Journal of Selection and Assessment* 14 (2006), pp. 113–30.

9.117 Marcus, B.; K. Lee; and M.C. Ashton. "Personality Dimensions Explaining Relationships Between Integrity Tests and Counterproductive Behavior: Big Five, or One in Addition?" *Personnel Psychology* 60 (2007), pp. 1–34; and Berry et al., "A Review of Recent Developments in Integrity Test Research."

9.118 Bernardin, H.J., and D.K. Cooke. "Validity of an Honesty Test in Predicting Theft among Convenience Store Employees." *Academy of Management Journal* 36 (1993), pp. 1097–1108.

9.119 Ones et al., "A Comprehensive Meta-Analysis."

9.120 Ibid.

9.121 Goffin, R.D., and N.D. Christiansen. "Correcting Personality Tests for Faking: A Review of Popular Personality Tests and an Initial Survey of Researchers." *International Journal of Selection and Assessment* 11 (2003), pp. 340–44.

9.122 Birkeland, S.A.; T.M. Manson; J.L. Kisamore; M.T. Brannick; and M.A. Smith. "A Meta-Analytic Investigation of Job Applicant Faking on Personality Measures." *International Journal of Selection and Assessment* 14 (2006), pp. 317–35; and Viswesvaran, C., and D.S. Ones. "Meta-Analysis of Fakability Estimates: Implications for Personality Measurement." *Educational and Psychological Measurement* 59 (1999), pp. 197–210.

9.123 Miner and Capps, *How Honesty Testing Works;* Cunningham, M.R.; D.T. Wong; and A.P. Barbee. "Self-Presentation Dynamics on Overt Integrity Tests: Experimental Studies of the Reid Report." *Journal of Applied Psychology* 79 (1994), pp. 643–58; and Ones, D.S., and C. Viswesvaran. "The Effects of Social Desirability and Faking on Personality and Integrity Assessment for Personnel Selection." *Human Performance* 11 (1998), pp. 245–69.

9.124 Ones, D.S.; S. Dilchert; C. Viswesvaran; and T.A. Judge. "In Support of Personality Assessment in Organizational Settings." *Personnel Psychology* 60 (2007), pp. 995–1027; and Tett, R.P., and N.D. Christiansen. "Personality Tests at the Crossroads: A Response to Morgeson, Campion, Dipboye, Hollenbeck, Murphy, and Schmitt (2007)." *Personnel Psychology* 60 (2007), pp. 967–93.

9.125 Cortina, J.M.; N.B. Goldstein; S.C. Payne; H.K. Davison; and S.W. Gilliland. "The Incremental Validity of Interview Scores over and above Cognitive Ability and Conscientiousness Scores." *Personnel Psychology* 53 (2000), pp. 325–51.

9.126 Schmidt, F.L., and J.E. Hunter. "Select on Intelligence." In *Blackwell Handbook of Principles of Organizational Behavior,* ed. E.A. Locke. Malden, MA: Blackwell, 2000, pp. 3–14.

9.127 Frauenheim, "The (Would-Be) King."

9.128 Rafter, M.V. "Assessment Providers Scoring Well." *Workforce Management,* January 19, 2009, pp. 24–25.

9.129 Overholt, "True or False."

9.130 Ibid.

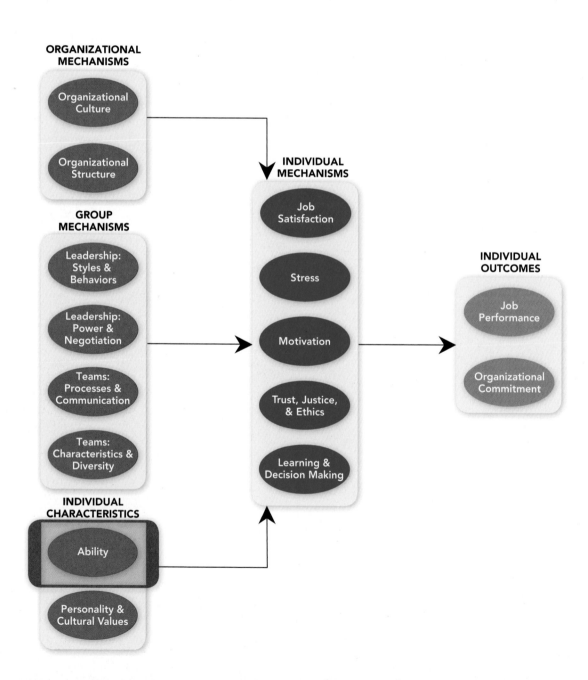

ORGANIZATIONAL MECHANISMS

Organizational Culture

Organizational Structure

GROUP MECHANISMS

Leadership: Styles & Behaviors

Leadership: Power & Negotiation

Teams: Processes & Communication

Teams: Characteristics & Diversity

INDIVIDUAL CHARACTERISTICS

Ability

Personality & Cultural Values

INDIVIDUAL MECHANISMS

Job Satisfaction

Stress

Motivation

Trust, Justice, & Ethics

Learning & Decision Making

INDIVIDUAL OUTCOMES

Job Performance

Organizational Commitment

LEARNING GOALS

After reading this chapter, you should be able to answer the following questions:

10.1 What is ability?

10.2 What are the various types of cognitive ability?

10.3 What are the various types of emotional ability?

10.4 What are the various types of physical ability?

10.5 How does cognitive ability affect job performance and organizational commitment?

10.6 What steps can organizations take to hire people with high levels of cognitive ability?

MICROSOFT

How long has it been since you last used a Microsoft product? Even if you're a hardcore Apple fan who doesn't use Windows, chances are that you've recently used programs in Microsoft's Office suite—Word to write a report, Excel to track numbers, or PowerPoint to prepare a presentation. In fact, Microsoft Office has a 95 percent market share, and 400 million copies of it are in use today.[1] Microsoft sells many other products and services as well, making it the number one company in the computer software industry, with revenues of more than $50 billion annually.[2] The computer software industry is extremely competitive, and each year, rival firms offer excellent alternatives to products provided by Microsoft, many of which cost less or are even free.[3]

So how has Microsoft continued to grow and thrive for more than 30 years in this tough competitive environment? According to CEO Steve Ballmer, the most important thing Microsoft does is hire great people.[4] Because technology is constantly changing, Microsoft can't hire on the basis of industry experience or what people have done in the past; instead, it relies on what employees are capable of doing in the future. Developing software requires new ideas and innovative solutions, so Microsoft only hires people whom it believes are exceptionally intelligent—the top 10 percent of the top 10 percent.[5] Each year, Microsoft receives about 144,000 job applications[6] for roughly 4,500 jobs,[7] so it can be quite selective in hiring people. You may be wondering exactly how Microsoft determines which people, from this huge pool of applicants, possess the desired qualities.

Applicants who are lucky enough to make it through the screening process are invited to Microsoft's headquarters in Redmond, Washington, where they face a day of intense interviews. However, in contrast to traditional interviews that focus on the past accomplishments of the applicant—"Tell me about a time when you had to solve a really difficult problem"—interviews at Microsoft consist of puzzles, riddles, and impossible questions.[8] Why ask applicants interview questions such as, "How would you move Mount Fuji?" "How do they make M&M's?" and "If you could remove any of the 50 U.S. states, which would it be?"[9] What's the logic behind these questions? Microsoft believes that the mental abilities involved in trying to solve such problems are the same ones required to develop and market computer software. Given Microsoft's success, it's not surprising that this approach to hiring has caught on with other companies in the high-tech industry that need world-class problem solvers. Although you might not look forward to the prospect of having to solve puzzles and answer impossible questions during an already stressful job interview, it's certainly something you might want to prepare for in the future.[10]

ABILITY

The topic of ability is probably already familiar to you. One reason is because "ability" is an everyday word in our language, and we've all developed a pretty good understanding of our own abilities. So if the topic is so familiar to you already, why would we write an entire chapter on it for this textbook? Well for one thing, there are many different abilities, some of which are important but might not be as familiar to you. Another reason we included a chapter on ability is that, although it might seem obvious that abilities are highly related to effectiveness in jobs, this relationship is truer in some circumstances than in others. Finally, it may be useful to understand how organizations use information about abilities to make good managerial decisions. Our chapter is organized around these three issues.

Ability refers to the relatively stable capabilities people have to perform a particular range of different but related activities.[11] In contrast to skills, which can be improved over time with training and experience, ability is relatively stable. Although abilities can change slowly over time with repeated practice and repetition, the level of a given ability generally limits how much a person can improve, even with the best training in the world. One reason for this stability relates to the "nature vs. nurture" question, an issue that has been much debated in OB (see Chapter 9 on Personality and Cultural Values for more discussion of such issues). Are abilities a function of our genes, or are they something we develop as a function of our experiences and surroundings?

As it turns out, abilities are a function of both genes and the environment, and the amount attributable to each source depends somewhat on the nature of the ability. Consider for a moment abilities that are physical in nature. Although training that involves weightlifting, dancing, and swimming can improve a person's strength, equilibrium, and endurance, there are limits to how much improvement is possible with such training. As an example, there are millions of people who take golf lessons and practice their swing for countless hours on a driving range, yet the vast majority of these people could never compete in a professional golf tournament because they can't hit the ball straight. As an example of abilities that are cognitive in nature, you likely know people who, even if they went to the best schools on earth, would have great difficulty doing well in jobs such as theoretical astrophysics that require a lot of brainpower.

For cognitive abilities, it appears that genes and the environment play roughly equal roles.[12] However, differences in cognitive abilities due to the environment become less apparent as people get older, which may be especially true for the effect of the family environment.[13] As an example, though neglect, abuse, and deprivation may have a negative impact on how children fare on standardized intelligence tests, that negative impact does not tend to carry over into adulthood. Beyond the family situation, what are some other factors in the environment that affect cognitive abilities? First, the quantity of schooling may be important because it provides opportunities for people to develop knowledge and critical thinking skills.[14] Second, there is evidence that our choice of occupations may influence our cognitive abilities. It appears that complex work develops and exercises our minds, which promotes higher performance on intelligence tests.[15] Third, certain biological factors are known to affect cognitive abilities

10.1
What is ability?

Few people have the physical abilities necessary to compete with professional golfers such as Annika Sorenstam.

negatively during childhood. Examples include malnutrition, exposure to toxins such as lead, and prenatal exposure to alcohol.

WHAT DOES IT MEAN FOR AN EMPLOYEE TO BE "ABLE"?

As the examples in the previous paragraph imply, there are different types of ability. Whereas the golf example refers to physical ability, the theoretical astrophysics example refers to cognitive ability. In fact, there are many different facets of ability, and they can be grouped into subsets by considering similarities in the nature of the activities involved. As we'll talk about in the sections to follow, abilities can be grouped into three general categories: cognitive, emotional, and physical. Taken together, these abilities refer to *what people can do*. That's in contrast to personality (the subject of Chapter 9), which refers to *what people are like*. As with personality, organizational personnel and hiring systems focus on finding an applicant whose abilities match the requirements of a given job.

10.2

What are the various types of cognitive ability?

COGNITIVE ABILITY

Cognitive ability refers to capabilities related to the acquisition and application of knowledge in problem solving.[16] Cognitive abilities are very relevant in the jobs most of you will be involved with—that is, work involving the use of information to make decisions and solve problems. Chances are good that your cognitive abilities have been tested several times throughout your life. For example, almost all children in the United States take standardized tests of intelligence at some point during elementary school. Although you might not remember taking one of these, you probably remember taking the Scholastic Assessment Test (SAT). And though you probably only thought about the SAT as a test that would have a major impact on where you could and could not go to college, the SAT is actually a test of cognitive ability.

You might also remember that the SAT included a variety of different questions; some tested your ability to do math problems, whereas other questions assessed your ability to complete sentences and make analogies. The different types of questions reflect that there are several specific types of cognitive ability that contribute to effectiveness on intellectual tasks. Table 10-1 lists many of these cognitive ability types, along with their specific facets and some jobs in which they're thought to be important. The information in this table, as well as that discussed in the following sections, comes from research that produced a public database called O*NET, which outlines requirements of employees in different types of jobs and occupations.[17]

VERBAL ABILITY. **Verbal ability** refers to various capabilities associated with understanding and

"I'm going to need to speak to someone from either personnel or maintenance."

TABLE 10-1	Types and Facets of Cognitive Ability	
TYPE	**MORE SPECIFIC FACET**	**JOBS WHERE RELEVANT**
Verbal	*Oral* and *Written Comprehension:* Understanding written and spoken words and sentences *Oral* and *Written Expression:* Communicating ideas by speaking or writing so that others can understand	Business executives; police, fire, and ambulance dispatchers; clinical psychologists
Quantitative	*Number Facility:* Performing basic math operations quickly and correctly *Mathematical Reasoning:* Selecting the right method or formula to solve a problem	Treasurers; financial managers; mathematical technicians; statisticians
Reasoning	*Problem Sensitivity:* Understanding when there is a problem or when something may go wrong *Deductive Reasoning:* Applying general rules to specific problems *Inductive Reasoning:* Combining specific information to form general conclusions *Originality:* Developing new ideas	Anesthesiologists; surgeons; business executives; fire inspectors; judges; police detectives; forensic scientists; cartoonists; designers
Spatial	*Spatial Orientation:* Knowing where one is relative to objects in the environment *Visualization:* Imagining how something will look after it has been rearranged	Pilots; drivers; boat captains; photographers; set designers; sketch artists
Perceptual	*Speed and Flexibility of Closure:* Making sense of information and finding patterns *Perceptual Speed:* Comparing information or objects with remembered information or objects	Musicians; fire fighters; police officers; pilots; mail clerks; inspectors

Sources: Adapted from E.A. Fleishman, D.P. Costanza, and J. Marshall-Mies, "Abilities," in *An Occupational Information System for the 21*st *Century: The Development of O*NET,* eds. N.G. Peterson, M.D. Mumford, W.C. Borman, P.R. Jeanneret, and E.A. Fleishman (Washington DC: American Psychological Association, 1999), pp. 175–95; and *O*NET Web site, The O*NET Content Model: Detailed Outline With Descriptions, http://www.onet center.org/content.html/1.a?d=1#cm_1.a (May 20, 2009).*

expressing oral and written communication. *Oral comprehension* is the ability to understand spoken words and sentences, and *written comprehension* is the ability to understand written words and sentences. Although these two aspects of verbal ability would seem highly related—that is, people who have high oral comprehension would tend to have high written comprehensive, and vice versa—it's not difficult to think of people who might be high on one ability but low on the other. As an example, it's been reported that as a result of his dyslexia, Tom Cruise has poor written comprehension and can only learn his lines after listening to them on tape.[18]

Two other verbal abilities are *oral expression,* which refers to the ability to communicate ideas by speaking, and *written expression,* which refers to the ability to communicate ideas in writing. Again, though it might seem that these abilities should be highly related, this is not necessarily so. You may have taken a class with a professor who has published

Tom Cruise has dyslexia, and so he struggles with written comprehension. He learns the lines for his movies by listening to them on tape.

several well-regarded books and articles but had a very difficult time expressing concepts and theories to students effectively. Although there could be many reasons why this might happen, one explanation is that the professor had high ability in terms of written expression but low ability in terms of oral expression.

Generally speaking, verbal abilities are most important in jobs in which effectiveness depends on understanding and communicating ideas and information to others. The effectiveness of business executives depends on their ability to consider information from reports and other executives and staff, as well as their ability to articulate a vision and strategy that promotes employee understanding. As another example, consider how important the verbal abilities of a 9-1-1 dispatcher might be if a loved one suddenly became ill and stopped breathing one evening.

QUANTITATIVE ABILITY. **Quantitative ability** refers to two types of mathematical capabilities. The first is *number facility,* which is the capability to do simple math operations (adding, subtracting, multiplying, and dividing). The second is *mathematical reasoning,* which refers to the ability to choose and apply formulas to solve problems that involve numbers. If you think back to the SAT, you can probably remember problems such as the following: "There were two trains 800 miles apart, and they were traveling toward each other on the same track. The first train began traveling at noon and averaged 45 miles per hour. The second train started off two hours later. At what speed did the second train average if the two trains smashed into each other at 10:00 p.m. of the same day"?

Although number facility may be necessary to solve this problem, mathematical reasoning is crucial because the test taker needs to know which formulas to apply. Although most of us wish that problems like this would be limited to test-taking contexts (especially this particular problem), there are countless situations in which quantitative abilities are important. For example, consider the importance of quantitative ability in jobs involving statistics, accounting, and engineering. Quantitative abilities may be important in less complex, lower-level jobs as well. Have you ever been at a fast-food restaurant or convenience store when the cash register wasn't working and the clerk couldn't manage to count out change correctly or quickly? If you have, you witnessed a very good example of low quantitative ability, and perhaps some very annoyed customers. For another example of a situation where quantitative abilities are important, see our **OB on Screen** feature.

REASONING ABILITY. **Reasoning ability** is actually a diverse set of abilities associated with sensing and solving problems using insight, rules, and logic. The first reasoning ability, *problem sensitivity,* is the ability to sense that there's a problem right now or likely to be one in the near future. Anesthesiology is a great example of a job for which problem sensitivity is crucial. Before surgeries, anesthesiologists give drugs to patients so that surgical procedures can take place without the patients experiencing pain. However, during the surgery, patients can have negative reactions to the drugs that might result in the loss of life. So the ability of the anesthesiologist to sense when something is wrong even before the problem is fully apparent can be a life-or-death matter.

The second type of reasoning ability is called *deductive reasoning.* This ability, which refers to the use of general rules to solve problems, is important in any job in which people

OB ON SCREEN

21

I'm pretty good with numbers.

With those words, Ben Campbell (Jim Sturgess) responds to some surprised customers after he mentally calculates their final bill for the purchase of several items of clothing, including discounts and sales tax. In fact, Ben's remarkable quantitative abilities take center stage in the film *21* (Dir.: Robert Luketic, Columbia Pictures, 2008). Ben is a senior at MIT who needs $300,000 to attend Harvard Medical School the following year. After he answers a very difficult question in a nonlinear math class, his professor, Micky Rosa (Kevin Spacey), provides him with an interesting opportunity to earn the money: join a team of blackjack players who win tons of money by counting cards. After some initial hesitation, Ben takes up Micky's offer. He learns that the team consists of "spotters" who sit at different tables, playing small amounts of money to keep track of the count (essentially, a point system that keeps track of the proportion of high cards in the deck to low cards), and "big players" who enter the game and place large bets after receiving a signal from a spotter that a table's count is favorable.

Ben quickly becomes the star big player on the team because he has an uncanny ability to keep track of the count himself while also playing the game correctly in a very stressful situation. Although there's nothing inherently wrong with players using superior numerical facility to win at blackjack, counting cards gives players a significant advantage over casinos, who employ security personnel to "rough-up" players suspected of the activity. As we learn in the film, quantitative ability is a key attribute for big players, but other abilities also may be necessary. As an example, Micky believes that Ben is born to count cards not only because of his exceptional cognitive abilities, but also because he stays composed and never becomes emotional.

are presented with a set of facts that need to be applied to make effective decisions. The job of a judge requires deductive reasoning because it centers on making decisions by applying the rules of law to make verdicts. In contrast, *inductive reasoning* refers to the ability to consider several specific pieces of information and then reach a more general conclusion regarding how those pieces are related. Inductive reasoning is required of police detectives and crime scene investigators who must consider things like tire tracks, blood spatter, fibers, and fingerprints to reach conclusions about perpetrators of crimes and causes of death.

Finally, *originality* refers to the ability to develop clever and novel ways to solve problems. Larry Page and Sergey Brin, the two founders of Google, provide good examples of originality. They not only developed the Internet search software that gave Google a competitive advantage, and created the first completely new advertising medium in nearly half a century, but they also refuse to follow conventional wisdom when it comes to managerial practices and business decisions.[19] Clearly, originality is important in a wide variety of occupations, but in some jobs, originality is the most critical ability. For example, a cartoonist, designer, writer, or advertising executive without originality would find it difficult to be successful.

SPATIAL ABILITY. There are two main types of **spatial ability**, or capabilities associated with visual and mental representation and manipulation of objects in space. The first is called *spatial orientation*, which refers to a good understanding of where one is relative to other things in the environment. A tourist with high spatial organization would have no trouble finding her way back to her hotel on foot after a long day of sightseeing, even without a map or help from anyone on the street. The second spatial ability is called *visualization*, which is the ability to imagine how separate things will look if they were put together in a particular way. If you're good at imagining how a room would look if it were rearranged, or if your friends are impressed that you can buy things that go together well, chances are that you would score high on visualization.

PERCEPTUAL ABILITY. **Perceptual ability** refers to being able to perceive, understand, and recall patterns of information. More specifically, *speed and flexibility of closure* refers to being able to pick out a pattern of information quickly in the presence of distracting information, even without all the information present. People who work for the Central Intelligence Agency likely need speed and flexibility of closure to break secret codes. Related to this ability is *perceptual speed*, which refers to being able to examine and compare numbers, letters, and objects quickly. If you can go into the produce section of a supermarket and choose the best tomatoes faster than the people around you, chances are you have high perceptual speed. Effectiveness in jobs in which people need to proofread documents, sort things, or categorize objects depends a lot on perceptual speed.

GENERAL COGNITIVE ABILITY. If you've read the preceding sections carefully, you probably thought about where you stand on the different types of cognitive abilities. In doing so, you may have also reached the conclusion that you're higher on some of these abilities and lower on others. Maybe you think of yourself as being smart in verbal abilities but not as smart in quantitative abilities. In fact, most people score more similarly across their cognitive abilities than they realize. People who are high on verbal abilities also tend to be high on reasoning, quantitative, spatial, and perceptual abilities, and people who are low on verbal abilities tend to be low on the other abilities. Although this consistency might not apply to everyone, it applies often enough that researchers have been trying to understand why this occurs for well over 100 years.[20]

The most popular explanation for the similarity in the levels of different cognitive abilities within people is that there is a **general cognitive ability**—sometimes called *g* or the *g factor*—that underlies or causes all of the more specific cognitive abilities we've discussed so far.[21] To understand what this ability means more clearly, consider the diagram in Figure 10-1 that depicts general cognitive ability as the area in common across the more specific cognitive abilities that we've discussed. This overlap exists because each of the specific abilities depends somewhat on the brain's ability to process information effectively. So, because some brains are capable of processing information more effectively than others, some people tend to score higher across the specific abilities, whereas others tend to score lower.

You're probably familiar with the intelligence quotient, which is known as IQ. Well, IQ was something originally used in educational contexts to diagnose learning disabilities, and accordingly, tests to measure IQ were developed using questions with which disabled students might struggle. IQ tests were then scaled as a percentage that indicated a person's mental age relative to his or her chronological age. IQ scores lower than 100 were interpreted as indicating a potential learning or educational deficiency, whereas scores higher than 100 were interpreted as indicating that someone was particularly bright for their age. However, it turns out that IQ tests and tests of general cognitive ability are often quite similar in terms of the types of questions included, and more importantly, scores on the two types of tests say pretty much the same thing about the people who take them.[22] Does a high IQ boost managerial effectiveness? Although we'll discuss this matter in some detail later, for now see our **OB at the Bookstore** feature for one author's perspective.

EMOTIONAL ABILITY

Michael Scott, as played by Steve Carell on NBC's *The Office,* believes that he's a great boss, multitalented, and super funny. He also believes that he's a people person; he thinks he really understands his employees and that his employees like and respect him. Unbeknownst to Michael though, he actually comes across to all but one of his employees as insensitive and incompetent to the point of being pathetic. Although entertaining to TV viewers, it shouldn't be too hard to imagine how a lack of self-awareness and an inability to read others' emotions could result in significant problems for bosses and employees. As a real-world example, consider the case of Dirk Snyder, who headed the

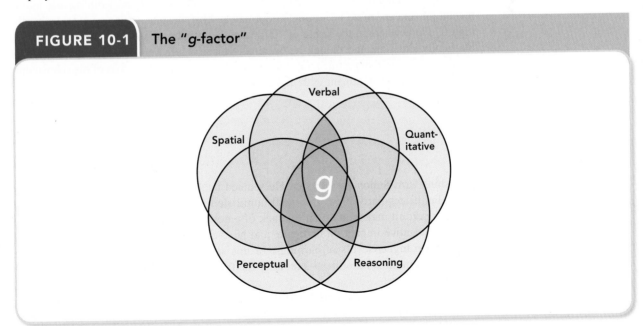

FIGURE 10-1   The "g-factor"

OB AT THE BOOKSTORE

OUTLIERS

by Malcolm Gladwell (New York: Little, Brown and Company, 2008).

Geniuses are the ultimate outliers. Surely there is nothing that can hold someone like that back? But is that true?

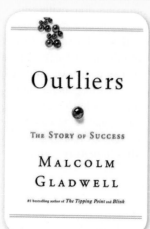

With those words, Malcolm Gladwell presents the question that he sets out to answer in his bestselling book. The central premise is that you don't have to have genius-level IQ to be an outlier, which Gladwell defines as someone who achieves extraordinary success. Rather, as long as *enough* IQ is present, other factors become much more important in determining whether someone becomes an outlier in most situations. So what are these "other" factors? As one example, Gladwell explains how people can become outliers because luck provides opportunities that others in a given field may lack. As another example, Gladwell believes that becoming an outlier takes experience and hard work (i.e., around 10,000 hours' worth).

Although the book is framed as an unbiased explanation of how outliers come to be, it also conveys a message that should be very appealing to most readers. Becoming an outlier isn't just for the very few people who are lucky enough to be born with genius-level IQ. Instead, people of reasonable intelligence can become outliers as long as they take advantage of the opportunities bestowed upon them, make opportunities for themselves, and work long and hard enough. However, the book also illustrates how the potential of intelligent people to become outliers can be thwarted by factors that are beyond their control. For example, Gladwell recounts the life of Chris Langdon, who bounced around from menial job to menial job and ended up becoming a doorman at a bar, despite having an extraordinarily high IQ (somewhere in the range of 200). Langdon was born into a very poor and unstable family situation, and though he eventually made it to a very prestigious college, his mother forgot to fill out a financial statement, which resulted in the loss of his scholarship and his deep disenchantment with higher education.

publishing firm Simon & Schuster. He seemed unable to control or perceive his emotions, and he regularly blew up at and humiliated his subordinates.[23] To make matters worse, he didn't understand that his lack of emotional control and understanding were having a negative impact on his team, and he eventually was fired, despite leading his company to higher levels of earnings. In this section of the chapter, we describe the concept of emotional abilities—precisely the type of ability that Michael Scott appears to lack.

So how are emotional abilities different than cognitive abilities? Most of us know someone who is very smart from a "cognitive ability" or IQ standpoint, but at the same time, the person just can't manage to be effective in real-world situations that involve

"I don't have to be smart, because someday I'll just hire lots of smart people to work for me."

other people. As an example, you may have played *Trivial Pursuit* with a group of friends and found someone at the table who could not only answer the majority of the questions correctly but also managed to say odd or inappropriate things throughout the game. You may also know someone who doesn't seem very "book smart" but always seems able to get things done and says the right things at the right time. In the context of the same *Trivial Pursuit* game, such a person might have answered most of the game questions incorrectly but, sensing how uncomfortable and angry people were becoming with the annoying player, made jokes to lighten things up.

In fact, for several decades now, researchers have been investigating whether there is a type of ability that influences the degree to which people tend to be effective in social situations, regardless of their level of cognitive abilities.[24] Although there has been some debate among these researchers,[25] many believe that there is a human ability that affects social functioning, called **emotional intelligence**.[26] Emotional intelligence is defined in terms of a set of distinct but related abilities, which we describe next.[27]

SELF-AWARENESS. The first type of emotional intelligence is **self-awareness**, or the appraisal and expression of emotions in oneself. This facet refers to the ability of an individual to understand the types of emotions he or she is experiencing, the willingness to acknowledge them, and the capability to express them naturally.[28] As an example, someone who is low in this aspect of emotional intelligence might not admit to himself or show anyone else that he's feeling somewhat anxious during the first few days of a new job. These types of emotions are perfectly natural in this job context, and ignoring them might increase the stress of the situation. Ignoring those emotions might also send the wrong signal to new colleagues, who might wonder, "Why isn't the new hire more excited about his new job?"

OTHER AWARENESS. The second facet of emotional intelligence is called **other awareness**, or the appraisal and recognition of emotion in others.[29] As the name of this facet implies, it refers to a person's ability to recognize and understand the emotions that other people are feeling. People who are high in this aspect of emotional intelligence are not only sensitive to the feelings of others but also can anticipate the emotions that people will experience in different situations. In contrast, people who are low in this aspect of emotional intelligence do not effectively sense the emotions that others are experiencing, and if the emotions are negative, this inability could result in the person doing something that worsens the situation. As an example, have you ever had a professor who couldn't sense that students in class didn't understand the material

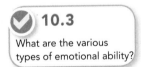

10.3

What are the various types of emotional ability?

"Other awareness" is one aspect of emotional intelligence that allows us to empathize with others and understand their feelings.

being presented in a lecture? When that professor continued to press on with the slides, oblivious to the fact that the students were becoming even more confused, it was poor other awareness in action. As another example, an accountant at Chemical Bank in New York recalls that his boss asked him to refine his skills in this aspect of emotional intelligence.[30] Although he was a good accountant, he needed help showing interest in other people's emotions so that discussions with clients were less contentious. As a final example, the CEO of Forte Hotels, a chain of luxury hotels in Europe, prizes employees who have the ability to understand the customer's emotions so they can react accordingly. "I know the most amazing waitress," he says. "She can look at a counterful of people eating breakfast and tell immediately who wants chatting up, who wants to be left alone. Uncanny. Just uncanny."[31]

EMOTION REGULATION. The third facet of emotional intelligence, **emotion regulation**, refers to being able to recover quickly from emotional experiences.[32] As an example of this aspect of emotional intelligence, consider the possible responses of someone on his way to work, who is driving just below the speed limit in his brand new Prius, who gets cut off by an aggressive driver who, as she passes by, throws a beer can and shouts an obscenity. If the Prius driver can regulate his emotions effectively, he recovers quickly from the initial anger and shock of the encounter. He would be able to get back to whatever he was listening to on the radio, and by the time he got to work, the incident would likely be all but forgotten. However, if this person were not able to regulate his emotions effectively, he might lose his temper, tailgate the aggressive driver, and then ram the new Prius into her rusted-out 1973 Ford pickup at the next stoplight. We hope it's obvious to you that the former response is much more appropriate than the latter, which could prove quite costly to the individual. Although this example highlights the importance of regulating negative emotions, we should also point out that this aspect of emotional intelligence also applies to positive emotions. Consider, for example, the response of someone who is told that she's about to receive a significant pay raise. If this person is unable to regulate her own emotions effectively, she might feel joyous and giddy the rest of the day and, as a consequence, not be able to accomplish any more work.

USE OF EMOTIONS. The fourth aspect of emotional intelligence is the **use of emotions**.[33] This capability reflects the degree to which people can harness emotions and employ them to improve their chances of being successful in whatever they're seeking to do. To understand this facet of emotional intelligence, consider a writer who's struggling to finish a book but is under a serious time crunch because of the contract with the publisher. If the writer was high in this aspect of emotional intelligence, she would likely psych herself up for the challenge and encourage herself to work hard through any bouts of writer's block. In contrast, if the writer is low in this aspect of emotional intelligence, she might begin to doubt her competence as a writer and think about different things she could do with her life. Because these behaviors will slow progress on the book even further, the number and intensity of self-defeating thoughts might increase, and ultimately, the writer might withdraw from the task entirely.

APPLYING EMOTIONAL INTELLIGENCE. Although you may appreciate how emotional intelligence can be relevant to effectiveness in a variety of interpersonal situations, you might be wondering whether knowledge of emotional intelligence can be useful to managers in their quest to make their organizations more effective. It turns out there is growing evidence that the answer to this question is "yes."[34] In fact, the U.S. Air Force studied recruiters and found that those recruiters who were high in some aspects of emotional intelligence were three times more likely to meet recruiting quotas than recruiters who scored lower in the same aspects of emotional intelligence.[35] Recruiters with high emotional intelligence were more effective because they projected positive emotions and could quickly sense and appropriately respond to recruits' concerns. Because these capabilities made recruiting easier, there was less pressure to meet performance quotas, which translated into fewer hours at the office, higher satisfaction, and ultimately higher retention. In fact, after the Air Force began requiring new recruiters to pass an emotional intelligence test, turnover among new recruiters dropped from 25 percent to 2 percent. Given that, on average, it costs about $30,000 to train a new recruiter, this lower turnover translated into about $2.75 million in savings a year.

As a second example, in the early 1990s, executives at IDS Life Insurance, a subsidiary of American Express, began experimenting with emotional intelligence training to increase the sales performance of their financial service advisors.[36] The executives believed that the most effective advisors had high emotional intelligence—they could easily put themselves in the shoes of prospective clients to build solid client–advisor relationships, they could better motivate themselves to sell insurance, and they could effectively manage their emotions in the face of all the disappointment that comes with trying to make sales. Apparently the IDS executives were correct, because in one early assessment of the training program involving only a small number of advisors, the increase in revenues attributable to the training amounted to tens of millions of dollars. To date, thousands of financial service advisors and other personnel at IDS and American Express have taken courses in emotional intelligence that range from a few hours to several days.

Although the two previous examples illustrate the usefulness of staffing and training practices based on emotional intelligence, there is some evidence that emotional intelligence may have a significantly stronger impact on the job performance of some people than others. One recent study, for example, found that emotional intelligence is a more important determinant of job performance for people with lower levels of cognitive intelligence.[37] The explanation for this relationship is easy to understand if you consider that, in many circumstances, high emotional intelligence can compensate somewhat for low cognitive intelligence. In other words, exceptional "people smarts" can, to some extent, make up for deficiencies in "book smarts." Finally, as the **OB Internationally** insert box discusses, emotional intelligence is the foundation for cultural intelligence, a type of intelligence that enables people to be effective in contexts in which they interact with people from different cultures.[38]

ASSESSING EMOTIONAL INTELLIGENCE. As we discussed previously, cognitive abilities are typically assessed using measures with questions such as those included in SAT or IQ tests. So how is emotional intelligence assessed? One type of emotional intelligence assessment is similar to a SAT-style test, because questions are scored as correct or incorrect. As the example items in Figure 10-2 illustrate, test takers are asked to describe the emotions of people depicted in pictures, predict emotional responses to different situations, and identify appropriate and inappropriate emotional responses. After a person takes the test, it gets sent back to the test publisher to be scored.

Another type of assessment asks people about behaviors and preferences that are thought to reflect emotional intelligence. One of the first tests of this type, the "Emotional

OB INTERNATIONALLY

What makes some people more or less effective in culturally diverse organizational contexts? According to some, the answer to this question is *cultural intelligence*,[39] or the ability to discern differences among people that are due to culture, and to understand what these differences mean in terms of the way people tend to think and behave in different situations. There are three sources of cultural intelligence that correspond to the "head," "body," and "heart."[40] The source of cultural intelligence that corresponds to the head is called *cognitive cultural intelligence.* This concept refers to the ability to sense differences among people due to culture and to use this knowledge in planning how to interact with others in anticipation of a cross-cultural encounter. The source of cultural intelligence that corresponds to the body is called *physical cultural intelligence,* which refers to the ability to adapt one's behavior when a cultural encounter requires it. Finally, the source of cultural intelligence that corresponds to the heart is called *emotional cultural intelligence.* This concept refers to the level of effort and persistence an individual exerts when trying to understand and adapt to new cultures.

Understanding cultural intelligence may be useful because it's an ability that can be improved through training.[41] Such a program could begin with an assessment to identify sources of cultural intelligence that may be weak. Consider, for example, an individual who was very knowledgeable about the customs and norms of another culture and was very willing to learn more but who just couldn't alter her body language and eye contact so that it was appropriate for the other culture. In this particular case, the aim of the training would be to improve physical cultural intelligence. The individual might be asked to study video that contrasts correct and incorrect body language and eye contact. The individual might also be asked to engage in role-playing exercises to model the appropriate behavior and receive feedback from an expert. Finally, the individual might be asked to take acting classes. Although such training may seem to be quite involved and expensive, the costs of poor performance in cross-cultural contexts can be devastating for both the employee and the organization.

Quotient Inventory (EQ-i),"[42] includes 133 such questions. Although the EQ-i has been used by many organizations in an attempt to improve managerial practices and organizational effectiveness, it has been criticized for measuring personality traits more than actual abilities.[43] More recently, a group of researchers published a very short and easy-to-score measure specifically designed to assess each of the four facets of emotional intelligence described in this section.[44] Although this assessment is similar in format to the EQ-i, the items don't appear to overlap as much with aspects of personality. You can take the test yourself in our **OB Assessments** feature to see where you stand in terms of emotional intelligence.

PHYSICAL ABILITIES

Physical abilities are likely very familiar to you because many of you took physical education classes early in your school career. Maybe you were evaluated on whether you could climb a rope to the ceiling of a gymnasium, run around a track several times, or kick a ball to a teammate who was running full stride. Or maybe you've applied for

FIGURE 10-2 | Sample Items from an Emotional Intelligence Test

1. Indicate how much of each emotion is expressed by this face:

	None				Very Much
a) Happiness	1	2	3	4	5
b) Anger	1	2	3	4	5
c) Fear	1	2	3	4	5
d) Excitement	1	2	3	4	5
e) Surprise	1	2	3	4	5

2. What mood(s) might be helpful to feel when meeting in-laws for the very first time?

	Not Useful			Useful	
a) Slight Tension	1	2	3	4	5
b) Surprise	1	2	3	4	5
c) Joy	1	2	3	4	5

3. Tom felt anxious, and became a bit stressed when he thought about all the work he needed to do. When his supervisor brought him an additional project, he felt _____.
(Select the best choice.)

a) Overwhelmed

b) Depressed

c) Ashamed

d) Self-conscious

e) Jittery

4. Debbie just came back from vacation. She was feeling peaceful and content. How well would each action preserve her mood?

Action 1: She started to make a list of things at home that she needed to do.

Very Ineffective 1   2   3   4   5 Very Effective

Action 2: She began thinking about where and when she would go on her next vacation.

Very Ineffective 1   2   3   4   5 Very Effective

Action 3: She decided it was best to ignore the feeling since it wouldn't last anyway.

Very Ineffective 1   2   3   4   5 Very Effective

Source: Copyright © 2006 J. Mayer, P. Salovey, and D. Caruso. Reprinted with permission.
Note that the photo in item 1 does not appear in the test published by Multi-Health Systems.

OB ASSESSMENTS

EMOTIONAL INTELLIGENCE

How high is your emotional intelligence? This assessment will tell you where you stand on the four facets of emotional intelligence discussed in this chapter—self-awareness, other awareness, emotion regulation, and emotion use. Answer each question using the response scale provided. Then follow the instructions below to score yourself. (For more assessments relevant to this chapter, please visit the Online Learning Center at www.mhhe.colquitt).

1 TOTALLY DISAGREE	2 DISAGREE	3 SOMEWHAT DISAGREE	4 NEUTRAL	5 SOMEWHAT AGREE	6 AGREE	7 TOTALLY AGREE

1. I have a good sense of why I have certain feelings most of the time. _____
2. I have a good understanding of my own emotions. _____
3. I really understand what I feel. _____
4. I always know whether or not I am happy. _____
5. I am a good observer of others' emotions. _____
6. I always know my friends' emotions from their behavior. _____
7. I am sensitive to the feelings and emotions of others. _____
8. I have a good understanding of the emotions of people around me. _____
9. I always set goals for myself and then try my best to achieve them. _____
10. I always tell myself I am a competent person. _____
11. I am a self-motivating person. _____
12. I would always encourage myself to try my best. _____
13. I am able to control my temper so that I can handle difficulties rationally. _____
14. I am quite capable of controlling my own emotions. _____
15. I can always calm down quickly when I am very angry. _____
16. I have good control over my own emotions. _____

SCORING AND INTERPRETATION

Self-Awareness: Sum up items 1–4. _____
Other Awareness: Sum up items 5–8. _____
Emotion Use: Sum up items 9–12. _____
Emotion Regulation: Sum up items 13–16. _____

If you scored 19 or above, then you are above average on a particular dimension. If you scored 18 or below, then you are below average on a particular dimension.

Sources: K.S. Law, C.S. Wong, and L.J. Song, "The Construct and Criterion Validity of Emotional Intelligence and its Potential Utility for Management Studies," *Journal of Applied Psychology* 89 (2004), pp. 483–96; and C.S. Wong and K.S. Law, "The Effects of Leader and Follower Emotional Intelligence on Performance and Attitude," *The Leadership Quarterly* 13 (2002), pp. 243–74.

a job and had to take a test that assessed your ability to manipulate and assemble small mechanical parts. As a final example, and the one likely to be most familiar, you've probably been subject to tests that measure the quality of your vision and hearing. Although these examples may not seem to be related, each refers to a different type of physical ability. In this section, we review a few important types of physical abilities, which are illustrated in Table 10-2.[45]

10.4

What are the various types of physical ability?

STRENGTH. Although **strength** generally refers to the degree to which the body is capable of exerting force, there are actually several different types of strength that are important, depending on the job. *Static strength* refers to the ability to lift, push, or pull very heavy objects using the hands, arms, legs, shoulders, or back. Static strength is involved in jobs in which people need to lift objects like boxes, equipment, machine parts, and heavy tools. With *explosive strength,* the person exerts short bursts of energy to move him- or herself or an object. Employees who are required to run, jump, or throw things at work depend on their explosive strength to be effective. The final type of strength, *dynamic strength,* refers to the ability to exert force for a prolonged period of time without becoming overly fatigued and giving out. Dynamic strength is involved in jobs in which the person has to climb ropes or ladders or pull him- or herself up onto platforms. Although jobs requiring physical strength may vary as to which category is important, there are also many jobs that require all three categories. Firefighters, for example, must typically pass grueling tests of strength before being hired. In Dublin, California, one part of the firefighter strength test involves climbing a long flight of stairs under time constraints without touching the rails while wearing a 50-pound vest and carrying another 25 pounds of equipment. Another part of the test involves safely moving a 165-pound dummy out of harm's way.[46]

STAMINA. **Stamina** refers to the ability of a person's lungs and circulatory system to work efficiently while he or she is engaging in prolonged physical activity. Stamina may be important in jobs that require running, swimming, and climbing. In fact, stamina is involved whenever the nature of the physical activity causes the heart rate to climb and the depth and rate of breathing to increase for prolonged periods of time. As you can imagine, the firefighter test described in the previous paragraph assesses stamina as well as strength.

FLEXIBILITY AND COORDINATION. Generally speaking, **flexibility** refers to the ability to bend, stretch, twist, or reach. When a job requires extreme ranges of motion—for example, when people need to work in a cramped compartment or an awkward position—the type of flexibility involved is called *extent flexibility.* If you've ever watched a person working inside the trunk of a car installing speakers, you've seen extent flexibility. When a job requires repeated and somewhat quick bends, stretches, twists, or reaches, the type of flexibility involved is called *dynamic flexibility.* To understand what dynamic flexibility involves, picture a house painter on a ladder trying to paint some trim just barely within reach.

In addition to flexibility, **coordination**, or the quality of physical movement, may be important in some jobs. *Gross body coordination* refers to the ability to synchronize the movements of the body, arms, and legs to do something while the whole body is in motion. In contrast, *gross body equilibrium* involves the ability to maintain the balance of the body in unstable contexts or when the person has to change directions. Jumping rope effectively requires gross body coordination; walking on a balance beam requires gross body equilibrium. Both types of coordination are important in contexts that involve quick movements. However, gross body equilibrium is more important when the work environment is artificially elevated and inherently unstable.

PSYCHOMOTOR ABILITIES. There are several different examples of **psychomotor abilities**, which generally refer to the capacity to manipulate and control objects. *Fine manipulative abilities* refer to the ability to keep the arms and hands steady while using the

TABLE 10-2	Physical Abilities	
TYPE	**MORE SPECIFIC FACET**	**JOBS WHERE RELEVANT**
Strength	*Static:* Lifting, pushing, pulling heavy objects *Explosive:* Exerting a short burst of muscular force to move oneself or objects *Dynamic:* Exerting muscular force repeatedly or continuously	Structural iron and steel workers; tractor trailer and heavy truck drivers; farm workers; firefighters
Stamina	Exerting oneself over a period of time without circulatory system giving out	Athletes; dancers; commercial divers; firefighters
Flexibility & Coordination	*Extent Flexibility:* Degree of bending, stretching, twisting of body, arms, legs *Dynamic Flexibility:* Speed of bending, stretching, twisting of body, arms, legs *Gross Body Coordination:* Coordinating movement of body, arms, and legs in activities that involve all three together *Gross Body Equilibrium:* Ability to regain balance in contexts where balance is upset	Athletes; dancers; riggers; industrial machinery mechanics; choreographers; commercial divers; structural iron and steel workers
Psychomotor	*Fine Manipulative Abilities:* Keeping hand and arm steady while grasping, manipulating, and assembling small objects *Control Movement Abilities:* Making quick, precise adjustments to a machine while operating it *Response Orientation:* Quickly choosing among appropriate alternative movements *Response Time:* Quickly responding to signals with body movements	Fabric menders; potters; timing device assemblers; jewelers; construction drillers; agricultural equipment operators; photographers; highway patrol pilots; athletes
Sensory	*Near and Far Vision:* Seeing details of an object up close or at a distance *Night Vision:* Seeing well in low light *Visual Color Discrimination:* Detecting differences in colors and shades *Depth Perception:* Judging relative distances *Hearing Sensitivity:* Hearing differences in sounds that vary in terms of pitch and loudness *Auditory Attention:* Focusing on a source of sound in the presence of other sources *Speech Recognition:* Identifying and understanding the speech of others	Electronic testers and inspectors; highway patrol pilots; tractor trailer, truck, and bus drivers; airline pilots; photographers; musicians and composers; industrial machine mechanics; speech pathologists

Source: Adapted from E.A. Fleishman, D.P. Costanza, and J. Marshall-Mies, "Abilities," in *An Occupational Information System for the 21*st *Century: The Development of O*NET,* eds. N.G. Peterson, M.D. Mumford, W.C. Borman, P.R. Jeanneret, and E.A. Fleishman (Washington DC: American Psychological Association, 1999), pp. 175–95; and *O*NET Web site, The O*NET Content Model: Detailed Outline With Descriptions, http://www.onet center.org/content.html/1.A?D=1#Cm_1.A (May 20, 2009).*

hands to do precise work, generally on small or delicate objects such as arteries, nerves, gems, and watches. *Control movement abilities* are important in tasks for which people have to make different precise adjustments, using machinery to complete the work effectively. Anyone who drills things for a living, whether it be wood, concrete, or teeth, needs this type of ability. The ability to choose the right action quickly in response to several different signals is called *response orientation*. It shouldn't be too difficult to imagine the importance of response orientation for an airline pilot who responds to the flashing lights, buzzers, and verbal information triggered during an in-flight emergency. The final psychomotor ability we describe is called *response time*. This ability reflects how quickly an individual responds to signaling information after it occurs. Returning to the previous example, most of us would feel more secure if our airline pilot had both a fast response orientation and a quick response time. After all, making the right decision may not be useful in this context if the decision is made too late!

SENSORY ABILITIES. **Sensory ability** refers to capabilities associated with vision and hearing. Examples of important visual abilities include the ability to see things up close and at a distance (*near and far vision*) or in low light contexts (*night vision*), as well as the ability to perceive colors and judge relative distances between things accurately (*visual color discrimination* and *depth perception*). There are many different jobs that emphasize only one or two of these visual abilities. For example, whereas effectiveness as a watch repairer depends on good near vision, effectiveness as an interior designer depends on visual color discrimination. However, there are other jobs in which effectiveness might depend on almost all categories of visual abilities. A fighter pilot needs near vision to read instruments and checklists, far vision and depth perception to see enemy targets and landmarks, night vision to conduct operations in low light, and visual color discrimination to interpret information from warning lights and computer readouts correctly.

Abilities related to hearing, also referred to as auditory abilities, include the capability to hear and discriminate sounds that vary in terms of loudness and pitch (*hearing sensitivity*), being able to focus on a single sound in the presence of many other sounds (*auditory attention*), and the ability to identify and understand the speech of another person (*speech recognition*). Perhaps the most obvious jobs for which auditory abilities would be important are musicians and composers (yes, we are going to ignore exceptions like Beethoven, who was deaf at the time he wrote his Ninth Symphony). However, with

Noel Lee founded Monster Cable after using his extraordinary auditory ability to identify which type of speaker wire sounds best.

these jobs, the emphasis would likely be on hearing sensitivity and auditory attention rather than speech recognition (who listens to lyrics these days?). Another job for which auditory abilities might be crucially important is bartending, especially if the bar is crowded and noisy. In this context, a bartender needs auditory attention and speech recognition to be able to isolate and understand the words of a single patron against the backdrop of the loud chatter. As an example of a company that exists because of auditory ability, consider the case of Monster Cable, the Brisbane, California–based manufacturer of audiovisual cables and accessories. Noel Lee, the company's founder, started out by comparing the sound of Tchaikovsky's 1812 Overture and Michael Jackson's "Liberian Girl" using different types of speaker wire.[47] He listened to the music over and over again and carefully considered the dynamics, loudness, bass response, and high frequencies of the music to determine which combination of wire thickness, composition, and braiding pattern sounded best.

SUMMARY: WHAT DOES IT MEAN FOR AN EMPLOYEE TO BE "ABLE"?

Thus far in the chapter, we have presented you with a fairly detailed description of the domain of human abilities, which are summarized in Figure 10-3. Although the list of abilities included in the figure may seem somewhat daunting, we hope that you can appreciate that this set of abilities describes each and every one of us. Moreover, as we have alluded to throughout the chapter, these abilities play an important role in determining how effective we can be at different tasks and jobs.

FIGURE 10-3   What Does It Mean for an Employee to Be "Able"?

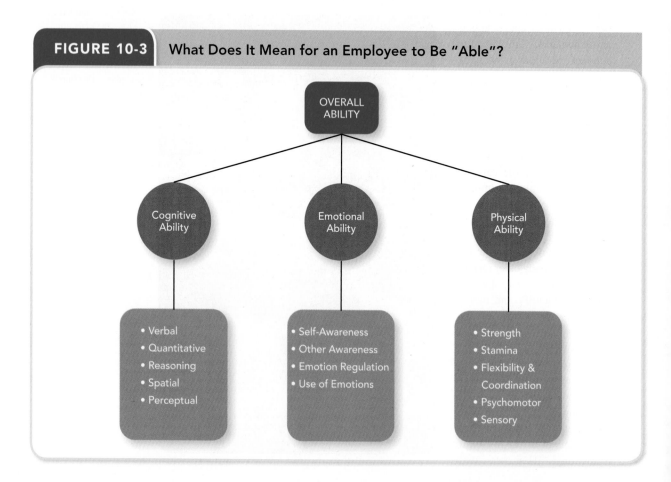

HOW IMPORTANT IS ABILITY?

So, now that you know what ability is and where it comes from, let's turn to the next important question: Does ability really matter? That is, does ability have a significant impact on job performance and organizational commitment—the two primary outcomes in our integrative model of OB? The answer to this question depends on what type of ability you are referring to—cognitive, emotional, or physical. We focus our discussion on general cognitive ability because it's the most relevant form of ability across all jobs and is likely to be important in the kinds of positions that students in an OB course will be pursuing. As it turns out, there is a huge body of research linking general cognitive ability to job performance, as summarized in Figure 10-4.[48]

 10.5

How does cognitive ability affect job performance and organizational commitment?

The figure reveals that general cognitive ability is a strong predictor of job performance—in particular, the task performance aspect. Across all jobs, smarter employees fulfill the

| FIGURE 10-4 | Effects of General Cognitive Ability on Performance and Commitment |

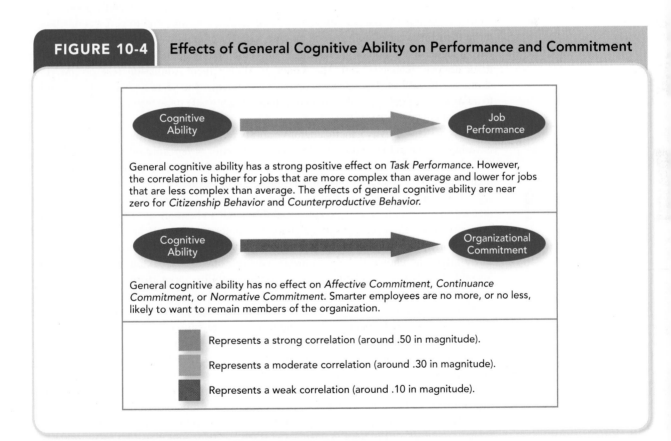

Sources: J.W. Boudreau, W.R. Boswell, T.A. Judge, and R.D Bretz, "Personality and Cognitive Ability as Predictors of Job Search Among Employed Managers," *Personnel Psychology* 54 (2001), pp. 25–50; S.M. Colarelli, R.A. Dean, and C. Konstans, "Comparative Effects of Personal and Situational Influences on Job Outcomes of New Professionals," *Journal of Applied Psychology* 72 (1987), pp. 558–66; D.N. Dickter, M. Roznowski, and D.A. Harrison, "Temporal Tempering: An Event History Analysis of the Process of Voluntary Turnover," *Journal of Applied Psychology* 81 (1996), pp. 705–16; and F.L. Schmidt and J. Hunter, "General Mental Ability in the World of Work: Occupational Attainment and Job Performance," *Journal of Personality and Social Psychology* 86 (2004), pp. 162–73.

requirements of their job descriptions more effectively than do less smart employees.[49] In fact, of all the variables discussed in this book, none has a stronger correlation with task performance than general cognitive ability. Thousands of organizations, and many that are quite well known, assess cognitive ability in an effort to select the best candidates available for specific jobs.[50] The use of cognitive ability tests for this purpose appears to be quite reasonable, given that scores on such tests have a strong positive correlation with measures of performance across different types of jobs.[51]

In fact, this relationship holds even for performance in academic contexts. We mentioned the Scholastic Assessment Test, or the SAT, several times in this chapter because it's likely to be quite familiar to you and because it largely reflects general cognitive ability.[52] Most colleges and universities in the United States take these scores into account when deciding which students to admit because they believe that higher scores increase the chances that students will be successful in college. But does the SAT really relate to how well someone does in college? Many of you are likely to be skeptical because you probably know someone who did extremely well on the SAT but performed poorly as a college student. Similarly, you probably know someone who didn't do that well on the SAT but who performed well as a college student. As it turns out, the SAT is actually good at predicting college performance. Students with higher SAT scores tend to perform much better in their first year of college, end up with a higher cumulative grade point average, and have a higher likelihood of graduating.[53] The same finding applies to predicting success in graduate-level school as well. The Graduate Management Admission Test, or GMAT, is similar to the SAT in structure and content, and students who score higher on this test prior to admission to graduate school tend to achieve better grade point averages over the course of their graduate program.[54]

So what explains why general cognitive ability relates to task performance? People who have higher general cognitive ability tend to be better at *learning and decision making*, (which we covered in detail in Chapter 8). They're able to gain more knowledge from their experiences at a faster rate, and as a result, they develop a bigger pool of knowledge regarding how to do their jobs effectively.[55] There are, however, three important caveats that we should mention. First, cognitive ability tends to be more strongly correlated with task performance than citizenship behavior or counterproductive behavior.[56] An increased amount of job knowledge helps an employee complete job tasks, but it doesn't necessarily affect the choice to help a coworker or refrain from breaking an important rule. Second, the positive correlation between cognitive ability and performance is even stronger in jobs that are complex or situations that demand adaptability.[57] Third, people may do poorly on a test of general cognitive ability for reasons other than a lack of cognitive ability. As an example, people who come from economically disadvantaged backgrounds may do poorly on such tests, not because they lack the underlying cognitive ability but because they may not have had the learning opportunities needed to provide the appropriate responses.

In contrast to relationships with job performance, research has not supported a significant linkage between cognitive ability and organizational commitment.[58] On the one hand, we might expect a positive relationship with commitment because people with higher cognitive ability tend to perform more effectively, and therefore, they might feel they fit well with their job. On the other hand, we might expect to see a negative relationship with commitment because people with higher cognitive ability possess more job knowledge, which increases their value on the job market, and in turn the likelihood that they would leave for another job.[59] In the end, knowing how smart an employee is tells us very little about the likelihood that he or she will remain a member of the organization.

APPLICATION: THE WONDERLIC

Given the strong relationship between general cognitive ability and job performance, it isn't surprising that many organizations apply the content of this chapter by using ability tests to hire new employees. One of the most widely used tests is the **Wonderlic Personnel Test**, a 12-minute test of general cognitive ability that consists of 50 questions. It's been in use for several decades now and has been given to more than 120 million people by thousands of organizations.[60] From the example items that appear in Figure 10-5, you should be able to see how the items correspond with many of the cognitive abilities that we've described previously.

People who take the test receive one point for each correct response, and those points are summed to give a total score that can be used as a basis for selecting people for different jobs. The Wonderlic User's Manual offers recommendations for minimum passing scores for different job families, some of which are included in Table 10-3. For example, a score of 17 is the minimum suggested score for unskilled laborer, a score of 21—which is the average for high school graduates and corresponds to an IQ of approximately 100—is the minimum suggested score for a firefighter. A score of 28 is the minimum suggested score for upper-level managerial and executive work and around the average for all college graduates.

You'll hear about the Wonderlic Personnel Test every March and April, because NFL football teams take Wonderlic scores into account when drafting college players. One question that people always debate during this time is whether scores on a test of cognitive ability are relevant to a football player's performance on the field. Although supporters of

 10.6

What steps can organizations take to hire people with high levels of cognitive ability?

TABLE 10-3	Suggested Minimum Wonderlic Scores for Various Jobs
JOB	**MINIMUM SCORES**
Mechanical Engineer	30
Attorney	29
Executive	28
Teacher	27
Nurse	26
Office Manager	25
Advertising Sales	24
Manager/Supervisor	23
Police Officer	22
Firefighter	21
Cashier	20
Hospital Orderly	19
Machine Operator	18
Unskilled Laborer	17
Maid-Matron	16

Source: *Wonderlic Personnel Test and Scholastic Level Exam: User's Manual* (Libertyville, IL: Wonderlic Personnel Test, Inc., 1992), pp. 28–29. Reprinted with permission.

FIGURE 10-5 | **Sample Wonderlic Questions**

1. Which of the following is the earliest date?

    A) Jan. 16, 1898   B) Feb. 21, 1889   C) Feb. 2, 1898   D) Jan. 7, 1898   E) Jan. 30, 1889

2. LOW is to HIGH as EASY is to ___?___ .

    J) **SUCCESSFUL**   K) **PURE**   L) **TALL**   M) **INTERESTING**   N) **DIFFICULT**

3. A featured product from an Internet retailer generated 27, 99, 80, 115 and 213 orders over a 5-hour period. Which graph below best represents this trend?

A

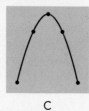
B

C

D

E

4. What is the next number in the series?   29   41   53   65   77   ___?___

    J) 75   K) 88   L) 89   M) 98   N) 99

5. *One word below appears in color. What is the OPPOSITE of that word?*
   She gave a complex answer to the question and we all agreed with her.

    A) long   B) better   C) simple   D) wrong   E) kind

6. Jose's monthly parking fee for April was $150; for May it was $10 more than April; and for June $40 more than May. His average monthly parking fee was ___?___ for these 3 months.

    J) $66   K) $160   L) $166   M) $170   N) $200

7. *If the first two statements are true, is the final statement true?*

    Sandra is responsible for ordering all office supplies.

    Notebooks are office supplies.

    Sandra is responsible for ordering notebooks.

    A) yes   B) no   C) uncertain

8. Which THREE choices are needed to create the figure on the left? Only pieces of the same color may overlap.

J

K

L

M

N

9. Which THREE of the following words have similar meanings?

    A) observable   B) manifest   C) hypothetical   D) indefinite   E) theoretical

10. Last year, 12 out of 600 employees at a service organization were rewarded for their excellence in customer service, which was ___?___ of the employees.

    J) 1%   K) 2%   L) 3%   M) 4%   N) 6%

Answers:

    1. E,   2. N,   3. D,   4. L,   5. C,   6. M,   7. A,   8. KLM,   9. CDE,   10. K

the Wonderlic's use in the NFL argue that cognitive ability is necessary to remember plays and learn complex offensive and defensive systems, many people wonder how the ability to answer questions like those listed in Figure 10-5 relates to a player's ability to complete a pass, run for a touchdown, tackle an opponent, or kick a field goal. Moreover, detractors of the Wonderlic wonder why a poor score should overshadow a record of superior accomplishments on the playing field.

Nevertheless, it appears that teams do take these scores seriously. As an example, after directing his Texas Longhorns to the national championship over the University of Southern California, quarterback Vince Young was one of the hottest players coming into the 2006 NFL draft. Before the draft, however, reports began circulating that he scored a 6 on the Wonderlic, a score thought to be too low for an NFL quarterback. Sportswriters then began to project that Young would end up being drafted after players with clearly inferior records of accomplishments on the field.[61] Later, Young retook the test and scored a 16. Although the score was considered low for quarterback prospects (who averaged 25.5 in 2005), it was enough of an improvement for the Tennessee Titans, who drafted him third overall that year. Someone on the Tennessee staff may have recalled that Dan Marino also scored a 16 on the way to his Hall-of-Fame–worthy career.[62]

TAKEAWAYS

10.1   Ability refers to the relatively stable capabilities of people to perform a particular range of different but related activities. Differences in ability are a function of both genes and the environment.

10.2   Cognitive abilities include verbal ability, quantitative ability, reasoning ability, spatial ability, and perceptual ability. General cognitive ability, or g, underlies all of these more specific cognitive abilities.

10.3   Emotional intelligence includes four specific kinds of emotional skills: self-awareness, other awareness, emotion regulation, and use of emotions.

10.4   Physical abilities include strength, stamina, flexibility and coordination, psychomotor abilities, and sensory abilities.

10.5   General cognitive ability has a strong positive relationship with job performance, due primarily to its effects on task performance. In contrast, general cognitive ability is not related to organizational commitment.

10.6   Many organizations use cognitive ability tests to hire applicants with high levels of general cognitive ability. One of the most commonly used tests is the Wonderlic Personnel Test.

KEY TERMS

- Ability   *p. 339*
- Cognitive ability   *p. 340*
- Verbal ability   *p. 340*
- Quantitative ability   *p. 342*
- Reasoning ability   *p. 342*
- Spatial ability   *p. 344*

chapter 11

Teams: Characteristics and Diversity

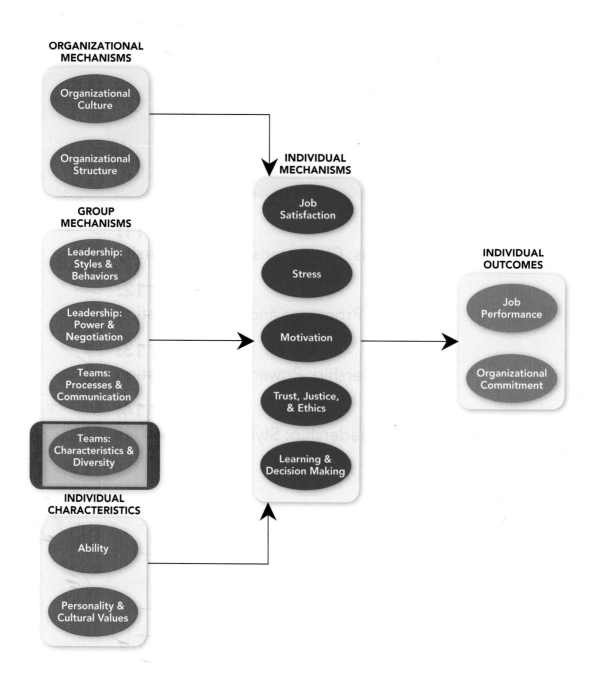

ORGANIZATIONAL MECHANISMS

- Organizational Culture
- Organizational Structure

GROUP MECHANISMS

- Leadership: Styles & Behaviors
- Leadership: Power & Negotiation
- Teams: Processes & Communication
- Teams: Characteristics & Diversity

INDIVIDUAL CHARACTERISTICS

- Ability
- Personality & Cultural Values

INDIVIDUAL MECHANISMS

- Job Satisfaction
- Stress
- Motivation
- Trust, Justice, & Ethics
- Learning & Decision Making

INDIVIDUAL OUTCOMES

- Job Performance
- Organizational Commitment

✅ LEARNING GOALS

After reading this chapter, you should be able to answer the following questions:

11.1 What are the five general team types and their defining characteristics?

11.2 What are the three general types of team interdependence?

11.3 What factors are involved in team composition?

11.4 What are the types of team diversity and how do they influence team functioning?

11.5 How do team characteristics influence team effectiveness?

11.6 How can team compensation be used to manage team effectiveness?

LOGITECH

When's the last time you used a computer mouse or keyboard? What about a universal remote for your home entertainment system, external speakers for your iPod, or a controller or racing wheel for your PlayStation 3? If you've used any of these things recently, chances are good that it was designed and manufactured by Logitech, a Swiss company known for highly innovative and reasonably priced "personal peripherals" involved in computer navigation, Internet communications, digital music, home entertainment control, and gaming. Founded in 1981, the company has experienced double-digit growth in sales each year for the past decade, with revenues of almost $2.5 billion per year.[1] Logitech's success can be attributed to its ability to bring a large number of highly innovative products to market. In a recent year, for example, Logitech introduced 130 new products, many of which were honored with industry awards for superior innovation and design.[2] Today, it ships approximately 165 million products to customers in more than 100 countries.[3]

So what gives Logitech the ability to offer such a large number of innovative products? One factor is that Logitech uses teams with highly specialized members who are dispersed across the globe, then manages the teams in such a way that they can accomplish work continuously.[4] Consider, for example, the team that developed and manufactured Logitech's mouse, the Revolution. Product design and mechanical engineering took place in Ireland, electrical engineering took place in Switzerland, tooling took place in Taiwan, manufacturing took place in China, and software engineering and quality assurance took place in California.[5] Although you might be inclined to believe that time zone differences would be a hindrance to this sort of team, Logitech turned it into a competitive advantage by letting the work *follow the sun*.[6] Specifically, work was accomplished continuously because members of a team who finished their workday in one country electronically handed off the work to team members in another country who had just arrived at the office. Because these electronic hand-offs occurred continuously, product development and other work needed to bring the mouse to market was completed much more quickly.

Although "follow the sun" teams are gaining attention in many companies that operate globally, there are some issues that need to be considered.[7] As one example, language and cultural differences among team members can create misunderstandings that prevent work from being accomplished effectively after it's been handed off. Moreover, beyond obvious language issues, just imagine how difficult it must be for members of this sort of dispersed team to find convenient times to communicate with one another. If a team member in California needed to meet virtually with the team on Friday at noon (Pacific Standard Time), it would be 8:00 p.m. Friday evening in Ireland and 4:00 a.m. Friday morning in Taiwan.

TEAM CHARACTERISTICS AND DIVERSITY

The topic of teams is likely familiar to almost anyone who might be reading this book. In fact, you've probably had firsthand experience with several different types of teams at different points in your life. As an example, most of you have played a team sport or two (yes, playing soccer in gym class counts). Most of you have also worked in student teams to complete projects or assignments for a course. Or perhaps you've worked closely with a small group of people to accomplish a task that was important to you—planning an event, raising money for a charity, or starting and running a small cash business. Finally, some of you have been members of organizational teams responsible for making a product, providing a service, or generating recommendations for solving company problems.

But what exactly is a team, and what is it that makes a team more than a "group"? A **team** consists of two or more people who work *interdependently* over some time period to accomplish *common goals* related to some *task-oriented purpose*.[8] You can think of teams as a special type of group, where a group is just a collection of two or more people. Teams are special for two reasons. First, the interactions among members within teams revolve around a deeper dependence on one another than the interactions within groups. Second, the interactions within teams occur with a specific task-related purpose in mind. Although the members of a friendship group may engage in small talk or in-depth conversations on a frequent basis, the members of a team depend on one another for critical information, materials, and actions that are needed to accomplish goals related to their purpose for being together.

The use of teams in today's organizations is widespread. National surveys indicate that teams are used in the majority of organizations in the United States, regardless of whether the organization is large or small.[9] In fact, some researchers suggest that almost all major U.S. companies are currently using teams or planning to implement them and that up to 50 percent of all employees in the United States work in a team as part of their job.[10] Thus, whereas the use of teams was limited to pioneers such as Procter & Gamble in the 1960s, teams are currently used in all types of industries to accomplish all the types of work necessary to make organizations run effectively.[11]

Why have teams become so widespread? The most obvious reason is that the nature of the work needed to be done requires them. As work has become more complex, interactions among multiple team members have become more vital, because they allow the team to pool complementary knowledge and skills. As an example, surgical teams consist of individuals who receive specialized training in the activities needed to conduct surgical procedures safely. The team consists of a surgeon who received training for the procedure in question, an anesthesiologist who received training necessary to manage patient pain, and an operating room nurse who was trained on how to provide overall

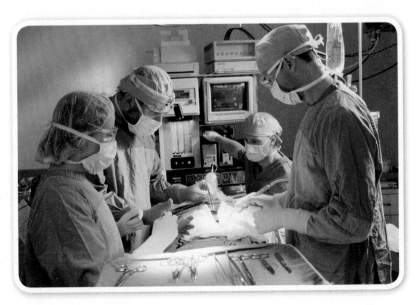

An action team, such as a surgical team, often performs tasks that are complex in execution but limited in duration.

care for the patient. Teams may also be useful to organizations in ways beyond just accomplishing the work itself. For example, one recent study revealed that problem-solving teams composed primarily of rank-and-file workers could boost productivity in steel mills by devising ways to increase the efficiency of production lines and quality control processes.[12] Although implementing teams often makes sense in settings such as these, for which the nature of the work and work-related problems are complex, teams vary a great deal from one another in terms of their effectiveness. The goal of this chapter, as well as the next, is to help you understand factors that influence team effectiveness.

WHAT CHARACTERISTICS CAN BE USED TO DESCRIBE TEAMS?

This is the first of two chapters on teams. This chapter focuses on team characteristics—the task, unit, and member qualities that can be used to describe teams and that combine to make some teams more diverse than others. Team characteristic provide a means of categorizing and examining teams, which is important because teams come in so many shapes and sizes. Team characteristics play an important role in determining what a team is capable of achieving and, as our **OB on Screen** feature illustrates, may influence the strategies and processes the team uses to reach its goals. Chapter 12 will focus on team processes and communication—the specific actions and behaviors that teams can engage in to achieve synergy. The concepts in that chapter will help explain why some teams are more or less effective than their characteristics would suggest they should be. For now, however, we turn our attention to this question: "What characteristics can be used to describe teams?"

TEAM TYPES

11.1

What are the five general team types and their defining characteristics?

One way to describe teams is to take advantage of existing taxonomies that place teams into various types. One such taxonomy is illustrated in Table 11-1. The table illustrates that there are five general types of teams and that each is associated with a number of defining characteristics.[13] The most notable characteristics include the team's purpose, the length of the team's existence, and the amount of time involvement the team requires of its individual members. The sections to follow review these types of teams in turn.

WORK TEAMS. **Work teams** are designed to be relatively permanent. Their purpose is to produce goods or provide services, and they generally require a full-time commitment from their members. Although all work teams have these defining characteristics, they can vary a great deal across organizations in other important ways. One way that work teams vary is in the degree to which members have autonomy in defining their roles and decision making. In traditional work teams, members have very specific sets of job duties, and their decision making is confined to the activities required by those duties. Members of self-managed work teams, in contrast, are not locked into specific jobs. Instead, they jointly decide how to organize themselves and carry out the team's work.

MANAGEMENT TEAMS. **Management teams** are similar to work teams in that they are designed to be relatively permanent; however, they are also distinct in a number of important ways. Whereas work teams focus on the accomplishment of core operational-level production and service tasks, management teams participate in managerial-level tasks that affect the entire organization. Specifically, management teams are responsible

OB ON SCREEN

WE ARE MARSHALL

We got a huge problem on the O line, coach.

With those words, Marshall University assistant football coach Red Dawson (Matthew Fox) sums up an obvious problem faced by his team in the movie *We Are Marshall* (Dir,: McG, Warner Brothers, 2006). In 1970, most of the players and coaches on the team died in a plane crash on the way home from a game. To field a team the following year, the university president hired Jack Lengyel (Matthew McConaughey) as head coach. Coach Lengyel's first task is to hire a new coaching staff and recruit new players. The recruits are predominantly freshman and "walk-ons" with no experience playing college football, and it doesn't take long to see that his new team has serious shortcomings.

Coach Lengyel is a big fan of an offensive system called the "power-I," and he plans to use it with his new team. However, after two weeks of practice, he realizes that the system will not work because his players don't possess the necessary capabilities. The players simply lack the size, strength, speed, knowledge, and skills necessary to make the system work. This gap is particularly serious for the players on the offensive line, who must block for the running backs and protect the team's only quarterback. Coach Lengyel calls a meeting with his coaching staff to find a solution to the problem, and after throwing the playbook in the trash can for dramatic effect, he asks the question: "What is the simplest offense that you have ever run and actually won a football game?" In essence, Coach Lengyel realizes that he has to find an offensive system that is compatible with the characteristics of his team. Coach Dawson suggests a system called the "veer," designed to take the focus off any single player, that seems well suited to teams with weak offensive lines. The team ultimately adopts the veer system and performs at a level that most likely surpasses what would have happened if Coach Lengyel had stuck with the power-I. How well does the team perform? You'll have to watch the movie to find out.

for coordinating the activities of organizational subunits—typically departments or functional areas—to help the organization achieve its long-term goals. Top management teams, for example, consist of senior-level executives who meet to make decisions about the strategic direction of the organization. It may also be worth mentioning that because

TABLE 11-1 | Types of Teams

TYPE OF TEAM	PURPOSE AND ACTIVITIES	LIFE SPAN	MEMBER INVOLVEMENT	SPECIFIC EXAMPLES
Work Team	Produce goods or provide services.	Long	High	Self-managed work team Production team Maintenance team Sales team
Management Team	Integrate activities of subunits across business functions.	Long	Moderate	Top management team
Parallel Team	Provide recommendations and resolve issues.	Varies	Low	Quality circle Advisory council Committee
Project Team	Produce a one-time output (product, service, plan, design, etc.).	Varies	Varies	Product design team Research group Planning team
Action Team	Perform complex tasks that vary in duration and take place in highly visible or challenging circumstances.	Varies	Varies	Surgical team Musical group Expedition team Sports team

Sources: S.G. Cohen and D.E. Bailey, "What Makes Teams Work: Group Effectiveness Research from the Shop Floor to the Executive Suite," *Journal of Management* 27 (1997), pp. 239–90; and E. Sundstrom, K.P. De Meuse, and D. Futrell, "Work Teams: Applications and Effectiveness." *American Psychologist* 45 (1990), pp. 120–33.

members of management teams are typically heads of departments, their commitment to the management team is offset somewhat by the responsibilities they have in leading their unit.

PARALLEL TEAMS.   **Parallel teams** are composed of members from various jobs who provide recommendations to managers about important issues that run "parallel" to the organization's production process.[14] Parallel teams require only part-time commitment from members, and they can be permanent or temporary, depending on their aim. Quality circles, for example, consist of individuals who normally perform core production tasks but also meet regularly to identify production-related problems and opportunities for improvement. As an example of a more temporary parallel team, committees often form to deal with unique issues or issues that arise only periodically.

PROJECT TEAMS.   **Project teams** are formed to take on "one-time" tasks that are generally complex and require a lot of input from members with different types of training and expertise.[15] Although project teams only exist as long as it takes to finish a project, some projects are quite complex and can take years to complete. Members of some project teams work full-time, whereas other teams only demand a part-time commitment. A planning team comprised of engineers, architects, designers, and builders, charged with designing a suburban town center, might work together full-time for a year or more. In contrast, the engineers and artists who constitute a design team responsible for creating an electric toothbrush might work together for a month on the project while also serving on other project teams.

ACTION TEAMS. **Action teams** perform tasks that are normally limited in duration. However, those tasks are quite complex and take place in contexts that are either highly visible to an audience or of a highly challenging nature.[16] Some types of action teams work together for an extended period of time. For example, sports teams remain intact for at least one season, and musical groups like AC/DC may

The Australian Band AC/DC, which was formed in 1973, is an example of an action team that has stayed together for an extended period of time

stick together for decades. Other types of action teams stay together only as long as the task takes to complete. Surgical teams and aircraft flight crews may only work together as a unit for a single two-hour surgery or flight.

SUMMARY. So how easy is it to classify teams into one of the types summarized in Figure 11-1? Well, it turns out that teams often fit into more than one category. As an example, consider the teams at Pixar, the company that has produced many computer-animated hit films, such as *Toy Story*, *Monster's Inc.*, *Finding Nemo*, *Cars*, *Wall-E*, and *Up*. On the one hand, because the key members of Pixar's teams have stuck together for each film the company has produced, it might seem like Pixar uses work teams.[17] On the other hand, because the creation of each film can be viewed as a project, and because members are likely involved in multiple ongoing projects, it might seem reasonable to say that Pixar uses project teams. It's probably most appropriate to say that Pixar teams have characteristics of both work teams and project teams.

VARIATIONS WITHIN TEAM TYPES

Even knowing whether a team is a project team, an action team, or some other type of team doesn't tell you the whole story. Often there are important variations within those categories that are needed to understand a team's functioning. For example, **virtual teams** are teams in which the members are geographically dispersed, and interdependent activity occurs through electronic communications—primarily e-mail, instant messaging, and Web conferencing. Although communications and group networking software is far from perfect, it has advanced to the point that it's possible for teams doing all sorts of work to function virtually. In fact, it's likely that there are tens of millions of virtual teams operating

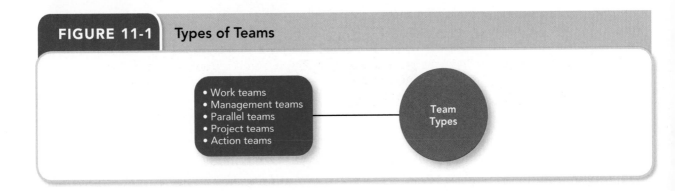

FIGURE 11-1 Types of Teams

- Work teams
- Management teams
- Parallel teams
- Project teams
- Action teams

Team Types

today. As we described in the chapter opening, virtual teams are not just an efficient way to accomplish work when members are geographically separated. Logitech and other companies in high-tech industries are using virtual teams to make continuous progress on work tasks without members having to work 24/7.

In addition to varying in their "virtuality," teams of any type can differ in the amount of experience they have working together. One way to understand this point is to consider what occurs in teams at different stages of their development as they progress from a newly formed team to one that's well-established. According to the most well-known theory, teams go through a progression of five stages shown in the top panel of Figure 11-2.[18] In the first stage, called **forming**, members orient themselves by trying to understand their boundaries in the team. Members try to get a feel for what is expected of them, what types of behaviors are out of bounds, and who's in charge. In the next stage, called **storming**, members remain committed to ideas they bring with them to the team. This initial unwillingness to accommodate others' ideas triggers conflict that negatively affects some interpersonal relationships and harms the team's progress. During the next stage, **norming**, members realize that they need to work together to accomplish team goals, and consequently, they begin to cooperate with one another. Feelings of solidarity develop as members work toward team goals. Over time, norms and expectations develop regarding what different members are responsible for doing. In the fourth stage of team development, which is called **performing**, members are comfortable working within their roles, and the team makes progress toward goals. Finally, because the life span of many teams is limited,

FIGURE 11-2 | Two Models of Team Development

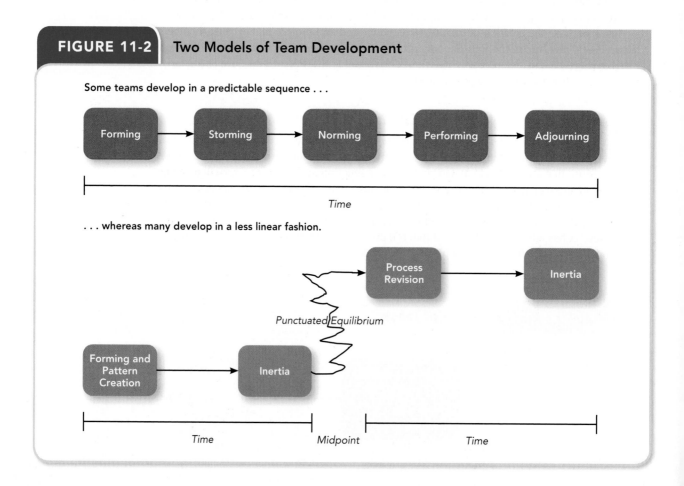

Some teams develop in a predictable sequence . . .

Forming → Storming → Norming → Performing → Adjourning

Time

. . . whereas many develop in a less linear fashion.

Forming and Pattern Creation → Inertia

Punctuated Equilibrium

Process Revision → Inertia

Time   Midpoint   Time

there is a stage called **adjourning.** In this stage, members experience anxiety and other emotions as they disengage and ultimately separate from the team.

But does this sequence of forming, storming, norming, performing, and adjourning apply to the development of all types of teams? Chances are that you've had some experience with teams that would lead you to answer this question with a "no." One situation in which this developmental sequence is less applicable is when teams are formed with clear expectations regarding what's expected from the team and its members. With action teams, for example, there are established rules and standard operating procedures that guide team members' behaviors and their interactions with one another. As a specific example, an aircraft flight crew doesn't have to go through the forming, storming, norming, and performing stages to figure out that the pilot flies the plane and the flight attendant serves the beverages. As another example, though the adjourning stage only happens once for each type of team, the implications are likely to be more significant for team types with longer life spans that require high member involvement. Dissolving a work team that's been together for four years is likely to trigger greater anxiety and stronger emotions among members than a situation in which a committee that meets briefly once a month for a year is disbanded.

A second situation in which the development sequence is less applicable may be in certain types of project teams that follow a pattern of development called **punctuated equilibrium.**[19] This sequence appears in the bottom panel of Figure 11-2. At the initial team meeting, members make assumptions and establish a pattern of behavior that lasts for the first half of its life. That pattern of behavior continues to dominate the team's behavior as it settles into a sort of inertia. At the midway point of the project—and this is true regardless of the length of the project—something remarkable happens: Members realize that they have to change their task paradigm fundamentally to complete it on time. Teams that take this opportunity to plan a new approach during this transition tend to do well, and the new framework dominates their behavior until task completion. However, teams that don't take the opportunity to change their approach tend to persist with their original pattern and may "go down with a sinking ship."

TEAM INTERDEPENDENCE

In addition to taxonomies of team types, we can describe teams by talking about the interdependence that governs connections among team members. In a general sense, you can think of interdependence as the way in which the members of a team are linked to one another. That linkage between members is most often thought of in terms of the interactions that take place as the team accomplishes its work. However, linkages among team members also exist with respect to their goals and rewards. In fact, you can find out where your student project team stands on different aspects of interdependence using our **OB Assessments** feature.

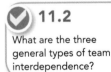

11.2

What are the three general types of team interdependence?

TASK INTERDEPENDENCE. **Task interdependence** refers to the degree to which team members interact with and rely on other team members for the information, materials, and resources needed to accomplish work for the team.[20] As Figure 11-3 illustrates, there are four primary types of task interdependence, and each requires a different degree of interaction and coordination.[21]

The type of task interdependence with the lowest degree of required coordination is **pooled interdependence.**[22] With this type of interdependence, group members complete their work assignments independently, and then this work is simply "piled up" to represent the group's output. Consider what pooled interdependence would be like on a fishing boat. Each fisherman would bait his or her own pole, drop the baited line into the water, reel the fish in, remove the fish from the hook, and, finally, throw the fish into a tank filled with ice and other fish. At the end of the day, the boat's production would be the weight of the total fish that were caught.

OB ASSESSMENTS

INTERDEPENDENCE

How interdependent is your student project team? This assessment is designed to measure three types of interdependence: task interdependence, goal interdependence, and outcome interdependence. Read each of the following questions with a relevant student team in mind. Answer each question using the response scale provided. Then follow the instructions below to score yourself. (For more assessments relevant to this chapter, please visit the Online Learning Center at www.mhhe.com/colquitt).

1 TOTALLY DISAGREE	2 DISAGREE	3 SOMEWHAT DISAGREE	4 NEUTRAL	5 SOMEWHAT AGREE	6 AGREE	7 TOTALLY AGREE

1. I cannot accomplish my tasks without information or materials from other members of my team. _____

2. Other members of my team depend on me for information or materials needed to perform their tasks. _____

3. Within my team, jobs performed by team members are related to one another. _____

4. My work goals come directly from the goals of my team. _____

5. My work activities on any given day are determined by my team's goals for that day. _____

6. I do very few activities on my job that are not related to the goals of my team. _____

7. Feedback about how well I am doing my job comes primarily from information about how well the entire team is doing. _____

8. Evaluations of my performance are strongly influenced by how well my team performs. _____

9. Many rewards from my work (e.g., pay, grades) are determined in large part by my contributions as a team member. _____

SCORING AND INTERPRETATION

Task Interdependence: Sum up items 1–3. _____
Goal Interdependence: Sum up items 4–6. _____
Outcome Interdependence: Sum up items 7–9. _____

If you scored 14 or above, then you are above average on a particular dimension. If you scored 13 or below, then your team is below average on a particular dimension.

Source: M.A. Campion, E.M. Papper, and G.J. Medsker, "Relations Between Work Team Characteristics and Effectiveness: A Replication and Extension," *Personnel Psychology* 49 (1996), pp. 429–52. Reprinted with permission of Wiley-Blackwell.

The next type of task interdependence is called **sequential interdependence**.[23] With this type of interdependence, different tasks are done in a prescribed order, and the group is structured such that the members specialize in these tasks. Although members in groups with sequential interdependence interact to carry out their work, the interaction only

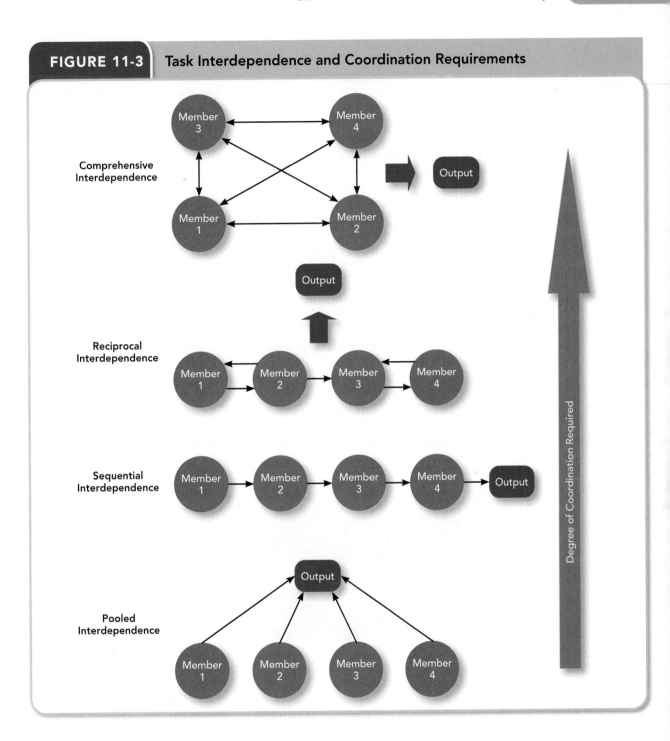

FIGURE 11-3 Task Interdependence and Coordination Requirements

occurs between members who perform tasks that are next to each other in the sequence. Moreover, the member performing the task in the latter part of the sequence depends on the member performing the task in the earlier part of the sequence, but not the other way around. The classic assembly line in manufacturing contexts provides an excellent example of this type of interdependence. In this context, an employee attaches a part to the unit being built, and once this is accomplished, the unit moves on to another employee who adds another part. The process typically ends with the unit being inspected and then packaged for shipping.

Reciprocal interdependence is the next type of task interdependence.[24] Similar to sequential interdependence, members are specialized to perform specific tasks. However, instead of a strict sequence of activities, members interact with a subset of other members to complete the team's work. To understand reciprocal interdependence, consider a team of people who are involved in a business that designs custom homes for wealthy clients. After meeting with a client, the salesperson would provide general criteria, structural and aesthetic details, and some rough sketches to an architect who would work up some initial plans and elevations. The architect then would submit the initial plans to the salesperson, who would review the plans with the customer. Typically, the plans need to be revised by the architect several times, and during this process, customers have questions and requests that require the architect to consult with other members of the team. For example, the architect and structural engineer may have to meet to decide where to locate support beams and load-bearing walls. The architect and construction supervisor might also have to meet to discuss revisions to a design feature that turns out to be too costly. As a final example, the salesperson might have to meet with the designers to assist the customer in the selection of additional features, materials, and colors, which would then need to be included in a revision of the plan by the architect.

Finally, **comprehensive interdependence** requires the highest level of interaction and coordination among members as they try to accomplish work.[25] In groups with comprehensive interdependence, each member has a great deal of discretion in terms of what they do and with whom they interact in the course of the collaboration involved in accomplishing the team's work. Teams at IDEO, arguably the world's most successful product design firm, function with comprehensive interdependence. These teams are composed of individuals from very diverse backgrounds, and they meet as a team quite often to share knowledge and ideas to solve problems related to their design projects.[26]

Face-to-face team meetings that involve comprehensive interdependence can consume a lot of time, yet these meetings are an important part of accomplishing work that requires collaboration.

It's important to note that there is no one right way to design teams with respect to task interdependence. However, it's also important to recognize the trade-offs associated with the different types. On the one hand, as the level of task interdependence increases, members must spend increasing amounts of time communicating and coordinating with other members to complete tasks. This type of coordination can result in decreases in productivity, which is the ratio of work completed per the amount of time worked. On the other hand, increases in task interdependence increase the ability of the team to adapt to new situations. The more members interact and communicate with other members, the more likely it is that the team will be able to devise solutions to novel problems it may face.

GOAL INTERDEPENDENCE. In addition to being linked to one another by task activities, members may be linked by their goals.[27] A high degree of **goal interdependence** exists when team members have a shared vision of the team's goal and align their individual goals with that vision as a result.[28] To understand the power of goal interdependence, visualize a small boat with several people on board, each with a paddle.[29] If each person on the boat wants to go to the exact same place on the other side of a lake, they will all row in the same direction, and the boat will arrive at the desired location. If, however, each person believes the boat should go someplace different, each person will row in a different direction, and the boat will have major problems getting anywhere.

So how do you create high levels of goal interdependence? One thing to do would be to ensure that the team has a formalized mission statement that members buy in to. Mission statements can take a variety of forms, but good ones clearly describe what the team is trying to accomplish in a way that creates a sense of commitment and urgency among team members.[30] Mission statements can come directly from the organization or team leaders, but in many circumstances, it makes more sense for teams to go through the process of developing their own mission statements. This process not only helps members identify important team goals and the actions the team needs to take to achieve these goals, but it also increases feelings of ownership toward the mission statement itself. Table 11-2 describes a set of recommended steps that teams can take to develop their own mission statements.[31]

Although you might believe that the mission for some team tasks is very obvious, all too often this isn't the case. In student teams, for example, you might expect that the obvious goal in the minds of the team members would be to learn the course material. However, it's often the case that students come to a team like this with individual goals that are drastically different. Some students might be more interested in "just getting by" with a passing grade because they already have a job and just need their degree. Others students might want to do well in the course, but are more concerned with maintaining balance with the demands of their lives outside of school. Finally, other students might be focused solely on their grades, perhaps because they want to get into a prestigious graduate school in an

TABLE 11-2	The Mission Statement Development Process

Steps in Mission Statement Development

1. The team should meet in a room where there can be uninterrupted discussion for 1–3 hours.

2. A facilitator should describe the purpose of a mission statement, along with important details that members of the team should consider. Those details may include the products, outcomes, or services that the team is responsible for providing, as well as relevant time constraints.

3. The team should brainstorm to identify potential phrases or elements to include in the mission statement.

4. If the team is large enough, subgroups should be formed to create "first draft" mission statements. Those mission statements should include action verbs and be no more than four sentences.

5. The subgroups should share the first drafts with one another.

6. The team should then try to integrate the best ideas into a single mission statement.

7. The resulting mission statement should be evaluated using the following criteria:
   Clarity—It should focus clearly on a single key purpose.
   Relevance—It should focus on something that is desired by the team members.
   Significance—If achieved, there are benefits that excite the members.
   Believability—It reflects something that members believe they can achieve.
   Urgency—It creates a sense of challenge and commitment.

8. The team should then revise any weak areas of the mission statement. The team should continue to work on the mission statement until there is consensus that it inspires dedication and commitment among members toward a common purpose.

Source: P.S. MacMillan, *The Performance Factor: Unlocking the Secrets of Teamwork* (Nashville, TN: Broadman & Holman Publishers, 2001), pp. 51–53. Copyright © 2001 B&H Publishing Group. Used by permission.

unrelated discipline. Of course, the problem here is that each of these goals is associated with a different approach to working in the team. Students who want to learn the course material will work hard on the team assignments and will want to spend extra time discussing assignment-related issues with teammates, students who just want to get by will do the minimum amount of work, students who want to maintain their work–life balance will look for the most efficient way to do things, and students who are focused on their grades would be willing to take shortcuts that might inhibit learning. Although trying to reach a consensus on a team mission may not be easy in a situation in which the members have goals that vary along these lines, research has shown that teams of students experience significantly greater effectiveness if they invest time and effort doing so soon after the team first forms.[32]

OUTCOME INTERDEPENDENCE. The final type of interdependence relates to how members are linked to one another in terms of the feedback and outcomes they receive as a consequence of working in the team.[33] A high degree of **outcome interdependence** exists when team members share in the rewards that the team earns, with reward examples including pay, bonuses, formal feedback and recognition, pats on the back, extra time off, and continued team survival. Of course, because team achievement depends on the performance of each team member, high outcome interdependence also implies that team members depend on the performance of other team members for the rewards that they receive. In contrast, low outcome interdependence exists in teams in which individual members receive rewards and punishments on the basis of their own performance, without regard to the performance of the team. Research into project teams involved in consulting, financial planning, and research and development shows that in teams in which members reflect on their performance, higher levels of outcome interdependence increase the amount of information shared among members, which promotes learning, and, ultimately, team performance.[34] As we discuss in the Application section at the end of this chapter, the way a team is designed with respect to outcome interdependence also has important implications for the level of cooperation and motivation in the team.

TEAM COMPOSITION

11.3

What factors are involved in team composition?

You probably already agree that team effectiveness hinges on **team composition**—or the mix of people who make up the team. If you've been a member of a particularly effective team, you may have noticed that the team seemed to have the right mix of abilities and personalities. Team members were not only capable of performing their role responsibilities effectively, but they also cooperated and got along fairly well together. In this section, we identify the most important characteristics to consider in team composition, and we describe how these elements combine to influence team functioning and effectiveness. As shown in Figure 11-4, five aspects of team composition are crucial: roles, ability, personality, diversity and team size.

MEMBER ROLES. A **role** is defined as a pattern of behavior that a person is expected to display in a given context.[35] In a team setting, there are a variety of roles that members can take or develop in the course of interacting with one another, and depending on the specific situation, the presence or absence of members who possess these roles may have a strong impact on team effectiveness.[36] One obvious way to distinguish roles is to consider the role of the leader and the role of members. In **leader–staff teams**, the leader makes decisions for the team and provides direction and control over members who perform assigned tasks, so this distinction makes sense in that the responsibilities of the leader and the rest of the team are distinct.[37] Typically, however, team members have some latitude with respect to the behaviors they exhibit. In these situations, team roles can be described in terms of three rather broad categories, which are shown in Table 11-3: team task roles, team building roles, and individualistic roles.[38]

FIGURE 11-4	Five Aspects of Team Composition

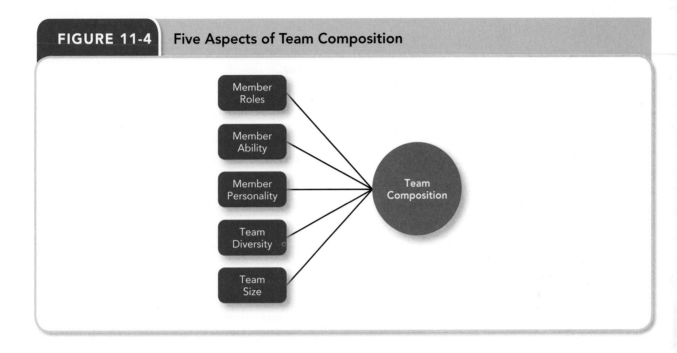

Team task roles refer to behaviors that directly facilitate the accomplishment of team tasks. Examples include the *orienter* who establishes the direction for the team, the *devil's advocate* who offers constructive challenges to the team's status quo, and the *energizer* who motivates team members to work harder toward team goals. As you may have realized, the importance of specific task-oriented roles depends on the nature of the work in which the team is involved. The orienter role may be particularly important in teams that have autonomy over how to accomplish their work. The devil's advocate role may be particularly important in team contexts in which decisions are "high stakes" in nature. Finally, the energizer role may be most important in team contexts in which the work is important but not intrinsically motivating.

In contrast to task-oriented roles, **team building roles** refer to behaviors that influence the quality of the team's social climate. Examples of team building roles include the *harmonizer* who steps in to resolve differences among teammates, the *encourager* who praises the work of teammates, and the *compromiser* who helps the team see alternative solutions that teammates can accept. As you might have gathered as you read these examples, the presence of members who take on social roles helps teams manage conflicts that could hinder team effectiveness.

Finally, whereas task roles and team building roles focus on activities that benefit the team, **individualistic roles** reflect behaviors that benefit the individual at the expense of the team. For example, the *aggressor* "puts down" or deflates fellow teammates. The *recognition seeker* takes credit for team successes. The *dominator* manipulates teammates to acquire control and power. If you've ever had an experience in a team in which members took on individualistic roles, you probably realize just how damaging they can be to the team. Individualistic role behaviors foster negative feelings among team members, which serves to hinder a team's ability to function and perform effectively.[39] As our **OB at the Bookstore** feature illustrates, team members who take on individualistic roles can cause real problems for a team.

| TABLE 11-3 | Team and Individualistic Roles |

TEAM TASK ROLES	DESCRIPTION
Initiator-contributor	Proposes new ideas
Coordinator	Tries to coordinate activities among team members
Orienter	Determines the direction of the team's discussion
Devil's advocate	Offers challenges to the team's status quo
Energizer	Motivates the team to strive to do better
Procedural-technician	Performs routine tasks needed to keep progress moving
TEAM BUILDING ROLES	**DESCRIPTION**
Encourager	Praises the contributions of other team members
Harmonizer	Mediates differences between group members
Compromiser	Attempts to find the halfway point to end conflict
Gatekeeper/expediter	Encourages participation from teammates
Standard setter	Expresses goals for the team to achieve
Follower	Accepts the ideas of teammates
INDIVIDUALISTIC ROLES	**DESCRIPTION**
Aggressor	Deflates teammates, expresses disapproval with hostility
Blocker	Acts stubbornly resistant and disagrees beyond reason
Recognition seeker	Brags and calls attention to him- or herself
Self-confessor	Discloses personal opinions inappropriately
Slacker	Acts cynically, nonchalantly, or goofs off
Dominator	Manipulates team members for personal control

Source: Adapted from K. Benne and P. Sheats, "Functional Roles of Group Members." *Journal of Social Issues* 4 (1948), pp. 41–49.

MEMBER ABILITY. Team members possess a wide variety of abilities (see Chapter 10 on Ability for more discussion of such issues). Depending on the nature of the tasks involved in the team's work, some of these may be important to consider in team design. For example, for teams involved in physical work, relevant physical abilities will be important to take into account. Consider the types of abilities that are required of pit crew members in stock car racing, where margins of victory can be one-tenth of a second. When a car pulls into pit row, pit crew members need to leap over the pit wall and lift heavy tires, jacks, and other equipment to get the race car back on the track—ideally in about 14 seconds. In this setting, flexibility, cardiovascular endurance, and explosive strength are required, and in fact, racing teams have hired professional trainers and even built gyms to improve these abilities of their pit crew members.[40]

It's also important to take cognitive abilities into account when designing teams. General cognitive ability is important to many different types of teams. In general, smarter teams perform better because teamwork tends to be quite complex.[41] Team members not

OB AT THE BOOKSTORE

BAD APPLES
by Brette McWhorter Sember & Terrence J. Sember (Avon, MA: Adams Business, 2009).

*A bad apple is bad for everyone, whether he causes an emotional drain on the people
on the team, a drain on resources, or negatively affects the company's bottom line.*

BAD APPLES

HOW TO MANAGE DIFFICULT EMPLOYEES,
ENCOURAGE GOOD ONES TO STAY,
AND BOOST PRODUCTIVITY

BRETTE MCWHORTER SEMBER AND TERRENCE J. SEMBER
FOREWORD BY ROSANNE T. DEE

With those words, Sember and Sember apply the cliché, "a
bad apple can spoil the whole barrel," to the problem of
a team member who is "particularly difficult, troublesome,
or hard to work with." Most of us have had experiences
with a teammate such as this, so it's easy to appreciate the
basic issue. That is, a team member who engages in certain types of individualistic behaviors can cause problems
that spread to negatively affect other team members as well
as the team itself. At a minimum, a bad apple contributes
less and distracts other members from the important tasks at
hand. However, it's often the case that bad apples engage in
behaviors that result in the spread of negative emotions and
thoughts to other members of the team.

A logical managerial response to bad apples is to fire
them. Unfortunately, there are many situations in which
doing so may not be feasible. For example, the bad apple might have skills or knowledge
needed in the team that would be difficult to replace if the person were terminated. As
another example, the bad apple might be politically connected, perhaps the nephew of
an owner of the business or a powerful executive. Whatever the reason, there are many
circumstances when it may be necessary to manage bad apples by trying to change
their behavior. So what's the best way to do this? The authors suggest that team leaders
or managers need to provide feedback to bad apples about specific behaviors that are
troublesome to the team. Gossiping, backstabbing, whining, lying, and being passive-
aggressive, combative, or narcissistic are classic examples of bad apple behavior. People
might not realize they are engaging in these behaviors or that their behavior hurts the
team; and even if they do, the feedback lets the offenders know that others are aware
of what they're doing and that it's a real problem. Of course, managing bad apples may
require more than just feedback, so the authors describe how various motivational and
disciplinary tactics could be used.

only have to be involved in several different aspects of the team's task, but they also have
to learn how best to combine their individual efforts to accomplish team goals.[42] In fact,
the more that this type of learning is required, the more important member cognitive ability
becomes. For example, research has shown that cognitive ability is more important to
teams when team members have to learn from one another to adapt to unexpected changes,
compared with contexts in which team members perform their assigned tasks in a routine
fashion.[43]

Of course, not every member needs high levels of these physical or cognitive abilities. If you've ever played Trivial Pursuit using teams, you might recall playing against
another team in which only one of the team members was smart enough to answer any

of the questions correctly. In fact, in tasks with an objectively verifiable best solution, the member who possesses the highest level of the ability relevant to the task will have the most influence on the effectiveness of the team. These types of tasks are called **disjunctive tasks**.[44] You may also recall situations in which it was crucial that everyone on the team possessed the relevant abilities. Returning to the pit crew example, stock cars cannot leave the pit area until all the tires are mounted, and so the length of the pit stop is determined by the physical abilities of the slowest crew member. Tasks like this, for which the team's performance depends on the abilities of the "weakest link," are called **conjunctive tasks**. Finally, there are **additive tasks**, for which the contributions resulting from the abilities of every member "add up" to determine team performance. The amount of money that a Girl Scout troop earns from selling Thin Mints and Samoas is the sum of what each Girl Scout is able to sell on her own.

MEMBER PERSONALITY. Team members also possess a wide variety of personality traits (see Chapter 9 on Personality and Cultural Values for more discussion of such issues). These personality traits affect the roles that team members take on,[45] as well as how teams function and perform as units.[46] For example, the agreeableness of team members has an important influence on team effectiveness.[47] Why? Because agreeable people tend to be more cooperative and trusting, and these tendencies promote positive attitudes about the team and smooth interpersonal interactions. Moreover, because agreeable people may be more concerned about their team's interests than their own, they should work hard on behalf of the team.[48] There is a caveat regarding agreeableness in teams, however. Because agreeable people tend to prefer harmony and cooperation rather than conflict and competition, they may be less apt to speak up and offer constructive criticisms that might help the team improve.[49] Thus, if a team is composed of too many highly agreeable members, there's a chance that the members will behave in a way that enhances harmony of the team at the expense of task accomplishment.[50]

As another example, team composition in terms of members' conscientiousness is important to teams.[51] After all, almost any team would benefit from having members who tend to be dependable and work hard to achieve team goals. What might be less obvious to you is the strong negative effect on the team of having even one member who is particularly low on conscientiousness.[52] To understand why this is true, consider how you would react to a team member who was not dependable and did not appear to be motivated

A task that can go only as quickly as the slowest team member, like a pit stop in a car race, is a conjunctive task.

to work hard toward team goals. If you're like most people, you would find the situation dissatisfying, and you would consider different ways of dealing with it. Some people might try to motivate the person to be more responsible and work harder; others might try to get the person ejected from the team.[53] The problem is that these natural reactions to a low conscientiousness team member not only divert attention away from accomplishing work responsibilities, but they also can result in some very uncomfortable and time-consuming interpersonal conflicts. Moreover, even if you and the other members of the team work harder to compensate for this person, it would be difficult for your team to perform as effectively as other teams in which all members are more interpersonally responsible and engaged in the team's work.

Finally, the personality characteristic of extraversion is relevant to team composition.[54] People who are extraverted tend to perform more effectively in interpersonal contexts and are more positive and optimistic in general.[55] Therefore, it shouldn't surprise you to hear that having extraverted team members is generally beneficial to the social climate of the group, as well as to team effectiveness in the eyes of supervisors.[56] At the same time, however, research has shown that having too many members who are very high on extraversion can hurt the team. The reason for this can be attributed to extraverts' tendency to be assertive and dominant. As you would expect when there are too many members with these types of tendencies, power struggles and unproductive conflict occur with greater frequency.[57]

DIVERSITY. Another aspect of team composition refers to the degree to which members are different from one another in terms of any attribute that might be used by someone as a basis of categorizing people. We refer to those differences as **team diversity**.[58] Trying to understand the effects of team diversity is somewhat difficult, because there are so many different characteristics that may be used to categorize people, and diversity on specific characteristics may matter more or less depending on the nature of the team and organizational context.[59] For example, you might imagine how the dynamics in a team consisting of both men and women could vary depending on whether the team is in an organization dominated by men (or women) or whether it is balanced in terms of the employees' sex. There are also several reasons diversity might influence team functioning and effectiveness, and some of these reasons seem contradictory.

The predominant theory that has been used to explain why diversity has positive effects is called the **value in diversity problem-solving approach**.[60] According to this perspective, diversity in teams is beneficial because it provides for a larger pool of knowledge and perspectives from which a team can draw as it carries out its work. Having greater diversity in knowledge perspectives stimulates the exchange of information, which in turn fosters learning among team members.[61] The knowledge that results from this learning is then shared and integrated with the knowledge of other members, ultimately helping the team perform more effectively.[62] Research has shown that these benefits of diversity are more likely to occur when the team includes members who are able and willing to put in the effort necessary to understand and integrate different perspectives.[63] Teams that engage in work that's relatively complex and requires creativity tend to benefit most from diversity, and research on teams that are diverse in terms of many different characteristics related to knowledge and perspectives—ethnicity, expertise, personality, attitudes—supports this idea.[64]

A theory that's been used widely to explain why diversity may have detrimental effects on teams is called the **similarity-attraction approach**.[65] According to this perspective, people tend to be more attracted to others who are perceived as more similar. People also tend to avoid interacting with those who are perceived to be dissimilar to reduce the likelihood of having uncomfortable disagreements. Consistent with this perspective, research has shown that diversity on attributes such as cultural background, race, and attitudes are associated with communication problems and ultimately poor team effectiveness.[66]

11.4

What are the types of team diversity and how do they influence team functioning?

Surface-level diversity can sometimes create issues for teams as they begin their tasks, but such problems usually disappear over time.

So it appears that there are two different theories about diversity effects that are relevant to teams, and each has been supported in research. Which perspective is correct? As it turns out, a key to understanding the impact of team diversity requires that you consider both the general type of diversity and the length of time the team has been in existence.[67] **Surface-level diversity** refers to diversity regarding observable attributes such as race, ethnicity, sex, and age.[68] Although this type of diversity may have a negative impact on teams early in their existence because of similarity-attraction issues, those negative effects tend to disappear as members become more knowledgeable about one another. In essence, the stereotypes that members have about one another based on surface differences are replaced with knowledge regarding underlying characteristics that are more relevant to social and task interactions.[69]

One complication here is that *faultlines* often occur in diverse groups, whereby informal subgroups develop based on similarity in surface-level attributes such as gender or other characteristics.[70] The problem with faultlines is that knowledge and information possessed by one subgroup may not be communicated to other subgroups in a manner that might help the entire team perform more effectively. Research has shown, however, that the detrimental effects of having subgroups can be offset with training that reinforces the idea that teams may benefit from their diversity.[71] Leadership or reward practices that reinforce the value of sharing information and promote a strong sense of team identity also help diverse teams perform more effectively.[72]

Deep-level diversity, in contrast, refers to diversity with respect to attributes that are less easy to observe initially but that can be inferred after more direct experience. Differences in attitudes, values, and personality are good examples of deep-level diversity.[73] In contrast to the effects of surface-level diversity, time appears to increase the negative effects of deep-level diversity on team functioning and effectiveness.[74] Over time, as team members learn more about one another, differences that relate to underlying values and goals become increasingly apparent. Those differences can therefore create problems among team members that ultimately result in reduced effectiveness. See our **OB Internationally** feature for a discussion of the challenges of managing deep-level diversity in teams that include members from different cultures.

We also should mention an important caveat here. Although personality is normally considered a deep-level diversity variable,[75] some specific personality types do not function this way.[76] In the previous section on personality, for example, we pointed out that though having team members who are extraverted and agreeable is generally a good thing, problems arise if a team has too many members with these attributes. So whereas diversity on most deep-level characteristics is problematic for teams, this claim does not apply to extraversion and agreeableness, because for these two personality characteristics, there are benefits to having a mix of members.

TEAM SIZE. Two adages are relevant to team size: "the more the merrier" or "too many cooks spoil the pot." Which statement do you believe is true in terms of how many members to include on a team? The answer, according to the results of one recent meta-analysis, is that having a greater number of members is beneficial for management and project teams but not for teams engaged in production tasks.[77] Management and project teams engage in work that's complex and knowledge intensive, and these teams therefore benefit from the additional resources and expertise contributed by additional members.[78]

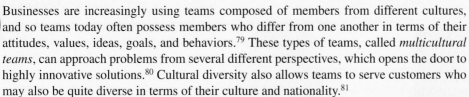

OB INTERNATIONALLY

Businesses are increasingly using teams composed of members from different cultures, and so teams today often possess members who differ from one another in terms of their attitudes, values, ideas, goals, and behaviors.[79] These types of teams, called *multicultural teams*, can approach problems from several different perspectives, which opens the door to highly innovative solutions.[80] Cultural diversity also allows teams to serve customers who may also be quite diverse in terms of their culture and nationality.[81]

Unfortunately, the attributes that give multicultural teams these advantages also give them disadvantages. As an example, people from different cultures communicate differently, which can lead to misunderstandings. For example, to people in the United States, the phrase "to table something" means to put it off until later, whereas in some European countries, it means discuss it right now.[82] Imagine your reaction if you didn't know this difference, and you told a team you were leading that you wanted to table something, and then one of your team members started to discuss options and recommendations about the issue. There are differences in the directness of communications as well. Westerners tend to be very direct and to the point, but to people in other countries, such as Japan, this directness may cause embarrassment and a sense of disrespect.[83] There are also cultural differences in decision-making processes.[84] In some cultures, decisions can be made only after careful consideration and reconsideration of all relevant issues, which is much different from the style in other cultures, such as the United States, where decisions are made rather quickly and with less analysis.[85] Although these differences might seem trivial, they often lead to misunderstandings that reduce the willingness of team members to cooperate. So how can multicultural teams be managed to ensure the advantages outweigh the disadvantages? Although there is no one best way to manage multicultural teams, one proven approach is to encourage teams to take the time to communicate openly about cultural differences and develop strategies to accommodate them.[86]

In contrast, production teams tend to engage in routine tasks that are less complex. Having additional members beyond what's necessary to accomplish the work tends to result in unnecessary coordination and communication problems. Additional members therefore may be less productive because there is more socializing, and they feel less accountable for team outcomes.[87] Although making a claim about the absolute best team size is impossible, research with undergraduate students concluded that team members tend to be most satisfied with their team when the number of members is between 4 and 5.[88] Of course, there are other rules of thumb you can use to keep teams size optimal. Jeff Bezos, the CEO of Amazon.com, uses the two-pizza rule: "If a team can't be fed by two pizzas, it's too large."[89]

SUMMARY: WHAT CHARACTERISTICS CAN BE USED TO DESCRIBE TEAMS?

The preceding sections illustrate that there are a variety of characteristics that can be used to describe teams. As Figure 11-5 illustrates, teams can be described using taxonomies of team types. For example, teams can be described by categorizing them as a work team, a management team, a parallel team, a project team, or an action team. Teams can also be described using the nature of the team's interdependence with regard to its task, goals, and outcomes. Finally, teams can be described in terms of their composition. Relevant member characteristics include member roles, member ability, member personality, member diversity, and team size.

FIGURE 11-5   What Characteristics Can Be Used to Describe Teams?

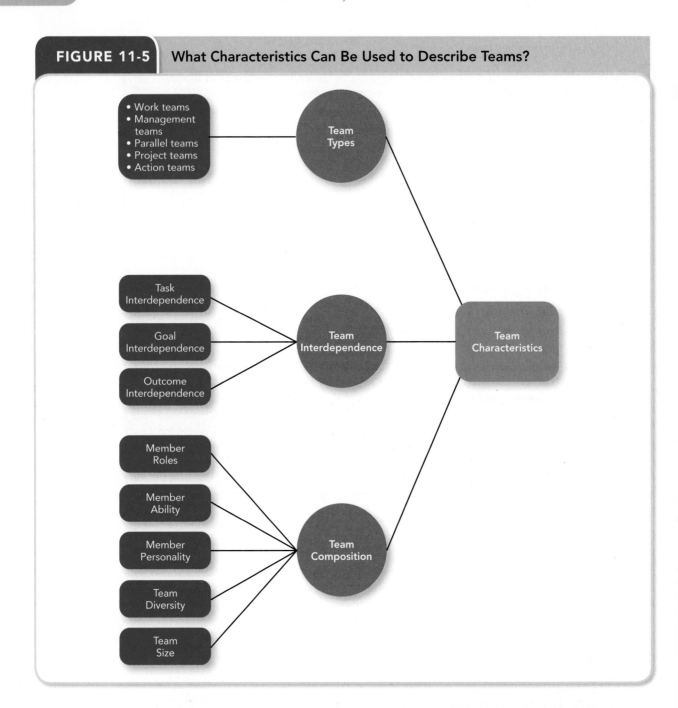

HOW IMPORTANT ARE TEAM CHARACTERISTICS?

In previous chapters, we have described individual characteristics and mechanisms and discussed how these variables affect individual performance and commitment. In this chapter, we're concerned with team characteristics, and so naturally, we're interested in how they influence team effectiveness. One aspect of team effectiveness is *team performance*, which may include metrics such as the quantity and quality of goods or services produced, customer satisfaction, the effectiveness or accuracy of decisions, victories, completed reports, and successful investigations. Team performance in the context of student project teams most often means the quality with which the team completes assignments and projects, as well as the grades they earn.

A second aspect of team effectiveness is team commitment, which is sometimes called team viability. **Team viability** refers to the likelihood that the team can work together effectively into the future.[90] If the team experience is not satisfying, members may become disillusioned and focus their energy on activities away from the team. Although a team with low viability might be able to work together on short-term projects, over the long run, a team such as this is bound to have significant problems.[91] Rather than planning for future tasks and working through issues that might improve the team, members of a team with low viability are more apt to be looking ahead to the team's ultimate demise.

Of course, it's difficult to summarize the relationship between team characteristics and team performance and commitment when there are so many characteristics that can be used to describe teams. Here we focus our discussion on the impact of task interdependence, because high task interdependence is one of the things that distinguishes true teams from mere groups of individuals. As Figure 11-6 shows, it turns out that the relationship between task interdependence and team performance is moderately positive.[92] That is, task performance tends to be higher in teams in which members depend on one another and have to coordinate their activities rather than when members work more or less independently. It's important to mention that the relationship between task interdependence and team performance is significantly stronger in teams that are responsible for completing complex knowledge work rather than simple tasks. When work is more complex, interdependence is necessary because there is a need for members to interact and share resources and information. When work is simple, sharing information and resources is less necessary because members can do the work by themselves.

In the lower portion of Figure 11-6, you can see that the relationship between task interdependence and team commitment is weaker.[93] Teams with higher task interdependence have only a slightly higher probability of including members who are committed to their team's continued existence. As with the relationship with team performance, task interdependence has a stronger effect on viability for teams doing complex knowledge work. Apparently, sharing resources and information in a context in which it's unnecessary is dissatisfying to members and results in a team with reduced prospects of continued existence.

11.5
How do team characteristics influence team effectiveness?

APPLICATION: TEAM COMPENSATION

Although all team characteristics have implications for managerial practices, outcome interdependence is particularly relevant for two reasons. First, outcome interdependence has obvious connections to compensation practices in organizations,[94] and most of us are interested in factors that determine how we get paid. If you work for an organization with compensation that has high outcome interdependence, a higher percentage of your pay will depend on how well your team does. If you work for an organization with compensation that has low outcome interdependence, a lower percentage of your pay will depend on how well your team does.

A second reason outcome interdependence is important to consider is that it presents managers with a tough dilemma. High outcome interdependence promotes higher levels of cooperation because members understand that they share the same fate—if the team

11.6
How can team compensation be used to manage team effectiveness?

| FIGURE 11-6 | Effects of Task Interdependence on Performance and Commitment |

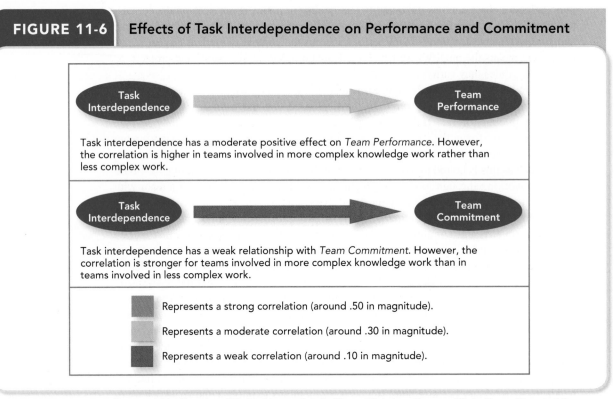

Task interdependence has a moderate positive effect on *Team Performance*. However, the correlation is higher in teams involved in more complex knowledge work rather than less complex work.

Task interdependence has a weak relationship with *Team Commitment*. However, the correlation is stronger for teams involved in more complex knowledge work than in teams involved in less complex work.

■ Represents a strong correlation (around .50 in magnitude).

■ Represents a moderate correlation (around .30 in magnitude).

■ Represents a weak correlation (around .10 in magnitude).

Sources: M.A. Campion, G.J. Medsker, and A.C. Higgs, "Relations Between Work Group Characteristics and Effectiveness: Implications for Designing Effective Work Groups," *Personnel Psychology* 46 (1993), pp. 823–49; M.A. Campion, E.M. Papper, and G.J. Medsker, "Relations Between Work Team Characteristics and Effectiveness: A Replication and Extension," *Personnel Psychology* 49 (1996), pp. 429–52; and G.L. Stewart, "A Meta-Analytic Review of Relationships Between Team Design Features and Team Performance," *Journal of Management* 32 (2006), pp. 29–54.

wins, everyone wins, and if the team fails, everyone fails.[95] At the same time, high outcome interdependence may result in reduced motivation, especially among higher performing members. High performers may perceive that they're not paid in proportion to what they contributed to the team and that their teammates are taking advantage of this inequity for their own benefit.[96]

One solution to this dilemma has been to design team reward structures with **hybrid outcome interdependence**, which means that members receive rewards that are dependent on both their team's performance and how well they perform as individuals.[97] In fact, the majority of organizations that use teams use some sort of hybrid outcome interdependence. But what percentage of team members' pay is typically based on team performance in business organizations? This is a difficult question to answer, because as we discussed earlier in the chapter, there are so many different types of teams doing so many different types of tasks, and also because organizations vary dramatically in their approaches to rewarding their employees. For example, the size of team-based pay in the goods and service sectors averages around 10–12 percent of an employee's base pay.[98] In contrast, production workers at Nucor, the Crawfordsville, Indiana–based steel company, earn team-based bonuses of 170 percent of their base pay, on average.[99] It's important to note that hybrid outcome interdependence, in and of itself, may not always be that effective in promoting team functioning and effectiveness. Research conducted at Xerox, for example, shows that service teams with hybrid outcome interdependence are less effective than service teams with very high or very low levels of outcome interdependence.[100] Part of the problem with hybrid outcome interdependence is that it can lead to uncertainty about which types of behaviors are being rewarded and how pay ultimately is determined. To make hybrid interdependence work, organizations need to ensure that the system makes sense to employees. At Nucor, most production workers know within one-tenth of 1 percent what the team's bonus is for the week, as well as which products will be produced next and how these future operations will likely affect their bonuses.[101]

One way to resolve the dilemma of outcome interdependence is to implement a level of team-based pay that matches the level of task interdependence. Members tend to be more productive in high task interdependence situations when there is also high outcome interdependence. Similarly, members prefer low task interdependent situations when there is low outcome interdependence.[102] To understand the power of aligning task and outcome interdependence, consider scenarios in which there is not a good match. For example, how would you react to a situation in which you worked very closely with your teammates on a team project in one of your classes, and thought your professor said the team's project was outstanding, yet she awarded an A to one of your team members, a B to another, and a C to you? Similarly, consider how you would react to a situation in which you scored enough points for an A on your final exam, but your professor averaged everyone's grades together and gave all students a C. Chances are you wouldn't be happy with either scenario.

TAKEAWAYS

11.1   There are several different types of teams—work teams, management teams, action teams, project teams, and parallel teams—but many teams in organizations have characteristics that fit in multiple categories and differ from one another in other ways.

11.2   Teams can be interdependent in terms of the team task, goals, and outcomes. Each type of interdependence has important implications for team functioning and effectiveness.

11.3   Team composition refers to the characteristics of the members who work in the team. These characteristics include roles, ability, personality, and member diversity, as well as the number of team members.

11.4   The effect of diversity on the team depends on time and whether the diversity is surface-level or deep-level. The effects of surface-level diversity tend to diminish with time, whereas the effects of deep-level diversity tend to increase over time.

11.5   Task interdependence has a moderate positive relationship with team performance and a weak relationship with team commitment.

11.6   Outcome interdependence has important effects on teams, which can be managed with compensation practices that take team performance into account.

KEY TERMS

DISCUSSION QUESTIONS

11.1   Prior to reading this chapter, would have you made a distinction between groups and teams? After reading this chapter, has your position changed, and if so, how?

11.2   In which types of teams have you worked? Were these teams consistent with the team types discussed in this chapter, or were they a combination of types?

11.3   Think about your student teams. Which aspects of both models of team development apply the most and least to teams in this context?

11.4   Think about a highly successful team with which you are familiar. What types of task, goal, and outcome interdependence does this team have? Describe how changes in task, goal, and outcome interdependence might have a negative impact on this team.

11.5   What type of roles do you normally take on in a team setting? Are there task or social roles that you simply don't perform well? If so, why do you think this is?

11.6   Do you think student teams function best in an additive, disjunctive, or conjunctive manner? What are the advantages and disadvantages of each structure?

11.7   What is the most important team composition factor in your student teams? If a student team has limitations in its composition, what can it do to improve?

CASE: LOGITECH

Logitech's success in bringing a large number of innovative products to market can be attributed to the type of teams they use to accomplish product development and manufacturing. The teams consist of members who are specialized in a given functional area and who are geographically dispersed across different countries and continents.[103] Work in these teams is accomplished continuously as members in one location use electronic communications to coordinate their efforts and hand off their work to members in other locations. Although this approach to accomplishing work has advantages and has enabled Logitech's remarkable growth over the last decade, there are some significant challenges to managing teams designed in this manner. For example, Peter Sheehan, a creative director from Ireland, noted that people tend to approach the work very differently based on their functional areas, which is a problem because the members of the Logitech teams are very specialized.[104] Although all members may understand that the ultimate goal is to develop a successful product, members from different areas may have different ideas about what "successful" means and what processes and outcomes need to be achieved to get there. Because of the geographical separation, inconsistencies in the way different members are approaching the work may not become apparent until significant problems occur.

Other companies in the electronics industry that use the "follow the sun" approach are struggling with similar issues. For example, IBM uses the approach in its chip design business, whereby design changes made during the day in North America get sent to India for additional work and physical implementation.[105] As noted by Mike Gruver, an IBM program manager, it's often difficult to tell whether someone from a different culture really understands what you're saying, and it's uncomfortable to keep on asking if they want you to restate something that you said.[106] As another example, Kathleen Gillam, a manager from Intel, noted that despite the positives from the use of globally distributed virtual teams, there are very simple things, such as having different holidays and working days, that make the process difficult.[107] In the end, the follow the sun approach to accomplishing work appears to have advantages, but there are also significant challenges having to do with managing differences among members in their functional and cultural backgrounds.

11.1   Describe the teams that Logitech uses to develop new products in terms of the characteristics outlined in this chapter. Do these teams fit into one of the "types" from the taxonomy presented in this chapter? If so, which one? If not, why?

11.2   In what ways are the teams at Logitech diverse? Describe the potential advantages and disadvantages of these types of diversity. Why might the advantages of these types of diversity outweigh the disadvantages in the context of the follow the sun teams?

11.3   If you were charged with creating a follow the sun team to develop a new product, what characteristics would you include in your design to ensure that the team is effective?

EXERCISE: PAPER PLANE CORPORATION

The purpose of this exercise is to analyze the advantages and disadvantages of sequential versus pooled interdependence on a team production project. This exercise uses groups, so your instructor will either assign you to a group or ask you to create your own group. The exercise has the following steps.

11.1 Your professor will supply you with the materials you need to create your final product (as many paper airplanes as you can fold to quality standards in three 5-minute rounds). Instructions for folding the paper airplanes and judging their quality are provided below. Before you start work on your airplanes, do the following:

a. As a group, select a team manager (who will supervise operations and get additional resources as needed) and a team inspector (who will judge the quality of the work on airplanes).

b. Familiarize yourself with how to make a paper airplane by folding one according to the instructions.

c. Be sure you are in a space where all of the team members can work comfortably.

d. To the extent possible, move away from other groups.

e. Familiarize yourself with the information about the Paper Plane Corporation.

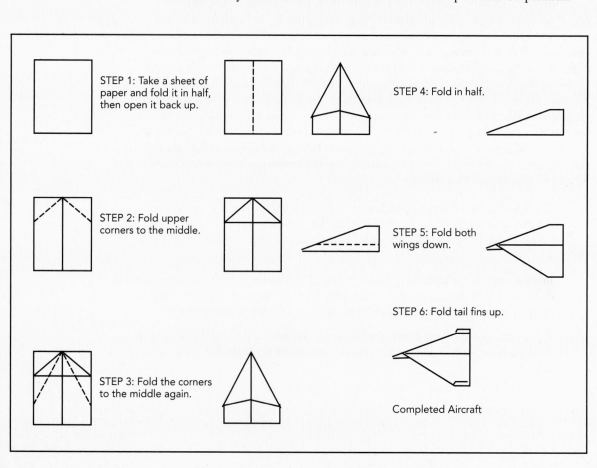

STEP 1: Take a sheet of paper and fold it in half, then open it back up.

STEP 2: Fold upper corners to the middle.

STEP 3: Fold the corners to the middle again.

STEP 4: Fold in half.

STEP 5: Fold both wings down.

STEP 6: Fold tail fins up.

Completed Aircraft

11.2 Your group is the complete workforce for the Paper Plane Corporation. Established in 1943, Paper Plane has led the market in paper plane production. Presently under new management, the company is contracting to make aircraft for the U.S. Air Force. You must determine the most efficient method for producing these aircraft. You must make your contract with the Air Force under the following conditions:

   a. The Air Force will pay $200,000 per airplane.

   b. The aircraft must pass a strict inspection by a quality control manager.

   c. A penalty of $250,000 per airplane will be subtracted for each failure to meet the production requirements.

   d. Labor and other overhead will be computed at $3,000,000.

   e. Cost of materials will be $30,000 per bid plane. If you bid for 10 but only make 8, you must pay the cost of materials for those you failed to make or those that did not pass inspection.

11.3 In the first round of airplane manufacturing process, the Air Force has asked you to focus on individuality. Each Paper Plane worker should manufacture his or her own planes from start to finish. When each plane is finished, it should be put in a central location for quality inspection. When time is called, you will record your team profit on the Summary Sheet.

11.4 In the second round of manufacturing, the Air Force has asked you to give each worker a specific job. In other words, the manufacturing process will take place in an assembly-line fashion. When planes come off the assembly line, they will be given directly to the quality control manager for inspection. When time is called, you will record your team profit on the Summary Sheet.

11.5 In the final round of manufacturing, the Air Force has asked your team to devise a manufacturing process that will maximize both efficiency and effectiveness. You may do whatever you like in terms of creating paper airplanes. You will have the same amount of time that you did in the two previous rounds. When time is called, you will record your team profit on the Summary Sheet.

11.6 Class discussion (whether in groups or as a class) should center on the following questions:

   a. Did pooled interdependence (Round 1) or sequential interdependence (Round 2) work better for your group in terms of the number of planes made correctly? Why do you think you got the result you did?

b. How did you change your work structure in Round 3? Did the changes you implemented help you achieve better productivity? Why or why not?

c. From your perspective, what are the advantages and disadvantages of pooled and/ or sequential interdependence?

Round 1
   Bid: _____ Aircraft @ $200,000 per aircraft = _____
   Results: _____ Aircraft @ $200,000 per aircraft = _____
   Subtract: $3,000,000 overhead + _____ × $30,000 cost of raw materials +
   _____ × $250,000 penalty for not completing a bid plane = _____
   Profit: _____

Round 2
   Bid: _____ Aircraft @ $200,000 per aircraft = _____
   Results: _____ Aircraft @ $200,000 per aircraft = _____
   Subtract: $3,000,000 overhead + _____ × $30,000 cost of raw materials +
   _____ × $250,000 penalty for not completing a bid plane = _____
   Profit: _____

Round 4
   Bid: _____ Aircraft @ $200,000 per aircraft = _____
   Results: _____ Aircraft @ $200,000 per aircraft = _____
   Subtract: $3,000,000 overhead + _____ × $30,000 cost of raw materials +
   _____ × $250,000 penalty for not completing a bid plane = _____
   Profit: _____

Sources: Adapted from J.M. Ivancevich, R. Konopaske, and M. Matteson, *Organizational Behavior and Management*, 7th ed. (Chicago: McGraw-Hill/Irwin, 2005). Original exercise by Louis Potheni in F. Luthans, *Organizational Behavior* (New York: McGraw-Hill, 1985), p. 555.

ENDNOTES

11.1 Logitech, "Annual Report 2008," http://ww3.ics.adp.com/ streetlink_data/dirLOGI/annual/ HTML2/default.htm (accessed June 20, 2009).

11.2 Logitech, corporate Web site, http://www.logitech.com/index. cfm/175/481&cl=us,en (accessed June 23, 2008).

11.3 Logitech, "Annual Report 2008."

11.4 Schiff, D. "Global Teams Rock around the Clock." *Electronic Engineering Times* 1435 (August 7, 2006), pp. 12, 20.

11.5 Ibid.

11.6 Godinez, V. "Sunshine 24/7: As EDS' Work Stops in One Time Zone, It Picks Up in Another." *Knight Ridder Tribune Business News,* January 2, 2007, ProQuest database (February 12, 2007); Schiff, "Global Teams Rock"; and Treinen and Miller-Frost, "Following the Sun: Case Studies in Global Software Development." *IBM Systems Journal* 45 (2006), pp. 773–83. "

11.7 Treinen and Miller-Frost, "Following the Sun."

11.8 Ilgen, D.R.; D.A. Major; J.R. Hollenbeck; and D.J. Sego. "Team

Research in the 1990s." In *Leadership Theory and Research: Perspectives and Directions,* ed. M.M. Chemers and R. Ayman. New York: Academic Press, Inc., 1993, pp. 245–70.

11.9 Devine, D.J.; L.D. Clayton; J.L. Philips; B.B. Dunford; and S.B. Melner. "Teams in Organizations: Prevalence, Characteristics, and Effectiveness." *Small Group Research* 30 (1999), pp. 678–711; Gordan, J. "Work Teams: How Far Have They Come?" *Training* 29 (1992), pp. 59–65; and Lawler, E.E., III; S.A. Mohrman; and G.E. Ledford Jr. *Creating High Performance Organizations: Practices and Results of Employee Involvement and Total Quality Management in* Fortune *1000 Companies.* San Francisco: Jossey-Bass, 1995.

11.10 Stewart, G.L.; C.C. Manz; and H.P. Sims Jr. *Team Work and Group Dynamics.* New York: John Wiley & Sons, 1999.

11.11 Ibid.

11.12 Boning, B; C. Ichniowski; and K. Shaw. "Opportunity Counts: Teams and the Effectiveness of Production Incentives." *Journal of Labor Economics* 25 (2007), pp. 613–50.

11.13 Cohen, S.G., and D.E. Bailey. "What Makes Teams Work: Group Effectiveness Research from the Shop Floor to the Executive Suite." *Journal of Management* 23 (1997), pp. 239–90.

11.14 Ibid.

11.15 Ibid.

11.16 Sundstrom, E.; M. McIntyre; T. Halfhill; and H. Richards. "Work Groups: From the Hawthorne Studies to Work Teams of the 1990s and Beyond." *Group Dynamics, Theory, Research, and Practice* 4 (2000), pp. 44–67.

11.17 Schlender, B. "The Man who Built Pixar's Incredible Innovation Machine." *Fortune*, November 15, 2004, p. 206. ProQuest database (May 28, 2007).

11.18 Tuckman, B.W. "Developmental Sequence in Small Groups." *Psychological Bulletin* 63 (1965), pp. 384–99; and Tuckman, B.W., and M.A.C. Jensen. "Stages of Small-Group Development Revisited." *Group and Organization Management* 2 (1977), pp. 419–27.

11.19 Gersick, C.J.G. "Time and Transition in Work Teams: Toward a New Model of Group Development." *Academy of Management Journal* 33 (1988), pp. 9–41; and Gersick, C.J.G. "Marking Time: Predictable Transitions in Task Groups." *Academy of Management Journal* 32 (1989), pp. 274–309.

11.20 Thompson, J.D. *Organizations in Action.* New York: McGraw-Hill, 1967; and Van de Ven, A.H.; A.L. Delbeccq; and R. Koenig. "Determinants of Coordination Modes within Organizations." *American Sociological Review* 41 (1976), pp. 322–38.

11.21 Ibid.

11.22 Thompson, *Organizations in Action.*

11.23 Ibid.

11.24 Ibid.

11.25 Van de Ven et al., "Determinants of Coordination Modes."

11.26 Kelley, T. *The Art of Innovation.* New York: Doubleday, 2001.

11.27 Saavedra, R.; P.C. Earley; and L. Van Dyne. "Complex

Interdependence in Task Perform-ing Groups." *Journal of Applied Psychology* 78 (1993), pp. 61–72.

11.28   Deutsch, M. *The Resolution of Conflict.* New Haven, CT: Yale University Press, 1973; and Wong, A.; D. Tjosvold; and Zi-you Yu. "Organizational Partner-ships in China: Self-Interest, Goal Interdependence, and Opportun-ism." *Journal of Applied Psychol-ogy* 90 (2005), pp. 782–91.

11.29   MacMillan, P.S. *The Performance Factor: Unlocking the Secrets of Teamwork.* Nashville, TN: Broad-man & Holman Publishers, 2001.

11.30   Ibid.

11.31   Ibid.

11.32   Mathieu, J.E., and T.L. Rapp. "The Foundation for Successful Team Performance Trajectories: The Roles of Team Charters and Performance Strategies. *Journal of Applied Psychology* 94 (2009), pp. 90–103.

11.33   Shea, G.P., and R.A. Guzzo. "Groups as Human Resources." In *Research in Personnel and Human Resources Management,* Vol. 5, eds. K.M. Rowland and G.R. Ferris. Greenwich CT: JAI Press, 1987, pp. 323–56.

11.34   De Dreu, C.K.W. "Outcome Inter-dependence, Task Reflexivity, and Team Effectiveness: Motivated Information Processing Perspec-tive." *Journal of Applied Psychol-ogy* 92 (2007), pp. 628–38.

11.35   Biddle, B.J. *Role Theory: Expecta-tions, Identities, and Behavior.* New York: Academic Press; and Katz, D., and R. L. Kahn. *The Social Psychology of Organizations.* 2nd ed. New York: John Wiley & Sons.

11.36   Humphrey, S.E.; F.P. Morgeson; and M. J. Mannor. "Developing

a Theory of the Strategic Core of Teams: A Role Composition Model of Team Performance." *Journal of Applied Psychology* 94 (2009), pp. 48–61.

11.37   Brehmer, B., and R. Hagafors. "Use of Experts in Complex Deci-sion Making: A Paradigm for the Study of Staff Work." *Orga-nizational Behavior and Human Decision Processes* 38 (1986), pp. 181–95.

11.38   Benne, K., and P. Sheats. "Func-tional Roles of Group Members." *Journal of Social Issues* 4 (1948), pp. 41–49.

11.39   Cole, M.S; F. Walter; and H. Bruch. "Affective Mechanisms Linking Dysfunctional Behavior to Performance in Work Teams: A Moderated Mediation Study." *Journal of Applied Psychology* 95 (2008), pp. 945–58.

11.40   Spencer, L. "Conditioning Has Become an Important Tool: Let's Get Physical." *Stock Car Racing.* http://www.stockcarracing.com/ howto/stock_car_pit_crew_ conditioning/ (accessed February 8, 2007).

11.41   Devine, D.J., and J.L. Philips. "Do Smarter Teams Do Better: A Meta-Analysis of Cognitive Abil-ity and Team Performance." *Small Group Research* 32 (2001), pp. 507–32; and Stewart, G.L. "A Meta-Analytic Review of Relationships Between Team Design Features and Team Perfor-mance." *Journal of Management* 32 (2006), pp. 29–54.

11.42   LePine, J.A.; J.R. Hollenbeck; D.R. Ilgen; and J. Hedlund. "Effects of Individual Differences on the Performance of Hierar-chical Decision-Making Teams: Much More than g." *Journal of*

Applied Psychology 82 (1997), pp. 803–11.

11.43 LePine, J.A. "Team Adaptation and Postchange Performance: Effects of Team Composition in Terms of Members' Cognitive Ability and Personality." *Journal of Applied Psychology* 88 (2003), pp. 27–39; and LePine, J.A. "Adaptation of Teams in Response to Unforeseen Change: Effects of Goal Difficulty and Team Composition in Terms of Cognitive Ability and Goal Orientation." *Journal of Applied Psychology* 90 (2005), pp. 1153–67.

11.44 Steiner, I.D. *Group Process and Productivity.* New York: Academic Press, 1972.

11.45 Stewart, G.L.; I.S. Fulmer; and M.R. Barrick. "An Exploration of Member Roles as a Multilevel Linking Mechanism for Individual Traits and Team Outcomes." *Personnel Psychology* 58 (2005), pp. 343–65.

11.46 Bell, S.T. "Deep Level Composition Variables as Predictors of Team Performance: A Meta-Analysis. *Journal of Applied Psychology* 92 (2007), pp. 395–415; and Peeters, M.A.G.; H.F.J.M Tuijl; C.G. van Rutte; and I.M.M.J. Reymen. "Personality and Team Performance: A Meta-Analysis." *European Journal of Personality* 20 (2006), pp. 377–96.

11.47 Ibid.

11.48 Comer, D.R. "A Model of Social Loafing in Real Work Groups." *Human Relations* 48 (1995), pp. 647–67; and Wagner, J.A., III. "Studies of Individualism–Collectivism: Effects on Cooperation in Groups." *Academy of Management Journal* 38 (1995), pp. 152–72.

11.49 LePine, J.A., and L. Van Dyne. "Voice and Cooperative Behavior as Contrasting Forms of Contextual Performance: Evidence of Differential Relationships with Personality Characteristics and Cognitive Ability." *Journal of Applied Psychology* 86 (2001), pp. 326–36.

11.50 McGrath, J.E. "The Influence of Positive Interpersonal Relations on Adjustment and Interpersonal Relations in Rifle Teams." *Journal of Abnormal and Social Psychology* 65 (1962), pp. 365–75.

11.51 Bell, "Deep Level Composition Variables"; Peeters et al., "Personality and Team Performance."

11.52 Barrick, M.R.; G.L. Stewart; M.J. Neubert; and M.K. Mount. "Relating Member Ability and Personality to Work-Team Processes and Team Effectiveness." *Journal of Applied Psychology* 83 (1998), pp. 377–91; LePine et al., "Effects of Individual Differences"; and Neuman, G.A., and J. Wright. "Team Effectiveness: Beyond Skills and Cognitive Ability." *Journal of Applied Psychology,* 84 (1999), pp. 376–89.

11.53 LePine, J.A., and L. Van Dyne. "Peer Responses to Low Performers: An Attributional Model of Helping in the Context of Work Groups." *Academy of Management Review* 26 (2001), pp. 67–84.

11.54 Bell, "Deep Level Composition Variables"; Peeters et al., "Personality and Team Performance."

11.55 Barrick, M.R., and M.K. Mount. "The Big Five Personality Dimensions and Job Performance: A Meta-Analysis." *Personnel Psychology* 44 (1991), pp. 1–26.

11.56 Barrick et al., "Relating Member Ability and Personality."

11.57 Barry, B., and G.L. Stewart. "Composition, Process, and Performance in Self-Managed Groups: The Role of Personality." *Journal of Applied Psychology* 82 (1997), pp. 62–78.

11.58 Williams, K., and C. O'Reilly. "The Complexity of Diversity: A Review of Forty Years of Research." In *Research in Organizational Behavior,* Vol. 21, eds. B. Staw and R. Sutton. Greenwich, CT: JAI Press, 1998, pp. 77–140.

11.59 Joshi, A., and H. Roh. "The Role of Context in Work Team Diversity Research: A Meta-Analytic Review. *Academy of Management Journal* 52 (2009), pp. 599–627.

11.60 Cox, T.; S. Lobel; and P. McLeod. "Effects of Ethnic Group Cultural Differences on Cooperative and Competitive Behavior on a Group Task." *Academy of Management Journal* 34 (1991), pp. 827–47; and Mannix, E., and M.A. Neal. "What Differences Make a Difference? The Promise and Reality of Diverse Teams in Organizations." *Psychological Science in the Public Interest* 6 (2005), pp. 31–55.

11.61 van Knippenberg, D.; C. K.W. DeDreu; and A.C. Homan. "Work Group Diversity and Group Performance: An Integrative Model and Research Agenda." *Journal of Applied Psychology* 89 (2004), pp. 1008–22.

11.62 Ibid.

11.63 Kearney, E.; D. Gebert; and S.C. Voelpel. "When and How Diversity Benefits Teams: The Importance of Team Members' Need for Cognition." *Academy of*

Management Journal 52 (2009), pp. 581–98.

11.64 Canella, A.A., Jr.; J.H. Park; and H.U. Lee. "Top Management Team Functional Background Diversity and Firm Performance: Examining the Roles of Team Member Colocation and Environmental Uncertainty." *Academy of Management Journal* 51 (2008), pp. 768–84; Gruenfeld, D.H.; E.A. Mannix; K.Y. Williams; and M.A. Neale. "Group Composition and Decision Making: How Member Familiarity and Information Distribution Affect Processes and Performance." *Organizational Behavior and Human Decision Processes* 67 (1996), pp. 1–15; Hoffman, L. "Homogeneity and Member Personality and Its Effect on Group Problem Solving." *Journal of Abnormal and Social Psychology* 58 (1959), pp. 27–32; Hoffman, L., and N. Maier. "Quality and Acceptance of Problem Solutions by Members of Homogeneous and Heterogeneous Groups." *Journal of Abnormal and Social Psychology* 62 (1961), pp. 401–7; Nemeth, C.J. "Differential Contributions of Majority and Minority Influence." *Psychological Review* 93 (1986), pp. 22–32; Stasster, G.; D. Steward; and G. Wittenbaum. "Expert Roles and Information Exchange During Discussion: The Importance of Knowing Who Knows What." *Journal of Experimental Social Psychology* 57 (1995), pp. 244–65; Triandis, H.; E. Hall; and R. Ewen. "Member Heterogeneity and Dyadic Creativity." *Human Relations* 18 (1965), pp. 33–55; and Watson, W.; K. Kuman; and I. Michaelsen. "Cultural Diversity's Impact on Interaction Process and Performance: Comparing Homogeneous and

Diverse Task Groups." *Academy of Management Journal* 36 (1993), pp. 590–602.

11.65 Byrne, D. *The Attraction Paradigm.* New York: Academic Press, 1971; and Newcomb, T.M. *The Acquaintance Process.* New York: Holt, Rinehart, and Wilson, 1961.

11.66 Byrne, D.; G. Clore; and P. Worchel. "The Effect of Economic Similarity-Dissimilarity as Determinants of Attraction." *Journal of Personality and Social Psychology* 4 (1996), pp. 220–24; Lincoln, J., and J. Miller. "Work and Friendship Ties in Organizations: A Comparative Analysis of Relational Networks." *Administrative Science Quarterly* 24 (1979), pp. 181–99; Triandis, H. "Cognitive Similarity and Interpersonal Communication in Industry." *Journal of Applied Psychology* 43 (1959), pp. 321–26; and Triandis, H. "Cognitive Similarity and Communication in a Dyad." *Human Relations* 13 (1960), pp. 279–87.

11.67 Jackson, S.E.; K.E. May; and K. Whitney. "Understanding the Dynamics of Diversity in Decision-Making Teams." In *Team Decision-Making Effectiveness in Organizations,* eds. R.A. Guzzo and E. Salas. San Francisco: Jossey-Bass, 1995, pp. 204–61; and Milliken, F.J., and L.L. Martins. "Searching for Common Threads: Understanding the Multiple Effects of Diversity in Organizational Groups." *Academy of Management Review* 21 (1996), pp. 402–33.

11.68 Harrison, D.A.; K.H. Price; and M.P. Bell. "Beyond Relational Demography: Time and the Effects of Surface- and Deep-Level Diversity on Work Group Cohesion." *Academy of Management Journal* 41 (1998), pp. 96–107; and Harrison, D.A.; K.H. Price; J.H. Gavin; and A.T. Florey. "Time, Teams, and Task Performance: Changing Effects of Surface- and Deep-Level Diversity on Group Functioning." *Academy of Management Journal* 45 (2002), pp. 1029–45.

11.69 Ibid.

11.70 Lau, D, and J. K. Murnighan. "Demographic Diversity and Faultlines: The Compositional Dynamics of Organizational Groups." *Academy of Management Review* 23 (1998), pp. 325–40; and Lau, D., and J.K. Murnighan. "Interactions with Groups and Subgroups: The Effects of Demographic Faultlines." *Academy of Management Journal* 48 (2005), pp. 645–59.

11.71 Homan, A.C.; D. van Knippenberg; G.A. Van Kleef; and C.K. W. De Dreu. "Bridging Faultlines by Valuing Diversity: Diversity Beliefs, Information Elaboration, and Performance in Diverse Work Groups." *Journal of Applied Psychology* 92 (2007), pp. 1189–99.

11.72 Homan, A.C.; J.R. Hollenbeck; S.E. Humphrey; D. Van Knippenberg; D.R. Ilgen; and G.A. Van Kleef. "Facing Differences with an Open Mind: Openness to Experience, Salience of Intragroup Differences, and Performance of Diverse Work Groups." *Academy of Management Journal* 51 (2008), pp. 1204–22; and Kearney, E., and D. Gebert. "Managing Diversity and Enhancing Team Outcomes: The Promise of Transformational Leadership." *Journal of Applied Psychology* 94 (2009), pp. 77–89.

11.73 Ibid.

11.74   Ibid.

11.75   Bell, "Deep Level Composition Variables."

11.76   Humphrey, S.E.; J.R. Hollenbeck; C.J. Meyer; and D.R. Ilgen. "Trait Configurations in Self-Managed Teams: A Conceptual Examination of Seeding for Maximizing and Minimizing Trait Variance in Teams." *Journal of Applied Psychology* 92 (2007), pp. 885–92.

11.77   Stewart, "A Meta-Analytic Review."

11.78   Kozlowski, S.W.J., and B.S. Bell. "Work Groups and Teams in Organization." In *Comprehensive Handbook of Psychology: Industrial and Organizational Psychology,* Vol. 12, eds. W.C. Borman, D.R. Ilgen, and R.J. Klimoski. New York: John Wiley & Sons, 2003, pp. 333–75.

11.79   Harris, M. *Cultural Anthropology.* 2nd ed. New York: Harper and Row, 1987; and Triandis, H.C. *Culture and Social Behavior,* Chicago: McGraw-Hill, 1994.

11.80   Gupta, S. "Mine the Potential of Multicultural Teams: Mesh Cultural Differences to Enhance Productivity." *HR Magazine* (October 2008), pp. 79–84.

11.81   Ibid.

11.82   Ibid.

11.83   Brett, J.; K. Behfar; and M.C. Kern. "Managing Multicultural Teams." *Harvard Business Review* 84 (November, 2006), pp. 84–91.

11.84   Ibid.

11.85   Ibid.

11.86   Ibid.

11.87   Gooding, R.Z., and J.A. Wagner III. "A Meta-Analytic Review of the Relationship Between Size and Performance: The Productivity and Efficiency of Organizations and Their Subunits." *Administrative Science Quarterly* 30 (1985), pp. 462–81; and Markham, S.E.; F. Dansereau; and J.A. Alutto. "Group Size and Absenteeism Rates: A Longitudinal Analysis." *Academy of Management Journal* 25 (1982), pp. 921–27.

11.88   Hackman, J.R., and N.J. Vidmar. "Effects of Size and Task Type on Group Performance and Member Reactions." *Sociometry* 33 (1970), pp. 37–54.

11.89   Yank, J.L. "The Power of Number 4.6." *Fortune* 153, no. 11 (June 12, 2006), p. 122. ProQuest database (May 28, 2007).

11.90   Sundstrom, E.; K.P. De Meuse; and D. Futrell. "Work Teams: Applications and Effectiveness." *American Psychologist* 45 (1990), pp. 120–33.

11.91   Stewart et al., *Team Work and Group Dynamics.*

11.92   Stewart, "A Meta-Analytic Review."

11.93   Campion, M.A.; G.J. Medsker; and A.C. Higgs. "Relations Between Work Group Characteristics and Effectiveness: Implications for Designing Effective Work Groups." *Personnel Psychology* 46 (1993), pp. 823–49; and Campion, M.A.; E.M. Papper; and G.J. Medsker. "Relations Between Work Team Characteristics and Effectiveness: A Replication and Extension." *Personnel Psychology* 49 (1996), pp. 429–52.

11.94   DeMatteo, J.S.; L.T. Eby; and E. Sundstrom. "Team-Based Rewards: Current Empirical Evidence and Directions for Future Research." *Research in*

Organizational Behavior 20 (1998), pp. 141–83.

11.95 Deutsch, M.A. "A Theory of Cooperation and Competition." *Human Relations* 2 (1949), pp. 199–231.

11.96 Williams, K.; S.G. Harkins; and B. Latane. "Identifiability as a Deterrent to Social Loafing: Two Cheering Experiments." *Journal of Personality and Social Psychology* 40 (1981), pp. 303–11.

11.97 Lawler, E.E. *Strategic Pay: Aligning Organizational Strategies and Pay Systems.* San Francisco: Jossey-Bass, 1990.

11.98 O'Dell, C. *People, Performance, Pay.* American Productivity Institute, 1987, cited in DeMatteo et al., "Team-Based Rewards."

11.99 Bolch, M. "Rewarding the Team: Make Sure Team-Oriented Compensation Plans Are Designed Carefully." *HR Magazine* (2007), pp. 91–95.

11.100 Wageman, R. "Interdependence and Group Effectiveness." *Administrative Science Quarterly* 40 (1995), pp. 145–80.

11.101 Bolch, "Rewarding the Team".

11.102 Johnson, D.W.; G. Maruyama; R. Johnson; D. Nelson; and L. Skon. "Effects of Cooperative, Competitive, and Individualistic Goal Structures on Achievement: A Meta-Analysis." *Psychological Bulletin* 89 (1981), pp. 47–62; Miller, L.K., and R.L. Hamblin. "Interdependence, Differential Rewarding and Productivity." *American Sociological Review* 28 (1963), pp. 768–78; and Rosenbaum, M.E. "Cooperation and Competition." In *Psychology of Group Influence,* ed. P.B. Paulus. Hillsdale, NJ: Lawrence Erlbaum, 1980.

11.103 Schiff, "Global Teams Rock"; Treinen and Miller-Frost, "Following the Sun."

11.104 Ibid.

11.105 Ibid.

11.106 Ibid.

11.107 Ibid.

chapter 12

Teams: Processes and Communication

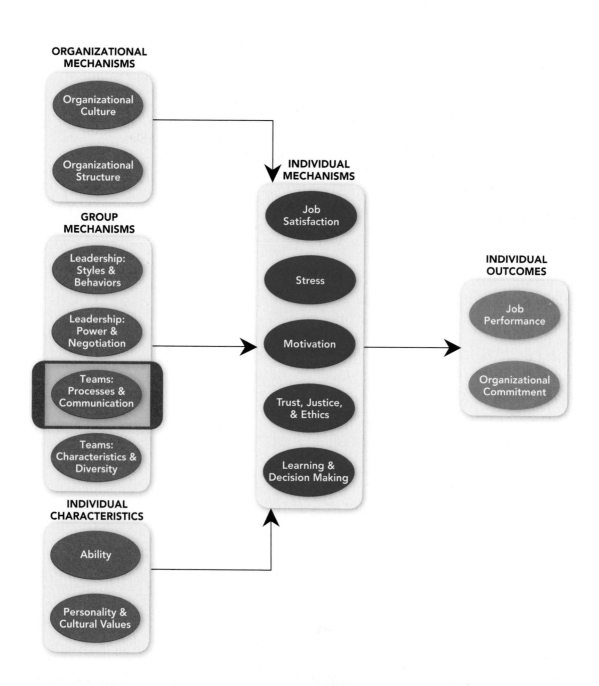

ORGANIZATIONAL
MECHANISMS

Organizational
Culture

Organizational
Structure

GROUP
MECHANISMS

Leadership:
Styles &
Behaviors

Leadership:
Power &
Negotiation

Teams:
Processes &
Communication

Teams:
Characteristics &
Diversity

INDIVIDUAL
CHARACTERISTICS

Ability

Personality &
Cultural Values

INDIVIDUAL
MECHANISMS

Job
Satisfaction

Stress

Motivation

Trust, Justice,
& Ethics

Learning &
Decision Making

INDIVIDUAL
OUTCOMES

Job
Performance

Organizational
Commitment

After reading this chapter, you should be able to answer the following questions:

12.1 What are taskwork processes, and what are some examples of team activities that fall into this process category?

12.2 What are teamwork processes, and what are some examples of team activities that fall into this process category?

12.3 What factors influence the communication process in teams?

12.4 What are team states, and what are some examples of the states that fall into this process category?

12.5 How do team processes affect team performance and team commitment?

12.6 What steps can organizations take to improve team processes?

UNITED AIRLINES

Even if you've never flown on United Airlines, chances are that you're familiar with the company—it's one of the oldest airlines in the world, with roots going back to the 1920s.[1] With its nearly 50,000 employees and a fleet of almost 400 aircraft that make more than 3,000 flights a day to over 200 domestic and international locations, it's also one of the world's largest airlines.[2] If you've gone online to a Web site like Expedia, Priceline, or Travelocity to find a flight, United Airlines was likely one of your options, especially if you needed to fly through San Francisco, Denver, Chicago, or Washington, DC, where United has major hubs. Of course, you also might be familiar with United Airlines because it's been in the news so much in the past decade. The most memorable news stories focused on the events of September 11, 2001, when terrorists hijacked two United Airlines jets—Flight 175, which crashed into the South Tower of the World Trade Center in New York City, and Flight 93, which crashed into a field in Pennsylvania.[3]

In part because of these hijackings, but also due to competition from low-cost rivals like Southwest, United Airlines filed for Chapter 11 bankruptcy protection in 2002.[4] United emerged from this bankruptcy in 2006 after taking some drastic and highly publicized steps to cut costs. For instance, United eliminated unprofitable routes and costly services such as free meals. The company also terminated its employees' pension plan,[5] and many United employees were laid off, furloughed, or forced to take pay cuts.[6] To improve its competitive position, United was faced with the difficult challenge of looking for ways to cut costs and improve services without further alienating its employees, whose efforts were needed to help the company make it through this difficult time period. One strategy involved reducing the amount of time it takes to "turn" an aircraft, or prepare it for its next departure. The job of turning an aircraft rests largely with the team of ramp workers who direct the aircraft into the gate after it lands, set up equipment to unload and reload passengers and cargo, and push it out of the gate for departure.[7] United figured that if it could reduce the amount of time between flights by 4 or 5 minutes, it might be able to schedule more than 100 additional flights a day without needing to purchase any additional aircraft.[8]

To put this plan into action, United identified the most efficient and consistent process that could be used to turn the planes, then trained its ramp workers in this process.[9] Part of the training was conducted at Pit Instruction and Training LLC—or "Pit Crew U," a school that teaches people how to become members of pit crews for automobile racing teams.[10] The job of a pit crew is to service a race car quickly and safely when it comes in for a pit stop during a race using a highly coordinated process. During the training, the ramp crew workers learned how to perform actual pit crew tasks, such as changing tires. However, the goal of the training was not to transform the ramp crew members into pit crew members. Rather, the training was intended to impart skills in the principles of teamwork, preparedness, and safety, that could be applied to the job of turning a plane more quickly. So how well has the training worked? The next time you're waiting for a flight at an airport, look out a window at a United Airlines gate and watch the ramp crews in action.

TEAM PROCESSES AND COMMUNICATION

As we described in Chapter 11 on Team Characteristics and Diversity, a team consists of two or more people who work interdependently over some time period to accomplish common goals related to some task-oriented purpose.[11] The effectiveness of organizations depends to a large extent on the activities and interactions that occur within teams as they move toward their task-related objectives. **Team process** is a term that reflects the different types of communication, activities, and interactions that occur within teams that contribute to their ultimate end goals.[12] Team characteristics, like member diversity, task interdependence, team size, and so forth, affect team processes and communication. Those processes, in turn, have a strong impact on team effectiveness.

Some of the team processes and forms of communication that we describe in this chapter are observable by the naked eye. An outside observer would be able to see members of United Airlines ramp crews communicating with one another to plan for the next arrival or solve a problem. Other processes, in contrast, are less visible. An outside observer wouldn't be able to see the sense of "cohesion" felt by the crew members or the shared "mental models" that cause them to work together so efficiently. Thus team processes include interactions among members that occur behaviorally, as well as the hard-to-see feelings and thoughts that coalesce as a consequence of member interactions.

WHY ARE SOME TEAMS MORE THAN THE SUM OF THEIR PARTS?

Take a second and try to think of a few teams that have been successful. It's likely that the success of some of these teams was expected because the team had members who are very talented and skilled. The success of other teams may be more difficult to understand just by looking at the rosters of their members. These teams might have members who appear to be less talented and skilled, but as they work together, they somehow became "more than the sum of their parts." Getting more from the team than you would expect according to the capabilities of its individual members is called **process gain**. This capability, which is synonymous with "synergy," is most critical in situations in which the complexity of the work is high or tasks require members to combine their knowledge, skills, and efforts to solve problems. In essence, process gain is important because it results in useful resources and capabilities that did not exist before the team created them.[13] Our **OB on Screen** feature illustrates vividly how a team that achieves process gain develops capabilities that help it achieve much more than what most people would rationally expect.

Having described process gain, we now consider its polar opposite. Consider this list of names: LeBron James, Dwyane Wade, Carmelo Anthony, Tim Duncan, and Allen Iverson. You don't have to be much more than a casual basketball fan to recognize those names as some of the best in professional basketball. Is that the roster of some all-NBA team? No, it's the roster of the USA Men's Basketball team that competed in the 2004 Olympics and 2006 World Championships. With a roster like that, it seems certain that the USA's "Dream Team" would've taken home gold in one or both of those events. Instead, they finished in third place in the 2004 Olympics, behind Argentina and Italy, and in third place again in the 2006 World Championship, behind Spain and Greece. What explains the poor showing? For some reason, the USA Men's Basketball team wound up being "less than the sum of its parts." That is, it seemed to be harmed by **process loss**, or getting less from the team than you would expect based on the capabilities of its individual members.

OB ON SCREEN

300

The world will know that free men stood against a tyrant, that few stood against many, and before this battle was over, that even a god-king can bleed.

With those words, King Leonidis (Gerard Butler) announces that his band of 300 Spartan soldiers is capable of pulling off a truly remarkable feat—standing against the Persian army led by Xerxes (Rodrigo Santoro) in the movie *300* (Dir. Zack Snyder, Warner Brothers, 2006). Why would that feat be so remarkable? Because the Persian army includes well over 100,000 soldiers (and a few mutated elephants and rhinos). The movie centers on the battle of Thermopylae, during which a small band of Spartans employed strategies and tactics that gave them the fighting capabilities of a much larger force. Those tactics represent a source of process gain, because the army was able to achieve more than you'd expect if you simply added up the capabilities of the individual soldiers.

Beyond simply illustrating the concept of process gain, the movie illustrates the role that team processes play in achieving it. The clearest example occurs when the Persian Army "darkens the sky" by launching tens of thousands of arrows simultaneously. When this happens, the Spartans immediately get into a tight formation, lift their shields, and then link them together in a manner that creates a collective shield over the entire formation (think a giant turtle shell, and you get the picture).

Although the movie vividly illustrates the power of process gain, it also alludes to its fragility. For example, as long as each and every soldier executes his part of the process of creating the collective shield, the tactic is effective, and the Spartans can withstand repeated onslaughts of countless arrows. However, if just one Spartan soldier fails to raise his shield on time, it creates a breach in the formation that will only widen as the soldier is struck down (thereby exposing the soldier next to him). Thus, a single soldier's failure in the team process could lead to the destruction of the entire army. This fact was not lost on King Leonidis, who in one scene rejects a volunteer for the Spartan army because the volunteer, though a fierce fighter, could not lift his shield over his head.

What factors conspire to create process loss? One factor is that in teams, members have to work to not only accomplish their own tasks but also coordinate their activities with the activities of their teammates.[14] Although this extra effort focused on integrating work is a necessary aspect of the team experience, it's called **coordination loss** because it consumes time and energy that could otherwise be devoted to task activity.[15] Such coordination losses are often driven by **production blocking**, which occurs when members have to wait on one another before they can do their part of the team task.[16] If you've ever worked in a team in which you felt like you couldn't get any of your own work done because of all the time spent in meetings, following up requests for information from other team members, and waiting on team members to do their part of the team task, you already understand how frustrating production blocking (and coordination loss) can be.

The second force that fosters process loss in team contexts is **motivational loss**, or the loss in team productivity that occurs when team members don't work as hard as they could.[17] Why does motivation loss occur in team contexts? One explanation is that it's often quite difficult to gauge exactly how much each team member contributes to the team. Members of teams can work together on projects over an extended period of time, and as a consequence, it's difficult to keep an accurate accounting of who does what. Similarly, members contribute to their team in many different ways, and contributions of some members may be less obvious than others. Finally, members of teams don't always work together at the same time as a unit. Regardless of the reasons for it, uncertainty regarding "who contributes what" results in team members feeling less accountable for team outcomes. Those feelings of reduced accountability, in turn, cause members to exert less effort when working on team tasks than they would if they worked alone on those same tasks. This phenomenon is called **social loafing**,[18] and it can significantly hinder a team's effectiveness.[19]

TASKWORK PROCESSES

Having described process gains and process losses, it's time to describe the particular team processes that can help teams increase their synergy while reducing their inefficiency. One relevant category of team processes is **taskwork processes**, which are the activities of team members that relate directly to the accomplishment of team tasks. In a general sense, taskwork occurs any time that team members interact with the tools or technologies that are used to complete their work. In this regard, taskwork is similar to the concept of task performance described in Chapter 2 on Job Performance. However, in the context of teams, especially those that engage in knowledge work, three types of taskwork processes are crucially important: creative behavior, decision making, and boundary spanning. These three taskwork processes are shown in Figure 12-1.

CREATIVE BEHAVIOR. When teams engage in creative behavior, their activities are focused on generating novel and useful ideas and solutions.[20] In Chapter 9 on Personality and Cultural Values, we noted that creative behavior is driven in part by the creativity of individual employees, because some employees are simply more original and imaginative than others. However, the team environment is also uniquely suited to fostering creative behavior.[21] As a consequence, organizations like Palo Alto–based IDEO, arguably the world's most successful product design firm, rely on teams to come together and combine their members' unique sets of knowledge and skill in a manner that results in novel and useful ideas.[22] However, achieving such outcomes depends on much more than just putting a diverse mix of people together and letting them go at it. In fact, creative behavior in teams can be fostered when members participate in a specific set of activities.

Perhaps the best-known activity that teams use to foster creative behavior is **brainstorming**. Generally speaking, brainstorming involves a face-to-face meeting of

12.1

What are taskwork processes, and what are some examples of team activities that fall into this process category?

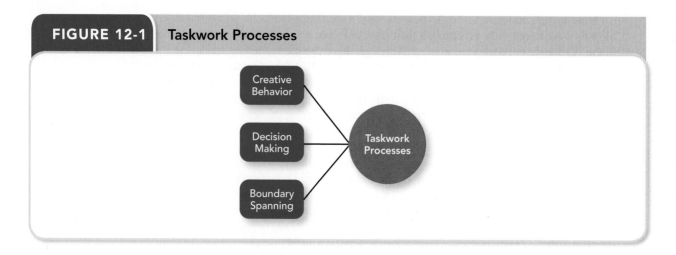

FIGURE 12-1 Taskwork Processes

team members in which each offers as many ideas as possible about some focal problem or issue.[23] Most brainstorming sessions center around the following rules:

1. Express all ideas that come to mind (no matter how strange).
2. Go for quantity of ideas rather than quality.
3. Don't criticize or evaluate the ideas of others.
4. Build on the ideas of others.

The theory is that if a team follows these rules, it will develop a large pool of ideas that it can use to address the issue at hand.[24] This concept sounds good in theory, and almost all of us have been in some sort of brainstorming meeting at some point. It may surprise you to learn then that such brainstorming sessions rarely work as well as intended. In fact, research suggests that team members would be better off coming up with ideas on their own, as individuals, before pooling those ideas and evaluating them to arrive at a solution.[25]

Why doesn't brainstorming work as well as individual idea generation? There appear to be at least three reasons.[26] First, there may be a tendency for people to social loaf in brainstorming sessions. That is, members may not work as hard thinking up ideas as they would if they had to turn in an individually generated list with their name on it. Second, though the brainstorming rules explicitly forbid criticizing others' ideas, members may be hesitant to express ideas that seem silly or not well thought-out. Third, brainstorming results in production blocking because members have to wait their turn to express their ideas. This waiting around consumes time that could otherwise be used by individuals to generate new ideas.

Given the problems associated with brainstorming, why do organizations continue to use it? One reason is that the general idea of brainstorming is well-known, and common sense leads people to believe that it works as advertised. Another reason is that there are benefits of brainstorming beyond just generating ideas. For example, brainstorming builds morale and results in the sharing of knowledge that might otherwise be locked inside the minds of the individual team members.[27] Although this knowledge may not be useful for the particular problem that's being debated, it might be useful for issues that arise in the future. To achieve the benefits of brainstorming, some companies take extra steps to ensure team members are fully engaged in the process of generating ideas. At IDEO, for example, brainstorming meetings often open with a warm-up session, typically a fast-paced word game to clear the minds of the participants.[28] Table 12-1 lists secrets of better brainstorming, as practiced at IDEO.

One offshoot of brainstorming that addresses some of its limitations is the **nominal group technique**.[29] Similar to a traditional brainstorming session, this process starts off by

TABLE 12-1	IDEO's Secrets for Brainstorming

WHAT TO DO	DESCRIPTION
Have a sharp focus	Begin the brainstorming with a clearly stated problem.
Playful rules	Encourage playfulness, but don't debate or critique ideas.
Number the ideas	Makes it easier to jump back and forth between ideas.
Build and jump	Build on and explore variants of ideas.
The space remembers	Use space to keep track of the flow of ideas in a visible way.
Stretch your brain	Warm up for the session by doing word games.
Get physical	Use drawings and props to make the ideas three-dimensional.
WHAT NOT TO DO	**DESCRIPTION**
The boss speaks first	Boss's ideas limit what people will say afterwards.
Give everybody a turn	Forcing equal participation reduces spontaneity.
Only include experts	Creative ideas come from unexpected places.
Do it offsite	You want creativity at the office too.
Limit the silly stuff	Silly stuff might trigger useful ideas.
Write down everything	The writing process can reduce spontaneity.

Source: T. Kelley and J. Littman, *The Art of Innovation* (New York: Doubleday, 2001).

bringing the team together and outlining the purpose of the meeting. The next step takes place on an individual level however, as members have a set period of time to write down their own ideas on a piece of paper. The subsequent step goes back into the team setting, as members share their ideas with the team in a round-robin fashion. After the ideas are recorded, members have a discussion intended to clarify the ideas and build on the ideas of others. After this, it's back to an individual environment; members rank order ideas on a card that they submit to a facilitator. A facilitator then tabulates the scores to determine the winning idea. From this description, you probably can guess how the nominal group technique addresses the problems with brainstorming. By making people write down ideas on their own, it decreases social loafing and production blocking. Although team members might still be hesitant about expressing wild ideas to the group, doing so might be less threatening than having nothing to contribute to the group. In addition, ranking items as individuals makes people less apprehensive about going "against the grain" of the group by voicing support for an unpopular idea.

DECISION MAKING. In Chapter 8 on Learning and Decision Making, we described how people use information and intuition to make specific decisions. In team contexts, however, decision making involves multiple members gathering and considering information that's relevant to their area of specialization, and then making recommendations to a team leader who is ultimately responsible for the final decision.[30] If you ever watched the TV show *The Apprentice,* you should be able to understand this process quite clearly. The show typically began with Donald Trump assigning two teams a fairly complex task. A member from each team then volunteered to be project leader, and this person assigned roles like marketing, logistics, and sales to the other team members. Throughout the project, members made suggestions and recommendations to the leader, who ultimately was responsible for making the decisions that determined the success of the project. Of course, project success was important because someone from the losing team—most often the project leader—got to hear Trump say those famous words: "You're fired."

What factors account for a team's ability to make effective decisions? At least three factors appear to be involved.[31] The first factor is **decision informity**, which reflects whether members possess adequate information about their own task responsibilities. Project teams on *The Apprentice* often failed, for example, because the team member in charge of marketing didn't gather information necessary to help the team understand the desires and needs of the client. The second factor is **staff validity**, which refers to the degree to which members make good recommendations to the leader. Team members can possess all the information needed to make a good recommendation but then fail to do so because of a lack of ability, insight, or good judgment. The third factor is **hierarchical sensitivity**, which reflects the degree to which the leader effectively weighs the recommendations of the members. Whom does the leader listen to, and whom does the leader ignore? Teams that make good decisions tend to have leaders that do a good job giving recommendations the weight they deserve. Together, these three variables play a large role in how effective teams are in terms of their decision making.[32]

The decision informity, staff validity, and hierarchical sensitivity concepts can be used to make specific recommendations for improving team decision making. For example, research shows that more experienced teams tend to make better decisions because they develop an understanding of the information that's needed and how to use it, and have leaders that develop an understanding of which members provide the best recommendations.[33] As another example, team decision making may be improved by giving members feedback about the three variables involved in the decision-making process.[34] For instance, a team can improve its decision making if the members are told that they have to share and consider additional pieces of information before making recommendations to the leader. Although this recommendation may seem obvious, all too often teams only receive feedback about their final decision. In addition, there may be a benefit to separating the process of sharing information from the process of making recommendations and final decisions, at least in terms of how information is communicated among members.[35] Whereas teams tend to share more information when they meet face-to-face, leaders do a better job considering recommendations and making final decisions when they're away from

Like many teams in the real world, the teams on the television show *The Apprentice* often struggled to make good decisions.

the members. Leaders who are separated don't have to deal with pressure from members who may be more assertive or better at articulating and defending their positions. Our **OB Internationally** feature describes additional considerations that need to be taken into account to improve decision making in culturally diverse teams.[36]

BOUNDARY SPANNING. The third type of taskwork process is **boundary spanning**, which involves three types of activities with individuals and groups other than those who are considered part of the team.[37] **Ambassador activities** refer to communications that are intended to protect the team, persuade others to support the team, or obtain important resources for the team. As you might have guessed from this description, members who engage in ambassador activities typically communicate with people who are higher up in the organization. For example, a member of a marketing team might meet with senior management to request an increase in the budget for an expanded television ad campaign. **Task coordinator activities** involve communications that are intended to coordinate task-related issues with people or groups in other functional areas. Continuing with the marketing team example, a member of the team might meet with someone from manufacturing to work out how a coupon might be integrated into the product packaging materials. Finally, **scout activities** refer to things team members do to obtain information about technology, competitors, or the broader marketplace. The marketing team member who meets with an engineer to seek information about new materials is engaging in scout activities. Taken

OB INTERNATIONALLY

In today's global economy, organizations have become increasingly reliant on multinational teams, or teams composed of individuals who do not share the same national identification.[38] One benefit of multinational teams is economic. Rather than having separate businesses or products in several different countries, organizations leverage economies of scale by establishing multinational teams to develop and manage global products.[39] A second benefit is that diversity in terms of national origin may result in business decisions that are more innovative. Such innovation stems from the team having a diverse set of experiences and perspectives from which to draw when trying to accomplish work.[40] However, along with these benefits are potential team process problems. The most obvious problem is language barriers that prevent team members from communicating effectively with one another. Beyond simple misunderstandings, communication barriers can result in difficulties in coordinating tasks and may hinder members from receiving or understanding the information they need to make good recommendations and decisions.[41] So what can multinational teams do to address some of these problems?

One solution is *group decision support systems,* which involve the use of computer technology to help the team structure its decision-making process.[42] As an example, team members might meet in a room where each member sits at a networked laptop. At different points during the meeting, members are directed to provide their ideas and recommendations into the computer. These inputs are then summarized and shared visually with the entire team on their computer screens. Advantages of this approach are that the system keeps the meeting focused squarely on the task, and information can be presented in a logical sequence at a pace that makes it easier to digest. Moreover, no single member can dominate the meeting. As a consequence of these advantages, team members may participate more uniformly in the meeting and develop a more consistent understanding of the information that was exchanged. Another advantage is that the technique can be modified and used when members are geographically dispersed.

together, research suggests that these boundary-spanning activities may be as important to determining team success as the processes that occur entirely within the team.[43]

TEAMWORK PROCESSES

12.2

What are teamwork processes, and what are some examples of team activities that fall into this process category?

Another category of team processes that helps teams increase their process gain while minimizing their process loss is teamwork processes. **Teamwork processes** refer to the interpersonal activities that facilitate the accomplishment of the team's work but do not directly involve task accomplishment itself.[44] You can think of teamwork processes as the behaviors that create the setting or context in which taskwork can be carried out. So what types of behaviors do teamwork processes involve? Figure 12-2 summarizes the set of teamwork processes discussed in this chapter.[45]

TRANSITION PROCESSES. Teamwork processes become important right when teams first begin their work. **Transition processes** are teamwork activities that focus on preparation for future work. For example, *mission analysis* involves an analysis of the team's task, the challenges that face the team, and the resources available for completing the team's work. *Strategy formulation* refers to the development of courses of action and contingency plans, and then adapting those plans in light of changes that occur in the team's environment. Finally, *goal specification* involves the development and prioritization of goals related to the team's mission and strategy. Each of these transition processes is relevant before the team actually begins to conduct the core aspects of its work. However, these transition processes also may be important between periods of work activity. For example, think about the halftime adjustments made by a basketball team that's losing a game badly. The team could consider the strengths of its opponent and develop a new strategy intended to neutralize them. In this way, teams may switch from transition processes to taskwork, then back to transition processes.

ACTION PROCESSES. Whereas transition processes are important before and between periods of taskwork, **action processes** are important as the taskwork is being accomplished. One type of action process involves *monitoring progress toward goals*. Teams that pay attention to goal-related information—perhaps by charting the team's performance relative to team goals—are typically in a good position to realize when they are "off-track" and need to make changes. *Systems monitoring* involves keeping track of things that the team needs to accomplish its work. A team that does not engage in systems monitoring may fail because it runs out of inventory, time, or other necessary resources. *Helping behavior* involves members going out of their way to help or back up other team members. Team members can provide indirect help to their teammates in the form of feedback or coaching, as well as direct help in the form of assistance with members' tasks and responsibilities.

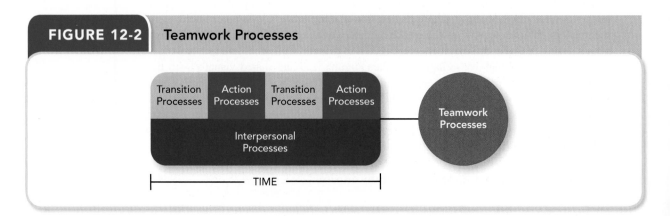

| FIGURE 12-2 | **Teamwork Processes** |

Helping behavior may be most beneficial when workload is distributed unequally among team members.[46] *Coordination* refers to synchronizing team members' activities in a way that makes them mesh effectively and seamlessly. Poor coordination results in team members constantly having to wait on others for information or other resources necessary to do their part of the team's work.[47]

INTERPERSONAL PROCESSES. The third category of teamwork processes is called **interpersonal processes**. The processes in this category are important before, during, or in between periods of taskwork, and each relates to the manner in which team members manage their relationships. The first type of interpersonal process is *motivating and confidence building*, which refers to things team members do or say that affect the degree to which members are motivated to work hard on the team's task. Expressions that create a sense of urgency and optimism are examples of communications that would fit in this category. Similarly, *affect management* involves activities that foster a sense of emotional balance and unity. If you've ever worked in a team in which members got short-tempered when facing pressure or blamed one another when there were problems, you have firsthand experience with poor affect management.

Another important interpersonal process is *conflict management*, which involves the activities that the team uses to manage conflicts that arise in the course of its work. Conflict tends to have a negative impact on a team, but the nature of this effect depends on the focus of the conflict as well as the manner in which the conflict is managed.[48] **Relationship conflict** refers to disagreements among team members in terms of interpersonal relationships or incompatibilities with respect to personal values or preferences. This type of conflict centers on issues that are not directly connected to the team's task. Relationship conflict is not only dissatisfying to most people, it also tends to result in reduced team performance. **Task conflict**, in contrast, refers to disagreements among members about the team's task. Logically speaking, this type of conflict can be beneficial to teams if it stimulates conversations that result in the development and expression of new ideas.[49] Research findings, however, indicate that task conflict tends to result in reduced team effectiveness unless two conditions are present.[50] First, members need to trust one another and be confident that they can express their opinions openly without fear of reprisals. Second, team members need to engage in effective conflict management processes. (For more discussion of conflict management issues, see Chapter 13 on Leadership: Power and Negotiation.)

What does effective conflict management involve? First, when trying to manage conflict, it's important for members to stay focused on the team's mission. If members do this, they can ratio-

For task conflict to be productive, team members must feel free to express their opinions and know how to manage conflict effectively.

nally evaluate the relative merits of each position.[51] Second, any benefits of task conflict disappear if the level of the conflict gets too heated, if parties appear to be acting in self-interest rather than in the best interest of the team, or if there is high relationship conflict.[52] Third, to effectively manage task conflict, members need to discuss their positions openly and be willing to exchange information in a way that fosters collaborative problem solving.[53] If you've ever had an experience in an ongoing relationship in which you tried to avoid uncomfortable conflict by ignoring it, you probably already understand that this strategy only tends to make things worse in the end.

COMMUNICATION

12.3

What factors influence the communication process in teams?

So far in this chapter, we've described the focus of the activities and interactions among team members as they work to accomplish the team's purpose. For example, taskwork processes involve members sharing ideas, making recommendations, and acquiring resources from parties outside the team. As another example, teamwork processes involve members planning how to do the team's work, helping other team members with their work, and saying things to lift team members' spirits. Now we shift gears a bit and focus our attention on **communication**, the process by which information and meaning gets transferred from a sender to a receiver.[54] Much of the work that's done in a team is accomplished interdependently and involves communication among members, and therefore, the effectiveness of communication plays an important role in determining whether there is process gain or process loss.

One way to understand communication is to consider the model depicted in Figure 12-3.[55] On the left side of the model is the source or *sender* of information. In a team that manufactures steel engine parts, for example, the sender might be a team member who wants to share information with another team member. More specifically, the sender might want to let another member know that the team has to work more quickly to reach a difficult performance goal. Generally speaking, senders may use verbal and written language, as well as nonverbal language and cues, to *encode* the information into a *message.* Continuing with our example, the sender may choose to quickly wave an arm up and down to convey the idea that the team needs to work faster. This encoded message is transmitted to a *receiver,* who needs to interpret or *decode* the message to form an understanding of the information it contains. In our example, the message is transmitted visually because the members are working face-to-face, but messages can be transmitted in written form, electronically, or even indirectly through other individuals. With this basic model of communication in mind, we can consider factors that may influence the effectiveness of this process.

COMMUNICATOR ISSUES. One important factor that influences the communication process is the communicators themselves. Communicators need to encode and interpret

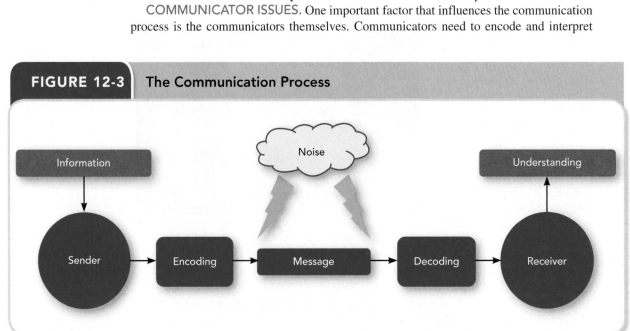

FIGURE 12-3　**The Communication Process**

Information → Sender → Encoding → Message → Decoding → Receiver → Understanding

Noise

messages, and it turns out that these activities can be major sources of communication problems.[56] In our example, the receiver may interpret the arm waving as a message that something is going wrong and that the team needs to slow down to cope with the problem. Of course, this interpretation is the exact opposite of what the sender intended to convey. The communication process may also suffer if the participants lack *communication competence*, which refers to the skills involved in encoding, transmitting, and receiving messages.[57] In fact, it may have already occurred to you that perhaps the sender in our example should have chosen an alternative way to communicate the idea that the team needs to work more quickly. Along the same lines, a receiver who isn't skilled in listening carefully to a sender's message may misinterpret a message or miss it altogether.

NOISE. A second factor that influences the communication process is the presence of *noise* that interferes with the message being transmitted.[58] Depending on how the message is being transmitted, noise can take on several different forms. In the context of our example, the sender and receiver may be working several feet from one another, and steam from the manufacturing process may make it difficult to see and appreciate the meaning of the gestures members make. As another example, you've probably had difficulty trying to hold a conversation with someone in a restaurant or bar because of blaring music or crowd noise. If so, you can understand that noise increases the effort that the communicators need to exert to make the communication process work. The sender has to talk louder and more clearly, and perhaps increase the use of alternative means of communicating, such as using hand gestures to help clarify messages. In addition, the receiver has to listen more carefully and think harder to fill in the spaces left by spoken words that are impossible to hear. If one of the two parties to the communication isn't willing to put in the extra effort to send and receive messages when there is noise, the conversation likely will not last very long.

INFORMATION RICHNESS. A third factor that influences the communication process is **information richness**, which is the amount and depth of information that gets transmitted in a message.[59] Messages that are transmitted through face-to-face channels have the highest level of information richness,[60] because senders can convey meaning through not only words but also their body language, facial expressions, and tone of voice. Face-to-face communication also achieves high information richness because it provides the opportunity for senders and receivers to receive feedback, which allows them to verify and ensure that their messages are received and interpreted correctly. At the opposite end of the information richness spectrum are computer-generated reports that consist largely of numbers.[61] Although these types of reports may include a lot of information, they're limited to information that's quantifiable, and there's an absence of additional cues that could provide context and meaning to the numbers. A personal written note is a good example of a message with a moderate level of information richness.[62] Although the information in a note is limited to the words written down on the page, the choice of words and punctuation can add meaning beyond the words themselves. For example, research shows that recipients of e-mails try to interpret the emotions of the sender from the content of the message, and unfortunately, they often mistakenly perceive the emotion as negative even when it's not.[63]

From our description, it may sound as though higher levels of information richness are preferable to lower levels. This assertion is true when the situation or task at hand is complex and difficult to understand.[64] In this case, the more cues that are available to the receiver, the more likely it is that the message will be understood the way the sender intended it to be. However, the benefits of information richness may overcomplicate the communication process when the task at hand is relatively simple and straightforward.[65] The additional information that needs to be interpreted by the receiver increases the chance that some of the cues will seem contradictory, and when this happens, receivers may feel like they're being sent "mixed messages." In summary, the appropriate level of information richness depends on the nature of the team's situation: The greater the level of complexity in the work being accomplished by the team, the more likely it is that the benefits of information richness outweigh its costs.

NETWORK STRUCTURE. So far in our discussion of communication, we've kept things simple by focusing on the flow of information between two people—a sender and a receiver. Of course, teams typically have more than just two people, so it's important at this point to consider the implications of this additional complexity. One way to understand communication in teams composed of more than two people is to consider the concept of **network structure**, which is defined as the pattern of communication that occurs regularly among each member of the team.[66]

As depicted in Figure 12-4, communication network patterns can be described in terms of *centralization,* or the degree to which the communication in a network flows through some members rather than others.[67] The more communication flows through fewer members of the team, the higher the degree of centralization. You can think of the circles in the figure as team members, and the lines between the circles represent the flow of communication back and forth between the two members. On the left side of the figure is the *all channel* network structure, which is highly decentralized. Every member can communicate with every other member. Student teams typically communicate using this type of structure. On the right side of the figure, at the other extreme, is the *wheel* network structure. This network structure is high centralized because all the communication flows though a single member. Teams that use a wheel structure often consist of an "official" leader who makes final decisions based on recommendations from members who have expertise in different fields. Although there are many other configurations you can easily think of, we also included the *circle* and *Y* structures to illustrate examples that fall between the extremes in terms of the level of centralization.

So why are network structures important to learn about? Quite a bit of research on this topic suggests that network structure has important implications for team effectiveness, though those implications depend on the nature of the team's work.[68] On the one hand, when the work is simple and straightforward, a centralized structure tends to result in faster solutions with fewer mistakes. On the other hand, when the work is complex and

FIGURE 12-4 Communication Network Structures

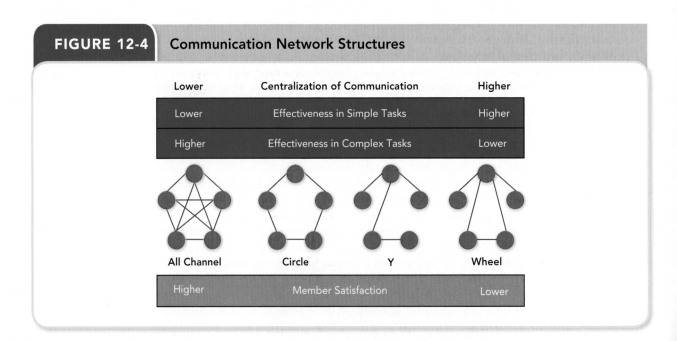

Lower	Centralization of Communication	Higher
Lower	Effectiveness in Simple Tasks	Higher
Higher	Effectiveness in Complex Tasks	Lower

All Channel   Circle   Y   Wheel

Higher	Member Satisfaction	Lower

difficult to understand, a decentralized structure tends to be more efficient. Apparently, when work is complex and difficult to understand, the team can benefit if members have the ability to communicate with anyone on the team to get assistance or resolve problems. When the work is simple and easy to understand, the additional communication channels afforded by a decentralized structure become unnecessary and divert members' attention from the task. It's important to mention, however, that members tend to prefer decentralized network structures. That is, they tend to be more satisfied with the team when they are "in the loop," even though their position in the loop might not help the team perform more effectively.

TEAM STATES

A fourth category of team processes that helps teams increase their process gain while minimizing their process loss is less visible to the naked eye. **Team states** refer to specific types of feelings and thoughts that coalesce in the minds of team members as a consequence of their experience working together. Although there are many types of team states that we could review in this chapter, Figure 12-5 summarizes the set of team states we discuss.

12.4

What are team states, and what are some examples of the states that fall into this process category?

COHESION. For a number of reasons, members of teams can develop strong emotional bonds to other members of their team and to the team itself. This emotional attachment, which is called **cohesion**,[69] tends to foster high levels of motivation and commitment to the team, and as a consequence, cohesiveness tends to promote higher levels of team performance.[70] But is a cohesive team necessarily a good team? According to researchers, the answer to this question is no. In highly cohesive teams, members may try to maintain harmony by striving toward consensus on issues without ever offering, seeking, or seriously considering alternative viewpoints and perspectives. This drive toward conformity at the expense of other team priorities is called **groupthink** and is thought to be associated with feelings of overconfidence about the team's capabilities.[71] Groupthink has been blamed for decision-making fiascos in politics as well as in business. Some famous examples include John F. Kennedy's decision to go forward with the Bay of Pigs invasion of Cuba,[72] NASA's decision to launch the space shuttle Challenger in unusually cold weather,[73] and Enron's Board of Directors' decisions to ignore illegal accounting practices.[74]

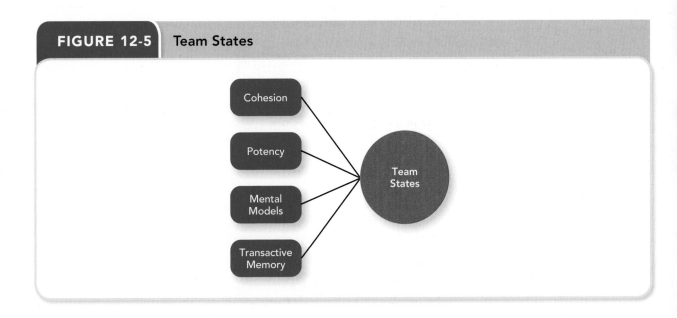

FIGURE 12-5 **Team States**

So how do you leverage the benefits of cohesion without taking on the potential costs? One way is to acknowledge that cohesion can potentially have detrimental consequences. A good first step in this regard would be to assess the team's cohesion using a scale such as the one in our **OB Assessments** feature. A high score on this sort of assessment indicates the team may be vulnerable to groupthink. A second step in preventing problems associated with cohesion would be to formally institute the role of devil's advocate. The person filling this role would be responsible for evaluating and challenging prevailing points of view in a constructive manner and also bringing in fresh perspectives and ideas to the team. Although the devil's advocate role could be filled by an existing team member, it's also possible that the team could bring in an outsider to fill that role.

POTENCY. The second team state, **potency**, refers to the degree to which members believe that the team can be effective across a variety of situations and tasks.[75] When a

---

OB ASSESSMENTS

COHESION

How cohesive is your team? This assessment is designed to measure cohesion—the strength of the emotional bonds that develop among members of a team. Think of your current student project team or an important team that you belong to in your job. Answer each question using the response scale provided. Then subtract your answers to the boldfaced questions from 8, with the difference being your new answers for those questions. For example, if your original answer for question 6 was "5", your new answer is "3" $(8 - 5)$. Then sum up your answers for the eight questions. (For more assessments relevant to this chapter, please visit the Online Learning Center at www.mhhe.com/colquitt).

1	2	3	4	5	6	7
STRONGLY DISAGREE	DISAGREE	SLIGHTLY DISAGREE	NEUTRAL	SLIGHTLY AGREE	AGREE	STRONGLY AGREE

1. If given a chance, I would choose to leave my team to join another.   _____

2. The members of my team get along well together.   _____

3. The members of my team will readily defend each other from criticism.   _____

4. I feel that I am really a part of my team.   _____

5. I look forward to being with the members of my team every day.   _____

6. I find that I generally do not get along with other members of my team.   _____

7. I enjoy belonging to this team because I am friends with many members.   _____

8. The team to which I belong is a close one.   _____

SCORING AND INTERPRETATION

If your scores sum up to 48 or above, you feel a strong bond to your team, suggesting that your team is cohesive. If your scores sum up to less than 48, you feel a weaker bond to your team, suggesting that your team is not as cohesive.

Source: G.H. Dobbins and S.J. Zacarro, "The Effects of Group Cohesion and Leader Behavior on Subordinate Satisfaction," *Group and Organization Management* 11 (1986), pp. 203–19. Copyright © 1986 by Sage Publications Inc. Journals. Reproduced via permission of Sage Publications Inc. Journals via Copyright Clearance Center.

team has high potency, members are confident that their team can perform well, and as a consequence, they focus more of their energy on team tasks and teamwork in hopes of achieving team goals.[76] When a team has low potency, members are not as confident about their team, and so they begin to question the team's goals and one another. Ultimately, this reaction can result in members focusing their energies on activities that don't benefit the team. In the end, research has shown that potency has a strong positive impact on team performance.[77] So how does high potency develop in teams? Team members' confidence in their own capabilities, their trust in other members' capabilities, and feedback about past performance are all likely to play a role.[78] Specifically, team potency is promoted in teams in which members are confident in themselves and their teammates and when the team has experienced success in the past.

MENTAL MODELS. **Mental models** refer to the level of common understanding among team members with regard to important aspects of the team and its task.[79] A team may have shared mental models with respect to the capabilities that members bring to the team as well as the processes the team needs to use to be effective.[80] How can these two types of mental models foster team effectiveness? When team members share in their understanding of one another's capabilities, they're more likely to know where to go for the help they might need to complete their work. In addition, they should be able to anticipate when another member needs help to do his or her work. When members have a shared understanding of which processes are necessary to help the team be effective, they can carry out these processes efficiently and smoothly. To help you understand why this is true, consider what would happen in a team of students who had different understandings about how the team should manage conflict. Few disagreements would get resolved if some of the members believed that direct confrontation was best, whereas others believed that avoidance was best.

TRANSACTIVE MEMORY. Whereas mental models refer to the degree to which the knowledge is shared among members, **transactive memory** refers to how specialized knowledge is distributed among members in a manner that results in an effective system of memory for the team.[81] This concept takes into account the idea that not everyone on a team has to possess the same knowledge. Instead, team effectiveness requires that members understand when their own specialized knowledge is relevant to the team and how their knowledge should be combined with the specialized knowledge of other members to accomplish team goals. If you've ever worked on a team that had effective transactive memory, you may have noticed that work got done very efficiently.[82] Everyone focused on his or her specialty and what he or she did best, members knew exactly where to go to get information when there were gaps in their knowledge, and the team produced synergistic results. Of course, transactive memory can also be fragile because the memory system depends on each and every member.[83] If someone is slow to respond to another member's request for information or forgets something important, the team's system of memory fails. Alternatively, if a member of the team leaves, you lose an important node in the memory system.

SUMMARY: WHY ARE SOME TEAMS MORE THAN THE SUM OF THEIR PARTS?

So what explains why some teams become more than the sum of their parts (whereas other teams become less)? As shown in Figure 12-6, teams become more than the sum of their parts if their team process achieves process gain rather than process loss. Teams can accomplish that goal by engaging in activities involved in effective taskwork processes, teamwork processes, communication, and team states. Important taskwork processes include creative behavior, decision making, and boundary spanning. Important teamwork processes include

FIGURE 12-6   Why Are Some Teams More than the Sum of Their Parts?

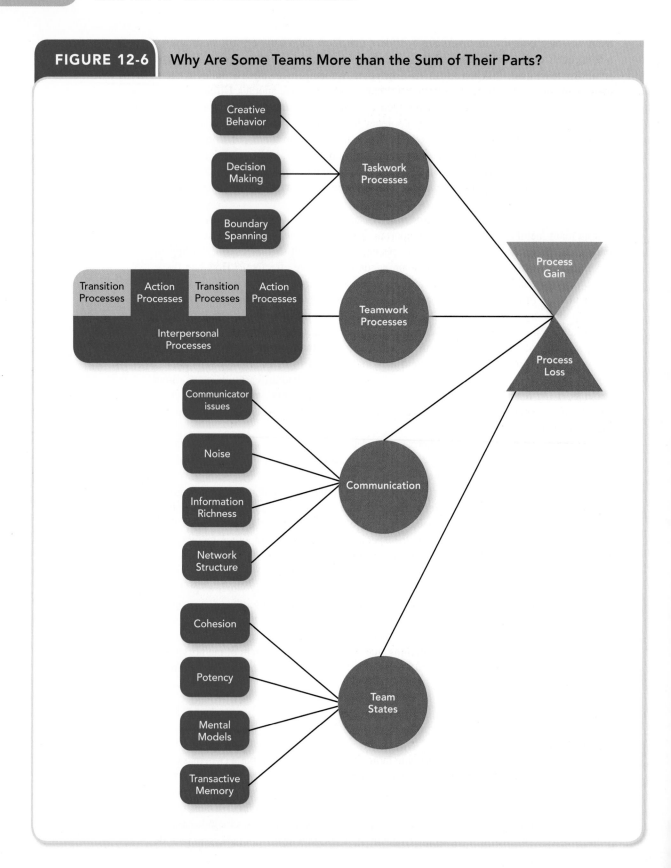

transition processes, action processes, and interpersonal processes. Communication can be enhanced by ensuring that members are competent communicators, noise is minimized, and appropriate levels of information richness and network complexity are chosen. Team states refer to variables such as cohesion, potency, mental models, and transactive memory. In contrast to the taskwork processes, teamwork processes, and communication, team states offer less visible and observable reasons for why some teams possess an effective synergy whereas others seem quite inefficient.

HOW IMPORTANT ARE TEAM PROCESSES?

Do team processes affect performance and commitment? Answering this question is somewhat complicated for two reasons. First, as in Chapter 11 on Team Characteristics and Diversity, when we say "performance and commitment," we are not referring to the performance of individuals or their attachment to the organization. Instead, we are referring to the performance of teams and the degree to which teams are capable of remaining together as ongoing entities. In the jargon of research on teams, this form of commitment is termed "team viability." Second, as we have described throughout this chapter, there are several different types of team processes that we could consider in our summary. In Figure 12-7, we characterize the relationship among team processes, performance, and commitment by focusing specifically on research involving teamwork processes. The figure therefore

12.5

How do team processes affect team performance and team commitment?

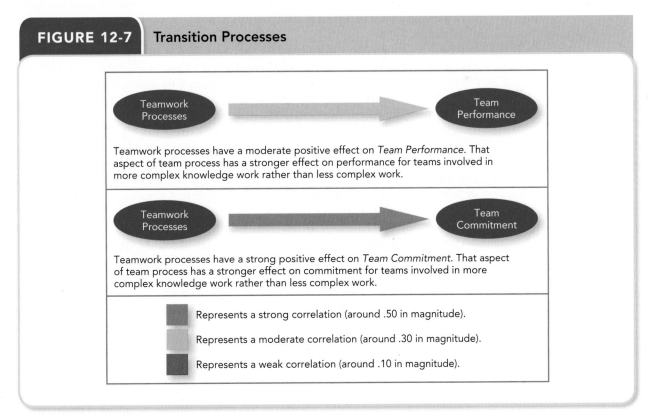

FIGURE 12-7 | **Transition Processes**

Teamwork processes have a moderate positive effect on *Team Performance*. That aspect of team process has a stronger effect on performance for teams involved in more complex knowledge work rather than less complex work.

Teamwork processes have a strong positive effect on *Team Commitment*. That aspect of team process has a stronger effect on commitment for teams involved in more complex knowledge work rather than less complex work.

Represents a strong correlation (around .50 in magnitude).

Represents a moderate correlation (around .30 in magnitude).

Represents a weak correlation (around .10 in magnitude).

Source: J.A. LePine, R.F. Piccolo, C.L. Jackson, J.E. Mathieu, and J.R. Saul, "A Meta-Analysis of Team Process: Towards a Better Understanding of the Dimensional Structure and Relationships with Team Effectiveness Criteria," *Personnel Psychology* 61 (2008), pp. 356–76.

A rare orchestra that performs without a conductor, the Orpheus Chamber Orchestra exhibits such teamwork and commitment that it has had a successful history of over 35 years of performance. While all members of the orchestra help refine the interpretation and execution of each work in its repertoire, they also select a concertmaster and principal players to lead each piece.

represents a summary of existing research on transition processes, action processes, and interpersonal processes.

Research conducted in a wide variety of team settings has shown that teamwork processes have a moderate positive relationship with team performance.[84] This same moderate positive relationship appears to hold true, regardless of whether the research examines transition processes, action processes, or interpersonal processes. Why might the relationships between these different types of processes and team performance be so similarly positive? Apparently, effectiveness with respect to a wide variety of interactions is needed to help teams achieve process gain and, in turn, perform effectively. The interpersonal activities that prepare teams for future work appear to be just as important as those that help members integrate their taskwork and those that build team confidence and a positive team climate. Researchers have also found that the importance of team processes to team performance may be more strongly positive in teams in which there are higher levels of interdependence.[85] This relationship can be explained quite easily: Activities that are meant to improve the integration of team members' work are simply more important in team contexts in which the work of team members needs to be integrated.

Research also indicates that teamwork processes have a strong positive relationship with team commitment.[86] In other words, teams that engage in effective teamwork processes tend to continue to exist together into the future. Why should teamwork and team commitment be so strongly related? One reason is that people tend to be satisfied in teams in which there are effective interpersonal interactions, and as a consequence, they go out of their way to do things that they believe will help the team stick together. Think about a team situation that you've been in when everyone shared the same goals for the team, work was coordinated smoothly, and everyone was positive, pleasant to be around, and willing to do their fair share of the work. If you've ever actually been in a situation like this—and we hope that you have—chances are that you did your best to make sure the team could continue on together. It's likely that you worked extra hard to make sure that the team achieved its goals. It's also likely that you expressed positive sentiments about the team and your desire for the team to remain together. Of course, just the opposite would be true in a team context in which members had different goals for the team, coordination was difficult and filled with emotional conflict, and everyone was pessimistic and disagreeable. Members of a team like this would not only find the situation dissatisfying but, also make it known that they would be very open to a change of scenery.

APPLICATION: TRAINING TEAMS

12.6

What steps can organizations take to improve team processes?

Team-based organizations invest a significant amount of resources into training that's intended to improve team processes. These types of investments seem to be a smart thing to do, given that team processes have a positive impact on both team performance and team commitment. In this section, we review several different approaches that organizations use to train team processes. Our **OB at the Bookstore** feature illustrates how some of these approaches may be used to address problems that teams often face.

OB AT THE BOOKSTORE

THE FIVE DYSFUNCTIONS OF A TEAM
by Patrick Lencioni (San Francisco: Jossey-Bass, 2002).

Like so many other aspects of life, teamwork comes down to mastering a set of behaviors that are at once theoretically uncomplicated, but extremely difficult to put into practice day after day. Success comes only for those groups that overcome the all-too-human behavioral tendencies that corrupt teams and breed dysfunctional politics within them.

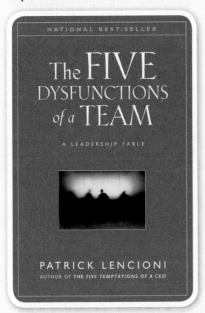

With those words, Lencioni argues in his book that teams face a relatively small number of natural pitfalls, and unless teams are prepared to face them, they often prove lethal. The book's lessons are centered on a parable of a newly hired 57-year-old CEO named Kathryn Petersen who turns around Decision Tech, a Silicon Valley technology firm that has gone through some tough times. She does so by helping the firm's executive committee overcome five crucial team dysfunctions: absence of trust, fear of conflict, lack of commitment, avoidance of accountability, and inattention to results. So how is Petersen able to accomplish this incredible feat? Beyond having exceptionally high performance standards and being supportive of her employees, Petersen uses several different types of team-building assessments, exercises, and guided discussions. In the end, it's easy to come away from the story impressed with the lessons that Petersen taught her team.

But how useful are those lessons in the real world? It turns out that the book has caught on in the business world, as well as in some rather unexpected places. For example, current and former National Football League head coaches such as Norv Turner, Marty Schottenheimer, Nick Saban, Romeo Crennel, and Marvin Lewis have read the book and applied its lessons to promote effective teamwork among players and coaching staff.[87]

And how do the five dysfunctions stack up against what we know from OB research? Lencioni based the book on his consulting work with CEOs and executive teams, so the dysfunctions were taken from commonsense knowledge gained from those experiences. Although OB scholars would agree that the dysfunctions are valid concerns for teams, there is no research that supports the idea that these five dysfunctions are the primary drivers of team functioning and effectiveness, that some are more important to overcome than others, or that the techniques Petersen used to approach the dysfunctions are optimal. Nevertheless, the book not only highlights common problems with team processes, it also identifies potential ways of dealing with them.

TRANSPORTABLE TEAMWORK COMPETENCIES

One approach to training teams is to help individual team members develop general competencies related to teamwork activities. Table 12-2 shows that this type of training could involve many different forms of knowledge, skills, and abilities.[88] Taken together, such knowledge, skills, and abilities are referred to as **transportable teamwork competences**.[89] This label reflects the fact that trainees can transport what they learn about teamwork from one team context and apply it in another. As a specific example of how this type of training might work, consider a recent study of teamwork training for naval aviators in an advanced pilot training program.[90] In this study, one group of pilots went through two days of training, during which they received instruction on preferred communication practices, communicating suggestions and asking questions, and communicating about potential problems. The pilots who went through the training believed that in addition to building teamwork knowledge and skills, the training would increase their mission effectiveness and flight safety. Most important, teams that were composed of pilots who went through the training were significantly more effective than teams composed of pilots who did not go through the training. Effectiveness was judged by performance in dangerous scenarios, such as ice buildup on the aircraft wings and instructions from the air traffic control tower that were conflicting or ambiguous.

TABLE 12-2	Teamwork Knowledge, Skills, and Abilities
COMPETENCY	**DESCRIPTION**
Conflict resolution	• Can distinguish between desirable and undesirable conflict. • Encourages desirable conflict and discourages undesirable conflict. • Uses win–win strategies to manage conflict.
Collaborative problem solving	• Can identify situations requiring participative problem solving. • Uses the appropriate degree of participation. • Recognizes and manages obstacles to collaborative problem solving.
Communications	• Understands communication networks. • Communicates openly and supportively. • Listens without making premature evaluations. • Uses active listening techniques. • Can interpret nonverbal messages of others. • Engages in ritual greetings and small talk.
Goal setting and performance management	• Helps establish specific and difficult goals for the team. • Monitors, evaluates, and provides performance-related feedback.
Planning and task coordination	• Coordinates and synchronizes activities among team members. • Establishes expectations to ensure proper balance of workload within the team.

Source: Adapted from M.J. Stevens and M.A. Campion, "The Knowledge, Skill, and Ability Requirements for Teamwork: Implications for Human Resource Management," *Journal of Management* 20 (1994), pp. 503–30.

CROSS-TRAINING

A second type of team training involves training members in the duties and responsibilities of their teammates. The idea behind this type of training, which is called **cross-training**,[91] is that team members can develop shared mental models of what's involved in each of the roles in the team and how the roles fit together to form a system.[92] What exactly does cross-training involve? Researchers have found that cross-training may involve instruction at three different levels of depth.[93] At the shallowest level, there is **personal clarification**. With this type of training, members simply receive information regarding the roles of the other team members. As an example, the highly specialized members of surgical teams—surgeons, anesthesiologists, operating room nurses—might meet so that they can learn about others' roles and how each contributes to the team's goal of achieving overall patient well-being.

At the next level of cross-training, there is **positional modeling**, which involves team members observing how other members perform their roles. In the case of the surgical teams, the surgeons might spend a day shadowing operating room nurses as they perform their duties. The shadowing not only helps the surgeons gain a better understanding of what the job of a nurse entails but also may provide insight into how the activities involved in their respective jobs could be integrated more effectively.

Finally, the deepest level of cross-training involves **positional rotation**. This type of training gives members actual experience carrying out the responsibilities of their teammates. Although this type of hands-on experience could expand skills of members so that they might actually perform the duties of their teammates if they had to, the level of training required to achieve proficiency or certification in many situations may be prohibitive. For example, because it takes years of specialized training to become a surgeon, it would be impractical to train an operating room nurse to perform this job for the purposes of positional rotation.

TEAM PROCESS TRAINING

Cross-training and training in transportable teamwork competencies focus on individual experiences that promote individual learning. **Team process training**, in contrast, occurs in the context of a team experience that facilitates the team being able to function and perform more effectively as an intact unit. One type of team process training is called **action learning**. With this type of training, which has been used successfully at companies such as Motorola and General Electric, a team is given a real problem that's relevant to the organization and then held accountable for analyzing the problem, developing an action plan, and finally carrying out the action plan.[94] How does this type of experience develop effective team processes? First, the team receives coaching to help facilitate more effective processes during different phases of the project. Second, there are meetings during which team members are encouraged to reflect on the team processes they've used as they worked on the project. In these meetings, the members not only discuss what they observed and learned from their experiences, but also what they would do differently in the future.

A second type of team process training involves experience in a team context when there are task demands that highlight the importance of effective teamwork processes. As an example, the chapter opening described how United Airlines used pit crew training for its ramp crews.[95] Although teams of ramp workers at an airline like United must work with luggage, belt loaders, and baggage carts, there are parallels with the work of NASCAR pit crews that work with tires, jacks, and air guns. Primarily, effective performance in both contexts means performing work safely within tight time constraints. Moreover, in both of these contexts, achieving goals requires teamwork, communication, and strict adherence to standardized team procedures. The real value of the pit crew training to the ramp crews is that it conveys the lessons of teamwork in a very vivid way. If a team fails to follow procedures and work together when trying to change tires, tools will be misplaced, parts will be dropped, and members will get in one another's way. As a consequence, a pit stop may last for minutes rather than seconds.

TEAM BUILDING

The fourth general type of team process training is called **team building**. This type of training normally is conducted by a consultant and intended to facilitate the development of team processes related to goal setting, interpersonal relations, problem solving, and role clarification.[96] The ropes course is a very popular task used in team building. It requires team members to work together to traverse wooden beams, ropes, and zip lines while dangling in a harness 20–50 feet in the air. Other examples include laser tag and paintball,[97] WhirlyBall (think lacrosse played in bumper cars with a whiffle ball and plastic scoops),[98] whitewater rafting, scavenger hunts, and beating drums in a drum circle.[99] Team-building activities such as these are hugely popular with organizations of all sizes, and they do seem like an awful lot of fun.

But can you really build effective teams by having them participate in enjoyable activities that seem so unrelated to their jobs? In fact, this was the basis for Senators Byron Dorgan's and Ron Wyden's request that the inspector general of the U.S. Postal Service be fired.[100] In their letter to the chairman of the Post Office Board of Governors, they wrote that the inspector general "has spent millions of agency dollars on expensive and silly 'team building' exercises, diverting massive resources from the task of finding waste and improving efficiency. . . . On tapes, you see images of public servants dressed up as the Village People, wearing cat costumes, doing a striptease, and participating in mock trials—all on official time, all at the public's expense."[101] Although it's somewhat difficult to gauge the effectiveness of team-building interventions because so many different types of exercises have been used, research has been conducted that provides mixed support for the senators' claim. The findings of one meta-analysis found that team building did not have a significant effect on team performance when performance was defined in terms of productivity.[102] However, the research found that team building is most likely to have positive effects for smaller teams and when the exercise emphasizes the importance of clarifying role responsibilities.

TAKEAWAYS

12.1   Taskwork processes are the activities of team members that relate directly to the accomplishment of team tasks. Taskwork processes include creative behavior, decision making, and boundary spanning.

12.2   Teamwork processes refer to the interpersonal activities that facilitate the accomplishment of the team's work but do not directly involve task accomplishment itself. Teamwork processes include transition processes, action processes, and interpersonal processes.

12.3   Communication is a process through which much of the work in a team is accomplished. Effectiveness in communication can be influenced by the communication competence of the sender and receiver, noise, information richness, and network structure.

12.4   Team states refer to specific types of feelings and thoughts that coalesce in the minds of team members as a consequence of their experience working together. Team states include cohesion, potency, mental models, and transactive memory.

12.5   Teamwork processes have a moderate positive relationship with team performance and a strong positive relationship with team commitment.

12.6   Organizations can use training interventions to improve team processes. Such interventions may include training in transportable teamwork competencies, cross-training, team process training, and team building.

KEY TERMS

• Team process	p. 413	• Relationship conflict	p. 421
• Process gain	p. 413	• Task conflict	p. 421
• Process loss	p. 413	• Communication	p. 422
• Coordination loss	p. 415	• Information richness	p. 423
• Production blocking	p. 415	• Network structure	p. 424
• Motivational loss	p. 415	• Team states	p. 425
• Social loafing	p. 415	• Cohesion	p. 425
• Taskwork processes	p. 415	• Groupthink	p. 425
• Brainstorming	p. 415	• Potency	p. 426
• Nominal group technique	p. 416	• Mental models	p. 427
• Decision informity	p. 418	• Transactive memory	p. 427
• Staff validity	p. 418	• Transportable teamwork	
• Hierarchical sensitivity	p. 418	competencies	p. 432
• Boundary spanning	p. 419	• Cross-training	p. 433
• Ambassador activities	p. 419	• Personal clarification	p. 433
• Task coordinator activities	p. 419	• Positional modeling	p. 433
• Scout activities	p. 419	• Positional rotation	p. 433
• Teamwork processes	p. 420	• Team process training	p. 433
• Transition processes	p. 420	• Action learning	p. 433
• Action processes	p. 420	• Team building	p. 434
• Interpersonal processes	p. 421		

DISCUSSION QUESTIONS

12.1   Before reading this chapter, how did you define teamwork? How did this definition correspond to the definition outlined in this book?

12.2   Think of a team you've worked in that performed poorly. Were any of the causes of the poor performance related to the forces that tend to create process loss? If so, which force was most problematic? What steps, if any, did your team take to deal with the problem?

12.3   Think of a team you've worked in that performed exceptionally well. What type of taskwork process did the team engage in? Which teamwork processes did the team seem to depend on most to produce the exceptional results?

12.4 Think about the team states described in this chapter. If you joined a new team, how long do you think it would take you to get a feel for those team states? Which states would you be able to gauge first? Which would take longer?

12.5 Describe the communication process in a student team of which you've been a member. Were there examples of "noise" that detracted from the team members' ability to communicate with one another? What was the primary mode of communication among members? Did this mode of communication possess an appropriate level of information richness? Which network structure comes closest to describing the one that the team used to communicate? Was the level of centralization appropriate?

12.6 Which types of teamwork training would your student team benefit most from? What exactly would this training cover? What specific benefits would you expect? What would prevent a team from training itself on this material?

CASE: UNITED AIRLINES

To improve its competitive position, United Airlines sought to reduce the amount of time its planes stay on the ground between flights. As one United Airlines senior executive stated, "Our airplanes don't earn money while they're sitting on the ground. . . . They need to be in the air. So if we can shave even four or five minutes off of every aircraft turn, we can fly well over a hundred more flights a day."[103] To achieve this goal, United decided to invest in training for employees who work in ramp crews, which are responsible for guiding planes to their gate and chocking their wheels after arrival, positioning the "jet bridge" that connects the airport gate with the door of the aircraft so that passengers can safely exit and board, setting up belt loaders so that baggage can be unloaded and loaded, performing various maintenance tasks, and keeping the ground free of debris that could get sucked up in the jet engines. So what type of training did the ramp crews receive? They were sent to "Pit Crew U," where they learned how to service a racing car during a pit stop. The task typically involves changing tires using a jack and air guns, pumping gas into the car, cleaning up spills, and washing the car's windshield. In a competitive race, all these tasks have to happen in about 13 seconds, without any mistakes that could cause damage to the car or injury to the driver, members of the pit crew, or spectators. So why did United Airlines believe that it could reduce the time it takes to turn an aircraft through training in an altogether different job?

United believed that the set of skills that promote the effectiveness of crews responsible for servicing a car during a pit stop is roughly the same as the set of skills that promote the effectiveness of ramp crews responsible for servicing a plane between flights. To accomplish the goal of a 13-second pit stop during a real race, pit crews must use a highly standardized and coordinated process. The members of the crew need to plan and prepare themselves and their tools for each and every pit stop. During the pit stop, the members follow their part of a standardized process, and when something unexpected happens—for example, when a tool breaks or fuel spills on the car and ignites—the members must communicate with one another and make adjustments to the process. Although the specific tasks, tools, and time constraints are different, ramp crews also need to follow a standardized and coordinated process to turn a plane for the next flight. Members of ramp crews should be prepared and ready to fulfill the requirements of their specific part of the crew's task. They also need to communicate effectively with one another and adapt to unusual circumstances—such as when a baggage cart breaks or an important tool is misplaced. Of course, there are some important issues that come to mind when considering the appropriateness of pit crew training for ramp crews. Most obviously, perhaps, the racing context might cause ramp crews to overemphasize the goal of increasing speed and underemphasize the important actions that protect the safety of the flight crew and passengers. We do not know of any specific examples in which this issue has caused a problem at United Airlines, however, it may be worthwhile to consider how training could be adapted to deal with the possibility.

12.1   Which specific types of team processes are most relevant to ramp crews? Which factors in the ramp crew context likely cause the majority of problems with communication?

12.2   Which type of team process training takes place at Pit Crew U? Which specific team processes and communication factors does the training emphasize?

12.3   What recommendations would you make to ensure that the ramp crews maintained their focus on safety? Are there additional types of team processes or communication training that should be incorporated to overcome potential issues having to do with the speed versus safety trade-off?

EXERCISE: WILDERNESS SURVIVAL

The purpose of this exercise is to experience team processes during a decision-making task. This exercise uses groups, so your instructor will either assign you to a group or ask you to create your own group. The exercise has the following steps:

12.1   Working individually, read the following scenario:

You have gone on a Boundary Waters canoe trip with five friends to upper Minnesota and southern Ontario in the Quetico Provincial Park. Your group has been traveling Saganagons Lake to Kawnipi Lake, following through Canyon Falls and Kennebas Falls and Kenny Lake. Fifteen to eighteen miles away is the closest road, which is arrived at by paddling through lakes and rivers and usually portaging (taking the land path) around numerous falls. Saganagons Lake is impossible to cross in bad weather, generally because of heavy rain. The nearest town is Grand Marais, Minnesota, 60 miles away. That town has plenty of camping outfitters but limited medical help, so residents rely on hospitals farther to the south.

The terrain is about 70 percent land and 30 percent water, with small patches of land here and there in between the lakes and rivers. Bears are not uncommon in this region. It's now mid-May, when the (daytime) temperature ranges from about 25° to 70°, often in the same day. Nighttime temperatures can be in the 20s. Rain is frequent during the day (nights, too) and can be life threatening if the temperature is cold. It's unusual for the weather to stay the same for more than a day or two. Generally, it will rain one day and be warm and clear the next, with a third day windy—and it's not easy to predict what type of weather will come next. In fact, it may be clear and warm, rainy and windy, all in the same day.

Your group was in two canoes going down the river and came to some rapids. Rather than taking the portage route on land, the group foolishly decided to shoot the rapids by canoe. Unfortunately, everyone fell out of the canoes, and some were banged against the rocks. Luckily no one was killed, but one person suffered a broken leg, and several others had cuts and bruises. Both canoes were damaged severely. Both were bent in half, one with an open tear of 18 inches, while the other suffered two tears of 12 and 15 inches long. Both have broken gunwales (the upper edges on both sides). You lost the packs that held the tent, most clothing, nearly all the food, cooking equipment, the fuel, the first aid kit, and the flashlight. Your combined possessions include the items shown in the table on the following page.

You had permits to take this trip, but no one knows for sure where you are, and the closest phone is in Grand Marais. You were scheduled back four days from now, so it's likely a search party would be sent out in about five days (because you could have been delayed a day or so in getting back). Just now it has started to drizzle, and it looks like rain will follow. Your task is to figure out how to survive in these unpredictable and possibly harsh conditions until you can get help.

12.2 Working individually, consider how important each of the items in the table would be to you in this situation. Begin with the most important item, giving it a rank of "1," and wind up with the least important item, giving it a rank of "14." Put your rankings in Column B.

12.3 In your groups, come to a consensus about the ranking of the items. Put those consensus rankings in Column C. Group members should not merely vote or average rankings together. Instead, try to get everyone to more or less agree on the rankings. When someone disagrees, try to listen carefully. When someone feels strongly, that person should attempt to use persuasive techniques to create a consensus.

12.4 The instructor will post the correct answers and provide the reasons for those rankings, according to two experts (Jeff Stemmerman and Ken Gieske of REI Outfitters, both of whom act as guides for many canoe trips in the Boundary Waters region). Put those expert rankings in Column D. At this point, the Individual Error scores in Column A can be computed by taking the absolute difference between Column B and Column D. The Group Error scores in Column E can also be computed by taking the absolute difference between Column C and Column D. Finally, the Persuasion scores can be computed by taking the absolute difference between Column B and Column C. Remember that all of the differences are absolute differences—there should not be any negative numbers in the table. After completing all these computations, fill in the three scores below the table: the Individual Score (total of Column A), the Group Score (total of Column E), and the Persuasion Score (total of Column F). The Persuasion score measures how much you are able to influence other group members to match your thinking.

12.5 The instructor will create a table similar to the one that follows in an Excel file in the classroom or on the chalkboard. All groups should provide the instructor with their

	A	B	C	D	E	F
	INDIVIDUAL ERROR (B – D)	YOUR RANKING	GROUP RANKING	EXPERT RANKING	GROUP ERROR (C – D)	PERSUASION SCORE (B – C)
Fanny pack of food (cheese, salami, etc.)						
Plastic-covered map of the region						
Six personal flotation devices						
Two fishing poles (broken)						
Set of clothes for three (wet)						
One yellow Frisbee						
Water purification tablets						
Duct tape (one 30' roll)						
Whiskey (one pint, 180 proof)						
Insect repellant (one bottle)						
Matches (30, dry)						
Parachute cord (35')						
Compass						
Six sleeping bags (synthetic)						

Individual Score: (Total all numbers in Column A): _____

Group Score: (Total all numbers in Column E): _____

Persuasion Score: (Total all numbers in Column F): _____

Average Member Score (the average of all of the Individual Scores for the group), the Group Score, their Best Member Score (the lowest of all the Individual Scores for the group), and that member's Persuasion Score (the Persuasion Score for the member who had the lowest Individual Score).

12.6 Fill in a "Yes" for the Process Gain row if the Group Score was lower than the Average Member Score. This score would reflect a circumstance in which the group

GROUPS	1	2	3	4	5	6	7	8
Average Member Score								
Group Score								
Best Member Score								
Best Member's Persuasion								
Process Gain? (Yes or No)								

discussion actually resulted in more accurate decisions—when "the whole" seemed to be more effective than "the sum of its parts." Fill in a "No" for the Process Gain row if the Group Score was higher than the Average Member Score. In this circumstance, the group discussion actually resulted in less accurate decisions—and the group would have been better off if no talking had occurred.

12.7 Class discussion (whether in groups or as a class) should center on the following questions: Did most groups tend to achieve process gain in terms of group scores that were better than the average individual scores? Were the group scores usually better than the best member's score? Why not; where did the groups that lacked synergy tend to go wrong? In other words, what behaviors led to process loss rather than process gain? What role does the best member's persuasion score play in all of this? Did groups that tended to listen more to the best member (as reflected in lower persuasion numbers) have more frequent instances of process gain?

Source: Adapted from D. Marcic, J. Selzer, and P. Vail. *Organizational Behavior: Experiences and Cases* (Cincinnati, OH: South-Western, 2001).

ENDNOTES

12.1　United Airlines, Corporate Web Site. "Era 1: 1910–1925." http://www.united.com/page/middle page/0,6823,2281,00.html (July 3, 2009).

12.2　United Airlines, Corporate Web Site. "Company Information." http://ir.united.com/phoenix.zhtml?c=83680&p=irol-homeProfile (July 3, 2009).

12.3　United Airlines, Corporate Web Site. "Company Information." http://www.united.com/page/article/0,6722,50100,00.html (July 3, 2009).

12.4　United Airlines, Corporate Web Site. "Company Information." http://www.united.com/page/middlepage/0,6823,50103,00.html (July 29, 2009)

12.5　MSNBC Online. "United Gets Approval to Shift Pension Plans." May 11, 2005. http://www.msnbc.msn.com/id/7804770/ (July 3, 2009).

12.6　Ibid.

12.7　Cary, S. "United Airlines Workers Go to School for Pit Crews." *The San Diego Union Tribune Online*,

March 25, 2006. http://www.signonsandiego.com/uniontrib/20060325/news_lz1n25read.html (July 5, 2009).

12.8 ABC News.com. "Corporations Send Employees to Pit Crew U." April 9, 2006. http://abcnews.go.com/print?id=1817896 (June 16, 2009).

12.9 Cary, "United Airlines Workers."

12.10 Ibid.

12.11 Ilgen, D.R.; D.A. Major; J.R. Hollenbeck; and D.J. Sego. "Team Research in the 1990s." In *Leadership Theory and Research: Perspectives and Directions,* eds. M.M. Chemers and R. Ayman. New York: Academic Press, Inc., 1993.

12.12 "Process." Merriam-Webster online dictionary, http://www.merriam-webster.com/dictionary/process (May 27, 2007).

12.13 Hackman, J.R. "The Design of Work Teams." In *Handbook of Organizational Behavior,* ed. J.W. Lorsch. Englewood Cliffs, NJ: Prentice Hall, 1987, pp. 315–42.

12.14 Steiner, I.D. *Group Processes and Productivity.* New York: Academic Press, 1972.

12.15 Hackman, "The Design of Work Teams."

12.16 Lamm, H., and G. Trommsdorff. "Group Versus Individual Performance on Tasks Requiring Ideational Proficiency (Brainstorming)." *European Journal of Social Psychology* 3 (1973), pp. 361–87.

12.17 Hackman, "The Design of Work Teams."

12.18 Latane, B.; K. Williams; and S. Harkins. "Many Hands Make Light the Work: The Causes and Consequences of Social Loafing." *Journal of Personality and Social Psychology* 37 (1979), pp. 822–32.

12.19 Latane et al., "Many Hands"; Jackson, C.L., and J.A. LePine. "Peer Responses to a Team's Weakest Link: A Test and Extension of LePine and Van Dyne's Model." *Journal of Applied Psychology* 88 (2003), pp. 459–75; and Sheppard, A. "Productivity Loss in Performance Groups: A Motivation Analysis." *Psychological Bulletin* 113 (1993), pp. 67–81.

12.20 Shalley, C.E.; J. Zhou; and G.R. Oldham. "The Effects of Personal and Contextual Characteristics on Creativity: Where Should We Go from Here?" *Journal of Management* 30 (2004), pp. 933–58.

12.21 Hirst, G.; D.V. Knippenberg; and J. Zhou. "A Cross-Level Perspective on Employee Creativity: Goal Orientation, Team Learning Behavior, and Individual Creativity." *Academy of Management Journal,* 52 (2009), pp. 280–93.

12.22 Kelley, T., and J. Littman. *The Art of Innovation* New York: Doubleday, 2001, p. 69.

12.23 Osborn, A.F. *Applied Imagination* (revised ed.). New York: Scribner, 1957.

12.24 Ibid.

12.25 Diehl, M., and W. Stroebe. "Productivity Loss in Brainstorming Groups: Toward a Solution of a Riddle." *Journal of Personality and Social Psychology* 53 (1987), pp. 497–509; and Mullen, B.; C. Johnson; and E. Salas. "Productivity Loss in Brainstorming Groups: A Meta-Analytic Investigation." *Basic and Applied Social Psychology* 12 (1991), pp. 3–23.

12.26　Diehl and Stroebe, "Productivity Loss."

12.27　Sutton, R.I., and A. Hargadon. "Brainstorming Groups in Context: Effectiveness in a Product Design Firm." *Administrative Science Quarterly* 41 (1996), pp. 685–718.

12.28　Kelley and Littman, *The Art of Innovation.*

12.29　Delbecq, A.L., and A.H. Van de Ven. "A Group Process Model for Identification and Program Planning." *Journal of Applied Behavioral Sciences* 7 (1971), pp. 466–92; and Geschka, H.; G.R. Schaude; and H. Schlicksupp. "Modern Techniques for Solving Problems." *Chemical Engineering,* August 1973, pp. 91–97.

12.30　Brehmer, B., and R. Hagafors. "Use of Experts in Complex Decision Making: A Paradigm for the Study of Staff Work." *Organizational Behavior and Human Decision Processes* 38 (1986), pp. 181–95; and Ilgen, D.R.; D. Major; J.R. Hollenbeck; and D. Sego. "Raising an Individual Decision Making Model to the Team Level: A New Research Model and Paradigm." In *Team Effectiveness and Decision Making in Organizations,* eds. R. Guzzo and E. Salas. San Francisco: Jossey-Bass, 1995, pp. 113–48.

12.31　Hollenbeck, J.R.; J.A. Colquitt; D.R. Ilgen; J.A. LePine; and J. Hedlund. "Accuracy Decomposition and Team Decision Making: Testing Theoretical Boundary Conditions." *Journal of Applied Psychology* 83 (1998), pp. 494–500; and Hollenbeck, J.R.; D.R. Ilgen; D.J. Sego; J. Hedlund; D.A. Major; and J. Phillips. "Multilevel Theory of Team Decision Making; Decision Performance in Teams Incorporating Distributed Expertise." *Journal of Applied Psychology* 80 (1995), pp. 292–316.

12.32　Humphrey, S.E.; J.R. Hollenbeck; C.J. Meyer; and D.R. Ilgen. "Hierarchical Team Decision Making." *Research in Personnel and Human Resources Management* 21 (2002), pp. 175–213.

12.33　Hollenbeck et al., "Multilevel Theory of Team Decision Making"; and Hollenbeck, J.R.; D.R. Ilgen; J.A. LePine; J.A. Colquitt; and J. Hedlund. "Extending the Multilevel Theory of Team Decision Making: Effects of Feedback and Experience in Hierarchical Teams." *Academy of Management Journal* 41 (1998), pp. 269–82.

12.34　Hollenbeck et al., "Extending the Multilevel Theory."

12.35　Hedlund, J.; D.R. Ilgen; and J.R. Hollenbeck. "Decision Accuracy in Computer-Mediated vs. Face-to-Face Decision Making Teams." *Organizational Behavior and Human Decision Processes* 76 (1998), pp. 30–47.

12.36　Ilgen, D.R.; J.A. LePine; and J.R. Hollenbeck. "Effective Decision Making in Multinational Teams." In *New Perspectives in International Industrial–Organizational Psychology,* eds. P.C. Earley and M. Erez. San Francisco: Jossey-Bass, 1997, pp. 377–409.

12.37　Ancona, D.G. "Outward Bound: Strategies for Team Survival in an Organization." *Academy of Management Journal* 33 (1990), pp. 334–65.

12.38　Dwyer, P.; P. Engardio; S. Schiller; and S. Reed. "The New Model: Tearing up Today's Organization Chart." *BusinessWeek,* November 18, 1994, pp. 80–90.

12.39 Cox, T.; S. Lobel; and P. McLeod. "Effects of Ethnic Group Cultural Differences on Cooperative and Competitive Behavior on a Group Task." *Academy of Management Journal* 34 (1991), pp. 827–47; and Mannix, E., and M.A. Neal. "What Differences Make a Difference? The Promise and Reality of Diverse Teams in Organizations." *Psychological Science in the Public Interest* 6 (2005), pp. 31–55.

12.40 Ilgen et al., "Effective Decision Making."

12.41 Prieto Zamora, J.M., and R. Martinez Arias. "Those Things Yonder Are not Giants, but Decision Makers in International Teams." In *New Perspectives on International Industrial and Organizational Psychology,* eds. P.C. Earley and M. Erez. San Francisco: New Lexington Press, 1997, pp. 410–45.

12.42 Ibid.; and Hollenbeck et al., "Accuracy Decomposition."

12.43 Ibid.; and Marrone, J.A.; P.E. Tesluk; and J.B. Carson. "A Multilevel Investigation of Antecedents and Consequences of Team Member Boundary-Spanning Behavior." *Academy of Management Journal* 50 (2007), pp. 1423–39.

12.44 LePine, J.A.; R.F. Piccolo; C.L. Jackson; J.E. Mathieu; and J.R. Saul. "A Meta-Analysis of Team Process: Towards a Better Understanding of the Dimensional Structure and Relationships with Team Effectiveness Criteria." *Personnel Psychology* 61 (2008), pp. 273–307; and Marks, M.A.; J.E. Mathieu; and S.J. Zaccaro. "A Temporally Based Framework and Taxonomy of Team Processes." *Academy of Management Review* 26 (2001), pp. 356–76.

12.45 Marks et al., "A Temporally Based Framework." This section on teamwork processes is based largely on their work.

12.46 Barnes, C.M.; J.R. Hollenbeck; D.T. Wagner; D.S. DeRue; J.D. Nahrgang; and K.M. Schwind. "Harmful Help: The Costs of Backing-Up Behavior in Teams." *Journal of Applied Psychology* 93 (2008), pp. 529–39.

12.47 Kozlowski, S.W.J., and B.S. Bell. "Work Groups and Teams in Organizations." In *Handbook of Psychology,* Vol. 12: Industrial and Organizational Psychology, eds. W.C. Borman; D.R. Ilgen; and R.J. Klimoski; Hoboken, NJ: John Wiley & Sons, Inc., 2003, pp. 333–75.

12.48 Behfar, K.J.; R.S. Peterson; E.A. Mannix; and W.M.K. Trochim. "The Critical Role of Conflict Resolution in Teams: A Close Look at the Links Between Conflict Type, Conflict Management Strategies, and Team Outcomes." *Journal of Applied Psychology* 93 (2008), pp. 170–88; and De Dreu, C.K.W., and L.R. Weingart. "Task Versus Relationship Conflict, Team Performance, and Team Member Satisfaction: A Meta-Analysis." *Journal of Applied Psychology* 88 (2003), pp. 741–49.

12.49 Jehn, K. "A Multimethod Examination of the Benefits and Detriments of Intergroup Conflict." *Administrative Science Quarterly* 40 (1995), pp. 256–82.

12.50 De Dreu and Weingart, "Task Versus Relationship Conflict."

12.51 Thompson, L.L. *Making the Team: A Guide for Managers,* 2nd ed. Upper Saddle River, NJ: Pearson Prentice Hall, 2004.

12.52   De Church, L.A., and M.A. Marks. "Maximizing the Benefits of Task Conflict: The Role of Conflict Management." *The International Journal of Conflict Management* 12 (2001), pp. 4–22; De Dreu and Weingart, "Task Versus Relationship Conflict"; and Van de Vliert, E., and M.C. Euwema. "Agreeableness and Activeness as Components of Conflict Behaviors." *Journal of Personality and Social Psychology* 66 (1994), pp. 674–87.

12.53   De Church and Marks, "Maximizing the Benefits"; and Van de Vliert and Euwema, "Agreeableness and Activeness."

12.54   Langan-Fox, J. "Communication in Organizations: Speed, Diversity, Networks, and Influence on Organizational Effectiveness, Human Health, and Relationships." In *Handbook of Industrial, Work, and Organizational Psychology*. Vol. 2, ed. N. Anderson, D.S. Ones; and H.K. Sinangil. Thousand Oaks, CA: Sage Publications, 2001, pp. 188–205.

12.55   Krone, K.J.; F.M. Jablin; and L.L. Putman. "Communication Theory and Organizational Communication: Multiple Perspectives." In *Handbook of Organizational Communication*, eds. F.M. Jablin, K.L. Putman, KH. Roberts, and L.W. Porter. Newbury Park, CA: Sage, 1987; and Shannon, C.E., and W. Weaver. *The Mathematical Theory of Communication.* Urbana: University of Illinois Press, 1964.

12.56   Ibid.

12.57   Jablin, F.M., and P.M. Sias. "Communication Competence." In *The New Handbook of Organizational Communication: Advances in Theory, Research, and Methods*, eds. F.M. Jablin and L.L. Putnam . Thousand Oaks, CA: Sage, 2001, pp. 819–64.

12.58   Krone et al., "Communication Theory and Organizational Communication"; and Shannon and Weaver, "The Mathematical Theory of Communication."

12.59   Daft, R.L., and R.H. Lengel. "Information Richness: A New Approach to Managerial Behavior and Organizational Design." In *Research in Organizational Behavior*, eds. B.M. Staw and L.L. Cummings. Greenwich, CT: JAI Press, 1984, pp. 191–233.

12.60   Ibid.

12.61   Ibid.

12.62   Ibid.

12.63   Byron, K. "Carrying Too Heavy a Load? The Communication and Miscommunication of Emotion by Email." *Academy of Management Review* 33 (2008), pp. 309–27.

12.64   Daft and Lengel, "Information Richness."

12.65   Ibid.

12.66   Leavitt, H.J. "Some Effects of Certain Communication Patterns on Group Performance." *Journal of Abnormal and Social Psychology* 436 (1951), pp. 38–50.

12.67   Glanzer, M., and R. Glaser. "Techniques for the Study of Group Structure and Behavior: II. Empirical Studies of the Effects of Structure in Small Groups." *Psychological Bulletin* 58 (1961), pp. 1–27.

12.68   Farace, R.V.; P.R. Monge; and H.M. Russell. "Communication in Micro-Networks." In *Organizational Communication*, 2nd ed., eds. F.D. Ferguson and S. Ferguson. New Brunswick, NJ:

Transaction Books, 1988, pp. 365–69.

12.69 Festinger, L. "Informal Social Communication." *Psychological Review* 57 (1950), pp. 271–82.

12.70 Beal, D.J.; R.R. Cohen; M.J. Burke; and C.L. McLendon. "Cohesion and Performance in Groups: A *Meta*-Analytic Clarification of Construct Relations." *Journal of Applied Psychology* 88 (2003), pp. 989–1004; and Mullen, B., and C. Copper. "The Relation Between Group Cohesiveness and Performance: An Integration." *Psychological Bulletin* 115 (1994), pp. 210–27.

12.71 Janis, I.L. *Victims of Groupthink: A Psychological Study of Foreign Policy Decisions and Fiascoes.* Boston, MA: Houghton Mifflin, 1972.

12.72 Ibid.

12.73 Hirokawa, R.; D. Gouran; and A. Martz. "Understanding the Sources of Faulty Group Decision Making: A Lesson from the *Challenger* Disaster." *Small Group Behavior* 19 (1988), pp. 411–33; Esser, J., and J. Linoerfer. "Groupthink and the Space Shuttle *Challenger* Accident: Toward a Quantitative Case Analysis." *Journal of Behavioral Decision Making* 2 (1989), pp. 167–77; and Moorhead, G.; R. Ference; and C. Neck. "Group Decision Fiascoes Continue: Space Shuttle *Challenger* and a Revised Groupthink Framework." *Human Relations* 44 (1991), pp. 539–50.

12.74 Stephens, J., and P. Behr. "Enron Culture Fed Its Demise." *Washington Post,* June 27, 2002, pp. A1–2.

12.75 Shea, G.P., and R.A. Guzzo. "Groups as Human Resources."

In *Research in Personnel and Human Resource Management,* Vol. 5, eds. K.M. Rowland and G.R. Ferris. Greenwich, CT: JAI Press, 1987, pp. 323–56.

12.76 Tasa, K.; S. Taggar; and G.H. Seijts. "Development of Collective Efficacy in Teams: A Multilevel and Longitudinal Perspective." *Journal of Applied Psychology* 92 (2007), pp. 17–27.

12.77 Gully, S.M.; K.A. Incalaterra; A. Joshi; and J.M. Beubien. "A Meta-Analysis of Team-Efficacy, Potency, and Performance: Interdependence and Level of Analysis as Moderators of Observed Relationships." *Journal of Applied Psychology* 87 (2002), pp. 819–32.

12.78 Tasa et al., ""Development of Collective Efficacy in Teams."

12.79 Klimoski, R.J., and S. Mohammed. "Team Mental Model: Construct or Metaphor?" *Journal of Management* 20 (1994), pp. 403–37.

12.80 Cannon-Bowers, J.A.; E. Salas; and S.A. Converse. "Shared Mental Models in Expert Team Decision Making." *Individual and Group Decision Making,* ed. N.J. Castellan. Hillsdale, NJ: Erlbaum, 1993, pp. 221–46.

12.81 Wegner, D.M. "Transactive Memory: A Contemporary Analysis of the Group Mind." In *Theories of Group Behavior,* ed. B. Mullen and G.R. Goethals. New York: Springer-Verlag, 1986, pp. 185–208.

12.82 Hollingshead, A.B. "Communication, Learning, and Retrieval in Transactive Memory Systems." *Journal of Experimental Social Psychology* 34 (1998), pp. 423–42.

12.83 Wegner, "Transactive Memory."

12.84 LePine et al., "A Meta-Analysis of Team Process."

12.85 Barrick, M.R.; B.H. Bradley; A.L. Kristoff Brown; and A.E. Colbert. "The Moderating Role of Top Management Team Interdependence: Implications for Real Teams and Working Groups." *Academy of Management Journal* 50 (2007), pp. 544–57.

12.86 LePine et al., "A Meta-Analysis of Team Process."

12.87 Jones, D. "Business Leadership Book Wins Fans in NFL." *USA Today,* November 29, 2005, http://www.usatoday.com/money/books/2005-11-27-nfl-book-usat_x.htm (May 29, 2007).

12.88 Stevens, M.J., and M.A. Campion. "The Knowledge, Skill, and Ability Requirements for Teamwork: Implications for Human Resource Management." *Journal of Management* 20 (1994), pp. 503–30.

12.89 Ibid.; and Ellis, A.P.J.; B. Bell; R.E. Ployhart; J.R. Hollenbeck; and D.R. Ilgen. "An Evaluation of Generic Teamwork Skills Training with Action Teams: Effects on Cognitive and Skill-Based Outcomes." *Personnel Psychology* 58 (2005), pp. 641–72.

12.90 Stout, R.J.; E. Salas; and J.E. Fowlkes. "Enhancing Teamwork in Complex Environments through Team Training." *Group Dynamics: Theory, Research, and Practice* 1 (1997), pp. 169–82.

12.91 Volpe, C.E.; J.A. Cannon-Bowers; E. Salas; and P.E. Spector. "The Impact of Cross-Training on Team Functioning: An Empirical Investigation." *Human Factors* 38 (1996), pp. 87–100.

12.92 Marks, M.A.; M.J. Sabella; C.S. Burke; and S.J. Zaccaro. "The Impact of Cross-Training on Team Effectiveness." *Journal of Applied Psychology* 87 (2002), pp. 3–13.

12.93 Blickensderfer, E.; J.A. Cannon-Bowers; and E. Salas. "Cross Training and Team Performance." In *Making Decisions Under Stress: Implications for Individual and Team Training,* eds. J.A. Cannon-Bowers and E. Salas. Washington, DC: APA Press, 1998, pp. 299–311.

12.94 Dotlich, D., and J. Noel. *Active Learning: How the World's Top Companies Are Recreating their Leaders and Themselves.* San Francisco: Jossey-Bass, 1998; and Marquardt, M. "Harnessing the Power of Action Learning." *T&D* 58 (June 2004), pp. 26–32.

12.95 Carey, S. "Racing to Improve; United Airlines Employees Go to School for Pit Crews to Boost Teamwork, Speed." *The Wall Street Journal,* Eastern Edition, March 24, 2006, p. B.1.

12.96 Salas, E.; D. Bozell; B. Mullen; and J.E. Driskell. "The Effect of Team Building on Performance: An Integration." *Small Group Research* 30 (1999), pp. 309–29.

12.97 Berman, D. "Zap! Pow! Splat!; Laser Tag and Paintball Can Enhance Teamwork, Communications, and Planning." *BusinessWeek,* February 9, 1998, p. ENT22. Proquest Database (April 19, 2007).

12.98 Rasor, M. "Got Game? Bring It On: WhirlyBall Helps Workers Develop Drive, Teamwork." *Knight Ridder Tribune Business News,* April 3, 2006, p. 1. Proquest Database (May 7, 2006).

12.99   Regan, M.P. "Team Players: From Drums to Daring Getaways, Workers Embark on Team-Building Exercises." *Gainesville Sun,* February 15, 2004, pp. 5G, 6G.

12.100   Ballard, T.N. "Postal IG Under Fire for Unusual 'Team-Building' Activities." GovernmentExecutive.com, 2003, http://www.govexec.com/

dailyfed/0503/050203t1.htm (October 15, 2003).

12.101   Dorgan, B.L., and R. Widen. "Letter to Chairman Fineman," May 1, 2003, http://www.govexec.com/pdfs/corcoran.pdf.

12.102   Salas et al., "The Effect of Team Building."

12.103   ABC News.com. "Corporations Send Employees to Pit Crew U." Cary, "United Airlines Workers."

Leadership: Power and Negotiation

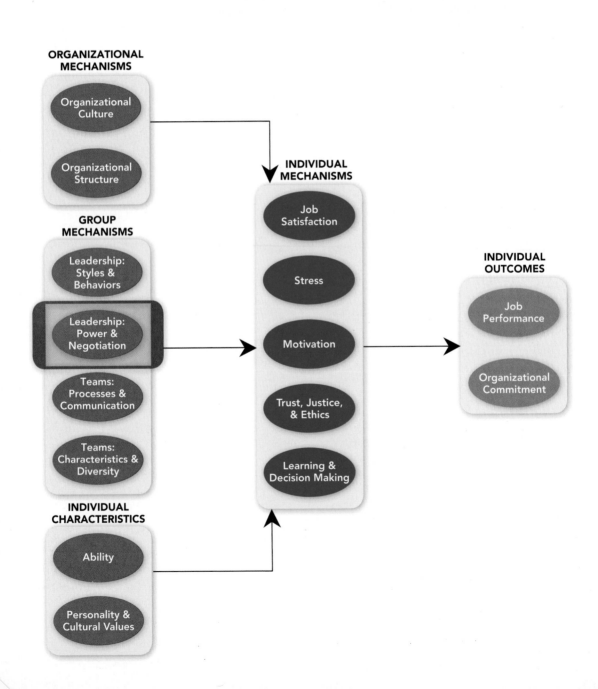

ORGANIZATIONAL
MECHANISMS

- Organizational Culture
- Organizational Structure

GROUP
MECHANISMS

- Leadership: Styles & Behaviors
- Leadership: Power & Negotiation
- Teams: Processes & Communication
- Teams: Characteristics & Diversity

INDIVIDUAL
CHARACTERISTICS

- Ability
- Personality & Cultural Values

INDIVIDUAL
MECHANISMS

- Job Satisfaction
- Stress
- Motivation
- Trust, Justice, & Ethics
- Learning & Decision Making

INDIVIDUAL
OUTCOMES

- Job Performance
- Organizational Commitment

✅ LEARNING GOALS

After reading this chapter, you should be able to answer the following questions:

13.1 What is leadership, and what role does power play in leadership?

13.2 What are the different types of power that leaders possess, and when can they use those types most effectively?

13.3 What behaviors do leaders exhibit when trying to influence others, and which of these is most effective?

13.4 What is organizational politics, and when is political behavior most likely to occur?

13.5 How do leaders use their power and influence to resolve conflicts in the workplace?

13.6 What are the ways in which leaders negotiate in the workplace?

13.7 How do power and influence affect job performance and organizational commitment?

HARPO

It might very well surprise you to see the face of Oprah Winfrey here in this chapter on leadership. After all, Winfrey is an actress and television talk show host—isn't she? Why yes, she certainly is, but she's a lot more than that as well. Winfrey is recognized as one of the leading businesspeople in the country and stands firmly in control at Harpo ("Oprah" spelled backward), an entertainment and media company with $345 million in sales in 2008 and 410 employees.[1] Winfrey currently ranks eighth in *Fortune* magazine's list of the most powerful women in business.[2] She also is one of only four women to have remained on the list since its inception in 1998.[3] She's proven to be an extremely shrewd leader and negotiator as chairperson of the organization she founded, earning the respect of not only those who watch her shows, read her magazine, listen to her radio channel, and purchase products that she endorses, but the employees of Harpo as well.

As you'll find in reading this chapter, Winfrey's power at Harpo doesn't come solely because she sits at the top of the organizational chart. Part of her power is celebrity driven, but this celebrity persona has been carefully managed and controlled by Winfrey herself. Winfrey owns every piece of her company: the content, the name brand, the studio, and all production facilities.[4] One of her most important negotiating victories came in 1988, when she acquired the rights to syndicate her own talk show (something that only Johnny Carson had done previously and few have done since).[5] Since that time, everything that has earned the Oprah stamp of approval has gone through careful consideration, and most potential opportunities get turned down. Winfrey recognizes that her approach to business is somewhat unique: "I don't care about money. It throws people off in business meetings. They start shuffling papers."[6] There are many examples of such behavior; she rejected a cosmetics company by asking, "Why would I do that?"[7] and she declined invitations from AT&T, Ralph Lauren, and Intel to sit on their corporate boards by saying, "Guys, I don't know what I'd be doing on your board."[8] This willingness to admit what she does and doesn't know has helped her not only influence the masses but also lead her organization and its employees. Winfrey is the first to admit that she knows little about the numbers side of the business; instead, she hands the operational duties of running the organization over to others. As a privately owned company, Harpo, Inc., can think long-term rather than worry about short-term numbers for shareholders, which can be a real benefit when the entire company is built on a set of core values that employees hold dear.

What Winfrey does know is how to entertain and influence through various forms of media, including a best-selling magazine (*O, The Oprah Magazine*), a satellite radio channel, and an award-winning Web site. Harpo is headquartered in several buildings in downtown Chicago, or "the campus" as Harpo employees like to call it. The campus has its own café, gym, and spa facilities. Harpo employees freely admit that Winfrey is incredibly demanding, but as Winfrey notes, "I don't yell at people. I don't mistreat people. I don't talk down to people, so no one else in this building, in this vicinity, has the right to do it. Treating people with respect is the most important thing to me. It's not just talk."[9] As OWN (the Oprah Winfrey Network) gets started in late 2009 or early 2010, Winfrey's presence, already seemingly everywhere, will only increase. OWN is a 50–50 joint venture between Harpo and Discovery Communications and will replace the previous Discovery Health channel, broadcasting to approximately 70 million homes.[10] It represents just one more form of influence that Winfrey will exert, and if history holds true, she'll make good use of it too.

LEADERSHIP: POWER AND NEGOTIATION

As evidenced by Harpo, Inc., leaders within organizations can make a huge difference to the success of an organization or group. It would be easy after reading the opening example to anoint Oprah Winfrey as a great leader and try to adopt her behavioral examples to follow in her footsteps. However, things aren't quite that simple. Many other leaders have exhibited similar behaviors and not been nearly as successful. Thankfully, leadership also isn't just about being a celebrity, or most of us would have to give up right now! As we'll discover in this and the next chapter, there are many different types of leaders, many of whom can excel, given the right circumstances.

There is perhaps no subject that's written about more in business circles than the topic of leadership. A quick search on Amazon.com for "leadership" will generate a list of more than 200,000 books! That number doesn't even count the myriad of videos, calendars, audio recordings, and other items, all designed to help people become better leaders. Given all the interest in this topic, a natural question becomes, "What exactly is a leader?" We define **leadership** as the use of power and influence to direct the activities of followers toward goal achievement.[11] That direction can affect followers' interpretation of events, the organization of their work activities, their commitment to key goals, their relationships with other followers, and their access to cooperation and support from other work units.[12] This chapter focuses on how leaders *get* the power and influence they use to direct others and the ways in which power and influence are utilized in organizations, including through negotiation. Chapter 14 will focus on how leaders actually *use* their power and influence to help followers achieve their goals.

✔ **13.1**

What is leadership, and what role does power play in leadership?

WHY ARE SOME LEADERS MORE POWERFUL THAN OTHERS?

What exactly comes to mind when you think of the term "power"? Does it raise a positive or negative image for you? Certainly it's easy to think of leaders who have used power for what we would consider good purposes, but it's just as easy to think of leaders who have used power for unethical or immoral purposes. For now, try not to focus on how leaders use power but instead on how they acquire it. **Power** can be defined as the ability to influence the behavior of others and resist unwanted influence in return.[13] Note that this definition gives us a couple of key points to think about. First, just because a person has the ability to influence others does not mean they will actually choose to do so. In many organizations, the most powerful employees don't even realize how influential they could be! Second, in addition to influencing others, power can be seen as the ability to resist the influence attempts of others.[14] This resistance could come in the form of the simple voicing of a dissenting opinion, the refusal to perform a specific behavior, or the organization of an opposing group of coworkers.[15] Sometimes leaders need to resist the influence of other leaders or higher-ups to do what's best for their own unit. Other times leaders need to resist the influence of their own employees to avoid being a "pushover" when employees try to go their own way.

ACQUIRING POWER

Think about the people you currently work with or have worked with in the past, or think of students that are involved in many of the same activities you are. Do any of those people seem to have especially high levels of power, meaning that they have the ability to influence your

13.2

What are the different types of power that leaders possess, and when can they use those types most effectively?

behavior? What is it that gives them that power? In some cases, their power may come from some formal position (e.g., supervisor, team leader, teaching assistant, resident advisor). However, sometimes the most powerful people we know lack any sort of formal authority. It turns out that power in organizations can come from a number of different sources. Specifically, there are five major types of power that can be grouped along two dimensions: organizational power and personal power.[16] These types of power are illustrated in Figure 13-1.

ORGANIZATIONAL POWER. The three types of organizational power derive primarily from a person's position within the organization. These types of power are considered more formal in nature.[17] **Legitimate power** derives from a position of authority inside the organization and is sometimes referred to as "formal authority." People with legitimate power have some title—some term on an organizational chart or on their door that says, "Look, I'm supposed to have influence over you." Those with legitimate power have the understood right to ask others to do things that are considered within the scope of their authority. When managers ask an employee to stay late to work on a project, work on one task instead of another, or work faster, they are exercising legitimate power. The higher up in an organization a person is, the more legitimate power they generally possesses. *Fortune* magazine provides rankings of the most powerful women in business. As shown in Table 13-1, all of those women possess legitimate power, in that they hold a title that affords them the ability to influence others.

Legitimate power does have its limits, however. It doesn't generally give a person the right to ask employees to do something outside the scope of their jobs or roles within the organization. For example, if a manager asked an employee to wash their car or mow their lawn, it would likely be seen as an inappropriate request. As we'll see later in this chapter, there's a big difference between having legitimate power and using it effectively. When used ineffectively, legitimate power can be a very weak form of power. In our opening example, Winfrey doesn't simply go bossing everyone in the organization around; she manages her legitimate power effectively to earn respect and get people to commit to their endeavors.

FIGURE 13-1   **Types of Power**

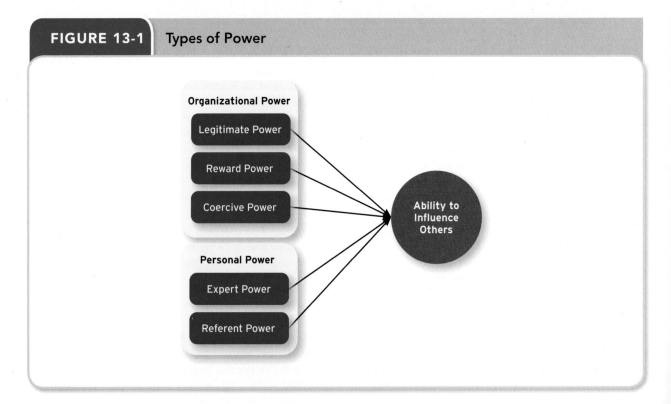

TABLE 13-1	*Fortune*'s 15 Most Powerful Women in Business in 2008

	NAME	COMPANY	POSITION	AGE
1	Indra Nooyi	PepsiCo	Chairman and CEO	52
2	Irene Rosenfeld	Kraft Foods	Chairman and CEO	55
3	Pat Woertz	Archer Daniels Midland	Chairman, President, and CEO	55
4	Anne Mulcahy	Xerox	Chairman and CEO	55
5	Angela Braly	Wellpoint	President and CEO	47
6	Andrea Jung	Avon Products	Chairperson and CEO	50
7	Susan Arnold	Procter & Gamble	President, Global Business Units	54
8	Oprah Winfrey	Harpo, Inc.	Chairperson	54
9	Brenda Barnes	Sara Lee	Chairman and CEO	54
10	Ursula Burns	Xerox	President	50
11	Ann Livermore	Hewlett-Packard	Executive Vice President	50
12	Anne Sweeney	Disney-ABC	Co-Chair, Disney Media Networks; President, Disney-ABC Television Group	50
13	Susan Desmond-Hellmann	Genentech	President, Product Development	51
14	Ginni Rometty	IBM	Senior Vice-President, Global Business Services	51
15	Ellen Kullman	Dupont	President	52

Source: J. Shambora and B. Kowitt, "The 50 Most Powerful Women," *Fortune*, October 13, 2008 (Vol. 158, No. 7/U.S. Edition), p. 165. Copyright © 2009 Time Inc. All rights reserved.

The next two forms of organizational power are somewhat intertwined with legitimate power. **Reward power** exists when someone has control over the resources or rewards another person wants. For example, managers generally have control over raises, performance evaluations, awards, more desirable job assignments, and the resources an employee might require to perform a job effectively. Those with reward power have the ability to influence others if those being influenced believe they will get the rewards by behaving in a certain way. **Coercive power** exists when a person has control over punishments in an organization. Coercive power operates primarily on the principle of fear. It exists when one person believes that another has the ability to punish him or her and is willing to use that power. For example, a manager might have the right to fire, demote, suspend, or lower the pay of an employee. Sometimes the limitations of a manager to impose punishments are formally spelled out in an organization. However, in many instances, managers have a considerable amount of leeway in this regard. Coercive power is generally regarded as a poor form of power to use regularly, because it tends to result in negative feelings toward those that wield it.

PERSONAL POWER. Of course, the women in Table 13-1 don't appear on that list just because they have some formal title that affords them the ability to reward and punish others. There's something else about them, as people, that provides them additional capabilities to influence others. Personal forms of power capture that "something else." **Expert power** derives from a person's expertise, skill, or knowledge on which others depend.

"Hank, when you're finished firing this gentleman I have some rather unfortunate news for you as well."

When people have a track record of high performance, the ability to solve problems, or specific knowledge that's necessary to accomplish tasks, they're more likely to be able to influence other people who need that expertise. Consider a lone programmer who knows how to operate a piece of antiquated software, a machinist who was recently trained to operate a new piece of equipment, or the only engineer who has experience working on a specific type of project. All of these individuals will have a degree of expert power because of what they individually bring to the organization. Pat Woertz, the CEO of Archer Daniels Midland (ADM), the Decatur, Illinois–based agricultural firm, appears third in Table 13-1 largely because of her expert power. ADM hired Woertz as CEO because it felt that her time at Chevron provided her with energy expertise that could help the firm in its push for renewable fuels.[18] There is perhaps no place where expert power comes into play more than in Silicon Valley, where it's widely perceived that the best leaders are those with significant technological experience and expertise. At Intel, CEO Andy Grove "fostered a culture in which 'knowledge power' would trump 'position power.' Anyone could challenge anyone else's idea, so long as it was about the idea and not the person—and so long as you were ready for the demand 'Prove it.'"[19]

Referent power exists when others have a desire to identify and be associated with a person. This desire is generally derived from affection, admiration, or loyalty toward a specific individual.[20] Although our focus is on individuals within organizations, there are many examples of political leaders, celebrities, and sports figures who seem to possess high levels of referent power. Barack Obama, Angelina Jolie, and Peyton Manning all possess referent power to some degree, because others want to emulate them. The same could be said of leaders in organizations who possess a good reputation, attractive personal qualities, or a certain level of charisma. Oprah Winfrey, as detailed in our opening chapter case, clearly wields an incredible amount of referent power. The people who watch her on TV or listen to her on satellite radio admire her views and often seek to emulate her actions. Just consider what happens when Winfrey mentions a book on her show—it rockets up the bestseller list almost immediately. If only she was looking for a good organizational behavior text. . . .

Of course, it's possible for a person to possess all of the forms of power at the same time. In fact, the most powerful leaders—like those in Table 13-1—have bases of power that include all five dimensions. From an employee's perspective, it's sometimes difficult to gauge what form of power is most important. Why exactly do you do what your boss asks you to do? Is it because the boss has the formal right to provide direction, because the boss controls your evaluations, or because you admire and like the boss? Many times, we don't know exactly what type of power leaders possess until they attempt to use it. Generally speaking, the personal forms of power are more strongly related to organizational commitment and job performance than are the organizational forms. If you think about the authorities for whom you worked the hardest, they probably possessed some form of expertise and charisma, rather than just an ability to reward and punish. Some useful guidelines for wielding each of the forms of power can be found in Table 13-2.

TABLE 13-2	Guidelines for Using Power

TYPE OF POWER	GUIDELINES FOR USE
Legitimate	• Make polite, clear requests. • Explain the reason for the request. • Don't exceed your scope of authority. • Follow up to verify compliance. • Insist on compliance if appropriate.
Reward	• Offer the types of rewards people desire. • Offer rewards that are fair and ethical. • Don't promise more than you can deliver. • Explain the criteria for giving rewards and keep it simple. • Provide rewards as promised if requirements are met. • Don't use rewards in a manipulative fashion.
Coercive	• Explain rules and requirements and ensure people understand the serious consequences of violations. • Respond to infractions promptly and without favoritism. • Investigate to get facts before following through. • Provide ample warnings. • Use punishments that are legitimate, fair, and commensurate with the seriousness of noncompliance.
Expert	• Explain the reasons for a request and why it's important. • Provide evidence that a proposal will be successful. • Don't make rash, careless, or inconsistent statements. • Don't exaggerate or misrepresent the facts. • Listen seriously to the person's concerns and suggestions. • Act confidently and decisively in a crisis.
Referent	• Show acceptance and positive regard. • Act supportive and helpful. • Use sincere forms of ingratiation. • Defend and back up people when appropriate. • Do unsolicited favors. • Make self-sacrifices to show concern. • Keep promises.

Source: Adapted and partially reprinted from G. Yukl, *Leadership in Organizations*, 5th ed. (Upper Saddle River, NJ: Prentice Hall, 2002).

CONTINGENCY FACTORS. There are certain situations in organizations that are likely to increase or decrease the degree to which leaders can use their power to influence others. Most of these situations revolve around the idea that the more other employees depend on a person, the more powerful that person becomes. A person can have high levels of expert and referent power, but if he or she works alone and performs tasks that nobody sees, the ability to influence others is greatly reduced. That being said, there are four factors that have an effect on the strength of a person's ability to use power to influence others.[21] These factors are summarized in Table 13-3. **Substitutability** is the degree to which people have alternatives in accessing resources. Leaders that control resources to which no one else has access can use their power to gain greater influence. **Discretion** is the degree to which managers have the right to make decisions on their own. If managers are forced to follow organizational policies and rules, their ability to influence others is reduced. **Centrality** represents how important a person's job is and how many people

TABLE 13-3	The Contingencies of Power
CONTINGENCY	**LEADER'S ABILITY TO INFLUENCE OTHERS INCREASES WHEN . . .**
Substitutability	There are no substitutes for the rewards or resources the leader controls.
Centrality	The leader's role is important and interdependent with others in the organization.
Discretion	The leader has the freedom to make his or her own decisions without being restrained by organizational rules.
Visibility	Others know about the leader and the resources he or she can provide.

depend on that person to accomplish their tasks. Leaders who perform critical tasks and interact with others regularly have a greater ability to use their power to influence others. **Visibility** is how aware others are of a leader's power and position. If everyone knows that a leader has a certain level of power, the ability to use that power to influence others is likely to be high.

Ken Loughridge, an information technology manager working for MWH Global—an environmental and engineering consulting firm based in England—took these ideas to heart when he changed jobs within the organization. He consulted a survey that the company had completed to map out the "social network" of the organization. He then used that network map to determine where his employees went for information, who possessed certain types of expertise, and who offered the most help to employees. He next met with each of the most well-connected individuals face-to-face. In a sense, he was seeking out and networking with the individuals in his organization who were likely to have the most power.[22] Companies are increasingly using such networking maps to understand the power structures in their organizations.

USING INFLUENCE

Up until now, we've discussed the types of power leaders possess and when their opportunities to use that power will grow or diminish. Now we turn to the specific strategies that leaders use to translate that power into actual influence.

Recall that having power increases our *ability* to influence behavior. It doesn't mean that we will use or exert that power. **Influence** is the use of an actual behavior that causes behavioral or attitudinal changes in others.[23] There are two important aspects of influence to keep in mind. First, influence can be seen as directional. It most frequently occurs downward (managers influencing employees) but can also be lateral (peers influencing peers) or upward (employees influencing managers). Second, influence is all relative. The absolute power of the "influencer" and "influencee" isn't as important as the disparity between them.[24]

INFLUENCE TACTICS. Leaders depend on a number of tactics to cause behavioral or attitudinal changes in others. In fact, there are at least ten types of tactics that leaders can use to try to influence others.[25] These tactics and their general levels of effectiveness are illustrated in Figure 13-2. The four most effective tactics have been shown to be rational persuasion, inspirational appeals, consultation, and collaboration. **Rational persuasion** is the use of logical arguments and hard facts to show the target that the request is a worthwhile one.

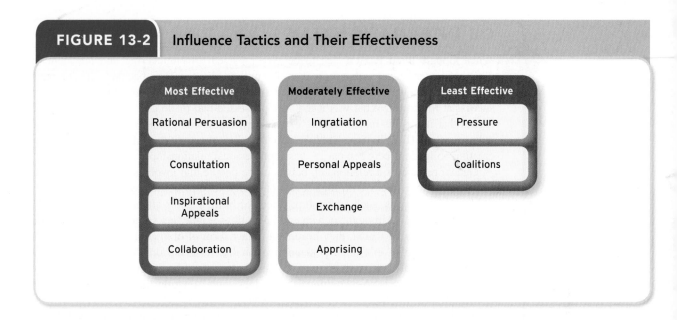

FIGURE 13-2 Influence Tactics and Their Effectiveness

Most Effective	Moderately Effective	Least Effective
Rational Persuasion	Ingratiation	Pressure
Consultation	Personal Appeals	Coalitions
Inspirational Appeals	Exchange	
Collaboration	Apprising	

Research shows that rational persuasion is most effective when it helps show that the proposal is important and feasible.[26] Rational persuasion is particularly important because it's the only tactic that is consistently successful in the case of upward influence.[27] At Hewlett-Packard, for example, Chairman and CEO Mark Hurd suggests that he uses this tactic most often to influence others and that it's the tactic that most often influences him when used by employees.[28] An **inspirational appeal** is a tactic designed to appeal to the target's values and ideals, thereby creating an emotional or attitudinal reaction. To use this tactic effectively, leaders must have insight into what kinds of things are important to the target. **Consultation** occurs when the target is allowed to participate in deciding how to carry out or implement a request. This tactic increases commitment from the target, who now has a stake in seeing that his or her opinions are valued. A leader uses **collaboration** by attempting to make it easier for the target to complete the request. Collaboration could involve the leader helping complete the task, providing required resources, or removing obstacles that make task completion difficult.[29]

Four other influence tactics are sometimes effective and sometimes not. **Ingratiation** is the use of favors, compliments, or friendly behavior to make the target feel better about the influencer. You might more commonly hear this referred to as "sucking up," especially when used in an upward influence sense. Ingratiation has been shown to be more effective when used as a long-term strategy and not nearly as effective when used immediately prior to making an influence attempt.[30] **Personal appeals** occur when the requestor asks for something based on personal friendship or loyalty. The stronger the friendship, the more successful the attempt is likely to be. As described in our **OB Internationally** feature, there are cultural differences when it comes to this kind of an appeal, as there are with other influence attempts. An **exchange tactic** is used when the requestor offers a reward or resource to the target in return for performing a request. This type of request requires that the requestor have something of value to offer.[31] Finally, **apprising** occurs when the requestor clearly explains why performing the request will benefit the target personally. It differs from rational persuasion in that it focuses solely on the benefit to the target as opposed to simple logic or benefits to the group or organization. It differs from exchange, in that the benefit is not necessarily something that the requestor gives to the target but rather something that results from the action.[32]

 13.3
What behaviors do leaders exhibit when trying to influence others, and which of these is most effective?

OB INTERNATIONALLY

When Google hired Kai-Fu Lee to be vice president of engineering and president of Google Greater China, with a more than $10 million compensation package, the company was counting on his continued ability to use the same skills that allowed him to be a huge success at Microsoft. What was it that Lee possessed that made him so worthwhile? Lee argues that it was his understanding of *guanxi* (pronounced gwan-she).[33] In the Chinese culture, guanxi (literally translated "relationships") is the ability to influence decisions by creating obligations between parties based on personal relationships.

Guanxi represents a relationship between two people that involves both sentiment and obligation.[34] Individuals with high levels of guanxi tend to be tied together on the basis of shared institutions, such as kinship, places of birth, schools attended, and past working relationships.[35] Although such shared institutions might "get someone in the door" in the United States, in China, they become a higher form of obligation. Influence through guanxi just happens—it's an unspoken obligation that must be addressed.[36] It is, in a sense, a blend of formal and personal relationships that exists at a different level than in the United States. There is no such thing as a "business-only" relationship, and the expectation is simply that if you take, you must also give back.[37]

American managers who go to work overseas must be conscious of these different but influential relationships. In addition to understanding the power of guanxi, evidence suggests that Chinese managers from different areas (e.g., Hong Kong, Taiwan, Mainland China) have different beliefs when it comes to which influence tactics are the most effective.[38] If anything, it goes to show that managers need to be acutely aware of both general and more specific cultural differences when trying to influence others in China.

The two tactics that have been shown to be least effective and could result in resistance from the target are pressure and coalitions. Of course, this statement doesn't mean that they aren't used or can't be effective at times. **Pressure** is the use of coercive power through threats and demands. As we've discussed previously, such coercion is a poor way to influence others and may only bring benefits over the short term. The last tactic is the formation of coalitions. **Coalitions** occur when the influencer enlists other people to help influence the target. These people could be peers, subordinates, or one of the target's superiors. Coalitions are generally used in combination with one of the other tactics. For instance, if rational persuasion is not strong enough, the influencer might bring in another person to show that that person agrees with the logic of the argument.

Two points should be noted about leaders' use of influence tactics. First, influence tactics tend to be most successful when used in combination.[39] Many tactics have some limitations or weaknesses that can be overcome using other tactics. Second, the influence tactics that tend to be most successful are those that are "softer" in nature. Rational persuasion, consultation, inspirational appeals, and collaboration take advantage of personal rather than organizational forms of power. Leaders that are the most effective at influencing others will generally rely on the softer tactics, make appropriate requests, and ensure the tactics they use match the types of power they have.

RESPONSES TO INFLUENCE TACTICS. As illustrated in Figure 13-3, there are three possible responses people have to influence tactics.[40] **Internalization** occurs when the target of influence agrees with and becomes committed to the influence request.[41] For

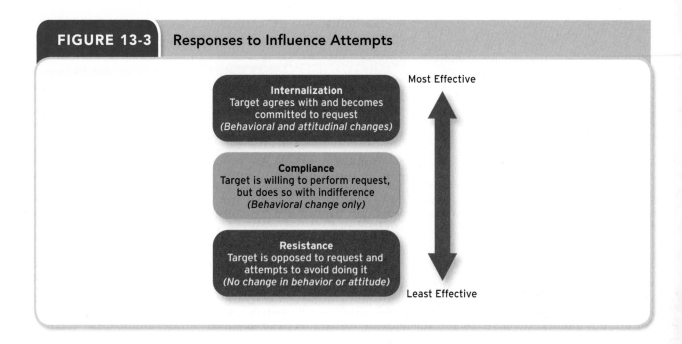

FIGURE 13-3 Responses to Influence Attempts

Internalization
Target agrees with and becomes committed to request
(Behavioral and attitudinal changes)

Compliance
Target is willing to perform request, but does so with indifference
(Behavioral change only)

Resistance
Target is opposed to request and attempts to avoid doing it
(No change in behavior or attitude)

Most Effective

Least Effective

a leader, this is the best outcome, because it results in employees putting forth the greatest level of effort in accomplishing what they are asked to do. Internalization reflects a shift in both the behaviors and the attitudes of employees. **Compliance** occurs when targets of influence are willing to do what the leader asks, but they do it with a degree of ambivalence. Compliance reflects a shift in the behaviors of employees but not their attitudes. This behavior is the most common response to influence attempts in organizations, because anyone with some degree of power who makes a reasonable request is likely to achieve compliance. That response allows leaders to accomplish their purpose, but it doesn't bring about the highest levels of employee effort and dedication. Still, it's clearly preferable to **resistance**, which occurs when the target refuses to perform the influence request and puts forth an effort to avoid having to do it. Employee resistance could come in the form of making excuses, trying to influence the requestor in return, or simply refusing to carry out the request. Resistance is most likely when the influencer's power is low relative to the target or when the request itself is inappropriate or unreasonable.[42]

POWER AND INFLUENCE IN ACTION

In this section, we look at two major areas in which leaders have the ability to use power to influence others. The first is through navigating the environment of organizational politics within the organization. The second is through using power and influence to help solve conflicts within the organization. As it turns out, it's easy for these two areas to coincide.

ORGANIZATIONAL POLITICS. If there was perhaps one term that had a more negative connotation than power, it might be politics. You've probably had people give you career advice such as, "Stay away from office politics" or "Avoid being seen as political." The truth is that you can't escape it; politics are a fact of life in organizations![43] Although you might hear company executives, such as former Vodaphone

13.4

What is organizational politics, and when is political behavior most likely to occur?

"You have no idea how political this place is."

CEO Sir Christopher Gent, make statements such as, "[When I was CEO], we were mercifully free of company politics and blame culture,"[44] you can be pretty sure that wasn't actually the case—especially given that England's Vodaphone is one of the world's largest mobile phone operators. Most leaders, such as Allison Young, vice president of Blue Cross and Blue Shield of Louisiana, will tell you that "You have to assess the political situation early on and make decisions on forward-looking strategy not only on the facts, but also the political landscape."[45] Whether we like it or not, organizations are filled with independent, goal-driven individuals who must take into account the possible actions and desires of others to get what they want.[46]

Organizational politics can be seen as actions by individuals that are directed toward the goal of furthering their own self-interests.[47] Although there's generally a negative perception of politics, it's important to note that this definition doesn't imply that furthering one's self-interests is necessarily in opposition to the company's interests. A leader needs to be able to push his or her own ideas and influence others through the use of organizational politics. Research has recently supported the notion that, to be effective, leaders must have a certain degree of political skill.[48] In fact, universities and some organizations such as Becton, Dickinson, and Company—a leading global medical technology company based in Franklin Lakes, New Jersey—are training their future leaders to be attuned to their political environment and develop their political skill.[49]

Political skill is the ability to effectively understand others at work and use that knowledge to influence others in ways that enhance personal and/or organizational objectives.[50] Two aspects of political skill are *networking ability*, or an adeptness at identifying and developing diverse contacts, and *social astuteness*, or the tendency to observe others and accurately interpret their behavior.[51] To see where you stand on these two dimensions, see our **OB Assessments** feature. Political skill also involves two other capabilities. *Interpersonal influence* involves having an unassuming and convincing personal style that's flexible enough to adapt to different situations.[52] *Apparent sincerity* involves appearing to others to have high levels of honesty and genuineness.[53] Taken together, these four skills provide a distinct advantage when navigating the political environments in organizations.

Although organizational politics can lead to positive outcomes, people's perceptions of politics are generally negative. This perception is certainly understandable, as anytime someone acts in a self-serving manner, it's potentially to the detriment of others.[54] In a highly charged political environment in which people are trying to capture resources and influence one another toward potentially opposing goals, it's only natural that some employees will feel stress about the uncertainty they face at work. Environments that are perceived as extremely political have been shown to cause lower job satisfaction, increased strain, lower job performance, and lower organizational commitment among employees.[55] In fact, high levels of organizational politics have even been shown to be detrimental to company performance as a whole.[56]

As a result, organizations (and leaders) do their best to minimize the perceptions of self-serving behaviors that are associated with organizational politics. This goal requires identifying the particular organizational circumstances that cause politics to thrive. As illustrated in Figure 13-4, organizational politics are driven by both personal characteristics

OB ASSESSMENTS

POLITICAL SKILL

How much political skill do you have? This assessment is designed to measure two dimensions of political skill. Please write a number next to each statement that indicates the extent to which it accurately describes your attitude toward work while you were on the job. Alternatively, consider the statements in reference to school rather than work. Answer each question using the response scale provided. Then sum up your answers for each of the dimensions. (For more assessments relevant to this chapter, please visit the Online Learning Center at www.mhhe.com/colquitt).

1	2	3	4	5
STRONGLY DISAGREE	DISAGREE	NEUTRAL	AGREE	STRONGLY AGREE

1. I spend a lot of time and effort networking with others. _____

2. I know a lot of important people and am well connected. _____

3. I am good at using my connections and networks to make things happen. _____

4. I have developed a large network of colleagues and associates whom I can call on for support when I really need to get things done. _____

5. I spend a lot of time making connections. _____

6. I always seem to instinctively know the right thing to say or do to influence others. _____

7. I have a good intuition or savvy about how to present myself to others. _____

8. I am particularly good at sensing the motivations and hidden agendas of others. _____

9. I pay close attention to people's facial expressions. _____

10. I understand people very well. _____

SCORING AND INTERPRETATION

Networking Ability: Sum up items 1–5. _____

Social Astuteness: Sum up items 6–10. _____

For networking ability, scores of 18 or more are above average and scores of 17 or less are below average. For social astuteness, scores of 19 or more are above average and scores of 18 or less are below average.

Source: Adapted from G.R. Ferris, D.C. Treadway, R.W. Kolodinsky, W.A. Hochwarter, C.J. Kacmar, C. Douglas, and D.D. Frink, "Development and Validation of the Political Skill Inventory," *Journal of Management* 31 (2005), pp. 126–52.

| FIGURE 13-4 | Factors That Foster Organizational Politics |

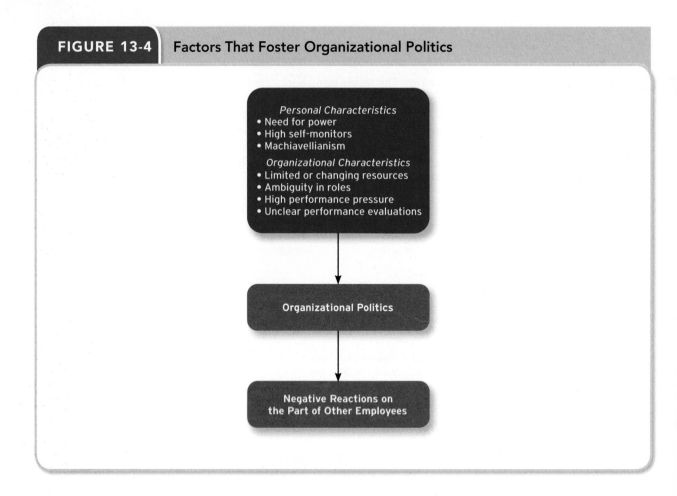

and organizational characteristics. Some employees have a strong need for power that provides them with an incentive to engage in political behaviors. Others are high in self-monitoring, meaning that they have a tendency to be closely guarded in their actions and behaviors.[57] Still others have "Machiavellian" tendencies, meaning that they're willing to manipulate and deceive others to acquire power.[58] There's no doubt that politics plays a role in organizational relationships; for a relatively self-serving take on this topic, check out this chapter's **OB at the Bookstore** feature.

Organizational factors that are the most likely to increase politics are those that raise the level of uncertainty in the environment. When people are uncertain about an outcome or event, they'll generally act in ways that help reduce that uncertainty. A number of events can trigger uncertainty, including limited or changing resources, ambiguity in role requirements, high performance pressures, or unclear performance evaluation measures.[59] These sorts of organizational factors generally have a much stronger effect on political behavior than do personal factors. That's actually a good thing for organizations, because it may be easier to clarify performance measures and roles than it is to change the personal characteristics of a workforce.

CONFLICT RESOLUTION. In addition to using their power to shape office politics, leaders can use their influence in the context of conflict resolution. Conflict arises when two or more individuals perceive that their goals are in opposition (see Chapter 12 on Team Processes and Communication for more discussion of such issues). Conflict and politics are

OB AT THE BOOKSTORE

I HATE PEOPLE!
by Jonathan Littman and Marc Hershon (New York: Little, Brown, 2009).

We hate people who play favorites, people who make the rules, people who don't give others a break. You know who we're talking about.

I HATE PEOPLE!

*Kick Loose from the Overbearing and
Underhanded Jerks at Work
and Get What You Want Out of Your Job*

JONATHAN LITTMAN & MARC HERSHON

With these words, Jonathan Littman and Marc Hershon express their anger at many of the people they believe you might be likely to run into on a regular basis at work. Such coworkers, whether consciously or unconsciously, are likely to ruin your career if you allow them to, through their various forms of political (or naively unpolitical) behavior. The authors describe these employees in detail using a "10 Least Wanted" list—stereotypes of coworkers who are the most likely to get in your way and prevent you from accomplishing your job effectively. The authors split these typecasts into three groups: Stumbling Blocks, Wrong Turns, and Time Wasters. A few examples:

Stop Signs: Individuals whose first answer is always "no."

Liar Liar: People who perpetually lie to hide their own shortcomings.

Switchblade: Coworkers who support you one moment and then stab you in the back the next.

Sheeple: Individuals who think like everyone else and won't try to do things differently.

The authors are adamant that to become successful at work, you need to become a "soloist." A soloist is independent, creative, original, and successful. Soloists practice "solocrafting," which involves identifying and avoiding the "10 Least Wanted" and spending time only with those who can help them accomplish their goals. As part of its premise, the book asserts that anytime there's more than one person assigned to a task, social loafing invariably corrupts the process. Overall, the book is a funny read, because we can all think of individuals who fit the stereotypes that the authors come up with. The authors certainly have some creative ideas about managing work environments: work at a coffee house where others can't disturb you, and use a Web site (www.slydial.com) to make sure your phone calls go directly to the voicemail of the person you are trying to call so you don't have to have a real conversation. Although some of these behaviors might be to your advantage every now and then, we can't help but believe that were you actually to start performing all of these (sometimes political) behaviors, you would have turned yourself into any number of the "10 Least Wanted" whom you are trying to avoid.

clearly intertwined, because the pursuit of one's own self-interests often breeds conflict in others. When conflict arises in organizations, leaders have the ability to use their power and influence to resolve it. As illustrated in Figure 13-5, there are five different styles a leader can use when handling conflict, each of which is appropriate in different circumstances.[60]

FIGURE 13-5	Styles of Conflict Resolution

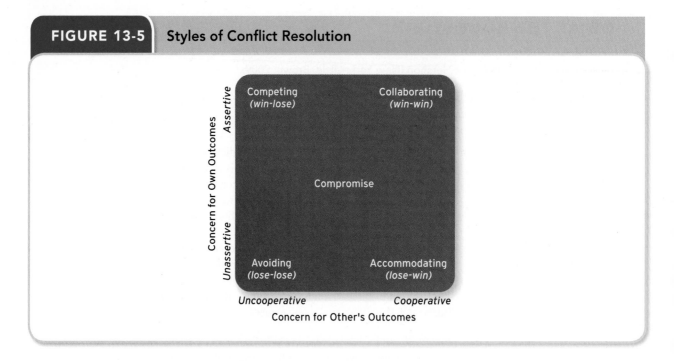

The five styles can be viewed as combinations of two separate factors: how *assertive* leaders want to be in pursuing their own goals and how *cooperative* they are with regard to the concerns of others.

Competing (high assertiveness, low cooperation) occurs when one party attempts to get his or her own goals met without concern for the other party's results. It could be considered a win–lose approach to conflict management. Competing occurs most often when one party has high levels of organizational power and can use legitimate or coercive power to settle the conflict. It also generally involves the hard forms of influence, such as pressure or coalitions. Although this strategy for resolving conflict might get the result initially, it won't win a leader many friends, given the negative reactions that tend to accompany such tactics. It's best used in situations in which the leader knows they are right and a quick decision needs to be made.

Avoiding (low assertiveness, low cooperation) occurs when one party wants to remain neutral, stay away from conflict, or postpone the conflict to gather information or let things cool down. Avoiding usually results in an unfavorable result for everyone, including the organization, and may result in negative feelings toward the leader. Most important, avoiding never really resolves the conflict. **Accommodating** (low assertiveness, high cooperation) occurs when one party gives in to the other and acts in a completely unselfish way. Leaders will typically use an accommodating strategy when the issue is really not that important to them but is very important to the other party. It's also an important strategy to think about when the leader has less power than the other party. If leaders know they are going to lose the conflict due to their lack of power anyway, it might be a better long-term strategy to give in to the demands from the other party.

Collaboration (high assertiveness, high cooperation) occurs when both parties work together to maximize outcomes. Collaboration is seen as a win–win form of conflict resolution. Collaboration is generally regarded as the most effective form of conflict

13.5

How do leaders use their power and influence to resolve conflicts in the workplace?

resolution, especially in reference to task-oriented rather than personal conflicts.[61] However, it's also the most difficult to come by because it requires full sharing of information by both parties, a full discussion of concerns, relatively equal power between parties, and a lot of time investment to arrive at a resolution. However, this style also results in the best outcomes and reactions from both parties. **Compromise** (moderate assertiveness, moderate cooperation) occurs when conflict is resolved through give-and-take concessions. Compromise is perhaps the most common form of conflict resolution, whereby each party's losses are offset by gains and vice versa. It is seen as an easy form of resolution, maintains relations between parties, and generally results in favorable evaluations for the leader.[62] For more discussion of when to use the various conflict resolution strategies, see Table 13-4.

One recent and unique example of conflict resolution is the One Laptop Per Child project. Nicolas Negroponte is the founder and chairperson of this nonprofit organization, whose mission is to give millions of $100 laptops to undereducated children in the world's poorest nations. Needless to say, manufacturing a $100 laptop (named the XO) is no small feat. Negroponte is leading a network of vastly different individuals, all working on their own time or on loan from other organizations, through a painstaking collaboration process of design and manufacturing. The process hasn't always been easy. Negroponte had to adopt a competing style of conflict resolution to make a custom wireless system for the laptop function. This competitive response upset a faction of volunteers who subsequently quit the project. However, Negroponte also has facilitated collaboration among very disparate groups. As a leader with varying degrees of power, Negroponte constantly has to balance the needs of the project with the needs of individuals and attempt to resolve conflict effectively.[63] Surprisingly, conflict arises most frequently with regard to the countries to which the project wants to give the laptops![64]

The One Laptop Per Child project intends to provide millions of $100 laptops for the world's poorest children. Founder and director Nicholas Negroponte has put together a large team of volunteers, "borrowed" workers from many different organizations, and worked to establish an effective collaboration among them by adopting a wide variety of conflict resolution strategies, even competing.

TABLE 13-4	When to Use the Various Conflict Resolution Styles
RESOLUTION STYLE	**USE DURING THE FOLLOWING SITUATIONS:**
Competing	• When quick decisive action is vital (i.e., emergencies). • On important issues for which unpopular actions need implementation. • On issues vital to company welfare when you know you're right. • Against people who take advantage of noncompetitive people.
Avoiding	• When an issue is trivial or more important issues are pressing. • When you perceive no chance of satisfying your concerns. • When potential disruption outweighs the benefits of resolution. • To let people cool down and regain perspective. • When gathering information supercedes an immediate decision. • When others can resolve the conflict more effectively. • When issues seem tangential or symptomatic of other issues.
Collaborating	• To find an integrative solution when both sets of concerns are too important to be compromised. • When your objective is to learn. • To merge insights from people with different perspectives. • To gain commitment by incorporating concerns into a consensus. • To work through feelings that have interfered with a relationship.
Accommodating	• When you find you are wrong, to allow a better position to be heard, to learn, and to show your reasonableness. • When issues are more important to others than yourself, to satisfy others and maintain cooperation. • To build social credits for later issues. • To minimize loss when you are outmatched and losing. • When harmony and stability are especially important. • To allow subordinates to develop by learning from mistakes.
Compromising	• When goals are important but not worth the effort of potential disruption of more assertive modes. • When opponents with equal power are committed to mutually exclusive goals. • To achieve temporary settlements to complex issues. • To arrive at expedient solutions under time pressure. • As a backup when collaboration or competition is unsuccessful.

Source: K.W. Thomas, "Toward Multi-Dimensional Values in Teaching: The Example of Conflict Behaviors," *Academy of Management Review* 2 (1977), pp. 484–90. Copyright © 1977 by Academy of Management. Reproduced via permission of Academy of Management via Copyright Clearance Center.

13.6

What are the ways in which leaders negotiate in the workplace?

NEGOTIATIONS

There is perhaps no better place for leaders to use their power, influence, political, and conflict resolution skills than when conducting negotiations. **Negotiation** is a process in which two or more interdependent individuals discuss and attempt to come to an agreement about their different preferences.[65] Negotiations can take place inside the organization or when dealing with organizational outsiders. Negotiations can involve settling a contract dispute between labor and management, determining a purchasing price for products, haggling over a performance review rating, or determining the starting salary for a new employee.

Clearly, negotiations are a critical part of organizational life, for both leaders and employees. Successful leaders are good at negotiating outcomes of all types, and doing it well requires knowledge of power structures, as well as how best to influence the other party.

NEGOTIATION STRATEGIES. There are two general strategies leaders must choose between when it comes to negotiations: distributive bargaining and integrative bargaining.[66] **Distributive bargaining** involves win–lose negotiating over a "fixed-pie" of resources.[67] That is, when one person gains, the other person loses (also known as a "zero-sum" condition). The classic example of a negotiation with distributive bargaining is the purchase of a car. When you walk into a car dealership, there's a stated price on the side of the car that's known to be negotiable. In these circumstances though, every dollar you save is a dollar the dealership loses. Similarly, every dollar the salesperson negotiates for, you lose. Distributive bargaining is similar in nature to a competing approach to conflict resolution. Some of the most visible negotiations that have traditionally been approached with a distributive bargaining tactic are union–management labor negotiations. Whether it be automobile manufacturers, airlines, or nurses at hospitals, the negotiations for these sessions are typically viewed through a win–lose lens. For an example of a man who always takes a distributive bargaining position, see this chapter's **OB on Screen** feature.

Many negotiations within organizations, including labor–management sessions, are beginning to occur with a more integrative bargaining strategy. **Integrative bargaining** is aimed at accomplishing a win–win scenario.[68] It involves the use of problem solving and mutual respect to achieve an outcome that's satisfying for both parties. Leaders who thoroughly understand the conflict resolution style of collaboration are likely to thrive in these types of negotiations. In general, integrative bargaining is a preferable strategy whenever possible, because it allows a long-term relationship to form between the parties (because neither side feels like the loser). In addition, integrative bargaining has a tendency to produce a higher level of outcome favorability when both parties' views are considered, compared with distributive bargaining.[69] However, not all situations are appropriate for integrative bargaining. Integrative bargaining is most appropriate in situations in which multiple outcomes are possible, there is an adequate level of trust, and parties are willing to be flexible.[70] Please don't approach your next used car purchase with an integrative bargaining strategy!

NEGOTIATION STAGES. Regardless of the strategy used, the actual negotiating process typically goes through a series of stages:[71]

- **Preparation.** Arguably the single most important stage of the negotiating process, during preparation, each party determines what its goals are for the negotiation and whether or not the other party has anything to offer. Each party also should determine its best alternative to a negotiated agreement, or **BATNA**. A BATNA describes each negotiator's bottom line. In other words, at what point are you willing to walk away? At the BATNA point, a negotiator is actually better off not negotiating at all. In their seminal book, *Getting to Yes: Negotiating Without Giving In*, Roger Fisher and William Ury state that people's BATNA is the standard by which all proposed agreements should be measured.[72]

- **Exchanging information.** In this nonconfrontational process, each party makes a case for its position and attempts to put all favorable information on the table. Each party also informs the other party how it has arrived at the conclusions it has and which issues it believes are important. When the other party is unfamiliar, this stage likely contains active listening and lots of questions. Studies show that successful negotiators ask many questions and gather much information during this stage.[73]

OB ON SCREEN

THERE WILL BE BLOOD

I have a competition in me. I want no one else to succeed.

With these words, Daniel Plainview (Daniel Day-Lewis) summarizes his view toward business, relationships, and life in *There Will Be Blood* (Dir.: Paul Thomas Anderson, Paramount, 2007). Daniel is an oil man through and through. He cares about nothing other than making money, will remove anyone who stands in his way, and eschews contact with other people unless it stands to benefit him somehow. As Daniel states at one point in the movie, "I look at people and I see nothing worth liking." He is the epitome of greed, and his approach to all conflict and negotiation adopts a win–lose philosophy.

Toward the beginning of the movie, Daniel appears in front of a group of townspeople with his "son and partner" H.W. Plainview (Dillon Freasier), trying to convince them why they should sell him a lease to drill for oil on their land. When the townspeople cannot come to an agreement quickly, Daniel finds someone willing to split from the group to lease him the rights to drill just on their property. He has little patience or need for compromise or collaboration. When executives from Standard Oil Company offer to make him rich beyond his wildest dreams, by buying the oil leases he has accumulated in California, Daniel simply cannot stand the thought of negotiating with a large conglomerate that might benefit from his hard work. Remember, he can't win if someone else does too. His goal is to make extraordinary amounts of money, all by himself, and at the expense of others. Daniel subsequently loses contact and significant relationships with anyone he has ever known. His nemesis is Eli Sunday (Paul Dano), an evangelical minister whose family and church lie on the land and in the town where Daniel wants to build a large series of oil derricks. The movie climaxes in a final negotiation between Daniel and Eli, featuring the now classic line, "I drink your milkshake!"

- **Bargaining.** This stage is the one most people imagine when they hear the term "negotiation." Success at this stage depends mightily on how well the previous two stages have proceeded. The goal is for each party to walk away feeling like it has gained something of value (regardless of the actual bargaining strategy). During this stage, both parties likely must make concessions and give up something to get something in return. To the degree that each party keeps the other party's concerns and motives in mind, this stage will go much more smoothly.

- **Closing and commitment.** This stage entails the process of formalizing an agreement reached during the previous stage. For large, complex negotiations such as labor contracts established between an organization and a union, it can be a very long stage. For others, such as a negotiation between two coworkers about how they might handle their future relationship, no formal documents or contracts are required, and a simple handshake might suffice. Ideally, there will be no issues or misconceptions about the agreement arrived at during the bargaining stage. If they do exist, the negotiation process can regress back into the bargaining stage, and the process starts all over again. The stage also might be simply a recognition that the parties ended at an impasse with no agreement! In this case, several options are still available, as we discuss in the Application section at the end of this chapter.

SUMMARY: WHY ARE SOME LEADERS MORE POWERFUL THAN OTHERS?

So what explains why some leaders are more powerful and influential than others? As shown in Figure 13-6, answering that question requires an understanding of the types of power leaders acquire, what kinds of influence tactics they have available to them, and how they can use that influence to alter the attitudes and behaviors of their employees. Leaders acquire both organizational (legitimate, reward, coercive) and personal (expert, referent) forms of power, which gives them the ability to influence others. They can then use that power to influence others through influence tactics. Those tactics can help achieve organizational goals or may be applied more specifically to dealing with organizational politics, conflict resolution, or negotiation situations. In the end, there are three possible responses to influence attempts: internalization, compliance, and resistance. The effectiveness of those attempts will depend on leaders' skill at performing them and how well they match the forms of power they have with the appropriate types of influence.

HOW IMPORTANT ARE POWER AND INFLUENCE?

 13.7

How do power and influence affect job performance and organizational commitment?

How important is a leader's ability to use power and influence? In other words, does a leader's power and influence correlate with job performance and organizational commitment? Figure 13-7 summarizes the research evidence linking power and influence to job performance and organizational commitment. The figure reveals that power and influence are moderately correlated with job performance. When used correctly and focused on task-related outcomes, power and influence can create internalization in workers, such that they are both behaviorally and attitudinally focused on high levels of task performance. That internalization also helps increase citizenship behavior, whereas the compliance associated with power and influence can decrease counterproductive behavior. These job performance benefits make sense given that the effective use of power and influence can increase the *motivation* levels of employees, whereas the ineffective use of power and influence can increase the *stress* levels of employees.

Figure 13-7 also reveals that power and influence are moderately related to organizational commitment. When a leader draws on personal sources of power, such as expert power and referent power, a stronger emotional bond can be created with the employee, boosting affective commitment. The effective use of such power should increase *job satisfaction* and a sense of *trust* in the leader, all of which are associated with increased commitment

FIGURE 13-6   Why Are Some Leaders More Powerful Than Others?

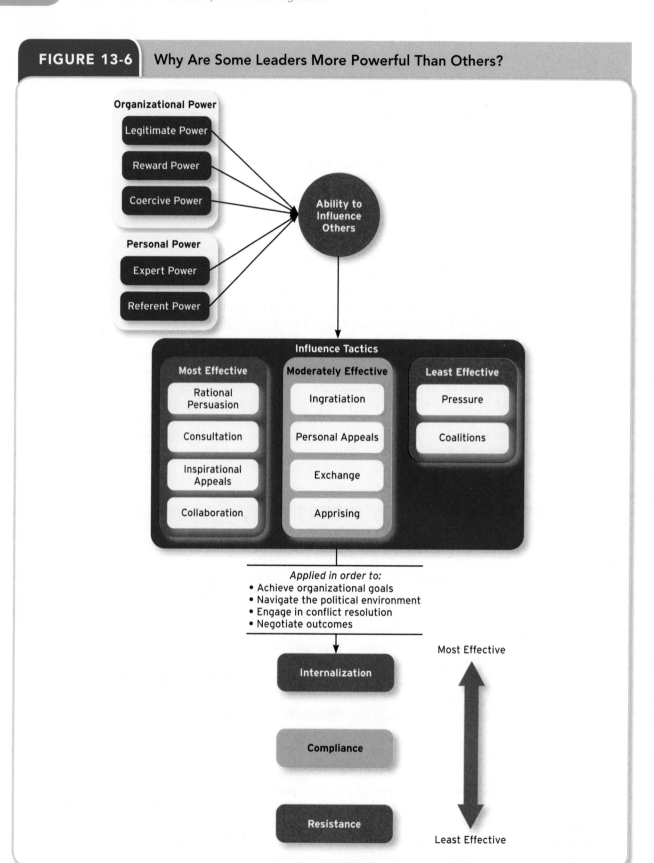

FIGURE 13-7 | Effects of Power and Influence on Performance & Commitment

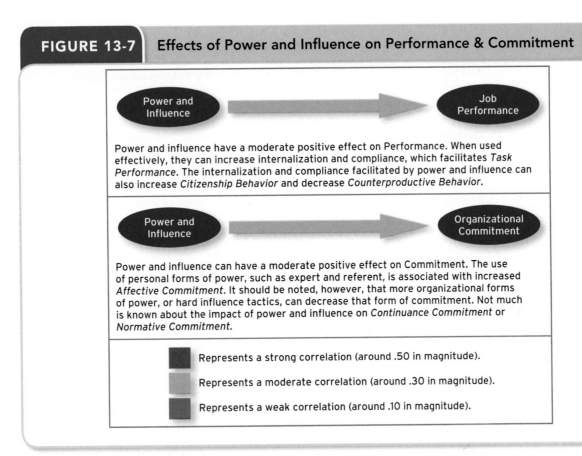

Power and Influence → **Job Performance**

Power and influence have a moderate positive effect on Performance. When used effectively, they can increase internalization and compliance, which facilitates *Task Performance*. The internalization and compliance facilitated by power and influence can also increase *Citizenship Behavior* and decrease *Counterproductive Behavior*.

Power and Influence → **Organizational Commitment**

Power and influence can have a moderate positive effect on Commitment. The use of personal forms of power, such as expert and referent, is associated with increased *Affective Commitment*. It should be noted, however, that more organizational forms of power, or hard influence tactics, can decrease that form of commitment. Not much is known about the impact of power and influence on *Continuance Commitment* or *Normative Commitment*.

Represents a strong correlation (around .50 in magnitude).

Represents a moderate correlation (around .30 in magnitude).

Represents a weak correlation (around .10 in magnitude).

Sources: R.T. Sparrowe, B.W. Soetjipto, and M.L. Kraimer, "Do Leaders' Influence Tactics Relate to Members' Helping Behavior? It Depends on the Quality of the Relationship," *Academy of Management Journal* 49 (2006), pp. 1194–1208; G. Yukl, H. Kim, and C.M. Falbe, "Antecedents of Influence Outcomes," *Journal of Applied Psychology* 81 (1996), pp. 309–17; and P.P. Carson, K.D. Carson, and C.W. Rowe, "Social Power Bases: A Meta-Analytic Examination of Interrelationships and Outcomes," *Journal of Applied Social Psychology* 23 (1993), pp. 1150–69.

levels. As with job performance, however, it's important to note that an ineffective use of power can also decrease commitment levels. In particular, repeated uses of coercive power or repeated reliance on hard influence tactics such as pressure or coalitions could actually decrease organizational commitment levels.

APPLICATION: ALTERNATIVE DISPUTE RESOLUTION

There is always the possibility that, despite a leader's best effort, negotiations and/or conflict management will result in an impasse between two parties. In many organizations, disputes that might escalate into actual legal battles are settled through alternative dispute resolution. **Alternative dispute resolution** is a process by which two parties resolve conflicts through the use of a specially trained, neutral third party. There are various types of alternative dispute resolution that offer each party more or less control over the outcomes in question.[74] Two of the most common forms are mediation and arbitration.

Mediation requires a third party to facilitate the dispute resolution process, though this third party has no formal authority to dictate a solution. In essence, a mediator plays the role of a neutral, objective party who listens to the arguments of each side and attempts to help two parties come to an agreement. In serious, potentially litigious situations, trained mediators offer a relatively easy and quick way out of difficult disputes. A more definite form of alternative resolution is the process of arbitration. **Arbitration** occurs when a third party determines a binding settlement to a dispute. The arbitrator can be an individual or a group (board) whose job is to listen to the various arguments and then make a decision about the solution to the conflict. In some ways, arbitration is much riskier for both parties, because the outcome of the dispute rests solely in the arbitrator's hands. The arbitrator's role isn't to make everyone happy but rather to arrive at the most equitable solution in their opinion. In conventional arbitration, the arbitrator can create a solution of their choosing, mixing and matching available alternatives. In contrast, in final-offer arbitration, each party presents its most fair offer, and the arbitrator chooses the offer identified as most reasonable.

The goal of dispute resolution is always to have the two parties come to a voluntary agreement. Traditionally, mediation is the first step in alternative dispute resolution; if the mediator cannot help the two parties come to an agreement, the process continues to arbitration. Recent research suggests though that an opposite approach might lead to better results. That is, the two parties undergo the arbitration process, and the arbitrator makes a decision, which they place in a sealed envelope. The two parties then go through the process of mediation; if they still can't come to an agreement, they turn to the arbiter's decision. Flipping the order resulted in significantly higher voluntary agreement rates between the two parties.[75]

TAKEAWAYS

13.1   Leadership is the use of power and influence to direct the activities of followers toward goal achievement. Power is the ability to influence the behavior of others and resist unwanted influence in return. Power is necessary, in that it gives leaders the ability to influence others.

13.2   Leaders have five major types of power. There are three organizational forms of power: Legitimate power is based on authority or position, reward power is based on the distribution of resources or benefits, and coercive power is based on the handing out of punishments. There are two personal forms of power: Expert power is derived from expertise and knowledge, whereas referent power is based on the attractiveness and charisma of the leader. These types of power can be used most effectively when leaders are central to the work process, highly visible, have discretion, and are the sole controllers of resources and information.

13.3   Leaders can use at least ten different influence tactics to achieve their objectives. The most effective are rational persuasion, consultation, inspirational appeals, and collaboration. The least effective are pressure and the forming of coalitions. Tactics with moderate levels of effectiveness are ingratiation, exchange, personal appeals, and apprising.

13.4   Organizational politics are individual actions that are directed toward the goal of furthering a person's own self-interests. Political behavior is most likely to occur in organizational situations in which individual outcomes are uncertain.

13.5 Leaders use power and influence to resolve conflicts through five conflict resolution styles: avoidance, competing, accommodating, collaborating, and compromising. The most effective, and most difficult, tactic is collaboration.

13.6 Leaders use both distributive and integrative bargaining strategies to negotiate outcomes. The process of negotiating effectively includes four steps: preparation, exchanging information, bargaining, and closing and commitment.

13.7 Power and influence have moderate positive relationships with job performance and organizational commitment. However, for these beneficial effects to be realized, leaders must wield their power effectively and rely on effective influence tactics in negotiating outcomes.

KEY TERMS

DISCUSSION QUESTIONS

13.1 Can a leader influence others without power? How exactly would that influence take place?

13.2 Which forms of power do you consider to be the strongest? Which types of power do you currently have? How could you go about obtaining higher levels of the forms that you're lacking?

13.3 Who is the most influential leader you have come in contact with personally? What forms of power did they have, and which types of influence did they use to accomplish objectives?

13.4 Think of a time when you resisted an influence attempt at work. What made you resist? Could the person attempting to influence you have done anything differently to get you to behave the way they wanted?

13.5 What would it take to have a "politically free" environment? Is that possible?

13.6 Think about the last serious conflict you had with a coworker or group member. How was that conflict resolved? Which approach did you take to resolve it?

13.7 Think of a situation in which you negotiated an agreement. Which approach did you take? Was it the appropriate one? How might the negotiation process have gone more smoothly?

CASE: HARPO

Having Oprah Winfrey as the owner and a cornerstone of a company confers many advantages. However, it's not without its drawbacks. As an organization whose entire existence relies on one person with extreme amounts of power and influence based on referent power, what if that power starts to fade? At the moment, Winfrey has the ability to influence presidential elections (some say she single-handedly pushed President Obama over the top in the race against Hillary Clinton) and boost the sales of books tenfold on *The New York Times* best-seller list.[76] What happens though if something goes wrong and the public's trust in her diminishes? One of the things for which Winfrey is well known is her generous charitable contributions, including a $40 million Leadership Academy for girls in South Africa. Yet Winfrey faced numerous criticisms about the way the school has been run, including a 2007 accusation that one of the teachers was sexually abusing students.[77] Although the controversy was handled fairly deftly, it raises concerns for Harpo.

One of Harpo's jobs—to control the content it disseminates—remains a challenge as well, because Winfrey not only creates much of the content but is the content itself. Every copy of *O Magazine* has her on the cover. Every television show created by the company lists Winfrey as a producer. Oprah is the brand. The lingering question for Harpo: What happens if something happens to Winfrey? Her stated intentions for the new OWN network is that it must live on beyond her, but whether people would tune in without Oprah represents a real dilemma for the organization.

13.1 What are the potential dangers of having one super-powerful leader of an organization?

13.2 How might Winfrey go about ensuring that Harpo survives after her departure or in the event of a loss of faith on the part of the public? Is it possible to have a true leadership succession plan in these circumstances?

13.3 As a holder of immense referent power, what types of concerns should Oprah Winfrey have in terms of influencing the employees around her?

EXERCISE: LOBBYING FOR INFLUENCE

The purpose of this exercise is to give you experience in using influence tactics to modify the behavior of others. Follow these steps:

13.1 During this exercise, your objective is to get other people in the class to give you their points. If you get more than 50 percent of the total number of points distributed to the whole class, you'll win. Each person in the class has a different number of points, as shown in the class list. You can keep or give away your points in whatever manner you choose, as long as you follow the rules for each round of the process. There are five rounds, described next.

Round 1. In this round, you will write memos to your classmates. You can say whatever you want in your memos, and write them to whomever you choose, but for the 10-minute writing period, there will be no talking, only writing. You will deliver all your messages at one time, at the end of the 10-minute writing period.

Round 2. In this round, you will respond in writing to the messages you received in the first round. You can also write new memos as you see fit. Again, there is to be no talking! At the end of 15 minutes, you can distribute your memos.

Round 3. In Round 3, you can talk as much as you like. You will have 15 minutes to talk with anyone about anything.

Round 4. In this round, you will create ballots to distribute your points any way you see fit. To distribute your points, put a person's name on an index card, along with the number of points you want that person to have. If you choose to keep any of your points, put your own name on the card, along with the number of points you want to keep. Do not hand in your cards until asked to do so by the professor.

Round 5. If there is no clear winner, Round 5 will be used to repeat steps 3 and 4.

13.2 Class discussion (whether in groups or as a class) should focus on the following questions:

- What kinds of social influence attempts did you make during this exercise?
- How successful were you at influencing others to go along with you?
- What kinds of influence did others use on you?
- What was the most successful way you saw someone else use influence during the memo-writing and discussion sections?
- What other factors determined how you voted?

Source: Adapted from "Voting for Dollars," in the Instructor's Manual for D.A. Whetten and K.S. Cameron, *Developing Management Skills,* 7th ed. (Englewood Cliffs, NJ: Prentice Hall, 2007).

ENDNOTES

13.1 http://www.hoovers.com (accessed June 26, 2009).

13.2 Shambora, J., and B. Kowitt. "50 Most Powerful Women." *Fortune,* October 13, 2008, pp. 165–73.

13.3 Sellers, P. "The Power 50." *Fortune,* October 15, 2007, p. 77.

13.4 Alleyne, S. "Oprah Means Business." *Black Enterprise* 18 (June 2008), pp. 117–28.

13.5   Ibid.

13.6   Ibid.

13.7   Ibid.

13.8   Sellers, P. "The Business of being Oprah." *Fortune*, April 1, 2002, pp. 50–58.

13.9   Alleyne, "Oprah Means Business."

13.10   Schechner, S. "TV Veteran Named CEO at Winfrey's Network." *The Wall Street Journal*, January 30, 2009, p. B5.

13.11   Yukl, G. *Leadership in Organizations*. 4th ed. Englewood Cliffs, NJ: Prentice-Hall, 1998.

13.12   Ibid.

13.13   McMurray, V.V. "Some Unanswered Questions on Organizational Conflict." *Organization and Administrative Sciences* 6 (1975), pp. 35–53; and Pfeffer, J. *Managing with Power.* Boston: Harvard Business School Press, 1992.

13.14   Cotton, J.L. "Measurement of Power-Balancing Styles and Some of their Correlates." *Administrative Science Quarterly* 21 (1976), pp. 307–19; and Emerson, R.M. "Power-Dependence Relationships." *American Sociological Review* 27 (1962), pp. 29–41.

13.15   Ashforth, B.E., and F.A. Mael. "The Power of Resistance." In *Power and Influence in Organizations,* eds. R.M. Kramer and M.E. Neal. Thousand Oaks, CA: Sage, 1998, pp. 89–120.

13.16   French, Jr., J.R.P., and B. Raven. "The Bases of Social Power." In *Studies in Social Power,* ed. D. Cartwright. Ann Arbor: University of Michigan, Institute for Social Research, 1959, pp. 150–67; and Yukl, G., and C.M. Falbe. "The Importance of Different Power Sources in Downward and Lateral Relations." *Journal of Applied Psychology* 76 (1991), pp. 416–23.

13.17   Yukl, G. "Use Power Effectively." In *Handbook of Principles of Organizational Behavior,* ed. E.A. Locke. Madden, MA: Blackwell, 2004, pp. 242–47.

13.18   Levenson, E.; C. Tkaczyk; and J.L. Yang. "Indra Rising," *Fortune* 154, no. 8 (2006), p. 145.

13.19   Tedlow, R.S. "The Education of Andy Grove." *Fortune,* December 12, 2005, pp. 117–38.

13.20   French and Raven, "The Bases of Social Power."

13.21   Hickson, D.J.; C.R. Hinings; C.A. Lee; R.E. Schneck; and J.M. Pennings. "A Strategic Contingencies Theory of Intraorganizational Power." *Administrative Science Quarterly* 16 (1971), pp. 216–27; Hinings, C.R.; D.J. Hickson; J.M. Pennings; and R.E. Schneck. "Structural Conditions of Intraorganizational Power." *Administrative Science Quarterly* 19 (1974), pp. 22–44; and Salancik, G.R., and J. Pfeffer. "Who Gets Power and How They Hold on to It: A Strategic Contingency Model of Power." *Organizational Dynamics* 5 (1977), pp. 3–21.

13.22   McGregor, J. "The Office Chart That Really Counts." *BusinessWeek,* February 27, 2006, pp. 48–49.

13.23   Somech, A., and A. Drach-Zahavy. "Relative Power and Influence Strategy: The Effects of Agent/Target Organizational Power on Superiors' Choices of Influence Strategies." *Journal of Organizational Behavior* 23 (2002), pp. 167–79; and Stahelski, A.J., and C.F. Paynton. "The Effects of Status Cues on Choices of Social Power and Influence Strategies." *Journal of Social Psychology* 135 (1995), pp. 553–60.

13.24   Yukl (1998), *Leadership in Organizations.*

13.25   Yukl, G.; C. Chavez; and C.F. Seifert. "Assessing the Construct Validity and Utility of Two New Influence Tactics." *Journal of Organizational Behavior* 26 (2005), pp. 705–25; and Yukl, G. *Leadership in Organizations,* 5th ed. Upper Saddle River, NJ: Prentice Hall, 2002.

13.26   Yukl, G.; H. Kim; and C. Chavez. "Task Importance, Feasibility, and Agent Influence Behavior as Determinants of Target Commitment." *Journal of Applied Psychology* 84 (1999), pp. 137–43.

13.27   Yukl (1998), *Leadership in Organizations.*

13.28   Hardy, Q. "The UnCarly." *Forbes,* March 12, 2007, pp. 82–90; and Malone, M.S. "Hurd Instinct." *The Wall Street Journal,* September 14, 2006, p. A20.

13.29   Yukl et al., "Task Importance."

13.30   Wayne, S.J., and G.R. Ferris. "Influence Tactics, Affect, and Exchange Quality in Supervisor–Subordinate Interactions: A Laboratory Experiment and Field Study." *Journal of Applied Psychology* 75 (1990), pp. 487–99.

13.31   Kelman, H.C. "Compliance, Identification, and Internalization: Three Processes of Attitude Change." *Journal of Conflict Resolution* 2 (1958), pp. 51–56.

13.32   Yukl et al., "Assessing the Construct Validity."

13.33   Buderi, R. "The Talent Magnet." *Fast Company* 106 (2006), pp. 80–84.

13.34   Chen, C.C.; Y.R. Chen; and K. Xin. "Guanxi Practices and Trust in Management: A Procedural Justice Perspective." *Organization Science* 15 (2004), pp. 200–209.

13.35   Yang, M.M. *Gifts, Favors, and Banquets: The Art of Social Relationships in China.* Ithaca, NY: Cornell University Press, 1994.

13.36   Fu, P.P.; T.K. Peng; J.C. Kennedy; and G. Yukl. "A Comparison of Chinese Managers in Hong Kong, Taiwan, and Mainland China." *Organizational Dynamics* 33 (2003), pp. 32–46.

13.37   Buderi, "The Talent Magnet."

13.38   Fu et al., "A Comparison."

13.39   Falbe, C.M.; and G. Yukl. "Consequences for Managers of Using Single Influence Tactics and Combinations of Tactics." *Academy of Management Journal* 35 (1992), pp. 638–52.

13.40   Yukl (2002), *Leadership in Organizations.*

13.41   Ibid.

13.42   Somech and Drach-Zahavy, "Relative Power and Influence Strategy"; Yukl (2002), *Leadership in Organizations*; Yukl, "Use Power Effectively."

13.43   Mintzberg, H. "The Organization as Political Arena." *Journal of Management Studies* 22 (1985), pp. 133–54.

13.44   Bryan-Low, C., and J. Singer. "Vodafone Group Life President Resigns over Management Flap." *The Wall Street Journal,* March 13, 2006, p. B3.

13.45   Ramel, D. "Protégé Profiles." *Computerworld* 39 (2005), p. 50.

13.46   Bacharach, S.B., and E.J. Lawler. "Political Alignments in Organizations." In *Power and Influence in Organizations,* eds. R.M. Kramer and M.E. Neal. Thousand

Oaks, CA: Sage, 1998, pp. 67–88.

13.47   Kacmar, K.M., and R.A. Baron. "Organizational Politics: The State of the Field, Links to Related Processes, and an Agenda for Future Research." In *Research in Personnel and Human Resources Management,* Vol. 17, ed. G.R. Ferris. Greenwich, CT: JAI Press, 1999, pp. 1–39.

13.48   Ferris, G.R.; D.C. Treadway; P.L. Perrewe; R.L. Brouer; C. Douglas; and S. Lux. "Political Skill in Organizations." *Journal of Management* 33 (2007), pp. 290–320; and Treadway, D.C.; G.R. Ferris; A.B. Duke; G.L. Adams; and J.B. Thatcher. "The Moderating Role of Subordinate Political Skill on Supervisors' Impressions of Subordinate Ingratiation and Ratings of Subordinate Interpersonal Facilitation." *Journal of Applied Psychology* 92 (2007), pp. 848–55.

13.49   Seldman, M., and E. Betof. "An Illuminated Path." *T + D* 58 (2004), pp. 34–39.

13.50   Ferris, G.R.; D.C. Treadway; R.W. Kolokinsky; W.A. Hochwarter; C.J. Kacmar; and D.D. Frink. "Development and Validation of the Political Skill Inventory." *Journal of Management* 31 (2005), pp. 126–52.

13.51   Ferris et al., "Political Skill in Organizations"; Ferris et al., "Development and Validation."

13.52   Ibid.

13.53   Ibid.

13.54   Ferris, G.R.; D.D. Frink; D.P.S. Bhawuk; J. Zhou; and D.C. Gilmore. "Reactions of Diverse Groups to Politics in the Workplace." *Journal of Management* 22 (1996), pp. 23–44.

13.55   Kacmar and Baron, "Organizational Politics"; Hochwarter, W.A. "The Interactive Effects of Pro-Political

Behavior and Politics Perceptions on Job Satisfaction and Commitment." *Journal of Applied Social Psychology* 33 (2003), pp. 1360–78; Randall, M.L.; R. Cropanzano; C.A. Bormann; and A. Birjulin. "Organizational Politics and Organizational Support as Predictors of Work Attitudes, Job Performance, and Organizational Citizenship Behavior." *Journal of Organizational Behavior* 20 (1999), pp. 159–74; and Witt, L.A. "Enhancing Organizational Goal Congruence: A Solution to Organizational Politics." *Journal of Applied Psychology* 83 (1998), pp. 666–74.

13.56   Eisenhardt, K.M., and L.J. Bourgeois. "Politics of Strategic Decision Making in High-Velocity Environments: Toward a Midrange Theory." *Academy of Management Journal* 31 (1988), pp. 737–70.

13.57   Biberman, G. "Personality and Characteristic Work Attitudes of Persons with High, Moderate, and Low Political Tendencies." *Psychological Reports* 60 (1985), pp. 1303–10; Ferris et al., "Reactions of Diverse Groups"; and O'Connor, W.E., and T.G. Morrison. "A Comparison of Situational and Dispositional Predictors of Perceptions of Organizational Politics." *Journal of Psychology* 135 (2001), pp. 301–12.

13.58   Valle, M., and P.L. Perrewe. "Do Politics Perceptions Relate to Political Behaviors? Tests of an Implicit Assumption and Expanded Model." *Human Relations* 53 (2000), pp. 359–86.

13.59   Fandt, P.M., and G.R. Ferris. "The Management of Information and Impressions: When Employees Behave Opportunistically." *Organizational Behavior and Human Decision Processes* 45 (1990), pp. 140–58; O'Connor and Morrison, "A Comparison of Situational and

Dispositional Predictors"; and Poon, J.M.L. "Situational Antecedents and Outcomes of Organizational Politics Perceptions." *Journal of Managerial Psychology* 18 (2003), pp. 138–55.

13.60 Lewicki, R.J., and J.A. Litterer. *Negotiations.* Homewood, IL: Irwin, 1985; and Thomas, K.W. "Conflict and Negotiation Processes in Organizations." In *Handbook of Industrial and Organizational Psychology.* 2nd ed., Vol. 3, eds. M.D. Dunnette and L.M. Hough. Palo Alto, CA: Consulting Psychologists Press, pp. 651–717.

13.61 Weingart, L., and K.A. Jehn. "Manage Intra-Team Conflict Through Collaboration." *Handbook of Principles of Organizational Behavior,* ed. E.A. Locke. Madden, MA: Blackwell, 2004, pp. 226–38.

13.62 Thomas, K.W. "Toward Multi-Dimensional Values in Teaching: The Example of Conflict Behaviors." *Academy of Management Review* 2 (1977), pp. 484–90; and de Dreu, C.K.W.; A. Evers; B. Beersma; E.S. Kluwer; and A. Nauta. "A Theory-Based Measure of Conflict Management Strategies in the Workplace." *Journal of Organizational Behavior* 22 (2001), pp. 645–68.

13.63 Fahey, J. "The Soul of a Laptop." *Forbes,* May 7, 2007, pp. 100–104.

13.64 Hamm, S.; G. Smith; and N. Lakshman. "Social Cause Meets Business Reality: The Misadventures of One Laptop per Child." *BusinessWeek,* June 16, 2008, p. 48.

13.65 Adapted from Neale, M.A., and M.H. Bazerman. "Negotiating Rationally: The Power and Impact of the Negotiator's Frame." *Academy of Management Executive* 2 (1992), pp. 42–51.

13.66 Bazerman, M.H., and M.A. Neale. *Negotiating Rationally.* New York:

The Free Press, 1992; and Pinkley, R.L.; T.L. Griffeth; and G.B. Northcraft. "Fixed Pie a la Mode: Information Availability, Information Processing, and the Negotiation of Suboptimal Agreements." *Organizational Behavior and Human Decision Processes* 50 (1995), pp. 101–12.

13.67 Pinkley et al., "Fixed Pie a la Mode."

13.68 Kolb, D.M., and J. Williams. "Breakthrough Bargaining." *Harvard Business Review,* February 2001, pp. 88–97.

13.69 Pinkley et al., "Fixed Pie a la Mode."

13.70 Thomas, "Conflict and Negotiation Processes."

13.71 Based on Shell, R. *Bargaining for Advantage: Negotiation Strategies for Reasonable People.* 2nd ed. New York: Penguin, 2006.

13.72 Fisher, R., and W. Ury. *Getting to Yes: Negotiating Agreement Without Giving In.* New York: Penguin Books, 1991..

13.73 Shell, *Bargaining for Advantage.*

13.74 Nugent, P.S. "Managing Conflict: Third-Party Interventions for Managers." *Academy of Management Executive* 16 (2002), pp. 139–54.

13.75 Conlon, D.E.; H. Moon; and K.Y. Ng. "Putting the Cart Before the Horse: The Benefits of Arbitrating Before Mediating." *Journal of Applied Psychology* 87 (2002), pp. 978–84.

13.76 Alleyne, S. "Oprah Means Business," *Black Enterprise* 18 (June 2008), pp. 117–28; and Sellers, P. "The Business of Being Oprah," *Fortune,* April 1, 2002, pp. 50–58.

13.77 Russell, A. "Shaken Oprah 'Cleans' Her Girls Academy," *Financial Times,* November 6, 2007, p. 8

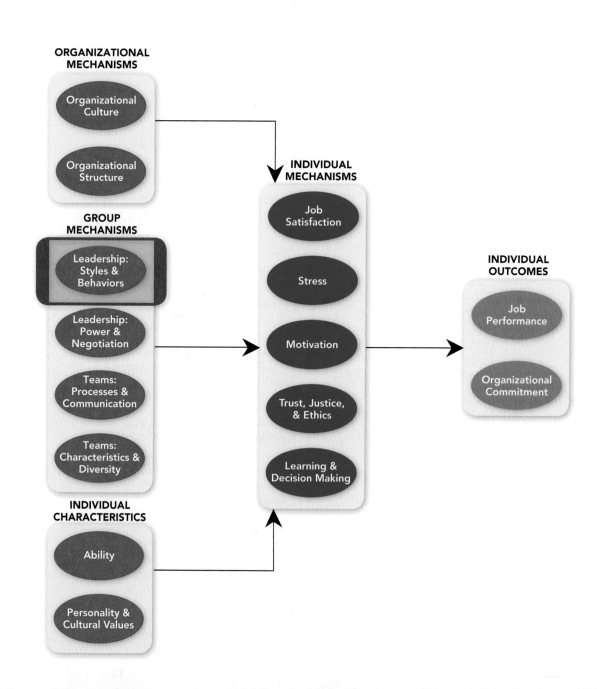

ORGANIZATIONAL MECHANISMS
- Organizational Culture
- Organizational Structure

GROUP MECHANISMS
- Leadership: Styles & Behaviors
- Leadership: Power & Negotiation
- Teams: Processes & Communication
- Teams: Characteristics & Diversity

INDIVIDUAL CHARACTERISTICS
- Ability
- Personality & Cultural Values

INDIVIDUAL MECHANISMS
- Job Satisfaction
- Stress
- Motivation
- Trust, Justice, & Ethics
- Learning & Decision Making

INDIVIDUAL OUTCOMES
- Job Performance
- Organizational Commitment

FORD

Alan Mulally is a leader in a unique, enviable, and somewhat daunting position. As the CEO of Ford Motor Company, he has the opportunity to turn around and save (his second) an American and global corporate icon. The first opportunity (and success) was at Boeing, where he spent almost 40 years, mainly as an aeronautical engineer, before moving up in the ranks because of his unique ability to lead large groups of people toward a common goal.[1] As CEO, Mulally led numerous aircraft programs, including the development of Boeing's 777 aircraft—widely considered the first airline success story of the twenty-first century—through extremely troubling times for the industry.[2] When he was chosen by then-Chairman and CEO William Ford to lead Ford in 2006, the decision was met with immense skepticism from every corner of the automotive industry.[3] Even Mulally's mother said, "But Alan, you're an airplane guy."[4] The transition, three years later, is still ongoing; in a recent meeting with Wall Street analysts, Mulally referred to the "Paris Air Show" when he meant to say "Paris Motor Show."[5]

Fortunately for Ford, good leadership has turned out to transcend industry. Part of the reason is that Mulally didn't charge into Ford like a bull in a china shop, imposing his will on everyone around. Instead, he came in with a much more subdued style, building consensus and using the team that was already in place.[6] Mulally is known for being incredibly optimistic, and Ford's head of manufacturing, Joe Hinrichs, says, "Alan brings infectious energy. This is a person people want to follow."[7] In a relatively short time, Mulally has transformed what had become known as one of the staunchest "me-first" corporate cultures in the world to a company focused on a singular vision of success as "One Ford."[8] To focus completely on Ford (and in contrast with most executives in Detroit), Mulally lives less than three minutes from his office so that, as he likes to say, "all the way home and all the way back here I can always see the blue oval on the side of buildings."[9] That focus also led Mulally to cut his own salary by 30 percent for 2009 and 2010 to show that upper management shares in the sacrifices that it has demanded of rank-and-file employees.[10]

Fortune magazine dubs his leadership style the "Mulally Method," defined as a "good-natured but relentless insistence on following what he has determined to be the correct course of action."[11] Mulally's style focuses on creating transparency; everyone knows everything so that management can react to issues proactively as a group. "Communicate, communicate, communicate. Everyone has to know the plan, its status, and areas that need special attention," says Mulally, summarizing the efforts to get Ford to think and work as a global brand as opposed to a set of regional fiefdoms, as had been the case for decades.[12] "Information should never be used as a weapon on a team," adds Mulally.[13] Aside from his focus on communication, Mulally is known for wearing off-the-rack suits, expressing humility, and having a good-natured demeanor. He's also very confident, however, always willing to make the difficult decision while being incredibly driven to win.[14] This Mulally Method leadership style may be different from what Ford has been used to, but it also seems to be exactly what Ford has needed.

LEADERSHIP: STYLES AND BEHAVIORS

This is the second of two chapters on **leadership**, defined as the use of power and influence to direct the activities of followers toward goal achievement.[15] That direction can affect followers' interpretation of events, the organization of their work activities, their commitment to key goals, their relationships with other followers, or their access to cooperation and support from other work units.[16] The last chapter described how leaders *get* the power and influence needed to direct others. In the case of Alan Mulally, his power derives from his formal role as Ford's CEO, his expertise and success in leading large projects, and his charisma. This chapter describes how leaders actually *use* their power and influence in an effective way. Since he took over Ford, automotive analysts have marveled at Mulally's ability to transform the culture so quickly in a company that always tended to reject outsiders.[17] Surprisingly, Ford has managed to maintain market share, differentiate itself from GM and Chrysler, and reduce its debt load during what might be the most difficult period the U.S. automotive industry has ever faced.[18]

14.1

What is leadership and what does it mean for a leader to be "effective"?

Of course, most leaders can't judge their performance by pointing to changes in debt load and market share. Fortunately, leader effectiveness can be gauged in a number of ways. Leaders might be judged by objective evaluations of unit performance, such as profit margins, market share, sales, returns on investment, productivity, quality, costs in relation to budgeted expenditures, and so forth.[19] If those sorts of indices are unavailable, the leader's superiors may judge the performance of the unit on a more subjective basis. Other approaches to judging leader effectiveness center more on followers, including indices such as absenteeism, retention of talented employees, grievances filed, requests for transfer, and so forth.[20] Those sorts of indices can be complemented by employee surveys that assess the perceived performance of the leader, the perceived respect and legitimacy of the leader, and employee commitment, satisfaction, and psychological well-being. The top panel of Table 14-1 provides one example of these sorts of measures.

One source of complexity when judging leader effectiveness, particularly with more subjective, employee-centered approaches, is "Whom do you ask?" The members of a given unit often disagree about how effective their leader is. **Leader–member exchange theory**, which describes how leader–member relationships develop over time on a dyadic basis, can explain why those differences exist.[21] The theory argues that new leader–member relationships are typically marked by a **role taking** phase, during which a manager describes role expectations to an employee and the employee attempts to fulfill those expectations with his or her job behaviors.[22] In this period of sampling and experimentation, the leader tries to get a feel for the talent and motivation levels of the employee. For some employees, that initial role taking phase may eventually be supplemented by **role making**, during which the employee's own expectations for the dyad get mixed in with those of the leader.[23] The role making process is marked by a free-flowing exchange in which the leader offers more opportunities and resources and the employee contributes more activities and effort.

Over time, the role taking and role making processes result in two general types of leader–member dyads, as shown in Figure 14-1. One type is the "high-quality exchange" dyad, marked by the frequent exchange of information, influence, latitude, support, and attention. Those dyads form the leader's "ingroup" and are characterized by higher levels of mutual trust, respect, and obligation.[24] The other type is the "low-quality exchange" dyad, marked by a more limited exchange of information, influence, latitude, support, and attention. Those dyads form the leader's "outgroup" and are characterized by lower levels of trust, respect, and obligation.[25] Tests of the theory suggest that employees who are competent, likable, and similar to the leader in personality will be more likely to end up in the leader's ingroup; those factors have even greater impact than age, gender, or racial similarity.[26] Leader–member exchange theory also suggests that judgments of leader effectiveness should gauge how effective the most critical leader–member dyads appear to be. The bottom panel of Table 14-1 provides one example of this sort of measure, with more agreement indicating a higher-quality exchange relationship and thus higher levels

TABLE 14-1	**Employee-Centered Measures of Leader Effectiveness**

Unit-Focused Approach

Ask all members of the unit to fill out the following survey items, then average the responses across the group to get a measure of leader effectiveness.

1. My supervisor is effective in meeting our job-related needs.

2. My supervisor uses methods of leadership that are satisfying.

3. My supervisor gets us to do more than we expected to do.

4. My supervisor is effective in representing us to higher authority.

5. My supervisor works with us in a satisfactory way.

6. My supervisor heightens our desire to succeed.

7. My supervisor is effective in meeting organizational requirements.

8. My supervisor increases our willingness to try harder.

9. My supervisor leads a group that is effective.

Dyad-Focused Approach

Ask members of the unit to fill out the following survey items in reference to their particular relationship with the leader. The responses are not averaged across the group; rather, differences across people indicate differentiation into "ingroups" and "outgroups" within the unit.

1. I always know how satisfied my supervisor is with what I do.

2. My supervisor understands my problems and needs well enough.

3. My supervisor recognizes my potential.

4. My supervisor would use his/her power to help me solve work problems.

5. I can count on my supervisor to 'bail me out' at his/her expense if I need it.

6. My working relationship with my supervisor is extremely effective.

7. I have enough confidence in my supervisor to defend and justify his/her decisions when he/she is not present to do so.

Sources: Adapted from B. Bass and B. Avolio, *MLQ Manual* (Menlo Park, CA: Mind Garden, Inc., 2004); and G.B. Graen and M. Uhl-Bien, "Relationship-Based Approach to Leadership: Development of Leader–Member Exchange (LMX) Theory of Leadership over 25 Years: Applying a Multi-Level Multi-Domain Perspective," *Leadership Quarterly* 6 (1995), pp. 219–47.

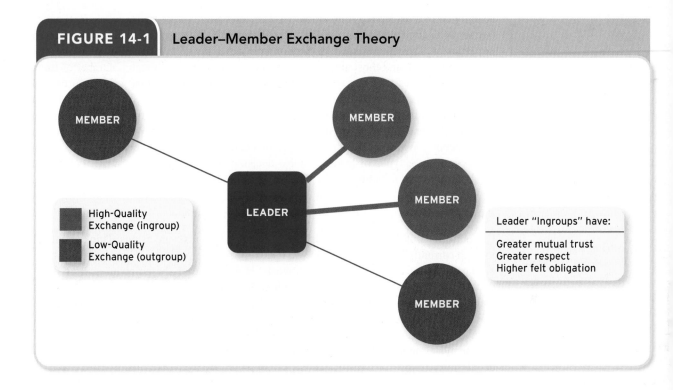

FIGURE 14-1 | **Leader–Member Exchange Theory**

of leader effectiveness on a dyadic basis.[27] A recent meta-analysis found that employees who have higher-quality exchange relationships are more likely to exhibit organizational citizenship behaviors.[28]

WHY ARE SOME LEADERS MORE EFFECTIVE THAN OTHERS?

For our purposes, **leader effectiveness** will be defined as the degree to which the leader's actions result in the achievement of the unit's goals, the continued commitment of the unit's employees, and the development of mutual trust, respect, and obligation in leader–member dyads. Now that we've described what it means for a leader to be effective, we turn to the critical question in this chapter: "Why are some leaders more effective than others?" That is, why exactly are some leaders viewed as more effective on a unitwide basis, and why exactly are some leaders better at fostering high-quality exchange relationships? Beginning as far back as 1904, research on leadership has attempted to answer such questions by looking for particular traits or characteristics of effective leaders.[29] The search for traits and characteristics is consistent with "great person" theories of leadership that suggest that "leaders are born, not made."[30] Early research in this area frequently focused on physical features (e.g., gender, height, physical attractiveness, energy level), whereas subsequent research focused more squarely on personality and ability (see Chapter 9 on Personality and Cultural Values and Chapter 10 on Ability for more discussion of such issues).

After a century of research, leadership scholars now acknowledge that there is no generalizable profile of effective leaders from a trait perspective.[31] In fact, most studies have concluded that traits are more predictive of **leader emergence** (i.e., who becomes a leader in the first place) than they are of leader effectiveness (i.e., how well people

14.2

What traits and characteristics are related to leader emergence and leader effectiveness?

actually do in a leadership role). Table 14-2 reviews some of the traits and characteristics frequently examined in organizational behavior research in general and leadership research in particular. The table draws a distinction between traits and characteristics that predict leader emergence and those that predict leader effectiveness. Although a number of traits and characteristics are relevant to leadership, two limitations of this work have caused leadership research to move in a different direction. First, many of the trait–leadership correlations are weak in magnitude, particularly when leader effectiveness serves as the outcome. Second, the focus on leader traits holds less practical relevance than a focus on leader actions. What exactly can leaders *do* that can make them more effective? This chapter reviews three types of leader actions: decision-making styles, day-to-day behaviors, and behaviors that fall outside of a leader's typical duties.

LEADER DECISION-MAKING STYLES

Of course, one of the most important things leaders do is make decisions. Think about the job you currently hold or the last job you had. Now picture your boss. How many decisions did he or she have to make in a given week? How did he or she go about making those decisions? A leader's decision-making style reflects the process the leader uses to generate and choose from a set of alternatives to solve a problem (see Chapter 8 on Learning and Decision Making for more discussion of such issues). Decision-making styles capture *how* a leader decides as opposed to *what* a leader decides.

The most important element of a leader's decision-making style is this: Does the leader decide most things for him- or herself, or does the leader involve others in the process?

TABLE 14-2	Traits/Characteristics Related to Leader Emergence and Effectiveness	
DESCRIPTION OF TRAIT/ CHARACTERISTIC	**LINKED TO EMERGENCE?**	**LINKED TO EFFECTIVENESS?**
High conscientiousness	√	
Low agreeableness	√	
Low neuroticism		
High openness to experience	√	√
High extraversion	√	√
High general cognitive ability	√	√
High energy level	√	√
High stress tolerance	√	√
High self-confidence	√	√

Sources: Adapted from T.A. Judge, J.E. Bono, R. Ilies, and M.W. Gerhardt, "Personality and Leadership: A Qualitative and Quantitative Review," *Journal of Applied Psychology* 87 (2002), pp. 765–80; T.A. Judge, A.E. Colbert, and R. Ilies, "Intelligence and Leadership: A Quantitative Review and Test of Theoretical Propositions," *Journal of Applied Psychology* 89 (2004), pp. 542–52; and G. Yukl, *Leadership in Organizations,* 4th ed. (Englewood Cliffs, NJ: Prentice-Hall, 1998).

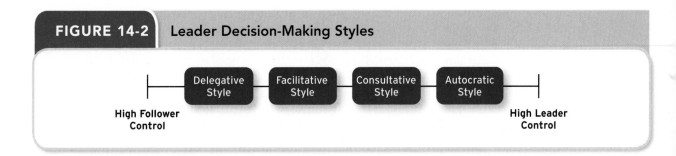

FIGURE 14-2 | **Leader Decision-Making Styles**

High Follower
Control

Delegative Style — Facilitative Style — Consultative Style — Autocratic Style

High Leader
Control

We've probably all had bosses (or professors, or even parents) who made virtually all decisions by themselves, stopping by to announce what had happened once the call had been made. We've probably also had other bosses (or professors, or parents) who tended to do the opposite—involving us, asking our opinions, or seeking our vote even when we didn't care about what was being discussed. It turns out that this issue of leader versus follower control can be used to define some specific decision-making styles. Figure 14-2 shows those styles, arranged on a continuum from high follower control to high leader control.

DEFINING THE STYLES. With an **autocratic style**, the leader makes the decision alone without asking for the opinions or suggestions of the employees in the work unit.[32] The employees may provide information that the leader needs but are not asked to generate or evaluate potential solutions. In fact, they may not even be told about the decision that needs to be made, knowing only that the leader wants information for some reason. This decision-making style seems to be a favorite of Massimo d'Amore, the brash and demanding CEO of PepsiCo. Americas. In 2008, when Pepsi sales were down 29 percent from 2000, d'Amore took drastic action: He went completely around the company's marketing group and created totally new ads and slogans for the company's seven biggest brands, including Pepsi and Gatorade, in just seven months.[33] To save time, everything, from logo design to package creation to shooting the television commercials, occurred simultaneously, and d'Amore injected himself throughout the creative process, making decisions with very little consultation from others.[34] His actions were vastly different from the way the once proud marketing group had operated in the past.[35] Some employees called it being "d'Amoralized."[36] Whether the initiative works for Pepsi is yet to be determined, but numerous key marketing and brand executives have left the company voluntarily as a result.[37]

The next two styles in Figure 14-2 offer more employee involvement. With a **consultative style**, the leader presents the problem to individual employees or a group of employees, asking for their opinions and suggestions before ultimately making the decision him- or herself.[38] With this style, employees do "have a

14.3

What four styles can leaders use to make decisions, and what factors combine to make these styles more effective in a given situation?

Massimo d'Amore, CEO of PepsiCo. Americas, used an autocratic leadership style to make a number of key decisions, including the redesign of the Pepsi logo.

"I'd like your honest, unbiased and possibly career-ending opinion on something."

GREGORY

Source: Copyright © The New Yorker Collection 2003 Alex Gregory from cartoonbank. com. All rights reserved.

say" in the process, but the ultimate authority still rests with the leader. That ultimate authority changes with a **facilitative style**, in which the leader presents the problem to a group of employees and seeks consensus on a solution, making sure that his or her own opinion receives no more weight than anyone else's.[39] With this style, the leader is more facilitator than decision maker. Disney CEO Bob Iger seems to embrace a combination of consultative and facilitative styles.[40] When he took over for Michael Eisner, Iger made his meetings with division heads less autocratic; whereas Eisner held court, Iger encourages conversation. Iger describes his style this way: "You put good people in jobs and give them room to run. . . . You involve yourself in a responsible way, but not to the point where you are usurping their authority. I don't have the time or concentration— and you could argue maybe even the talent—to do that."[41] This facilitative style has allowed Iger to mend fences with employees frustrated by the Eisner era and allowed him—through a relationship with Steve Jobs and other executives—to purchase Pixar Studios in 2009, an acquisition that some regard as one of the shrewdest moves Disney has ever made.[42]

With a **delegative style**, the leader gives an individual employee or a group of employees the responsibility for making the decision within some set of specified boundary conditions.[43] The leader plays no role in the deliberations unless asked, though he or she may offer encouragement and provide necessary resources behind the scenes. Phil Knight, the chairman of Nike, the Oregon–based athletic apparel company, often embraces a delegative style.[44] A quiet and enigmatic figure, Knight has been described as the ultimate delegator, with executives interpreting his silences and nods as the freedom to make their own decisions, even when those decisions take the company in different directions. It's a mystery to employees what Knight actually does in his managing role at Nike, other than to serve as a father figure and visionary. When the copresident of the Nike brand was asked how frequently he met with Knight, he estimated, "Once a week . . . and we probably did that twice a month."[45] The management style that has defined Knight's approach over the past 40 years is straightforward: Find people who care about the product and let them handle the details. Given his delegative style, it's ironic that Knight has sometimes had trouble ceding the CEO position to others during his tenure at Nike.[46]

WHEN ARE THE STYLES MOST EFFECTIVE? Which decision-making style is best? As you may have guessed, there is no one decision-making style that's effective across all situations, and all styles have their pluses and minuses. There are many factors to consider when leaders choose a decision-making style.[47] The most obvious consideration is the quality of the resulting decision, because making the correct decision is the ultimate means of judging the leader. However, leaders also have to consider whether employees will accept and commit to their decision. Research studies have repeatedly shown that allowing employees to participate in decision making increases their job satisfaction.[48] Such participation also helps develop employees' own decision-making skills.[49]

Of course, such participation has a downside for employees because it takes up time. Many employees view meetings as an interruption of their work. One recent study found that employees spend, on average, six hours a week in scheduled meetings and that time spent in meetings relates negatively to job satisfaction when employees don't depend on others in their jobs, focus on their own task accomplishment, and believe meetings are run ineffectively.[50] Diane Bryant, CIO at Intel, argues that "You need people who are critical to making the decisions on the agenda, not people who are there only because they'll be impacted. At Intel, if we see someone who doesn't need to be there, people will say, 'Bob, I don't think we need you here. Thanks for coming.'"[51] According to Chairman Bill Ford, prior to Alan Mulally's arrival, Ford managers convened "pre-meetings," during which they would work to get their stories straight before meeting with their bosses. Mulally's focus on information transparency eliminated these meetings.[52] And GM is working through many of the same issues. Under then-CEO Rick Wagoner, it recognized that it needed to make decisions more quickly and initiated a program called "GoFast." Managers held workshops that focused on the idea of making decisions more quickly. The problem was that across the company, more than 7,000 GoFast workshops took place, leading one executive to complain that "the whole premise of GoFast became going slow."[53]

How can leaders effectively manage their choice of decision-making styles? The **time-driven model of leadership** offers one potential guide.[54] It suggests that the focus should shift away from autocratic, consultative, facilitative, and delegative *leaders* to autocratic, consultative, facilitative, and delegative *situations*. More specifically, the model suggests that seven factors combine to make some decision-making styles more effective in a given situation and other styles less effective. Those seven factors include:

- *Decision significance:* Is the decision significant to the success of the project or the organization?
- *Importance of commitment:* Is it important that employees "buy in" to the decision?
- *Leader expertise:* Does the leader have significant knowledge or expertise regarding the problem?
- *Likelihood of commitment:* How likely is it that employees will trust the leader's decision and commit to it?
- *Shared objectives:* Do employees share and support the same objectives, or do they have an agenda of their own?
- *Employee expertise:* Do the employees have significant knowledge or expertise regarding the problem?
- *Teamwork skills:* Do the employees have the ability to work together to solve the problem, or will they struggle with conflicts or inefficiencies?

Figure 14-3 illustrates how these seven factors can be used to determine the most effective decision-making style in a given situation. The figure asks whether the levels of each of the seven factors are high (H) or low (L). The figure functions like a funnel, moving from left to right, with each answer taking you closer to the recommended style (dashes mean that a given factor can be skipped for that combination). Although the model seems complex at first glance, the principles within it are straightforward. Autocratic styles are reserved for decisions that are insignificant or for which employee commitment is unimportant. The only exception is when the leader's expertise is high and the leader is trusted. An autocratic style in these situations should result in an accurate decision that makes the most efficient use of employees' time. Delegative styles should be reserved for circumstances in which employees have strong teamwork skills and are not likely to commit blindly to whatever decision the leader provides. Deciding between the remaining two styles—consultative and facilitative—is more nuanced and requires a more complete consideration of all seven factors.

Recently ousted GM CEO, Fritz Henderson, took over the bankrupt company in early 2009 and became known for making quick, autocratic decisions. When presented with three potential names for a new car model, he made the decision overnight. When a customer focus group didn't like a new model that already had moved far along the production process, he killed the entire program within hours.[55] Henderson perceived tremendous amounts of time pressure, and he cared little about the commitment level of those underneath him; they needed to change too for the company to survive. Before his departure from GM, Henderson stated, "We need to be faster, without any doubt. As a company we should take more risks. Part of it is how you behave. It starts at the top and moves down the organization. When people realize speed has real value, they will change."[56] For Henderson, decision significance is high, importance of commitment is low, and leader expertise is high, so he adopts an autocratic decision style. However, if we were to return to the example of Massimo d'Amore, the demanding CEO of PepsiCo. Americas, we recognize that for decisions about the rebranding of Pepsi's beverages, decision significance is high, importance of commitment is questionable, and the leader does not appear to have expertise in the subject matter of the decisions. As a result, his autocratic style led to major fallout among his employees, including high levels of turnover (perhaps he did need their commitment after all!). A key point about Figure 14-3 is that unless a leader is an expert with regard to the focus of the decision, autocratic decisions are not the right style to choose.

Research tends to support many of the time-driven model's propositions, particularly when it uses practicing managers as participants.[57] For example, one study asked managers to recall past decisions, the context surrounding those decisions, and the eventual successes (or failures) of their decisions.[58] When managers used the decision-making styles recommended by the model, those decisions were rated as successful 68 percent of the time. When managers went against the model's prescriptions, their decisions were only rated as successful 22 percent of the time. It's also interesting to note that studies suggest that managers tend to choose the style recommended by the model only around 40 percent of the time and exhibit less variation in styles than the model suggests they should.[59] In particular, managers seem to overuse the consultative style and underutilize autocratic and facilitative styles.

DAY-TO-DAY LEADERSHIP BEHAVIORS

Leaving aside how they go about making decisions, what do leaders *do* on a day-to-day basis? When you think about bosses that you've had, what behaviors did they tend to perform as part of their daily leadership responsibilities? A series of studies at Ohio State in the 1950s attempted to answer that question. Working under grants from the Office of Naval Research and the International Harvester Company, the studies began by generating a list of all the behaviors leaders engage in—around 1,800 in all.[60] Those behaviors were

FIGURE 14-3 | The Time-Driven Model of Leadership

START HERE → | END HERE →

Decision Significance	Importance of Commitment	Leader Expertise	Likelihood of Commitment	Shared Objectives	Employee Expertise	Teamwork Skills	
H	H	H	H	-	-	-	Autocratic
H	H	H	L	H	H	H	Delegative
H	H	H	L	H	H	L	Consultative
H	H	H	L	H	L	-	
H	H	H	L	L	-	-	
H	H	L	H	H	H	H	Facilitative
H	H	L	H	H	H	L	
H	H	L	H	H	L	-	Consultative
H	H	L	H	L	-	-	
H	H	L	L	H	H	H	Facilitative
H	H	L	L	H	H	L	
H	H	L	L	H	L	-	Consultative
H	H	L	L	L	-	-	
H	L	H	-	-	-	-	Autocratic
H	L	L	-	H	H	H	Facilitative
H	L	L	-	H	H	L	
H	L	L	-	H	L	-	Consultative
H	L	L	-	L	-	-	
L	H	-	H	-	-	-	Autocratic
L	H	-	L	-	H	-	Delegative
L	H	-	L	-	L	-	Facilitative
L	L	-	-	-	-	-	Autocratic

Source: Adapted from V.H. Vroom, "Leadership and the Decision-Making Process," *Organizational Dynamics* 28 (2000), pp. 82–94.

trimmed down to 150 specific examples, then grouped into several categories, as shown in Table 14-3.[61] The table reveals that many leaders spend their time engaging in a mix of initiating, organizing, producing, socializing, integrating, communicating, recognizing, and representing behaviors. Although eight categories are easier to remember than 1,800 behaviors, further analyses suggested that the categories in Table 14-3 really boil down to just two dimensions: initiating structure and consideration.[62]

Initiating structure reflects the extent to which the leader defines and structures the roles of employees in pursuit of goal attainment.[63] Leaders who are high on initiating structure play a more active role in directing group activities and prioritize planning, scheduling, and trying out new ideas. They might emphasize the importance of meeting deadlines, describe explicit standards of performance, ask employees to follow formalized procedures, and criticize poor work when necessary.[64] **Consideration** reflects the extent to which leaders create job relationships characterized by mutual trust, respect for employee ideas, and consideration of employee feelings.[65] Leaders who are high on consideration create a climate of good rapport and strong, two-way communication and exhibit a deep concern for the welfare of employees. They might do personal favors for employees, take

14.4

What two dimensions capture most of the day-to-day leadership behaviors in which leaders engage?

TABLE 14-3	Day-to-Day Behaviors Performed by Leaders

BEHAVIOR	DESCRIPTION
Initiating Structure	
Initiation	Originating, facilitating, and sometimes resisting new ideas and practices
Organization	Defining and structuring work, clarifying leader versus member roles, coordinating employee tasks
Production	Setting goals and providing incentives for the effort and productivity of employees
Consideration	
Membership	Mixing with employees, stressing informal interactions, and exchanging personal services
Integration	Encouraging a pleasant atmosphere, reducing conflict, promoting individual adjustment to the group
Communication	Providing information to employees, seeking information from them, showing an awareness of matters that affect them
Recognition	Expressing approval or disapproval of the behaviors of employees
Representation	Acting on behalf of the group, defending the group, and advancing the interests of the group

Source: J.K. Hemphill and A.E. Coons, "Development of the Leader Behavior Description Questionnaire," in *Leader Behavior: Its Description and Measurement,* eds. R.M. Stogdill and A.E. Coons. (Columbus, OH: Bureau of Business Research, Ohio State University, 1957), pp. 6–38.

time to listen to their problems, "go to bat" for them when needed, and treat them as equals.[66]

The Ohio State studies argued that initiating structure and consideration were (more or less) independent concepts, meaning that leaders could be high on both, low on both, or high on one and low on the other. That view differed from a series of studies conducted at the University of Michigan during the same time period. Those studies identified concepts similar to initiating structure and consideration, calling them production-centered (or task-oriented) and employee-centered (or relations-oriented) behaviors.[67] However, the Michigan studies framed their task-oriented and relations-oriented concepts as two ends of one continuum, implying that leaders couldn't be high on both dimensions.[68] In fact, a recent meta-analysis of 78 studies showed that initiating structure and consideration are only weakly related—knowing whether a leader engages in one brand of behavior says little about whether he or she engages in the other brand.[69] To see how much initiating structure and consideration you engage in during leadership roles, see our **OB Assessments** feature.

After an initial wave of research on initiating structure and consideration, leadership experts began to doubt the usefulness of the two dimensions for predicting leadership

OB ASSESSMENTS

INITIATING STRUCTURE AND CONSIDERATION

How do you act when you're in a leadership role? This assessment is designed to measure initiating structure and consideration. Please write a number next to each statement that reflects how frequently you engage in the behavior described. Then subtract your answers to the boldfaced questions from 6, with the difference being your new answer for that question. For example, if your original answer for question 16 was "4," your new answer is "2" (6 – 4). Then sum up your answers for each of the dimensions. (For more assessments relevant to this chapter, please visit the Online Learning Center at www.mhhe.com/colquitt).

1	2	3	4	5
NEVER	SELDOM	OCCASIONALLY	OFTEN	ALWAYS

1. I let group members know what is expected of them. _____
2. I encourage the use of uniform procedures. _____
3. I try out my ideas in the group. _____
4. I make my attitudes clear to the group. _____
5. I decide what shall be done and how it shall be done. _____
6. I assign group members to particular tasks. _____
7. I make sure that my part in the group is understood by the group members. _____
8. I schedule the work to be done. _____
9. I maintain definite standards of performance. _____
10. I ask group members to follow standard rules and regulations. _____
11. I am friendly and approachable. _____
12. I do little things to make it pleasant to be a member of the group. _____
13. I put suggestions made by the group into operation. _____
14. I treat all group members as equals. _____
15. I give advance notice of changes. _____
16. **I keep to myself.** _____
17. I look out for the personal welfare of group members. _____
18. I am willing to make changes. _____
19. **I refuse to explain my actions.** _____
20. **I act without consulting the group.** _____

SCORING AND INTERPRETATION

Initiating Structure: Sum up items 1–10. _____
Consideration: Sum up items 11–20. _____

For initiating structure, scores of 38 or more are high. For consideration, scores of 40 or more are high.

Source: R.M. Stogdill, *Manual for the Leader Behavior Description Questionnaire–Form XII* (Columbus, OH: Bureau of Business Research, The Ohio State University, 1963).

effectiveness.[70] More recent research has painted a more encouraging picture, however. A meta-analysis of 103 studies showed that initiating structure and consideration both had beneficial relationships with a number of outcomes.[71] For example, consideration had a strong positive relationship with perceived leader effectiveness, employee motivation, and employee job satisfaction. It also had a moderate positive relationship with overall unit performance. For its part, initiating structure had a strong positive relationship with employee motivation and moderate positive relationships with perceived leader effectiveness, employee job satisfaction, and overall unit performance.

Although initiating structure and consideration tend to be beneficial across situations, there may be circumstances in which they become more or less important. The **life cycle theory of leadership** (sometimes also called the situational model of leadership) argues that the optimal combination of initiating structure and consideration depends on the readiness of the employees in the work unit.[72] **Readiness** is broadly defined as the degree to which employees have the ability and the willingness to accomplish their specific tasks.[73] As shown in Figure 14-4, the theory suggests that readiness varies across employees and can be expressed in terms of four important snapshots: R1–R4. To find the optimal combination of leader behaviors for a particular readiness snapshot, put your finger on the relevant R, then move it straight down to the recommended combination of behaviors.

The description of the first two R's has varied over time and across different formulations of the theory. One formulation described the R's as similar to stages of group development.[74] R1 refers to a group of employees who are working together for the first time and are eager to begin, but they lack the experience and confidence needed to perform their roles. Here the optimal combination of leader behaviors is **telling**—high initiating structure and low consideration—in which case the leader provides specific instructions and

FIGURE 14-4 | The Life Cycle Theory of Leadership

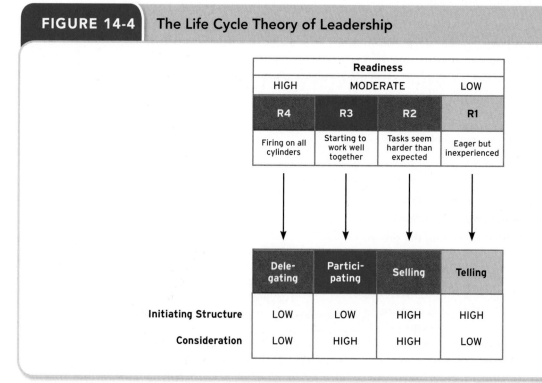

Source: Adapted from P. Hersey and K. Blanchard, "Revisiting the Life-Cycle Theory of Leadership." *Training and Development* January 1996, pp. 42–47.

closely supervises performance. The lion's share of the leader's attention must be devoted to directing followers in this situation, because their goals and roles need to be clearly defined. In the R2 stage, the members have begun working together and, as typically happens, are finding that their work is more difficult than they had anticipated. As eagerness turns to dissatisfaction, the optimal combination of leader behaviors is **selling**—high initiating structure and high consideration—in which the leader supplements his or her directing with support and encouragement to protect the confidence levels of the employees.

As employees gain more ability, guidance and direction by the leader become less necessary. At the R3 stage, employees have learned to work together well, though they still need support and collaboration from the leader to help them adjust to their more self-managed state of affairs. Here **participating**—low initiating structure and high consideration—becomes the optimal combination of leader behaviors. Finally, the optimal combination for the R4 readiness level is **delegating**—low initiating structure and low consideration—such that the leader turns responsibility for key behaviors over to the employees. Here the leader gives them the proverbial ball and lets them run with it. All that's needed from the leader is some degree of observation and monitoring to make sure that the group's efforts stay on track.

Estimates suggest that the life cycle theory has been incorporated into leadership training programs at around 400 of the firms in the *Fortune* 500, with more than one million managers exposed to it annually.[75] Unfortunately, the application of the theory has outpaced scientific testing of its propositions, and the shifting nature of its terminology and predictions has made scientific testing somewhat difficult.[76] The research that has been conducted supports the theory's predictions only for low readiness situations, suggesting that telling and selling sorts of behaviors may be more effective when ability, motivation, or confidence are lacking.[77] When readiness is higher, these tests suggest that leader behaviors simply matter less, regardless of their particular combinations. Tests also suggest that leaders only use the recommended combinations of behaviors between 14 and 37 percent of the time,[78] likely because many leaders adhere to the same leadership philosophy regardless of the situation. It should also be noted that tests of the theory have been somewhat more supportive when conducted on an across-job, rather than within-job, basis. For example, research suggests that the performance of lower ranking university employees (e.g., maintenance workers, custodians, landscapers) depends more on initiating structure and less on consideration than the performance of higher ranking university employees (e.g., professors, instructors).[79]

Although the scientific validity of the life cycle theory remains in question, its predictions often seem to play out in professional sports. General managers often hire coaches with a "hands-on" directive philosophy for youthful teams with several rookies or new starters. Over time, those teams mature and become more experienced, at which point the coach's style begins to wear on the veterans. The general managers then bring in coaches with a more "hands-off" style (often referred to as a "player's coach"). This same dynamic recently played out at Home Depot, the Atlanta-based hardware retailer. Controversial CEO Bob Nardelli agreed to resign after a six-year tenure, with one observer noting, "the fact is that this retail organization never really embraced his leadership style."[80] That style was focused on cutting costs as opposed to customer service.[81] Nardelli had been described as a detail-obsessed manager devoted to building a disciplined corps predisposed to following orders.[82] He believed in a command-and-control sort of environment and was fond of saying, "Facts are friendly."[83] You can probably already guess the adjectives associated with Nardelli's replacement: The cofounder of Home Depot described new CEO Frank Blake as more "people oriented," lacking Nardelli's sharp edges while playing the role of consensus builder.[84]

TRANSFORMATIONAL LEADERSHIP BEHAVIORS

By describing decision-making styles and day-to-day leader behaviors, we've covered a broad spectrum of what it is that leaders do. Still, something is missing. Take a small piece of scrap paper and jot down five people who are famous for their effective leadership. They can come from inside or outside the business world and can be either living people or historical figures. All that's important is that their name be practically synonymous with great leadership. Once you've compiled your list, take a look at the names. Do they appear on your list because they tend to use the right decision-making styles in the right situations and engage in effective levels of consideration and initiating structure? What about the case of Alan Mulally? Do decision-making styles and day-to-day leadership behaviors explain his importance to the fortunes of Ford?

The missing piece of this leadership puzzle is what leaders do to motivate their employees to perform beyond expectations. **Transformational leadership** involves inspiring followers to commit to a shared vision that provides meaning to their work while also serving as a role model who helps followers develop their own potential and view problems from new perspectives.[85] Transformational leaders heighten followers' awareness of the importance of certain outcomes while increasing their confidence that those outcomes can be achieved.[86] What gets "transformed" is the way followers view their work, causing them to focus on the collective good more than just their own short-term self-interests and to perform beyond expectations as a result.[87] Former President Dwight D. Eisenhower once noted, "Leadership is the ability to decide what is to be done, and then to get others to want to do it."[88] Former President Harry S Truman similarly observed, "A leader is a man who has the ability to get other people to do what they don't want to do, and like it."[89] Both quotes capture a transformation in the way followers view their work and what motivates them on the job.

Transformational leadership is viewed as a more motivational approach to leadership than other managerial approaches. Figure 14-5 contrasts various approaches to leadership according to how active or passive they are and, ultimately, how effective they prove to be. The colored cubes in the figure represent five distinct approaches to motivating employees, and the depth of the cubes represent how much a leader prioritizes each of the approaches. The figure therefore represents an optimal leadership approach that prioritizes more effective and more active behaviors. That optimal approach includes low levels of **laissez-faire**

Mother Teresa's inspiring humanitarian work with India's sick and poor, and her founding of the influential Missionaries of Charity, became known around the world and suggest that she was a transformational leader. She was awarded the Nobel Peace Prize in 1979.

| FIGURE 14-5 | Laissez-Faire, Transactional, and Transformational Leadership |

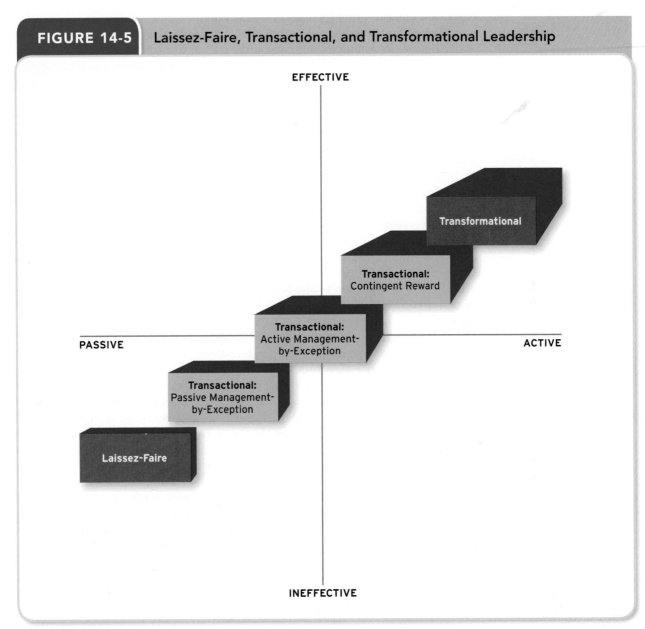

Source: Adapted from B.M. Bass and R.E. Riggio, *Transformational Leadership,* 2nd ed. (Mahwah, NJ: Lawrence Erlbaum Associates, 2006).

(i.e., hands-off) leadership, represented by the red cube, which is the avoidance of leadership altogether.[90] Important actions are delayed, responsibility is ignored, and power and influence go unutilized. One common measure of leadership reflects laissez-faire styles with this statement: "The leader avoids getting involved when important issues arise."[91]

The three yellow cubes represent **transactional leadership**, which occurs when the leader rewards or disciplines the follower depending on the adequacy of the follower's performance.[92] With **passive management-by-exception**, the leader waits around for mistakes and errors, then takes corrective action as necessary.[93] After all, "if it ain't broke, don't fix it!"[94] This approach is represented by statements like: "The leader takes no action until complaints are received."[95] With **active management-by-exception**, the leader arranges to monitor mistakes and errors actively and again takes corrective action when required.[96] This approach is represented by statements like: "The leader directs attention toward failures to meet standards."[97] **Contingent reward** represents a more active and effective brand of transactional leadership, in which the leader attains follower agreement on what needs to be done using promised or actual rewards in exchange for adequate performance.[98] Statements like "The leader makes clear what one can expect to receive when performance goals are achieved" exemplify contingent reward leadership.[99]

Transactional leadership represents the "carrot-and-stick" approach to leadership, with management-by-exception providing the "sticks" and contingent reward supplying the "carrots." Of course, transactional leadership represents the dominant approach to motivating employees in most organizations, and research suggests that it can be effective. A meta-analysis of 87 studies showed that contingent reward was strongly related to follower motivation and perceived leader effectiveness[100] (see Chapter 6 on Motivation for more discussion of such issues). Active management-by-exception was only weakly related to follower motivation and perceived leader effectiveness, however, and passive management-by-exception seems actually to harm those outcomes.[101] Such results support the progression shown in Figure 14-5, with contingent reward standing as the most effective approach under the transactional leadership umbrella.

Finally, the green cube represents transformational leadership—the most active and effective approach in Figure 14-5. How effective is transformational leadership? Well, we'll save that discussion for the "How Important Is Leadership" section that concludes this chapter, but suffice it to say that transformational leadership has the strongest and most beneficial effects of any of the leadership variables described in this chapter. It's also the leadership approach that's most universally endorsed across cultures, as described in our **OB Internationally** feature. In addition, it probably captures the key qualities of the famous leaders we asked you to list a few paragraphs back. To understand why it's so powerful, we need to dig deeper into the specific kinds of actions and behaviors that leaders can utilize to become more transformational. It turns out that the full spectrum of transformational leadership can be summarized using four dimensions: idealized influence, inspirational motivation, intellectual stimulation, and individualized consideration. Collectively, these four dimensions of transformational leadership are often called "the Four I's."[102] For our discussion of transformational leadership, we'll use Steve Jobs, CEO of Apple, widely recognized as one of the most transformational leaders in the corporate world, as a running example. Estimates predict that Apple would lose 25 percent of its market share were Jobs to leave—a troubling prediction given Jobs's medical issues related to pancreatic cancer.[103]

Idealized influence involves behaving in ways that earn the admiration, trust, and respect of followers, causing followers to want to identify with and emulate the leader.[104] Idealized influence is represented by statements like: "The leader instills pride in me for being associated with him/her."[105] Idealized influence is synonymous with *charisma*—a Greek word that means "divinely inspired gift"—which reflects a sense among followers that the leader possesses extraordinary qualities.[106] Charisma is a word often associated with Steve Jobs. One observer noted that even though Jobs could be very difficult to work with, his remarkable charisma created a mysterious attraction that drew people to him, keeping them loyal to his collective sense of mission.[107]

To some extent, discussions of charisma serve as echoes of the "great person" view of leadership that spawned the trait research described in Table 14-2. In fact, research suggests

14.5

How does transformational leadership differ from transactional leadership, and which behaviors set it apart?

OB INTERNATIONALLY

Does the effectiveness of leader styles and behaviors vary across cultures? Answering that question is one of the objectives of Project GLOBE's test of culturally endorsed implicit leadership theory, which argues that effective leadership is "in the eye of the beholder" (see Chapter 9 on Personality and Cultural Values for more discussion of such issues).[108] To test the theory, researchers asked participants across cultures to rate a number of leader styles and behaviors using a 1 (very ineffective) to 7 (very effective) scale. The figure below shows how three of the styles and behaviors described in this chapter were rated across 10 different regions (note that the term "Anglo" represents people of English ethnicity, including the United States, Great Britain, and Australia).

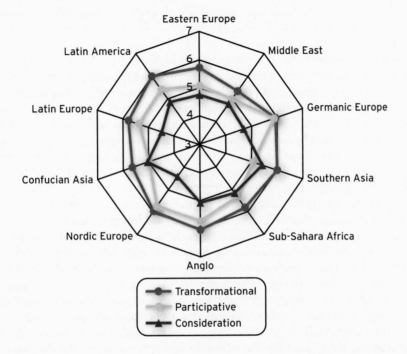

It turns out that transformational leadership is the most universally accepted approach to leadership of any of the concepts studied by Project GLOBE,[109] receiving an average rating near 6 in every region except the Middle East. That appeal is likely explained by the fact that transformational leaders emphasize values like idealism and virtue that are endorsed in almost all countries.[110] The figure also shows that a participative style is favorably viewed in most countries, though more variation is evident. Even more variation is seen with consideration behaviors, which are endorsed a bit less across the board but especially in Europe. Understanding these kinds of results can help organizations select and train managers who will fit the profile of an effective leader in a given region.

that there is a genetic component to charisma specifically and to transformational leadership more broadly. Studies on identical twins reared apart show that such twins have very similar charismatic profiles, despite their differing environments.[111] Indeed, such research suggests that almost 60 percent of the variation in charismatic behavior can be explained by genes. One explanation for such findings is that genes influence the personality traits that give rise to charisma. For example, research suggests that extraversion, openness to experience, and agreeableness have significant effects on perceptions of leader charisma,[112] and all three of those personality dimensions have a significant genetic component (see Chapter 9 on Personality and Cultural Values for more discussion of such issues).

Inspirational motivation involves behaving in ways that foster an enthusiasm for and commitment to a shared vision of the future.[113] That vision is transmitted through a sort of "meaning-making" process in which the negative features of the status quo are emphasized while highlighting the positive features of the potential future.[114] Inspirational motivation is represented by statements like: "The leader articulates a compelling vision of the future."[115] At Apple, Steve Jobs is renowned for spinning a "reality distortion field" that reshapes employees' views of the current work environment.[116] One Apple employee explained, "Steve has this power of vision that is almost frightening. When Steve believes in something, the power of that vision can literally sweep aside any objections, problems, or whatever. They just cease to exist."[117]

Intellectual stimulation involves behaving in ways that challenge followers to be innovative and creative by questioning assumptions and reframing old situations in new ways.[118] Intellectual stimulation is represented by statements like: "The leader gets others to look at problems from many different angles."[119] Intellectual stimulation has been a staple of Jobs's tenure at Apple. He pushed for a different power supply on the Apple II so that the fan could be removed, preventing it from humming and churning like other computers of the time. Years later, he insisted on removing the floppy drive from the iMac because it seemed silly to transfer data one megabyte at a time, a decision that drew merciless criticism when the iMac debuted.

Individualized consideration involves behaving in ways that help followers achieve their potential through coaching, development, and mentoring.[120] Not to be confused with the consideration behavior derived from the Ohio State studies, individualized consideration represents treating employees as unique individuals with specific needs, abilities, and aspirations that need to be tied into the unit's mission. Individualized consideration is represented by statements like: "The leader spends time teaching and coaching."[121] Of the four facets of transformational leadership, Steve Jobs seems lowest on individualized consideration. Employees who are not regarded as his equals are given a relatively short leash and sometimes face an uncertain future in the company. In fact, some Apple employees resist riding the elevator for fear of ending up trapped with Jobs for the ride between floors. As one observer describes it, by the time the doors open, you might have had your confidence undermined for weeks.[122] To see an example of high individualized consideration (not to mention high levels of the other "Four I's"), see our **OB on Screen** feature.

One interesting domain for examining transformational leadership issues is politics. Many of the most famous speeches given by U.S. presidents include a great deal of transformational content. Table 14-4 includes excerpts from speeches given by presidents that rank highly on transformational content based on scientific and historical study.[123] One theme that's notable in the table is the presence of a crisis, as many of the presidents were attempting to steer the country through a difficult time in history (e.g., World War II, the Cold War, the Civil War). That's not a coincidence, in that times of crisis are particularly conducive to the emergence of transformational leadership.[124] Times of stress and turbulence cause people to long for charismatic leaders, and encouraging, confident, and idealistic visions resonate more deeply during such times. Some support for this suggestion comes from President George W. Bush's speeches before and after the tragedies on 9/11. Coding of his major speeches, public addresses, and radio addresses shows a significant increase in the transformational content of his rhetoric after the 9/11 attacks, including more focus on a collective mission and more articulation of a values-based vision.[125]

OB ON SCREEN

STAR TREK

Your father was captain of a starship for 12 minutes. He saved 800 lives—including your mother's, and yours. I dare you to do better.

With those words, Captain Christopher Pike (Bruce Greenwood) of the *U.S.S. Enterprise* challenges a young Jim Kirk (Chris Pine) to do more with his life in *Star Trek* (Dir.: J.J. Abrams, Paramount, 2009). Pike has just been summoned to the scene of a fight between Kirk and some Starfleet cadets stationed in his hometown. As he looks at the mess that's been made at the local bar, Pike recognizes the guilty party as the son of George Kirk—a man who sacrificed his own life to save the crew of the *U.S.S. Kelvin*, not to mention his wife and infant son.

Nowadays, Jim has drifted away from the promising career path exemplified by his father. When Pike conducts a quick check of Kirk's profile, he sees aptitude scores that are off the charts. At that moment, he decides to intervene in Kirk's life, to prevent him from becoming the first "genius-level repeat offender" in the Midwest. Pike's goal is to change the way Kirk thinks about his life, and he uses transformational leadership to do it. First, he references Kirk's father as a source of idealized influence, challenging him to live up to that role model. Second, he engages in individualized consideration by building a mentor-style rapport, noting to Kirk, "You can settle for less in ordinary life, or do you feel like you were meant for something better? Something special?" Third, he even throws in some inspirational motivation by suggesting that Kirk could become an officer within four years, and captain his own ship within eight. Kirk's now sufficiently motivated response? "Four years? I'll do it in three."

As future research is conducted, we're fairly confident that President Barack Obama's speeches will be described similarly, as many of his campaign and postelection speeches are high in transformational content. In fact, President Obama is known for being a very charismatic leader in terms of both the messages he delivers and the mannerisms that go along with them.[126] Indeed, evidence suggests that it is these types of leaders that followers are the most attracted to in times of crisis and uncertainty, which could be one of the reasons why Obama was elected over John McCain.[127]

TABLE 14-4		Transformational Rhetoric among U.S. Presidents	
PRESIDENT	**TERM**	**REMARK**	**WHICH "I"?**
Abraham Lincoln	1861–1865	"Fourscore and seven years ago our forefathers brought forth on this continent, a new nation, conceived in Liberty, and dedicated to the proposition that all men are created equal."	Idealized influence
Franklin Roosevelt	1933–1945	"First of all, let me assert my firm belief that the only thing we have to fear is fear itself—nameless, unreasoning, unjustified terror which paralyzes needed efforts to convert retreat into advance."	Inspirational motivation
John F. Kennedy	1961–1963	"And so, my fellow Americans . . . ask not what your country can do you for you—ask what you can do for your country. My fellow citizens of the world: Ask not what America will do for you, but what together we can do for the freedom of man."	Intellectual stimulation
Lyndon Johnson	1963–1969	"If future generations are to remember us more with gratitude than sorrow, we must achieve more than just the miracles of technology. We must also leave them a glimpse of the world as it was created, not just as it looked when we got through with it."	Idealized influence
Ronald Reagan	1981–1989	"General Secretary Gorbachev, if you seek peace, if you seek prosperity for the Soviet Union and Eastern Europe, if you seek liberalization: Come here to this gate! Mr. Gorbachev, open this gate! Mr. Gorbachev, tear down this wall!"	Idealized influence
Bill Clinton	1993–2001	"To realize the full possibilities of this economy, we must reach beyond our own borders, to shape the revolution that is tearing down barriers and building new networks among nations and individuals, and economies and cultures: globalization. It's the central reality of our time."	Intellectual stimulation

Sources: J.S. Mio, R.E. Riggio, S. Levin, and R. Reese, "Presidential Leadership and Charisma: The Effects of Metaphor," *Leadership Quarterly* 16 (2005), pp. 287–94; http://www.usa-patriotism.com/quotes/_list.htm.

SUMMARY: WHY ARE SOME LEADERS MORE EFFECTIVE THAN OTHERS?

So what explains why some leaders are more effective than others? As shown in Figure 14-6, answering that question requires an understanding of the particular styles that leaders use to make decisions and the behaviors they perform in their leadership role. In terms of decision-making styles, do they choose the most effective combination of leader and follower control in terms of the autocratic, consultative, facilitative, and delegative styles, particularly considering the importance of the decision and the expertise in the unit? In

FIGURE 14-6   Why Are Some Leaders More Effective Than Others?

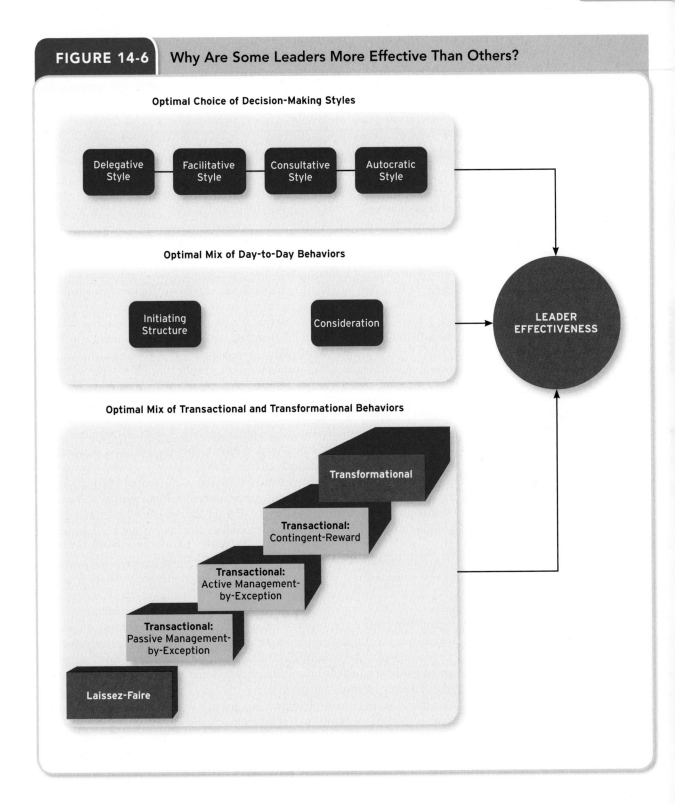

terms of day-to-day behaviors, do they engage in adequate levels of initiating structure and consideration? Finally, do they utilize an effective combination of transactional leadership behaviors, such as contingent reward, and transformational leadership behaviors, such as idealized influence, inspirational motivation, intellectual stimulation, and individualized consideration?

HOW IMPORTANT IS LEADERSHIP?

How important is leadership? As with some other topics in organizational behavior, that's a complicated question because "leadership" isn't just one thing. Instead, all of the styles and behaviors summarized in Figure 14-6 have their own unique importance. However, transformational leadership stands apart from the rest to some extent, with particularly strong effects in organizations. For example, transformational leadership is more strongly related to unit-focused measures of leadership effectiveness, like the kind shown in the top panel of Table 14-1.[128] Units led by a transformational leader tend to be more financially successful and bring higher quality products and services to market at a faster rate.[129] Transformational leadership is also more strongly related to dyad-focused measures of leader effectiveness, like the kind shown in the bottom panel of Table 14-1. Transformational leaders tend to foster leader–member exchange relationships that are of higher quality, marked by especially strong levels of mutual respect and obligation.[130]

14.6

How does leadership affect job performance and organizational commitment?

What if we focus specifically on the two outcomes in our integrative model of OB: performance and commitment? Figure 14-7 summarizes the research evidence linking transformational leadership to those two outcomes. The figure reveals that transformational leadership indeed affects the job performance of the employees who report to the leader. Employees with transformational leaders tend to have higher levels of task performance and engage in higher levels of citizenship behaviors.[131] Why? One reason is that employees with transformational leaders have higher levels of *motivation* than other employees.[132] They feel a stronger sense of psychological empowerment, feel more self-confident, and set more demanding work goals for themselves.[133] They also *trust* the leader more, making them willing to exert extra effort even when that effort might not be immediately rewarded.[134]

Figure 14-7 also reveals that employees with transformational leaders tend to be more committed to their organization.[135] They feel a stronger emotional bond with their organization and a stronger sense of obligation to remain present and engaged in their work.[136] Why? One reason is that employees with transformational leaders have higher levels of *job satisfaction* than other employees.[137] One study showed that transformational leaders can make employees feel that their jobs have more variety and significance, enhancing intrinsic satisfaction with the work itself.[138] Other studies have shown that charismatic leaders express positive emotions more frequently and that those emotions are "caught" by employees through a sort of "emotional contagion" process.[139] For example, followers of transformational leaders tend to feel more optimism and less frustration during their workday, which makes it a bit easier to stay committed to work.[140]

Although leadership is very important to unit effectiveness and the performance and commitment of employees, there are contexts in which the importance of the leader can be reduced. The **substitutes for leadership model** suggests that certain characteristics of the situation can constrain the influence of the leader, making it more difficult for the leader to influence employee performance.[141] Those situational characteristics come in two varieties, as shown in Table 14-5. **Substitutes** reduce the importance of the leader while simultaneously providing a direct benefit to employee performance. For example, a cohesive work

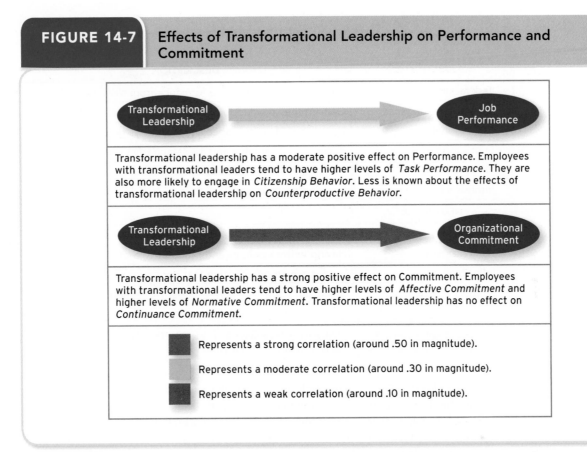

FIGURE 14-7 Effects of Transformational Leadership on Performance and Commitment

Sources: T.A. Judge and R.F. Piccolo, "Transformational and Transactional Leadership: A Meta-Analytic Test of Their Relative Validity," *Journal of Applied Psychology* 89 (2004), pp. 755–68; J.P. Meyer, D.J. Stanley, L. Herscovitch, and L. Topolnytsky, "Affective, Continuance, and Normative Commitment to the Organization: A Meta-Analysis of Antecedents, Correlates, and Consequences," *Journal of Vocational Behavior* 61 (2002), pp. 20–52; and P.M. Podsakoff, S.B. MacKenzie, J.B. Paine, and D.G. Bachrach, "Organizational Citizenship Behaviors: A Critical Review of the Theoretical and Empirical Literature and Suggestions for Future Research," *Journal of Management* 26 (2000), pp. 513–63.

group can provide its own sort of governing behaviors, making the leader less relevant, while providing its own source of motivation and job satisfaction. **Neutralizers**, in contrast, only reduce the importance of the leader; they themselves have no beneficial impact on performance.[142] For example, spatial distance lessens the impact of a leader's behaviors and styles, but distance itself has no direct benefit for employee job performance.

The substitutes for leadership model offers a number of prescriptions for a better understanding of leadership in organizations. First, it can be used to explain why a leader who seemingly "does the right things" doesn't seem to be making any difference.[143] It may be that the leader's work context possesses high levels of neutralizers and substitutes. Second, it can be used to explain what to do if an ineffective person is in a leadership role with no immediate replacement waiting in the wings.[144] If the leader can't be removed, perhaps the organization can do things to make that leader more irrelevant. Studies of the substitutes for leadership model have been inconsistent in showing that substitutes and neutralizers actually make leaders less influential in the predicted manner.[145] What is more clear is that the substitutes in Table 14-5 have beneficial effects on the job performance and

TABLE 14-5	Leader Substitutes and Neutralizers

SUBSTITUTES	DESCRIPTION
Task feedback	Receiving feedback on performance from the task itself
Training & experience	Gaining the knowledge to act independently of the leader
Professionalism	Having a professional specialty that offers guidance
Staff support	Receiving information and assistance from outside staff
Group cohesion	Working in a close-knit and interdependent work group
Intrinsic satisfaction	Deriving personal satisfaction from one's work
NEUTRALIZERS	
Task stability	Having tasks with a clear, unchanging sequence of steps
Formalization	Having written policies and procedures that govern one's job
Inflexibility	Working in an organization that prioritizes rule adherence
Spatial distance	Being separated from one's leader by physical space

Source: Adapted from S. Kerr and J.M. Jermier, "Substitutes for Leadership: Their Meaning and Measurement," *Organizational Behavior and Human Performance* 22 (1978), pp. 375–403.

organizational commitment of employees. In fact, the beneficial effects of the substitutes is sometimes even greater than the beneficial effects of the leader's own behaviors and styles. Some leadership experts even recommend that leaders set out to create high levels of the substitutes in their work units wherever possible, even if the units might ultimately wind up "running themselves."[146]

APPLICATION: LEADERSHIP TRAINING

Given the importance of leadership, what can organizations do to maximize the effectiveness of their leaders? One method is to spend more time training them. As mentioned in Chapter 8, organizations spent $134.39 billion on employee learning and development in 2007, and much of that was devoted to management and supervisory training.[147] One training analyst explains the increasing emphasis on leadership training this way: "The biggest problem that companies face today is an acute shortage of midlevel managers. They look around and just don't have enough qualified people." The same analyst notes that hiring leaders away from competitors isn't an option "because they probably don't have enough managers either."[148]

14.7

Can leaders be trained to be more effective?

Leadership training programs often focus on very specific issues, like conducting more accurate performance evaluations, being a more effective mentor, structuring creative problem solving, or gaining more cultural awareness and sensitivity.[149] However, training programs can also focus on much of the content covered in this chapter. For example, content could focus on contextual considerations that alter the effectiveness of decision-making styles or particular leader behaviors, such as initiating structure and consideration. What about transformational leadership? Given how dependent charisma is on personality and genetic factors, is it possible that transformational leaders can only be born, not made? See our **OB at the Bookstore** feature for one answer to that question.

OB AT THE BOOKSTORE

THE LEADERSHIP CHALLENGE
4th ed., by James M. Kouzes and Barry Z. Posner (San Francisco, CA: Jossey Bass, 2007).

Good leadership is an understandable and universal process. Though each leader is a unique individual, there are patterns to the practice that are shared. And that can be learned.

With those words, Kouzes and Posner lay out their "field guide for leaders"—a book that describes five practices of exemplary leadership, provides case studies of real people who use those practices, and offers specific recommendations for learning how to use them. So what exactly are the five practices? They include:

1. *Model the Way:* Be a model of the behavior you expect of others in order to gain commitment.

2. *Inspire a Shared Vision:* Forge a unity of purpose by describing a dream that is for the common good.

3. *Challenge the Process:* Be willing to step out into the unknown to innovate, grow, and improve.

4. *Enable Others to Act:* Foster a sense of collaboration and trust to build teamwork.

5. *Encourage the Heart:* Create a culture of celebration to show appreciation for contributions.

A quick glance at the five practices reveals that Kouzes and Posner's exemplary leadership has much in common with the "Four I's" of transformational leadership. In particular, the first three practices are quite similar to idealized influence, inspirational motivation, and intellectual stimulation.

The book devotes two chapters to each of the five practices, with each chapter describing eight specific steps to take to get better at a given practice. For example, some of the steps involved in inspiring a shared vision include reading a biography of a visionary leader, determining the "something" you want to do, writing a vision statement, expanding your communication skills, and learning to be a better listener. In all, the book includes 80 specific steps that can be taken to become a more transformational leader. The book also includes information on the Leadership Practices Inventory (LPI), which can offer a "before and after" look at your proficiency with the five practices. The popularity of Kouzes and Posner's book is testament to the view that transformational leaders can indeed be made, not just born.

It turns out that many training programs focus on transformational leadership content, and research suggests that those programs can be effective.[150] One study of transformational leadership training occurred in one of the largest bank chains in Canada.[151] Managers at all of the branches in one region were randomly assigned to either a transformational training group or a control group. The managers in the training group took part in a one-day training session that began by asking them to describe the best and worst leaders they had ever encountered. Where applicable, the behaviors mentioned as belonging to the best leaders were framed around transformational leadership. The transformational dimensions were then described in a lecture-style format. Participants set goals for how they could behave more transformationally and engaged in role-playing exercises to practice those behaviors. The managers then created specific action plans, with progress on those plans monitored during four "booster sessions" over the next month. The results of the study showed that managers who participated in the training were rated as more transformational afterward. More importantly, their employees reported higher levels of organizational commitment, and their branches enjoyed better performance in terms of personal loan sales and credit card sales.

TAKEAWAYS

14.1 Leadership is defined as the use of power and influence to direct the activities of followers toward goal achievement. An "effective leader" improves the performance and well-being of his or her overall unit, as judged by profit margins, productivity, costs, absenteeism, retention, employee surveys, and so forth. An "effective leader" also cultivates high-quality leader–member exchange relationships on a dyadic basis through role taking and role making processes.

14.2 Leader emergence has been linked to a number of traits, including conscientiousness, disagreeableness, openness, extraversion, general cognitive ability, energy level, stress tolerance, and self-confidence. Of that set, the last six traits also predict leader effectiveness.

14.3 Leaders can use a number of styles to make decisions. Beginning with high leader control and moving to high follower control, they include autocratic, consultative, facilitative, and delegative styles. According to the time-driven model of leadership, the appropriateness of these styles depends on decision significance, the importance of commitment, leader expertise, the likelihood of commitment, shared objectives, employee expertise, and teamwork skills.

14.4 Most of the day-to-day leadership behaviors that leaders engage in are examples of either initiating structure or consideration. Initiating structure behaviors include initiation, organization, and production sorts of duties. Consideration behaviors include membership, integration, communication, recognition, and representation sorts of duties.

14.5 Transactional leadership emphasizes "carrot-and-stick" approaches to motivating employees, whereas transformational leadership fundamentally changes the way employees view their work. More specifically, transformational leadership inspires employees to commit to a shared vision or goal that provides meaning and challenge to their work. The specific behaviors that underlie transformational leadership include the "Four I's": idealized influence, inspirational motivation, intellectual stimulation, and individualized consideration.

14.6 Transformational leadership has a moderate positive relationship with job performance and a strong positive relationship with organizational commitment. It has stronger effects on these outcomes than other leadership behaviors.

14.7   Leaders can be trained to be effective. In fact, such training can be used to increase transformational leadership behaviors, despite the fact that charisma is somewhat dependent on personality and genetic factors.

KEY TERMS

DISCUSSION QUESTIONS

14.1   Before reading this chapter, which statement did you feel was more accurate: "Leaders are born" or "Leaders are made"? How do you feel now, and why do you feel that way?

14.2   The time-sensitive model of leadership argues that leaders aren't just concerned about the accuracy of their decisions when deciding among autocratic, consultative, facilitative, and delegative styles; they're also concerned about the efficient use of time. What other considerations could influence a leader's use of the four decision-making styles?

14.3   The time-sensitive and life cycle models of leadership both potentially suggest that leaders should use different styles and behaviors for different followers. Can you think of any negative consequences of that advice? How could those negative consequences be managed?

14.4   Consider the four dimensions of transformational leadership: idealized influence, inspirational motivation, intellectual stimulation, and individualized consideration. Which of those dimensions would you respond to most favorably? Why?

14.5   Can you think of any potential "dark sides" to transformational leadership? What would they be?

CASE: FORD

In 2009, Ford was the lone member of the Big 3 U.S. automakers not to take a handout from the U.S. government to sustain its operations during the financial crisis. There were a number of reasons for this choice, but one of the main ones was Alan Mulally's great desire to differentiate Ford from the other two big carmakers: General Motors and Chrysler. The strategy seems to be paying off, as consumers have shied away from purchasing cars from the two automakers that declared bankruptcy. It also has put Ford in a good position for the future. John Casesa, an automotive industry analyst, argues, "The speed with which Mulally has transformed Ford into a more nimble and healthy operation has been one of the more impressive jobs I've seen. It probably would have been game over for Ford already but for the changes he has brought."[152] When Mulally took over, Ford was a huge conglomeration of automobiles and designs. Mulally was adamant about getting rid of non-Ford brands and thus sold off Jaguar, Land Rover, and Aston Martin just at the right time, before the market collapsed. However, this decision was a particularly difficult one, because the culture at Ford previously had designated working on the "Ford" brand as a career killer. It was not where the best and brightest wanted to spend their time.[153]

Mulally's vision for the company has been to revitalize the Ford brand, because he believed brand loyalty could not be replaced. When he first arrived at Ford, he asked for a product lineup and was surprised to discover the Taurus line had been canceled and renamed the Five Hundred. Mulally responded, "Well, you've got until tomorrow to find a vehicle to put the Taurus name on because that's why I'm here. Then you have two years to make the coolest vehicle that you can possibly make."[154] He is betting the proverbial farm on the 2010 Taurus, and thus far, it has garnered extremely positive reviews, despite a price tag over $30,000. His push during the past three years—to build cars that will sell globally—represents a new method for Ford and goes completely against the grain of the company's previous market segmentation strategies. European-developed small cars, such as the Fiesta and the Focus, are on their way to the U.S. market, which Mulally believes is the future of the company. At 63 years of age, Mulally doesn't appear to be slowing down; more than ever, he seems excited about coming in to work every day.[155]

14.1   What do you think makes Alan Mulally an effective leader at this point in Ford's history?

14.2   Would you consider Mulally a transformational leader? Why or why not?

14.3   If Ford had been forced to take money from the federal government to sustain its operations, would your opinion of his leadership change?

EXERCISE: TAKE ME TO YOUR LEADER

The purpose of this exercise is to explore the commonalities in effective leadership across different types of leaders. This exercise uses groups, so your instructor will either assign you to a group or ask you to create your own group. The exercise has the following steps:

14.1   Imagine that a space alien descended down to Earth and actually uttered the famous line, "Take me to your leader!" Having read a bit about leadership, your group knows that leaders come in a number of shapes and sizes. Instead of showing the alien just one leader, your group decides it might be beneficial to show the alien a whole variety of leaders. Each member should choose one type of leader from the table to focus on (each member must choose a different type). Try to choose examples that are personally interesting but that also maximize the diversity within the group.

Orchestra Conductor	Fashion Designer	Drummer in Rock Band
Coach	Personal Tax Accountant	Point Guard in Basketball
Film Director	Night Club DJ	Bartender
College Professor	Fitness Trainer	Sheriff
Talk Show Host	Prison Guard	Millionaire Philanthropist
Stock Broker	Real Estate Broker	Agent
Psychotherapist	MBA Program Director	Auditor
Campaign Manager	Construction Project Supervisor	CEO
Diplomat	Sports Color Commentator	Vice President of Marketing

14.2   Individually, jot down some thoughts that highlight for the alien what is truly distinctive about "leadership" for this type of leader. For example, if you were showing the alien a coach, you might call attention to how coaches cannot control the game itself very much but instead must make their influence felt on the practice field by instilling skills while being anticipatory in their thinking. You might also call attention to how coaches need to be creative and adapt quickly during the game itself.

14.3   Share the thoughts you've jotted down in your groups, going from member to member, with each person describing what "leadership" means for the given types of leaders.

14.4   Once all these thoughts about the various types of leaders have been shared, think about whether there are certain traits, styles, or behaviors that are universal across all the types. For example, maybe all of the types have some kind of organizing quality to them (e.g., leaders need to be organized, leaders need to do things to help others be organized). Create a list of four "leadership universals."

14.5   Now consider the situational challenges faced by the types of leaders you discussed, including challenges rooted in the task, their followers, or the surrounding work context. For example, the fact that the coach has little direct impact on the game is a situational challenge. Do other leader types also grapple with lack of direct control? Create a list of four "situational challenges" faced by multiple types of leaders.

14.6   Elect a group member to write the group's four universals and four challenges on the board.

14.7   Class discussion (whether in groups or as a class) should center on whether the theories described in the chapter discuss some of the leadership universals identified by the groups. Are there theories that also include some of the situational challenges uncovered? Which leadership theory seems best equipped for explaining effective leadership across a wide variety of leader types?

Source: Adapted from D. Marcic, J. Seltzer, and P. Vail, *Organizational Behavior: Experiences and Cases.* (Cincinnati, OH: South-Western, 2001).

ENDNOTES

14.1   Kelly, K. M. "A Leader When Detroit Needs One." *Automotive Design & Production*, May 2009, p. 40; and Mecham, M., and A.L. Velocci Jr. "Find a Way." *Aviation Week & Space Technology*, January 1, 2007, p. 50.

14.2   Mecham and Velocci, "Find a Way."

14.3   Reed, J., and B. Simon. "The Drive to Transform." *Financial Times*, October 25, 2008, p. 9.

14.4   Mecham and Velocci, "Find a Way."

14.5   Kiley, D. "Ford's Saviour?" *BusinessWeek*, March 16, 2009, pp. 30–34.

14.6   Ibid.

14.7   Taylor, A., III. "Fixing up Ford." *Fortune*, May 25, 2009, pp. 44–51.

14.8   Kiley, "Ford's Saviour?"

14.9   Reed and Simon, "The Drive to Transform."

14.10 Simon, B., and A. Ward. "Ford Chiefs Take 30% Salary Cut This Year." *Financial Times*, February 25, 2009, p. 27.

14.11 Taylor, "Fixing up Ford."

14.12 Ibid.

14.13 Kiley, "Ford's Saviour?"

14.14 Taylor, "Fixing up Ford."

14.15 Yukl, G. *Leadership in Organizations,* 4th ed. Englewood Cliffs, NJ: Prentice-Hall, 1998.

14.16 Ibid.

14.17 Kiley, D. "Ford Heads Out on a Road of its Own" *BusinessWeek,* January 19, 2009, p. 47.

14.18 Freeland, C., and J. Reed. "View From the Top." *Financial Times*, January 16, 2009, p. 10.

14.19 Yukl, *Leadership in Organizations.*

14.20 Ibid.

14.21 Dansereau, F., Jr.; G. Graen; and W.J. Haga. "A Vertical Dyad Linkage Approach to Leadership Within Formal Organizations: A Longitudinal Investigation of the Role Making Process." *Organizational Behavior and Human Performance* 13 (1975), pp. 46–78; Graen, G.; M. Novak; and P. Sommerkamp. "The Effects of Leader-Member Exchange and Job Design on Productivity and Satisfaction: Testing a Dual Attachment Model." *Organizational Behavior and Human Performance* 30 (1982), pp. 109–31; Graen, G.B., and M. Uhl-Bien. "Relationship-Based Approach to Leadership: Development of Leader-Member Exchange (LMX) Theory of Leadership over 25 Years: Applying a Multi-Level Multi-Domain Perspective." *Leadership Quarterly* 6 (1995), pp. 219–47; and Liden, R.C.; R.T. Sparrowe; and S.J. Wayne. "Leader–Member Exchange Theory: The Past and Potential for the Future." In *Research in Personnel and Human Resources Management,* Vol. 15, ed. G.R. Ferris. Greenwich, CT: JAI Press, 1997, pp. 47–119.

14.22 Graen, G.B., and T. Scandura. "Toward a Psychology of Dyadic Organizing." In *Research in Organizational Behavior,* Vol. 9, eds. L.L. Cummings and B.M. Staw. Greenwich, CT: JAI Press, 1987, pp. 175–208.

14.23   Ibid.

14.24   Graen and Uhl-Bien, "Relationship-Based Approach to Leadership."

14.25   Ibid.

14.26   Bauer, T.N., and S.G. Green. "Development of Leader–Member Exchange: A Longitudinal Test." *Academy of Management Journal* 39 (1996), pp. 1538–67; Gerstner, C.R., and D.V. Day. "Meta-Analytic Review of Leader–Member Exchange Theory: Correlates and Construct Issues." *Journal of Applied Psychology* 82 (1997), pp. 827–44; and Liden, R.C.; S.J. Wayne; and D. Stillwell. "A Longitudinal Study on the Early Development of Leader–Member Exchanges." *Journal of Applied Psychology* 78 (1993), pp. 662–74.

14.27   Graen and Uhl-Bien, "Relationship-Based Approach to Leadership."

14.28   Ilies, R.; J.D. Nahrgang; and F.P. Morgeson. "Leader–Member Exchange and Citizenship Behaviors: A Meta-Analysis." *Journal of Applied Psychology* 92 (2007), pp. 269–77.

14.29   Stogdill, R.M. "Personal Factors Associated with Leadership: A Survey of the Literature." *Journal of Applied Psychology* 54 (1948), pp. 259–69.

14.30   Den Hartog, D.N., and P.L. Koopman. "Leadership in Organizations." In *Handbook of Industrial, Work, and Organizational Psychology,* Vol. 2, eds. N. Anderson, D.S. Ones, H.K. Sinangil, and C. Viswesvaran. Thousand Oaks, CA: Sage, 2002, pp. 166–87.

14.31   Yukl, *Leadership in Organizations;* and Zaccaro, S.J.

"Trait-Based Perspectives of Leadership." *American Psychologist* 62 (1998), pp. 6–16.

14.32   Vroom, V.H. "Leadership and the Decision-Making Process." *Organizational Dynamics* 28 (2000), pp. 82–94; and Yukl, *Leadership in Organizations.*

14.33   Zmuda, N., and E.B. York. "Marketing Meddling Sparks Brain Drain at Chaotic Pepsi." *Advertising Age*, August 10, 2009, pp. 1–2.

14.34   Helm, B. "Blowing Up Pepsi." *BusinessWeek*, April 27, 2009, pp. 32–36.

14.35   Zmuda and York, "Marketing Meddling."

14.36   Helm, "Blowing Up Pepsi."

14.37   Zmuda and York, "Marketing Meddling."

14.38   Vroom, "Leadership and the Decision-Making Process"; and Yukl, *Leadership in Organizations.*

14.39   Ibid.

14.40   Grover, R. "How Bob Iger Unchained Disney." *BusinessWeek,* February 5, 2007, pp. 74–79.

14.41   Ibid.

14.42   Siklos, R. "Bob Iger Rocks Disney." *Fortune*, January 19, 2009, pp. 80–86.

14.43   Vroom, "Leadership and the Decision-Making Process"; and Yukl, *Leadership in Organizations.*

14.44   Roth, D. "Can Nike Still Do It Without Phil Knight?" *Fortune,* April 4, 2005, pp. 59–68.

14.45   Ibid.

14.46   Holmes, S. "Inside the Coup at Nike." *BusinessWeek,* February 6, 2006, pp. 34–37.

14.47 Vroom, "Leadership and the Decision-Making Process."

14.48 Miller, K.I., and P.R. Monge. "Participation, Satisfaction, and Productivity: A Meta-Analytic Review." *Academy of Management Journal* 29 (1986), pp. 727–53; and Wagner, J.A., III. "Participation's Effects on Performance and Satisfaction: A Reconsideration of Research Evidence." *Academy of Management Review* 19 (1994), pp. 312–30.

14.49 Vroom, "Leadership and the Decision-Making Process."

14.50 Rogelberg, S.G.; D.J. Leach; P.B. Warr; and J.L. Burnfield. "'Not Another Meeting!' Are Meeting Time Demands Related to Employee Well-Being?" *Journal of Applied Psychology* 91 (2006), pp. 86–96.

14.51 Yang, J.L. "What's the Secret to Running Great Meetings?" *Fortune*, October 27, 2008, p. 26.

14.52 Kiley, "Ford's Saviour?"

14.53 Taylor, A., III. "It's Clutch Time for Fritz Henderson and GM." *Fortune*, October 12, 2009, p. 64.

14.54 Vroom, "Leadership and the Decision-Making Process"; Vroom, V.H., and A.G. Jago. *The New Leadership: Managing Participation in Organizations.* Englewood Cliffs, NJ: Prentice Hall, 1988; Vroom, V.H., and A.G. Jago. "Decision Making as a Social Process: Normative and Descriptive Models of Leader Behavior." *Decision Sciences* 5 (1974), pp. 743–69; and Vroom, V.H., and P.W. Yetton. *Leadership and Decision Making.* Pittsburgh, PA: University of Pittsburgh Press, 1973.

14.55 Taylor, "It's Clutch Time."

14.56 Ibid.

14.57 Aditya, R.N.; R.J. House; and S. Kerr. "Theory and Practice of Leadership: Into the New Millennium." In *Industrial and Organizational Psychology: Linking Theory with Practice,* eds. C.L. Cooper and E.A. Locke. Malden, MA: Blackwell, 2000, pp. 130–65; House, R.J., and R.N. Aditya. "The Social Scientific Study of Leadership: Quo Vadis?" *Journal of Management* 23 (1997), pp. 409–73; and Yukl, *Leadership in Organizations.*

14.58 Vroom, V.H., and A.G. Jago. "On the Validity of the Vroom-Yetton Model." *Journal of Applied Psychology* 63 (1978), pp. 151–62. See also Vroom and Yetton, *Leadership and Decision Making;* Vroom and Jago, *The New Leadership;* and Field, R.H.G. "A Test of the Vroom-Yetton Normative Model of Leadership." *Journal of Applied Psychology* 67 (1982), pp. 523–32.

14.59 Vroom and Yetton, *Leadership and Decision Making.*

14.60 Hemphill, J.K. *Leader Behavior Description.* Columbus, OH: Ohio State University, 1950. Cited in Fleishman, E.A.; E.F. Harris; and H.E. Burtt. *Leadership and Supervision in Industry: An Evaluation of a Supervisory Training Program.* Columbus, OH: Bureau of Educational Research, Ohio State University, 1955.

14.61 Hemphill, J.K., and A.E. Coons. "Development of the Leader Behavior Description Questionnaire." In *Leader Behavior: Its Description and Measurement,* eds. R.M. Stogdill and A.E. Coons. Columbus, OH: Bureau of Business Research, Ohio State University, 1957, pp. 6–38.

14.62 Fleishman, E.A. "The Description of Supervisory Behavior." *Journal of Applied Psychology* 37 (1953), pp. 1–6; Fleishman et al., *Leadership and Supervision in Industry;* Hemphill and Coons, "Development of the Leader Behavior Description Questionnaire"; Halpin, A.W., and B.J. Winer. *Studies in Aircrew Composition: The Leadership Behavior of the Airplane Commander* (Technical Report No. 3). Columbus, OH: Personnel Research Board, Ohio State University, 1952. Cited in Fleishman et al., *Leadership and Supervision in Industry.*

14.63 Fleishman, "The Description of Supervisory Behavior"; Fleishman et al., *Leadership and Supervision in Industry;* and Fleishman, E.A., and D.R. Peters. "Interpersonal Values, Leadership Attitudes, and Managerial 'Success.'" *Personnel Psychology* 15 (1962), pp. 127–43.

14.64 Yukl, *Leadership in Organizations.*

14.65 Fleishman, "The Description of Supervisory Behavior"; Fleishman et al., *Leadership and Supervision in Industry;* and Fleishman and Peters, "Interpersonal Values."

14.66 Yukl, *Leadership in Organizations.*

14.67 Katz, D.; N. Maccoby; and N. Morse. *Productivity, Supervision, and Morale in an Office Situation.* Ann Arbor, MI: Institute for Social Research, University of Michigan, 1950; Katz, D.; N. Maccoby; G. Gurin; and L. Floor. *Productivity, Supervision, and Morale among Railroad Workers.* Ann Arbor, MI: Survey Research Center, University of Michigan, 1951; Katz, D.; and R.L. Kahn. "Some Recent Findings in Human-Relations Research in Industry." In *Readings in Social Psychology,* eds. E. Swanson, T. Newcomb, and E. Hartley. New York: Holt, pp. 650–65; Likert, R. *New Patterns of Management.* New York: McGraw-Hill, 1961; and Likert, R. *The Human Organization.* New York: McGraw-Hill, 1967.

14.68 Fleishman, E.A. "Twenty Years of Consideration and Structure." In *Current Developments in the Study of Leadership,* eds. E.A. Fleishman and J.G. Hunt. Carbondale, IL: Southern Illinois Press, 1973, pp. 1–37.

14.69 Judge, T.A.; R.F. Piccolo; and R. Ilies. "The Forgotten Ones? The Validity of Consideration and Initiating Structure in Leadership Research." *Journal of Applied Psychology* 89 (2004), pp. 36–51.

14.70 Aditya et al., "Theory and Practice of Leadership"; Den Hartog and Koopman, "Leadership in Organizations"; House and Aditya, "The Social Scientific Study of Leadership"; Korman, A.K. " 'Consideration,' 'Initiating Structure,' and Organizational Criteria—A Review." *Personnel Psychology* 19 (1966), pp. 349–61; Yukl, *Leadership in Organizations;* and Yukl, G., and D.D. Van Fleet. "Theory and Research on Leadership in Organizations." In *Handbook of Industrial and Organizational Psychology,* Vol. 3, eds. M.D. Dunnette and L.M. Hough. Palo Alto, CA: Consulting Psychologists Press, 1992, pp. 147–97.

14.71 Judge et al., "The Forgotten Ones?"

14.72 Hersey, P., and K.H. Blanchard. "Life Cycle Theory of Leadership." *Training and Development Journal,*

May 1969, pp. 26–34; Hersey, P., and K.H. Blanchard. "So You Want to Know Your Leadership Style?" *Training and Development Journal,* February 1974, pp. 22–37; Hersey, P., and K.H. Blanchard. "Revisiting the Life-Cycle Theory of Leadership." *Training and Development,* January 1996, pp. 42–47. and Hersey, P., and K.H. Blanchard. *Management of Organizational Behavior: Leading Human Resources.* 9th ed. Upper Saddle River, NJ: Pearson, 2008.

14.73   Hersey and Blanchard, *Management of Organizational Behavior.*

14.74   Hersey and Blanchard, "Revisiting the Life-Cycle Theory of Leadership."

14.75   Fernandez, C.F., and R.P. Vecchio. "Situational Leadership Revisited: A Test of an Across-Jobs Perspective." *Leadership Quarterly* 8 (1997), pp. 67–84.

14.76   Graeff, C.L. "Evolution of Situational Leadership Theory: A Critical Review." *Leadership Quarterly* 8 (1997), pp. 153–70.

14.77   Vecchio, R.P. "Situational Leadership Theory: An Examination of a Prescriptive Theory." *Journal of Applied Psychology* 72 (1987), pp. 444–51; and Norris, W.R., and R.P. Vecchio. "Situational Leadership Theory: A Replication." *Group and Organization Management* 17 (1992), pp. 331–42.

14.78   Vecchio, "Situational Leadership Theory"; Norris and Vecchio, "Situational Leadership Theory: A Replication"; and Blank, W.; J.R. Weitzel; and S.G. Green. "A Test of Situational Leadership Theory." *Personnel Psychology* 43 (1990), pp. 579–97.

14.79   Fernandez and Vecchio, "Situational Leadership Theory Revisited."

14.80   Grow, B. "Out at Home Depot." *BusinessWeek,* January 15, 2007, pp. 56–62.

14.81   McGregor, J. "Putting Home Depot's House in Order." *BusinessWeek*, May 18, 2009.

14.82   Grow, B. "Renovating Home Depot." *BusinessWeek,* March 6, 2006, pp. 50–58.

14.83   Ibid.; and Grow, "Out at Home Depot."

14.84   Sellers, P. "Six Sigma Man: Another GE Vet Atop Home Depot." *Fortune,* January 22, 2007, p. 30; and Grow, "Renovating Home Depot."

14.85   Bass, B.M., and R.E. Riggio. *Transformational Leadership,* 2nd ed. Mahwah, NJ: Lawrence Erlbaum Associates, 2006; Bass, B.M. *Leadership and Performance Beyond Expectations.* New York: The Free Press, 1985; and Burns, L.M. *Leadership.* New York: Harper & Row, 1978.

14.86   Bass, *Leadership and Performance Beyond Expectations.*

14.87   Ibid.

14.88   Larson, A. *The President Nobody Knew.* New York: Popular Library, 1968, p. 68. Cited in Ibid.

14.89   Truman, H.S. *Memoirs.* New York: Doubleday, 1958. Cited in Bass, *Leadership and Performance Beyond Expectations.*

14.90   Bass and Riggio, *Transformational Leadership.*

14.91   Ibid.; and Bass, B.M., and B.J. Avolio. *MLQ: Multifactor Leadership Questionnaire.* Redwood City, CA: Mind Garden, 2000.

14.92   Bass and Riggio, *Transformational Leadership;* Bass, *Leadership and Performance Beyond Expectations;* Burns, *Leadership.*

14.93 Bass and Riggio, *Transformational Leadership.*

14.94 Bass, *Leadership and Performance Beyond Expectations.*

14.95 Bass and Riggio, *Transformational Leadership;* and Bass and Avolio, *MLQ.*

14.96 Bass and Riggio, *Transformational Leadership.*

14.97 Ibid.; and Bass and Avolio, *MLQ.*

14.98 Bass and Riggio, *Transformational Leadership.*

14.99 Ibid.; and Bass and Avolio, *MLQ.*

14.100 Judge, T.A., and R.F. Piccolo. "Transformational and Transactional Leadership: A Meta-Analytic Test of their Relative Validity." *Journal of Applied Psychology* 89 (2004), pp. 755–68.

14.101 Ibid.

14.102 Bass and Riggio, *Transformational Leadership.*

14.103 Collingwood, H. "Do CEO's Matter?" *The Atlantic*, June 2009, pp. 54–60.

14.104 Bass and Riggio, *Transformational Leadership.*

14.105 Ibid.; and Bass and Avolio, *MLQ.*

14.106 Conger, J.A. "Charismatic and Transformational Leadership in Organizations: An Insider's Perspective on these Developing Research Streams." *Leadership Quarterly* 10 (1999), pp. 145–79.

14.107 Young, J.S., and W.L. Simon. *iCon: Steve Jobs—The Greatest Second Act in the History of Business.* Hoboken, NJ: Wiley, 2005.

14.108 House, R.J.; P.J. Hanges; M. Javidan; P.W. Dorfman; and V. Gupta. *Culture, Leadership, and Organizations.* Thousand Oaks, CA: Sage, 2004. and Dorfman,

P.W.; P.J. Hanges; and F.C. Brodbeck. "Leadership and Cultural Variation: The Identification of Culturally Endorsed Leadership Profiles." In *Culture, Leadership, and Organizations,* eds. R.J. House, P.J. Hanges, M. Javidan, P.W. Dorfman, and V. Gupta. Thousand Oaks, CA: Sage, 2004, pp. 669–720.

14.109 Javidan, M.; R.J. House; and P.W. Dorfman. "A Nontechnical Summary of GLOBE Findings." In *Culture, Leadership, and Organizations,* eds. R.J. House, P.J. Hanges, M. Javidan, P.W. Dorfman, and V. Gupta. Thousand Oaks, CA: Sage, 2004, pp. 29–48.

14.110 Dorfman et al., "Leadership and Cultural Variation."

14.111 Johnson, A.M.; P.A. Vernon; J.M. McCarthy; M. Molso; J.A. Harris; and K.J. Jang. "Nature vs. Nurture: Are Leaders Born or Made? A Behavior Genetic Investigation of Leadership Style." *Twin Research* 1 (1998), pp. 216–23.

14.112 Judge, T.A., and J.E. Bono. "Five-Factor Model of Personality and Transformational Leadership." *Journal of Applied Psychology* 85 (2000), pp. 751–65.

14.113 Bass and Riggio, *Transformational Leadership.*

14.114 Conger, "Charismatic and Transformational Leadership in Organizations."

14.115 Bass and Riggio, *Transformational Leadership;* and Bass and Avolio, *MLQ.*

14.116 Young and Simon, *iCon.*

14.117 Ibid.

14.118 Bass and Riggio, *Transformational Leadership.*

14.119 Ibid.; and Bass and Avolio, *MLQ.*

14.120 Bass and Riggio, *Transformational Leadership.*

14.121 Ibid.; and Bass and Avolio, *MLQ.*

14.122 Young and Simon, *iCon.*

14.123 Mio, J.S.; R.E. Riggio; S. Levin; and R. Reese. "Presidential Leadership and Charisma: The Effects of Metaphor." *Leadership Quarterly* 16 (2005), pp. 287–94.

14.124 Conger, "Charismatic and Transformational Leadership in Organizations."

14.125 Bligh, M.C.; J.C. Kohles; and J.R. Meindl. "Charisma under Crisis: Presidential Leadership, Rhetoric, and Media Responses before and after the September 11th Terrorist Attacks." *Leadership Quarterly* 15 (2004), pp. 211–39.

14.126 Bligh, M.C., and J.C. Kohles. "The Enduring Allure of Charisma: How Barack Obama Won the Historic 2008 Presidential Election." *Leadership Quarterly* 20 (2009), pp. 483–92.

14.127 Ibid.

14.128 Lowe, K.B.; K.G. Kroeck; and N. Sivasubramaniam. "Effectiveness Correlates of Transformational and Transactional Leadership: A Meta-Analytic Review of the MLQ Literature." *Leadership Quarterly* 7 (1996), pp. 385–425.

14.129 Howell, J.M., and B.J. Avolio. "Transformational Leadership, Transactional Leadership, Locus of Control, and Support for Innovation: Key Predictors of Consolidated-Business-Unit Performance." *Journal of Applied Psychology* 78 (1993), pp. 891–902; Howell, J.M.; D.J. Neufeld; and B.J. Avolio. "Examining the Relationship of Leadership and Physical Distance with Business Unit Performance." *Leadership*

Quarterly 16 (2005), pp. 273–85; Keller, R.T. "Transformational Leadership, Initiating Structure, and Substitutes for Leadership: A Longitudinal Study of Research and Development Project Team Performance." *Journal of Applied Psychology* 91 (2006), pp. 202–10; and Waldman, D.A.; G.G. Ramirez; R.J. House; and P. Puranam. "Does Leadership Matter? CEO Leadership Attributes and Profitability under Conditions of Perceived Environmental Uncertainty." *Academy of Management Journal* 44 (2001), pp. 134–43.

14.130 Howell, J.M., and K.E. Hall-Merenda. "The Ties That Bind: The Impact of Leader–Member Exchange, Transformational and Transactional Leadership, and Distance on Predicting Follower Performance." *Journal of Applied Psychology* 84 (1999), pp. 680–94; Piccolo, R.F., and J.A. Colquitt. "Transformational Leadership and Job Behaviors: The Mediating Role of Core Job Characteristics." *Academy of Management Journal* 49 (2006), pp. 327–40; and Wang, H.; K.S. Law; R.D. Hackett; D. Wang; and Z.X. Chen. "Leader–Member Exchange as a Mediator of the Relationship Between Transformational Leadership and Followers' Performance and Organizational Citizenship Behavior." *Academy of Management Journal* 48 (2005), pp. 420–32.

14.131 Judge and Piccolo, "Transformational and Transactional Leadership"; Podsakoff, P.M.; S.B. MacKenzie; J.B. Paine; and D.G. Bachrach. "Organizational Citizenship Behaviors: A Critical Review of the Theoretical and Empirical Literature and Suggestions for Future Research."

Journal of Management 26 (2000), pp. 513–63.

14.132 Judge and Piccolo, "Transformational and Transactional Leadership."

14.133 Avolio, B.J.; W. Zhu; W. Koh; and P. Bhatia. "Transformational Leadership and Organizational Commitment: Mediating Role of Psychological Empowerment and Moderating Role of Structural Distance." *Journal of Organizational Behavior* 25 (2004), pp. 951–68; Kirkpatrick, S.A., and E.A. Locke. "Direct and Indirect Effects of Three Core Charismatic Leadership Components on Performance and Attitudes." *Journal of Applied Psychology* 81 (1996), pp. 36–51; and Shamir, B.; E. Zakay; E. Breinin; and M. Popper. "Correlates of Charismatic Leader Behaviors in Military Units: Subordinates' Attitudes, Unit Characteristics, and Superiors' Appraisals of Leader Performance." *Academy of Management Journal* 41 (1998), pp. 387–409.

14.134 Podsakoff, P.M.; S.B. MacKenzie; and W.H. Bommer. "Transformational Leader Behaviors and Substitutes for Leadership as Determinants of Employee Satisfaction, Commitment, Trust, and Organizational Citizenship Behaviors." *Journal of Management* 22 (1996), pp. 259–98; Podsakoff, P.M.; S.B. MacKenzie; R.H. Moorman; and R. Fetter. "Transformational Leader Behaviors and their Effects on Followers' Trust in Leader, Satisfaction, and Organizational Citizenship Behaviors." *Leadership Quarterly* 1 (1990), pp. 107–42; and Shamir et al., "Correlates of Charismatic Leader Behaviors."

14.135 Meyer, J.P.; D.J. Stanley; L. Herscovitch; and L. Topolnytsky.

"Affective, Continuance, and Normative Commitment to the Organization: A Meta-Analysis of Antecedents, Correlates, and Consequences." *Journal of Vocational Behavior* 61 (2002), pp. 20–52.

14.136 Walumbwa, F.O.; B.J. Avolio; and W. Zhu. "How Transformational Leadership Weaves Its Influence on Individual Job Performance: The Role of Identification and Efficacy Beliefs." *Personnel Psychology* 61 (2008), pp. 793–825.

14.137 Judge and Piccolo, "Transformational and Transactional Leadership."

14.138 Piccolo and Colquitt, "Transformational Leadership and Job Behaviors." See also Bono, J.E., and T.A. Judge. "Self-Concordance at Work: Toward Understanding the Motivational Effects of Transformational Leaders." *Academy of Management Journal* 46 (2003), pp. 554–71; and Shin, S.J., and J. Zhou. "Transformational Leadership, Conservation, and Creativity: Evidence from Korea." *Academy of Management Journal* 46 (2003), pp. 703–14.

14.139 Bono, J.E., and R. Ilies. "Charisma, Positive Emotions, and Mood Contagion." *Leadership Quarterly* 17 (2006), pp. 317–34; and McColl-Kennedy, J.R., and R.D. Anderson. "Impact of Leadership Style and Emotions on Subordinate Performance." *Leadership Quarterly* 13 (2002), pp. 545–59.

14.140 Bono, J; H.J. Foldes; G. Vinson; and J.P. Muros. "Workplace Emotions: The Role of Supervision and Leadership." *Journal of Applied Psychology* 92 (2007), pp. 1357–67.

14.141 Kerr, S., and J.M. Jermier. "Substitutes for Leadership: Their

Meaning and Measurement." *Organizational Behavior and Human Performance* 22 (1978), pp. 375–403.

14.142 Howell, J.P.; P.W. Dorfman; and S. Kerr. "Moderator Variables in Leadership Research." *Academy of Management Review* 11 (1986), pp. 88–102.

14.143 Kerr and Jermier, "Substitutes for Leadership"; and Jermier, J.M., and S. Kerr. "'Substitutes for Leadership: Their Meaning and Measurement': Contextual Recollections and Current Observations." *Leadership Quarterly* 8 (1997), pp. 95–101.

14.144 Howell, J.P.; D.E. Bowen; P.W. Dorfman; S. Kerr; and P.M. Podsakoff. "Substitutes for Leadership: Effective Alternatives to Ineffective Leadership." *Organizational Dynamics* Summer 1990, pp. 21–38.

14.145 Podsakoff, P.M., and S.B. MacKenzie. "Kerr and Jermier's Substitutes for Leadership Model: Background, Empirical Assessment, and Suggestions for Future Research." *Leadership Quarterly* 8 (1997), pp. 117–25; Podsakoff, P.M.; B.P. Niehoff; S.B. MacKenzie; and M.L. Williams. "Do Substitutes for Leadership Really Substitute for Leadership? An Empirical Examination of Kerr and Jermier's Situational Leadership Model." *Organizational Behavior and Human Decision Processes* 54 (1993), pp. 1–44; Podsakoff et al., "Transformational Leadership Behaviors and Substitutes for Leadership"; and Podsakoff, P.M.; S.B. MacKenzie; M. Ahearne; and W.H. Bommer.

"Searching for a Needle in a Haystack: Trying to Identify the Illusive Moderators of Leadership Behavior." *Journal of Management* 21 (1995), pp. 422–70.

14.146 Howell et al., "Substitutes for Leadership: Effective Alternatives."

14.147 Paradise, A. "Investment in Learning Remains Strong." *T + D* 62 (November 2008), pp. 44–51.

14.148 Kranz, G. "A Higher Standard for Managers." *Workforce,* June 11, 2007, pp. 21–26.

14.149 Gist, M.E., and D. McDonald-Mann. "Advances in Leadership Training and Development." In *Industrial and Organizational Psychology: Linking Theory with Practice,* ed. C.L. Cooper and E.A. Locke. Malden, MA: Blackwell, 2000, pp. 52–71.

14.150 Ibid.; Dvir, T.; D. Eden; B.J. Avolio; and B. Shamir. "Impact of Transformational Leadership on Follower Development and Performance: A Field Experiment." *Academy of Management Journal* 45 (2000), pp. 735–44; and Barling, J.; T. Weber; and E.K. Kelloway. "Effects of Transformational Leadership Training on Attitudinal and Financial Outcomes: A Field Experiment." *Journal of Applied Psychology* 81 (1996), pp. 827–32.

14.151 Barling et al., "Effects of Transformational Leadership Training."

14.152 Kiley, "Ford's Savior?"

14.153 Ibid.

14.154 Taylor, "Fixing Up Ford."

14.155 Ibid.

chapter 15

Organizational Structure

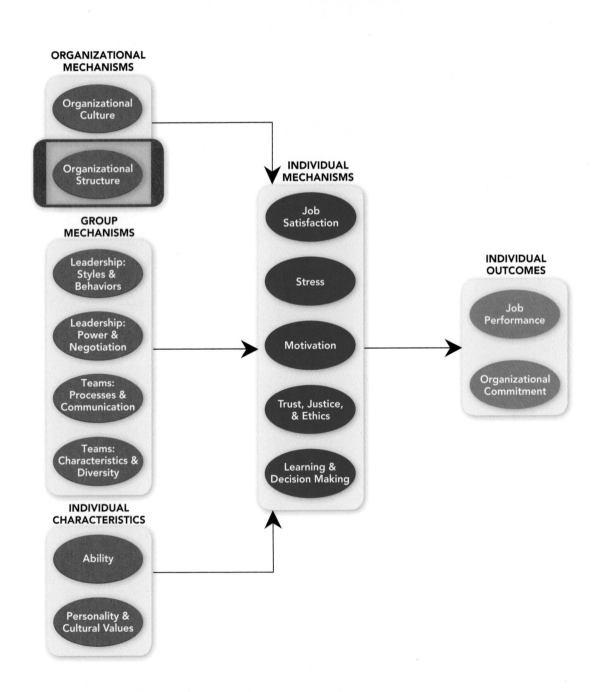

ORGANIZATIONAL MECHANISMS

Organizational Culture

Organizational Structure

GROUP MECHANISMS

Leadership: Styles & Behaviors

Leadership: Power & Negotiation

Teams: Processes & Communication

Teams: Characteristics & Diversity

INDIVIDUAL CHARACTERISTICS

Ability

Personality & Cultural Values

INDIVIDUAL MECHANISMS

Job Satisfaction

Stress

Motivation

Trust, Justice, & Ethics

Learning & Decision Making

INDIVIDUAL OUTCOMES

Job Performance

Organizational Commitment

✓ LEARNING GOALS

After reading this chapter, you should be able to answer the following questions:

15.1 What is an organization's structure, and what does it consist of?

15.2 What are the major elements of an organizational structure?

15.3 What is organizational design, and what factors does the organizational design process depend on?

15.4 What are some of the more common organizational forms that an organization might adopt for its structure?

15.5 When an organization makes changes to its structure, how does that restructuring affect job performance and organizational commitment?

15.6 What steps can organizations take to reduce the negative effects of restructuring efforts?

CISCO SYSTEMS

Cisco Systems, based in San Jose, California, is the world's largest provider of Internet networking and communications equipment and also an employer of more than 65,000 persons. The company plays the role of the "plumber of the technology world,"[1] because three-quarters of its business comes from routers, switches, and other networking products, all designed to keep information flowing around the globe. John Chambers, the CEO of Cisco Systems, states, "From a business-model and leadership perspective, we're seeing a massive shift from management by command and control to management by collaboration and teamwork. You could almost say this shift is as revolutionary as the assembly line. Business processes are being turned upside down to better compete in a global environment."[2] So how has Cisco met this challenge head on? By making changes to its organizational structure that allow its employees and executives to gain "speed, skill, and flexibility."[3]

These organizational changes are many, from adopting matrix structures in which employees report to more than one boss to instituting highly developed and formalized cross-functional teams at multiple levels within the organization. The transition hasn't been easy. The restructuring required immense collaboration between employees and executives, who were used to a more traditional, hierarchical structure. The new system receives support from the compensation system, which rewards collaborative abilities instead of individual performance.[4] Approximately 20 percent of Cisco's top managers were not cut out for the change—according to Chambers, "It's not that they weren't successful working on their own or that that they weren't good people; they just couldn't collaborate effectively."[5] The goal for the reorganization has been to spread leadership and decision making throughout the company, to such a wide level that people and teams feel as if they have the authority to move ahead with important initiatives.[6] For example, Cisco's three-year-old Emerging Technologies Group already has generated eight products, each expected to earn around $1 billion in revenue.[7] And, says Chambers, "We now have a whole pool of talent who can lead these working groups, like mini CEOs and COOs."[8]

Although some parts of this reorganization have been informal, many of the structural changes represent formal initiatives. Major priorities are no longer managed at the top but rather through "councils" and "boards" that consist of multiple executives and managers.[9] For example, Cisco's engineering organization (one-third of its employee base) reports to a "Development Council," which comprises nine senior vice presidents. The combination of multiple managers from various disciplines across the organization attempts to reduce the silo mentality that keeps people from developing a broad picture, allowing them to make better and faster decisions. Cisco says that this team structure enabled it to make a decision about a major acquisition in a mere eight days—something that would have been impossible under the old structure.[10] Despite the constant state of flux, Cisco maintains at least 10 boards and more than 30 councils (the councils target $10 billion plus market opportunities).[11] In this sense, Cisco's ability to adjust to an ever-changing technology market appears better than ever.

ORGANIZATIONAL STRUCTURE

As the preceding example illustrates, an organization's structure can have a significant impact on its financial performance and ability to manage its employees. The decisions that John Chambers has made regarding Cisco's organizational structure will have an impact on how employees communicate and cooperate with one another, how power is distributed, and how individuals view their work environment. In fact, an organization's structure dictates more than you might think. We've spent a great deal of time in this book talking about how employee attitudes and behaviors are shaped by individual characteristics, such as personality and ability, and group mechanisms, such as teams and leaders. In this and the following chapter, we discuss how the organization as a whole affects employee attitudes and behavior.

"No, now all of our pillaging is done electronically from a centralized office."

Source: Copyright © The New Yorker Collection 2003 Christopher Weyant from cartoonbank.com. All rights reserved.

Think about some of the jobs you've held in the past (or perhaps the job you hope to have after graduation). What types of employees did you interact with on a daily basis? Were they employees who performed the same tasks that you performed? Or maybe they didn't do exactly what you did, but did they serve the same customer? How many employees did your manager supervise? Was every decision you made scrutinized by your supervisor, or were you given a "long leash"? The answers to all of these questions are influenced by organizational structure. An **organizational structure** formally dictates how jobs and tasks are divided and coordinated between individuals and groups within the company. Organizational structures can be relatively simple when a company only has 5–20 employees but grow incredibly complex in the case of Cisco's 65,000 employees who produce thousands of different kinds of products.

 15.1

What is an organization's structure, and what does it consist of?

WHY DO SOME ORGANIZATIONS HAVE DIFFERENT STRUCTURES THAN OTHERS?

One way of getting a feel for an organization's structure is by looking at an organizational chart. An **organizational chart** is a drawing that represents every job in the organization and the formal reporting relationships between those jobs. It helps organizational members and outsiders understand and comprehend how work is structured within the company.

FIGURE 15-1   Two Sample Organizational Structures

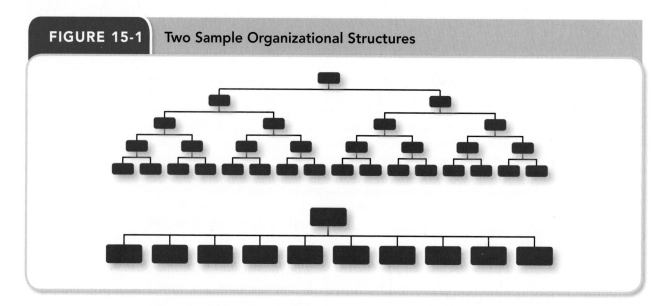

Figure 15-1 illustrates two sample organizational charts. In a real chart, the boxes would be filled with actual names and job titles. As you can imagine, as companies grow larger, their organizational charts get more complex. Can you imagine drawing an organizational chart that included every one of Cisco's 65,000 employees? Not only would that require a lot of boxes and a lot of paper, it would probably take a couple of years to put together (plus, as soon as someone left the organization, it would be time to update the chart!).

ELEMENTS OF ORGANIZATIONAL STRUCTURE

The organizational charts described in this chapter are relatively simple and designed to illustrate specific points (if you want to see how complex some of these charts can get, do a search on the Internet for "organizational chart," and you'll begin to see how varied organizations can be in the way they design their company). Specifically, charts like those in Figure 15-1 can illustrate the five key elements of an organization's structure. Those five key elements, summarized in Table 15-1, describe how work tasks, authority relationships,

TABLE 15-1   Elements of Organizational Structure

ORGANIZATIONAL STRUCTURE DIMENSION	DEFINITION
Work Specialization	The degree to which tasks in an organization are divided into separate jobs.
Chain of Command	Answers the question of "who reports to whom?" and signifies formal authority relationships.
Span of Control	Represents how many employees each manager in the organization has responsibility for.
Centralization	Refers to where decisions are formally made in organizations.
Formalization	The degree to which rules and procedures are used to standardize behaviors and decisions in an organization.

and decision-making responsibilities are organized within the company. These elements will be discussed in the next several sections.

WORK SPECIALIZATION. **Work specialization** is the way in which tasks in an organization are divided into separate jobs. In some organizations, this categorization is referred to as a company's division of labor. How many tasks does any one employee perform? To some degree, work specialization is a never-ending trade-off among productivity, flexibility, and worker motivation. Take an assembly line worker at Ford as an example. Henry Ford was perhaps the earliest (and clearly most well-known) believer in high degrees of work specialization. He divided tasks among his manufacturing employees to such a degree that each employee might only perform one single task, over and over again, all day long. Having only one task to perform allowed those employees to be extremely productive at doing that one thing. It also meant that training new workers was much easier when replacements were needed.

However, there are trade-offs when organizations make jobs highly specialized. Highly specialized jobs can cause organizations to lose the ability associated with employees who can be flexible in what they do. By spending all their time performing specialized tasks well, employees fail to update or practice other skills. Accounting majors, for example, might specialize in taxes or auditing. Some larger companies might hire these graduates for their ability to do either auditing or tax—but not both. Other companies might be looking for an accountant who can perform either aspect well, depending on how they divide up accounting duties within their organization. Still other companies might want to hire "general managers" who understand accounting, finance, management, marketing, and operations as a part of their job. Thus, high levels of specialization may be acceptable in larger firms with more employees but can be problematic in smaller firms in which employees must be more flexible in their job duties. Aetna, the Hartford, Connecticut–based health insurer, publishes more than 1,300 different job titles, each of which has its own list of the competencies that employees in those jobs must perform.[12]

Organizations may also struggle with employee job satisfaction when they make jobs highly specialized. If you recall from Chapter 4 on Job Satisfaction, we discussed five core characteristics of jobs that significantly affect satisfaction. One of those characteristics was variety, or the degree to which the job requires a number of different activities involving a number of different skills and talents.[13] Employees tend to be more satisfied with jobs that require them to perform a number of different kinds of activities. Even though you might be

Charlie Chaplin in *Modern Times* (1932) has a job with an extremely high degree of work specialization.

very efficient and productive performing a job with only one task, how happy would you be to perform that job on a daily basis? One of the most famous films in early motion picture history was *Modern Times,* a film in which Charlie Chaplin was relegated to performing the same task over and over, very quickly. The movie ridiculed work specialization and the trend of treating employees as machines.

CHAIN OF COMMAND. The **chain of command** within an organization essentially answers the question "Who reports to whom?" Every employee in a traditional

15.2

What are the major elements of an organizational structure?

organizational structure has one person to whom they report. That person then reports to someone else, and on and on, until the buck stops with the CEO (though in a public company, even the CEO is responsible to the Board of Directors). The chain of command can be seen as the specific flow of authority down through the levels of an organization's structure. Organizations depend on this flow of authority to attain order, control, and predictable performance.[14] Some newer organizational structures make this chain of command a bit more complex. It has become common to have positions that report to two or more different managers. For example, Intel placed two people apiece in charge of the two largest divisions of their organization. Questions have arisen as to how their duties will be split up and whether employees will know who it is they report to.[15] For an interesting chain of command restructuring, see this chapter's **OB on Screen** feature.

SPAN OF CONTROL. A manager's **span of control** represents how many employees he or she is responsible for in the organization. The organizational charts in Figure 15-1 provide an illustration of the differences in span of control. In the top chart, each manager is responsible for leading two subordinates. In most instances, this level would be considered a narrow span of control. In the bottom chart, the manager is responsible for 10 employees. Typically, this number would be considered a wide span of control. Of course, the key question in many organizations is how many employees one manager can supervise effectively. Answering that question requires a better understanding of the benefits of narrow and wide spans of control.

Narrow spans of control allow managers to be much more hands-on with employees, giving them the opportunity to use directive leadership styles while developing close mentoring relationships with employees. A narrow span of control is especially important if the manager has substantially more skill or expertise than the subordinates. Early writings on management assumed that the narrower the span of control, the more productive employees would become.[16] However, a narrow span of control requires organizations to hire many managers, which can significantly increase labor costs. Moreover, if the span of control becomes too narrow, employees can become resentful of their close supervision and long for more latitude in their day-to-day decision making. In fact, current research suggests that a moderate span of control is best for an organization's productivity.[17] This relationship is illustrated in Figure 15-2. Note that organizational performance increases as span of control increases, but only up to the point that managers no longer have the ability to coordinate and supervise the large numbers of employees underneath them. Most organizations work hard to try to find the right balance, and this balance differs for every organization, depending on its unique circumstances. However, there is no question that spans of control in organizations have increased significantly in recent years.[18] Organizations such as Coca-Cola have vice presidents with up to 90 employees reporting to them![19]

An organization's span of control affects how "tall" or "flat" its organizational chart becomes. For example, the top panel of Figure 15-1 depicts a tall structure with many hierarchical levels and a narrow span of control, whereas the bottom panel depicts a flat organization with few levels and a wide span of control. Think about what happens when an organization becomes "taller." First, more layers of management means having to pay more management salaries. Second, communication in the organization becomes more complex as each new layer becomes one more point through which information must pass when traveling upward or downward. Third, the organization's ability to make decisions becomes slower, because approval for decisions has to be authorized at every step of the hierarchy.

Throughout the 1990s and into the 2000s, organizations worked to become flatter to reduce the costs associated with multiple layers of management and increase their ability to adapt to their environment. Intel, for example, recently announced a reduction

OB ON SCREEN

THE DEPARTED

Queenan's compartmentalizing everything in SIU, which is the right thing to do. Personally I don't trust half the troopers out there anymore. Bottom line, we think we might have a problem. We think Costello's got a rat in the state police.

With those words, Colin Sullivan (Matt Damon) informs his newly created subunit of officers about the organizational structure within the Massachusetts State Police's Special Investigation Unit (SIU) in *The Departed* (Dir.: Martin Scorsese, Warner Bros., 2006). The twist is that Sullivan, who has been put in charge of finding the leak within the department, is actually the rat (don't worry if you haven't seen the movie, we aren't giving anything away here). Recruited at a young age by mob boss Frank Costello (Jack Nicholson) to infiltrate the police, Sullivan provides information to Costello about police operations to help him avoid getting arrested. Sullivan would love to have access to all the information that Police Captain Queenan (Martin Sheen) controls, because the state police have an officer by the name of Billy Costigan (Leonardo DiCaprio) who has infiltrated Costello's organization to provide information that they hope will bring Costello to justice. If that wasn't confusing enough, Costello knows he has a cop informant working in his crew, and the police know that Costello has a rat inside the police department!

Captain Queenan and his trusted aide Sergeant Dignam (Mark Wahlberg) are the only two people on the police force who know that Billy is actually a police officer. To hide Costigan's identity, they constitute a special unit within the SIU that controls its own actions and information and only shares what it thinks is necessary with the rest of SIU. To find the rat, SIU gives Sullivan his own subunit, with its own reporting structure, that only answers to Captain Ellerby (Alec Baldwin), as well as wide latitude to get things done. Most organizations constantly try to break down the communication barriers that an organizational structure and reporting relationships erect; the SIU is using organizational structure to create communication barriers that will keep information from being spread to those who shouldn't have it.

| FIGURE 15-2 | Span of Control and Organizational Performance |

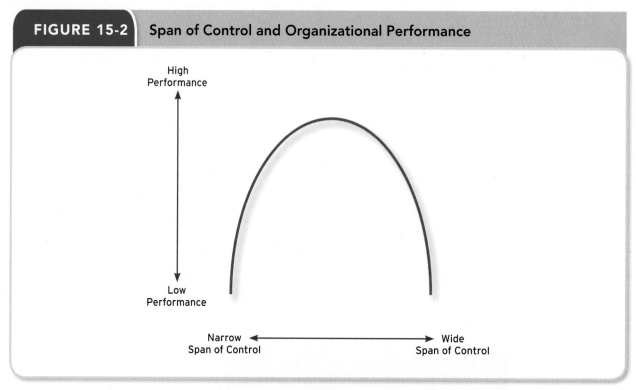

Source: Adapted from N.A. Theobald and S. Nicholson-Crotty, "The Many Faces of Span of Control: Organizational Structure Across Multiple Goals," *Administration and Society* 36 (2005), pp. 648–60.

in its managerial ranks of 1,000 positions (or 1 percent of its 100,000 employees). A spokesperson from Intel announced that "This [layoff] is designed to improve costs and improve decision making and communications across the company."[20] Putnam Investment Company also went through a flattening of its organization recently, reducing the workforce by 11 percent—including 25 of its 50 highest-paid executives. Putnam CEO Ed Haldeman noted, "To attract and retain the best people, it's necessary to provide them with the autonomy and independence to make decisions."[21]

CENTRALIZATION. **Centralization** reflects where decisions are formally made in organizations. If only the top managers within a company have the authority to make final decisions, we would say that the organization has a highly "centralized" structure. In contrast, if decision-making authority is pushed down to lower-level employees and these employees feel empowered to make decisions on their own, an organization has a "decentralized" structure. Decentralization becomes necessary as a company grows larger. Sooner or later, the top management of an organization will not be able to make every single decision within the company. Centralized organizational structures tend to concentrate power and authority within a relatively tight group of individuals in the firm, because they are the ones who have formal authority over important decisions.

Many organizations are moving toward a more decentralized structure. A manager can't have 20 employees reporting to him or her if those employees aren't allowed to make some decisions on their own. Cisco Systems, in the opening vignette, is a perfect example, as is Yahoo. When Yahoo undertook its recent decentralization restructuring, CEO Carol Bartz was moved to observe, "Organizations can get in the way of innovation, because if people are all bound up, and if they don't know if they get to make the decision or somebody else, and if they do, what happens to them, and so on and so forth. There's a freeing when you organize around the fact that you're clearly in charge and go for it. It's really a fantastic group of people, and just cleaner lines and cleaner responsibility, and freedom to make mistakes, and have some fun."[22]

However, it's also important to realize that some organizations might choose to centralize a few functions while leaving other decisions in the hands of lower-level managers. Chicago–based Aon Insurance is a perfect example of this approach. Through a series of mergers and acquisitions over the past 20 years, Aon had grown to a size of 47,000 employees in 500 locations around the world. Each of those offices had the authority to make its own decisions regarding human resource practices, such as whom to hire and how to pay people. This decentralization led to employees being treated differently depending on the location where they worked, creating feelings of animosity and unfairness. These inconsistent decisions could have been made more efficiently by the organization as a whole. Aon recently elected to centralize certain employee-related decisions within the organization.[23] Have the organizations where you've worked been largely centralized or decentralized? See our **OB Assessments** feature to find out.

FORMALIZATION. A company is high in **formalization** when there are many specific rules and procedures used to standardize behaviors and decisions. Although not something you can necessarily see on an organizational chart, the impact of formalization is felt throughout the organization. Rules and procedures are a necessary mechanism for control in every organization. Although the word "formalization" has a somewhat negative connotation, think about your reaction if every McDonald's made its French fries in different ways at each location. Or think about this: Would it bother you if every time you called Dell for technical support, you got an operator who treated you differently and gave you conflicting answers? Formalization is a necessary coordination mechanism that organizations rely on to get a standardized product or deliver a standardized service.

Alcoa's Michigan Casting Center, a leading automotive part supplier, was plagued by the fact that it could have two machine operators running the same machine on two different shifts and get up to a 50 percent performance difference in output and quality between the workers. The company conducted a study to identify the best practices for each machine in its plant. These best practices became standard operating procedures for each worker, and that formalization allowed the company to get a more predictable level of output.[24] Companies such as W.L. Gore, the Newark, Delaware–based manufacturer of Gore-Tex, fall at the other extreme when it comes to formalization. Whereas most companies have titles for their jobs and job descriptions that specify the tasks each job is responsible for, Bill Gore (company founder) felt that such formalization would stifle communication and creativity. After one of his employees mentioned that she needed to put some kind of job title on a business card to hand out at an outside conference, Gore replied that she could put "supreme commander" on the card for all he cared. She liked the title so much that she followed through on his suggestion, and it became a running joke throughout the company.[25]

ELEMENTS IN COMBINATION. You might have noticed that some elements of an organization's structure seem to go hand-in-hand with other elements. For example, wide spans of control tend to be associated with decentralization in decision making. A high level of work specialization tends to bring about a high level of formalization. Moreover, if you take a closer look at the elements, you might notice that many of the elements capture the struggle between efficiency and flexibility. **Mechanistic organizations** are efficient, rigid, predictable, and standardized organizations that thrive in stable environments. Mechanistic organizations are typified by a structure that relies on high levels of formalization, a rigid and hierarchical chain of command, high degrees of work specialization, centralization of decision making, and narrow spans of control. In contrast,

OB ASSESSMENTS

CENTRALIZATION

Have you experienced life inside an organization with a highly centralized structure? This assessment is designed to measure two facets of what would be considered a centralized organizational structure. Those two facets are *hierarchy of authority*, which reflects the degree to which managers are needed to approve decisions, and *participation in decision making*, which reflects how involved rank-and-file employees are in day-to-day deliberations. Think about the last job you held (even if it was a part-time or summer job). Alternatively, think about a student group of yours that seems to have a definite "leader." Then answer each question using the response scale provided. (For more assessments relevant to this chapter, please visit the Online Learning Center at www.mhhe.com/colquitt).

1	2	3	4	5
STRONGLY DISAGREE	DISAGREE	UNCERTAIN	AGREE	STRONGLY AGREE

1. There can be little action here until a supervisor approves a decision.   _____

2. A person who wants to make his or her own decisions would be quickly discouraged.   _____

3. Even small matters have to be referred to someone higher up for a final answer.   _____

4. I have to ask my boss before I do almost anything.   _____

5. Any decision I make has to have my boss's approval.   _____

6. I participate frequently in the decision to adopt new programs.   _____

7. I participate frequently in the decision to adopt new policies and rules.   _____

8. I usually participate in the decision to hire or adopt new group members.   _____

9. I often participate in decisions that affect my working environment.   _____

SCORING AND INTERPRETATION

Hierarchy of Authority: Sum up items 1–5.   _____
Participation in Decision Making: Sum up items 6–9.   _____

A centralized structure would be one in which Hierarchy of Authority is high and Participation in Decision Making is low. If your score is above 20 for Hierarchy of Authority and below 8 for Participation in Decision Making, your organization (or student group) has a highly centralized structure.

Source: Adapted from M. Schminke, R. Cropanzano, and D.E. Rupp, "Organization Structure and Fairness Perceptions: The Moderating Effects of Organizational Level," *Organizational Behavior and Human Decision Processes* 89 (2002), pp. 881–905.

organic organizations are flexible, adaptive, outward-focused organizations that thrive in dynamic environments. Organic organizations are typified by a structure that relies on low levels of formalization, weak or multiple chains of command, low levels of work specialization, and wide spans of control. Table 15-2 sums up the differences between the two types of organizations.

If you think about the differences between the two types, it probably wouldn't be too difficult to come up with a few companies that fall more toward one end of the continuum or the other. Where would you place Cisco Systems? Evidence indicates that a mechanistic or organic culture can have a significant effect on the types of employee practices a company adopts, such as selection, training, recruitment, compensation, and performance systems.[26] However, it's important to remember that few organizations are perfect examples of either extreme. Most fall somewhere near the middle, with certain areas within the organization having mechanistic qualities and others being more organic in nature. Although it's tempting to label mechanistic as "bad" and organic as "good," this perception is not necessarily true. Being mechanistic is the only way for many organizations to survive, and it can be a highly appropriate and fruitful way to structure work functions. To find out why that's the case, we need to explore why organizations develop the kinds of structures they do.

ORGANIZATIONAL DESIGN

Organizational design is the process of creating, selecting, or changing the structure of an organization. Ideally, organizations don't just "let" a structure develop on its own; they proactively design it to match their specific circumstances and needs. However, some organizations aren't that proactive and find themselves with a structure that has unintentionally developed on its own, without any careful planning. Those organizations may then be forced to change their structure to become more effective. A number of factors

 15.3

What is organizational design, and what factors does the organizational design process depend on?

TABLE 15-2	Characteristics of Mechanistic vs. Organic Structures
MECHANISTIC ORGANIZATIONS	**ORGANIC ORGANIZATIONS**
High degree of work specialization; employees are given a very narrow view of the tasks they are to perform.	Low degree of work specialization; employees are encouraged to take a broad view of the tasks they are to perform.
Very clear lines of authority; employees know exactly whom they report to.	Although there might be a specified chain of command, employees think more broadly in terms of where their responsibilities lie.
High levels of hierarchical control; employees are not encouraged to make decisions without their manager's consent.	Knowledge and expertise are decentralized; employees are encouraged to make their own decisions when appropriate.
Information is passed through vertical communication between an employee and his or her supervisor.	Lateral communication is encouraged, focusing on information and advice as opposed to orders.
Employees are encouraged to develop firm-specific knowledge and expertise within their area of specialization.	Employees are encouraged to develop knowledge and expertise outside of their specialization.

Source: Adapted from T. Burns and G.M. Stalker, G.M. *The Management of Innovation* (London: Tavistock, 1961).

influence the process of organizational design. Those factors include the environment in which the organization does business, its strategy and technology, and the size of the firm.

BUSINESS ENVIRONMENT. An organization's **business environment** consists of its customers, competitors, suppliers, distributors, and other factors external to the firm, all of which have an impact on organizational design. One of the biggest factors in an environment's effect on structure is whether the outside environment is stable or dynamic. Stable environments don't change frequently, and any changes that do occur happen very slowly. Stable environments allow organizations to focus on efficiency and require little change over time. In contrast, dynamic environments change on a frequent basis and require organizations to have structures that are more adaptive.[27] Sony made a well-publicized corporate mistake when it failed to meet the needs of its changing business environment to match Apple's iPod.[28] Because it took it so long to recognize and adapt to this environmental shift, Sony has struggled to be profitable. Some would argue that the world is changing so fast that the majority of companies can no longer keep up.

Partially due to its organizational structure, Sony was unable to adjust to its changing business environment, allowing Apple to dominate the portable music player market with its innovative line of iPods.

COMPANY STRATEGY. A **company strategy** describes an organization's objectives and goals and how it tries to capitalize on its assets to make money. Although the myriad of organizational strategies is too involved to discuss here, two common strategies revolve around being either a low-cost producer or a differentiator.[29] Companies that focus on a low-cost producer strategy rely on selling products at the lowest possible cost. To do this well, they have to focus on being as efficient as they can be. Such companies are more likely to take a mechanistic approach to organizational design. Other companies might follow a differentiation strategy. Rather than focusing on supplying a product or service at the lowest cost, these companies believe that people will pay more for a product that's unique in some way. It could be that their product has a higher level of quality or offers features that a low-cost product doesn't. A differentiation strategy often hinges on adjusting to changing environments quickly, which often makes an organic structure more appropriate.

TECHNOLOGY. An organization's **technology** is the method by which it transforms inputs into outputs. Very early on in the study of organizations, it was assumed that technology was the major determinant of an organization's structure.[30] Since then, the picture has become less clear regarding the appropriate relationship between technology and structure.[31] Although not completely conclusive, research suggests that the more routine a technology is, the more mechanistic a structure should be. In many ways, this suggestion makes perfect sense: If a company makes the exact same thing over and over, it should focus on creating that one thing as efficiently as possible by having high levels of specialization, formalization, and centralization. However, if technologies need to be changed or altered to suit the needs of various consumers, it follows that decisions would be more decentralized and the rules and procedures the organization relies on would need to be more flexible.

COMPANY SIZE. There is no question that there is a significant relationship between **company size**, or the total number of employees, and structure.[32] As organizations become larger, they need to rely on some combination of specialization, formalization, and centralization to control their activities, thereby becoming more mechanistic in nature. When it comes to organizational performance, however, there is no definite answer as to when an organization's structure should be revised, or "how big is too big."[33] As many organizations get bigger, they attempt to create smaller units within the firm to create a "feeling of smallness." W.L. Gore did just that by attempting to prevent any one location in the company from having more than 150 employees. Top management was convinced that a size of 150 would still allow all the employees to talk to one another in the hallways. However, even Gore hasn't been able to maintain that goal; the company has grown to encompass 7,300 employees in 45 locations.[34]

COMMON ORGANIZATIONAL FORMS

Our discussion of organizational design described how an organization's business environment, strategy, technology, and size conspire to make some organizational structures more effective than others. Now we turn our attention to a logical next question: What structures do most organizations utilize? The sections that follow describe some of the most common organizational forms. As you read their descriptions, think about whether these forms would fall on the mechanistic or organic side of the structure continuum. You might also consider what kinds of design factors would lead an organization to choose that particular form.

15.4

What are some of the more common organizational forms that an organization might adopt for its structure?

SIMPLE STRUCTURES. **Simple structures** are perhaps the most common form of organizational design, primarily because there are more small organizations than large ones. In fact, more than 80 percent of employing organizations have fewer than 19 employees.[35] Small accounting and law firms, family-owned grocery stores, individual-owned retail outlets, independent churches, and landscaping services are all organizations that are likely to use a simple structure. Figure 15-3 shows a simple structure for a manager-owned restaurant. The figure reveals that simple structures are just that: simple. Simple structures are generally used by extremely small organizations in which the manager, president, and owner are all the same person. A simple structure is a flat organization with one person as the central decision-making figure; it is not large enough to have a high degree of formalization and will only have very basic differences in work specialization.

A simple structure makes perfect sense for a small organization, because employees can come and go with no major ripple effects on the organization. However, as the business grows, the coordinating efforts on the part of the owner/manager become increasingly more complex. In the case of our restaurant, let's assume that the growth of the restaurant requires the owner to spend time doing lots of little things to manage the employees. Now the manager has lost the ability to spend time focusing on the actual business at hand. The manager then decides to add a supervisor to handle all of the day-to-day organizing of the restaurant. This arrangement works well until the owner decides to open a second restaurant that needs to have its own supervisor. Now let's assume that this second restaurant is much larger, leading the owner to decide to have separate supervisors directly in charge of the waitstaff and the kitchen. All of a sudden, our little restaurant has three layers of management!

FIGURE 15-3   An Organizational Structure for a Small Restaurant

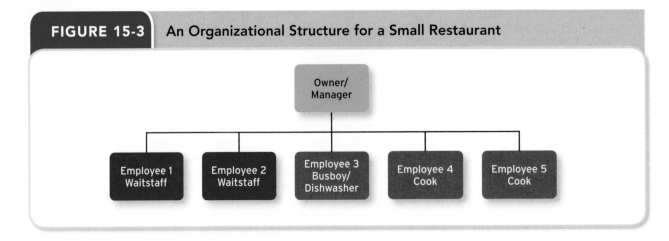

BUREAUCRATIC STRUCTURES. When you think of the word "bureaucracy," what thoughts come to mind? Stuffy, boring, restrictive, formal, hard to change, and needlessly complex are some of the terms that have a tendency to be associated with bureaucracies. Those unflattering adjectives aside, chances are very good that you either currently work in a bureaucracy or will after you graduate. A **bureaucratic structure** is an organizational form that exhibits many of the facets of the mechanistic organization. Bureaucracies are designed for efficiency and rely on high levels of work specialization, formalization, centralization of authority, rigid and well-defined chains of command, and relatively narrow spans of control. As mentioned previously, as an organization's size increases, it's incredibly difficult not to develop some form of bureaucracy.

There are numerous types of bureaucratic structures on which we might focus. The most basic of these is the **functional structure**. As shown in Figure 15-4, a functional structure groups employees by the functions they perform for the organization. For example, employees with marketing expertise are grouped together, those with finance duties are grouped together, and so on. The success of the functional structure is based on the efficiency advantages that come with having a high degree of work specialization that's centrally coordinated.[36] Managers have expertise in an area and interact with others with the same type of expertise to create the most efficient solutions for the company. As illustrated in our previous example of the fast-growing restaurant, many small companies naturally evolve into functionally based structures as they grow larger.

However, small companies experiencing rapid growth are not the only organizations to benefit from a functional structure. Smurfit-Stone Container Corporation, the Chicago–based paper and packaging manufacturer with 25,000 employees at 140 locations, is moving toward a more traditional functional structure. Smurfit-Stone was organized like other companies in the paper industry, with a structure relying on a large number of plants operating under different general managers. CEO Patrick Moore made the decision to move toward a more functional structure, noting that the move "allows us to drive a standardization of operating practices within the organization, which is critical. In addition, it allows us to drive scale and efficiency, which has suffered with the series of acquisitions that provided too many smaller, inefficient plants."[37] Smurfit-Stone hopes that the efficiencies generated by the change in structure will afford it enough cost savings to get a jump on its competitors.

Functional structures are extremely efficient when the organization as a whole has a relatively narrow focus, fewer product lines or services, and a stable environment. The biggest weaknesses of a functional structure tend to revolve around the fact that individuals within each function get so wrapped up in their own goals and viewpoints that they lose

FIGURE 15-4 | Functional and Multi-Divisional Structures

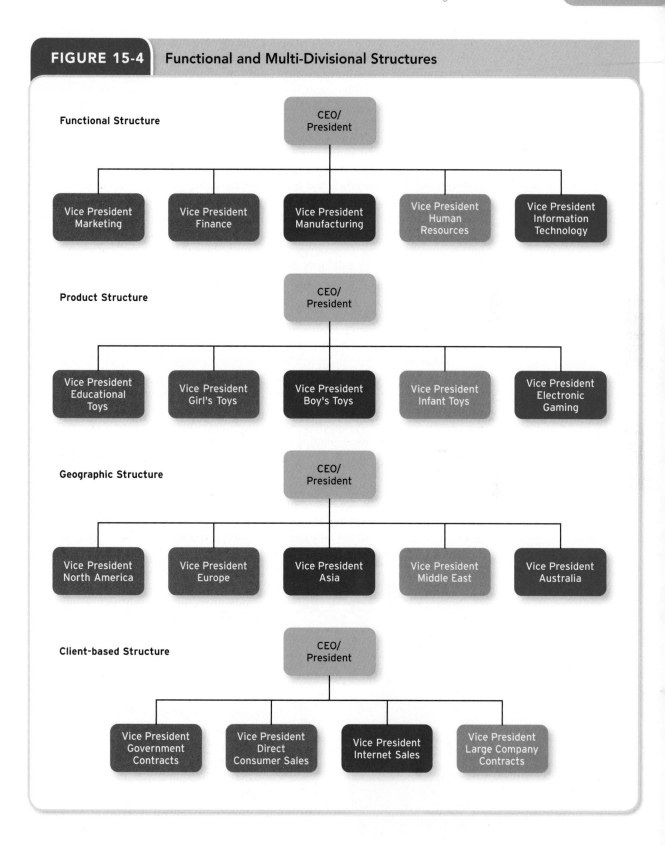

Functional Structure

CEO/President

- Vice President Marketing
- Vice President Finance
- Vice President Manufacturing
- Vice President Human Resources
- Vice President Information Technology

Product Structure

CEO/President

- Vice President Educational Toys
- Vice President Girl's Toys
- Vice President Boy's Toys
- Vice President Infant Toys
- Vice President Electronic Gaming

Geographic Structure

CEO/President

- Vice President North America
- Vice President Europe
- Vice President Asia
- Vice President Middle East
- Vice President Australia

Client-based Structure

CEO/President

- Vice President Government Contracts
- Vice President Direct Consumer Sales
- Vice President Internet Sales
- Vice President Large Company Contracts

sight of the bigger organizational picture. In other words, employees don't communicate as well across functions as they do within functions. Cisco struggled with this problem, which prompted it to make the structural changes described in the opening vignette. The Sony example also highlights this danger, in that hardware engineers failed to communicate with software developers, which prevented the hardware and software people from seeing all the pieces of the puzzle.[38]

In contrast to functional structures, **multi-divisional structures** are bureaucratic organizational forms in which employees are grouped into divisions around products, geographic regions, or clients (see Figure 15-4). Each of these divisions operates relatively autonomously from the others and has its own functional groups. Multi-divisional structures generally develop from companies with functional structures whose interests and goals become too diverse for that structure to handle. For example, if a company with a functional structure begins to add customers that require localized versions of its product, the company might adopt a geographic structure to handle the product variations. Which form a company chooses will likely depend on where the diversity in its business lies.

Product structures group business units around different products that the company produces. Each of those divisions becomes responsible for manufacturing, marketing, and doing research and development for the products in its own division. Boeing, Procter & Gamble, Hewlett-Packard, and Sony are companies that have developed product structures. Product structures make sense when firms diversify to the point that the products they sell are so different that managing them becomes overwhelming. CEO Mark Hurd changed Hewlett-Packard's organizational structure to become more product-based. He was inspired to do so because his sales force (in a centralized functional structure) simply had way too many products to sell (from the largest servers to the smallest printers). Shifting the sales force into three different product-based divisions allowed the salespeople to concentrate on a core set of products, reinvigorating the Hewlett-Packard sales force.[39]

However, there are downsides to a product structure. One of those downsides arises when the products are not really that different. Mattel ran into this problem with its product-based structure. The El Segundo, California–based toy company was organized into girl's brands (Barbie), boy's brands (Hot Wheels), the American Girl line, and Fisher-Price (educational toys, Dora the Explorer). When Mattel CEO Robert Eckert took over the company, he found that each of the divisions not only had its own unique culture and ways of doing business, but they were actually competing against one another! Mattel has since combined three of

Mattel recently centralized its operations by combining three of its four divisions. CEO Robert Eckert hopes the new organization will reduce competition between divisions and make the company more profitable.

the four divisions to push a "One Mattel" philosophy, hoping the more centralized and functional structure will help the company become more profitable.[40] Not all companies feel that competition is bad though. Fiat-Chrysler CEO Sergio Marchionne recently reorganized so that Dodge, Jeep and Chrysler are essentially operating as separate companies each with its own CEO. These companies are being forced to compete with each other for marketing and development resources. Marchionne is hoping that the competition will help to turn all three car brands around.[41]

Geographic structures are generally based around the different locations where the company does business. The functions required to serve a business are placed under a manager who is in charge of a specific location. Reasons for developing a geographic structure revolve around the different tastes of customers in different regions, the size of the locations that need to be covered by different salespeople, or the fact that the manufacturing and distribution of a product are better served by a geographic breakdown. When the Regus Group (a U.K. company) and HQ Global Work-places (a U.S. company) merged, they came together to form the world's largest supplier of meeting spaces and office suites. The new Regus group now has 750 office suite facilities in 350 cities across 60 countries. When they merged, HQ and Regus had different structures. Considering the necessarily geographic-based business (i.e., the distances between facilities and the range of customers), the new Regus group is structured by geographic region.[42] Many global companies are also organized by geographic location. IBM was one of the first, but that might be changing, as described in our **OB Internationally** feature.

One last form of multi-divisional structure is the **client structure**. When organizations have a number of very large customers or groups of customers that all act in a similar way, they might organize their businesses around serving those customers. For example, small banks traditionally organize themselves into divisions such as personal banking, small business banking, personal lending, and commercial lending. Similarly, consulting firms

OB INTERNATIONALLY

Traditionally, IBM has structured its 200,000-employee organization along geographic lines. Some might argue that IBM was the company that pioneered the first multinational geographic structure by setting up mini-IBMs in countries around the globe. Each country in which IBM operated had its own workforce and management team that reacted to the clients for whom it provided services in that country. The structure made perfect sense in a world in which consultants needed to be on location with their clients when those customers were having software or computer issues. However, IBM's environmental factors are changing rapidly. Competitors, especially those coming out of India, are providing many of the same services for significantly less money.

To change along with its competitors and respond to the "flattening world," IBM is reorganizing its workforce by creating and utilizing what it calls "competency centers." These centers will group employees from around the world on the basis of the specific skill sets that they have to offer clients. Some workers will be grouped into one location that can service clients all over the world through the use of technology. In Boulder, Colorado, IBM employs 6,200 professionals as part of a "call center" that monitors clients' computing functions worldwide. If something goes wrong in one of IBM's 426 data centers, employees in Boulder will more than likely be the ones to handle it or send it to someone who can. Other IBM workers will be grouped by broader geographic locations so that they can still be in relatively close proximity to their customers. When these employees are needed by a client, IBM has a computer database that allows it to put together teams of highly specialized consultants by examining the skill sets listed on 70,000 IBM resumes.

Does this change in structure sound familiar to you? It should—though IBM is maintaining some of it geographical structure, its organizational structure is becoming more functional. As the world becomes flatter through technology, clients expect the best talent from around the world, not just the best talent that happens to be sitting in their city. These structural changes will allow IBM to give clients just that. For IBM, these are the necessary changes that come with being a global company. It's not just about structure though, according to IBM Senior Vice President Robert W. Moffat Jr.: "Globalization is more than that. Our customers need us to put the right skills in the right place at the right time."[43]

often organize themselves into divisions that are responsible for small business clients, large business clients, and federal clients.

Matrix structures are more complex designs that try to take advantage of two types of structures at the same time. Companies such as Xerox, General Electric, and Dow Corning were among the first to adopt this type of structure.[44] Figure 15-5 provides an example of a matrix structure. In this example, employees are distributed into teams or projects within the organization on the basis of both their functional expertise and the product that they happen to be working on. Thus, the matrix represents a combination of a functional structure and a product structure. There are two important points to understand about the matrix structure. First, the matrix allows an organization to put together very flexible teams based on the experiences and skills of their employees.[45] This flexibility enables the organization to adjust much more quickly to the environment than a traditional bureaucratic structure would.

Second, the matrix gives each employee two chains of command, two groups with which to interact, and two sources of information to consider. This doubling of traditional structural elements can create high stress levels for employees if the demands of

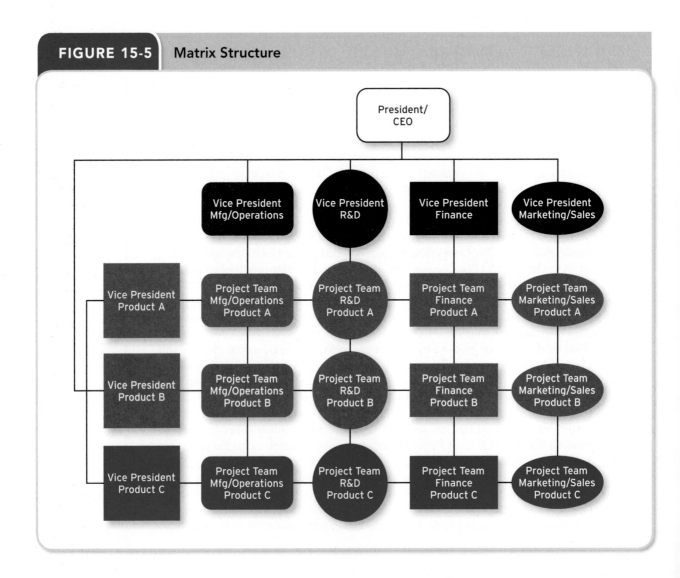

FIGURE 15-5   **Matrix Structure**

their functional grouping are at odds with the demands of their product- or client-based grouping.[46] The situation can become particularly stressful if one of the two groupings has more power than the other. For example, it may be that the functional manager assigns employees to teams, conducts performance evaluations, and decides raises—making that manager more powerful than the product- or client-based manager.[47] Although matrix structures have been around for an extremely long time, the number of organizations using them is growing as teams become a more common form of organizing work. They have also become more common in global companies, with the functional grouping balanced by a geographic grouping. For example, Areva NP, a French company that designs and builds nuclear power plants, has a matrix structure based on products (plants, fuel, services, and equipment) and geographical locations (France, Germany, and North America).[48]

SUMMARY: WHY DO SOME ORGANIZATIONS HAVE DIFFERENT STRUCTURES THAN OTHERS?

So why do some organizations have different structures? As shown in Figure 15-6, differences in the business environment, company strategy, technology, and firm size cause some organizations to be designed differently than others. These differences create variations in the five elements of organizational structure: work specialization, chain of command, span of control, centralization, and formalization. These elements then combine to form one of a number of common organizational forms, including: (1) a simple structure; (2) a bureaucratic structure, which may come in functional, product, geographic, or client forms; or (3) a matrix structure. Some of these forms are more mechanistic, whereas others are more organic. Taken together, these structures explain how work is organized within a given company.

HOW IMPORTANT IS STRUCTURE?

To some degree, an organization's structure provides the foundation for almost everything in organizational behavior. Think about some of the things that organizational structure affects: communication patterns between employees, the tasks an employee performs, the types of groups an organization uses, the freedom employees have to innovate and try new things, how power and influence are divided up in the company . . . we could go on and on. Picture the walls of a house. The occupants within those walls can decorate or personalize the structure as best they can. They can make it more attractive according to their individual preferences by adding and taking away furniture, but at the end of the day, they are still stuck with that structure. They have to work within the confines that the builder envisioned (unless they are willing to tear down walls or build new ones at considerable time, effort, and expense!). Organizational structures operate in much the same way for employees and their managers. A given manager can do many things to try to motivate, inspire, and set up an effective work environment so that employees have high levels of performance and commitment. At the end of the day, however, that manager must work within the structure created by the organization.

Given how many organizational forms there are, it's almost impossible to give an accurate representation of the impact of organizational structure on job performance. In fact, we might even say that an organization's structure determines what job performance is supposed to look like! In addition, the elements of structure are not necessarily good or bad for performance. For example, a narrow span of control is not necessarily better than a broad one; rather, the organization must find the optimal solution based on its environment

15.5

When an organization makes changes to its structure, how does that restructuring affect job performance and organizational commitment?

FIGURE 15-6 | Why Do Some Organizations Have Different Structures Than Others?

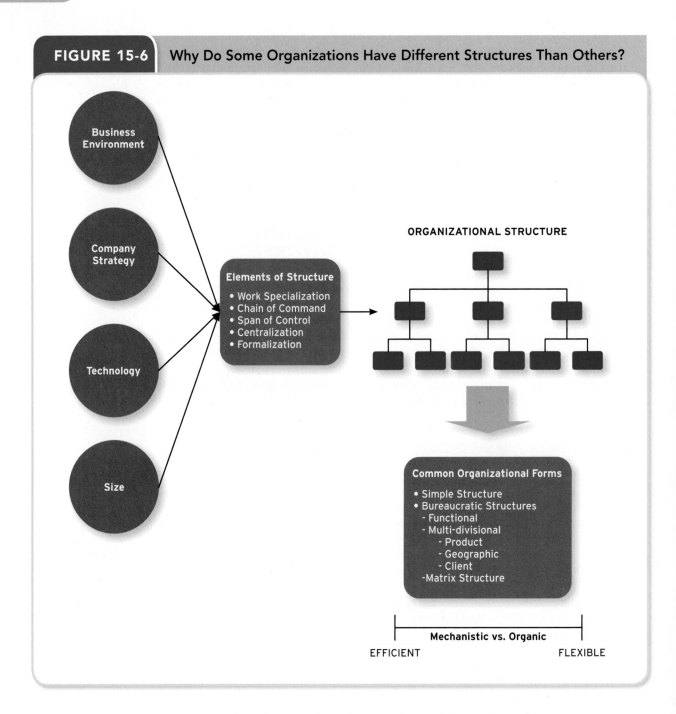

and culture. One thing we can say, as illustrated in Figure 15-7, is that changes to an organization's structure can have negative effects on the employees who work for the company, at least in the short term. The process of changing an organization's structure is called **restructuring**. Research suggests that restructuring has a small negative effect on task performance, likely because changes in specialization, centralization, or formalization may lead to confusion about how exactly employees are supposed to do their jobs, which hinders *learning* and *decision making*. Restructuring has a more significant negative effect on organizational commitment, however. Restructuring efforts can increase *stress* and

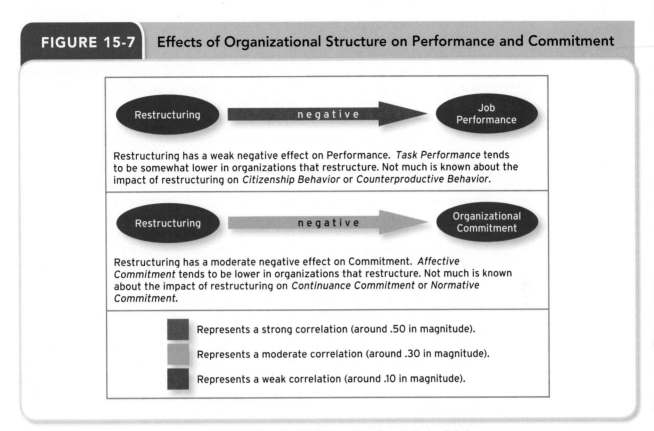

FIGURE 15-7   **Effects of Organizational Structure on Performance and Commitment**

Restructuring has a weak negative effect on Performance. *Task Performance* tends to be somewhat lower in organizations that restructure. Not much is known about the impact of restructuring on *Citizenship Behavior* or *Counterproductive Behavior.*

Restructuring has a moderate negative effect on Commitment. *Affective Commitment* tends to be lower in organizations that restructure. Not much is known about the impact of restructuring on *Continuance Commitment* or *Normative Commitment.*

Represents a strong correlation (around .50 in magnitude).

Represents a moderate correlation (around .30 in magnitude).

Represents a weak correlation (around .10 in magnitude).

Sources: C. Gopinath and T.E. Becker, "Communication, Procedural Justice, and Employee Attitudes: Relationships under Conditions of Divestiture," *Journal of Management* 26 (2000), pp. 63–83; and J. Brockner, G. Spreitzer, A. Mishra, W. Hockwarter, L. Pepper, and J. Weinberg, "Perceived Control as an Antidote to the Negative Effects of Layoffs on Survivors' Organizational Commitment and Job Performance," *Administrative Science Quarterly* 49 (2004), pp. 76–100.

jeopardize employees' *trust* in the organization. There is some evidence that the end result is a lower level of affective commitment on the part of employees, because they feel less emotionally attached to the firm.

APPLICATION: RESTRUCTURING

As you've read through our discussion of organizational structure, you may have noticed how important it is for organizations to adapt to their environment. The first step in adapting is recognizing the need to change. The second (and sometimes much more problematic) step is actually adapting through restructuring. Organizations attempt to restructure all the time—in fact, it's difficult to pick up a copy of *BusinessWeek* or *Fortune* without reading about some organization's restructuring initiatives. General Motors has undertaken a massive restructuring effort no less than eight times over the past 25 years![49] (And look where that got them. . .!) Most of the examples we put into this chapter pertain to organizations that were restructuring.

Restructuring efforts come in a variety of shapes and sizes. Organizations may change from a product-based structure to a functional structure, from a functional structure to a

15.6

What steps can organizations take to reduce the negative effects of restructuring efforts?

geographic-based structure, and on and on. However, the most common kind of restructuring in recent years has been a "flattening" of the organization. Why do so many organizations do this? Primarily to show investors that they are reducing costs to become more profitable. Think back to our discussion of tall and flat organizational hierarchies, in which we noted that taller organizations have more layers of management. Many restructuring efforts are designed to remove one or more of those layers to reduce costs. Of course, removing such layers doesn't just mean deleting boxes on an organizational chart; there are actual people within those boxes! Thus, efforts to flatten require organizations to lay off several of the managers within the company.

When employees get a sense that their company might be getting ready to restructure, it causes a great deal of stress because they become worried that they will be one of those to lose their jobs. When ex-CEO Carly Fiorina decided to restructure Hewlett-Packard, it caused widespread fear and panic among employees. For the 60 days prior to the actual restructuring announcement, work came to a standstill at the company—tales of high stress, low motivation, political battles, and power struggles abounded.[50] It's estimated that Hewlett-Packard as a company lost an entire quarter's worth of productivity.[51] Not a great way to run a business, especially when, not two years later, the new CEO Mark Hurd essentially undid everything that had previously been restructured! He unmerged units that had been merged, decentralized the company where it had been centralized, and flattened the layers of management from 11 to 8 levels.[52]

One of the ways in which managers can do their best to help a restructuring effort succeed is to help manage the layoff survivors (i.e., employees who remain with the company following a layoff). Many layoff survivors are known to experience a great deal of guilt and remorse following an organization's decision to remove some employees from the company.[53] Researchers and practitioners recently have been trying to understand layoff survivors better, as well as how to help them adjust more quickly. One of the major problems for layoff survivors is the increased job demands placed on them. After all, that coworker or boss the employee had was doing *something*. Layoff survivors are generally burdened with having to pick up the leftover tasks that used to be done by somebody else.[54] This burden creates a sense of uncertainty and stress. Recent research suggests that one of the best ways to help layoff survivors adjust is to do things that give them a stronger sense of control.[55] Allowing survivors to have a voice in how to move forward or help set the plans about how to accomplish future goals are two ways managers can help employees feel more in control. In addition, honest and frequent communication with layoff survivors greatly helps reduce their feelings of uncertainty and stress.[56] This communication is especially necessary when the organization is hiring at the same time it's firing. For instance, Boeing planned to cut 9,000 jobs in 2009, but in the same year, it had more than 1,500 current and anticipated job openings.[57] Many other employers, such as Microsoft, AT&T, and Time Warner, have experienced something similar.[58] This conflict sends mixed messages to those being laid off, as well as to the survivors. One sobering fact is that the survivors never know whether the restructuring will be a great idea, like Cisco's, that leads to success, or if it's simply a process of grasping at straws to avoid the ultimate demise of the company—a topic discussed in this chapter's **OB at the Bookstore**. For a restructuring to be truly successful, it requires more than simply changing lines on an organizational chart; it demands a different way of working for employees.[59]

OB AT THE BOOKSTORE

HOW THE MIGHTY FALL
by Jim Collins (New York: Harper Collins, 2009).

Reorganizations and restructurings can create a false sense that you're actually doing something productive. Companies are in the process of reorganizing themselves all the time; that's the nature of institutional evolution. But when you begin to respond to data and warning signs with reorganization as a primary strategy, you may well be in denial. It's a bit like responding to a severe heart condition or a cancer diagnosis by rearranging your living room.

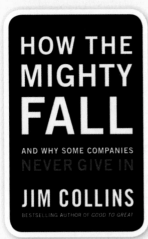

With those words, Jim Collins derides the process of reorganization as a tool for fixing a failing company. In the first chapter of this book, we reviewed Jim Collins' bestselling book *Good To Great*, in which he outlines how some companies make the leap from being above-average to being exceptional. His latest book, also a *New York Times* bestseller, takes a look at the opposite question: What causes extremely successful companies to fail? He finds that failing companies typically follow a five-stage path to failure:

1. *Hubris born of success.* Early success causes leaders to believe that they are entitled to future success.

2. *Undisciplined pursuit of more.* Growing in directions away from the core business and faster than highly talented people can be hired to manage it.

3. *Denial of risk and peril.* While results are still strong, signs that things might not be going well are written off or ignored and blamed on unique one time situations.

4. *Grasping for salvation.* Companies look for a "silver bullet" to try to turn things around—a new leader, a radical transformation, or a new product that will save the day.

5. *Capitulation to irrelevance or death.* Leaders throw in the towel when financial strength diminishes and the hope of a turnaround is lost.

One consistent theme through the book, especially in Stages 3 and 4, is that companies seem to think a reorganization will help them avoid the inevitable or solve their problems. Collins lists numerous example of companies that reorganize incessantly, hoping that by moving lines on an organizational chart, their business will turn around. His analysis of 11 companies suggests that there is no perfect organizational structure and that all structures have trade-offs. This revelation doesn't mean that restructuring is always bad; Collins details several companies that "turned around" out of Stage 4 to become successful once again, mostly by restructuring along the way. The final lesson should probably be that restructuring should happen only after a lot of thought, for the right reasons, and to solve real underlying problems in the organization, not just to make it look to outsiders or employees like something is being done.

TAKEAWAYS

15.1 An organization's structure formally dictates how jobs and tasks are divided and coordinated between individuals and groups within the organization. This structure, partially illustrated through the use of organizational charts, provides the foundation for organizing jobs, controlling employee behavior, shaping communication channels, and providing a lens through which employees view their work environment.

15.2 There are five major elements to an organization's structure: work specialization, chain of command, span of control, centralization of decision making, and formalization. These elements can be organized in such a way as to make an organization more mechanistic in nature, which allows it to be highly efficient in stable environments, or more organic in nature, which allows it to be flexible and adaptive in changing environments.

15.3 Organizational design is the process of creating, selecting, or changing the structure of an organization. Factors to be considered in organizational design include a company's business environment, its strategy, its technology, and its size.

15.4 There are literally thousands of organizational forms. The most common is the simple structure, which is used by most small companies. Larger companies adopt a more bureaucratic structure. This structure may be functional in nature, such that employees are grouped by job tasks, or multi-divisional, such that employees are grouped by product, geography, or client. Organizations may also adopt a matrix structure that combines functional and multi-divisional grouping.

15.5 Organizational restructuring efforts have a weak negative effect on job performance. They have a more significant negative effect on organizational commitment, because employees tend to feel less emotional attachment to organizations that are restructuring.

15.6 To reduce the negative effects of restructuring, organizations should focus on managing the stress levels of the employees who remain after the restructuring. Providing employees with a sense of control can help them learn to navigate their new work environment.

KEY TERMS

DISCUSSION QUESTIONS

15.1 Is it possible to be a great leader of employees in a highly mechanistic organization? What special talents or abilities might be required?

15.2 Why do the elements of structure, such as work specialization, formalization, span of control, chain of command, and centralization, have a tendency to change together? Which of the five do you feel is the most important?

15.3 Which is more important for an organization: the ability to be efficient or the ability to adapt to its environment? What does this say about how an organization's structure should be set up?

15.4 Which of the organizational forms described in this chapter do you think leads to the highest levels of motivation among workers? Why?

15.5 If you worked in a matrix organization, what would be some of the career development challenges that you might face? Does the idea of working in a matrix structure appeal to you? Why or why not?

15.6 Should an organization consult with rank-and-file employees before it restructures? Should it be open about its intentions to restructure or more secretive about key details? Why?

CASE: CISCO SYSTEMS

Prior to its reorganization, Cisco Systems had a reputation for having a kind of "cowboy culture" in which people with the most aggressive and strong personalities pushed and shoved to try to gain John Chambers's approval. Those who controlled the most resources had the most power, and they used that power for personal gain instead of the best interest of the company.[60] Now the company exhibits a sense of pride in managers who do something to help others succeed, even if they don't receive explicit or instant credit for it. John Chambers will be the first to tell you that the current collaborative structure could not have emerged without the systems put in place to facilitate communication between employees spread across the globe. Cisco had to figure out a way to allow everyone to work together without hopping on a plane every time they needed a meeting. Therefore, the company developed a technology called "TelePresence," which Chambers calls "a lifelike, ultra-high-definition videoconferencing system that enables meetings so realistic that they truly feel like everyone is in the same room even if they're thousands of miles away."[61] The technology seems to provide a competitive advantage to Cisco, though for $300,000, it will set up the very same system for anyone who wants one!

An issue that keeps popping up, however, is what happens when Chambers (who, at age 59, is recognized as one of the top CEOs in the world) retires. The current structure is mainly a result of his influence, though he also argues that the new structure minimizes his importance. The succession plan remains up in the air.[62] One thing is for certain though: The nimble decision-making ability of Cisco's councils and boards might be put to use very shortly, because as of late 2009, Cisco had $26 billion in cash laying around, waiting to be spent.[63]

15.1 Given the technology available at Cisco, is it possible for other companies to emulate its organizational structure? What might prevent other companies from doing so?

15.2   Evaluate Cisco's organizational structure in terms of its ability to compete effectively with its competitors. What specific advantages does it provide?

15.3   What types of employees is Cisco likely to attract with the structure it has put in place? Does this prediction bode well or ill for the future?

EXERCISE: CREATIVE CARDS, INC.

The purpose of this exercise is to demonstrate the effects of structure on organizational efficiency. This exercise uses groups, so your instructor will either assign you to a group or ask you to create your own group. The exercise has the following steps:

15.1   Creative Cards, Inc., is a small but growing company, started 10 years ago by Angela Naom, a graphic designer. The company has added many employees over the years but without a master plan. Now Angela wants to reorganize the company. The current structure of Creative Cards, Inc., is shown in the figure. Review the organizational chart and identify at least 10 problems with the design of Creative Cards, Inc. Be sure to consider work specialization, chain of command, span of control, centralization, and formalization in developing your answer.

15.2   Create a new organizational design that you think would help the company operate more efficiently and effectively.

15.3   Class discussion, whether in groups or as a class, should center on how Creative Cards could best manage such a significant restructuring.

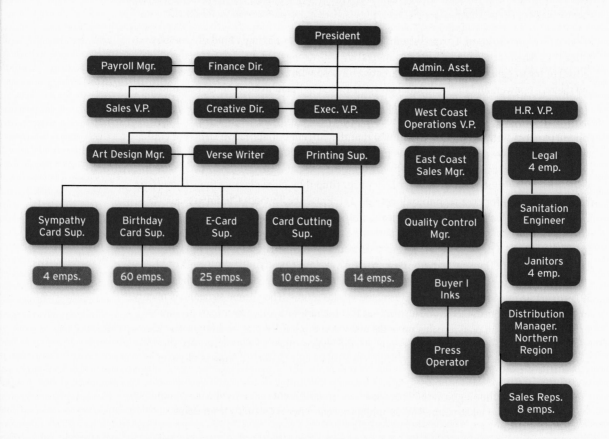

ENDNOTES

15.1 McGirt, E. "Revolution in San Jose." *Fast Company*, January 2009, p. 88.

15.2 Fryer, B., and T.A. Stewart. "Cisco Sees the Future." *Harvard Business Review,* November 2008, pp. 72–79.

15.3 Kimes, M. "Cisco Layers It On." *Fortune*, December 8, 2008, p. 24.

15.4 Fryer and Stewart, "Cisco Sees the Future."

15.5 Ibid.

15.6 McGirt, "Revolution in San Jose."

15.7 "50 of the World's Most Innovative Companies." *Fast Company*, March 2009, p. 52.

15.8 McGirt, "Revolution in San Jose."

15.9 Fryer and Stewart, "Cisco Sees the Future."

15.10 Kimes, "Cisco Layers It On."

15.11 Ibid.

15.12 Kranz, G. "Aetna's Odyssey Comes Full Circle." *Workforce Management Online*, March 2009, http://www.workforce.com/archive/feature/26/26/53/index.php?ht= (accessed June 18, 2009).

15.13 Hackman, J.R., and G. R. Oldham. *Work Redesign.* Reading, MA: Addison-Wesley, 1980.

15.14 Simon, H. *Administrative Behavior.* New York: Macmillan, 1947.

15.15 Edwards, C. "Shaking Up Intel's Insides." *BusinessWeek,* January 31, 2005, p. 35.

15.16 Meier, K.J., and J. Bohte. "Ode to Luther Gulick: Span of Control and Organizational Performance." *Administration and Society* 32 (2000), pp. 115–37.

15.17 Theobald, N.A., and S. Nicholson-Crotty. "The Many Faces of Span of Control: Organizational Structure Across Multiple Goals." *Administration and Society* 36 (2005), pp. 648–60.

15.18 Child, J., and M. McGrath. "Organizations Unfettered: Organizational Forms in an Information-Intensive Economy." *Academy of Management Journal* 44 (2001), pp. 1135–48.

15.19 Hymowitz, C. "Today's Bosses Find Mentoring Isn't Worth the Time and Risks." *The Wall Street Journal,* March 13, 2006, p. B1.

15.20 Nuttal, C. "Intel Cuts 1,000 Management Jobs." *Financial Times,* July 14, 2006, p. 23.

15.21 Marquez, J. "Taking a Longer View." *Workforce Management,* May 22, 2006, pp. 18–22.

15.22 Swisher, K. "A Question of Management." *The Wall Street Journal*, June 2, 2009, p. R4.

15.23 Marquez, J. "Many Businesses, but One Mission." *Workforce Management,* June 12, 2006, pp. 32–36.

15.24 Groszkiewicz, D.; and B. Warren. "Alcoa's Michigan Casting Center Runs the Business from the Bottom Up." *Journal of Organizational Excellence,* Spring 2006, pp. 13–23.

15.25 Kiger, P. "Power of the Individual." *Workforce Management*, February 27, 2006, pp. 1, 22–27.

15.26 Toh, S.M.; F.P. Morgeson; and M.A. Campion. "Human Resource Configurations: Investigating Fit Within the Organizational Context."

Journal of Applied Psychology 93 (2008), pp. 864–82.

15.27   Scott, W.R., and G.F. Davis. *Organizations and Organizing: Rational, Natural, and Open System Perspectives.* Englewood Cliffs, NJ: Pearson Prentice Hall, 2007.

15.28   Kane, Y.I., and P. Dvorak. "Howard Stringer, Japanese CEO." *The Wall Street Journal,* March 3, 2007, pp. A1, A6; and Singer, M. "Stringer's Way." *The New Yorker,* June 5, 2006, pp. 46–57.

15.29   Porter, M. *Competitive Strategy.* New York: The Free Press, 1980.

15.30   Woodward, J. *Industrial Organization: Theory and Practice.* London: Oxford University Press, 1965.

15.31   Miller, C.C.; W.H. Glick; Y. Wang; and G.P. Huber. "Understanding Technology–Structure Relationships: Theory Development and Meta-Analytic Theory Testing." *Academy of Management Journal* 34 (1991), pp. 370–99.

15.32   Gooding, J.Z., and J.A. Wagner III. "A Meta-Analytic Review of the Relationship Between Size and Performance: The Productivity and Efficiency of Organizations and their Subunits." *Administrative Science Quarterly* 30 (1985), pp. 462–81. See also Bluedorn, A.C. "Pilgrim's Progress: Trends and Convergence in Research on Organizational Size and Environments." *Journal of Management* 21 (1993), pp. 163–92.

15.33   Lawler, E.E., III. "Rethinking Organizational Size." *Organizational Dynamics,* 26 (1997), pp. 24–35.

15.34   Kiger, "Power of the Individual."

15.35   Scott and Davis, *Organizations and Organizing.*

15.36   Miles, R.E., and C.C. Snow. *Organizational Strategy, Structure, and Process.* New York: McGraw-Hill, 1978.

15.37   Shaw, M. "Boxing It Up the Right Way." *Pulp & Paper,* September 2006, pp. 31–34.

15.38   Singer, "Stringer's Way."

15.39   Lashinsky, A. "The Hurd Way: How a Sales-Obsessed CEO Rebooted HP." *Fortune,* April 17, 2006, pp. 92–102.

15.40   Ruiz, G. "Shaking up the Toyshop." *Workforce Management,* June 26, 2006, pp. 27–34.

15.41   Welch, D.; D. Kiley; and C. Matlack. "Tough Love at Chrysler." *BusinessWeek,* August 24 & 31, 2009, pp. 26-28.

15.42   Hosford, C. "Behind the Regus–HQ Merger: A Clash of Cultures That Wasn't." *Sales and Marketing Management,* March 2006, pp. 47–48.

15.43   Hamm, S. "Big Blue Shift." *BusinessWeek,* June 5, 2006, pp. 108–10.

15.44   Burns, L.R., and D.R. Wholey. "Adoption and Abandonment of Matrix Management Programs: Effects of Organizational Characteristics and Interorganizational Programs." *Academy of Management Journal* 36 (1993), pp. 106–38.

15.45   Hackman, J.R. "The Design of Work Teams." In *Handbook of Organizational Behavior,* ed. J.W. Lorsch. Englewood Cliffs, NJ: Prentice Hall, 1987, pp. 315–42.

15.46   Larson, E.W., and D.H. Gobeli. "Matrix Management: Contradictions and Insight." *California Management Review* 29 (1987), pp. 126–38.

15.47   Rees, D.W., and C. Porter. "Matrix Structures and the Training Implications." *Industrial and*

Commercial Training 36 (2004), pp. 189–93.

15.48 http://www.areva-np.com (accessed April 26, 2007).

15.49 Taylor, A., III. "GM and Me." *Fortune*, December 8, 2008, pp. 92–100; and Taylor, A., III. "GM Gets Its Act Together. Finally." *Fortune,* April 5, 2004, pp. 136–46.

15.50 Gopinath, C. "Businesses in a Merger Need to Make Sense Together." *Businessline,* June 26, 2006, p. 1.

15.51 Hamm, J. "The Five Messages Leaders Must Manage." *Harvard Business Review,* May 2006, pp. 114–23.

15.52 Lashinsky, "The Hurd Way."

15.53 Noer, D.M. *Healing the Wounds.* San Francisco: Jossey-Bass, 1993; and Mishra, K.; G.M. Spreitzer; and A. Mishra. "Preserving Employee Morale During Downsizing." *Sloan Management Review* 39 (1998), pp. 83–95.

15.54 Conlin, M. "The Big Squeeze on Workers; Is There a Risk to Wringing More from a Smaller Staff?" *BusinessWeek,* May 13, 2002, p. 96.

15.55 Brockner, J.; G. Spreitzer; A. Mishra; W. Hockwarter; L. Pepper; and J. Weinberg. "Perceived Control as an Antidote to the Negative Effects of Layoffs on Survivors' Organizational Commitment and Job Performance." *Administrative Science Quarterly* 49 (2004), pp. 76–100.

15.56 Brockner, J. "The Effects of Work Layoffs on Survivors: Research, Theory and Practice." In *Research in Organizational Behavior,* Vol. 10, eds. B.M. Staw and L.L. Cummings. Berkeley: University of California Press, 1988, pp. 213–55.

15.57 Tuna, C. "Many Companies Hire as They Fire." *The Wall Street Journal*, May 11, 2009, p. B6.

15.58 Ibid.

15.59 Porras, J.I., and P.J. Robertson. "Organizational Development: Theory, Practice, and Research." In *Handbook of Industrial and Organizational Psychology.* Vol. 3, 2nd ed., ed. M.D. Dunnette and L.M. Hough. 1992, Palo Alto: Consulting Psychologists Press, pp. 719–822.

15.60 McGirt, "Revolution in San Jose."

15.61 Fryer and Stewart, "Cisco Sees the Future."

15.62 McGirt, "Revolution in San Jose."

15.63 Kimes, "Cisco Layers It On."

chapter 16

Organizational Culture

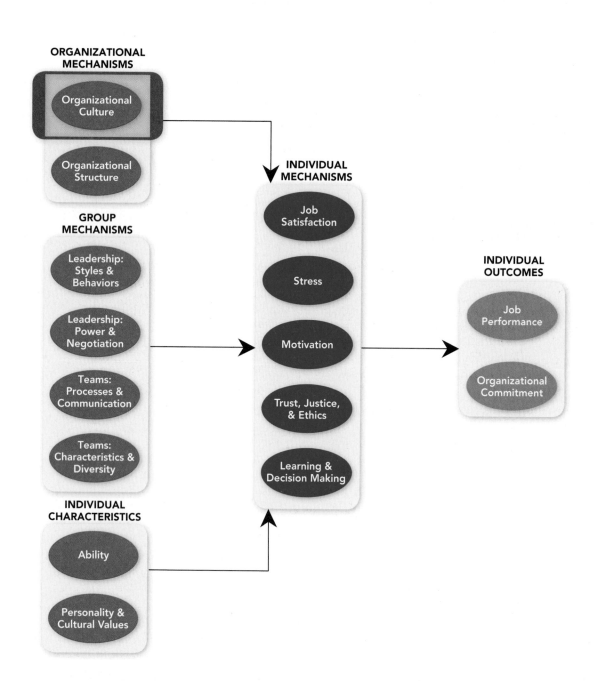

ORGANIZATIONAL MECHANISMS

- Organizational Culture
- Organizational Structure

GROUP MECHANISMS

- Leadership: Styles & Behaviors
- Leadership: Power & Negotiation
- Teams: Processes & Communication
- Teams: Characteristics & Diversity

INDIVIDUAL CHARACTERISTICS

- Ability
- Personality & Cultural Values

INDIVIDUAL MECHANISMS

- Job Satisfaction
- Stress
- Motivation
- Trust, Justice, & Ethics
- Learning & Decision Making

INDIVIDUAL OUTCOMES

- Job Performance
- Organizational Commitment

✅ LEARNING GOALS

After reading this chapter, you should be able to answer the following questions:

16.1 What is organizational culture, and what are its components?

16.2 What general and specific types can be used to describe an organization's culture?

16.3 What makes a culture strong, and is it always good for an organization to have a strong culture?

16.4 How do organizations maintain their culture and how do they change it?

16.5 What is person–organization fit and how does it affect job performance and organizational commitment?

16.6 What steps can organizations take to make sure that newcomers will fit with their culture?

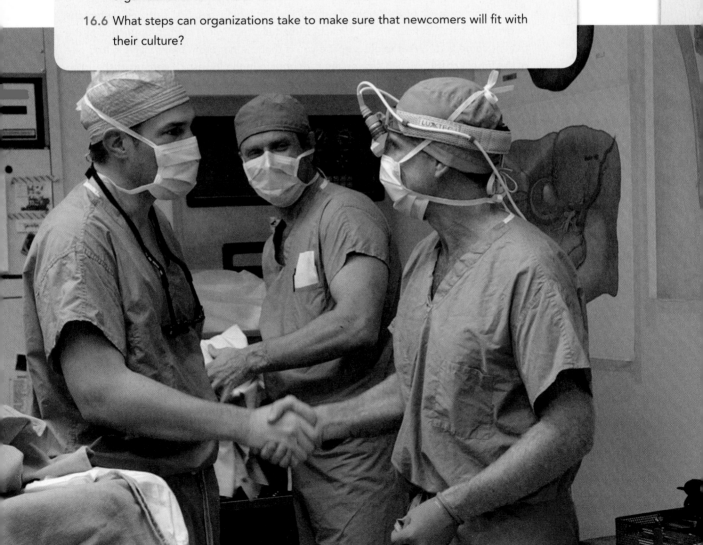

THE MAYO CLINIC

The Mayo Clinic, headquartered in Rochester, Minnesota, but with facilities in Arizona and Florida as well, is considered one of the single best healthcare-providing systems in the country. Every day, more than 42,000 persons work on one of its three campuses, all following a single mantra: "Put the patient first."[1] Although you wouldn't think it, within the healthcare industry, Mayo provides a surprisingly unique environment focused singularly on patient care. William and Charles Mayo, the original founders of the Mayo Clinic, established a core set of values in the early 1900s that, through significant effort, continue to thrive today.[2] These values are embodied in the way current employees treat and react to patients and have made the Mayo Clinic world-renowned for its service excellence. In an industry that has its own set of rules and regulations, the Mayo Clinic stands apart. Why? The answer is very clear: organizational culture.

The Mayo Clinic has established a customer service–oriented culture that permeates every aspect of its business: the organization's structure, the types of employees it hires, the way in which it organizes work, and how it manages its people.[3] Although it goes against almost everything the outside medical community practices and incentivizes, the Mayo Clinic puts all of its employees on salary (including doctors), focuses them on a single goal, and practices what it preaches—namely, regardless of cost, the needs of the patient come first.[4] What might surprise you is that the nonprofit Mayo Clinic is also one of the lowest costing health care systems, operating in the lowest 15 percent of spending per patient.[5] By encouraging doctors to work as a team, the hospital actually performs significantly fewer expensive scans and procedures. Denis Cortese, CEO of the Mayo Clinic, claims, "When doctors put their heads together in a room, when they share expertise, you get more thinking and less testing."[6]

As the clinic's culture thrived in Minnesota, most experts believed that it couldn't survive in other locations when it expanded. Those experts turned out to be wrong. The Mayo Clinic's two other major healthcare facilities, in Florida and Arizona (two of the most expensive states for healthcare), are excelling with the same culture in place.[7] Part of the reason is that the Mayo Clinic has set up a "service infrastructure" that allows its culture to survive virtually anywhere.[8] This infrastructure finds ways to engage physicians, focuses front-line employees on providing good first impressions, raises awareness of and education about the Mayo Service Values, and finds ways to measure and improve service processes continuously.[9] You can see its culture at all three locations by the way the buildings are built, by the stories the employees tell, by the symbols they hold up to others, and by what the company celebrates as an organization.[10] The Mayo Clinic's culture is what differentiates it from other healthcare providers.

ORGANIZATIONAL CULTURE

In almost every chapter prior to this point, we have simply given you definitions of important topics. However, in this case, it's important for you to understand that there are just about as many definitions of organizational culture as there are people who study it. In

"I don't know how it started, either. All I know is that it's part of our corporate culture."

fact, research on organizational culture has produced well over 50 different definitions![11] It seems that the term "culture" means a great many things to a great many people. Definitions of culture have ranged from as broad as, "The way we do things around here"[12] to as specific as . . . well, let's just suffice it to say that they can get complicated. Not surprisingly, the various definitions of organizational culture stem from how people have studied it. Sociologists study culture using a broad lens and anthropological research methods, like those applied to study tribes and civilizations. Psychologists tend to study culture and its effects on people using survey methods. In fact, many psychologists actually prefer the term "climate," but for our purposes, we'll use the two terms interchangeably. In this chapter, we define **organizational culture** as the shared social knowledge within an organization regarding the rules, norms, and values that shape the attitudes and behaviors of its employees.[13]

This definition helps highlight a number of facets of organizational culture. First, culture is social knowledge among members of the organization. Employees learn about most important aspects of culture through other employees. This transfer of knowledge might be through explicit communication, simple observation, or other, less obvious methods. In addition, culture is shared knowledge, which means that members of the organization understand and have a degree of consensus regarding what the culture is. Second, culture tells employees what the rules, norms, and values are within the organization. What are the most important work outcomes to focus on? What behaviors are appropriate or inappropriate at work? How should a person act or dress while at work? Indeed, some cultures even go so far as to say how employees should act when they aren't at work. Third, organizational culture shapes and reinforces certain employee attitudes and behaviors by creating a system of control over employees.[14] There is evidence that your individual goals and values will grow over time to match those of the organization for which you work.[15] This development really isn't that hard to imagine, given how much time employees spend working inside an organization.

16.1

What is organizational culture, and what are its components?

WHY DO SOME ORGANIZATIONS HAVE DIFFERENT CULTURES THAN OTHERS?

One of the most common questions people ask when you tell them where you are employed is, "So, tell me . . . what's it like there?" The description you use in your response is likely to have a lot to do with what the organization's culture is all about. In calculating your response to the question, you might consider describing the kinds of people who work at your company. More than likely, you'll do your best to describe the work atmosphere on a regular day. Perhaps you'll painstakingly describe the facilities you work in or how you feel the employees are treated. You might even go so far as to describe what it is that defines "success" at your company. All of those answers give clues that help organizational outsiders understand what a company is actually like. To give you a feel for the full range of potential answers to the "what's it like there?" question, it's necessary to review the facets of culture in more detail.

CULTURE COMPONENTS

There are three major components to any organization's culture: observable artifacts, espoused values, and basic underlying assumptions. You can understand the differences among these three components if you view culture like an onion, as in Figure 16-1. Some components of an organization's culture are readily apparent and observable, like the skin of an onion. However, other components are less observable to organizational outsiders or newcomers. Such outsiders can observe, interpret, and make conclusions based on what they see on the surface, but the inside remains a mystery until they can peel back the outside layers to gauge the values and assumptions that lie beneath. The sections that follow review the culture components in more detail.

FIGURE 16-1   The Three Components of Organizational Culture

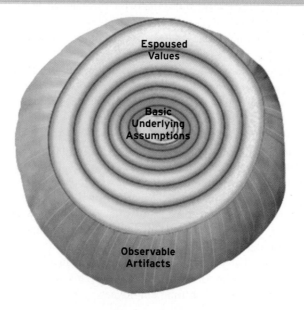

OBSERVABLE ARTIFACTS. **Observable artifacts** are the manifestations of an organization's culture that employees can easily see or talk about. They supply the signals that employees interpret to gauge how they should act during the workday. Artifacts supply the primary means of transmitting an organization's culture to its workforce. It's difficult to overestimate the importance of artifacts, because they help show not only current employees but also potential employees, customers, shareholders, and investors what the organization is all about. There are six major types of artifacts: symbols, physical structures, language, stories, rituals, and ceremonies.[16]

Symbols can be found throughout an organization, from its corporate logo to the images it places on its Web site to the uniforms its employees wear. Think about what Nike's "swoosh" represents: speed, movement, velocity. What might that symbol convey about Nike's culture? Or consider Apple Computer's "apple" logo. That symbol brings to mind Newton's discovery of gravity under the apple tree, conveying the importance of innovation within Apple's culture. When you think of the words "dark suit, white shirt, tie," what company do you think of? For many, the symbol represents IBM because that summarizes the company's long-standing dress code. Even though that dress code hasn't been in place at IBM for 10 years, it still symbolizes a formal, bureaucratic, and professional culture.

Physical structures also say a lot about a culture. Is the workplace open? Does top management work in a separate section of the building? Is the setting devoid of anything unique, or can employees express their personalities? Bloomberg, an information services, news, and media company based in New York, built its new headquarters in Manhattan primarily out of steel and glass, resembling what workers call a "beehive." It has no private offices, no cubicles, and even the conference rooms have glass walls. CEO Lex Fenwick sits on the third floor, surrounded by his sales and customer service staff. He believes this setup leads to instantaneous communication among employees.[17] IDEO, a creative design firm, also has an open office environment, though IDEO lets employees set up their offices however they like. When you walk around their work areas, you'll be walking underneath bicycles hanging over your head and crazy objects and toys in every direction.[18]

The ability to set up your own work space, as at the design firm IDEO, is a hallmark of an open corporate culture. Would this environment suit your working style?

Language reflects the jargon, slang, and slogans used within the walls of an organization. Do you know what a CTR, CPC, or Crawler is? Chances are you don't. If you worked for Yahoo, however, those terms would be second nature to you: CTR stands for click-through rate, CPC stands for cost-per-click, and a Crawler is a computer program that gathers information from other Web sites. Home Depot maintains a "stack it high and watch it fly" slogan, which reflects its approach to sales. Yum Brands Inc., which owns Pizza Hut, Taco Bell, KFC, and other fast-food restaurants, expects employees to be "customer maniacs"[19]—language that conveys its culture for customer interaction.

Stories consist of anecdotes, accounts, legends, and myths that are passed down from cohort to cohort within an organization. Telling stories can be a major mechanism through which leaders and employees describe what the company values or finds important. For example, Howard Schultz, CEO of Starbucks, tells the story of how (to improve quality) he forbade the common practice of resteaming milk. What this rule inadvertently created was the loss of millions of dollars of milk, as thousands of gallons of lukewarm liquid poured down the drain. One of his store managers came up with a simple, brilliant suggestion: Put etched lines inside the steaming pitchers so baristas would know how much milk to pour for the drink size they were making, instead of just guessing.[20] Paul Wiles, President/CEO of Novant Health in Winston-Salem, North Carolina, believes strongly in the power of storytelling to foster culture; he claims, "Talk about numbers, and people's eyes glaze over; talk about one child who died unnecessarily, and no one can walk away from that."[21]

Rituals are the daily or weekly planned routines that occur in an organization. Employees at New Belgium Brewing in Colorado, home of Fat Tire Ale, receive a case of beer a week after a year on the job, conveying the importance of both employees and the company's product.[22] At UPS, every driver and package handler attends a mandatory "three-minute meeting" with their managers to help with communication. The 180-second time limit helps enforce the importance of punctuality in the UPS culture. The Men's Wearhouse pays managers quarterly bonuses when theft (referred to as "shrink") is kept low. That ritual sends a message that "when workers steal from you, they are stealing from themselves and their colleagues."[23]

Ceremonies are formal events, generally performed in front of an audience of organizational members. In the process of turning around the company, Continental Airlines held a ceremony to burn an employee-despised 800-page policy manual. Gordon Bethune, then-CEO of Continental, put together a task force that came up with a new 80-page manual.[24] Other types of ceremonies revolve around celebrations for meeting quality goals, reaching a certain level of profitability, or launching a new product.

ESPOUSED VALUES. **Espoused values** are the beliefs, philosophies, and norms that a company explicitly states. Espoused values can range from published documents, such as a company's vision or mission statement, to verbal statements made to employees by executives and managers. Examples of some of Whole Foods Market's outward representations of espoused values can be found in Table 16-1. What do each of these statements tell you about Whole Foods and what it cares about?

It's certainly important to draw a distinction between espoused values and enacted values. It's one thing for a company to outwardly say something is important; it's another thing for employees to consistently act in ways that support those espoused values. When a company holds to its espoused values over time and regardless of the situations it operates in, the values become more believable both to employees and outsiders. However, in times of economic downturns, staying true to espoused values isn't always easy. Marriott International has been struggling in the most recent economic downturn, like many of its

TABLE 16-1 | The Espoused Values of Whole Foods

Below is a list of the 7 core values that Whole Foods believes lays the foundation for its organizational culture. The company believes that these values set it apart from competing organizations, show others why Whole Foods is a great place to work, and will always be the reasons for the company's existence regardless of how large it grows. More details about each value can be found on the company's Web site.

1. Selling the highest-quality natural and organic products available.
2. Satisfying and delighting our customers.
3. Supporting team member happiness and excellence.
4. Creating wealth through profits and growth.
5. Caring about our communities and our environment.
6. Creating ongoing win–win partnerships with our suppliers.
7. Promoting the health of our stakeholders through healthy-eating education.

Source: www.wholefoodsmarket.com/company/corevalues.php (accessed November 1, 2009).

competitors in the lodging/travel business. It has been very tempting for the company to do everything it can to slash expenses, but its espoused value of always treating its people right prevents cuts that would harm employee benefits. J.W. "Bill" Marriott Jr., the company's chairperson and CEO, states, "If the employees are well taken care of, they'll take care of the customer and the customer will come back. That's basically the core value of the company."[25]

BASIC UNDERLYING ASSUMPTIONS. **Basic underlying assumptions** are the taken-for-granted beliefs and philosophies that are so ingrained that employees simply act on them rather than questioning the validity of their behavior in a given situation.[26] These assumptions represent the deepest and least observable part of a culture and may not be consciously apparent, even to organizational veterans. Edgar Schein, one of the preeminent scholars on the topic of organizational culture, uses the example of safety in an engineering firm. He states, "In an occupation such as engineering, it would be inconceivable to deliberately design something that is unsafe; it is a taken-for-granted assumption that things should be safe."[27] Whatever a company's underlying assumptions are, its hidden beliefs are those that are the most likely to dictate employee behavior and affect employee attitudes. They're also the aspects of an organizational culture that are the most long-lasting and difficult to change.[28]

GENERAL CULTURE TYPES

If we can consider the combination of an organization's observable artifacts, espoused values, and underlying assumptions, we can begin to classify its culture along various dimensions. Of course, there are many different types of organizational cultures, just like there are many different types of personalities. Many researchers have tried to create general typologies that can be used to describe the culture of any organization. For instance, one popular general typology divides organizational culture along two dimensions: solidarity and sociability. Solidarity is the degree to which group members think and act alike, and sociability represents how friendly employees are to one another.[29] Figure 16-2 shows how we might

 16.2

What general and specific types can be used to describe an organization's culture?

FIGURE 16-2   A Typology of Organizational Culture

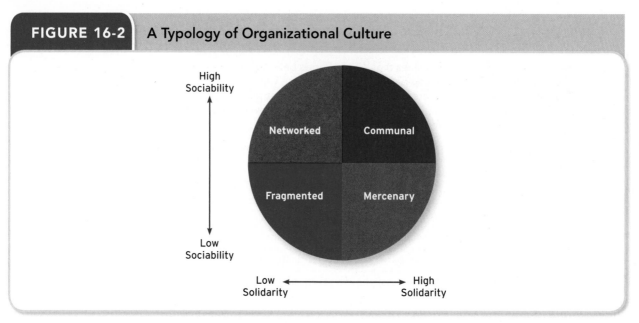

Source: Adapted from R. Goffee and G. Jones, *The Character of a Corporation* (New York: Harper Business, 1998).

describe organizations that are either high or low on these dimensions. Organizations that are low on both dimensions have a **fragmented culture** in which employees are distant and disconnected from one another. Organizations that have cultures in which employees think alike but aren't friendly to one another can be considered **mercenary cultures**. These types of organizations are likely to be very political, "what's in it for me" environments. One example of a mercenary culture can be found in this chapter's **OB at the Bookstore**. Cultures in which all employees are friendly to one another, but everyone thinks differently and does his or her own thing, are **networked cultures**. Many highly creative organizations have a networked culture. Organizations with friendly employees who all think alike are **communal cultures.** There is some evidence that organizations have a tendency to move through the cultures as they get larger. Small organizations generally start out as communal cultures oriented around the owner and founder. As companies grow, they tend to move toward a networked culture, because solidarity is harder to foster when groups get really large.[30] Although we like to think of culture as being stable, it can change, as we discuss later in this chapter.

SPECIFIC CULTURE TYPES

The typology in Figure 16-2 is general enough to be applied to almost any organization. However, there are obviously other ways to classify an organization's culture. In fact, many organizations attempt to manipulate observable artifacts and espoused values to create specific cultures that help them achieve their organizational goals. Some of these specific cultures are more relevant in some industries than in others. Although the number of specific cultures an organization might strive for are virtually endless, we focus on four examples: customer service cultures, safety cultures, diversity cultures, and creativity cultures.

Many organizations try to create a **customer service culture** focused on service quality. After all, 65 percent of the gross domestic product in the United States is generated by service-based organizations.[31] Organizations that have successfully created a service culture have been shown to change employee attitudes and behaviors toward customers.[32] These changes in attitudes and behaviors then manifest themselves in

OB AT THE BOOKSTORE

HOUSE OF CARDS
by William D. Cohan (New York: Doubleday, 2009).

"Our first desire is to promote from within. If somebody with an MBA degree applies for a job, we will certainly not hold it against them, but we are looking for people with PSD degrees"—that is, those who were poor and smart, with a deep desire to become rich.

That statement, taken from a memo to the Bear Stearns's partners written by Ace Greenberg, its CEO, effectively summarizes a key reason for the downfall of the fifth largest investment bank in the United States: its mercenary and overwhelmingly greedy culture. Cohan outlines in great detail the last 10 days of the 85-year-old firm that was worth $170 a share in 2007, before being sold to JPMorgan Chase for less than the value of the office building in which it resided ($2/share).

Although the investment banking industry as a whole is known for being aggressive, Bear Stearns was notorious as the worst of the bunch. Its culture was extremely political, opportunistic, and greedy. Those values were encouraged by those at the top during its final years, most notably by Greenberg and the most recent CEO, Jimmy Cayne, the championship-level bridge player who continued to attend tournaments during the company's most trying times. The book as a whole offers a great history of exactly what occurred in the 2008 financial meltdown, but it also recounts, in almost painful detail, a culture that was highly insular and clearly at least partially responsible for its final demise. The overall lesson in the story isn't that mercenary cultures can't be effective—Bear Stearns and many others just like it enjoyed great success for a very long period of time. Rather, it shows that organizational culture is highly influenced by the leadership in a company and that even when the environment shifts dramatically, it's difficult for people in organizations with strong cultures to change their behavior.

higher levels of customer satisfaction and sales.[33] Figure 16-3 illustrates the process of creating a service culture and the effects it has on company results. Numerous companies claim that the sole reason for their continued existence is their ability to create a service culture in their organization when it wasn't originally present.[34] In our chapter's opening example, a customer- (patient-) oriented culture has helped the Mayo Clinic become a world-renowned healthcare provider and differentiated it from its competitors. Companies might go out of their way to hire customer-oriented employees, but research also clearly shows that a customer service culture can lead to even more customer-oriented behaviors on the part of their employees and a larger bottom-line profit as a result.[35]

It's not uncommon for manufacturing or medical companies to go through a string of accidents or injuries that potentially harm their employees. For these organizations, creating a **safety culture** is of paramount importance. There is a clear difference between organizations in terms of the degree to which safe behaviors at work are viewed as expected

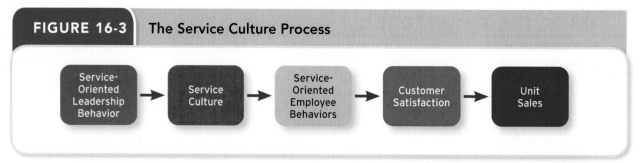

FIGURE 16-3   The Service Culture Process

Service-Oriented Leadership Behavior → Service Culture → Service-Oriented Employee Behaviors → Customer Satisfaction → Unit Sales

Source: Adapted from B. Schneider, M.G. Ehrhart, D.M. Mayer, J.L. Saltz, and K. Niles-Jolly, "Understanding Organization–Customer Links in Service Settings," *Academy of Management Journal* 48 (2005), pp. 1017–32.

and valued.[36] A positive safety culture has been shown to reduce accidents and increase safety-based citizenship behaviors.[37] A safety culture also reduces treatment errors in medical settings.[38] General Electric recently instigated an investigation into some of its service centers that were suffering unacceptable levels of accidents and injuries. Plants that were having problems underwent a process to energize their safety cultures through a series of two-day meetings that identified safety problems and potential solutions. Although GE does not expect all of its problems to be fixed overnight, it's so satisfied with the new culture created at these plants that it's working on rolling out similar programs in all of its 67 service centers across the United States.[39] As with many changes, it's very important that management's actions match its words. One study found that employees were highly cynical of a safety program when they perceived a mismatch between espoused and enacted safety values by management.[40] What also becomes clear in a recent meta-analysis is that having a safety-oriented culture means higher levels of safety performance and fewer injuries and accidents for an organization.[41]

There are a number of reasons why an organization might want to foster a **diversity culture**. What images come to mind when you think of Denny's? Do you think of the nation's largest family-style, full-service restaurant chain in the country and the Grand Slam breakfast, or do you think of race discrimination? Although the lawsuits that charged company discrimination against African Americans were settled back in 1994, the stigma of Denny's discrimination complaints still lingers. Since 1994, Denny's has maintained

Denny's has worked hard to recover from lawsuits charging it discriminated against minorities. In the process it developed techniques to encourage diversity that other firms have now adopted.

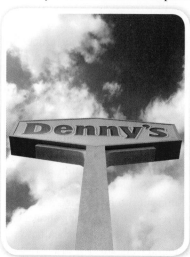

a position within the company of chief diversity officer, whose sole responsibility is to help create a culture of diversity. Denny's has since become a prime example of how to aggressively lead a charge toward a diversity culture. What used to be an all-white, all-male organization has tried to transform itself by hiring a large number of new minority managers and franchise owners, replacing half of the all-male board of directors with women, conducting diversity sensitivity training sessions, and performing a whole host of other symbolic actions. Many of the techniques used by Denny's are now recognized as key elements in successful corporate diversity initiatives.[42]

Given the importance of new ideas and innovation in many industries, it's understandable that some organizations focus on fostering a **creativity culture**. Creativity cultures affect both the quantity and quality of creative ideas within an organization.[43] Google recently put policies in place that will allow its engineers to spend 20 percent of their working time pursuing projects that they feel passionate about to foster innovation at the organization.[44] In part to foster a culture of creativity, Pfizer Canada has banned all e-mails and voice mails on weekends and after 6:00 p.m. on weekdays to keep their employees fresh while they're on the job. The company feels this 12-hour break has led to a higher-quality flow of ideas and provided a morale boost to go along with it.[45] SAS, the business analytics software firm based in North Carolina, has a full-blown infant day center, a Montessori school, and an after-school program to allow employees to spend more time thinking about creative solutions to problems and less time worrying about their kids.[46] To see whether you've spent time working in a creativity culture, see our **OB Assessments** feature.

CULTURE STRENGTH

Although most organizations seem to strive for one, not all companies have a culture that creates a sense of definite norms and appropriate behaviors for their employees. If you've worked for a company and can't identify whether it has a strong culture or not, it probably doesn't. A high level of **culture strength** exists when employees definitively agree about the way things are supposed to happen within the organization (high consensus) and when their subsequent behaviors are consistent with those expectations (high intensity).[47] As shown in Figure 16-4, a strong culture serves to unite and direct employees. Weak cultures

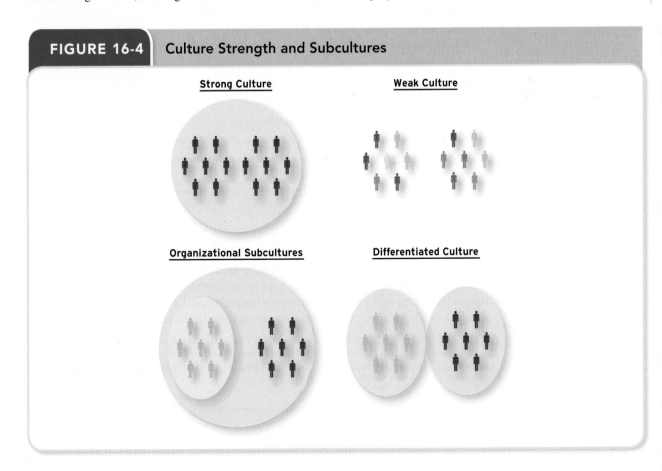

FIGURE 16-4 Culture Strength and Subcultures

Strong Culture

Weak Culture

Organizational Subcultures

Differentiated Culture

OB ASSESSMENTS

CREATIVITY CULTURE

Have you experienced a creativity culture? This assessment is designed to measure two facets of that type of culture. Think of your current job, or the last job that you held (even if it was a part-time or summer job). If you haven't worked, think of a current or former student group that developed strong norms for how tasks should be done. Answer each question using the response scale provided. Then subtract your answers to the boldfaced questions from 6, with the difference being your new answer for that question. For example, if your original answer for question 7 was "4," your new answer is "2" (6 – 4). Then sum up your scores for the two facets. (For more assessments relevant to this chapter, please visit the Online Learning Center at www.mhhe.com/colquitt).

1 STRONGLY DISAGREE	2 DISAGREE	3 UNCERTAIN	4 AGREE	5 STRONGLY AGREE

1. New ideas are readily accepted here. _____

2. This company is quick to respond when changes need to be made. _____

3. Management here is quick to spot the need to do things differently. _____

4. This organization is very flexible; it can quickly change procedures to meet new conditions and solve problems as they arise. _____

5. People in this organization are always searching for new ways of looking at problems. _____

6. It is considered extremely important here to follow the rules. _____

7. **People can ignore formal procedures and rules if it helps to get the job done.** _____

8. Everything has to be done by the book. _____

9. **It is not necessary to follow procedures to the letter around here.** _____

10. **Nobody gets too upset if people break the rules around here.** _____

SCORING AND INTERPRETATION

Innovation: Sum up items 1-5. _____

Formalization: Sum up items 6-10. _____

If your score is 22 or above for either facet, your organization or workgroup is high on that particular dimension. Creative cultures tend to be high on innovation and low on formalization. So if your score was 22 or above for innovation and 21 or below for formalization, then chances are you've experienced a strong creativity culture.

Source: M.G. Patterson, M.A. West, V.J. Shackleton, J.F. Dawson, R. Lawthom, S. Maitlis, D.L. Robinson, and A.M. Wallace, "Validating the Organizational Climate Measure: Links to Managerial Practices, Productivity and Innovation," *Journal of Organizational Behavior* 26 (2005), pp. 379–408. Reprinted with permission of Wiley-Blackwell.

exist when employees disagree about the way things are supposed to be or what's expected of them, meaning that there is nothing to unite or direct their attitudes and actions.

Strong cultures take a long time to develop and are very difficult to change. Individuals working within strong cultures are typically very aware of it. However, this discussion brings us to an important point: "Strong" cultures are not always "good" cultures. Strong cultures guide employee attitudes and behaviors, but that doesn't always mean that they guide them toward the most successful organizational outcomes. As such, it's useful to recognize some of the positive and negative aspects of having a strong organizational culture. Table 16-2 lists some of the advantages and disadvantages.[48] You might have noticed that all of the advantages in the left-hand column of Table 16-2 allow the organization to become more efficient at whatever aspect of culture is strong within the organization. The right-hand column's disadvantages all lead toward an organization's inability to adapt.

In some cases, the culture of an organization is not really strong or weak. Instead, there might be **subcultures** that unite a smaller subset of the organization's employees. These subgroups may be created because there is a strong leader in one area of the company that engenders different norms and values or because different divisions in a company act independently and create their own cultures. As shown in Figure 16-4, subcultures exist when the overall organizational culture is supplemented by another culture governing a more specific set of employees. Subcultures are more likely to exist in large organizations than they are in small companies.[49] Most organizations don't mind having subcultures, as long as they don't interfere with the values of the overall culture. In fact, subcultures can be very useful for organizations if there are certain areas of the organization that have different demands and needs for their employees.[50] However, when their values don't match those of the larger organization, we call subcultures **countercultures**. Countercultures can sometimes serve a useful purpose by challenging the values of the overall organization or signifying the need for change.[51] In extreme cases however, countercultures can split the organization's culture right down the middle, resulting in the differentiated culture in Figure 16-4. See this chapter's **OB on Screen** for an example of a subculture within a larger culture.

 16.3

What makes a culture strong, and is it always good for an organization to have a strong culture?

MAINTAINING AN ORGANIZATIONAL CULTURE

Clearly an organization's culture can be described in many ways, from espoused values and underlying assumptions, to general dimensions such as solidarity or sociability, to more specific types such as service cultures or safety cultures. No matter how we describe an

16.4

How do organizations maintain their culture and how do they change it?

TABLE 16-2	Pros and Cons of a Strong Culture

ADVANTAGES OF A STRONG CULTURE	DISADVANTAGES OF A STRONG CULTURE
Differentiates the organization from others	Makes merging with another organization more difficult
Allows employees to identify themselves with the organization	Attracts and retains similar kinds of employees, thereby limiting diversity of thought
Facilitates desired behaviors among employees	Can be "too much of a good thing" if it creates extreme behaviors among employees
Creates stability within the organization	Makes adapting to the environment more difficult

OB ON SCREEN

NEW IN TOWN

This will be an exciting utilization of new branding for capitalizing on a highly profitable demographic.

With those words, mid-level executive Lucy Hill (Renee Zellweger) tells a group of employees at a food processing plant in New Ulm, Minnesota (pop. 13,595), that change is coming in *New in Town* (Dir.: Jonas Elmer, Columbia Pictures, 2009). Her "fancy" words and corporate attitude don't go over well with the plant's employees—especially once they find out what that "change" really means. Lucy is a hard-driving Miami businesswoman in a large food conglomerate, accustomed to the "numbers mean everything" and "people are objects" culture that the corporate offices exude. Somewhat against her wishes (but willing to do whatever it takes to succeed), Lucy gets sent to Minnesota to downsize and run a small-town plant that is losing money. What she runs into is a section of the company that she can hardly believe exists. The small town plant is a completely different culture than what she's used to.

The first people she butts heads with are Stu Kopenhafer (J.K. Simmons) and the union representative, Ted Mitchell (Harry Connick Jr.). Stu is a crusty old manager who likes things the way they are and has a high level of distrust toward corporate employees and outsiders in general. To say Stu is skeptical of Lucy's goals for the plant would be a huge understatement. Lucy's run-ins with Stu and Ted near the beginning of the movie help highlight the differences between the plant and the corporate atmosphere that Lucy knows so well. One of the central struggles Lucy faces thus pertains to deciding which of the two cultures actually provides a better fit for her. The New Ulm plant is a definite subculture within the overall company, but whether that subculture is useful to the organization, or instead really a counterculture, you'll have to decide for yourself.

organization's culture, however, that culture will be put to the test when an organization's founders and original employees begin to recruit and hire new members. If those new members don't fit the culture, then the culture may become weakened or differentiated. However, two processes can conspire to help keep cultures strong: attraction–selection–attrition and socialization.

ATTRACTION–SELECTION–ATTRITION (ASA). The **ASA framework** holds that potential employees will be attracted to organizations whose cultures match their own personality, meaning that some potential job applicants won't apply due to a perceived lack of fit.[52] In addition, organizations will select candidates based on whether their personalities fit the culture, further weeding out potential "misfits." Finally, those people who still don't fit will either be unhappy or ineffective when working in the organization, which leads to attrition (i.e., voluntary or involuntary turnover).

Several companies can provide an example of ASA in action. FedEx has worked hard to create a culture of ethics. The executives at FedEx believe that a strong ethical culture will attract ethical employees who will then strengthen moral behavior at FedEx.[53] The Cheesecake Factory believes that selection is where maintaining a culture begins. Management suggests that its heavily service-oriented culture calls for certain types of employees; teaching people how to perform regular restaurant duties is possible, but teaching people to have the right personality and attitudes is not. As a company, it therefore consistently tries to identify the traits that allow employees to thrive in a Cheesecake Factory environment.[54] Of course, attraction and selection processes don't always align employees' personalities with organizational culture—one reason voluntary and involuntary turnover occurs in every organization.

SOCIALIZATION. In addition to taking advantage of attraction–selection–attrition, organizations also maintain an organizational culture by shaping and molding new employees. Starting a new job with a company is a stressful, complex, and challenging undertaking for both employees and organizations.[55] In reality, no outsider can fully grasp or understand the culture of an organization simply by looking at artifacts visible from outside the company. A complete understanding of organizational culture is a process that happens over time. **Socialization** is the primary process by which employees learn the social knowledge that enables them to understand and adapt to the organization's culture. It's a process that begins before an employee starts work and doesn't end until an employee leaves the organization.[56] What is it that an employee needs to learn and adapt to in order to be socialized into his or her new role within an organization? Most of the important information can be grouped into six dimensions, highlighted in Figure 16-5.[57] Research shows that each of these six dimensions is an important area in the process of socialization. Each has unique contributions to job performance, organizational commitment, and person–organization fit.[58]

Socialization happens in three relatively distinct stages. The **anticipatory stage** happens prior to an employee spending even one second on the job. It starts the moment a potential employee hears the name of the organization. When you see the company name "Microsoft," what does it make you think about? What are the images that come to your mind? Anticipatory socialization begins as soon as a potential employee develops an image of what it must be like to work for a given company. The bulk of the information acquired during this stage occurs during the recruitment and selection processes that employees go through prior to joining an organization. Relevant information includes the way employees are treated during the recruitment process, the things that organizational insiders tell them about the organization, and any other information employees acquire about what the organization is like and what working there entails.

The **encounter stage** begins the day an employee starts work. There are some things about an organization and its culture that can only be learned once a person becomes an organizational insider. During this stage, new employees compare the information they acquired as outsiders during the anticipatory stage with what the organization is really like now that they're insiders. To the degree that the information in the two stages is similar, employees will have a smoother time adjusting to the organization. Problems occur when

FIGURE 16-5   Dimensions Addressed in Most Socialization Efforts

Source: G.T. Chao, A.M. O'Leary-Kelly, S. Wolf, H.J. Klein, and P.D. Gardner, "Organizational Socialization: Its Content and Consequences," *Journal of Applied Psychology* 79 (1994), pp. 730–43. Copyright © 1994 by the American Psychological Association. Adapted with permission. No further reproduction or distribution is permitted without written permission from the American Psychological Association.

the two sets of information don't quite match. This mismatch of information is called **reality shock**. Reality shock is best exemplified by hearing an employee say something to the effect of, "Working at this company is not nearly what I expected it to be." Surveys suggest that as many as one-third of new employees leave an organization within the first 90 days as a result of unmet expectations.[59] The goal of the organization's socialization efforts should be to minimize reality shock as much as possible. We'll describe some ways that organizations can do this effectively in our Application section that concludes this chapter.

The final stage of socialization is one of **understanding and adaptation**. During this stage, newcomers come to learn the content areas of socialization and internalize the norms and expected behaviors of the organization. The important part of this stage is change on the part of the employee. By looking back at the content areas of socialization in Figure 16-5, you can begin to picture what a perfectly socialized employee looks like. The employee has adopted the goals and values of the organization, understands what the organization has been through, and can converse with others in the organization using technical language and specific terms that only insiders would understand. In addition, the employee enjoys and gets along with other employees in the organization, knows who to go to in order to make things happen, and understands and can perform the key functions of his or her job. Talk about the perfect employee! Needless to say, that's quite a bit of information to gain—it's not a process that happens overnight. Some would say that this last stage of socialization never truly ends, as an organization's culture continues to change and evolve over time.[60] However, organizations also know that the more quickly and effectively an employee is socialized, the sooner that employee becomes a productive worker within the organization.

It's important to note that the length of the socialization process varies depending on the characteristics of the employee, not just the company. For example, some employees might progress more rapidly through the stages because of the knowledge they possess, their ability to recognize cultural cues, or their adaptability to their environment. In fact, there is growing evidence that proactivity on the part of employee being socialized has a significant effect on socialization outcomes.[61] Some organizations might help their employees socialize more quickly because they have stronger cultures or cultures that are more easily understandable. The biggest difference though is that some organizations simply work harder at socializing their employees than others.

CHANGING AN ORGANIZATIONAL CULTURE

Given all the effort it takes to create and maintain a culture, changing a culture once one has been established is perhaps even more difficult. In fact, estimates put the rate of successful major culture change at less than 20 percent.[62] At eBay, CEO John Donahoe and chief technology officer Mark Carges are trying to change the culture to avoid the sense that every little decision must be an exercise in bureaucracy, with careful examination of all permutations of a possible outcome before acting. "Now we're actually going to put something out before we've got all the answers," claims Carges.[63] Their goal is to get eBay's employees to think about technology differently—a major culture shift for the company and many of its analytically inclined employees. One way they're initiating this shift is by moving employees who traditionally would not interact together in the workplace, such as making business staffers and software developers sit next to one another.[64] Changes like this can send a loud signal about what's going to be important in the future, even in the midst of massive change. In practice though, two other ways are more common methods to change a culture: changes in leadership and mergers or acquisitions.

CHANGES IN LEADERSHIP. There is perhaps no bigger driver of culture than the leaders and top executives of organizations. Just as the founders and originators of organizations set the tone and develop the culture of a new company, subsequent CEOs and presidents leave their mark on the culture. Many times, leaders are expected simply to sustain the culture that has already been created.[65] At other times, leaders have to be a driving force for change as the environment around the organization shifts. This expectation is one of the biggest reasons organizations change their top leadership. For example, Nortel Networks recently hired two former Cisco executives into the roles of chief operating officer and chief technology officer. It is Nortel's hope that these executives will help bring some of Cisco's culture of aggressiveness to Nortel and thus allow it to compete more effectively in the high-technology industry environment.[66]

MERGERS AND ACQUISITIONS. Merging two companies with two distinct cultures is a surefire way to change the culture in an organization. The problem is that there is just no way to know what the culture will look like after the merger takes place. What the new culture will resemble is a function of both the strength of the two cultures involved in the merger and how similar they are to each other.[67] Ideally, a new culture would be created out of a compromise in which the best of both companies is represented by the new culture. There are many stories that have arisen from the mergers of companies with very different cultures: AOL/Time Warner, Exxon/Mobil, HP/Compaq, and RJR/Nabisco, to name a few. Unfortunately, very few of these stories are good ones. Mergers rarely result in the strong culture that managers hope will appear when they make the decision to merge. In fact, most merged companies operate under a differentiated culture for an extended period of time. Some of them never really adopt a new identity, and when they do, many of them are seen as failures by the outside world. This perception is especially true in global mergers, in which each of the companies not only has a different organizational culture but is from a different country as well, as our **OB Internationally** box details. Every now and then though, a merger happens in which the leadership focuses on culture from the start, such was the case with the merger of Delta and Northwest Airlines. Rather than risk creating a fragmented culture, Delta CEO Richard Anderson went to the extreme of changing the ID numbers on every employee's security badge, so that employees could not tell whether a colleague started with Delta or Northwest. According to Anderson, he wanted to avoid a situation in which "employees were constantly sizing up which side you were on."[68]

Merging two different cultures has major effects on the attitudes and behaviors of organizational employees. Companies merge for many different strategic reasons, and

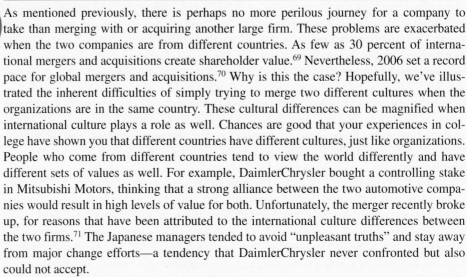

OB INTERNATIONALLY

As mentioned previously, there is perhaps no more perilous journey for a company to take than merging with or acquiring another large firm. These problems are exacerbated when the two companies are from different countries. As few as 30 percent of international mergers and acquisitions create shareholder value.[69] Nevertheless, 2006 set a record pace for global mergers and acquisitions.[70] Why is this the case? Hopefully, we've illustrated the inherent difficulties of simply trying to merge two different cultures when the organizations are in the same country. These cultural differences can be magnified when international culture plays a role as well. Chances are good that your experiences in college have shown you that different countries have different cultures, just like organizations. People who come from different countries tend to view the world differently and have different sets of values as well. For example, DaimlerChrysler bought a controlling stake in Mitsubishi Motors, thinking that a strong alliance between the two automotive companies would result in high levels of value for both. Unfortunately, the merger recently broke up, for reasons that have been attributed to the international culture differences between the two firms.[71] The Japanese managers tended to avoid "unpleasant truths" and stay away from major change efforts—a tendency that DaimlerChrysler never confronted but also could not accept.

There are many stories of failed international mergers, and one of the greatest reasons for them is that corporations fail to recognize the impact that national culture differences (in addition to organizational culture differences) have on their ability to be successful. One such merger that doesn't intend to fall victim to this issue is the creation of a joint venture between the telecommunication giants Nokia (Finland) and Siemens (Germany). This merger between two very different firms is projected to earn annual sales of $20 billion. The CEOs of the two companies (Siemens's Klaus Kleinfeld and Nokia's Olli-Pekka Kallasvuo) are determined not to let differences in their national or organizational cultures cause the merger fatal problems. Toward this end, cultural integration has been at the forefront of their minds. Although much of the main business will be located in Germany, headquarters for the new company will be in Helsinki. Both CEOs are determined for each company to learn from the other.[72]

though many managers and executives may realize its importance, whether the cultures will match is rarely the deciding criterion.[73] Slightly less troublesome but still a major hurdle to overcome are acquisitions. In most instances, the company doing the acquiring has a dominant culture to which the other is expected to adapt. A recent example is the acquisition of Anheuser-Busch by the Belgian-based firm InBev. InBev and its CEO Carlos Brito are known for their heavy-handed, cost-cutting ways; Anheuser-Busch is known for its free-spending atmosphere, in which employees get free admission to the company's theme parks and two cases of free beer each month. One industry analyst joked that the Budweiser Clydesdales get better treatment than the average InBev employee.[74] Another example comes from the acquisition of Mail Boxes Etc. by UPS. Strategically, the acquisition had many advantages that supposedly would allow UPS to compete better with FedEx and the U.S. Postal Service. However, the culture clash between the efficiency and rigidness of UPS and the entrepreneurial spirit of Mail Boxes Etc. franchisees has caused UPS some major headaches.[75] We've noted how difficult it is to get just one person to adapt to an established culture through the socialization process. Can you imagine how difficult it is to change an entire organization, all at one time?

One of the major reasons that one company purchases another is simply to acquire the technology that it has. In such cases, the acquired company usually is expected to change to fit the buyer's culture. However, a new approach being used by several companies, including Hewlett-Packard, Yahoo, and Cisco, is to buy companies with the intention of infusing their different culture into their own.[76] Under CEO Mark Hurd, HP is pursuing smaller, more nimble, and more creative companies to jumpstart its own stagnant, bureaucratic culture. Although this process of "innovation via absorption" looks good on paper, it's very difficult, and companies need to think twice about changing the fundamental cultures they have built.

SUMMARY: WHY DO SOME ORGANIZATIONS HAVE DIFFERENT CULTURES THAN OTHERS?

So why do some organizations have different cultures than others? As shown in Figure 16-6, attraction–selection–attrition processes, socialization, changes in leadership, and mergers and acquisitions shape the three components of organizational culture: basic underlying assumptions, espoused values, and observable artifacts. Specific combinations of those culture components then give rise to both general and specific culture types. For example, cultures can be categorized on the basis of solidarity and sociability into fragmented, mercenary, communal, and networked types. Cultures can also be categorized into more specific types, such as customer service, safety, diversity, and creativity. Finally, those general and specific types can be further classified according to the strength of the culture. Taken together, these processes explain "what it's like" within the hallways of a given organization.

HOW IMPORTANT IS ORGANIZATIONAL CULTURE?

Normally, this section is where we summarize the importance of organizational culture by describing how it affects job performance and organizational commitment—the two outcomes in our integrative model of OB. However (similar to organizational structure in Chapter 15), it's difficult to summarize the importance of culture in this way because there

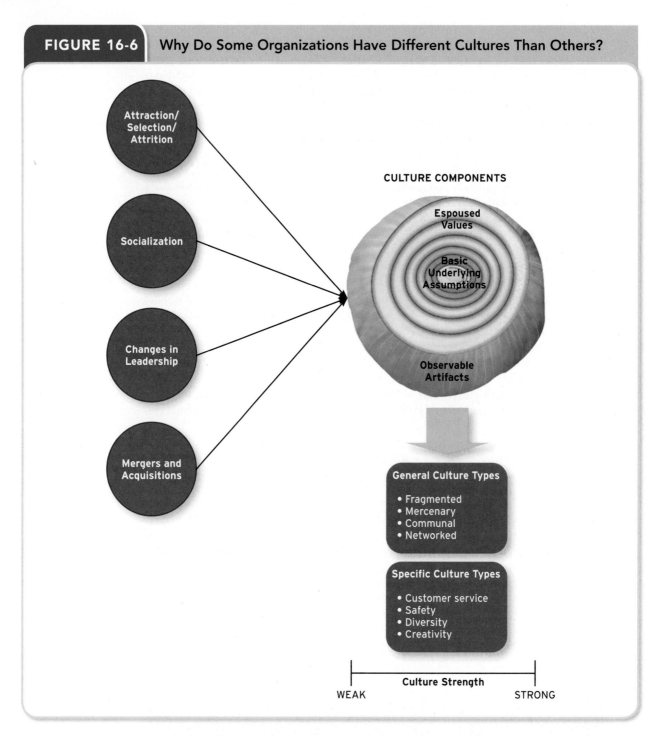

FIGURE 16-6   Why Do Some Organizations Have Different Cultures Than Others?

Attraction/
Selection/
Attrition

Socialization

Changes in
Leadership

Mergers and
Acquisitions

CULTURE COMPONENTS

Espoused
Values

Basic
Underlying
Assumptions

Observable
Artifacts

General Culture Types

- Fragmented
- Mercenary
- Communal
- Networked

Specific Culture Types

- Customer service
- Safety
- Diversity
- Creativity

Culture Strength

WEAK   STRONG

are so many different types and dimensions of the concept. High solidarity cultures, high sociability cultures, diversity cultures, creativity cultures, and so forth all have different effects on performance and commitment—effects that likely vary across different types of organizations and industries.

Regardless of the type of culture we're talking about however, one concept remains important for any employee in any business: fit. Think for a moment about working for an organization whose culture doesn't match your own values. Maybe you work for an organization that produces a product that you don't believe in or that might be harmful to others, such as Phillip Morris, Budweiser, or Harrah's casinos. Maybe your employer is an organization that expects you to perform questionable behaviors from an ethical standpoint or produces a product that's of poor quality. **Person–organization fit** is the degree to which a person's personality and values match the culture of an organization. Employees judge fit by thinking about the values they prioritize the most, then judging whether the organization shares those values. Table 16-3 provides a set of values that many people have used to judge fit. Which of these values would you say are the most important to you?

Two recent meta-analyses illustrate the importance of person–organization fit to employees.[77] When employees feel that their values and personality match those of the organization, they experience higher levels of *job satisfaction* and feel less *stress* about their day-to-day tasks. They also feel higher levels of *trust* toward their managers. Taken together, those results illustrate why person–organization fit is so highly correlated with organizational commitment, one of the two outcomes in our integrative model of OB (see Figure 16-7). When employees feel they fit with their organization's culture, they're much more likely to develop an emotional attachment to the company. The effects of fit on job performance are weaker, however. In general, person–organization fit is more related to citizenship behaviors than to task performance. Employees who sense a good fit are therefore more likely to help their colleagues and "go the extra mile" to benefit the company.

16.5

What is person–organization fit and how does it affect job performance and organizational commitment?

APPLICATION: MANAGING SOCIALIZATION

Most organizations recognize the importance of having employees adapt to the culture of their organization quickly. Luckily, there are a number of actions that organizations can take to help their employees adapt from the first day they walk in the door. Table 16-4 highlights some of the different tactics organizations can use when socializing their employees. Note that companies can take two very different approaches to the socialization process. The left-hand column represents a view of socialization in which the goal of the process is to have newcomers adapt to the organization's culture. This view assumes that the organization has a strong culture and definite norms and values that it wants employees to adopt, which is not always the case. Some organizations don't have a strong culture that they want employees to adapt to, or they might be trying to change their culture and want new employees to come in and "shake things up." The socialization tactics listed in the right-hand column of Table 16-4 might be more appropriate in such circumstances. In addition to the socialization tactics listed in the table, there are three other major ways in which organizations routinely and effectively help speed up the socialization process of newcomers: realistic job previews, orientation programs, and mentoring.

REALISTIC JOB PREVIEWS. One of the most inexpensive and effective ways of reducing early turnover among new employees is through the use of **realistic job previews**.[78] Realistic job previews (RJPs) occur during the anticipatory stage of socialization during the recruitment process. They involve making sure a potential employee has an accurate picture of what working for an organization is going to be like by highlighting both the positive *and* the negative aspects of the job.[79] Kal Tire, a leading Canadian automotive retail outlet, allows job candidates to spend an entire day inside the company becoming familiar with the organization and the job for which they're applying. By

16.6

What steps can organizations take to make sure that newcomers will fit with their culture?

TABLE 16-3	Values Used to Judge Fit with a Culture

Flexibility	Adaptability
Stability	Predictability
Being innovative	Take advantage of opportunities
A willingness to experiment	Risk taking
Being careful	Autonomy
Being rule oriented	Being analytical
Paying attention to detail	Being precise
Being team oriented	Sharing information freely
Emphasizing a single culture	Being people oriented
Fairness	Respect for the individual's rights
Tolerance	Informality
Being easy going	Being calm
Being supportive	Being aggressive
Decisiveness	Action orientation
Taking initiative	Being reflective
Achievement orientation	Being demanding
Taking individual responsibility	High expectations for performance
Opportunities for growth	High pay for good performance
Security of employment	Offers praise for good performance
Low level of conflict	Confronting conflict directly
Developing friends at work	Fitting in
Working in collaboration with others	Enthusiasm for the job
Working long hours	Not being constrained by rules
Having an emphasis on quality	Being distinctive from others
Having a good reputation	Being socially responsible
Being results oriented	Having a clear guiding philosophy
Being competitive	Being highly organized

Source: C.A. O'Reilly, J.A. Chatman, and D.F. Caldwell, "People and Organizational Culture: A Profile Comparison Approach to Assessing Person–Organization Fit," *Academy of Management Journal* 34 (1991), pp. 487–516. Copyright © 1991 Academy of Management. Reproduced with permission of Academy of Management via Copyright Clearance Center.

allowing applicants to see what the organization's idea of customer service is and the job demands of road tire repairs, Kal Tire is effectively reducing the likelihood of significant reality shock and shortening the encounter stage that generally accompanies initial employment.[80]

| FIGURE 16-7 | Effects of Person–Organization Fit on Performance and Commitment |

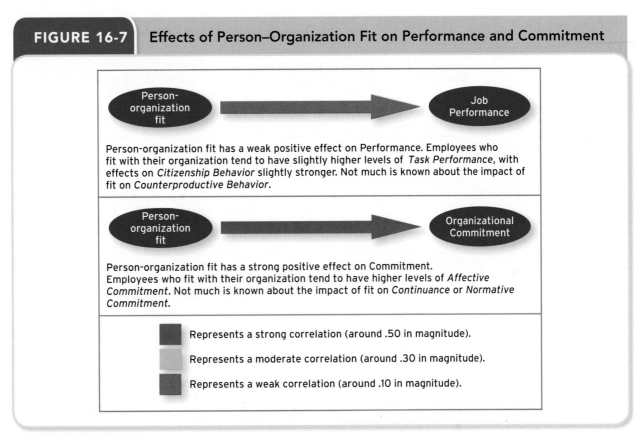

Sources: W. Arthur Jr., S.T. Bell, A.J. Villado, and D. Doverspike, "The Use of Person-Organization Fit in Employment Related Decision Making: An Assessment of Its Criterion-Related Validity," *Journal of Applied Psychology* 91 (2007), pp. 786–801; and A.L. Kristof-Brown, R.D. Zimmerman, and E.C. Johnson, "Consequences of Individuals' Fit at Work: A Meta-Analysis of Person–Job, Person–Organization, Person–Group, and Person–Supervisor Fit," *Personnel Psychology* 58 (2005), pp. 281–342.

ORIENTATION PROGRAMS. One effective way to start the socialization process is by having new employees attend some form of **newcomer orientation** session. Apparently most organizations agree, given that 64–93 percent of all organizations use some form of orientation training process.[81] Not all orientation programs are alike however, and different types of orientation training can be more effective than others.[82] Orientation programs have been shown to be effective transmitters of socialization content, such that those employees who complete orientation have higher levels of satisfaction, commitment, and performance than those who don't.[83] General Motors has a unique orientation program set up for its new hires in the Michigan area, called JumpStart. The program is designed to indoctrinate new employees into the GM culture, which GM believes will allow these employees to become productive much more quickly. Each new employee is able to join up to five different committees that represent a different aspect of GM's culture, in which they learn about key values, network with employees from different areas of the country, and interact with business leaders.[84]

MENTORING. One of the most popular pieces of advice given to college students as they begin their careers is that they need to find a mentor or coach within their organization.[85] **Mentoring** is a process by which a junior-level employee (protégé) develops a deep and long-lasting relationship with a more senior-level employee (mentor) within the

TABLE 16-4	Tactics Organizations Use to Socialize New Employees

TACTICS DESIGNED TO *ENCOURAGE* ADAPTATION TO THE ORGANIZATION'S CULTURE	TACTICS DESIGNED TO *DISCOURAGE* ADAPTATION TO THE ORGANIZATION'S CULTURE
Orient new employees along with a group of other new employees.	Orient new employees by themselves.
Put newcomers through orientation apart from current organizational members.	Allow newcomers to interact with current employees while they are being oriented.
Provide hurdles that are required to be met prior to organizational membership.	Allow organizational membership regardless of whether any specific requirements have been met.
Provide role models for newcomers.	Use no examples of what an employee is supposed to be like.
Constantly remind newcomers that they are now part of a group and that this new group helps define who they are.	Constantly affirm to newcomers that they are to be themselves and that they were chosen for the organization based on who they are.

Source: Adapted from G.R. Jones, "Socialization Tactics, Self-Efficacy, and Newcomers' Adjustments to Organizations," *Academy of Management Journal* 29 (1986), pp. 262–79; J. Van Maanen and E.H. Schein, "Toward a Theory of Organizational Socialization," *Research in Organizational Behavior* 1 (1979), pp. 209–64.

organization. The mentor can provide social knowledge, resources, and psychological support to the protégé both at the beginning of employment and as the protégé continues his or her career with the company. Mentoring has always existed in companies on an informal basis. However, as organizations continue to learn about the strong benefits of these relationships, they're more frequently instituting mentoring programs that formally match newcomers with mentors.[86] Formal programs allow the company to provide consistent information, train mentors, and ensure that all newcomers have the opportunity to develop one of these fruitful relationships. The Chubb Group of insurance companies based in New Jersey plans to start a group mentoring program among female employees in which multiple protégés meet regularly with multiple mentors.[87] This process has worked well for Budco, a marketing services and distribution firm that works with GM and Disney, which pairs four protégés with two mentors and has them meet twice a month. Group mentoring at the 850-employee company has significantly reduced turnover among new hires.[88]

TAKEAWAYS

16.1   Organizational culture is the shared social knowledge within an organization regarding the rules, norms, and values that shape the attitudes and behaviors of its employees. There are three components of organizational culture: observable artifacts, espoused values, and basic underlying assumptions. Observable artifacts include symbols, physical structures, language, stories, rituals, and ceremonies.

16.2 An organization's culture can be described on dimensions such as solidarity and sociability to create four general culture types: networked, communal, fragmented, and mercenary. Organizations often strive to create a more specific cultural emphasis, as in customer service cultures, safety cultures, diversity cultures, and creativity cultures.

16.3 Strong cultures have the ability to influence employee behaviors and attitudes. Strong cultures exist when employees agree on the way things are supposed to happen and their behaviors are consistent with those expectations. Strong cultures are not necessarily good or bad. Generally, a culture's effectiveness depends on how well it matches the company's outside environment. To this degree, adaptive cultures can be very useful.

16.4 Organizations maintain their cultures through attraction, selection, and attrition processes and socialization practices. Organizations change their cultures by changing their leadership or through mergers and acquisitions.

16.5 Person–organization fit is the degree to which a person's values and personality match the culture of the organization. Person–organization fit has a weak positive effect on job performance and a strong positive effect on organizational commitment.

16.6 There are a number of practices organizations can utilize to improve the socialization of new employees, including realistic job previews, orientation programs, and mentoring.

KEY TERMS

- Organizational culture — p. 557
- Observable artifacts — p. 559
- Symbols — p. 559
- Physical structures — p. 559
- Language — p. 560
- Stories — p. 560
- Rituals — p. 560
- Ceremonies — p. 560
- Espoused values — p. 560
- Basic underlying assumptions — p. 561
- Fragmented cultures — p. 562
- Mercenary cultures — p. 562
- Networked cultures — p. 562
- Communal cultures — p. 562
- Customer service culture — p. 562
- Safety culture — p. 563
- Diversity culture — p. 564
- Creativity culture — p. 565
- Culture strength — p. 565
- Subcultures — p. 567
- Countercultures — p. 567
- ASA framework — p. 569
- Socialization — p. 569
- Anticipatory stage — p. 569
- Encounter stage — p. 569
- Reality shock — p. 570
- Understanding and adaptation — p. 570
- Person–organization fit — p. 575
- Realistic job previews — p. 575
- Newcomer orientations — p. 577
- Mentoring — p. 577

DISCUSSION QUESTIONS

16.1 Have you or a family member worked for an organization that you would consider to have a strong culture? If so, what made the culture strong? Did you or they enjoy working there? What do you think led to that conclusion?

16.2   Is it possible for an employee to have personal values that are inconsistent with the values of the organization? If so, how is this inconsistency likely to affect the employee's behavior and attitudes while at work?

16.3   If you had to describe the culture of your university, what would it be like? What observable artifacts are present to be perceived by students? Are there any underlying assumptions that guide your behavior at your university?

16.4   How can two companies with very different cultures that operate in the same industry both be successful? Shouldn't one company's culture automatically be a better fit for the environment?

16.5   If an organization wanted to foster a diversity culture, what steps might management take to ensure that employees will support the new culture? What observable artifacts might a company change to instill this culture?

16.6   When you think of the U.S. Postal Service's culture, what kinds of words come to mind? Where do these impressions come from? Do you think your impressions are accurate? What has the potential to make them inaccurate?

16.7   Think about the last job you started. What are some unique things that companies might do to reduce the amount of reality shock that new employees encounter? Are these methods likely to be expensive?

CASE: THE MAYO CLINIC

One of the Mayo Clinic's continual struggles is to make sure that the people it hires fit into its organization's culture and match its values.[89] One high-level administrator estimates that the Mayo Clinic hits that target approximately 80 percent of the time. The Mayo Clinic's voluntary turnover rate is far below that for the rest of the service industry; for physicians, this rate sits at approximately 2.5 percent, and for nonphysician employees, it is 5 percent.[90] Luckily for Mayo, its culture is widely known, and people come from all over the world wanting to work in it. Doctors accept lower salaries than they could make working in private practice to work in the patient-oriented environment that the Mayo Clinic provides. For example, R.J. Karnes completed his surgery residency at the Mayo Clinic, went to work somewhere else, and then came back, mainly due to the sense of collegiality he enjoyed among the staff. "That easy exchange of knowledge helps afford us the ability to provide the highest level of care for our patients", Karnes says.[91] As it expands, making sure that new employees integrate into the culture effectively is of paramount importance. To help focus new hires on things they might not know and to strengthen the culture, the Clinic sends new employees through an orientation program that focuses heavily on the values, history, and culture of Mayo.[92]

Needless to say, the healthcare industry in the United States is going through massive turbulence and upheaval. The Mayo Clinic is being held up as an example for others of what healthcare could be, if done with the right culture and system. Officials at Mayo believe that they're in a good position to weather whatever healthcare storms might be coming; indeed, they could very well be the model for reform. As such, they're working hard to ensure that their three campuses act and react as one entity and that they continue to improve their healthcare delivery and healthcare management processes.

16.1   Is Mayo's corporate culture something that other healthcare systems can copy? Would it be possible to develop a national healthcare system modeled on the Mayo Clinic? Explain.

16.2 Under most scenarios, companies work hard to keep their culture unique so that it gives them a competitive advantage over others. Do you think Mayo should follow this philosophy? Why or why not?

16.3 Do you think it's possible that the Mayo Clinic's culture could fall to the wayside under the enormous amounts of outside pressure that would occur if healthcare were standardized in the United States? What can it do to keep this collapse from happening?

EXERCISE: UNIVERSITY CULTURE

The purpose of this exercise is to explore how organizational culture is transmitted through observable artifacts. This exercise uses groups, so your instructor will either assign you to a group or ask you to create your own group. The exercise has the following steps:

16.1 Using the table below, consider the observable artifacts that transmit the organizational culture of your university.

Symbols	Think about the logo and images associated with your university. What message do they convey about the university's culture?
Physical Structures	Think about the most visible physical structures on campus. What do those structures say about your university's culture?
Language	Think about the jargon, slang, slogans, and sayings associated with your university. What insights do they offer into the university's culture?
Stories	What anecdotes, accounts, legends, and myths are associated with your university? What messages do they convey about your university's culture?
Rituals	What are the daily or weekly routines that occur at your university, and what do they say about the culture?
Ceremonies	What are the formal events and celebrations that occur at your university, and what cultural signals do they convey?

16.2 Consider the sorts of values listed in Table 16-3. If you consider the symbols, physical structures, language, stories, rituals, and ceremonies identified in Step 1, what core values seem to summarize your university's culture? Using a transparency, laptop, or chalkboard, list the one value that seems to be most central to your university's culture. Then list the three cultural artifacts that are most responsible for transmitting that core value. Present your results to the class.

16.3 Class discussion (whether in groups or as a class) should center on the following topics: Do you like how your university's culture is viewed, as represented in the group presentations? Why or why not? If you wanted to change the university's culture to represent other sorts of values, what process would you use?

ENDNOTES

16.1 Berry, L.L., and K.D. Seltman. *Management Lessons from Mayo Clinic*. New York: McGraw Hill, 2008.

16.2 Finkel, E. "Brand of Brothers." *Modern Healthcare*, March 23, 2009, pp. H4–5.

16.3 Berry and Seltman, *Management Lessons from Mayo Clinic*.

16.4 Gawande, A. "The Cost Conundrum: What a Texas Town Can Teach Us about Health Care." *New Yorker*, June 1, 2009, pp. 36–44.

16.5 Ibid.

16.6 Ibid.

16.7 Berry and Seltman, *Management Lessons from Mayo Clinic*.

16.8 Frey, K.A.; J.A. Leighton; and K.K. Cecala. "Building a Culture of Service Excellence." *Physician Executive* 31 (2005), pp. 40–44.

16.9 Ibid.

16.10 Berry and Seltman, *Management Lessons from Mayo Clinic*.

16.11 Verbeke, W.; M. Volgering; and M. Hessels. "Exploring the Conceptual Expansion within the Field of Organizational Behavior: Organizational Climate and Organizational Culture." *Journal of Management Studies* 35 (1998), pp. 303–29.

16.12 Deal, T.E., and A.A. Kennedy. *Corporate Cultures: The Rites and Rituals of Corporate Life*. Reading, MA: Addison-Wesley, 1982.

16.13 Adapted from O'Reilly, C.A., III; J. Chatman; and D.L. Caldwell. "People and Organizational Culture: A Profile Comparison Approach to Assessing Person–Organization Fit."*Academy of Management Journal* 34 (1991), pp. 487–516; and Tsui, A.S.; Z. Zhang; W. Hui; K.R. Xin, and J.B. Wu. "Unpacking the Relationship between CEO Leadership Behavior and Organizational Culture." *The Leadership Quarterly* 17 (2006), pp. 113–37.

16.14 O'Reilly, C.A., and J.A. Chatman. "Culture as Social Control: Corporations, Cults, and Commitment." In *Research in Organizational Behavior*, Vol. 18, eds. B.M. Staw and L.L. Cummings. Stamford, CT: JAI Press, 1996, pp. 157–200.

16.15 Chatman, J.A. "Matching People and Organizations: Selection and Socialization in Public Accounting Firms." *Administrative Science Quarterly* 36 (1991), pp. 459–84.

16.16 Trice, H.M., and J.M. Beyer. *The Cultures of Work Organizations*. Englewood Cliffs, NJ: Prentice Hall, 1993.

16.17 Kaihla, P. "Best-Kept Secrets of the World's Best Companies." *Business 2.0* 7 (2006), pp. 82–87.

16.18 Stibbe, M. "Mothers of Invention." *Director* 55 (2002), pp. 64–68.

16.19 Shuit, D. P. "Yum Does a 360." *Workforce Management*, April 2005, pp. 59–60.

16.20 Berfield, S. "Howard Schultz Versus Howard Schultz." *BusinessWeek*, August 17, 2009, pp. 28–33.

16.21 Birk, S. "Creating a Culture of Safety: Why CEO's Hold the Key to Improved Outcomes." *Healthcare Executive*, March/April 2009, pp. 15–22.

16.22 Jacobson, D. "Extreme Extras." *Money Magazine*, April 7, 2006, p. 99.

16.23 Kaihla, "Best Kept Secret."

16.24 Higgins, J.M., and C. McAllaster. "If You Want Strategic Change, Don't Forget to Change Your Cultural Artifacts." *Journal of Change Management* 4 (2004), pp. 63–74.

16.25 Gunther, M. "Marriott Gets a Wake-Up Call." *Fortune*, July 6, 2009, pp. 62–66.

16.26 Schein, E.H. "Organizational Culture." *American Psychologist* 45 (1990), pp. 109–19.

16.27 Schein, E. H. *Organization Culture and Leadership.* San Francisco, CA: Jossey-Bass, 2004.

16.28 Schein, E.H. "What Is Culture?" In *Reframing Organizational Culture,* ed. P.J. Frost, L.F. Moore, M.R. Louis, C.C. Lundberg, and J. Martin. Beverly Hills, CA: Sage, 1991, pp. 243–53.

16.29 Goffee, R., and G. Jones. *The Character of a Corporation.* New York: Harper Business, 1998.

16.30 Ibid.

16.31 Lum, S.; and B.C. Moyer. "Gross Product by Industry, 1995–1997." *Survey of Current Business,* November 1998, pp. 20–40.

16.32 Schneider, B.; D.E. Bowen; M.G. Ehrhart; and K.M. Holcombe. "The Climate for Service: Evolution of a Construct." In *Handbook of Organizational Culture and Climate,* eds. N.M. Ashkanasy, C. Wilderom, and M.F. Peterson. Thousand Oaks, CA, Sage, 2000, pp. 21–36.

16.33 Schneider, B.; M.G. Ehrhart; D.M. Mayer; J.L. Saltz; and K. Niles-Jolly. "Understanding Organization–Customer Links in Service Settings." *Academy of Management Journal* 48 (2005), pp. 1017–32.

16.34 du Gay, P., and G. Salaman. "The Cult(ure) of the Customer." In *Strategic Human Resource Management,* eds. C. Mabey, G. Salaman, and J. Storey. London: Sage, 1998, pp. 58–67.

16.35 Grizzle, J.W.; A.R. Zablah; T.J. Brown; J.C. Mowen; and J.M. Lee. "Employee Customer Orientation in Context: How the Environment Moderates the Influence of Customer Orientation on Performance Outcomes." *Journal of Applied Psychology* 94 (2009), pp. 1227–42.

16.36 Zohar, D., and G. Luria. "Climate as a Social-Cognitive Construction of Supervisory Safety Practices: Scripts as a Proxy of Behavior Patterns." *Journal of Applied Psychology* 89 (2004), pp. 322–33.

16.37 Hofmann, D.A.; F.P. Morgeson; and S.J. Gerras. "Climate as a Moderator of the Relationship Between Leader-Member Exchange and Content Specific Citizenship: Safety Climate as an Exemplar." *Journal of Applied Psychology* 88 (2003), pp. 170–78.

16.38 Katz-Navon, T.; E. Naveh; and Z. Stern. "Safety Climate in Healthcare Organizations: A Multi-Dimensional Approach." *Academy of Management Journal* 48 (2005), pp. 1075–89.

16.39 Liss, H.J., and R.J. Wagner. "GE's Crash Course in Culture Change." *Occupational Hazards,* September 2004, pp. 83–88.

16.40 Clarke, S. "Perceptions of Organizational Safety: Implications for the Development of Safety Culture." *Journal of Organizational Behavior* 20 (1999), pp. 185–98.

16.41 Christian, M.S.; J.C. Bradley; J.C. Wallace; and M.J. Burke. "Workplace Safety: A Meta-Analysis of the Roles of Person and Situation Factors." *Journal of Applied Psychology* 94 (2009), pp. 1103–27.

16.42 Speizer, I. "Diversity on the Menu." *Workforce Management,* November 2004, pp. 41–45.

16.43 McLean, L.D. "Organizational Culture's Influence on Creativity and Innovation: A Review of the Literature and Implications for Human Resource Development." *Advances in Developing Human Resources* 7 (2005), pp. 226–46.

16.44 Frauenheim, E. "On the Clock but Off on Their Own: Pet-Project Programs Set to Gain Wider Acceptance." *Workforce Management,* April 24, 2006, pp. 40–41.

16.45 Poulton, T. "Got a Creative Creative Process? Fostering Creativity in an ROI-Focused Cubicle-Ridden Environment Ain't Easy. Here's How to Get your Team's Juices Flowing." *Strategy,* April 2006, p. 11.

16.46 Tkaczyk, C. "No. 20, SAS; Offer Affordable (Awesome) Day Care." *Fortune*, August 17, 2009, p. 26.

16.47 O'Reilly, C.A. "Corporations, Culture, and Commitment: Motivation and Social Control in Organizations." *California Management Review* 31 (1989), pp. 9–25.

16.48 O'Reilly et al., "People and Organizational Culture."

16.49 Schein, E.H. "Three Cultures of Management: The Key to Organizational Learning." *Sloan Management Review* 38 (1996), pp. 9–20.

16.50 Boisner A., and J. Chatman. "The Role of Subcultures in Agile Organizations." In *Leading and Managing People in Dynamic Organizations,* eds. R. Petersen and E. Mannix. Mahwah, NJ: Lawrence Erlbaum Associates, 2003.

16.51 See Howard-Grenville, J.A. "Inside the 'BLACK BOX': How Organizational Culture and Subcultures Inform Interpretations and Actions on Environmental Issues." *Organization & Environment* 19 (2006), pp. 46–73; and Jermier, J.; J. Slocum; L. Fry; and J. Gaines. "Organizational Subcultures in a Soft Bureaucracy: Resistance Behind the Myth and Façade of an Official Culture." *Organizational Science* 2 (1991), pp. 170–94.

16.52 Schneider, B.; H.W. Goldstein; and D.B. Smith. "The ASA Framework: An Update." *Personnel Psychology* 48 (1995), pp. 747–73.

16.53 Graf, A.B. "Building Corporate Cultures." *Chief Executive,* March 2005, p. 18.

16.54 Ruiz, G. "Tall Order." *Workforce Management,* April 2006, pp. 22–29.

16.55 For good summaries of socialization, see Fisher, C.D. "Organizational Socialization: An Integrative View." *Research in Personnel and Human Resource Management* 4 (1986), pp. 101–45; Bauer, T.N.; E.W. Morrison; and R.R. Callister. "Organizational Socialization: A Review and Directions for Future Research." In *Research in Personnel and Human Resource Management,* Vol. 16, ed. G.R. Ferris. Greenwich, CT: JAI Press, 1998, pp. 149–214.

16.56 Cable, D.M.; L. Aiman-Smith; P.W. Mulvey; and J.R. Edwards. "The Sources and Accuracy of Job Applicants' Beliefs about Organizational Culture." *Academy of Management Journal* 43 (2000), pp. 1076–85; and Louis, M.R. "Surprise and Sense-Making: What Newcomers Experience in Entering Unfamiliar Organizational Settings." *Administrative Science Quarterly* 25 (1980), pp. 226–51.

16.57 Chao, G.T.; A. O'Leary-Kelly; S. Wolf; H.J. Klein; and P.D. Gardner. "Organizational Socialization: Its Content and Consequences." *Journal of Applied Psychology* 79 (1994), pp. 450–63.

16.58 Ibid.; Klein, H.; and N. Weaver. "The Effectiveness of an Organizational-Level Orientation Training Program in the Socialization of New Hires." *Personnel Psychology,* Spring 2000, pp. 47–66; Wesson, M.J.; and C.I. Gogus. "Shaking Hands with a Computer: An Examination of Two Methods of Organizational Newcomer Orientation." *Journal of Applied Psychology* 90 (2005), pp. 1018–26.

16.59 Gravelle, M. "The Five Most Common Hiring Mistakes and How to Avoid Them." *The Canadian Manager* 29 (2004), pp. 11–13.

16.60 Van Maanen, J., and E.H. Schein. "Toward a Theory of Organizational Socialization." *Research in Organizational Behavior* 1 (1979), pp. 209–64.

16.61 Ashford, S.J., and J.S. Black. "Proactivity During Organizational Entry: The Role of Desire for Control." *Journal of Applied Psychology* 81 (1996), pp. 199–214; and Kim, T.; D.M. Cable; and S. Kim. "Socialization Tactics, Employee Proactivity, and Person–Organization Fit." *Journal of Applied Psychology* 90 (2005), pp. 232–41.

16.62 Mourier, P., and M. Smith. *Conquering Organizational Change: How to Succeed Where Most Companies Fail.* Atlanta: CEP Press, 2001.

16.63 MacMillan, D. "Can eBay Get It's Tech Savvy Back?" *BusinessWeek,* June 22, 2009, pp. 48–49.

16.64 Ibid.

16.65 Schein, *Organization Culture and Leadership.*

16.66 Gubbins, E. "Nortel's New Execs Bring Cisco Experience." *Telephony,* April 11, 2005, pp. 14–15.

16.67 Weber, Y. "Measuring Cultural Fit in Mergers and Acquisitions." In *Handbook of Organizational Culture and Climate,* eds. N.M. Ashkanasy, C. Wilderom, and M.F. Peterson. Thousand Oaks, CA; Sage, pp. 309–20.

16.68 Foust, D. "Pulling Delta Out of a Nosedive." *BusinessWeek,* May 25, 2009, pp. 36–37.

16.69 Brahy, S. "Six Solution Pillars for Successful Cultural Integration of International M&As." *Journal of Organizational Excellence,* Autumn 2006, pp. 53–63.

16.70 Platt, G. "Global Merger Activity Sets Record Pace." *Global Finance* 20 (2006), p. 60.

16.71 Edmondson, G. "Auf Wiedersehen, Mitsubishi." *BusinessWeek,* November 11, 2005, http://www.businessweek.com (February 9, 2007); and Bremmer, B. "A Tale of Two Auto Mergers." *BusinessWeek,* April 29, 2004, http://www.businessweek.com (February 9, 2007).

16.72 Ewing, J. "Nokia and Siemens: Exciting the Market." *BusinessWeek,* June 19, 2006.

16.73 Stahl, G.K., and M.E. Mendenhall. *Mergers and Acquisitions: Managing Culture and Human Resources.* Stanford, CA: Stanford University Press, 2005.

16.74 Foust, D.; J. Ewing; and G. Smith. "Looks Like a Beer Brawl." *BusinessWeek,* July 28, 2008, p. 52.

16.75 Gibson, R. "Package Deal: UPS's Purchase of Mail Boxes Etc. Looked Great on Paper. Then

Came the Culture Clash." *The Wall Street Journal,* May 8, 2006, p. R13.

16.76   Jana, R. "Putting the i into HiP." *BusinessWeek*, November 26, 2007, p. 10.

16.77   Arthur, W., Jr.; S.T. Bell; A.J. Villado; and D. Doverspike. "The Use of Person–Organization Fit in Employment Decision Making: An Assessment of Its Criterion-Related Validity." *Journal of Applied Psychology* 91 (2007), pp. 786–801; and Kristof-Brown, A.L.; R.D. Zimmerman; and E.C. Johnson, "Consequences of Individuals' Fit at Work: A Meta-Analysis of Person–Job, Person–Organization, Person–Group, and Person–Supervisor Fit," *Personnel Psychology* 58 (2005), pp. 281–342.

16.78   Barber, A.E. *Recruiting Employees: Individual and Organizational Perspectives.* Thousand Oaks, CA: Sage, 1998.

16.79   Wanous, J.P. *Organizational Entry: Recruitment, Selection, Orientation and Socialization of Newcomers.* Reading, MA: Addison-Wesley, 1992.

16.80   Gravelle, "The Five Most Common Hiring Mistakes."

16.81   Anderson, N.R.; N.A. Cunningham-Snell; and J. Haigh. "Induction Training as Socialization: Current Practice and Attitudes to Evaluation in British Organizations." *International Journal of Selection and Assessment* 4 (1996), pp. 169–83.

16.82   Wesson and Gogus, "Shaking Hands with a Computer."

16.83   Ibid.; Klein and Weaver, "The Effectiveness."

16.84   Marquez, J. "Despite Job Cuts, GM May Expand New-Hire Networking Program." *Workforce Management,* March 27, 2006, p. 16.

16.85   Wanberg, C.R.; E.T. Welsh; and S.A. Hezlett. "Mentoring Research: A Review and Dynamic Process Model." *Research in Personnel and Human Resources Management* 22 (2003), pp. 39–124.

16.86   Allen, T.D.; L.T. Eby; M.L. Poteet; E. Lentz; and L. Lima. "Outcomes Associated with Mentoring Protégés: A Meta-Analysis." *Journal of Applied Psychology* 89 (2004), pp. 127–36.

16.87   Tahmincioglu, E. "Group Mentoring: A Cost Effective Option." *Workforce Management Online,* December 2004 (March 2, 2007).

16.88   Ibid.

16.89   Berry and Seltman, *Management Lessons from Mayo Clinic*; Gawande, "The Cost Conundrum"

16.90   Berry and Seltman, Management Lessons from Mayo Clinic

16.91   Bendix, J. "Mayo Clinic." *Medical Economics*, March 6, 2009, p. 27

16.92   Hicks, S. "Orientation Redesign." *T + D*, July 2006, pp. 43–45.

Glossary

A

ability Relatively stable capabilities of people for performing a particular range of related activities.

ability to focus The degree to which employees can devote their attention to work.

absenteeism A form of physical withdrawal in which employees do not show up for an entire day of work.

abuse Employee assault or endangerment from which physical and psychological injuries may occur.

abusive supervision The sustained display of hostile verbal and nonverbal behaviors on the part of supervisors, excluding physical contact.

accommodating A conflict resolution style by which one party gives in to the other and acts in a completely unselfish way.

accomplishment striving A strong desire to accomplish task-related goals as a means of expressing one's personality.

action learning Team process training in which a team has the opportunity to work on an actual problem within the organization.

action processes Teamwork processes, such as helping and coordination, that aid in the accomplishment of teamwork as the work is actually taking place.

action team A team of limited duration that performs complex tasks in contexts that tend to be highly visible and challenging.

activation The degree to which moods are aroused and active, as opposed to unaroused and inactive.

active management-by-exception When the leader arranges to monitor mistakes and errors actively and takes corrective action when required.

adaptive task performance Thoughtful responses by an employee to unique or unusual task demands.

additive tasks Tasks for which the contributions from every member add up to determine team performance.

adjourning The final stage of team development, during which members experience anxiety and other emotions as they disengage and ultimately separate from the team.

affect-based trust Trust that depends on feelings toward the authority that go beyond any rational assessment of trustworthiness.

affective commitment An employee's desire to remain a member of an organization due to a feeling of emotional attachment.

affective events theory A theory that describes how workplace events can generate emotional reactions that impact work behaviors.

agreeableness One of the "Big Five" dimensions of personality reflecting traits like being kind, cooperative, sympathetic, helpful, courteous, and warm.

alternative dispute resolution A process by which two parties resolve conflicts through the use of a specially trained, neutral third party.

ambassador activities Boundary-spanning activities that are intended to protect the team, persuade others to support the team, or obtain important resources for the team.

anticipatory stage A stage of socialization that begins as soon as a potential employee develops an image of what it would be like to work for a company.

apathetics Employees with low commitment levels and low task performance levels who exert the minimum amount of effort needed to keep their jobs.

apprising An influence tactic in which the requestor clearly explains why performing the request will benefit the target personally.

arbitration A process by which a third party determines a binding settlement to a dispute between two parties.

ASA framework A theory (Attraction–Selection–Attrition) that states that employees will be drawn to organizations with cultures that match their personality, organizations will select employees that match, and employees will leave or be forced out when they are not a good fit.

autocratic style A leadership style where the leader makes the decision alone without asking for opinions or suggestions of the employees in the work unit.

autonomy The degree to which a job allows individual freedom and discretion regarding how the work is to be done.

availability bias The tendency for people to base their judgments on information that is easier to recall.

avoiding A conflict resolution style by which one party wants to remain neutral, stay away from conflict, or postpone the conflict to gather information or let things cool down.

B

bargaining The third stage of the negotiation process, during which each party gives and takes to arrive at an agreement.

basic underlying assumptions The ingrained beliefs and philosophies of employees.

BATNA A negotiator's best alternative to a negotiated agreement.

behavior modeling training A formalized method of training in which employees observe and learn from employees with significant amounts of tacit knowledge.

behavioral coping Physical activities used to deal with a stressful situation.

behavioral modeling When employees observe the actions of others, learn from what they observe, and then repeat the observed behavior.

behaviorally anchored rating scales (BARS) Use of examples of critical incidents to evaluate an employee's job performance behaviors directly.

benevolence The belief that an authority wants to do good for an employee, apart from any selfish or profit-centered motives.

benign job demands Job demands that are not appraised as being stressful.

Big Five The five major dimensions of personality including conscientiousness, agreeableness, neuroticism, openness to experience, and extraversion.

boosterism Positively representing the organization when in public.

boundary spanning Interactions among team members and individuals and groups who are not part of the team.

bounded rationality The notion that people do not have the ability or resources to process all available information and alternatives when making a decision.

brainstorming A team process used to generate creative ideas.

bureaucratic structure An organizational form that exhibits many of the facets of a mechanistic organization.

burnout The emotional, mental, and physical exhaustion from coping with stressful demands on a continuing basis.

business environment The outside environment, including customers, competitors, suppliers, and distributors, which all have an impact on organizational design.

C

causal inference The establishment that one variable does cause another, based on covariation, temporal precedence, and the elimination of alternative explanations.

centrality How important a person's job is and how many people depend on that person to accomplish their tasks.

centralization Refers to where decisions are formally made in organizations.

ceremonies Formal events, generally performed in front of an audience of organizational members.

chain of command Answer to the question of "who reports to whom?" and signifies formal authority relationships.

challenge stressors Stressors that tend to be appraised as opportunities for growth and achievement.

citizens Employees with high commitment levels and low task performance levels who volunteer to do additional activities around the office.

citizenship behavior Voluntary employee behaviors that contribute to organizational goals by improving the context in which work takes place.

civic virtue Participation in company operations at a deeper-than-normal level through voluntary meetings, readings, and keeping up with news that affects the company.

clear purpose tests Integrity tests that ask about attitudes toward dishonesty, beliefs about the frequency of dishonesty, desire to punish dishonesty, and confession of past dishonesty.

client structure An organizational form in which employees are organized around serving customers.

climate for transfer An organizational environment that supports the use of new skills.

closing and commitment The fourth and final stage of the negotiation process, during which the agreement arrived at during bargaining gets formalized.

coalitions An influence tactic in which the influencer enlists other people to help influence the target.

coercive power A form of organizational power based on the ability to hand out punishment.

cognition-based trust Trust that is rooted in a rational assessment of the authority's trustworthiness.

cognitive abilities Capabilities related to the use of knowledge to make decisions and solve problems.

cognitive coping Thoughts used to deal with a stressful situation.

cognitive distortion A reevaluation of the inputs an employee brings to a job, often occurring in response to equity distress.

cognitive moral development As people age and mature, they move through several states of moral development, each more

mature and sophisticated than the prior one.

cohesion A team state that occurs when members of the team develop strong emotional bonds to other members of the team and to the team itself.

collaboration Seen as both a conflict resolution style and an influence tactic whereby both parties work together to maximize outcomes.

communal cultures An organizational culture type in which employees are friendly to one another and all think alike.

communication The process by which information and meaning is transferred from a sender to a receiver.

communion striving A strong desire to obtain acceptance in personal relationships as a means of expressing one's personality.

communities of practice Groups of employees who learn from one another through collaboration over an extended period of time.

company size The number of employees in a company.

company strategy An organization's objectives and goals and how it tries to capitalize on its assets to make money.

comparison other Another person who provides a frame of reference for judging equity.

compensatory forms model A model indicating that the various withdrawal behaviors are negatively correlated; engaging in one

type of withdrawal makes one less likely to engage in other types.

competence The capability to perform work tasks successfully.

competing A conflict resolution style by which one party attempts to get his or her own goals met without concern for the other party's results.

compliance When targets of influence are willing to do what the leader asks but do it with a degree of ambivalence.

comprehensive interdependence A form of task interdependence in which team members have a great deal of discretion in terms of what they do and with whom they interact in the course of the collaboration involved in accomplishing the team's work.

compromise A conflict resolution style by which conflict is resolved through give-and-take concessions.

conjunctive tasks Tasks for which the team's performance depends on the abilities of the team's weakest link.

conscientiousness One of the "Big Five" dimensions of personality reflecting traits like being dependable, organized, reliable, ambitious, hardworking, and persevering.

consensus Used by decision makers to attribute cause; whether other individuals behave the same way under similar circumstances.

consideration A pattern of behavior where the leader creates job relationships characterized by mutual trust, respect for employee ideas, and consideration of employee feelings.

consistency Used by decision makers to attribute cause; whether this individual has behaved this way before under similar circumstances.

consultation An influence tactic whereby the target is allowed to participate in deciding how to carry out or implement a request.

consultative style A leadership style where the leader presents the problem to employees asking for their opinions and suggestions before ultimately making the decision him- or herself.

contingencies of reinforcement Four specific consequences used by organizations to modify employee behavior.

contingent reward When the leader attains follower agreement on what needs to be done using rewards in exchange for adequate performance.

continuance commitment An employee's desire to remain a member of an organization due to an awareness of the costs of leaving.

continuous reinforcement A specific consequence follows each and every occurrence of a certain behavior.

coordination The quality of physical movement in terms of synchronization of movements and balance.

coordination loss Process loss due to the time and energy it takes to coordinate work activities with other team members.

coping Behaviors and thoughts used to manage stressful demands and the emotions associated with the stressful demands.

corporate social responsibility A perspective that acknowledges that the responsibility of a business encompasses the economic, legal, ethical, and citizenship expectations of society.

correlation The statistical relationship between two variables. Abbreviated r, it can be positive or negative and range from 0 (no statistical relationship) to 1 (a perfect statistical relationship).

countercultures When a subculture's values do not match those of the organization.

counterproductive behavior Employee behaviors that intentionally hinder organizational goal accomplishment.

courtesy Sharing important information with coworkers.

coworker satisfaction Employees' feelings about their coworkers, including their abilities and personalities.

creative task performance. The degree to which individuals develop ideas or physical outcomes that are both novel and useful.

creativity culture A specific culture type focused on fostering a creative atmosphere.

crisis situation A change—sudden or evolving—that results in an urgent problem that must be addressed immediately.

cross-training Training team members in the duties and responsibilities of their teammates.

cultural values Shared beliefs about desirable end states or modes of conduct in a given culture that influence the expression of traits.

culture The shared values, beliefs, motives, identities, and interpretations that result from common experiences of members of a society and are transmitted across generations.

culture strength The degree to which employees agree about how things should happen within the organization and behave accordingly.

customer service culture A specific culture type focused on service quality.

cyberloafing A form of psychological withdrawal in which employees surf the Internet, e-mail, and instant message to avoid doing work-related activities.

D

daily hassles Minor day-to-day demands that interfere with work accomplishment.

daydreaming A form of psychological withdrawal in which one's work is interrupted by random thoughts or concerns.

decision informity The degree to which team members possess adequate information about their own task responsibilities.

decision making The process of generating and choosing from a set of alternatives to solve a problem.

deep-level diversity Diversity of attributes that are inferred through observation or experience, such as one's values or personality.

delegating When the leader turns responsibility for key behaviors over to employees.

delegative style A leadership style where the leader gives the employee the responsibility for making decisions within some set of specified boundary conditions.

differential exposure Being more likely to appraise day-to-day situations as stressful, thereby feeling that stressors are encountered more frequently.

differential reactivity Being less likely to believe that one can cope with the stressors experienced on a daily basis.

discretion The degree to which managers have the right to make decisions on their own.

disjunctive tasks Tasks with an objectively verifiable best solution for which the member with the highest level of ability has the most influence on team effectiveness.

disposition-based trust Trust that is rooted in one's own personality, as opposed to a careful assessment of the trustee's trustworthiness.

distinctiveness Used by decision makers to attribute cause; whether the person being judged acts in a similar fashion under different circumstances.

distributive bargaining A negotiation strategy in which one person gains and the other person loses.

distributive justice The perceived fairness of decision-making outcomes.

diversity culture A specific culture type focused on fostering or taking advantage of a diverse group of employees.

E

economic exchange Work relationships that resemble a contractual agreement by which employees fulfill job duties in exchange for financial compensation.

embeddedness An employee's connection to and sense of fit in the organization and community.

emotion regulation The ability to recover quickly from emotional experiences.

emotional contagion The idea that emotions can be transferred from one person to another.

emotional cues Positive or negative feelings that can help or hinder task accomplishment.

emotional intelligence A set of abilities related to the understanding and use of emotions that affect social functioning.

emotional labor When employees manage their emotions to complete their job duties successfully.

emotional support The empathy and understanding that people receive from others that can be used to alleviate emotional distress from stressful demands.

emotion-focused coping Behaviors and cognitions of an individual intended to help manage emotional reactions to the stressful demands.

emotions Intense feelings, often lasting for a short duration, that

are clearly directed at someone or some circumstance.

encounter stage A stage of socialization beginning the day an employee starts work, during which the employee compares the information as an outsider to the information learned as an insider.

engagement A term commonly used in the contemporary workplace to summarize motivation levels.

equity distress An internal tension that results from being over-rewarded or underrewarded relative to some comparison other.

equity theory A theory that suggests that employees create a mental ledger of the outcomes they receive for their job inputs, relative to some comparison other.

erosion model A model that suggests that employees with fewer bonds with coworkers are more likely to quit the organization.

escalation of commitment A common decision-making error in which the decision maker continues to follow a failing course of action.

espoused values The beliefs, philosophies, and norms that a company explicitly states.

ethics The degree to which the behaviors of an authority are in accordance with generally accepted moral norms.

ethnocentrism One who views his or her cultural values as "right" and values of other cultures as "wrong."

evidence-based management A perspective that argues

that scientific findings should form the foundation for management education.

exchange tactic An influence tactic in which the requestor offers a reward in return for performing a request.

exchanging information The second stage of the negotiation process, during which each party makes the strongest case for its position.

exit A response to a negative work event by which one becomes often absent from work or voluntarily leaves the organization.

expectancy The belief that exerting a high level of effort will result in successful performance on some task.

expectancy theory A theory that describes the cognitive process employees go through to make choices among different voluntary responses.

expert power A form of organizational power based on expertise or knowledge.

expertise The knowledge and skills that distinguish experts from novices.

explicit knowledge Knowledge that is easily communicated and available to everyone.

external comparison Comparing oneself to someone in a different company.

extinction The removal of a positive outcome following an unwanted behavior.

extraversion One of the "Big Five" dimensions of personality reflecting traits like being talkative, sociable, passionate, assertive, bold, and dominant.

extrinsic motivation Desire to put forth work effort due to some contingency that depends on task performance.

F

facilitative style A leadership style where the leader presents the problem to a group of employees and seeks consensus on a solution, making sure that his or her own opinion receives no more weight than anyone else's.

faking Exaggerating responses to a personality test in a socially desirable fashion.

family time demands The amount of time committed to fulfilling family responsibilities.

feedback In job characteristics theory, it refers to the degree to which the job itself provides information about how well the job holder is doing. In goal setting theory, it refers to progress updates on work goals.

financial uncertainty Uncertainties with regard to the potential for loss of livelihood, savings, or the ability to pay expenses.

fixed interval schedule Reinforcement occurs at fixed time periods.

fixed ratio schedule Reinforcement occurs following a fixed number of desired behaviors.

flexibility The ability to bend, stretch, twist, or reach.

flow A state in which employees feel a total immersion in the task at hand, sometimes losing track of how much time has passed.

focus of commitment The people, places, and things that inspire a desire to remain a member of an organization.

forced ranking A performance management system in which managers rank subordinates relative to one another.

formalization The degree to which rules and procedures are used to standardize behaviors and decisions in an organization.

forming The first stage of team development, during which members try to get a feel for what is expected of them, what types of behaviors are out of bounds, and who's in charge.

fragmented cultures An organizational culture type in which employees are distant and disconnected from one another.

four-component model A model that argues that ethical behaviors result from the multistage sequence of moral awareness, moral judgment, moral intent, and ethical behavior.

functional structure An organizational form in which employees are grouped by the functions they perform for the organization.

fundamental attribution error The tendency for people to judge others' behaviors as being due to internal factors such as ability, motivation, or attitudes.

G

general cognitive ability The general level of cognitive ability that plays an important role in determining the more narrow cognitive abilities.

geographic structure An organizational form in which employees are grouped around the different locations where the company does business.

goal commitment The degree to which a person accepts a goal and is determined to reach it.

goal interdependence The degree to which team members have a shared goal and align their individual goals with that vision.

goal setting theory A theory that views goals as the primary drivers of the intensity and persistence of effort.

gossiping Casual conversations about other people in which the facts are not confirmed as true.

groupthink Behaviors that support conformity and team harmony at the expense of other team priorities.

growth need strength The degree to which employees desire to develop themselves further.

H

harassment Unwanted physical contact or verbal remarks from a colleague.

helping Assisting coworkers who have heavy workloads, aiding them with personal matters, and showing new employees the ropes when they are first on the job.

heuristics Simple and efficient rules of thumb that allow one to make decisions more easily.

hierarchical sensitivity The degree to which the team leader effectively weighs the recommendations of the members.

hindrance stressors Stressors that tend to be appraised as thwarting progress toward growth and achievement.

history A collective pool of experience, wisdom, and knowledge created by people that benefits the organization.

human resource management Field of study that focuses on the applications of OB theories and principles in organizations.

hybrid outcome interdependence When team members receive rewards based on both their individual performance and that of the team to which they belong.

hypotheses Written predictions that specify relationships between variables.

I

idealized influence When the leader behaves in ways that earn the admiration, trust, and respect of followers, causing followers to want to identify with and emulate the leader.

identity The degree to which a job offers completion of a whole, identifiable piece of work.

impact The sense that a person's actions "make a difference"—that progress is being made toward fulfilling some important purpose.

incivility Communication that is rude, impolite, discourteous, and lacking in good manners.

independent forms model A model that predicts that the various withdrawal behaviors are uncorrelated; engaging in one type of withdrawal has little bearing on engaging in other types.

individualism–collectivism The degree to which a culture has a loosely knit social framework (individualism) or a tight social framework (collectivism).

individualistic roles Behaviors that benefit the individual at the expense of the team.

individualized consideration When the leader behaves in ways that help followers achieve their potential through coaching, development, and mentoring.

influence The use of behaviors to cause behavioral or attitudinal changes in others.

information richness The amount and depth of information that is transmitted in a message.

informational justice The perceived fairness of the communications provided to employees from authorities.

ingratiation The use of favors, compliments, or friendly behavior to make the target feel better about the influencer.

inimitable Incapable of being imitated or copied.

initiating structure A pattern of behavior where the leader defines and structures the roles of employees in pursuit of goal attainment.

inspirational appeal An influence tactic designed to appeal to one's values and ideals, thereby creating an emotional or attitudinal reaction.

inspirational motivation When the leader behaves in ways that foster an enthusiasm for and commitment to a shared vision of the future.

instrumental support The help people receive from others that can be used to address a stressful demand directly.

instrumentality The belief that successful performance will result in the attainment of some outcome(s).

integrative bargaining A negotiation strategy that achieves an outcome that is satisfying for both parties.

integrity The perception that an authority adheres to a set of acceptable values and principles.

integrity tests Personality tests that focus specifically on a predisposition to engage in theft and other counterproductive behaviors (sometimes also called "honesty tests").

intellectual stimulation When the leader behaves in ways that challenge followers to be innovative and creative by questioning assumptions and reframing old situations in new ways.

interests Expressions of personality that influence behavior through preferences for certain environments and activities.

internal comparisons Comparing oneself to someone in your same company.

internalization A response to influence tactics where the target agrees with and becomes committed to the request.

interpersonal citizenship behavior Going beyond normal job expectations to assist, support, and develop coworkers and colleagues.

interpersonal justice The perceived fairness of the interpersonal treatment received by employees from authorities.

interpersonal processes Teamwork processes, such as motivating and confidence building, that focus on the management of relationships among team members.

intrinsic motivation Desire to put forth work effort due to the sense that task performance serves as its own reward.

intuition An emotional judgment based on quick, unconscious, gut feelings.

J

job analysis A process by which an organization determines requirements of specific jobs.

job characteristics theory A theory that argues that five core characteristics (variety, identity, significance, autonomy, and feedback) combine to result in high levels of satisfaction with the work itself.

job enrichment When job duties and responsibilities are expanded to provide increased levels of core job characteristics.

job performance Employee behaviors that contribute either positively or negatively to the accomplishment of organizational goals.

job satisfaction A pleasurable emotional state resulting from the appraisal of one's job or job experiences. It represents how a person feels and thinks about his or her job.

justice The perceived fairness of an authority's decision making.

K

knowledge and skill The degree to which employees have the aptitude and competence needed to succeed on their job.

knowledge of results A psychological state indicating the extent to which employees are aware of how well or how poorly they are doing.

knowledge transfer The exchange of knowledge between employees.

knowledge work Jobs that primarily involve cognitive activity versus physical activity.

L

laissez-faire leadership When the leader avoids leadership duties altogether.

language The jargon, slang, and slogans used within an organization.

leader effectiveness The degree to which the leader's actions result in the achievement of the unit's goals, the continued commitment of the unit's employees, and the development of mutual trust, respect, and obligation in leader–member dyads.

leader emergence The process of becoming a leader in the first place.

leader–member exchange theory A theory describing how leader–member relationships develop over time on a dyadic basis.

leadership The use of power and influence to direct the activities of followers toward goal achievement.

leader–staff teams A type of team that consists of members who make recommendations to the leader who is ultimately responsible for team decisions.

learning A relatively permanent change in an employee's knowledge or skill that results from experience.

learning orientation A predisposition or attitude according to which building competence is deemed more important by an employee than demonstrating competence.

legitimate power A form of organizational power based on authority or position.

life cycle theory of leadership A theory stating that the optimal combination of initiating structure and consideration depends on the readiness of the employees in the work unit.

life satisfaction The degree to which employees feel a sense of happiness with their lives in general.

locus of control Whether one believes the events that occur around him or her are driven by him- or herself or the external environment.

lone wolves Employees with low commitment levels and high task performance levels who focus on their own career rather than what benefits the organization.

long breaks A form of physical withdrawal in which employees take longer-than-normal lunches or breaks to spend less time at work.

looking busy A form of psychological withdrawal in which one attempts to appear consumed with work when not performing actual work tasks.

loyalty A passive response to a negative work event in which one publicly supports the situation but privately hopes for improvement.

M

management by objectives (MBO) A management philosophy that bases employee evaluations on whether specific performance goals have been met.

management team A relatively permanent team that participates in managerial-level tasks that affect the entire organization.

masculinity–femininity The degree to which a culture values stereotypically male traits (masculinity) or stereotypically female traits (femininity).

matrix structure A complex form of organizational structure that combines a functional and multidivisional grouping.

maximum performance Performance in brief, special circumstances that demand a person's best effort.

meaning of money The idea that money can have symbolic value (e.g., achievement, respect, freedom) in addition to economic value.

meaningfulness (of work) A psychological state reflecting one's feelings about work tasks, goals, and purposes, and the degree to which they contribute to society and fulfill one's ideals and passions.

mechanistic organizations Efficient, rigid, predictable, and standardized organizations that thrive in stable environments.

mediation A process by which a third party facilitates a dispute resolution process but with no formal authority to dictate a solution.

mental models The degree to which team members have a shared understanding of important aspects of the team and its task.

mentoring The process by which a junior-level employee develops a deep and long-lasting relationship with a more senior-level employee within the organization.

mercenary cultures An organizational culture type in which employees think alike but are not friendly to one another.

meta-analysis A method that combines the results of multiple scientific studies by essentially calculating a weighted average correlation across studies (with larger studies receiving more weight).

Method of Authority Knowing something because a respected official, agency, or source has said it is so.

Method of Experience Knowing something because it is consistent with one's own experience and observations.

Method of Intuition Knowing something because it seems obvious or self-evident.

Method of Science Knowing something because scientific studies have replicated the result using a series of samples, settings, and methods.

missing meetings A form of physical withdrawal in which employees neglect important work functions while away from the office.

moods States of feeling that are mild in intensity, last for an extended period of time, and are not directed at anything.

moonlighting A form of psychological withdrawal in which employees use work time and resources to do nonwork-related activities.

moral awareness When an authority recognizes that a moral issue exists in a situation.

moral attentiveness The degree to which people chronically perceive and consider issues of morality during their experiences.

moral identity The degree to which a person views him- or herself as a moral person.

moral intensity The degree to which an issue has ethical urgency.

moral intent An authority's degree of commitment to the moral course of action.

moral judgment When an authority can accurately identify the "right" course of action.

moral principles Prescriptive guides for making moral judgments.

motivation A set of energetic forces that determine the direction,

intensity, and persistence of an employee's work effort.

motivational loss Process loss due to team members' tendency to put forth less effort on team tasks than they could.

multi-divisional structure An organizational form in which employees are grouped by product, geography, or client.

Myers-Briggs type indicator (MBTI) A personality framework that evaluates people on the basis of four types or preferences: extraversion versus introversion, sensing versus intuition, thinking versus feeling, and judging versus perceiving.

N

needs Groupings or clusters of outcomes viewed as having critical psychological or physiological consequences.

negative affectivity A dispositional tendency to experience unpleasant moods such as hostility, nervousness, and annoyance.

negative emotions Employees' feelings of fear, guilt, shame, sadness, envy, and disgust.

negative life events Events such as a divorce or death of a family member that tend to be appraised as a hindrance.

negative reinforcement An unwanted outcome is removed following a desired behavior.

neglect A passive, destructive response to a negative work event in which one's interest and effort in work decline.

negotiation A process in which two or more interdependent individuals

discuss and attempt to reach agreement about their differences.

network structure The pattern of communication that occurs regularly among each member of a team.

networked cultures An organizational culture type in which employees are friendly to one another, but everyone thinks differently and does their own thing.

neuroticism One of the "Big Five" dimensions of personality reflecting traits like being nervous, moody, emotional, insecure, jealous, and unstable.

neutralizers Situational characteristics that reduce the importance of the leader and do not improve employee performance in any way.

newcomer orientations A common form of training during which new hires learn more about the organization.

nominal group technique A team process used to generate creative ideas, whereby team members individually write down their ideas and then take turns sharing them with the group.

nonprogrammed decision Decisions made by employees when a problem is new, complex, or not recognized.

normative commitment An employee's desire to remain a member of an organization due to a feeling of obligation.

norming The third stage of team development, during which members realize that they need to work together to accomplish team goals and consequently begin to cooperate.

numerous small decisions People making many small decisions every day that are invisible to competitors.

O

observable artifacts Aspects of an organization's culture that employees and outsiders can easily see or talk about.

Occupational Information Network (O*NET) An online database containing job tasks, behaviors, required knowledge, skills, and abilities.

openness to experience One of the "Big Five" dimensions of personality reflecting traits like being curious, imaginative, creative, complex, refined, and sophisticated.

organic organizations Flexible, adaptive, outward-focused organizations that thrive in dynamic environments.

organizational behavior (OB) Field of study devoted to understanding, explaining, and ultimately improving the attitudes and behaviors of individuals and groups in organizations.

organizational chart A drawing that represents every job in the organization and the formal reporting relationships between those jobs.

organizational citizenship behavior Going beyond normal expectations to improve operations of the organization, as well as defending the organization and being loyal to it.

organizational commitment An employee's desire to remain a member of an organization.

organizational culture The shared social knowledge within an organization regarding the rules, norms, and values that shape the attitudes and behaviors of its employees.

organizational design The process of creating, selecting, or changing the structure of an organization.

organizational politics Individual actions directed toward the goal of furthering a person's own self-interests.

organizational structure Formally dictates how jobs and tasks are divided and coordinated between individuals and groups within the company.

other awareness The ability to recognize and understand the emotions that other people are feeling.

outcome interdependence The degree to which team members share equally in the feedback and rewards that result from the team achieving its goals.

P

parallel team A team composed of members from various jobs within the organization that meets to provide recommendations about important issues.

participating When the leader shares ideas and tries to help the group conduct its affairs.

passive management-by-exception When the leader waits around for mistakes and errors, then takes corrective action as necessary.

past accomplishments The level of success or failure with similar job tasks in the past.

pay satisfaction Employees' feelings about the compensation for their jobs.

perceived organizational support The degree to which employees believe that the organization values their contributions and cares about their well-being.

perceptual ability The capacity to perceive, understand, and recall patterns of information.

performance-avoid orientation A predisposition or attitude by which employees focus on demonstrating their competence so that others will not think poorly of them.

performance-prove orientation A predisposition or attitude by which employees focus on demonstrating their competence so that others think favorably of them.

performing The fourth stage of team development, during which members are comfortable working within their roles, and the team makes progress toward goals.

personal aggression Hostile verbal and physical actions directed toward other employees.

personal appeals An influence tactic in which the requestor asks for something based on personal friendship or loyalty.

personal clarification Training in which members simply receive information regarding the roles of the other team members.

personal development Participation in activities outside of work that foster growth and learning.

personality The structures and propensities inside a person that explain his or her characteristic patterns of thought, emotion, and behavior. Personality reflects what people are like and creates their social reputation.

person–organization fit The degree to which a person's values and personality match the culture of the organization.

physical structures The organization's buildings and internal office designs.

physical withdrawal A physical escape from the work environment.

pleasantness The degree to which an employee is in a good versus bad mood.

political deviance Behaviors that intentionally disadvantage other individuals.

political skill The ability to understand others and the use of that knowledge to influence them to further personal or organizational objectives.

pooled interdependence A form of task independence in which group members complete their work assignments independently, and then their work is simply added together to represent the group's output.

positional modeling Training that involves observations of how other team members perform their roles.

positional rotation Training that gives members actual experience carrying out the responsibilities of their teammates.

positive affectivity A dispositional tendency to experience pleasant, engaging moods such as enthusiasm, excitement, and elation.

positive emotions Employees' feelings of joy, pride, relief, hope, love, and compassion.

positive life events Events such as marriage or the birth of a child that tend to be appraised as a challenge.

positive reinforcement When a positive outcome follows a desired behavior.

potency A team state reflecting the degree of confidence among team members that the team can be effective across situations and tasks.

power The ability to influence the behavior of others and resist unwanted influence in return.

power distance The degree to which a culture prefers equal power distribution (low power distance) or an unequal power distribution (high power distance).

pressure An influence tactic in which the requestor attempts to use coercive power through threats and demands.

preparation The first stage of the negotiation process, during which each party determines its goals for the negotiation.

primary appraisal Evaluation of whether a demand is stressful and, if it is, the implications of the stressor in terms of personal goals and well-being.

problem-focused coping Behaviors and cognitions of an individual intended to manage the stressful situation itself.

procedural justice The perceived fairness of decision-making processes.

process gain When team outcomes are greater than expected based on the capabilities of the individual members.

process loss When team outcomes are less than expected based on the capabilities of the individual members.

product structure An organizational form in which employees are grouped around different products that the company produces.

production blocking A type of coordination loss resulting from team members having to wait on each other before completing their own part of the team task.

production deviance Intentionally reducing organizational efficiency of work output.

programmed decision Decisions that are somewhat automatic because the decision maker's knowledge allows him or her to recognize the situation and the course of action to be taken.

progression model A model indicating that the various withdrawal behaviors are positively correlated; engaging in one type of withdrawal makes one more likely to engage in other types.

Project GLOBE A collection of 170 researchers from 62 cultures who examine the impact of culture on the effectiveness of leader attributes, behaviors, and practices.

project team A team formed to take on one-time tasks, most of which tend to be complex and require input from members from different functional areas.

projection bias The faulty perception by decision makers that others think, feel, and act the same way as they do.

promotion satisfaction Employees' feelings about how the company handles promotions.

property deviance Behaviors that harm the organization's assets and possessions.

psychological contracts Employee beliefs about what employees owe the organization and what the organization owes them.

psychological empowerment An energy rooted in the belief that tasks are contributing to some larger purpose.

psychological withdrawal Mentally escaping the work environment.

psychomotor ability Capabilities associated with manipulating and controlling objects.

punctuated equilibrium A sequence of team development

during which not much gets done until the halfway point of a project, after which teams make necessary changes to complete the project on time.

punishment When an unwanted outcome follows an unwanted behavior.

Q

quantitative ability Capabilities associated with doing basic mathematical operations and selecting and applying formulas to solve mathematical problems.

quitting A form of physical withdrawal in which employees voluntarily leave the organization.

R

rational decision-making model A step-by-step approach to making decisions that is designed to maximize outcomes by examining all available alternatives.

rational persuasion The use of logical arguments and hard facts to show someone that a request is worthwhile.

readiness The degree to which employees have the ability and the willingness to accomplish their specific tasks.

realistic job previews The process of ensuring that a potential employee understands both the positive and negative aspects of the potential job.

reality shock A mismatch of information that occurs when an employee finds that aspects of working at a company are not what the employee expected it to be.

reasoning ability A diverse set of abilities associated with sensing and solving problems using insight, rules, and logic.

reciprocal interdependence A form of task interdependence in which group members interact with only a limited subset of other members to complete the team's work.

referent power A form of organizational power based on the attractiveness and charisma of the leader.

relational contracts Psychological contracts that focus on a broad set of open-ended and subjective obligations.

relationship conflict Disagreements among team members with regard to interpersonal relationships or incompatibilities in personal values or preferences.

reputation The prominence of an organization's brand in the minds of the public and the perceived quality of its goods and services.

resistance When a target refuses to perform a request and puts forth an effort to avoid having to do it.

resource-based view A model that argues that rare and inimitable resources help firms maintain competitive advantage.

responsibility for outcomes A psychological state indicating the degree to which employees feel they are key drivers of the quality of work output.

restructuring The process of changing an organization's structure.

reward power A form of organizational power based on the control of resources or benefits.

RIASEC model An interest framework summarized by six different personality types including realistic, investigative, artistic, social, enterprising, and conventional.

rituals The daily or weekly planned routines that occur in an organization.

role The behavior a person is generally expected to display in a given context.

role ambiguity When an individual has a lack of direction and information about what needs to be done.

role conflict When others have conflicting expectations of what an individual needs to do.

role making The phase in a leader–follower relationship when a follower voices his or her own expectations for the relationship, resulting in a free-flowing exchange of opportunities and resources for activities and effort.

role overload When an employee has too many demands to work effectively.

role taking The phase in a leader–follower relationship when a leader provides an employee with job expectations and the follower tries to meet those expectations.

routine task performance Well-known or habitual responses by employees to predictable task demands.

Rule of One-Eighth The belief that at best one-eighth or 12 percent of organizations will actually do what is required to build profits by putting people first.

S

S.M.A.R.T. goals Acronym that stands for Specific, Measurable, Achievable, Results-Based, Time-Sensitive goals.

sabotage Purposeful destruction of equipment, organizational processes, or company products.

safety culture A specific culture type focused on the safety of employees.

satisfaction with the work itself Employees' feelings about their actual work tasks.

satisficing When a decision maker chooses the first acceptable alternative considered.

schedules of reinforcement The timing of when contingencies are applied or removed.

scout activities Boundary-spanning activities that are intended to obtain information about technology, competitors, or the broader marketplace.

secondary appraisal When people determine how to cope with the various stressors they face.

selective perception The tendency for people to see their environment only as it affects them and as it is consistent with their expectations.

self-awareness The ability to recognize and understand the emotions in oneself.

self-determination A sense of choice in the initiation and continuation of work tasks.

self-efficacy The belief that a person has the capabilities needed to perform the behaviors required on some task.

self-serving bias When one attributes one's own failures to external factors and success to internal factors.

self-set goals The internalized goals that people use to monitor their own progress.

selling When the leader explains key issues and provides opportunities for clarification.

sensory ability Capabilities associated with vision and hearing.

sequential interdependence A form of task interdependence in which group members perform different tasks in a prescribed sequence, and members only depend on the member who comes before them in the sequence.

service work Providing a service that involves direct verbal or physical interactions with customers.

short-term vs. long-term orientation The degree to which a culture stresses values that are past and present-oriented (short-term orientation) or future-oriented (long-term orientation).

significance The degree to which a job really matters and impacts society as a whole.

similarity-attraction approach A theory explaining that team diversity can be counter-productive because people tend to avoid interacting with others who are unlike them.

simple structure An organizational form that features one person as the central decision-making figure.

situational strength The degree to which situations have clear behavioral expectations, incentives, or instructions that make differences between individuals less important.

social exchange Work relationships that are characterized by mutual investment, with employees willing to engage in "extra mile" sorts of behaviors because they trust that their efforts will eventually be rewarded.

social identity theory A theory that people identify themselves based on the various groups to which they belong and judge others based on the groups they associate with.

social influence model A model that suggests that employees with direct linkages to coworkers who leave the organization will themselves become more likely to leave.

social learning theory Theory that argues that people in organizations learn by observing others.

social loafing A type of motivational loss resulting from members feeling less accountable for team outcomes relative to independent work that results in individually identifiable outcomes.

social support The help people receive from others when they are confronted with stressful demands.

socialization The primary process by which employees learn the social knowledge that enables them to understand and adapt to the organization's culture.

socializing A form of psychological withdrawal in which one verbally chats with coworkers about nonwork topics.

socially complex resources Resources created by people, such as culture, teamwork, trust, and reputation. The source of competitive advantage is known, but the method of replicating the advantage is unclear.

span of control Represents how many employees each manager in the organization has responsibility for.

spatial ability Capabilities associated with visual and mental representation and manipulation of objects in space.

specific and difficult goals Goals that stretch an employee to perform at his or her maximum level while still staying within the boundaries of his or her ability.

sportsmanship Maintaining a positive attitude with coworkers through good and bad times.

staff validity The degree to which team members make good recommendations to the team leader.

stamina The ability of a person's lungs and circulatory system to work efficiently while he or she is engaging in prolonged physical activity.

stars Employees with high commitment levels and high task performance levels who serve as role models within the organization.

status striving A strong desire to obtain power and influence within a social structure as a means of expressing one's personality.

stereotype Assumptions made about others based on their social group membership.

stories Anecdotes, accounts, legends, and myths passed down from cohort to cohort within an organization.

storming The second stage of team development, during which conflict occurs due to members' ongoing commitment to ideas they bring with them to the team.

strains Negative consequences of the stress response.

strategic management Field of study devoted to exploring the product choices and industry characteristics that affect an organization's profitability.

strength The degree to which the body is capable of exerting force.

stress The psychological response to demands when there is something at stake for the individual, and where coping with these demands would tax or exceed the individual's capacity or resources.

stressors Demands that cause the stress response.

subculture A culture created within a small subset of the organization's employees.

substance abuse The abuse of drugs or alcohol before coming to work or while on the job.

substitutability The degree to which people have alternatives in accessing the resources a leader controls.

substitutes Situational characteristics that reduce the importance of the leader while simultaneously providing a direct benefit to employee performance.

substitutes for leadership model A model that suggests that characteristics of the situations can constrain the influence of the leader, which makes it more difficult for the leader to influence employee performance.

supervision satisfaction Employees' feelings about their boss, including his or her competency, communication, and personality.

surface-level diversity Diversity of observable attributes such as race, gender, ethnicity, and age.

symbols The images an organization uses, which generally convey messages.

T

tacit knowledge Knowledge that employees can only learn through experience.

tardiness A form of physical withdrawal in which employees arrive late to work or leave work early.

task complexity The degree to which the information and actions needed to complete a task are complicated.

task conflict Disagreements among members about the team's task.

task coordinator activities Boundary-spanning activities that are intended to coordinate task-related issues with people or groups in other functional areas.

task interdependence The degree to which team members interact with and rely on other team members for information, materials, and resources needed to accomplish work for the team.

task performance Employee behaviors that are directly involved in the transformation of organizational resources into the goods or services that the organization produces.

task strategies Learning plans and problem-solving approaches used to achieve successful performance.

taskwork processes The activities of team members that relate directly to the accomplishment of team tasks.

team Two or more people who work interdependently over some time period to accomplish common goals related to some task-oriented purpose.

team building Fun activities that facilitate team problem solving, trust, relationship building, and the clarification of role responsibilities.

team building roles Behaviors that influence the quality of the team's social climate.

team composition The mix of the various characteristics that describe the individuals who work in the team.

team diversity The degree to which team members are different from one another.

team process The different types of activities and interactions that occur within a team as the team works toward its goals.

team process training The use of team experiences that facilitates the team's ability to function and perform more effectively as an intact unit.

team states Specific types of feelings and thoughts that coalesce in the minds of team members as a consequence of their experience working together.

team task roles Behaviors that directly facilitate the accomplishment of team tasks.

team viability Team commitment; the likelihood a team can work together effectively into the future.

teamwork processes The interpersonal activities that promote the accomplishment of team tasks but do not involve task accomplishment itself.

technology The method by which an organization transforms inputs to outputs.

telling When the leader provides specific instructions and closely supervises performance.

theft Stealing company products or equipment from the organization.

theory A collection of verbal and symbolic assertions that specify how and why variables are related, as well as the conditions in which they should (and should not) be related.

360-degree feedback A performance evaluation system that uses ratings provided by supervisors, coworkers, subordinates, customers, and the employees themselves.

time pressure The sense that the amount of time allotted to do a job is not quite enough.

time-driven model of leadership A model that suggests that seven factors, including the importance of the decision, the expertise of the leader, and the competence of the followers, combine to make some decision-making styles more effective than others in a given situation.

training A systematic effort by organizations to facilitate the learning of job-related knowledge and behavior.

trait activation The degree to which situations provide cues that trigger the expression of a given personality trait.

traits Recurring trends in people's responses to their environment.

transactional contracts Psychological contracts that focus on a narrow set of specific monetary obligations.

transactional leadership A pattern of behavior where the leader rewards or disciplines the follower based on performance.

transactional theory of stress A theory that explains how stressful demands are perceived and appraised, as well as how people respond to the perceptions and appraisals.

transactive memory The degree to which team members' specialized knowledge is integrated into an effective system of memory for the team.

transfer of training Occurs when employees retain and demonstrate the knowledge, skills, and behaviors required for their job after training ends.

transformational leadership A pattern of behavior where the leader inspires followers to commit to a shared vision that provides meaning to their work while also serving as a role model who helps followers develop their own potential and view problems from new perspectives.

transition processes Teamwork processes, such as mission analysis and planning, that focus on preparation for future work in the team.

transportable teamwork competencies Team training that involves helping people develop general teamwork competencies that they can transport from one team context to another.

trust The willingness to be vulnerable to an authority based on positive expectations about the authority's actions and intentions.

trust propensity A general expectation that the words, promises, and statements of individuals can be relied upon.

trustworthiness Characteristics or attributes of a person that inspire trust, including competence, character, and benevolence.

type A behavior pattern People who tend to experience more stressors, appraise more demands as stressful, and be prone to experiencing more strains.

typical performance Performance in the routine conditions that surround daily job tasks.

U

uncertainty avoidance The degree to which a culture tolerates ambiguous situations (low uncertainty avoidance) or feels threatened by them (high uncertainty avoidance).

understanding and adaptation The final stage of socialization, during which newcomers come to learn the content areas of socialization and internalize the norms and expected behaviors of the organization.

use of emotions The degree to which people can harness emotions and employ them to improve their chances of being successful in whatever they are seeking to do.

V

valence The anticipated value of the outcome(s) associated with successful performance.

value in diversity problem-solving approach A theory that supports team diversity because it provides a larger pool of knowledge and perspectives.

value-percept theory A theory that argues that job satisfaction depends on whether the employee perceives that his or her job supplies those things that he or she values.

values Things that people consciously or unconsciously want to seek or attain.

variable interval schedule Reinforcement occurs at random periods of time.

variable ratio schedule Behaviors are reinforced after a varying number of them have been exhibited.

variety The degree to which a job requires different activities and skills.

veiled purpose tests Integrity tests that do not directly ask about dishonesty, instead assessing more general personality traits associated with dishonest acts.

verbal ability Various capabilities associated with understanding and expressing oral and written communication.

verbal persuasion Pep talks that lead employees to believe that they can "get the job done."

vicarious experiences Observations of and discussions with others who have performed some work task.

virtual team A team in which the members are geographically dispersed, and interdependent activity occurs through e-mail, Web conferencing, and instant messaging.

visibility How aware others are of a leader and the resources that leader can provide.

voice When an employee speaks up to offer constructive suggestions for change, often in reaction to a negative work event.

W

wasting resources Using too many materials or too much time to do too little work.

whistle-blowing When employees expose illegal actions by their employer.

withdrawal behavior Employee actions that are intended to avoid work situations.

Wonderlic Personnel Test A 12-minute test of general cognitive ability used to hire job applicants.

work complexity The degree to which job requirements tax or just exceed employee capabilities.

work responsibility The number and importance of the obligations that an employee has to others.

work specialization The degree to which tasks in an organization are divided into separate jobs.

work team A relatively permanent team in which members work together to produce goods and/or provide services.

work–family conflict A form of role conflict in which the demands of a work role hinder the fulfillment of the demands in a family role (or vice versa).

Z

zero acquaintance Situations in which two people have just met.

Chapter 1

Page 5: Courtesy of Apple; page 11: © AP Photo/Paul Sakuma; page 12 © AP Photo/Dave Martin; page 18: © Corbis/SYGMA; page 20: Book cover of *Good to Great* by Jim Collins, HarperCollins. Photo of cover: © Roberts Publishing Services; page 22: © Chris Rank/Bloomberg News/Landov.

Chapter 2

Page 33: © AP Photo; page 39: AP Photo/Eric Gay; page 40: © AP Photo/Steven Day; page 46: © Banana Stock/Punch Stock/DAL; page 48: © Photofest/Sony Pictures; page 51: Book cover of *Getting Things Done* by David Allen, Penguin Books. Photo of cover: © Roberts Publishing Services; page 53: © AP Photo/Marcus R. Donner.

Chapter 3

Page 67: Courtesy of Accenture; page 72: © Liquidlibrary/JupiterImages/DAL; page 75: © AP Photo/Morry Gash; page 77: © Disney/Pixar/Photofest; page 88: Courtesy of Harvard Business Press; page 89: © Lou Dematteis/Reuters/Corbis.

Chapter 4

Page 103: © 2008 Zappos.com, Inc.; page109: Courtesy of Quik Trip Convenience Stores; page 112: Book cover of *The Three Signs of a Miserable Job* by Patrick Lencioni, Jossey Bass Publishers. Photo of cover: © Roberts Publishing Services; page 116: © Nick White/Digital Vision/Getty Images/DAL; page 127: © Warner Bros./Photofest.

Chapter 5

Page 141: © AP Photo/Andy King - Coyne Public Relations; page 146: © Digital Vision/Flying Colours/Getty Images/RF; page 147: © Twentieth Century Fox/Photofest; page 152: © Manchan/Getty Images/DAL; page155: © Jonathan Daniel/Getty Images; page 157: © Ryan McVay/Getty Images/DAL; page 163: Book cover of *The Four-Hour Workweek* by Timothy Ferriss, Hyperion Publishers. Photo of cover: © Roberts Publishing Services; page 165: © William McCoy-Rainbow/Science Faction/Corbis.

Chapter 6

Page 177: © AP Photo/James A. Finley; page 179: Book cover of *Talent is Overrated* by Geoff Colvin, Portfolio Publishers, Penguin Group. Photo of cover: © Roberts Publishing Services; page180 (left): © Royalty-Free/Corbis/DAL; page 180 (right): © Royalty-Free/Corbis/DAL; page186: © Warner Bros./Photofest; page191:© Kimimasa Mayama/Bloomberg News/Landov; page 199: © AP Photo/Namas Bhojani.

Chapter 7

Page 217: © AP Photo/Namas Bhojani; page 223: © Brand X Pictures/PunchStock/DAL; page 225: © Warner Bros./Photofest; page 231: © Steven Brahms/Bloomberg News/Landov; page 236: © AP Wide World Photos; page 243 : © Simon & Schuster, Inc.

Chapter 8

Page 257: Courtesy of Xerox Corporation; page 260: © Dynamic Graphics/JupiterImages/DAL; page 262: © Digital Vision/DAL; page 265: © Warner Bros./Photofest; page 266: © AP Photo/Battle Creek Enquirer, John Grap; page 271: Courtesy of Little Brown Publishing. All rights reserved; page 277: © Kevin Moloney/The New York Times/Redux.

Chapter 9

Page 293: Courtesy of Kronos, Incorporated; page 298: © Royalty-Free/Corbis/DAL; page 301: © Universal Studios/Photofest;

page 306: © Royalty-Free/Corbis/DAL; page 307: © AP Photo/Battle Creek Enquirer, John Grap; page 318: Book cover of *Strengths Finder 2.0* by Tom Rath, Gallup Press. Photo of cover: © Roberts Publishing Services.

Chapter 10

Page 337: © AP Photo/Paul Sakuma; page 339: © AP Photo/John Gress; page 342: © Columbia Pictures/Photofest; page 343: © Columbia Pictures/Photofest; page 346: Courtesy of Little Brown Publishing. All rights reserved; page 348: © Digital Vision/DAL; page 351: © AP Photo/Mark J. Terrill; page 355: Photo by Markham Johnson.

Chapter 11

Page 373: © AP Photo/Keystone/Lauurent Gillieron; page 375: © Stockbyte/Getty Images/DAL; page 377: © Warner Bros./Photofest; page 379: © Robert Vos/Corbis; page 384: © Digital Vision/Getty Images/DAL; page 389: Book cover of *Bad Apples* by Brette McWhorter Sember and Terrence J. Sember, Avon Books. Photo of cover: © Roberts Publishing Services; page 390: © George Tiedmann/Corbis; page 392: © Bethean/Corbis/DAL.

Chapter 12

Page 411: © Penni Gladstone/San Francisco Chronicle/Corbis; page 414: © Warner Bros./Photofest; page 418: © TRUMP PROD. / THE KOBAL COLLECTION; page 421: © SuperStock; page 430: © The New York Times/Redux; page 431: Copyright © William James Warren, 2007. All rights are reserved.

Chapter 13

Page 449: © Spencer Platt/Newsmakers/Getty Images; page 463: Courtesy of Little Brown Publishing. All rights reserved; page 465:

Courtesy of One Laptop per Child; page 468: © Paramount Pictures/Photofest.

Chapter 14

Page 481: © AP Photo/Carlos Osorio; page 487: © Philippe Lopez/AFP/Getty Images; page 496: © Tim Graham/Getty Images; page 501: © Paramount Pictures/Photofest; page 507: *The Leadership Challenge 4/e* by Jim Kouzes and Barry Posner. Copyright

© 2008. Reprinted with permission of John Wiley & Sons, Inc.

Chapter 15

Page 525: © AP Photo/Paul Sakuma; page 529: © Sunset Boulevard/Corbis; page 531: © Warner Bros./Photofest; page 536: © AP Photo/Paul Sakuma; page 540: © Yoshikazu Tsuno/AFP/Getty Images/Getty Images; page 547: Book cover of *How the Mighty Fall* by Jim Collins, HarperCollins. Photo

of cover: © Roberts Publishing Services.

Chapter 16

Page 555: © AP Photo/Joey McLeister, Pool; page 559: © IDEO / Nicholas Zurcher; page 563: Book cover of *House of Cards* by William D. Cohan, Doubleday. Photo of cover: © Roberts Publishing Services; page 564: © James Cheadle/Alamy; page 568: © Warner Bros./Photofest.

Company Index

Subject Index

OB AT THE BOOKSTORE:

Bad Apples

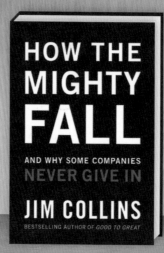

How the Mighty Fall

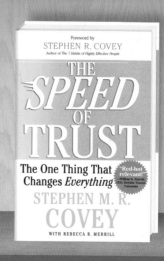

The Speed of Trust

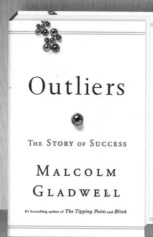

Outliers

StrengthsFinder 2.0

Talent is Overrated